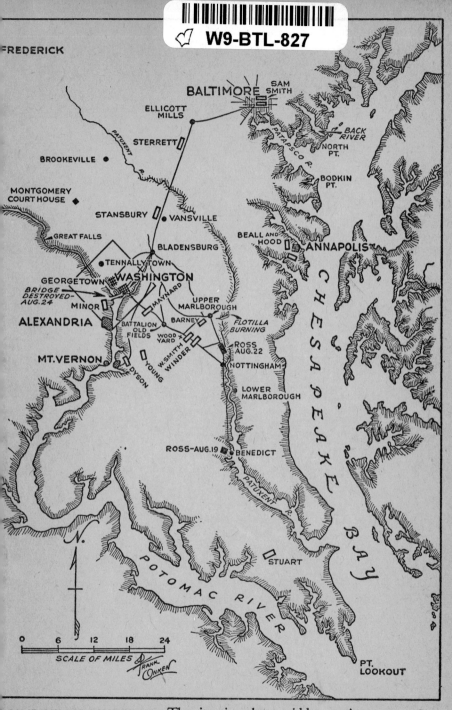

FREDERICK

W9-BTL-827

BALTIMORE · SAM SMITH

ELLICOTT MILLS

STERRETT

BROOKEVILLE

PATUXENT R.

BACK RIVER

PATAPSCO R.

NORTH PT.

BODKIN PT.

MONTGOMERY COURT HOUSE

STANSBURY · VANSVILLE

GREAT FALLS

BLADENSBURG

BEALL AND HOOD · ANNAPOLIS

TENNALLYTOWN

GEORGETOWN · WASHINGTON

BRIDGE DESTROYED—AUG. 24

MINOR

MAYNARD

UPPER MARLBOROUGH

ALEXANDRIA

BATTALION OLD FIELDS

BARNEY

FLOTILLA BURNING

WOOD YARD

ROSS AUG. 22

W. SMITH WINDER

NOTTINGHAM

MT. VERNON

YOUNG

DYSON

LOWER MARLBOROUGH

C H E S A P E A K E   B A Y

ROSS—AUG. 19 · BENEDICT

PATUXENT R.

STUART

N

P O T O M A C   R I V E R

0   6   12   18   24

SCALE OF MILES

FRANK ONKEN

PT. LOOKOUT

CAMPAIGN FOR WASHINGTON—The situation about midday on August 22, 1814.

THE PERILOUS FIGHT

By Neil H. Swanson

MAJOR GENERAL SAM SMITH
Ironmaster—merchant—soldier—politician

THE
PERILOUS
FIGHT

*being a little known and much abufed chapter
of our national hiftory in our*

SECOND WAR OF INDEPENDENCE

and a true narrative of

THE BATTLE OF GODLY WOOD

and The Attack on Fort McHenry more fuitably defcribed as

The Battle of Baltimore

*the whole conftituting the firft complete account of the
fkillful, and fuccefsful defenfe of that city by*

SAM'L SMITH

*then in his 62nd year, againft Lord Wellington's Invincibles fup-
ported by a powerful fleet, together with a* REFUTATION *of thofe*

TRADUCERS OF AMERICAN COURAGE

who have made fmall of the citizen foldiers who, lately
defeated and routed, marched again to face the conquerors of
Napoleon in fuperior numbers in the open field

☆

TO WHICH IS ADDED

some notice of the circumstances attending the writing of

The
Star Spangled
Banner

with particular reference to the remarkable errors of those
who, wholly without warrant of fact, have belittled the significance
of our national anthem by describing it as
"a song nobody can sing, about an
event of no importance."

★ ★ ★ ★

★ ★ ★

Recounted mainly from Contemporary Records

BY
NEIL H. SWANSON

Illustrated by JOHN G. STEES
Maps by FRANK ONKEN

FARRAR AND RINEHART, *Incorporated*
New York   Toronto

To Hildegarde, my wife, with love

and to the memory of the citizen soldiers of her divided family, who fought on opposite sides in our first War of Independence—

Captain Jonathan Sterling, Maryland Loyalist Regiment
Lieutenant William Sterling, Maryland Loyalist Regiment
Henry Sterling, Annemessex (Maryland) Militia
Isaac Sterling, Sussex (Maryland) Volunteers resisting Tory uprising, and Second Regiment of the Maryland Line, Continental Army

CONTENTS

x   *Contents*

Truth Is Stranger Than History

History, BEING A DEVICE IN-
vented by human beings to illuminate their past, is heir to all
human weakness.

It is an imperfect device, affected by the flaws of prejudice
and carelessness, cynicism and credulity, laziness, lapses of memory, selfishness and honest mistakes. The brightest light casts
shadows. Even when the lamp of history burns with its clearest
flame, it often highlights one side of a fact and leaves the other
sides in darkness. The result is frequently distortion. Sometimes
it is paradox.

Probably not one American in five hundred thousand has
ever heard of the battle of Godly Wood. But if that battle had
not been planned and fought "The Star-Spangled Banner"
might never have been written.

The whole story of the nation's anthem, in terms of historical significance and the courage of ordinary men, has never
been told in any one place. Even in fragments, it has seldom
been told accurately. In illuminating the birth scene of the
anthem—the defense of Baltimore in 1814—history has thrown
its highlight on the naval action and left Godly Wood in
shadow. By "the rockets' red glare, the bombs bursting in air"
you can see the brick-and-sod fort squatting on the end of
Whetstone Point. But you cannot see the rockets' red glare
and the shrapnel bursting in the woods on North Point, just
across the water; you cannot see militiamen, once soundly
beaten, standing up again to the Invincibles who beat them.
In illuminating the conclusion of our so-called Second War of
Independence, history has thrown its highlight on the battle of

New Orleans and has left this strangely similar and more important battle paradoxically misshapen and diminished.

But the real paradox is that for a hundred and thirty years, without warrant of truth, history has managed to leave "The Star-Spangled Banner" associated with defeat, futility and cowardice.

Even in Maryland, where the anniversary of the land battle is a legal holiday, there exists a notion that the whole thing was a trifling incident, inglorious in action and insignificant in result. Baltimoreans, who yield to no one in their pride of birthplace, are inclined to be apologetic when a stranger asks them to explain the holiday. Few know the truth.

This book is an attempt to place the birth of the national anthem in its actual setting of events. It is an attempt to describe those events exactly as they occurred, without the distortions and omissions, the braggings and the apologies, the half-truths and the carelessly perpetuated errors that have blurred them. And because the whole truth can be told only in terms of the human beings who took part in these events, this book is also an attempt to tell what the late summer days of 1814 meant to the men and women who lived through them.

Through almost four years of our greatest war, the first notes of "The Star-Spangled Banner" have been bringing America's millions to their feet in simple and instinctive fervor. It seemed to me that at this time it is possible to tell this story without shrinking from the natural emotion it arouses. It may not always be possible to tell it thus, without apology. When wars end, reaction comes. The fervor dies. The cynics mock. Ideals become shameful, love of country is a tin horn, courage is a coin lost in a muddy gutter, and self-sacrifice is folly.

I have not forgotten—I cannot forget—the cynics' carnival that followed World War I. I cannot forget my own bewilderment that all the values we had held so high should suddenly turn cheap and shoddy. We were still young when we came home from France—not young enough, perhaps, to be excused for not knowing that the cynics lied, but young enough to be fooled and disillusioned and to believe that it had all been wasted.

Those days will come again. They should not, but they will. When they come, I shall be glad that I have written this book: it is my retraction of my own disillusionment. I shall be even more glad than I now am that I have reached an age at which I have no shame in saying what I believe and am not afraid to write history with the emotion that gives life and meaning to the past because emotion holds the essence of the truth.

I have not forgotten—I shall not forget as long as I live— a rain-streaked twilight in a small French town, a small wet column of American infantry going up to the lines for the first time, and the band that a tough and wise old colonel turned out to play us away with "The Star-Spangled Banner." I am not sure yet that it was strictly GI. But God love him for it! It would have meant even more to me if I had known then, as I know now, what the words of the anthem stand for— if I had known then, as I have tried to express in this book, the quality of courage that made the anthem possible.

For the words of "The Star-Spangled Banner" might not have been written if another tough old colonel named Sam Smith had been less wise, and if a few hundred ordinary Americans, the citizen soldiers of another day, had not possessed the kind of courage that goes back for more after one dreadful licking.

Neil H. Swanson

THE PERILOUS FIGHT

1

THE FALL OF A CITY

The PRESIDENT OF THE UNITED States was a fugitive, wandering the country roads on horseback.

Behind him, Washington was burning. Fire was licking through the windows of the presidential palace. The halls of congress were in flames. The north end of the Potomac River bridge was burning. The new warships in the navy yard were burning. The treasury, the war department and the arsenal were burning.[1]

Through the summer night, hot, stifling, black with thunderheads,[2] the American army that had been too little until too late also wandered the back roads. That afternoon—the afternoon of August

24, 1814—it had met an invading enemy, inferior in numbers, near
the little town of Bladensburg in Maryland. The American army
had been beaten. It had never truly been an army. It was nothing,
now, but fragments.

They were sullen and bewildered fragments, scuffing on
through breathless heat and suffocating dust. Sodden with sweat,
sodden with sleeplessness, sodden with the shame of a defeat so
shocking and complete that it was hard to comprehend, they had
yet a little energy to dispute, to bicker, to prove—each man—that
his was not the blame. They had yet a little anger to curse the
carriage that came drifting past them on the dust-hushed road, a
shadow only a little blacker than the night, crowding them off
into the brittling weeds and the honeysuckle tangles from which
more dust whipped up to rankle in their eyes and throats and
grit between their teeth.

In the carriage a woman they could not see—a big-faced, imperious woman—rode with her body tensed against the ceaseless
jolting. Now and again the ruts and chuckholes set her reticule to
clinking; now and again they threw the portmanteau against her
leg. In the reticule were silver spoons snatched from the president's
table.[3] In the portmanteau—so the legend has it—was a roll of parch-
ment filled with bold handwriting, filled with fifty-six names written just as boldly but not quite so legibly. The president's wife—
so the legend says—had saved not only the spoons but also the
Declaration of Independence.

The legend is wrong. The Declaration of Independence was
not in Dolly Madison's carriage. It was in a "coarse linen" sack,
in a pile of similar sacks in a farmer's wagon bumping down the
road to Leesburg in Virginia.[4] But there were many, that night,
who would have wondered whether it was worth the saving. There
were some who wondered whether the Second War of Independence had not been lost that afternoon. There were some, well informed, who might wonder whether the Declaration would much
longer have any value except as a curiosity or as a trophy to be
displayed, perhaps, in the Tower of London along with the prayer-
ful prophecy of the *Times* of London concerning the United
States: "That ill-organized association is on the eve of dissolution,
and the world is speedily to be delivered of the mischievous example of the existence of a government founded on democratic
rebellion."

Dissolution was in the air. The army summoned at the twelfth hour to defend Washington had dissolved. The government had dissolved. The cabinet had at last put to practical use its favorite principle of administration: it had scrambled into the saddle and ridden off in all directions.[5] Seven hundred infantrymen of a foreign nation, with one puny fieldpiece and two grasshoppers,[6] held possession of the capital of the United States in the midst of a region whose first militia quotas called for thirty thousand troops. The nearest reinforcements for the fleeing army were cut off: the long bridge spanning the Potomac was on fire at both ends now: American soldiers on the Virginia shore had fired their end of it as the best means of keeping themselves out of danger.

In Baltimore, forty miles away, the people stood in the streets or leaned out at their dormer windows or climbed to the rooftops to watch the glare that pulsed and wavered in the southern sky. They told one another that it looked to be a raght good far—which, being literally translated from the native Bal'morese, means a right good fire, which in turn is Bal'more idiom for a bad fire.

Baltimore liked fires. It liked the noise and the commotion that went with them, the running, jostling, hollering excitement. It was a lusty, rambunctious upstart of a town.

Big and prosperous it might be—and even cultured and naïvely boastful of the culture. But in the community of American cities it was still the brawny young apprentice. It took its liquor straight and its excitement in the simplest, most direct forms. It liked to see itself in crowds. It liked not only fires but also shiplaunchings and mass picnics and parades and its swift private warships casting off to raid the English Channel and the Irish Sea and coming home again past Lazaretto Light with the flags of a dozen prizes hanging like the week's wash in their rigging. It liked to hear the guns of the homing privateersmen popping off in exuberant salutes to the little red-brick-and-green-sod fort on Whetstone Point.

It liked to see the Franklin Artillery and the Baltimore Yagers, the Blues and the Sharp Shooters and the Baltimore Light Infantry tramping through the streets to drill on Loudenslager's hill, with the town dogs and the town boys yapping behind and the drums rattling louder than the Jamaica rum kegs trundling across the planks of McEldery's wharf. It liked good, hearty noises.

But Baltimore was not noisy, that night of August 24th in the year 1814. The people in the streets made little groups, not crowds. They talked, but in low tones of apprehension. Even the householders trading their opinions from one dormer to another kept their voices calm—as calm as their anxiety would let them. The town was trying hard to keep its self-control. It was not excited. Its emotions had passed beyond excitement.

For part of Baltimore was gone. The best part, some people said. Those who said it probably were relatives and friends and therefore prejudiced, although the whole town took a deep pride in Joe Sterrett's swanky Fifth regiment and in Will Pinkney's Rifles. Two days ago the Fifth Maryland had struck its tents and marched away from Elk Ridge Landing, at the edge of town, on fifteen minutes' notice.[7] With it had gone three companies of the city rifleman battalion and two batteries of field guns—the American Artillerists under Captain Dick Magruder and the Franklins with Joe Myers riding at their head. No telling where they were now. No telling what had happened. All that the town knew, for certain, was that Maryland had been invaded—that the overwhelming hostile fleet in Chesapeake Bay had been powerfully reinforced, that it had entered the Patuxent River, that it had put ashore an army somewhere near the little town of Benedict.

Nobody knew how big that army was. Five thousand, so one story had it. But another made it twenty thousand. Rumors ran wild. The invading troops were marching northward, up the valley of Patuxent; they had passed Nottingham; they were coming to take Baltimore, to plunder it and burn it, wipe it out completely.

On one thing only the stories were agreed. The hostile army was made up of veterans, of the finest troops in Europe, of the soldiers who had swept the French eagles out of Spain, crushed Napoleon, captured Paris and sent the great conqueror into exile at a place called Elba. An island, the papers said it was.

All day Baltimore had watched and listened—listened for the grump of cannon, watched the Ellicott Mills road for the flying witch's-brooms of dust that would mean a horseman galloping in from McCoy's.

McCoy's tavern, thirteen miles away, was the nearest station on the horse-telegraph line that Henry Thompson had set up.[8] The line stretched off southward through the rolling hills to Washington and on across the broad tobacco plantings, past the meager backwoods clearings, through the piney barrens to Ross tavern. Early in the morning there had been one rider from McCoy's, but the news he carried had been two days old, and bad. Joshua Barney's flotilla —one sloop and seventeen gunboats, cockboats, little more than rowboats—had done all it could to play the David. It had tried hard, fighting, running, stopping, turning to fight again. But this was no single combat: this Goliath came with battleships and cruisers and a swarm of lesser vessels, and he was too powerful. The flotilla had fought and fled and fought and fled until the shallowing Patuxent gripped its bottoms. There was no flotilla left now. It had blown itself up.

That was all. But the war was coming close to home when something happened to Josh Barney. Josh was a Bal'more boy; he had hoed corn on his father's farm, out Bear Creek way; he had clerked in old man Ashburner's cluttered store on Long street and had been a prentice on the Bal'more pilot boat; when he was sixteen he had strutted through the streets as proud as a three-decker, carrying the first striped flag the town had ever seen, drumming up a crew for the little old *Hornet*—the first warship Baltimore sent to join the first navy of the new U. States. Now, in this new war, a good share of the men who manned his little gunboats had been Baltimore men; they had been the sailing masters and the mates and the able seamen off the merchant vessels lying idle in the Basin, shut off from the sea by the blockading fleet that held the Chesapeake.

Nobody knew what had happened to Josh Barney and his men. Nobody knew how many had been killed and wounded. They had simply vanished as completely as the Fifth and Will Pinkney's riflemen and Dick Magruder's and Joe Myers's gunners. They were out yonder somewhere under the flame-lighted sky, nobody knew where. Nobody knew what caused the fire or even what was burning. Nobody knew anything.

But Baltimore could guess. In midafternoon there had been another horse-telegraph dispatch. Before suppertime, by word of mouth, the news had got around. Most of Baltimore had heard one version or another of the message:

Aug. 24th 1814
M[c]Coys 13 miles from Balt[re]. and 1st.
Telegraphic Station from Balt[re].
11 A.M. Wednesday

Dear Gen[l].

I send this by Jn[o]. Howard, who states that Winder has fallen back on Washington & that his position at the old Fields was occupied by the enemy yesterday. Stansbury's Brigade & the 5th. Reg[t]. left Ross' this morning at 2 A.M. for Washington. . . .

I am with resp^t. Dear Genl. Your ob^t Servt Howard left Ross'
this morning   R. Patterson

Director of the Telegraphic Station at McCoys
Brig^r. Genl. Stricker, Baltimore [9]

Baltimore read that message in its own way: it was not a military dispatch, it was a personal letter. It said that Jim Caldwell and Nick Brice and Reverdy Hays and Elie Clagett and the Levering boys had been waked up at two o'clock this morning. It said that, while Baltimore was sleeping, Peregrine Janvier and Alex Gould and Nat Kimberly and young Tony Faulac and eight hundred other weary militiamen had been retreating toward the town that now was burning.[10] It said that foreign soldiers with death in their hands had been pressing close upon Ben Norris and Bill Tilyard and Phil Eulon and Sebastian Sultzer, upon the Blues and the Yagers and the Baltimore Light Infantry and all the town companies that used to go swinging down Market street in their bright, high-collared coats.

But not at two in the morning. They always came home to supper. Almost always. Sometimes they took their lunch. Rations, they called it. But they always came home to sleep. Oh . . . don't! Let's don't talk about it. Let's talk about something else. I'll go crazy if we don't. Alex was always so sleepy in the morning; he hated so to get up.

To the mothers and fathers in Baltimore, to the sweethearts, to the young wives crumpling the flounces of their fine madras gowns in the fine, tall parlors in Charles street, crumpling their cheap calicoes in hot hands in the small, hot houses in Brandy Alley and Sharping Lane, it was as if the enemy had peered in at the window. And that cold, sharp feeling in the stomach's pit was like the touch of cold, sharp bayonets upon a dear, loved body. *Alex, where are you? Did you get any sleep at all? Are you dreadfully tired? Have you had your supper tonight? Alex, are you all right? Are you? Oh, this awful waiting . . . waiting . . .*

The first stain of fire crept up into the sky along toward half past nine.[11] It was no brighter, then, than afterglow of the hot summer sunset. There were arguments about it. Nine and a half o'clock was late for afterglow, but what else could it be? There's nothing over there but the Patapsco River; you can't burn a river. All it means is that tomorrow'll be another scorcher.

The glare increased. The arguments died down. By half past

eleven there was no doubt left. A wave of fire more furious than those before it surged into the sky. It beat against the piled-up storm clouds and the clouds writhed as if wind was in them. From the Bal'more rooftops or even from John Eager Howard's hilltop beyond the north end of the town, a man couldn't tell for certain which part was smoke and which was thunderheads. But out on the horse-telegraph line—on the end of it that still was working—James Carroll was riding for McCoy's and writing a message in his mind so that he could scratch it off on paper quickly:

> I left Vanhorns about 8 o'Clock when on the Road to McCoy's Tavern an hour after I heard two or three heavy Explosions, it was considered by the Company with me as a Renewal of the Engagement but in a little Time a Light appeared in the Horizon in the Direction of the City of Washington which encreased until the Smoke and Flame were distinctly seen this Light continues to encrease to the present Hour & I have no doubt but that the British are burning the public Buildings at Washington.[12]

Ahead of Carroll on the road to Baltimore, Captain Henry Thompson's videttes had halted other frantic messengers and handed their dispatches over to fresh relay riders waiting in their saddles. In Baltimore, the first big drops of rain began to fall. They made a noise like galloping across the roofs.

In Market street a sound of galloping grew louder. The shower had not been hard enough to wet a man through, but the horse and rider from McCoy's were drenched. The horse was spent and trembling when it pulled up in the courthouse square, and the rider too was trembling when he pulled the sweat-damp fold of paper from his pocket. The militia officer who snatched it from him set off on a run for General John Stricker's quarters. Stricker's eyes took in the three lines at a glance:

> Washington ½ past 3
> The British have driven us from Bladensb^g. Some kill'd & wounded on both sides. We have retreated to Washington. Steretts regiment behaved very well.   Y^r.
>
> J. E. Howard J^r.[13]

There was a sound of running in the streets, a sound of voices, anxious and demanding. Townsfolk who had heard the hoofs or seen the horseman pass swarmed into courthouse square. They took possession of the relay rider and they had the news as soon as the brigade commander had it.

At McCoy's tavern, at "½ after 12 o'clock," R. Patterson had scribbled a postscript at the bottom of the note James Carroll had just written:

> From the report of several Horsemen come in during the night, who left our party after the defeat at Bladensburg, it seems they fled mostly on the Montgomery road, some stragglers of our army are progressing this way.
>
> R. Patterson

12½ o'Clock
Brig^r. Genl. Stricker, Baltimore [14]

In Baltimore that night nobody doubted that the enemy would follow. It was Baltimore he called "a doomed town." If the government of the United States was powerless to save its capital from destruction, what could one city do alone? What could Baltimore do, with its best troops already beaten and turned into stragglers? What could anybody do, with two invading armies splitting the United States up into pieces, with the blue-light [15] politicians talking treason, with New England politicians talking openly of splitting the United States up into pieces themselves, with men who loved politics more than their country talking openly about secession? [16]

There was the writing, plain on the wall, in Biblical letters of fire. Anybody who knew his Bible could read what it said: *Mene, mene, tekel upharsin.* The young country, weighed in the balance, found wanting. Democracy weighed and found wanting. Liberty and the pursuit of happiness weighed and found wanting. The temple already on fire, the roof cracking, the enemy's hands on the pillars.

The glare faded out. With appropriate offstage noises, thunder and lightning, the curtain closed on the first act of the melodrama titled "The Burning of Washington."

But the act is not over: there is an epilogue. A carriage buckets along "in the midst of a great cavalcade of teams of all descriptions, moving as rapidly as possible into Maryland." In the background, seen dimly through the stage rain, there is a crossroads tavern. In the wings, a woman is speaking.

She is telling a story. Her name is Polly Kemp; she is a Maryland girl, born on the Eastern Sho'; she has been visiting her uncle in Washington, but she is not in Washington now; she is one of the fugitives. Listen. Her words run together:

"It began to rain in great torrents, the lightning and thunder adding to the terrors of a dark night, our man walked ahead with a lantern, the outhouses and stable were so full that our poor tired rain-beaten horse had to be tied to the trees and remain out in the rain for hours, we were made as comfortable as was possible in our wet garments, and had been seated scarcely an hour when there was a loud rap upon the door and the great rough tavern keeper made it known to us in an angry voice that the intruder was Dolly Madison, as he attempted to push her away from the door. Father indignantly sprang to the door and pushing aside the angry keeper, went out into the rain to find that lady walking away in that terrible rain. Taking her arm he led her back into the house. The keeper began denouncing the President as the cause of the war and the destruction of the capital; many of the occupants murmured against admitting her, but father was determined that she should remain and remain she did: we took her under our special protection.

"We sat silently until 3 or 4 o'clock in the morning, when a rap came upon the door, one of our party opened the door and who should walk in but President Madison himself and several gentlemen, but the President did not remain long. An hour later a messenger announced to the President that the enemy was coming that way, he quickly drew on his great cloak and kissing his wife went out again into the storm followed by his faithful followers.

"By daybreak, Mrs. Madison became restless and could not stand the suspense any longer and started out with her coachman. . . . After they had gone some of the people in the tavern who were under the influence of liquor, were very angry with father for admitting them. How very sorry we were for Queen Dolly. . . . During all these indignities she spoke not a word." [17]

2

A CARNIVAL OF ASSES

O<small>N</small> FRIDAY, TWO DAYS AFTER THE
disastrous battle at Bladensburg, Dick Magruder walked down to
Ebenezer French's printing shop at No. 29 South Calvert street and
put an ad in the Baltimore *Patriot*:

American Artillerists

The members of this company who were in the late engagement at Bladensburg, and have returned to Baltimore, are ordered
forthwith to report themselves to me at my quarters, No. 53, South
Charles-street.

Those who are wounded, if any, will notify me of it through
some of their friends.

R. B. MAGRUDER, Captain

aug. 26 d4t

Peter Foy, lieutenant of the Fell's Point Riflemen and now commanding the company in Captain Bill Dyer's place, put in a similar want ad. It ordered the Fell's Point men to report "at my encampment, on Clem's Lot, head of Market street," and it, too, asked for news of the wounded.

WANTED—an army! LOST—somewhere between the village of Bladensburg and the Blue Ridge Mountains, most of our soldiers! Not drums, not bugle calls. Classified ads to rally a beaten, disorganized army!

When the paper came out on the evening of August 26th, the outlook was as dark as the night of the 24th had been when the glare faded out of the sky. All day the rumors had run like lightning on a wet rail fence. Wellington's Invincibles were marching on Baltimore. They were already halfway to McCoy's. The city had been left to its fate . . . General Winder was abandoning Baltimore . . . Charlie Ridgley's squadron of cavalry had orders from Winder to make all haste to the westward . . . what was left of the army was still in retreat, it was falling back on Frederick Town . . . Winder was not even thinking of making a stand until he had fallen back forty miles.[1]

Most of the rumors were wrong, but the town didn't know that. The newspapers didn't know it either; they didn't print all the rumors; they denied some of them, but they couldn't keep up with all the wild stories that went galloping through the streets. The *Patriot* did the best it could with the rumors, the pieces of truth, the half-truths, the half-falsehoods, the honest mistakes, and the downright lies:

"Many of those who were in the engagement at Bladensburg, have arrived in the city. No satisfactory account of the affair is received, as each was too much engaged at the time, and too much exhausted since, with fatigue and extraordinary privations, to give a distinct account.

"We learn generally, that on Wednesday, in the forenoon, a severe action took place at Bladensburg, which is six miles from Washington. Upon the approach of the enemy, our artillery and infantry, opened upon them, with briskness; and did considerable execution, as numbers were seen to fall. The enemy marched steadily forward, in close column, apparently disregarding the fire, and reserving their own, until our troops began to retreat, when they let drive at them. . . .

"Our troops not being one quarter equal to the enemy in number, received orders to retire, and fled in all directions. The enemy pursued their course to Washington. . . .

"Commodore Barney, with his gallant flotilla crew, bravely disputed the entrance of the enemy into the city. They fought most desperately; but like the rest were overpowered by numbers, literally ten to one.

"The Baltimore troops, in the first instance, bore the brunt of the battle, and behaved with the utmost coolness and courage—Twice they bore so hard on the enemy as to 'stagger his progress'.

"It is believed Gen. Winder has taken a position near Fredericktown.

"As yet we have not ascertained our loss—Reports, as usual, have exaggerated it; as several have been reported to be among the slain, who have arrived among us. It is certain, General Stansbury, Commodore Barney, Major Pinkney and Captain Sterrett are among the wounded—the brave Commodore very severely. The President of the United States, the Secretary of State and the Secretary of War, were in view of the enemy, when they advanced.

———

"Since the above was prepared, we are informed Com. Barney was wounded slightly in the shoulder, and also through the thigh; by which last shot his horse was killed under him.

———

"From Ross' Tavern

"August 25, 10 o'clock, A.M.—No English on this side of Bladensburg. They are employed in removing the wounded and burying the dead, which are believed to be numerous. No houses are injured.

"3 o'clock, P.M.—Nothing further.'

"6 o'clock, P.M.—Ditto ditto."

The story was full of mistakes. The American army had not been outnumbered by four to one: its infantry had outnumbered the enemy's infantry roughly (but not roughly enough) by seven to five, its cavalry had outnumbered the enemy's makeshift cavalry ten to one, its artillery had outnumbered the British artillery by twenty-six guns to three; only one of the three was in action.[2] The enemy hadn't disregarded the American fire and withheld his own; the silent, unswerving charge was only one phase of the battle, along toward the end; there had been plenty of shooting before that. General Winder had not fallen back to Frederick; he was at Montgomery Court House, trying to pick up the pieces of his army.[3]

The wonder is not that the story was full of mistakes: the wonder is that it contained any truth at all, considering that even the commanding general himself had no very clear idea about what had happened.[4] But if the account in the *Patriot* was not quite correct, it was at least highly appropriate; there would have been something almost indecent, something sarcastic and disrespectful, about an accurate story of a battle so filled with mistakes. The real wonder is that so many mistakes could have been packed into any one battle, that so many blunders could have been committed in one five-day campaign. The *Patriot* said:

"We would with earnestness and deference recommend to all *our friends*, who we know, are all *friends to the Country*, to suspend opinions, as to recent events, and to unite cordially, in the public cause. We give this as a general answer to sundry suggestions."

There were reasons for that "general answer." Some of the sundry suggestions had come from cheap politicians who thought less of the public cause than they did about lining up future jobs by besmearing the men who now held them. Other suggestions had come from defeatists and blue lights and others from loose-tongued he-gossips, from plain scandalmongers smacking their lips while they nibbled at reputations. They say Winder behaved like a frightened old woman . . . they say the president . . . they say Major Pinkney . . .

The scandalmongers went to work with a will on Major Pinkney, commanding officer of the Baltimore Rifle battalion. He was too good a target not to be sniped at: successful, distinguished, one-time attorney general of the United States, drafter of the declaration of war, minister to the Court of St. James's, and now painfully wounded at Bladensburg. They say Pinkney was a coward. They say Pinkney ran away. They say he was shot in the back. They say . . . they say . . . they say . . .

The truth came slowly to Baltimore. With it came a slow, fierce anger. Opposition politicians, gleeful, said the whole campaign had been a comedy of errors. Ordinary Baltimoreans failed to see the humor of it: there had been too many senseless, needless, asinine mistakes. The campaign had been an asses' carnival. Now, when it was too late, everyone could see that the carnival of asses had begun a long way back. It had begun more than a year ago, when the enemy's battleships—bigger than any American ship afloat—had taken possession of Chesapeake Bay. Even then, in July of 1813, a Maryland general had appealed to Congress to issue arms to its own members and to the people of the District of Columbia for the defense of Washington.[5] The committee on military affairs reported the next day that they had "examined into the state of preparation, naval and military, made to receive the enemy, and are satisfied that the preparation is, in every respect, adequate to the emergency, and that no measures are necessary, on the part of the House, to make it more complete."[6] Whatever "examining" it did was done overnight. And Congress did nothing at all. Congress and the president and the war department apparently counted upon God and Napoleon Bonaparte to protect fools and children.

Only fools or children could have been so fatheaded or so naïve. The emperor of Russia and the Duke of Wellington had entered conquered Paris five months ago, on March 31st. Napoleon had abdicated and had been packed off to exile in May. By the end of June the whole country knew that a fleet of transports, crammed with regiments that had helped to smash Napoleon's grand army, were sailing from the Garonne to settle the American war and the American hash.[7] For nearly five months the United States had been alone against the British Empire, and still the government at Washington had done next to nothing.

Not until mid-July, not until the hostile fleet in the Chesapeake was powerfully reinforced, did the secretary of war get around to transmitting an order to call out the Maryland militia. And even then Mr. Secretary Armstrong, having stuck one toe into the icy water of war, hastily pulled it out again. Don't call out the militia, he cautioned fatuously, except "in the event of invasion."[8] Even as late as August, at the beginning of this month of disaster, the secretary of war "could not be made to believe, when the enemy was almost at the door of the capital, that Washington City was his object. 'What the devil will he do here?' was his question to one who expressed a belief that the capital was in danger."[9]

Pennsylvania was finally called on for fourteen thousand militia. But Pennsylvania found an error in its militia law.[10] Pennsylvania was very sorry, but Pennsylvania wouldn't be able to go to war until sometime this fall. The war will keep, won't it?

The cabinet was as happy as an idiot child. It was busy cutting out paper dolls—an army on paper. It was busy drawing lines on a map—a new military district. The map looked lovely. See?

We're safe now. No army can cross those lines. We're as snug as a bug in a biscuit or an ostrich with his head in the sand. The cabinet, sitting there fast asleep, dreaming with its eyes wide open, felt very military and very heroic. It would have fitted admirably into the burlesque role of that other cabinet minister who took it upon himself to criticize a general's tactics. "I think," said the minister, tracing a route on a map with his finger, "you might have crossed the river here." "Yes, my lord, if your finger had been a bridge." [11]

The cabinet gave a name to the region inside its nice black lines: the Tenth Military District. The district was turned over to Brigadier General William H. Winder, lines and all—or rather, lines and nothing else. He "accepted the command without means and without time to create them; he found the district without magazines of provision or forage, without transport, tools or implements, without a commissariat or efficient quartermaster's department, without a general staff, and finally without troops." [12] Even in Maryland, with the enemy on its coast and its coast vulnerable at a hundred places and already harried at a dozen, poor Winder was authorized only to play with the cabinet's paper dolls. He could put blue coats on the dolls—if he could find any crayons. He could organize and equip Maryland's quota of six thousand militia—if he could find any equipment. But he was forbidden to call them to duty "until the 10th district should be actually invaded or menaced with invasion." [13]

General Winder, Maryland born, descended from stout-hearted early Maryland settlers, energetic and distinguished at the bar, energetic but less distinguished in the luckless American invasion of Canada, captured and lately exchanged,[14] spent his energy to the utmost. He rode from one threatened point to another, with a map in his hands and with apprehension growing into a sick certainty in his mind.[15] His hands were tied. All he could use them for was to write letters. He bombarded Washington with letters:

"The enemy's fleet has now spent more than a twelvemonth in the waters of the Chesapeake; and during that time has visited almost every river falling into the bay; and must be presumed to have such accurate information, that whatever expedition may be destined to these waters, will have a definite object, to the execution of which, on its arrival, it will proceed with the utmost promptitude and dispatch. Should Washington, Baltimore, or Annapolis, be their object, what possible chance will there be of collecting a force, after the arrival of the enemy, to interpose between them and either of those places? They can proceed, without dropping anchor, to within three hours' rowing and marching of Baltimore; within less of Annapolis; and upon arriving off South River, can debark and be in Washington in a day and a half . . . he can be in Washington, Baltimore, or Annapolis, in four days from entering the Capes. But allowing liberally for all causes of detention, he can be in either of those places in ten days from his arrival.

"What time will this allow us to hear of his arrival, to disseminate through the intricate and winding channels the various orders to the militia, for them to assemble, have their officers designated, their arms, accoutrements, and ammunition delivered, the necessary supplies provided, or for the commanding officer to learn the different corps and detachments, so as to issue orders with the promptitude and certainty so necessary in active operations? If the enemy's force should be strong, which, if it comes at all, it will be, sufficient numbers of the militia could not be warned and run together, even as a disorderly crowd, without arms, ammunition, or organization, before the enemy would already have given his blow.

"Would it not, then, be expedient to increase the force of my command, by immediately calling out a portion of the militia; so that, by previously selecting the best positions for defence, and increasing . . . the natural advantages of these positions, the advance of the enemy might be retarded, his force crippled, and time and opportunity thus gained for drawing together whatever other resources of defence might be competent to resist the enemy? . . . Allow me, sir, respectfully to propose that 4,000 militia be called out without delay. . . ."

The letter never was answered. The urgent, anxious, obviously sensible recommendations were ignored.

The Tenth Military District—all of Maryland, the District of Columbia, and all of Virginia north of the Rappahannock—awaited the onslaught of Wellington's Invincibles with a defending force of 612 men! [16] The War Department actually had contributed two regiments of regulars to this host, but the "regiments" mustered a total of 330. Of the rest, 194 were manning the red-brick fort in Baltimore harbor, 39 were divided between Fort Severn and Fort Madison at Annapolis, and 49 made up the garrison of Fort Washington, fondly envisioned as the guardian of the Potomac and bulwark of the nation's capital. Not until the last week of July were the paper dolls taken out of the box: the governor of Maryland called out three thousand militia.[17] Not the United States—the state of Maryland. General Winder was in the federal service; he couldn't touch the new paper dolls.

On August 15th, the transports bearing the Invincibles were in the Chesapeake. By the 19th they were as far up the Patuxent River as their keels could go, and their boats and barges were pouring the troops ashore near the village of Benedict, forty miles from Washington across country and fifty, perhaps, by road. At nine o'clock that morning, Joshua Barney sent Washington its warning in a dispatch from Nottingham, higher up the Patuxent:

> One of my officers has this moment arrived from the mouth of the Patuxent, and brings the enclosed account. I haste to forward it to you; the Admiral said he would dine in Washington on Sunday, after having destroyed the flotilla, etc.
>
> Yours, respectfully,
JOSHUA BARNEY
>
> "Hon. William Jones [18]
>
> One eighty or ninety gun ship, flag at the main.
> Four seventy-four gun ships, one flag at mizzen.
> Six frigates.
> Ten ships about thirty-two guns.
> Five small ships.
> Two brigs.
> One large schooner, sixteen guns.
> Two smaller schooners about ten guns.
> Thirteen large bay craft.
>
> A large number of small boats are now under way, standing up the Patuxent, with a number of men, with a determination to go to Washington, as they said yesterday.

For the invading army, the campaign of Bladensburg was only a six-day affair. For the defending army, it was an even shorter campaign: it lasted one day less, because it began a day later. Not until August 19th, with a hostile force ashore, was Winder permitted to open the boxes of paper soldiers and take out some of them—not all of them, only some. And when he reached out to Virginia, where the paper-doll cutters had said there would be twelve hundred militia, he found only seven hundred. He found, too, that the politicians who cut out the dolls forgot to put guns on their shoulders: the seven hundred Virginia militia either lacked muskets or lacked the flints to make the muskets go off.[19] Winder could hardly believe it. The situation was so fantastic it seemed unreal.

If it were not real, it would be broad comedy. It would be a farce. It would be burlesque. It has all the sure-fire ingredients: it is the silk-hatted gentleman who forgot to put on his trousers: it is the Coney Island fun-house and the girls' skirts blowing up, except that this time it is the politicians' skirts—and schemes—that blow up. It is George Bungle and Casper Milquetoast. It is the universal prat fall.

That is why the battle of Bladensburg is going to be a natural for the wisecrackers. That is why it is going to be such a good joke to the politicians who don't like the president. That is why it is going to seem so funny to historians who have never been shot at. But men will be killed in messy, unpleasant ways. The men who die for their country will die without honor. They will lie dead without dignity. They will be buried as quickly as possible and forgotten as quickly as possible because politicians regret their mistakes and would like to forget the whole thing in the shortest possible time. Mistakes, found out and remembered, are very bad politics.

3

FOR A PAPER ARMY,
A PAPER GENERAL

If THE BATTLE OF GETTYSBURG IS a fishhook of Pennsylvania hills and the battle of Waterloo is the letter A laid down on the Belgian fields, the battle of Bladensburg is the letter Y with a tail that is sixty miles long.

The Y is made of three roads. The old road from Georgetown comes in from the west toward Bladensburg village in one short stroke. The new turnpike from Washington is the other short stroke, coming up from the southwest. They meet just west of the thickety bank of a shallow stream that is known as the eastern branch of the Potomac River; and the village stands on the opposite, eastern bank. The tail of the Y is the continuation of these two joined roads.

There is a kink in the tail just after it leaves the junction of the Georgetown and Washington pikes, just after it leaves the angle of the Y and begins to become a tail. It crosses the stream on a little bridge and sticks out through the town stiffly, as if the bridge and the town hold it up. After that, it hangs down through southern Maryland all the way to Benedict Town.

On the 20th of August[1] the invading army was marching northward up the tail of the Y from Benedict. The road ran fairly straight, paralleling the Patuxent River, till it came to Nottingham; there it began to turn westward on a long, slow curve that carried it through Upper Marlborough to Bladensburg; across the shallow eastern branch of the Potomac, and so on to Washington. At intervals of a few miles were side roads; they branched off in several directions, all of them inviting to the enemy.

The American commander had to make one prime decision—to attack the British army or to wait and be attacked. For Winder, the decision was instinctive. It was probably subconscious: he was a man foredoomed to the defensive by his nature. To him, now, there was but one problem: where would the attack come?

The British had five possible objectives. The road by which they were advancing led to Nottingham and the American flotilla under Barney. It went on to Bladensburg and forked there: the invaders could turn north toward Baltimore or south to Washington. And other highways led northeastward to Annapolis and westward or southwestward to Fort Washington on the Potomac, guarding the capital against a fleet that might come up from Chesapeake Bay. They also led to Washington itself, but the east branch of the Potomac was too wide and deep there to be crossed by infantry without boats; if two bridges were blown up or burned, the river would protect the city from direct attack.

As Winder saw the situation, he must be prepared to guard all five of these objectives. But his troops were widely scattered. On the 20th of August his potential army was nine unrelated fragments strewn across the Maryland and Virginia landscape:

Annapolis—in and near the town, but thirty-five miles from the enemy, there were "various detachments"[2] of the Maryland militia. They were not a unit, and they were not under one commander. These fragments of a fragment were parts of two regiments under Colonels Beall and Hood, amounting to seven hundred and fifty men, and a small battalion of one hundred fifty led by Major Henry Waring of the Prince George's regiment.[3]

Baltimore—in the city or camped in its outskirts there were at least seven regiments of infantry, a regiment of artillery, and a rifle battalion.[4] This force was the most homogeneous fragment of all; it had the most artillery; part of it was by far the best trained. It could take the field with more than five thousand men and upwards of thirty cannon. But on the 20th of August only two of the seven regiments of infantry were in motion and those two, under Brigadier General Tobias Stansbury, were neither the best nor the oldest in service.[5] Only fifteen hundred and fifty men, out of more than five thousand available, had been ordered to march to the front that had taken on unmistakable form in southern Maryland. The best disciplined infantry, the riflemen, the fast-moving horse artillery—the very troops that were needed most to harass and delay the advancing enemy—were left idle and useless, thirty miles from the nearest other fragment of the army at Annapolis, forty miles from imperiled Washington, sixty miles from the foe.

Washington—in the city there were two regiments of George-town and District of Columbia militia, one thousand and seventy men with twelve six-pounder field guns. They began to move on the afternoon of the 20th, toward Nottingham, and by nightfall had managed to march almost five miles. When they went into bivouac, it was "ascertained there was a great deficiency of necessary camp equipage, the public stores being exhausted; many of the troops were compelled to lie out in the open field; and of the essential article of flints, upon a requisition of one thousand, only two hundred could be had." [6]

Virginia—across the Potomac from Washington was a regiment of six hundred militia infantry and a hundred mounted men; they were not only motionless but useless, "completely unarmed."

Somewhere between Washington and Fort Washington—a so-called "brigade" of militia that included a troop of cavalry, a battery of three small brass fieldpieces, and infantry from Alexandria and other Virginia towns. Whatever these five hundred men were doing, they were not becoming a part of a concentrated army; they were supposed to be guarding the "approaches" to Fort Washington, but they took no part in the Bladensburg campaign.

Somewhere between Washington and a place called the Wood Yard—still another fragment made up of lesser fragments: two regiments of United States regulars, the 36th and the 38th, which between them could muster no more than three hundred men; "various companies" of volunteer cavalry scratched together from Maryland, Virginia and the District and amounting in all to no more than three hundred; and one stout oddment of a hundred and twenty United States marines with five heavy cannon. This "brigade" also moved on the 20th in the general direction of Nottingham, but probably was not much nearer the enemy than the militia brigade that marched out of Washington in the afternoon.

Somewhere—probably still in Washington, one hundred and twenty-five untrained recruits who were called, on paper, United States dragoons; and eighty men of the 12th United States Infantry.

Somewhere Else—An undersize battalion of militia—one hundred and fifty men under Major Maynard, and sundry other "detachments" amounting to two hundred and forty men under Lieutenant Colonel Kramer.

Nottingham—Joshua Barney's flotilla crews, not part of the army at all. On the second day of invasion, they were the only American fighting men within reach of the enemy. Overwhelmingly outnumbered by the seamen and marines in the swarm of boats on the Patuxent River and by the infantry marching up the Nottingham road, they were falling back and were in imminent danger of being cut off and destroyed.

To call these nine assemblages an army is inaccurate. To call most of these men troops is to misname them: nine-tenths were civilians. It is equally inaccurate to call the disposition of these forces a deployment. Their arrangement was political, not military. Most of the militia units, for their comfort and the reassurance of the voters, were still in or near their home communities.

But on the second day of the invasion, Winder had almost ten thousand men at his disposal. He had—or he could have had—no less than fifty field guns. And the arrangement of his forces, although fortuitous, was not too bad. They were distributed around three-quarters of a flattened circle that was ninety miles long, north to south, and forty east to west.

The British army was inside the circle. If it tightened quickly, it might be a trap. All the fragments of Will Winder's army, concentrated, would outnumber the invaders more than two to one; in artillery their fire power would be overwhelming. But the circle was so large, yet, that the enemy could move inside it freely. If it did not tighten quickly, it could easily be broken; all its fragments could be beaten piecemeal; already, on the 20th of August, the flotilla was beyond help. But defense of the four other possible objectives was by no means hopeless. The American commander faced a situation that called for the rapid concentration of nine widely separated forces. If he acted promptly and decisively, the nine could be brought close enough together to support each other and yet cover the approaches to Annapolis, to Baltimore, to Washington and to the fort on the Potomac.

But there was a tenth force in the field. Its numbers were small. Its strength was incalculable. It was composed of James Madison, president of the United States, of James Monroe, secretary of state, of John Armstrong, secretary of war, William Jones, secretary of the navy, George Campbell, secretary of the treasury, and Richard Rush, the attorney general. They were face to face now with the awful results of their do-nothing folly, their months of political hush-hush. But with the jobholder's instinct to hide his mistakes from the public, which pays for them, they still would not let the people know how deadly the danger was. They still would not upset the voters by calling out all the militia. Instead, they took over the army.

On the American side, this campaign has all the merciless, inevitable logic of a Greek tragedy. For a paper army, a paper general.

The politicians infested the camps. They filled Winder's headquarters, plucked at his coattails, alarmed him with information, stuffed him with advice, and even dictated his tactics. Their notions of tactics were silly. No two bits of advice were alike. And the information was wrong.

The secretary of state helped himself to a troop of dragoons and galloped away as a scout. He was—for he said so himself—"in sight of the enemy's squadron lying before Benedict" by ten o'clock on the morning of August 20th, and he "continued to be a spectator of their movements until after the action at Bladensburg." [7] As a self-appointed intelligence officer, Colonel-Secretary Monroe left a good deal to be desired—especially intelligence. His dispatches—often addressed not to the commanding general but to the president—were interesting enough as travelogues and they had enough capital I's in them to build a fine picket fence, but they were distinctly unhelpful.

Monroe was at Aquasco Mills, seven miles from Benedict, at eight o'clock on the morning of the 20th. By one in the afternoon

he had managed to get "a view" of the enemy's ships "but being at
the distance of three miles, and having no glass," he could not
count them. As to the number of hostile troops, he had "not obtained any satisfactory information," but he assured Madison that
"we shall take better views in the course of the evening."

From Horse Head, the next day, he sent a dragoon galloping
to Washington with the vital intelligence that he had "quartered
last night near Charlotte Hall," that he had "no correct information"
concerning the enemy's movements, and that "the intelligence of
the enemy's force in the Potomac varies here as much as in Washington" and he "had no means of forming a correct estimate of
it." [8] That evening, from Nottingham, he favored Winder with
a dispatch advising him to send "five or six hundred men" because
the hostile force in sight was "not considerable." Then came a
postscript: "Ten or twelve more barges in view. There are but
two muskets in town. . . ." And then another: "Thirty or forty
barges are in view."

By that time he had lost the invading army entirely. He
found it late in the evening "in the rear of the town" but he still
had no information concerning the number of troops in the
column, "having seen its head only."

Someone else, in the meantime, had managed to see it all.
Colonel Beall, veteran of the Revolution and commander of part of
the militia left idle at Annapolis, was reconnoitering on his own
account; he had counted the 4,270 men in the British column and
had come close to the truth. He sent word to Winder that Ross
had four thousand troops; [9] he also gave the same figure to Colonel
Monroe, who promptly turned it into "between four and five
thousand," added a suppositious thousand men in the British barges
on the Patuxent, and decided that "the whole force of the enemy
might be estimated at about six thousand men." [10] He thereupon
"hastened" to Winder.[11] So did Beall.[12] Others, unnamed, told
Winder that no less than twelve thousand British were marching
against him.[13] Beall stuck to his four thousand, but his commander
ignored him.

"The better opinion," Winder decided, fixed the enemy's
force at "from five to seven thousand." [14] Monroe was with him;
Monroe was a member of the cabinet; his word carried weight;
Monroe was the "better opinion."

But there were other thumbs in the soup besides his. There
were both of John Armstrong's thumbs: the secretary of war could

not make up his mind which one of his blundering thumbs was best: he dipped them in alternately and sometimes so rapidly that it is almost impossible to tell which one is which. Armstrong had not gone scouting, he was close to Winder, he could breathe on poor Winder's neck; being secretary of war, he was Winder's superior, and when he had an idea—no matter how pompous, how vague, how impossible to execute, or how contrary to the idea just before it—the commanding general of the army felt obliged to accept the idea as pure wisdom and carry it out as an order.

Having delayed for two years any sensible measures of defense and having frustrated for almost two months every attempt Winder made to create an army, the secretary of war was now all promptness and vigor. On the first day of invasion, he ordered Winder "to take a position near the enemy." [15] With what, he didn't say. Most of his other ideas were equally helpful. In one breath he informed Winder that "the numbers, equipments, and movements of an enemy best indicated his object"; in the next he said that "of these, in the present case, we know too little to speak with any degree of assurance" and thereupon he proceeded to speak with assurance. [16]

He assured the commanding general that, "with the exception of landing troops at Benedict," the enemy's naval force and the direction of the enemy's movement indicated that Baltimore was the objective of the invasion. [17] A trifling exception! The British army was ashore in Maryland, it was moving north on a road that opened half a dozen gates to Washington at distances ranging from forty to twenty miles; it was at least seventy miles from Baltimore; and the fleet, regardless of the "direction of movement," was in a river that didn't lead to Baltimore, a river so shallow that even the smaller transports had run aground and the troops had to be rowed upriver several miles before they could land at Benedict.

But Armstrong had more good ideas. No matter whether the enemy's objective was Baltimore, the flotilla or Washington, he told Winder, "our course is a plain one: assemble as large a force as we can; place it speedily at Nottingham, or other point on the Patuxent; clear the road between that and Benedict of horses and cattle; break down bridges; abbatis the route, when leading through woods; select strong points for defense; and, as soon as his movement begins, harass his front and flanks by small attacks made by night and by day, while Stuart operates in the same way in his rear." [18]

There were only two minor factors to complicate the exquisite plainness of this course laid out for Winder by Armstrong. Even on the second day of invasion, Winder had less than eighteen hundred troops on hand with which to do all the things that John Armstrong proposed so glibly. And the Stuart who was to do all these same things in the enemy's rear was no Jeb Stuart with veteran raiders to wield like a single blade: he was the Maryland congressman and militia general who had tried in vain, more than a year ago, to persuade Congress to arm its own members for the defense of Washington: he was the commander now of a few badly organized, badly armed, incompetent militia raised in the southern counties and theoretically "looking toward the Potomac."

Aside from these trifling flaws, Armstrong's plan of campaign was admirable. Armstrong himself admired it. "A plan of this kind," he told Winder, "strictly pursued, will soon enable you to judge of the enemy's strength, equipment, and objects. If the first be small and the second scanty, his objects can not be great nor many—probably confined to an attack on Barney's flotilla. If, on the other hand, he shows a respectable park of artillery, with baggage and provision train, his object may be Baltimore or Washington." [19]

Unfortunately, Major General Robert Ross was not familiar with John Armstrong's formula. He had no respectable park of artillery: he had nothing but three puny, hand-drawn pieces. He had no baggage, he had no provision train. He did not have even a detachment of cavalry to protect him on the march, excepting two or three dozen men mounted on commandeered farm nags with blankets for saddles and ropes for reins and stirrups. [20] But, lacking Armstrong's guidance, he knew no better than to march on Washington.

The route he chose was not the shortest, but it was at once the easiest and the most obvious. He was making for the fords of the east branch of the Potomac, where his march could not be halted by destruction of the bridges. He was moving at his leisure up the long tail of the Y that led to Bladensburg.

Slowly as the British moved, Will Winder moved more slowly. He saw the danger in the enemy maneuver. He saw, also, how to meet it. But he was the kind of man who grasps a thistle gently. It was his weakness to see clearly what should be done—and then fail to do it. He had seen the utterly defenseless state of the Tenth Military District; he had argued, warned and pleaded; but he had accomplished nothing. His unanswered letters to the War Department are the sum of William Winder. He is measured by his own half measures.

Now, seeing Bladensburg the key to the defense of Washington, he decided to put one brigade there. But he called no more troops. He chose, for the point of danger, Tobias Stansbury's two regiments of drafted men who were already on the road. They were county levies; they lacked even rudimentary militia training; they had no artillery. Behind them, in Baltimore, five regiments of infantry were waiting with eight batteries of field guns. But Will Winder could not bring himself to grasp the situation firmly. He could not make up his mind to concentrate the army.

The invaders had been marching across Maryland for three days, unopposed, before Winder ventured to upset the citizens of Baltimore by calling for a part of their militia. Even then, he asked for fewer than a thousand. He could have had three times as many, but he did not "deem it practicable to reconcile the people of Baltimore to march a greater number." [21] His timidity was groundless. The town went to war the way it went to fires and picnics, with a noisy gusto.

The departure of the troops was gay and gaudy, it was "stuffed with any quantity of romance." [22] To John Kennedy, eighteen years old, a private in the Dandy Fifth, it was "a day of glorious anticipation." He had foresight and imagination: he was going to a party. When the Fifth had "beaten the British army and saved Washington," John was certain that James Madison could do no less than summon the whole regiment to a grand ball in the presidential palace. That much was imagination. But he had his dancing slippers in his knapsack. That was foresight.

Johnny marched in "the ecstacy of a vision of glory." For "the populace were cheering and huzzahing at every corner" as the column "hurried along in brisk step to familiar music, with banners fluttering in the wind and bayonets flashing in the sun. The pavements were crowded; the windows were filled with women; friends were rushing to the ranks to bid us goodbye; handkerchiefs were waving from the fair hands at the windows" and "some few of the softer sex" were shedding deliciously romantic and becoming tears.

Private Kennedy, thrilled to the toes of the army boots that fitted his martial mood much better than they fitted his feet, could hardly believe his luck: he was in "a real army marching to a real war." But there was little in that Sunday afternoon excursion to suggest reality. War was so little urgent that the Fifth, the Rifles and Joe Myers and Dick Magruder's batteries were halted for the night at Elk Ridge Landing, on the bank of the Patapsco River. Colonel Joseph Sterrett of the Fifth, commanding the detachment, had no orders to go farther. The march had been much more like a Sabbath outing than a military movement, the camp was more like a picnic than a prelude to a battle. Half the town, it seemed, had come along.

The militiamen experimented gaily with the novelty of cooking pork in commissary kettles over fires of fence rails. When they burned the pork into a "mess resembling black soap in a semi-liquid state" they whooped and hollered with delight and dumped out the "compost of charred bones . . . plated over with the scales of iron which the heat had brought off in flakes from the kettle." Then they rambled off to find the private groceries they had thoughtfully stowed in the baggage wagons. They hired cooks on the spot from the crowd of admiring camp followers that had trailed them from the city, and they dined on white bread and "ham in abundance," washed down with chocolate or coffee.

And then Johnny Kennedy—and others like him—met the first of a succession of small, personal realities that were to change his notions about war. He was equipped with dancing pumps but he could not be bothered with the nuisance of a blanket. The day had been blistering hot; now the evening turned suddenly chilly, the grass was a cold bath of dew. The troops wandered about the countryside, borrowing bedclothes, and went to sleep late in the splendor of bright-colored comforts.

They loafed half of Monday away. It was almost noon—fifteen minutes after eleven—when marching orders reached the Landing. They were strangely urgent orders. Officers who read them wondered. *Why? What's happened? Stansb'ry got his orders Sat'day. We were ready then, too . . . long sight readier than he was . . . whole brigade's been waiting two days.* It didn't make sense. Two days had been wasted. Two nights, cool for marching, had been wasted. *Now they want us in a hurry, but they don't want all of us.* That didn't make sense either. Four full regiments were being wasted, left behind in Baltimore. Six batteries were being wasted. *If something's gone wrong . . . if they need us so bad . . .*

Almost everything had gone wrong. While the Baltimore militia took their Sunday afternoon stroll, British infantry was marching into Nottingham. Josh Barney, trapped and helpless, had abandoned his flotilla and was cutting across country with four hundred of his sailors, hunting for Will Winder's army. When he found it at the Wood Yard, twelve miles from Nottingham, it was only half the size of Ross's column; Winder, on the third day of invasion, had succeeded in uniting only two of his nine scattered forces.[23] While Joe Sterrett fretted the forenoon away at Elk Ridge Landing, waiting for his orders, Winder was advancing upon Nottingham without the slightest notion that the enemy had spent the night there. He was riding out in front of his small army with Monroe, his willing helper. The colonel-secretary had somehow been interrupted in his role of "continuous spectator," but now it was thrust upon him. For the British army, moving out from Nottingham, turned suddenly into the road that the Americans were using. There was no collision: Winder sent back orders to retreat so promptly that most of his men saw nothing of the redcoats. But Monroe scrawled an excited message to the president:

> The enemy are advanced six miles on the road to the Wood Yard, and our troops are retiring. Our troops were on the march to meet them, but in too small a body to engage. General Winder proposes to retire till he can collect them in a body. The enemy are in full march for Washington. Have materials prepared to destroy the bridges.
>
> J. Monroe
>
> You had better remove the records.

The dispatch was wrong. The British were not in full march for Washington. General Ross, having moved his column into the Wood Yard road, halted for an hour or so to see what the Americans would do about it. When he saw that they intended to do nothing except back away, he turned around and leisurely resumed his northward march.

But that brief British feint had shocked Will Winder badly. When he stopped retreating, he was at Battalion Old Fields, only eight miles east of Washington, and his fragment of an army was worn out with useless marching and disheartened by the knowledge that it had run away from an enemy it had not seen—an enemy whose remote, invisible existence had been terrible enough to chase it more than ten miles.

In Washington, the shock was worse. The last line of Monroe's dispatch caused panic. Remove the records! War was serious when it put the precious files in danger. Washington loved its official papers. It was fascinated by them. Lose its filing cases? Never! Government officials waylaid army wagons coming in for rations.[24] They seized some that were already loaded. Food for the army? Dump it! We can get another army, but these papers are important. The commissary was already scandalously bad; in four days it had managed to produce but two days' rations.[25] Now it practically vanished. Winder's weary soldiers would go hungry at the Old Fields.

Colonel Sterrett, fifty miles away, knew nothing about what had happened. All he knew was that his men were needed—evidently needed badly. Within fifteen minutes after he received his orders, the Fifth and the guns and the Rifles swung out on the Bladensburg road. They were only militia, and they were civilian-soft. But they made, in the next thirty hours,[26] a forced march that tough veterans might have been proud of.

The road was deep sand; the sand slid; it was slippery and slick as hot grease. The sun burned like a fire in a grate. The dust was a smothering blanket. But Sterrett began to press them. *Close up! Close up, men! Close up!* They had winter uniforms on. They had helmets as big as buckets, made of jacked leather as thick as the sole of a boot. They had water at first, but they drank it. The dust caked their lips and their sweat turned the dust into mud. They licked the salt mud. Their mouths dried. Their tongues were like stoppers in empty canteens. The sweat soaked their winter pants and the dust in their pants turned to mud and the creased wool was gritty and stiff. The grit turned the creases to saws that cut into their legs. There was sand in their shoes. There was sand in their socks. Sand—and blood. They began to sweat blood in their shoes. *Close up, men! Close up there! Close up!*

4

A DISTINGUISHED SERVICE

OF ALL THE OFFICERS AND SOLDIERS
in the field in Maryland on Monday, August 22nd, the man who
performed the most distinguished service for the United States was
Robert Ross, commander of the British army. The service was a
simple one. He halted.

By so doing, he presented the invaded country with its anthem.
He set in motion the sequence of minor incidents that made Francis
Scott Key a witness to the attack on Baltimore three weeks later.

It was one o'clock when his advance guard came upon a "straggling and wide" village.[1] Gentle hills enclosed it; great trees
rose above neat cottages set far apart from one another and each

"ornamented with flower-beds and shrubberies." A stream wound through the valley. One young officer was sure that he had "never looked upon a landscape more pleasing or more beautiful." He was "no lover of the American character or nation then" but he "could not behold this peaceful scene without experiencing sincere regret that it should suffer profanation from the presence of a hostile force." Neither he nor his commanding general ever knew the final consequences of that profanation.

Ross, too, liked the village and the valley. He was looking for a place to rest his troops before he struck out, hard and swift, for Washington. His successful feint that morning had been reassuring: until Winder's column turned tail, Ross had been a bit uneasy.[2] After all, invading this enormous, sprawling country with four thousand infantry and a few sailors had seemed devilishly risky. It might still be risky, but at least there seemed to be no danger of immediate attack. He decided to go into camp for twenty-four hours of "leisure and repose."

There, in the almost deserted little town of Upper Marlborough, begins the story of "The Star-Spangled Banner." The narrator is an Englishman—an officer in the invading army.

The next morning young George Robert Gleig, lieutenant in the 85th Foot, woke up refreshed from four days of campaigning. He strolled through the village to make "a renewed search after people and other living creatures." With him was a young subaltern soon to die in action. This is George Gleig's story, the first chapter in the story of the poem that was to become the anthem of the country he was fighting:

"The only inhabitants whom we found abiding in his house was a Doctor Bean, a medical practitioner, and the proprietor of a valuable farm in the neighborhood. The Doctor was, in point of fact, a Scotchman; that is to say, he had migrated about twenty years ago from some district of North Britain, and still retained his native dialect in all its doric richness. He professed, moreover, to retain the feelings as well as the language of his boyish days. He was a Federalist—in other words, he was hostile to the war with England, which he still persisted in regarding as his mother country.[3] Such, at least, were the statements with which he favoured us, and we believed him the more readily, that he seemed really disposed to treat us as friends.

"There was nothing about his house or farm to which he made us not heartily welcome; and the wily emigrant was no loser by his

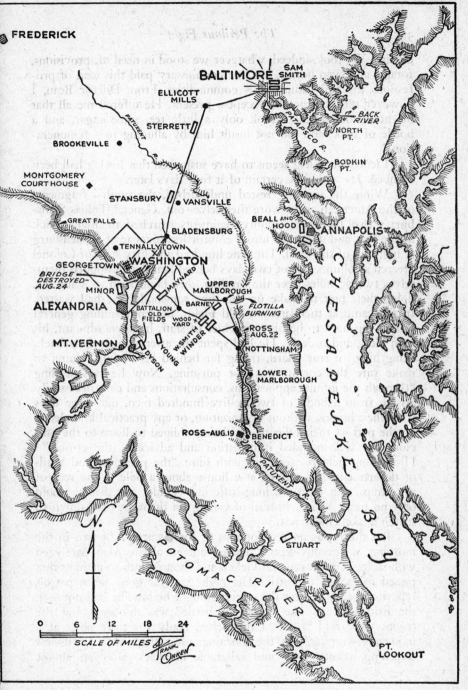

FREDERICK

BALTIMORE · SAM SMITH

ELLICOTT MILLS

STERRETT

BROOKEVILLE

MONTGOMERY COURT HOUSE

STANSBURY · VANSVILLE

GREAT FALLS

BLADENSBURG

TENNALLYTOWN

GEORGETOWN · WASHINGTON

BRIDGE DESTROYED— AUG.24

MINOR

ALEXANDRIA

MAYNARD

UPPER MARLBOROUGH

BARNEY

BATTALION OLD FIELDS

WOOD YARD

W.SMITH WINDER

FLOTILLA BURNING

ROSS AUG.22

NOTTINGHAM

MT. VERNON

DYSON

YOUNG

LOWER MARLBOROUGH

ROSS—AUG.19 · BENEDICT

BEALL and HOOD

ANNAPOLIS

BACK RIVER

NORTH PT.

BODKIN PT.

PATAPSCO R.

PATUXENT R.

C H E S A P E A K E

B A Y

STUART

P O T O M A C R I V E R

PT. LOOKOUT

N.

0   6   12   18   24

SCALE OF MILES

Frank ONKEN

THE CAMPAIGN FOR WASHINGTON—The situation about midday on August 22, 1814.

civility. We took, indeed, whatever we stood in need of, provisions, forage, and even horses; but our commissary paid this man of professions the full value of his commodities. From Doctor Bean, I however scrupled not to accept a present. He offered me all that his house contained; I took only a little tea, some sugar, and a bottle of milk; and did not insult him by alluding to a remuneration."

Lieutenant Gleig seems to have suspected that his leg had been climbed. He would be certain of it four days later.

While the invaders rested undisturbed, the sundry fragments of the American army wore themselves out. General Tobias Stansbury's two Baltimore County regiments marched themselves sick in the heat and staggered into a comfortless bivouac at Bladensburg at nightfall of the 22nd. The nine hundred and fifty men of Colonel Sterrett's column, almost two days behind Stansbury, flogged themselves twenty miles over the broiling, dust-blind road to Vansville, doing their best to make up the time somebody else had wasted. In the camp at the Battalion Old Fields, the commanding general was trying hard to be his own chief of staff, his own adjutant, his own clerk and orderly. He had spent the afternoon on horseback, being his own rear guard, riding far behind his fleeing column to make sure the enemy was not pursuing. Now he was wading "through the infinite applications, consultations and calls necessarily arising from a body of twenty-five hundred men, not three days from their homes, without organization, or any practical knowledge on the part of their officers, and being obliged to listen to the officious but well-intended information and advice of the crowd." [4] His willing helpers were still with him: "the president and heads of departments had arrived at a house about a mile in the rear of the camp." But even the long-suffering Winder felt that he could bear no more advice. Instead of calling on them, he "lay down to snatch a moment of rest."

But there was no rest for him or for his army. At two in the morning, a nervous sentry bawled out an alarm. Men paralyzed with sleep were shoved and kicked and shouted into something that passed for a line of battle. The night was far gone when patrols reported that, whatever the sentry thought he saw, he had not seen the British army. The "order of battle" was dismissed, but the troops were told "to hold themselves ready for their posts at a moment's warning." In the morning, after three days of useless marching, scanty food and miserable bivouacs, after an almost sleepless night, they were herded into line again and "were reviewed by the president and suite." It was doubtless thrilling and inspiring —to the president and suite.

Winder, too, received fresh inspiration. "At sunrise" he rode dutifully to call on the politicians and discovered that John Armstrong had invented a new set of tactics—the third set in three days. The secretary of war delivered an oration, highly patriotic, about Lexington and Concord. And then, having lectured Winder on the Minutemen's achievements, he explained that what they did would be all wrong now. He announced that if he were in command— and he was, being Winder's superior—he would "assemble my force in [the enemy's] front, fall quietly back to the Capitol, giving only that degree of resistance that invites pursuit. When arrived . . . I would immediately put in battery my twenty pieces of artillery . . . fill the upper part of the house and the adjacent buildings with infantry, regulars and militia, amounting to five thousand men, while my three hundred cavalry held themselves in reserve for a charge the moment a recoil appeared in the British columns of attack. On the success of this plan against the best-executed coup de main I would pledge both life and reputation, and earnestly recommend it to your adoption." [5] The enemy's "front" was at Upper Marlborough, more than twelve miles eastward; the "Capitol" was twelve miles westward. The secretary of war did not explain why Winder should advance east for the purpose of retreating west.

But Winder listened and "appeared to be pleased." [6] He decided to concentrate "all the troops within his reach" near Marlborough.

Off to Bladensburg galloped a courier with orders to Tobias Stansbury to advance toward Marlborough and "take a position in the road . . . seven miles from that place and four from the Old Fields." [7] Colonel Sterrett's column was still on the road, a full day's march behind Stansbury; but Winder hopefully sent orders that Sterrett, too, should move to within seven miles of Marlborough. Then, from his own force, he chose the eight hundred men who had made the longest advance and the longest retreat on Monday; they were ordered to approach the enemy "as near as possible without running too much risk." The rest of his own fragment of the army—seventeen hundred men—was left behind at the Battalion Old Fields under General Walter Smith, commanding officer of the Washington brigade. Winder himself, with a troop of cavalry, dashed off toward the road—the nearest of the two roads—that led from Upper Marlborough to Bladensburg. He hoped "to meet

General Stansbury, to make closer observations upon the road direct from the enemy to Bladensburg, and to establish more thoroughly a concert between Stansbury and Smith's command; to be also nearer to Beall, to give him also a direction toward the enemy on the road leading into Marlborough from the north, if my intelligence should continue to justify it, and to draw down Lieutenant Colonel Sterrett, with his force, as soon as I should ascertain where he was."

In other words, the commanding general was trying to be his own liaison patrol between the scattered segments of his army.

It was a hopeless undertaking. Now, on the fifth day of the invasion—on the day before the battle—Winder's army was still strewn across the countryside in seven pieces. Walter Smith's seventeen hundred men were still in camp at the Battalion Old Fields, motionless. The exhausted detachment of eight hundred, under Major George Peter, was feeling its way cautiously toward Upper Marlborough; just what it was expected to accomplish is not readily apparent. The seven hundred Virginia militia under Colonel Minor were still south of the Potomac. Young's five hundred were still guarding the "approaches" to Fort Washington; they were far out of touch and motionless and useless. The nine hundred under Beall and Hood and Waring were still near Annapolis and they, too, were motionless. Except for Major Peter's small force, only two bodies of American troops were moving in this last-minute "concentration." Sterrett's nine hundred and fifty Baltimoreans were marching hard from Vansville but the deep sand was dragging at them, holding them back maddeningly; they were still seven hours away. Tobias Stansbury was supposed to be advancing from Bladensburg toward Upper Marlborough with his whole brigade, but when Winder reached the highway it was empty: there was no sign of Stansbury and his fourteen hundred. Why? Where were they? What had happened? Winder was uneasy. The order to advance had been sent early in the morning. It was after noon, now.

What had happened was that a new thread had appeared in the dark pattern of disaster. This curious thread of General Stansbury's behavior has gone almost unnoticed in the crazy-quilt design of the campaign. The truth is that by the afternoon of August 23rd it had begun to dominate the pattern.

At ten o'clock in the forenoon a horseman brought to Stansbury on Lowndes's hill at Bladensburg a written order signed by the commanding general. It put Colonel Sterrett's reinforcements under Stansbury's control, it directed Stansbury to advance toward Upper Marlborough with all the troops he had,[8] and it notified him that Winder intended to join him on the road that day. Stansbury's two regiments were "instantly put in motion" toward Marlborough.

They did not move far. "After proceeding about one mile," General Stansbury "met Captain Moses Tabbs riding express" with information that the British "with their whole force" had left Marlborough, were "distant about six miles," and were marching up the road toward Bladensburg. "Toward me," General Stansbury put it. He did not set down the time of this meeting with Captain Tabbs, but it can be established with reasonable accuracy *if* Tabbs's information had any basis in truth. Two-thirds of the captain's news was wrong: the British were not marching toward Bladensburg or Stansbury—about whose presence they knew precisely nothing—and they were not "distant about six miles." The fact is that the British did not get within eight or ten miles of General Stansbury's force at any time that day. But if they had actually left Marlborough at the time Moses Tabbs set out to ride express, a curious fact appears between the lines of Stansbury's official report, like invisible writing suddenly made visible.

For the British, by their own accounts and others', rested at Marlborough until after noon; their advanced patrols were not in contact with Winder's outposts until after one o'clock. Marlborough was more than fifteen miles from Bladensburg by either the upper or the lower road. If the invading army actually was in motion when Captain Tabbs began his ride, the speed with which General Stansbury obeyed Winder's order to advance becomes very slow speed indeed. He received Winder's written order "about 10 o'clock a.m." He said that his brigade "was instantly put in motion" and "the march commenced toward Marlborough"; but he also says that he met Tabbs "after proceeding about one mile." The question arises: How long is instantly? Assuming that Captain Tabbs was correct in reporting that the enemy was on the march, it had taken Stansbury from ten o'clock in the morning until at least one o'clock in the afternoon—and probably until two o'clock or even later—to accomplish a march of one mile. While Winder sat his horse in the dusty road four or five miles southeast of Bladensburg and worried about Stansbury's missing brigade, Tobias Stansbury was retreating. So far as his official report discloses, he sent no word to his commanding general that, contrary to his orders, he was falling back.

While Winder watched and waited and his alarm increased,

three of his cavalry videttes came riding up with prisoners. They
had come upon a British scouting party and snatched two men out
of it. From the answers to his anxious questions, Winder came to
the conclusion that the enemy was still at Upper Marlborough and
had no intention of advancing that day. However, to make doubly
sure, he sent part of his own escort down the road toward Marlborough.

Presently, in the direction in which the dragoons had vanished,
there was a quick burst of firing. It ceased almost as suddenly as it
began. Then, somewhere to the south and east, more firing broke
out; it was heavier and it lasted longer. Winder, still looking vainly
northward for some sign of Stansbury's advance, decided that Major
Peter's column had run into other British scouting parties. But
again the distant *bump-bump* of the muskets died out. It had been,
he thought, a small collision of patrols; it wasn't serious. But the
matter of the lost brigade was deadly serious. Winder's anxiety
would not let him wait. He galloped off toward Bladensburg, hoping
every moment to see the dust of Stansbury's oncoming column.

Mile after mile the road stretched empty. The only dust upon
it was the dust that swirled up around Winder and his own small
escort. He was less than five miles from Bladensburg [9] when the
bad news reached him—from behind.

That second brief outburst of firing had been an affair of
patrols—Major Peter and General Ross's. But the British patrols had
four thousand men behind them, and Peter's had eight hundred.
The whole invading army was on the march. It had left Upper
Marlborough, it had moved straight west toward Washington. It
was already only three miles from the American camp at the Old
Fields. It had already thrust itself almost between the pieces of
Winder's army. John Armstrong's third plan of campaign was already falling apart: the intended last-minute concentration *before*
the intended retreat on Washington was already impossible. If the
troops at the Old Fields were ordered to join Stansbury—still out
of touch but presumably somewhere in the direction of Bladensburg—they would have to run the risk of passing in column across
the head of the British advance. If Stansbury could be found and
ordered to join Smith at the Old Fields, Stansbury's two regiments
would have to run the same risk.

Winder gave up his search for those two missing regiments.
He left two detachments of cavalrymen on the Bladensburg-Marl-

borough road to protect the regiments that he couldn't find, and then he rode hard for the camp at the Battalion Old Fields. The pounding hoofs in the soft dust of the road beat with a dull foreboding: too late . . . too late . . . too late.

5

WINDER GIVES AN ORDER
–FOUR TIMES

BATTLE MAPS ARE LIARS. THEY make chaos look as if it had been built to order from a scaled plan. The maps of the fight at Bladensburg, especially, give false impressions with their ruler-drawn exactness. The little blocks that represent the companies and regiments are smooth and clean-edged. Even the little guns, each gun a pen stroke with a shorter stroke on each side for the wheels, are ranged in lines as perfect as a drawing board can make them.

But there are no gullies on a drawing board. The hills are flat; the little blocks can climb them without panting. The symbols have a spurious authority. Looking at them, it is easy to forget that each of those neat symbols is made up of human beings . . . sweaty, hungry, frightened and bewildered human beings . . . men pitched overnight from comfort into danger . . . men with belly cramps and sun scald . . . men with blistered feet and crotches chafed raw by their woolen britches.

Bladensburg was chaos. It was fought without plan. But the fault was not Will Winder's.

Winder had a plan of battle. In spite of Armstrong's ever-changing, ever-silly notions, he had seen the point of danger clearly. He had seen, almost from the beginning, that the rambling village on the east branch of Potomac was the place he *must* hold. The army that controlled its five roads and its shallow fords controlled the situation. His own indecision, aggravated by the harassments of the politicians, had prevented proper concentration of the army. But on the afternoon of August 23rd, when the news reached him that the British were advancing, he acted instantly, decisively and firmly. He sent to Tobias Stansbury the order that would put his plan of battle into execution.

His plan was not carried out. General Stansbury, on whom he depended for its execution, either disobeyed the order or forgot it or misunderstood it or did not receive it.

The order was carried by one of Winder's own aides. It directed Stansbury to reverse his advance toward Marlborough—if he had begun to advance—and to "fall back and take the best position *in advance of Bladensburg,* and unite Lieutenant Colonel Sterrett with him should he arrive at Bladensburg, as . . . expected, that evening; and should he be attacked, to resist as long as possible, and if obliged to retire, to retreat toward the city.[1]

As Winder recalled the order afterward, it was the clearest, most direct, most nearly complete order issued in the whole campaign. Everything was in it—the situation, the movement to be executed, the position to be taken, the instructions and the authority to take command of the reinforcements from Baltimore, the positive instructions to fight "as long as possible," the direction of retirement if retreat became necessary, and—clearly implied if not stated in so many words—the rendezvous for the retreating troops, Washington. If that order had been carried out as Winder set it down in his report of the campaign . . .

There are so many *ifs* in the campaign that one more can scarcely be regarded as the hinge upon which to hang the issue of victory or defeat. But if there was a turning point, that order was the hinge on which it turned. The order was not obeyed.

The amazing fact is that General Stansbury had chosen *and occupied* the position Winder wanted him to take, *in advance of Bladensburg,* at least eighteen hours before Winder sent him the order to resist there to the utmost. He was still holding the position more than thirty hours after he first occupied it—more than twelve hours after Winder sent the order. And then he abandoned it almost immediately after receiving, by his own acknowledgment, a second message from Winder telling him that he was expected to resist as long as possible.[2]

General Stansbury had reached Bladensburg at seven o'clock on the evening of August 22nd with his two regiments of militia infantry. At that hour, the British army was in camp at Upper Marlborough and Winder's brigade was in camp at the Battalion Old Fields after its fruitless advance and its disheartening retreat. If Stansbury had any information concerning the position of the enemy or of the rest of the American army, he did not include it in his official report. But he felt perfectly safe—so safe that he divided his force of less than fourteen hundred men.[3] One regiment crossed the east branch of the Potomac by the Bladensburg bridge and encamped on Lowndes's hill, a thousand yards east of the stream; the other stayed on the western side of the branch, northwest of the town—a position certainly not much less than a thousand yards from the bridge. With no certainty about the enemy's whereabouts or intentions, these two weary regiments of militia were bivouacked a mile apart, with a town and a stream between them.

The next morning, when Stansbury examined the terrain, he liked Lowndes's hill better than the rising ground behind him on the west side of the stream. The hill commanded the roads by which the enemy might be expected to advance. The northernmost of the two roads from Upper Marlborough breasted the eastern slope of the hill and cut straight across its crest; the other, by which the British might come through the Wood Yard and the Old Fields, crossed a small ravine at the south end of Lowndes's hill and skirted the reverse slope until it joined the upper road at right angles at the edge of town. Field guns on the hill could wreak bloody damage on an enemy approaching over those roads. Stansbury had no field guns, but Colonel Sterrett's column was coming down from Baltimore and Sterrett had two batteries. Stansbury ordered his rear regiment to cross the branch and join the other on Lowndes's hill.

Thus, immediately upon his arrival at Bladensburg, he had chosen the commanding position *in advance of* the town and occupied it with part of his strength; now, early the next morning, he held it with his whole available force. He had selected, on his own responsibility and judgment, the position in which Winder, a few hours later, wanted him to be. He must have seen some merit in it.

When Stansbury reached Bladensburg, his brigade became the left wing of the army. It was potentially the stronger wing: it had prospects of being reinforced by at least eighteen hundred men— Sterrett's on the road from Vansville, and Beall, Hood and Waring's from Annapolis. The right wing was the twenty-five hundred men at the Battalion Old Fields. The two forces were farther apart than Winder wanted them to be, and the quick British thrust from Marlborough on the afternoon of August 23rd had forestalled a one army by a competent officer—if he had obedient and compejunction. But they were close enough together to be wielded as tent brigade commanders.

Stansbury had been neither prompt nor vigorous in obeying Winder's order to advance to a position seven miles from Marlborough. And, having marched one mile, he turned around and marched back to Bladensburg when Captain Tabbs alarmed him with false information. Thus, almost at the moment when Will Winder made the definite decision to give battle with his left wing *in advance of Bladensburg,* the commander of the left wing was retreating.

Fortuitously, this retreat anticipated Winder's order. But when Stansbury decided to fall back, he did not know what the right wing was doing; and, apparently, he made no effort to find out. In his official report he said merely that Tabbs's information "made me determine to avail myself of the high grounds I occupied in the morning, to which I immediately returned, and made the necessary preparations to receive the enemy."

Thus, for the third time within eighteen or twenty hours, General Stansbury demonstrated by his actions that he saw military advantages in occupying the high ground in advance of Bladensburg. He reversed his column and fell back to Lowndes's hill, first sending Moses Tabbs off toward Marlborough to "reconnoitre the enemy" and fetch back "every information." Already, at the time he began his laggardly advance toward Marlborough, he had dispatched his aide-de-camp, Major Woodyear, to find General Winder and to "communicate all the information which he might require as to my force; to receive particular orders as to the position I should take in the vicinity of Marlborough; and to obtain a knowledge of the country, and of the situation of the enemy." If, after he began to move away from Marlborough instead of toward it, he communicated that vital information to his superior, he did not record any such act.

Tabbs returned "about 4 o'clock p.m." with the news that his first report had been wrong, that the enemy was not moving toward Stansbury but "on leaving Marlborough had taken a different route." And "soon after," Major Woodyear also returned "from General Winder" with information that the "intelligence" which Stansbury had received concerning the enemy's movements was "in part incorrect" and that Winder still wanted Stansbury's troops to take a position "on the direct road from Bladensburg to Marlborough, at about seven miles distant from the latter place." Major Woodyear obviously had talked with Winder before the distant sound of musketry revealed the British advance and before Winder made the decision to give battle with Stansbury's brigade in front of Bladensburg. Winder obviously had been under the impression that Stansbury was moving toward the enemy. General Stansbury, on Lowndes's hill eight miles from where Winder's instructions to Woodyear would have put him, and informed by two officers that the "direct road" to Marlborough was clear of the enemy, did nothing. He stayed where he was.

Early in the day he had sent a courier galloping up the road toward Baltimore with orders to Colonel Sterrett "to move on with all possible expedition." The Fifth and the guns and the Rifles slogged into Bladensburg a little before sunset on the 23rd so tired they could scarcely stand, so hungry their bellies ached, so sick from the scorching sun and the choking dust that their empty bellies writhed at the first trickle of brine from the salty government-issue beef they had tried to eat raw. They had not halted to cook; they had marched forty miles in thirty hours; they were ready to drop in their tracks. But they were not given time to rest or even to make paste-soup of the musty flour that came with the doubtful beef. They were hurried across the Bladensburg bridge and out through the end of town to Lowndes's hill and into position with Ragan and Schutz's regiments as part of Stansbury's "necessary preparations to receive the enemy." They were kept under arms "nearly the whole of the night, without any sleep or food."

It was General Stansbury's intention, so he said, to reverse himself the next morning and to advance again toward Marlborough "at reveille." But this intention itself was quickly reversed. "At about 8 o'clock p.m., a militia captain who resided near Bladensburg, came into camp, attended by one of my sentinels, and informed me he was from General Winder's camp at the Battalion Old Fields; that General Winder was not in camp when he left it, and it was apprehended he had been taken prisoner, as he had gone out to reconnoitre the enemy and had not returned; that a detachment from the army had skirmished that day with the British; and that Brigadier-general Smith, of the District of Columbia, had taken command of the army, and would certainly join me in the course of the night." Stansbury set down this whole hodgepodge of fact, rumor, falsehood and imagination in his official report; he did not set down what disposition he made of the unnamed rumormonger who, on the face of things, had left the army and come home, spreading alarm as he came.

The probability is that nothing whatever happened to the anonymous militia captain, for hard on his heels came Mr. Colonel Monroe to stamp his tall tales with a phony authenticity. The secretary of state was still industriously fulfilling his self-appointed role of mischief maker, collector of false information and spreader-in-chief of alarm. "About 11 o'clock p.m., the Secretary of State, Colonel Monroe," was in General Stanbury's tent and "as well as [Stansbury could] recollect" was announcing that he had just come from Washington, that "he had been at, or heard from the camp of General Winder; that there was an alarming silence with respect to General Winder . . . and it was feared he was taken; that General Smith had, by persuasion, taken the command, and that they would move toward and join me before morning, he expected, from the Battalion Old Fields, and advised vigilance to prevent surprise."

There was one other piece of gratuitous advice that did not find its way into General Stansbury's report; it seemed, perhaps, too much at variance with the course of action that he chose to follow. But Monroe recorded it; he seemed, in fact, almost proud of it. Having done about as much as anyone could to upset Stansbury with talk of "alarming silence" and a missing commanding general (who of course wasn't missing), Monroe advised him "to fall forthwith on the enemy's rear."

Stansbury didn't know where the enemy's rear was—or where his front was, either, or his middle. Nine hundred of his twenty-one hundred men were worn to a frazzle from their forced march; they had just reached Bladensburg, had scarcely had time to pour the sand out of their shoes; they were in no condition for a night march in strange country or a night attack on an enemy whose whereabouts was unknown and whose strength was still supposed to be three times as great as Stansbury's.

General Stansbury did not "fall," either on the enemy's rear or for Monroe's advice. But Monroe had harrowed his mind and planted the seed of alarm. And the secretary of state had scarcely departed, his mischief done, when muskets began to go off.

Pickets on the upper road to Marlborough cut loose with a fusillade at a noise in the dark—a cow, or a dog pursuing a rabbit, or a wandering haystack, or perhaps another militia captain coming home from the wars. The firing jerked the whole camp to its feet. Exhausted men who could sleep through gunfire were yanked awake by their sergeants. "In a few moments [the] whole command were under arms and prepared for action"—so Stansbury said, and perhaps the statement is true. Comparatively, it probably *is* true. Even in the inevitable confusion of a night alarm in a militia bivouac, the troops on Lowndes's hill were probably better prepared for action than they were at noon the next day. For everything that happened in the twelve hours between Monroe's departure and the battle made them less and less prepared to fight successfully.

Young John Kennedy, for one, was acutely unhappy. Standing in line in the dark, he was acutely aware that his feet were swollen and sore from marching "in boots such as none but a green soldier would ever have put on." He had taken his boots off in camp and had put on his dancing pumps. When the flurry of shots woke him up and the long roll throbbed "from every drum in the camp," a messmate lighted a candle only to have it "stolen away by some neighbor." [4] In the excited confusion "some got the wrong boots, others a coat that didn't fit, some could not find their cross-belts." Now Johnny had sand in his dancing slippers. The sand hurt his feet. It wasn't romantic at all. It put right much strain on a man to feel like his country's defender at half past one in the morning, in pumps.

But Private Kennedy wasn't the only unhappy man on Lowndes's hill. The excitable pickets, shooting up innocent darkness, had made General Stansbury even more nervous than Colonel Monroe had left him.

The firing was on the direct road from Marlborough, the road by which Stansbury "expected the enemy" to come. Off toward Marlborough went Lieutenant Colonel Frisby Tilghman's detachment of volunteer Maryland cavalry, weary men on weary horses. Off toward the Battalion Old Fields went one of Tilghman's troops under Captain John C. Herbert. Waiting, watching and listening with apprehension, General Stansbury was laboring under three misapprehensions. First, he "expected the enemy" by the upper road from Marlborough, although Captain Moses Tabbs had told him in the late afternoon that the British army "had taken a different route" and although the information brought to him by both Major Woodyear and the anonymous militia captain indicated that the enemy had moved by way of the lower road in the direction of the Old Fields. Second, he believed that Winder's force was still at the Battalion Old Fields, even though Winder himself was reported to be missing and perhaps a prisoner. Third, he was "supposing" that his right and rear were "covered" by Winder's brigade. The facts were these:

The British were not on the upper road by which Stansbury, for some unknown reason, expected them. Winder's brigade was not at the Battalion Old Fields: it was in the outskirts of Washington, behind the eastern branch of the Potomac, after its retreat. And even if Winder's troops had still been at the Old Fields, they could not have covered General Stanbury's right and rear at Bladensburg: there was a road by which the British army could by-pass the Old Fields and advance on Bladensburg over the highway that came into town behind Lowndes's hill. But Stansbury "felt no apprehensions of surprise there, and no expectation that the enemy, without first beating General Winder, could approach . . . either by the Battalion or river road." (These two roads were in fact one road; they came together a mile south of Bladensburg.)

It was after two o'clock in the morning, and the troops on Lowndes's hill had been under arms for nearly three hours, when the cavalry patrols came back with information that the pickets had been shooting up the landscape: there were no British to be found on any road within miles. Stansbury dismissed the troops with orders "to be ready to turn out at a moment's warning."

The warning was not long in coming. The exhausted militiamen scarcely had time to crawl into their blankets—if they had any

—before they were hauled out again. At half past two, Major William Bates spurred into camp from Washington with news and orders. The news: Winder was not a prisoner, but neither was he at the Old Fields . . . Winder and his whole brigade had fallen back across the eastern branch . . . Winder had ordered the bridges burned behind him. The orders: the commanding general expected Stansbury to "resist the enemy as long as possible" if the British army moved by way of Bladensburg.

The news was heeded, but the orders weren't.

Stansbury was bitter about it: "Thus was my expectation of security from the Battalion and river roads cut off, my right flank and rear uncovered, and liable to be attacked and turned, without the possibility of securing it in the position I then lay." He "instantly" called a council of war—Colonel Schutz, Colonel Ragan, Colonel Sterrett of the Fifth Maryland, Major Pinkney of the Rifles. He "stated to them the information and orders . . . just received from General Winder, and [the] situation with respect to the enemy." The manner and the light in which the situation was presented may be surmised from his own state of mind. The result he set forth in his own words: "They were unanimous in opinion that our situation on that hill could not be defended with the force then under my command, worn down by hunger and fatigue as they were, and that it was indispensably necessary for the security of the army that we should immediately retire across the bridge of Bladensburg, and take a position on the road between Bladensburg and the city which we could defend. . . . Orders were instantly given to strike tents and prepare to march, and in about thirty minutes, without noise or confusion, the whole were in motion, and about half past three o'clock in the morning passed the bridge at Bladensburg leading to the City of Washington.

"Securing our rear from surprise, we halted in the road until the approach of day, with a view of finding some place where water could be had, in order that the men might cook their provisions and refresh themselves for a few moments. . . . At daylight I moved on to the foot of a hill near a brick-yard, and there ordered the troops to refresh themselves. This was about one and a half miles from Bladensburg."

The language is impressive. But the facts are not.

Stansbury himself had chosen the position on Lowndes's hill. To borrow the word he used so impressively, he chose the position "instantly"—he stationed his strongest regiment there as soon as it reached Bladensburg on the evening of August 22nd. He confirmed the choice next morning by placing his whole force on Lowndes's hill, and he confirmed it again that night by putting all his reinforcements in the same position. For a night and a day and most of a second night, he had been where his commanding general wanted him to be—*in advance* of Bladensburg and *between* the enemy and the upper crossings of the east branch of the Potomac.

Now, at half past two o'clock on the morning of the 24th, he had orders from General Winder to resist as long as possible if the enemy advanced in the direction of Bladensburg. He did not obey the orders. He retreated.

At two o'clock, he had "felt no expectation" that the enemy could approach him by the south road "without first beating General Winder." Less than an hour later, with the situation reversed, with Winder expecting Stansbury to prevent the enemy from approaching him by way of Bladensburg as long as possible, Stansbury was falling back.

At half past two, Stansbury knew that Winder had ordered the destruction of the bridges across the eastern branch of the Potomac to prevent the enemy from crossing the stream there. But at half past three, Stansbury and his whole force had "passed the bridge at Bladensburg," leaving the bridge itself intact and the shallow, easily fordable crossings of the east branch undefended at the very place where the enemy would approach them if he used the roads which Stansbury found so menacing.

A little after half past two in the morning, Stansbury's regimental and detachment commanders were "unanimous in opinion" that their men were so worn down by hunger and fatigue that they could not defend Lowndes's hill. At three, these men were breaking camp, loading wagons, falling into column, marching. They were being made more fit to defend some other position, not yet found, by being alternately marched and halted from three-thirty until after daylight, still without food.

At half past two, Stansbury was convinced that his right flank and rear were uncovered and in danger of being attacked and turned, although he was in the position he himself had chosen as the best available, although his officers had had at least some opportunity to familiarize themselves with the terrain, although the ground he held commanded both roads by which the enemy might approach, although his whole force had been formed in line of battle from eleven until after two, although he had patrols of cavalry on both the roads, although he had his six field guns in battery. But some time after three o'clock, with his whole force no longer drawn up for battle but halted in march-column in the darkness on a strange road, with his guns hitched, with the same menacing roads uncovered behind him, he was somehow convinced that he had succeded in "securing" the rear against surprise.

The battle of Bladensburg was lost that night, ten hours before it started.

Perhaps it had been lost before Tobias Stansbury gave up Lowndes's hill . . . days, weeks, months, even years before. Perhaps the delays, the inertia and the cocksureness of the federal administration had decided the campaign before the British transports sailed from the Garonne. Perhaps the meddlers and the mischief-makers and the three-plans-in-three-days strategists had made the loss of any battle certain. But if there remained, that last night, any chance of victory, it died out as the sound of tired boots died out on the bridge at Bladensburg, it was smothered as the deep dust of the road to Washington smothered the noise of the retreating gun wheels, it vanished as the rearguard vanished in the darkness on the west side of the river.

About three o'clock in the afternoon of August 23rd, General Wnider had decided where the battle *should* be fought.

About three o'clock in the morning of August 24th, General Stansbury—without knowing what he was doing—decided where the battle *would* be fought.[5]

Between those hours, General Winder followed what was probably the soundest course available. On the assumption that General Stansbury would obey orders and, by resisting as long as possible, would at least delay the enemy in any advance by way of Bladensburg, Winder placed his right wing in a position from which he could best meet any move the enemy might make. At sundown he ordered the troops at the Old Fields to fall back across the eastern branch of the Potomac. He gave orders also for preparations to destroy both of the bridges across the branch the moment they were threatened by the enemy's advance.

But the retreat was the beginning of panic. There had been no fighting except a few insignificant meetings of patrols, so trifling, so quickly broken off that they could scarcely be given the dignity of skirmishes. There was no pursuit: the invading army did not move from the position it occupied at three o'clock in the afternoon: it went into bivouac three miles from the camp that Winder was abandoning. But the American retreat became almost a rout. The march to the rear was "extremely rapid, yet orders were occasionally given to the captains of companies to hurry on their men. The march . . . literally became a run of eight miles . . . which unnecessarily fatigued and dispirited the men.[6] The troops, "much wearied and exhausted, encamped late at night" in Washington.

If his militiamen's nerves were on edge, Winder's were jangling alarm. If his troops were exhausted, they could at least lie down and rest during the night, but there was no more than "an hour or

two" of rest for Winder. He was as weary as any of his men; he had been in the saddle for days; his "harassing and perplexing embarrassments" had let him sleep only in snatches. He had worn out two horses, but now he borrowed another and rode to the president's house. He found Madison, but he had expected that he "should probably have found the secretary of war and other heads of departments there" and he failed to find them: "they had respectively retired to their homes.[7] John Armstrong, who had given him three plans of campaign in three days, was not at hand in this crisis. And Winder did not know that Mr. Colonel Monroe had managed to accomplish one more piece of mischief by riding to

Bladensburg and urging General Stansbury "to fall forthwith on the enemy's rear." [8] There is at least a suspicion that the president himself had a share in this piece of meddling: he, too, had ridden to Bladensburg on the evening of the 23rd. If either the president or the secretary of state had taken the trouble to tell Winder what they had done and said or even what they had seen at Bladensburg, he would have had a chance, at least, to avert the consequences: he would have known, some eight or ten hours before he finally found out, that his orders to General Stansbury had not been obeyed.

But the administration that had harassed him with impracticable instructions and perplexed him with false information did not bother to give him the one vital bit of information it possessed— that Stansbury had not taken a position *in advance* of Bladensburg, but had fallen back a mile *behind* the town. It did not bother to tell Winder that the secretary of state, with the president at hand, had advised Stansbury to leave Bladensburg altogether, to make a night march with already exhausted troops, to attack a supposedly vastly superior enemy, and to do all these things without the support of the rest of the army and even without the knowledge of the commanding general.

It was just as well for Winder's peace of mind that he didn't know what had been done behind his back. He was a pitiable figure as he left the president's house that night. The borrowed horse gave out and he left it at M'Keowin's hotel. Alone and lonely, he trudged back to camp on foot. He looked for the officer in command of the brigade, but Walter Smith was not there. Nobody seemed to know anything. There seemed to be nobody on whom he could depend to do anything. Still alone and on foot, he set out to make sure that his orders concerning the bridges had been obeyed. They hadn't.

At the first bridge, he found thirty men with axes but no combustibles and no preparations to get them; by the time thirty men finished hacking at the bridge, a fast-moving enemy could be across it and in the camp. There was no outposts to give warning of a surprise attack, no troops to protect the bridge wreckers. Winder scratched together a few volunteers and hurried them off to the upper bridge with orders to burn it at once; he roused out a few regulars and hurried them across the lower bridge as an outpost; he roused out a battery of field guns to cover it. There was a rumor that "some persons" at the navy yard were doing something about powder and combustibles to destroy the bridges. Convinced by this time—and with ample reason—that he could trust no one but himself to carry out the simplest mission, Winder trudged off to the navy yard.

In the dark, in his absorbed perplexity of mind, he missed his footing and fell headlong into a ditch or gully. He didn't know what he had fallen into, but he knew that he had bruised himself, had turned his ankle, and had wrenched his right arm. He was painfully hurt, but he went on.

At the navy yard, the commodore was asleep. Winder got him out of bed. Yes, there were "several casks" of powder, waiting in boats to be sent to blow up the bridge "when necessary." Winder was frantic. He was begging, now. For God's sake, give him enough powder to do the work. Give him material to burn the bridges. Don't leave it waiting in boats. Send it now! Haven't we had our fill of too little too late? We can't blow up bridges with powder a mile away. We can't burn bridges with firewood that hasn't been gathered. We won't need it "when necessary." It will be too late "when necessary." Do it now . . . now . . . *now!*

His arm ached. His ankle was torment. His mind was in an agony of apprehension. Back he tramped to the bridge, limping from one outpost to another, from guns to axemen to sentries, making sure they were where they had been told to be, making sure they knew why they were there. He was unable now to take anybody's word for anything.

It was three or four o'clock in the morning when he lay down at last to snatch a little sleep. Before sunrise, he was up again. He was sorting out his staff from the clutter of inert figures on the ground, he was shaking his aides awake, he was wondering how much longer their spent horses could keep going before they dropped. He was peering across Captain Benjamin Burch's six-pounders toward the east end of the branch bridge, peering northward across the huddled disorder of the bivouac toward the Bladensburg road, staring into the wan twilight for the first glimpse of couriers galloping down from Stansbury. He was waiting anxiously for news of the enemy last seen three miles east of the Old Fields, for news of his own left wing eight miles away at Bladensburg—supposedly in position in front of Bladensburg, supposedly prepared for battle to the end of its endurance.

He waited for hours. When the news came, he could hardly believe it. His orders disobeyed . . . the left wing not in position in advance of Bladensburg . . . Bladensburg abandoned . . . Stansbury's twenty-one hundred troops in retreat toward Washington without fighting, without even a sight of the enemy, without orders to retreat, with orders in fact precisely to the contrary.

And then, on the heels of that incredible and shocking information, came the news that the enemy was in full march for Bladensburg.

The British army was doing exactly what Will Winder had expected it to do. It was striking at the place where Winder had known the battle should be fought—the place where he had chosen the position to be held—the place where he had ordered Stansbury to resist to the last limit of endurance. And Stansbury had disobeyed.

Tobias Stansbury's retreat threw out of gear the whole mechanism of Winder's tactical defense. It left the road to Baltimore uncovered. It left the vulnerable upper crossings of the east branch unprotected. It widened the gap between Stansbury's troops and Beall's infantry coming down from Annapolis. It left these two forces—potentially the strongest segment of the army—without a rendezvous, without a plan of action and without a notion as to where they were to fight. It created an opportunity for the enemy to thrust himself between Beall and the rest of the army, and the fact is that Beall's column escaped being cut off by no more than thirty breathless minutes.

Indeed, Stansbury's withdrawal seems to have left him and his regimental commanders without any intention of fighting. For "early in the morning" of the 24th, Stansbury was sending Major Woodyear off to Washington to find Winder and inform him "of the exhausted state of the troops, and the impracticability of their meeting the enemy, in their present fatigued state, with any prospect of success, unless re-enforced." It was scarcely the message of an officer determined to fight until beaten to protect the rest of the army, as Stansbury himself had expected Winder to fight until beaten to protect him.

At daylight, a mile and a half to the west of Bladensburg, Stansbury had not yet found that nebulous "position on the road . . . which we could defend."

Between three o'clock and daylight, he had given up no less than five defensible positions—not including the position in which his three infantry regiments finally gave battle. In quick succession he abandoned Lowndes's hill, the town of Bladensburg, the west bank of the river, a curving ravine fifteen hundred yards from

Bladensburg bridge, and a second ravine five hundred yards behind the first.

All these natural lines of resistance had been given up. Stansbury's troops had been halted at "the foot of a hill . . . about one and a half miles from Bladensburg" and had been dismissed from ranks to "refresh themselves." Stansbury himself rode "to the top of the hill to examine the country," but he rode down again without having found a position he was willing to defend. When he returned to the foot of the hill, a horseman met him with a "note" from Winder. Not "orders," as General Stansbury recorded the message, but a "note," a "letter." By whatever name it may be called, it was certainly in writing and it was plain enough for Stansbury to understand that it was a message from the commanding general "directing" him "to oppose the enemy as long as [he] could should [the enemy] attempt a passage by the way of Bladensburg."

It was the second such order sent by Winder and admittedly received by Stansbury; by Winder's positive and detailed statement, it was the third such order sent. But Stansbury did not obey it; he "presumed" that it had been written without knowledge of his movements. Instead of obeying, he called another council of war. The officers present—Sterrett, Ragan, Pinkney—"urged the propriety of moving farther on the road toward the city, with a view of taking a stand on some more favorable ground for defence." Certainly, having left behind them five defensible positions, they were in a bad one now; with their troops dispersed at the foot of a hill, they were in no "position" at all. Certainly they were right in deciding that they must find "some more favorable ground." How right they were in deciding that the more favorable ground must exist "farther on the road," that it was some imagined place not yet examined nor even glimpsed, is another matter. Stansbury agreed with them; he "could not but admit the correctness of their views." Holding in his hand his commanding general's written orders to fight, he decided to continue the retreat: he "ordered the wagons to move slowly toward the city, intending to follow on with the troops." Searching for a defendable position but with no clear notion about where he was to find it, he intended to move slowly!

The intention was jarred out of him abruptly. At the moment when he gave the order, Major Woodyear galloped up.

Major Woodyear had been in Washington, he had been at army headquarters in the bivouac of the right wing, he had broken to

General Winder the dismaying news that the left wing, "instead of holding a position during the night in advance of Bladensburg, had taken one about a mile in its rear." (Even that was an understatement, since the only "position" Stansbury had taken was, first, a halt in column on the road and, second, a halt "at the foot of a hill.") The commanding general had listened with amazement. Winder was a gentleman before he was a general. He was to bear with dignity and restraint the unfair criticism and the brutal ridicule heaped on him after the campaign; his restraint was to be so rigid that he would refuse to use in his own defense the sharp-edged weapon of the truth that he might well have turned upon Monroe and Armstrong and the president; his self-control was to be so firm that he would describe his feelings about Stansbury's withdrawal as "considerable mortification" and would ascribe that officer's conduct to "misunderstanding or some other cause." Even such gentlemanly language indicates that Winder doubted the "misunderstanding."

But when Woodyear had concluded his report of Stansbury's unauthorized retreat, he found himself confronting a thoroughly angry man. The words Winder used were blunt and vigorous. Even in the mouth of Stansbury's own aide-de-camp, Winder's language was strong enough to bring Stansbury up short in his retreat and turn him around. The commanding general had sent Stansbury "an order to resume his position at Bladensburg; to post himself to the best advantage; make the utmost resistance, and to rely upon my supporting him if the enemy should move upon that road."

The instructions, as Woodyear delivered them, were vigorous enough to make Stansbury regard them as "positive orders." But somewhere in the seven or eight miles between Winder's headquarters and the foot of the hill where Stansbury was preparing to resume his retreat, the positive orders had undergone a change. Was it in Woodyear's memory as he delivered Winder's orders? Was it in Stansbury's mind as he listened to them? Winder said flatly that he ordered Stansbury *to resume his position at Bladensburg.* Stansbury had held only one "position"—*in advance of Bladensburg.* Winder had wanted him to be in only one position—*in advance of Bladensburg.* When Major Woodyear rode to Washington to report to Winder the beginning of the retreat, it was from the position *in advance of Bladensburg* that Stansbury was then beginning to withdraw. But as Stansbury acknowledged Winder's positive orders in his official report, they were "to give the enemy battle *at* Bladensburg."

The fact is that Stansbury did not *resume his position*. What he did was to order his troops "to retrace their steps *to* Bladensburg." But even this order was not completed in the literal meaning of his own words. The troops did not return *to* Bladensburg. General Stansbury did not give battle in *advance* of Bladensburg or *at* Bladensburg or even in the best available position *behind* Bladensburg. He halted the bulk of his troops four or five hundred yards west of the river and a little farther from the bridge. If he intended to occupy the third of the defensible positions he had given up—the river line—the intention was never carried into execution by the actual movement of his infantry regiments into that position. The three infantry regiments made up four-fifths of Stansbury's whole strength, but they were never in position to resist a crossing of the river. They were never within musket shot of the nearest bank . . . never within four hundred and fifty yards of the river at its nearest point . . . never within five hundred yards of the bridge.

The bridge, if not the only means of crossing the stream, was certainly the easiest, the handiest and the most obvious means. If not the only key to the position Stansbury at last selected, it was the best key. General Stansbury said that he detailed forty cavalrymen with axes to cut away the bridge and that he "saw them with the axes." But the bridge was not destroyed.

Stansbury said he posted his artillery so that it "commanded the pass into Bladensburg and the bridge." There is no other technical jargon that can be more impressive or more misleading than the technical language of war. There was no "pass" in any ordinary meaning of the word: there was no defile, no straitening of the terrain, no narrow passage by which the enemy was constrained to deliver his attack. So long as the bridge was undestroyed, the enemy might use it if he chose, but there was no necessity to choose it: the whole reach of the east branch above the bridge was shallow, fordable.

The guns "commanded" the stream and the bridge in the sense that they were on slightly higher ground. Some of them might have been placed where they could enfilade the stream, where infantry in battle line, advancing through the shallows, could be raked from one flank to the other. But they were not so placed. Some of them might have been placed to sweep the bridge from end to end. But they were not so posted: they could hit it only from an angle. From the position in which they fought, they could not command either the bridge or the river in the sense of controlling the crossing. Stansbury said that he intended to support the guns and guard their flanks with his whole force of infantry. But when the fighting began, the three infantry regiments were "several hundred yards" behind the artillery,[9] they were never close enough to fire a shot in its support. The fault was not Stansbury's. His intentions were good, but he was not permitted to carry out these last, best good intentions.

Now, with Major Woodyear's report of the commanding general's "mortification" burning in his ears, he gave the order to march.

6

THE CONFUSION OF TONGUES

Thin haze hung above the turn-pike. All the dust stirred up by the retreating regiments had not had time to settle.

In the dark, they had not seen it: they could only feel it, taste it, eat it. Now, where the turnpike dropped into the woods, the fine dust was spread across the road like spiders' webs spun overnight and stretched from tree to tree. With the sun striking through it, the haze even shimmered like a spider's web in early morning. It was goldeny and shining. When the first files came on, it swirled and eddied, it made halos for their leather-bucket helmets. But the men were in no mood for halos. The taste of dust did not improve with daylight.

Back down the turnpike tramped the weary and bewildered column. It churned up the dirt that it already had churned once, until it moved half hidden in another of those blinding, choking clouds that had become its constant torment. The woods wavered by, distorted in the drifting dust, half seen through bloodshot eyes. The left wing—the two thousand infantry, the horses, the caissons, the cannon and the cannoneers—moved like the tired ghost of an army wandering a ghostly forest. But ghosts do not sweat. The smothered column did. The August heat began to add its now familiar torture to the dust.

The woods dwindled and were left behind. The sun could do its worst. Men began to drop out.

The suffering column came presently to an extensive orchard that stretched for nearly a quarter of a mile along the left side of the road. As the head of each infantry regiment dragged itself abreast the orchard, it was turned off; the leading files squeezed their eyes small, crooked their arms across their faces, and plunged through the matted banks of weeds. The weeds, crusted thick with red dirt, exploded into clouds of reddish dust that bellied upwards and hung like the smoke of shell bursts with the fire still in them. The long, disordered ranks slumped to a halt between the orderly long ranks of trees.

Only the two batteries of Baltimore field artillery and the three companies of Baltimore riflemen kept the column. The road pitched toward the river and the little town. The guns came down the slope, the traces slack, the limbers crowding on the wheelers' heels, the cannoneers afoot to spare the weary horses. Just past the southeast corner of the orchard, the drivers swung their teams. Fresh clouds of dust exploded. The guns jolted down into the ditch and up again and went bouncing, yawing, sliding sidewise downhill, across the open ground. After them trailed the rifles.

Rifles and field guns, they came to a panting halt. There were, for a moment, no more commands. They could look around, they could wonder. They couldn't be certain . . . they couldn't be sure, in that moment, after so many marchings and countermarchings . . . but they could suspect. This was the morning and this was the place . . . the day and the field of battle . . . of the battle already lost. The pattern was working out.

The pattern was smaller, now, but it had not changed. It was still the letter Y. Four days ago, the strategic outline of the campaign had been a Y with a tail absurdly long, contained in the arc of a circle—all but encompassed by three-fourths of a flattened circle on which the American army was strung in bits and pieces.

At daylight this morning, the outline had shrunk a good deal, but it kept its essential form . . . the American army still scattered, but some of the fragments closer together . . . Colonel Beall's militia no longer at Annapolis but marching toward Bladensburg . . . Stansbury and the left wing a mile and a half west of Bladensburg . . . Winder and the right wing seven miles farther away to the west and south . . . the circle constricted, the lower end of the arc still trailing off toward Fort Washington and General Young's small brigade and the disorganized militia still farther away between the Patuxent and Potomac rivers . . . all those troops below Winder's bivouac useless now, out of reach . . . and the invading army, though no American knew it, pressing still deeper into the circle. At almost the same hour that General Stansbury began his retreat from Lowndes's hill, the British army had begun to advance again. By four o'clock in the morning it had passed through Winder's abandoned camp at the Battalion Old Fields; [1] an hour later it had reached a road fork from which one highway led almost due west toward Washington and Winder's right wind behind the two long bridges over the east branch of the Potomac, and a second highway led straight north toward Bladensburg. At that hour, Bladensburg was abandoned, the bridge and the fords uncovered; Stansbury's left wing was halted in column on the Washington turnpike with its rear toward the enemy. The British general had made use of the road fork as the basis of another ruse: he took the road that led straight west to Washington and held it until his whole army had passed the junction, then he reversed his column, countermarched, and took the road to Bladensburg. [2]

At sunrise—while General Stansbury was a mile and a half on his way to Washington and planning to continue his retreat, and while General Winder was hearing for the first time that Stansbury had fallen back without orders—General Ross had marched at least one of the ten miles that lay between the road fork and the bridge and fords at Bladensburg.

Now, in midforenoon, the strategic shape of the five-day campaign was becoming the tactical shape of the battle. The British army was marching up the tail of the Y; it still had six miles to march. Stansbury's 2,150 men were inside the arms of the Y; they were waiting to be attacked, but they didn't know where the enemy was or what he was doing; they were waiting to be reinforced, but they didn't know where Colonel Beall's militia was or what it was doing and they didn't know whether Winder was coming or not.

The ground where the Baltimore guns and the Baltimore rifle-men stopped was a neat triangular field—the apex of the Y. One side was the Washington turnpike, the other the Georgetown road. The base was the hill where the orchard spread and the infantry regiments flung themselves down to rest in the long, dry grass.

On the north side of the triangle and close to the Georgetown road, the field had been gouged up to make an earthwork—a bar-bette, they called it—a bank of dirt with a ditch in front. A hundred and fifty yards from the face of this fortification, the Georgetown road and the turnpike joined; from that point, the tail of the Y ran crookedly on for another two hundred yards to cross the Bladens-burg bridge. The earthwork had been constructed for heavy can-non, not for the light field guns of the Baltimore horse artillery. But it fixed the line of battle: Stansbury ordered the batteries to take their position there.

Major Will Pinkney's three companies of riflemen were drawn up between the barbette and the turnpike; down from the orchard where the three regiments were resting came two disappointed companies of infantry, detached to protect the left flank of the guns. The two companies of infantry were drafted men; they were supposed to be riflemen, but they had been equipped with muskets;[3] they were no more riflemen than the raw-recruit regular cavalry or the militia horsemen of that campaign were chasseurs or hussars or dragoons or any of the other impressive-sounding things they called themselves.

The artillery unlimbered. The drivers led the horses to the rear. The gunners wheeled their guns up to the bank of earth and found that they could shoot at nothing but their own position: the bank of earth was higher than the muzzles of their guns.

The Franklin Artillery and the American Artillerists had fine blue tunics and skin-fitting breeches, they had helmets with tall pom-pons on them. Whether they possessed that fundamental of good cannoneers—the hairy ears—their records do not say. Hairy or not, they all had dirty ears that morning, and a dirty job. The riflemen and infantry might flop down on the ground, but there was no rest for Captain Joe Myers's cannoneers nor for Captain Dick Magruder's. Off came the tunics—not so fine now as they were three days ago; off came shirts and undershirts. Half naked in the broiling sun, half hidden in the boiling dust, the swank artillerists attacked the earthwork with their spades and mattocks. They dug out embrasures, piled the dirt between them higher, ran the guns up into battery by strength of back and language. They threw down the spades and mattocks, snatched up axes, and cut underbrush and saplings in the thicket by the river, carried them across the field in armloads, stuck them up in the embankment. It was not good camouflage; leaves wilted quickly, their pale undersides betrayed as much as they concealed. But the earthwork, in the open field, did not look quite so naked and exposed. It looked, to those amateur warriors, just a little more like a position and less like a target.

It was still a target, natural and tempting: the six field guns—all the guns there were, in midforenoon—pushed out ahead of the main force with only five small companies to cover them. Altogether, cannoneers, riflemen and infantry, there were four hundred men to meet the first shock of the British army, the first shock of the Invincibles. Of how many Invincibles? Seven thousand? Nine thousand? Or that imagined irresistible twelve thousand? Even to the real British army, not much more than half as large as the smallest of those estimates and rumors, the guns would be an instant and inevitable objective.

For the guns were placed as if they were intended to be bait. Unsupported, that was all they could be. But no tactical trap had been set into which the enemy might be lured and caught. No ambush had been prepared, no masked counterblow had been devised or even thought of. There was no disposition of troops, either actual or contemplated, for which the precious guns and the four hundred men could serve as useful bait, as a deliberate sacrifice to tempt the enemy to his destruction. But there they were, set out like bait . . . six small, slow-firing guns . . . four hundred men. Live bait.

The embrasures and the camouflage were finished. There was time now for the cannoneers to sprawl out on the ground, to wander down the field into the hot shade of the thickets, to ease off up the hill into the edges of the orchard. It was hot everywhere. Even sitting still, a man could feel the sweat ooze out of him. The sweating turned the red dirt on him into mud. He could try to slap the dirt out of his pants and see that all the slapping did was rub the dirt in and make it solider; he could give it up and try to wipe his hands clean on his pants instead. That worked a little better, but not much.

When his hands were anyways a little cleaner, he could try to wipe the dirt and sweat off of his face, and feel the bristles of his three-day beard. He could make a stab at wiping the dirt and sweat off his chest and belly, and see the white smeared marks his fingers left, like weals, between the streaks of muck. He could look at the man sprawled next to him, and realize that his own face must look like that—the same red-rimmed eyes, the same stubbled chin, the same sun-scalded lump of red meat for a nose, the same white finger streaks across the grimy cheeks like war paint on a Nanticoke. They looked like dirty, painted savages, the lot of them. They surely didn't look like gentlemen.

They didn't even look like the Franklin Artillery and the American Artillerists. There wasn't a smidgin of resemblance between them and the gunners standing rammer-straight beside the shining black six-pounders in the Gay street gun house, drill nights, or squiring the girls at the battery dances. *If the girls could see us now. . . .* It's a damn' good thing they can't. *It's a damn' good thing they can't smell us, either. Jehosaphat, how we stink!* We surely do. If we stink as bad as this after three-four days, I'd hate to smell us, myself, after three-four months. *Don't worry about that. You'll be used to it then, you won't mind it. And you can buy cologne for the girls.* The hell we can. There ain't that much cologne in the world. Hey, Joe . . . *beg pardon, sir; I know; I forgot . . .* Captain Myers, we'd feel a lot better if we could peel off these festerin' britches an' take a runnin' jump into the branch. D'you think there'd be time, Joe . . . sir? Does the captain suppose we could? There was time, but they couldn't.

There was time, too, in the orchard behind the guns. The infantry had no embrasures to dig, it had no cannon to wrestle. There was no need for the infantry to hack and whack, to fetch and carry, to transplant bushes and saplings. It had all the shade it needed, and all the concealment as well: the orchard had been there a right long time: the trees were old and broadbacked and round-shouldered, they were thick with the summer's growing and bent with the summer's fruit: their branches were laced and mingled together. This wasn't a half-bad place.

The Fifth Maryland felt right snug, sprawled out on the matted grass, under the sprawling trees. This wasn't so different from lying under the trees in the picnic grove at Rutter's Spring, 'way back to Bal'more. If you closed your eyes so you couldn't see the dirty, unshaved, bleary-eyed faces around you, you could almost fool yourself, you could almost make yourself think that the pain in your middle was too much fried chicken and too much potato salad and too many watermelon pickles and too many toasts to the ladies. If you closed your eyes and closed your mind against the sweaty-wool smell of yourself and put your arm around your knapsack and blanket roll, you could almost fool yourself into thinking the blanket roll was a girl.

There was time to think about every girl you had ever known. There was time to trace a girl's name with your finger tip in the dust on the broad, round top of your leather shako. The leather showed up clean and glinty-black, it had a sheen like the wide, waiting, wondering pupils of a girl's dark eyes, close, coming closer. There was time to sit there cross-legged and look at the name and think, until the sergeant came along and raised blue bloody hell and you had to swab the dust off, name and all. It wasn't the sergeant's shako. It wasn't the sergeant's girl, either. *Oh, what the hell!* Let's get out of here. It's too hot to sleep. The God-damned sergeants and crickets and things won't let a man sleep or think. I don't want to think. I don't want to sleep. *There's something about this day . . .*

There was time to wander down through the orchard, ducking and twisting under the low-bent limbs, until you came to the edge of the trees, on the brow of the hill. There was time to figure how far you had marched in three days . . . how far you had marched for nothing . . . to count up the hours you had stayed awake for nothing. We passed this place yesterday, coming in from Bal'more. We passed it again about half past three this morning, marching the other way. If they wanted us here, why the devil didn't they say so? What is there about this place that's better than any other? How the hell do you know a battlefield when you see one? It doesn't look like a battlefield to me.

It was just ordinary-looking. It was just mildly pleasant and placid and stupid-still hot. Except for its triangle shape, the field in front of the orchard was an ordinary field, a little shabby and threadbare with August, patched here and there with weeds. Off to the left behind the guns, between the north corner of the orchard and the Georgetown road, a big barn stood in the corner of the field—weathered and raw and drab, about as ordinary as a barn could be. The road to Georgetown ran out of sight behind it and came into sight again, climbing up the hill. Still farther off to the left, across the road and about on a line with the guns, there was a little mill—a story-and-a-half affair with a lean-to snuggled against it—and a little creek and a milldam. The creek slid past the mill, over the dam, and ran down to the river that wasn't much more than a good-sized creek itself.

Down front, where the field came into a point and the roads came together, a sentry stood smack in the crossroads, smack in the blazing sun. In the flat ground this side of the little river, the thickets looked almost as hot as the sentry. The willows and larches had put on a sick-and-tired look. They looked droopy and breathless and limp in the dead-still heat. Over the thickety growth and through it, a man could see the gleam of the river—a smooth, still shine in the deeper pools and little, wrinkled shimmers along the bars. Down there to the right, the road squirmed away from the point of the field like a snake—a dusty, coppery-bodied snake—and crawled across the bridge and up to the town on the other side. The stream crawled under the bridge, not seeming to move any more than the road was moving, and curved in toward the thickets. The thickets got deeper and taller, there below the bridge; they turned into woods, and the woods crowded close to the stream and mostly hid it. But the far bank was level and clear. You could see the town, strung out along one street. You could see the road crawl up to it, about in its middle, and you could see both ends of the town pull back, away from it, as if the road was a snake sure enough and the town didn't want to get bit. But the road crawled right between the brick houses and turned itself into the main street until it came to the far east end of the town, out toward the rise of Lowndes's hill. There it squirmed again and turned south. You could see it for quite a ways, not squirming nor wriggling sidewise now but humping itself over the little swells of the ground, going off toward Battalion Old Fields, following along the river but keeping two hundred and fifty or three hundred yards away.

There was a queer thing about the town. The sun had climbed well up into the sky, there wasn't a scrap of cloud, but the town looked dull, it wasn't bright and shiny-looking the way it had been an hour or so ago. The upstairs windows along the opposite side of the strung-out street had had bright glints on their little panes, an hour or so ago. They had looked right cheerful. But most of the glints were gone, now; window by window, six small panes at a time, the houses across the street had turned sort of blank; it was downright odd. You figured it out, afterwhile. It meant that the sun was getting hot, down there in the little town.

The sun didn't strike the windows across the street, it struck the ones on this side, the windows you couldn't see: the reflections had kindled the fiery glints in the ones on the opposite side of the street. Now the sun was burning into the windows on this side and the women were closing the shutters against it, the reflections were going out.

It wasn't noon. It wasn't eleven, quite. But something was going to happen. There were feathers of dust on the roads across the Potomac branch—on the river road, south toward the Old Fields, and east on the road that came over Lowndes's hill. They were small, too small to be raised by a sizable column.

The feathers of dust came fast, they didn't rise high, there was no wind to lift them. The two horses came into the town like two scuttering hens with two brown-dust roosters behind them and feathers flying. They weren't a minute apart when they skurried over the bridge. It was like a race, and the horse from the eastward won it; the both of them went out of sight, past the orchard somewheres, or in it. And then pretty soon another horseman . . . with the dust on his clothes, you couldn't tell what he was, chasseur or dragoon or officer or man from the ranks . . . was tearing downhill from the orchard and over the bridge and up the main street of the village and breasting Lowndes's hill, and another was galloping up the Washington pike toward the rear. Now what's *that* about?

Part of the news sifted down to the company officers, after a while, and on down to the men. The British were coming. No mistake, this time: they were on the river road, they were heading for Bladensburg, they were only three and a half miles away. But the rest of the news did not reach the first line, it did not reach even the infantry colonels. Colonel Beall with his seven hundred and fifty Anne Arundel militia was coming down from Annapolis, he was coming in on the road that intersected the river road at the eastern end of the town, he was five miles away. It was going to be a race. It was going to be a race in dead earnest, with the finish line right over there in the village. But Major Pinkney wasn't told, and the consequence was another needless—though harmless—alarm.

And neither Major Pinkney nor the regimental commanders knew—so they said—until after the battle was over, that this was a three-horse race. They were not informed that Winder's troops, too, were racing for Bladensburg now. Winder needed **no** galloping courier from Stansbury to tell him the enemy was moving north on the river road. He had known it since ten o'clock, and his own troops were marching up the west side of the Potomac branch while the British marched up the east side. At eleven o'clock the American left wing, slogging north on the Washington pike as hard as it could slog, was a little farther from Bladensburg than the enemy's column was, and not quite so far distant as Beall's men on their forced march from Annapolis.

As the sun crept toward the zenith, the three dust clouds crept toward Bladensburg and toward each other. The circle was growing smaller. The pattern was shrinking swiftly now, but it was still unchanged. All the men with guns in their hands were moving in toward the apex of the Y.

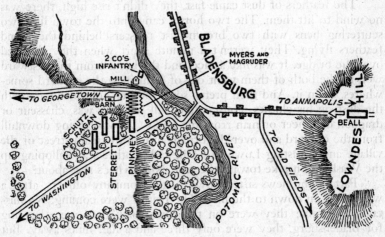

STANSBURY'S DEPLOYMENT—about 11:30 a.m., August 24.

Sometime between eleven o'clock and noon, Stansbury took his second—and last—step toward giving physical shape to the plan he had formed in his mind. It was not a long step. Orders went to the infantry colonels. The drummers slung their drums. The long roll throbbed through the orchard. Men heard it and groaned; they roused themslves from their sleep or gave up, with a kind of relief, the futile effort to sleep; they scrabbled around in the brittle dead grass for shoes and canteens and the oddments that fall out of knapsacks; they straggled into irregular ranks, buttoning their clothes as they came. The ranks marched a few yards and halted. And stood. And waited.

In the matted orchard, the infantry couldn't see what was going on. But down in the field, the gunners could see, and Will Pinkney's Rifles could see. What was going on was nothing.

It went on endlessly, through minutes that stretched like hours . . . like days . . . like weeks . . . like a whole damned calendar of weeks and months. Just a somnolent, placid town. Just the empty roads. Just the woods that moped in the sun. Just nothing . . . forever . . . amen.

And then, at last, something . . . something far down the valley, a kind of impalpable quiver above the woods . . . something far eastward across the valley, too, a place where the sun-burnished sky turned dull, a thin shiver and shake of something that might be only the heat haze but might be dust. Cannoneers, hunched in the dwindling shade of embrasures, got to their feet to look. Riflemen, sprawled in the stubbled field, stood up to watch, their heads turning south and then east and then south again. By Godfrey, it *was* dust! Dust on the river road, dust on the upper road. What did it mean? Were the British coming from *two* directions?

While the cloud on the river road was still faint, its movement scarcely to be discerned, the cloud to the east grew darker and larger. It traveled fast. The head of a column broke the sky-line above Lowndes's hill, and Will Pinkney began to give orders. The riflemen picked themselves up from the stubble, fell into ranks, moved down to the foot of the field. There were bushes there; a fence ran along the slope of the bank that ended the field. Part of the rifles spread out in a line behind the fence, the others climbed over and pushed on down toward the bridge. Will Pinkney took his stand at the top of the bank, in the open field, with the battalion adjutant and the sergeant major beside him. The adjutant's name was Will Pinkney, too, with "junior" attached. Father and son, they watched the advancing troops pour over the crest of Lowndes's hill.

But the troops were not British. The hurrying column was Beall's. It had gained in the race with Ross, but the finish was going to be tight.

Stouthearted, tough-minded, old Revolution soldier, Colonel William Dent Beall had disobeyed Stansbury's orders. But not to escape from danger . . . to face it. The messenger Stansbury sent at eleven o'clock had carried a warning to Beall that the British were coming on and had given him counsel of caution. Stansbury had heard that somewhere off to the left was "an old road." File off the main road, he urged Beall; don't try to reach Bladensburg; cross the branch somewhere above the town and take a position on the high ground to the north or northwest.⁴ But Colonel Beall was taking no chances on a roundabout road that Stansbury "understood" was available. He preferred the risk of meeting the enemy to the risk of being too late. He sent his baggage off to hunt for the by-pass, but he matched his militiamen's legs against the legs of the British.⁵ He had five miles or a little less to go, then; the British had three and a half. His men had covered eleven miles or more already this morning, the British eight or nine. But now Beall found a will in his troops to match his own will. He urged them along so stoutly, cajoled them or drove them, kept them so well closed up, that the motley militia outmarched the Invincibles.

By noon the enemy column was plainly visible, a mile or more down the valley from Lowndes's hill. But the dust of Beall's column was rising like smoke in the eastern end of the town.

Sweat-soaked, staggering-tired, panting with mouths wide open to suck in the choking dust, his militia came down the street at a shambling run. They turned left at the bend of the town, they flooded across the bridge, they came up the pike in disorderly, strung-out files. They weren't running now; they had won the race. They climbed the hill in a daze of exhaustion; their dirt-masked faces stared straight ahead at the climbing road; they passed, grotesque and unreal, and vanished beyond the orchard.⁶

Will Pinkney called his companies back from the fence and the bushes. They threw themselves down again in the open field. It was anticlimax. It was anteclimax as well. That quivering, thickening cloud on the river road wasn't reinforcements; it couldn't be reinforcements; a thing like that didn't happen twice. Well, it *could*. The riflemen argued about it. *There's more men than just us in this army. There must be. What's become of the Washington men? They say Winder's got a brigade. Washington's their town, ain't it? Then whyn't they come out an' fight?* They are coming. But no one has taken the trouble to tell the Maryland troops that Winder's brigade is hurrying up the turnpike.

The two batteries and the rifles and the two companies of infantry were still the first line, alone. That was all they knew. They could wait. They could wonder. There was still time to wonder how you were going to feel when the first gun went off . . . to wonder how soon it would happen . . . to wonder how Dick Magruder would measure up to the job of handling a battery under

fire and how he was feeling now. Captain Dick was all right, he
was good at drill, he was hell on keeping the guns shined up. But
he hadn't been in a battle, he never had laid a gun on a column of
men coming toward him with bayonets fixed. You couldn't help
wondering whether six small guns could stop a bayonet charge.
You looked at them . . . six black guns in a row behind a barbette
about seven sizes too big. That was likely the reason the guns
looked littler than common, the earthwork being so big. They
were loaded in earnest now. Each one had a round iron ball in its
throat, an iron ball that was supposed to weigh just six pounds and
possibly did . . . but it probably didn't, too [7] . . . and when you
laid the match to the touchhole the ball would likely as not go
farther than you intended, or not so far.

You ought to could hit that bridge down there with a six-
pound ball. But suppose you missed . . . could the bayonets cross
that field before you could load again? If they did. . . . You swallowed . . . anyways you tried to and couldn't. The six iron guns
weren't the only things that had six-pound lumps in their throats.

You couldn't help wondering why the army was staying back
there in the orchard. The three infantry regiments couldn't give the
guns and the rifles much help from back there. They couldn't give
any help at all, 'way back there. *Well, now . . . well . . . look at
that . . . they're moving. The infantry's coming out of the orchard.
That's more like it . . . that's better.* The cannoneers and the riflemen took a deep breath of comfort.

The three regiments were moving at last. Monroe had arrived
on the field.

Mr. Colonel Monroe was still energetic, still playing his dashing role. He had been at Winder's headquarters when, about ten
o'clock, the videttes brought definite news that the British had
stopped playing tricks and were marching for Bladensburg. The
president and most of the cabinet had been at headquarters too—the
secretary of war, the secretary of the treasury, the attorney general and the secretary of the navy, as well as the secretary of state.
They had been indulging in a "rather desultory" conversation in
which "no idea seemed to be entertained that it was necessary to
come instantly to a decision how we should act, and to set immediately about it." The president noted that Mr. Campbell, his secretary of the treasury, was "in a very languid state"—not too languid,
however, to tell Madison he was "grieved" because the secretary of
war felt that "it might not be delicate" to furnish General Winder

with advice based on his "military knowledge and experience."
John Armstrong had not been too delicate to give Winder four
plans of campaign in four days; indeed, on this very morning, he
had given Winder a fifth plan. He had even taken it upon himself
to give orders to Winder's troops: he had "advised" Joshua Barney
to "join the army at Bladensburg, and ordered Minor's regiment
to that place." He had also "advised" Winder "to leave Barney and
the Baltimore brigade upon the enemy's rear and right flank, while
he put himself in front with all the rest of his force." One trifling
flaw in this new plan of campaign was that Armstrong did not
know which was the enemy's rear and which was his front, he did
not know that since dawn, or earlier, the enemy had been marching north to force the Potomac branch crossing.

But President Madison took Mr. Campbell's grief to heart.
He assured the secretary of the treasury that he would speak to
the secretary of war "explicitly on the subject," and "turning my
horse to him, expressed to him my concern and the surprise at the
reserve he showed at the present crisis, and at the scruples I understood he had at offering his advice or opinion . . . and that I
thought it proper particularly that he should proceed to Bladensburg and give any aid to General Winder that he could." The
president added that, "if any difficulty on the score of authority
should arise," he himself would be at hand "to remove it" because
he intended "to have the members of the cabinet together in
Bladensburg, where it was expected General Winder would be,
and in consultation with him to decide on the arrangements suited
to the posture of things."

In other words, the president and the cabinet had taken command of the army.

As for Monroe, he was off at full tilt while Campbell was
"grieving" and Madison was expressing "concern and surprise" to
Armstrong. No sooner did word reach Winder's headquarters that
the British were moving on Bladensburg than Monroe "offered
his services to proceed to that place and join General Stansbury."
Both the president and the commanding (?) general expressed "a
wish that he would do so" and he "lost not a minute in complying
with their desire." The fathead was in the fire.

Sometime between eleven and twelve o'clock, the colonel-
secretary of state was galloping gallantly down the pike. He was
in the orchard. He was "assisting" General Stansbury to post his

troops. Stansbury didn't know it. Monroe didn't bother to tell him.[8]

In the orchard, the drums began to beat. They were muffled drums: the matted trees dulled their sound and the drummers were not the best drummers an army ever had. But they made their meaning plain: *Fall in!* The long roll throbbed and throbbed on the noon-hot, dead-still air.

The two Baltimore county regiments—Schutz's and Ragan's—fell in with militia commotion. They jostled, dug elbows in neighbors' ribs, craned their heads at the bulges and sags in the ranks; they straightened the ranks a little. The ranks didn't look too soldierly even when straight: there weren't many uniforms in them. These were drafted men: these were the soldiers-on-paper: these two regiments were part of the paper army that Armstrong had put in a box and forbidden Winder to touch until the last minute. It wasn't their fault they were paper soldiers. It wasn't their fault there hadn't been coats enough to make them all the same color, as even paper-doll soldiers should be. They wore seersucker coats or Sunday frock coats or coatees or no coats at all, they wore farmyard smocks or overalls or their best go-to-meeting breeches, they wore any hat that was handy. But they formed ranks as best they knew how and they shuffled out of the orchard, ducking their heads underneath the low boughs and wondering what it was all about. Around the six too-small cannon behind the too-big barbette, the artillerymen also wondered. *Look a' that! Where the hell is the infantry going? It isn't coming down here to support the guns, it's going the other way! And look there . . . across the bridge . . . !*

The cannoneers looked and gulped. While they had been puzzling about the infantry, the dust cloud over the river road had come closer, had come alive. Past the foot of Lowndes's hill crawled a thing with a thousand legs . . . with four thousand, eight thousand legs . . . a creeping caterpillar kind of thing that carried a brown-dust cocoon on its back . . . a mile-long, undulant thing that was scarlet in spots and steel-bright in other spots. *There they are! There they are!* The British column didn't look much like Beall's, it didn't move the way Beall's had moved, half running, higgledy-piggledly, streaming along the road like volunteer fire companies running to a fire and all mixed up with the crowd. The British column looked hard and solid, it had a slow, deliberate way of moving, a kind of relentless, unstoppable way. *So that's what a real army looks like. Well, this is it. We're in for*

*it now. It's going to happen . . . it's going to happen in just a few
minutes now. What's our infantry doing? My God, our whole
army's pulling out!*

The two infantry regiments, more than half of Stansbury's
strength, were marching away to the rear; they were already a
hundred and fifty yards up the hill behind the orchard. Stansbury,
down in the triangle field giving last-minute orders to Captain Magruder and Captain Joe Myers, watched with indignant amazement.
The winding militia column trudged on up the hill. Two hundred
and fifty yards to the rear of the orchard and almost a quarter mile
in the rear of the guns, the two regiments stopped, started again,
spread out, formed a straggling line on the open slope of the hill.
"Thus uncovered by the trees of the orchard, their situation and
numbers were clearly seen by the enemy from Lowndes's hill, and
the flanks of the artillery and riflemen unprotected and laid liable
to be turned, our main body being placed too far off to render
them any aid." [9]

Stansbury galloped up hill to the new-formed line. Who moved
these troops? Who stationed them here, of all places? Who gave
the order . . . who dared to give such an order? If anyone knew
the answer, he kept it to himself. What Stansbury got was an
indirect answer that was no answer at all: General Winder was
on the field. Where? Off to the left there, somewhere, off toward
the mill. Turning his horse to seek the commanding general, Stansbury met Brigadier General Smith of the District of Columbia
brigade; they talked for some moments—about which of them was
the senior and who outranked whom. There was also "some conversation . . . concerning the order of battle." Then Stansbury
rode down the hill and across the Georgetown road to the little
mill; he found Winder there "reconnoitering the position of the
enemy." While they talked, Stansbury saw the Fifth Maryland—the
last of his infantry regiments—"taken out of the orchard, marched
up the hill, and stationed on the left of Colonel Schutz's regiment,
that of Colonel Ragan being on the right, its right resting on the
main road [the Washington turnpike] but . . . the whole at so
great a distance from the artillery and riflemen" that even the
rawest recruit could wonder why the six guns and the four hundred men had been left alone, a quarter of a mile in front of the
nearest troops, to face the attack of the whole British army across
the stream.[10]

"Whose plan this was," Stansbury said later, "I know not; it was not mine, nor did it meet with my approbation." His own plan of battle had been destroyed. Someone had taken command of his troops and moved them into a position so obviously bad that it had nothing to recommend it and everything to condemn it. His instructions to his colonels had been countermanded, his order of battle had been torn up and tossed away like a scrap of worthless paper. But Stansbury, having given up the opportunity to defend Lowndes's hill, the town, and the river itself, now gave up the opportunity to save what was left of the line he had finally picked to defend. He said not one word to Winder about his disrupted plan, about the helplessness of the infantry on the hill to support the guns and the rifles, about the now perilous, hopeless position of the two Baltimore batteries. There are times when being a gentleman, possessing a gentleman's self-control and reserve and a gentleman's nice sense of precedence, is as deadly a handicap as being deaf, blind and dumb. This was one of the times. Stansbury had been on this ground for hours, he had been close enough to observe it on three successive days, he had chosen what he believed was the best position, he had made his plans to hold it. He saw, now, a fatal mistake . . . and was silent. Why?

It was not too late to correct the blunder. The British column had halted in the river road with its leading regiment at the foot of Lowndes's hill; it was waiting, motionless, while patrols slipped cautiously toward the town, fully expecting to find it defended. By Stansbury's own account, the Fifth Maryland was not moved until *after* he had met Winder and was "in conversation with him." There was time for the Fifth to come out of the orchard, to climb the hill, to move across the front of the two Baltimore county regiments, to go into line on the extreme left flank. By Winder's account, there was still time to bring up "two or three pieces" of field artillery and a company of riflemen from the Washington brigade to protect the left flank of the Fifth *after* it had taken its new position. These guns and riflemen were at least half a mile to the rear when Winder sent orders for them to move up to support the Fifth; they had to march more than half a mile to reach the extreme left flank. There was time also to move two more pieces of Washington artillery up to the right of the new line. But while all this was going on, Stansbury kept his silence. Why?

Perhaps he was embarrassed, sitting there in the saddle, face to face with the commanding general whose successive orders he had failed to obey; but if he was, he never confessed it. He considered his conduct impeccable: "finding a superior officer on the field," he concluded that General Winder had ordered the three regiments out of the orchard and into line on the exposed slope of the hill and "consequently did not interfere." A question, asked to confirm his conclusion, would scarcely have been interference. But the question went unasked. Why?

The answer is James Monroe.

Tobias Stansbury, Maryland gentleman with a gentleman's self-restraint, declined to accept the responsibility for the blunder but also declined to set down the blunderer's name. William Winder, Maryland gentleman with the same self-restraint, accepted most of the blame that came his way but declined this particular blame. He did not even call the blunder a blunder except indirectly, in his official report. "If I had had longer time," he wrote, "or to repeat the action of Bladensburg, I could correct several errors, which might materially have affected the issue of that battle. The advanced force ought to have been nearer to the creek, along the edge of the low ground, where they would have been skirted with bushes, and have avoided the inconvenience of the cover which the orchard afforded the enemy. The edge of the low grounds on the right of the road ought to have been lined with musketry, and a battery of cannon also planted in the field on the right of the road, directly fronting the bridge; and if Commodore Barney's heavy artillery, with his more expert artillerists, had occupied the position which the advanced artillerists did, and these posts had been obstinately defended, the enemy would not have crossed the river at that point, but would have been obliged to have made a circuit around to his right, and have crossed above and at the upper end of the town; or, if the whole force had been posted at the position of the second line, with all the advantage it afforded, and have acted with tolerable courage and firmness, the event might have been different." By "the second line," General Winder meant the position where Barney's guns finally fought, not the line where Stansbury's infantry regiments had been placed by somebody . . . the somebody whom Stansbury did not name.

Major Pinkney, commanding the rifle companies, was blunter than Winder. "The Fifth regiment," he said, "had now, to the great disparagement of my companies and of the artillery, been made to retire to a hill several hundred yards in our rear, but visible, nevertheless, to the enemy, where it could do little more than display its gallantry." But Will Pinkney, Maryland gentleman with a gentleman's self-restraint—the ex-cabinet member, the ex-ambassador, the diplomat-politician—also declined to name the "busy and blundering tactician" who took command of Stansbury's infantry.

But Winder named him. Not avoiding blame himself nor seeking to place it, but casually in the course of his formal report, General Winder said what Pinkney and Stansbury would not say. When Winder met Stansbury on the field, he "found him and Colonel Monroe together" and Monroe informed Winder "that he had been aiding General Stansbury to post his command."

Sterrett also named him. Lieutenant Colonel Joe Sterrett, commanding the Fifth, said "the first line formed on the battle-ground was changed under the direction of Colonel Monroe."

There it is—Monroe's thumb in the soup, the soup thoroughly spilled, the stain of it plain to be seen. The stain is still there, where it doesn't belong, on the courage of men who fled from a hopelessly bad position, from a needlessly bad position in which they should not have been placed. Worse, the stain has been spread to the courage of men who did not run away but who fell back under orders, reluctant and cursing the orders. Politicians found the stain useful to distract attention from their own shortcomings, their own almost-criminal follies; they rubbed the stain in. Careless historians, copying what they said, have rubbed it in deeper yet.

But Monroe was deft with his thumb: he popped it into his mouth and it came out looking clean: there is scarcely a trace of the soup, there is only a smell: he licked his thumb quickly with words. Even while he was giving Sterrett the orders that moved the Fifth Maryland, he was saying, "Although you see I am active, you will please bear in mind that this is not my plan." Those may not be precisely the words he used: Colonel Sterrett was not quite certain, but he was certain enough about the sense of the words. And when Monroe set down his own account of his doings, he said that the withdrawal of Sterrett's regiment was "a measure taken with reluctance and in haste" and then added innocently that General Winder arrived on the field "after General Stansbury had made this disposition." The innocent, casual phrase puts the blame on Stansbury. It says, in effect, that Stansbury lied.

But Monroe was not accusing, he was not placing blame: he could neither blame nor accuse, because he did not admit that what had been done was a grotesque tactical blunder. Nothing so crude about Colonel Monroe. The phrase by which he shifted the responsibility to Stansbury has the familiar sound of a politician's alibi-innuendo. It is the sort of indirect accusation which, if proved wrong, can be disarmingly defended: it was only polite and courteous to imply that General Stansbury had been in full command of his troops: it would have been rude and cruel to say that somebody found it necessary to take his authority out of his hands on the field of battle. Nevertheless, it was a flat contradiction of what General Stansbury said. Did Stansbury himself, as Monroe remarked, make "this disposition"? Aside from that one sly phrase, there is not the slightest evidence to support the charge. Stansbury was utterly frank in admitting, over his own signature, that he had not obeyed successive orders received from Winder. He was almost naïve about it. To believe Monroe's phrase is to believe that Stansbury was guilty of falsehood—and there is nothing to support such belief.

Was there any truth in what Monroe said? Did somebody else order Stansbury's three regiments into that new, useless position? Did somebody else tell Colonel Monroe to transmit the order? The truth is elusive. The gremlins are nimble. But they left their tracks, and the tracks go back, on this morning of battle, to General Winder's camp near Washington. The sequence in which the tracks were made becomes important. And the sequence can be established.

President Madison and Secretary of State Monroe were with General Winder in his headquarters when definite news arrived that the British were marching on Bladensburg. Monroe galloped off to join Stansbury. Then Attorney General Rush arrived at headquarters, and "not long afterward" came Secretary of the Navy Jones. Then Winder, having "put his troops in motion," followed Monroe toward Bladensburg. "When he had left the house," the secretary of war and the secretary of the treasury appeared there —so said the attorney general. The secretary of war had a slightly different version: he said that Winder "was on the point of joining the troops at Bladensburg" but he made it plain that he gave Winder no orders because he "took it for granted that [Winder] had received the counsel he required." Only after Winder's departure did the "languid" secretary of the treasury complain to Madison that the secretary of war was "taking no part on so critical an occasion"; only then did Madison tell his secretary of war that "he should proceed to Bladensburg and give any aid to General Winder that he could" and that the president himself would be at hand to settle "any difficulty on the score of authority." Thereupon, Armstrong also rode off toward Bladensburg. Winder, of course, knew nothing about this arrangement: he was only the commanding general: it wasn't important for him to know that he was to be superseded in military command on the battlefield by a cabinet member. A little while after Armstrong had left, the president followed with his escort of department heads.

There they are, strung out on the Washington turnpike—Monroe far out in front, then Winder, then Armstrong, then Madison and his suite. They reached the field in that order. Colonel Monroe arrived when "the enemy was about three miles from Bladensburg." Winder got there in time to ride down to the mill and look at the enemy, and in time to send back for field guns to support the flanks of Stansbury's infantry regiments in their new position. Secretary of War Armstrong arrived when he "had barely time to reconnoitre the march of the enemy, or to inform myself of our own arrangements." Madison was so far behind that before he "could reach the town, the forces of the enemy had possession of it." Somewhere along the road, Madison had had a change of heart or mind: he would not supersede the commanding general after all. For when Armstrong "again met the president" on the field, Madison told him that "he had come to a new determination, and that the military functionaries should be left to the discharge of their own duties, on their own responsibilities." Therefore the secretary of war "now became, of course, a mere spectator of the combat." [11]

Who, then, conceived the tactical plan which Monroe disclaimed even while he was putting it into execution? There are numerous witnesses to testify on this point—the cabinet members who gathered at Winder's Washington headquarters. They left firsthand accounts of the "rather desultory" discussion there, and these accounts make one fact unmistakably clear. Neither before Monroe rushed off toward Bladensburg nor after he left did anyone at Winder's headquarters have any "plan" for the disposition of the American troops. The plain fact is that it was impossible for anyone at Winder's headquarters, that morning, to have a plan for arranging the American line of battle: nobody there knew what the situation was: nobody knew where Stansbury's regiments were. And the sequence of arrivals on the field makes it clear that Monroe, and only Monroe, had the opportunity to disarrange Stansbury's plan of action and to move his troops.

In justice both to General Winder and to Colonel Monroe, it must be said that Monroe was not the only busy helper on the field. Winder already had seen some of them, even before he found Monroe and Stansbury together. The harassed commander, about to fight a battle on ground where he had not meant to fight it, with an army just now coming together for the first time, "became greatly annoyed" by "numerous self-constituted contributors of advice." They swarmed around him as he rode toward Tournecliffe's bridge—"suggesters of position, intermeddlers with command, gentlemen of respectability and good will, committees, a whole democracy of commanders"—all of them industriously help-

FRANCIS SCOTT KEY

ing "to mar all singleness of purpose and unity of action." There were other less offensive bystanders, among them Alexander McKim, the Baltimore member of Congress, on one of his fast trotting horses. McKim was "a rich merchant who said that, having voted for war, he could not find it in his conscience, if not to fight for it, at least to stand by those who did." [12] He knew his place and kept it. But Winder saw "several gentlemen, among the rest, Mr. Francis S. Key, not only recommending, but showing where they thought the troops ought to be posted, riding to the spots designated and confounding the outset."

If Mr. Key had a place that day, he had somehow mislaid it. He was an elegant young gentleman of Georgetown—poet, lawyer, heir to comfort, kinsman to some very definitely "right" people. He was, or at least he had been, a lieutenant-quartermaster of a swank society militia outfit, Major George Peter's battery of field artillery. Major Peter was a former regular who knew his business [13] —and his place. Mr. Key knew neither. His military experience had been confined to buying his tight blue militia uniform, attending a few drills and a president's review, and "campaigning" against Cockburn's marauders [14] who, if they knew about it, did not mind at all. He had seen two of these campaigns—one twelve days long in 1813, and one two months ago that lasted for a fortnight. [15] He had "come a cropper from his horse into the river" and also had been "struck in the face by a piece of salt pork." [16] His other qualifications for advising generals in the deployment of an army were not readily apparent. General Winder was most unappreciative of Mr. Key's attempts at helpfulness. His comment, in his official report, was sour; even when he decided that amateur artilleryman might have been carrying instructions from Brigadier General Walter Smith, he merely made a footnote of it and let the comment stand. The wonder is that he did not order Mr. Key back to his battery forthwith. There is no record to show that the young man rejoined it when his exciting excursion into tactics ended.

Into this chaos of meddle and muddle came the whole right wing of Winder's army. Sweating and swearing and straggling and stumbling-tired, the Washington militia infantry streamed down the hill where Stansbury's troops had halted at daybreak and Stansbury himself had searched in vain for a position he thought worth defending. Behind them came Barney's guns, the flotillamen and the marines . . . the sweat-black, red-mucked horses spinning the heavy cannon at a trot [17] . . . the eighteen-pounders slewing and swaying through the deep ruts . . . the lumbering ammunition wagons lost in a boiling cloud of dust as if the powder that they carried had exploded . . . the seamen sturdily running in the ditches alongside their guns . . . the sailors-turned-soldier clutching bayoneted muskets across their chests as they ran.

Now, at almost the last minute, with time for scarcely more than a glance at the terrain, the right wing fell into a position made defensible by nature. It was a position through which the left wing had marched twice this morning but which had not impressed itself on either Stansbury or the officers present at his council of war. But now, just ahead, Joshua Barney saw the turnpike drop brusquely to a ravine and a creek six hundred yards in front of him. A short, narrow, unrailed bridge spanned the little stream. To a sailor's eye, the ground was broken like a heavy sea tormented by a cross chop. But for a broad space between the higher ground and the ravine, there was a field of fire . . . there was a chance to rake the road, the bridge . . . a chance to swing the guns and sweep the lip of the ravine on either side . . . to swing them farther yet and sweep the slopes that formed, just here, an angle into which an enemy attacking from the front must come. There was a chance, too, for cross fire, if another battery could be brought into action on the north side of the pike.

The place had possibilities. Others had already seen them. The right flank was covered: Barney could see a substantial body of in-

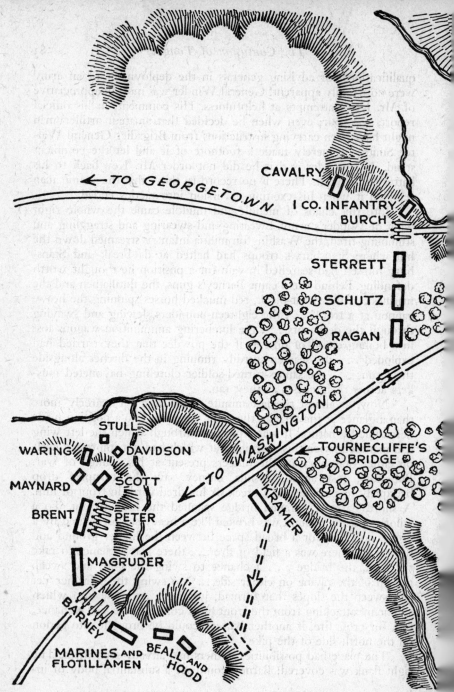

THE BATTLE OF BLADENSBURG—The final deployment of the Americ
approach

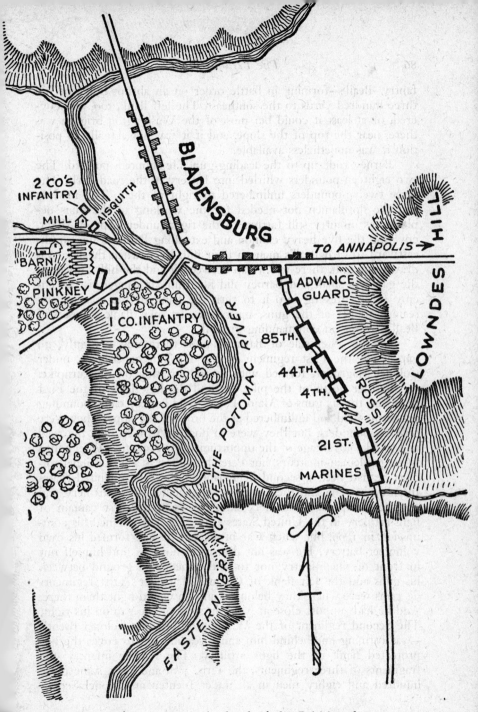

2 CO'S INFANTRY

MILL

AISQUITH

BARN

PINKNEY

I CO. INFANTRY

BLADENSBURG

TO ANNAPOLIS →

ADVANCE GUARD

85TH.

44TH.

4TH.

ROSS

21ST.

MARINES

LOWNDES HILL

EASTERN BRANCH OF THE POTOMAC RIVER

N

...ny at 12:30 p.m., August 24, as the head of the British column
...adensburg.

fantry—Beall's—forming in battle order on an abrupt bulge of hill three hundred yards to the southeast. The left flank, too, was covered, or at least it could be: most of the Washington brigade was there, near the top of the slope, and if it was not actually in position it was nonetheless available.

Barney rode up to the leading gun. He shouted, pointed. The two eighteen-pounders whirled into battery in the road itself. The three twelve-pounders unlimbered to right of them. The marines and the flotillamen not needed for the working of the guns deployed as infantry still farther to the right, under Captain Miller, covering the five heavy cannon and extending Barney's line southeastward toward Beall's men on their hill. Even when the line was drawn out thin, there was a gap between it and the hill. However, the gap was small and Barney did not think it dangerous: an enemy force, pressing into it to turn the flank of the marines and seamen to get at the guns, must leave its own flank exposed to Beall's troops on commanding ground.

On the other side of Barney's guns there was, presently, no gap at all: the First regiment of the Washington brigade, under Colonel Magruder, formed with its right resting on the turnpike.

Farther north of the pike, beyond the left flank of the First regiment, the six guns of Major Peter's field battery came pounding across the field and unlimbered at the brow of the slope. They were only six-pounders, but they were in position to help rake the road and to take advantage of the opportunity for cross fire. Peter's men were gentlemen-amateurs, but Peter himself was a professional soldier; he had been a second lieutenant in the Ninth United States Infantry in 1799 and then, successively, lieutenant of artillery and engineers, captain of artillery and, by 1808, the first captain of light artillery in the United States army. He had resigned his commission in 1809, but when war broke out he had formed his own volunteer battery. He was not dismayed, now, to find himself out in front of the infantry nor to find unoccupied ground between his guns and the left flank of Colonel Magruder's First regiment: his guns were where they belonged and he would fight them there. And he had support close at hand, in spite of the gap on his right. The Second regiment of the Washington brigade—Colonel Brent's —was forming line behind him and spreading out to cover the unprotected flank of the light artillery. The regular infantry—the fragments of three regiments, the 12th, 36th and 38th, some three hundred and eighty men in all under Lieutenant Colonel Scott—

extended Brent's line to the north, still behind Peter's guns but overhanging them on the left just as the right flank of Brent's regiment overhung them to the south.

Behind the regulars, Major Henry Waring's slim battalion of one hundred and fifty Maryland militia formed a second line. Major Samuel Maynard's equally thin battalion of militia probably was part of that second line. The slope in front of the American position bent back sharply to the west, here, still confronting the ravine, which also bent. Waring's battalion and its supporting detachments were in position to meet a flanking movement coming up the ravine or through the fields beyond it. But the ravine itself, while it would serve as an obstacle to disarrange the enemy's advance, would also serve to cover such a turning movement. North of the turnpike bridge, it flattened into a small, grassy glade through which an attacking force could move swiftly and easily northwestward around the American left. But it was dominated by another abrupt bulge of ground just as the opposite flank was dominated by the hill now held by Beall's men; to this bulge, two companies of the Washington brigade were hurried, under Captains Stull and Davidson. Stull's men were in no pleasant mood: enlisted as riflemen, presumably because they had some qualifications and experience in the use of firearms, they had been refused rifles by the secretary of war: angered, they had at first peremptorily declined to march unless the government kept its bargain. But they had marched; and they marched, now, into a key position where rifles would have been extremely useful.

And finally, down the slope in front of Barney's guns and across the open ground to the right of the turnpike, sped Lieutenant Colonel Kramer's small battalion of Maryland militia. Two hundred and forty strong, it went into line on the edge of the ravine below the bridge, four hundred yards in advance of Beall's hilltop position and almost three hundred yards in advance of the nearest troops on the brow of the slope.

The right wing was in battle order. In despite of chaos and confusion and the "democracy of commanders," it was in better order than it could reasonably have been expected to be. The position was not bad. If it was not the best of the five positions which Stansbury successively abandoned in his night retreat, it was nevertheless a position in which green troops backed by good artillery could make a stand; it was infinitely better than the position that Colonel Monroe foisted upon Stansbury. And the troops of the right wing were not badly disposed. True, Colonel Kramer's battalion on the edge of the ravine masked part of Barney's field of fire and part of Peter's also; but, as the story of the battle itself unfolds, it will be seen that Kramer's raw troops fought stoutly in their advanced position and that they drew back, still fighting, to a new position in time to give the guns a chance. True, too, the cavalry that had been mostly with the right wing was now huddled together in a stubble field on the extreme left of Stansbury's line, apparently without orders and certainly with a fence between it and the enemy; but the cavalry, inexperienced, undisciplined and now worn out—men and horses alike—by days and nights of singularly ineffective scouting, probably was so useless that it might as well have been kept off the battlefield entirely.

The flaw in the position and the disposition of the right wing was no minor matter of a small battalion thrust out in front of the main line and the guns, nor of a small body of cavalry mishandled. The flaw was fundamental: the right wing was not to be united with the left wing even in the climax of battle. The two wings, the two halves of the army—Stansbury's Maryland brigade and Smith's Columbian brigade—were not brought into position to operate as an army. They fought as two separate armies. The only support the third line gave the second was the five pieces of artillery and the one company of riflemen—armed with muskets—sent forward and divided between Stansbury's flanks. The two wings fought two separate battles.

They fought, in fact, three separate battles. For the first line —the Baltimore artillery and the three rifle companies, with their slender infantry reinforcement—was left to fight the day's first engagement alone. Until that opening engagement was over, until it was thoroughly lost, the only support the first line received from the second line was the long-range fire of Ben Burch's two detached guns on the turnpike and a single ineffectual volley fired by an unidentified infantry company.

General Winder sensed the fatal weakness in the position of Major Pinkney's hopeless "forlorn hope." "A few minutes before the action commenced," Surgeon Hanson Catlett delivered to Pinkney an order from Winder "to take the most judicious position with his riflemen to protect the artillery at the battery." Up to that point, it left everything to the judgment of the Rifles' commander; then, however, it added that Pinkney should place part of his command "upon the left of the battery" and the major accordingly pulled Captain Edward Aisquith's whole company out of his forming line and hurried it across the triangle field toward the Georgetown road. This company was almost immediately replaced on the right of the guns by a company of infantry which reported to Pinkney, who placed it on the right of his shortened line.

Neither Winder's order nor the resulting hasty shift of troops is important except as it sets the pattern for what is to come . . . except as it shows Winder's judgment in action . . . except as it offers additional proof that Winder had plenty of time to correct Monroe's blunders if he had comprehended how fatal the blunders were. Arriving upon the field, he had been uneasy about Stansbury's line: he had time to send back for Captain Burch's five guns and for infantry to protect them. Now, uneasy about Pinkney's line, he had time to disrupt it, to shift a third of its strength from the right to the left, to replace the shifted rifle company with a detachment of infantry. True, the left flank of the Baltimore batteries needed protection badly; after Monroe moved Stansbury's regiments to the rear, the only troops on the left of the guns were the two infantry companies which Stanbury had placed "near, and protected by, the barn" and "intended to defend the road leading by the mill, on the left of the battery, into the field." But the barn was *behind* the guns, their left flank was still unprotected; they needed Aisquith's Sharp Shooters; they needed, in fact, all the men who could have been sent.

The half-naked roustabouts at the Baltimore guns begin to put on their shirts and their coats and their crossbelts. They are Maryland gentlemen, they dress for battle as if they were dressing for dinner. They button their high-collared tunics up to their chins, they tug the straps of their helmets tight under their chins.

All that Winder's order achieved was to weaken Pinkney's line, already too weak, at the point where the first blow fell . . . at the obvious danger point in front of the Bladensburg bridge. It split Pinkney's command, divided the rifle battalion. It did nothing at all to correct the blunder Monroe had made, nor the blunder Stansbury had made. It added only a handful of raw troops to the first line; it left the second line where it was, too far to the rear to support the first or protect the guns; it did nothing at all to retrieve the blunder of leaving the fordable river undefended—the blunder that Winder saw later and said he would have corrected.

Obediently, the riflemen moved down the field again to the

fence and the fringe of the undergrowth. The newly arrived infantry company went into position "near to the main road, under cover of some bushes" and another fence. If these men of the first line saw plainly that they had been left to meet the first shock of the battle alone, if they saw plainly that the rest of their brigade was too far away to help them, they had at least the advantage of knowing how bad their situation was. The riflemen "went to their posts with cheerfulness, although they were about to contend . . . with veteran troops, greatly superior in numbers." [16]

Back in the second line, the three infantry regiments also knew only what they could see, but they could see less: the orchard concealed most of what was about to happen. The regimental commanders did not even know that the other half of the army was on the field. General Winder had time to send to the various regiments a piece of news that reached him on the field—news of "a signal victory obtained by General Izard over the enemy, in which one thousand of the enemy were slain, and many prisoners taken." He did not take time to let his troops know that the whole Washington brigade, with five heavy guns and the battle-tried flotillamen, was at hand and preparing for action.

7

THE PAPER AND THE WIND

IT IS TWELVE AND A HALF O'CLOCK.
The sky is as clean as a scalded plate. The sun is as bright and hot as the polished brass knob of an andiron. Across the gray-drooping, heat-sick tops of the willows, across the stream and the village roofs, at the far east end of the crooked street, the dust cloud over the river road has settled a little, has drifted a little aside. The enemy stands in plain sight.

The enemy looks different. *What's he look different from?* Oh, I don't know . . . nothing in partic'lar . . . only I didn't expect . . . Well, just diff'rent.

The enemy, seen for the first time, always looks different.

Those red-jacketed men over there are no longer a word of

contempt in a holiday orator's mouth, no longer an angry phrase in the *Patriot* or the *National Intelligencer*. They are no longer even a false report fetched in by one of Charlie Ridgley's videttes, no longer a rumor well yeasted with imagination and kneaded by tongue after tongue until it rises and swells like dough. Those men over there look sort of ordinary, they don't look any bigger than other men. There are a lot of them, though. The column stretches away down the river road as if it went clear to the Old Fields or clear to Marlb'rough or clear to England, maybe. To the cannoneers and the riflemen, left alone in the triangle field, the British column looks as if the most swollen rumors were true. It looks like all the twelve thousand men it was reported to be.

The British, watching the three lines of men on the opposite side of the branch, believe they are facing nine thousand American troops.

There are, on paper, 5,938 Americans. There are, on paper, 4,270 British.[1]

Both those figures are probably high, for neither takes into account the sick and the stragglers. Both armies had suffered attrition,[2] the strength of both had been ground down on the hard, hot grindstone of Maryland's August sun.

There are four good, veteran regiments over there on the river road . . . the 85th . . . the Fourth, the King's Own . . . the 44th, the East Essex Foot . . . the 21st, the Royal North British Fusiliers. Now that the dust has thinned, a man can see that the column is not all red: there are streaks and patches of blue. Besides the four infantry regiments, there are two hundred sailors from the fleet and six hundred royal marines; there is a company of a hundred Negroes "lately armed and disciplined" in Bermuda; there is a detachment of sappers and miners and a detachment of rocket troops.[3] Half the sailors are hauling ammunition and stores, half are dragging the guns by hand . . . one six-pounder and two little grasshoppers taking a three-pound ball. There are two-wheeled powder carts and tumbrils loaded with rockets. There is even a troop of cavalry . . . infantry mounted on Maryland farm nags . . . riding with blanket saddles, with reins and stirrups of rope. The long column waits, silent, solid, closed up, the men six abreast in the road. Where the river road touches the town, a small block of scarlet waits by itself . . . the advance guard . . . fifty men of the 85th.

The waiting is almost over. Little figures go scuttling up the main street, back to the column, back to the cluster of officers on the green slope of Lowndes's hill. The advance guard moves. The column behind it stirs with a sudden flash, with a sudden ripple of light as the bayonets lift, as the muskets go to the carry. Here they come. *Here they come!*

The leading company of the 85th passes out of sight between the farthest houses, it swings left into the street, it is steady and brisk. Behind the raw bank of earth and the wilted camouflage, the Baltimore gunpointers stoop to their guns. They know how the guns are laid; they are sure, but they have to make sure. In the gun corporals' hands, the slow matches smolder and glow. The glow trembles a little. We've never shot at a man, we've never tried to blow a man's insides out with a six-pound chunk of iron. When they get to the corner of that house . . . when the front rank takes six more steps . . . four more . . . Number One . . . *fire!*

The little gun roars and jumps. The trail digs a gouge in the dirt. The embrasure is roily with smoke. Number Two . . . *fire!*

But the neat red block is gone from the village street. It has split apart like a billet of wood when the ax comes down on the block. The two halves are huddled against the walls of the houses on either side of the street. There are only chips left in the street, three chips in scarlet jackets. One lies still, the other two wriggle and squirm.[4] *So that's it. So that's what it's like.*

The second six-pound ball only plows up the empty street, it only throws dirt on the chips.

The advance guard is moving again, it halted for only a moment. But it isn't marching now, it isn't in proper column. The split-apart halves haven't come together, they seem content to stay split. They are two long files on either side of the street, pressed close to the fronts of the houses. The files move in jerks. A man runs, you can see him swerve around the front steps of a house; when he comes to the next house, he drops to his knees and crouches, half hidden behind its steps. Three more men, flattened against a red-brick wall, peel themselves away from the wall and begin to run along the edge of the roadway; they move heavily, their run is a jouncing trot; you can see their knapsacks jounce up and down on their backs. Two of them slip out of sight behind the corner of a house; the third flattens himself again to its wall. Jerkily, in no kind of drill formation, with spurts and pauses, with no neat drill-ground spaces between the men but with irregular gaps, the advance company worms its way down the street toward the elbow-bend of the town. It makes a poor target. It makes no target at all.

Behind it, on the river road, a long section has broken loose from the column halted below Lowndes's hill. The whole first brigade of the British army is moving into the village. It moves in a strong, steady current . . . the ranks are closed up . . . the men are still six abreast. But the current breaks when it touches the town. It doesn't flow down the street. It turns into two small rivulets, trickling along the gutters.

The frustrated gunners swear. *What the hell? What in hell are they up to? What kind of fumadiddle is that? The British don't fight like that. They fight in the open; that's how we licked 'em before. God damn it, the British stand up, they don't hide; that's how Braddock got licked. They come at you in double ranks . . . in columns of double ranks . . . in thick columns of companies. You can mow 'em down.* But they don't. And you can't.

The Baltimore guns are firing smoothly. The crews are well drilled, they move with a gun-house precision. The six-pound balls are making big splashes of dust in the street, they are knocking bricks out of the houses, they are knocking holes in the walls.[5] But they are doing the enemy almost no damage at all. They can't stop the steady trickle of infantry down through the town.

For this battle was fought hours ago, when Stansbury gave up Lowndes's hill and the village itself. We are fighting it now with guns, but the guns don't count. This opening phase of the battle was fought when Stansbury picked this position "under cover of the town." Now, one by one, the blunders made in preparing the battle fall on the men who must fight it.

The town is not "cover" for either the guns or the rifles. It is almost perfect cover for the advancing British, filtering through the back yards and between the houses, seeping along the street. The Baltimore guns are banging away, but "only occasionally" can the crews find "an object" to shoot at. The British infantry is flopping down in the gutters, lying flat in the gardens, squatting behind the big trees.[6] These are hard-bitten men, they have faced flying iron before. They crack jokes when the brick dust showers them. The tough old-campaigner jokes help to steady the few young recruits who came out from England after the fighting in France was over. But a man is hit, now and then. A six-pound ball strikes a boy stretched out on his belly between two subalterns. It smashes his leg and grinds it completely off. The boy looks at his lieutenant with a "peculiar expression . . . as much as to ask how, under such circumstances, he ought to behave." The lieutenant can "not help laughing." [7]

The British have not fired a shot. The battle, so far, belongs to the Baltimore guns. But their fire is slackening; the cartridge chests aren't too full; they can't afford to waste powder. Major Pinkney stood behind the guns till the second round was fired, but he is down at the end of the open field, now; he has gone forward again to his observation post in front of the batteries, to the top of the bank where the field drops down to the thicketed bottoms. His men—the two companies left here at the apex of the Y, the hundred men of Bill Dyer and Dominic Bader's companies—are sifting down through the bushes, down toward the edge of the stream, toward the bridge. Even then they are still out of range, their rifles still out of the fight.

But the Baltimore guns have, presently, a target. Just north of the bend of the town, a warehouse juts out from the row of houses. Now, from the warehouse . . . close under the partial concealment of its wall or inside, through a window . . . springs a flash and a noise. The noise is a strange, roaring whoos-shh. The flash is a stream of flame. A streak of something leaps across the river. It spits fire backwards, it trails fire behind it. It looks a good deal like a comet and it's near of a size, with a comet low down in the sky. Only comets don't jump at you out of somebody's yard. They don't come straight at you, either. This thing is coming straight for the guns. It rises, arches, clears the tops of the willows. The wind of it stirs the willows, the fiery sparks drip on the leaves. But it's dropping now, it's curving down toward the field, it's beginning to wobble. You can see a stick, swishing behind it, in and out of the sparks. It hits the ground a good way in front of the guns and kicks up a jet of dirt. It lies there . . . not long, only a second . . . a man can see it quiver. As if it had taken a good deep breath, it wooshes again . . . it darts off to one side with smoke and fire spurting out of its tail . . . it bounces and jumps . . . it darts this way and that . . . it acts like a crazy thing, like a hen with its head chopped off. It leaves a scorched trail in the weeds, a crazily crooked trail with feathers of smoke drifting down. When it lies still at last, you can see an eight-foot pole attached to a kind of tube with a pointed nose. The pole, too, is scorched.

Another flash springs from the warehouse . . . another harsh, rushing roar . . . another fire-spitting streak. Then several together, a volley of rockets, a whole skein of fire threads weaving and interweaving. The cannoneers watch them come. Their bodies go tense, they can't help shrinking a little. The riflemen make themselves small in the bushes, they stare with a fixed fascination. This is the unknown . . . this is the strange new weapon . . . this is the poison gas at Ypres . . . the tanks at Cambrai . . . the flame thrower . . . the incendiary bomb of its day . . . the Stuka . . . the screaming dive bomber . . . the flaming onion . . . the bazooka, the katiusha. Its primary purpose is terror. It can burn ships, explode magazines, set towns on fire. But against living things, it depends more on fear than on fire; its target is minds more than bodies; its flaming trail sets fire to imaginations. It can rout a cavalry charge by stampeding the horses, break up a column of field guns galloping into action; the rocket troops themselves, when furnished with horses, must leave the teams far to the rear; horses can become accustomed to gunfire but not to these fiery monsters, not to this tearing sound, half gargle, half strangled whoop.[8]

There is something personal about these hurtling, fire-spouting things. You can see them come. They are aimed straight at you . . . at *you*. The truth is that aiming is largely a matter of hope and intention. This new weapon is at least as inaccurate as it is fear-inspiring. What a flight of rockets will do in a little wind is almost beyond prediction; they have been known to turn in mid-air and plunge down on the troops who discharged them.[9] Even now, in the dead-still calm, they fly every which way. But that is part of their terror: you never can tell: you can't tell what the crazy thing will do when it starts to wobble, you can't guess where it is going; even when it falls and lies still, its nose pointed away, you can't be sure that it's dead, you can't know that it won't gush flame in your face and take three idiotic leaps and come darting back to bury its red-hot metal tip in your guts.[10] It doesn't. Not often, at least. But the thought of it leaves your guts weak.

The volley of rockets falls harmless. The gunners stay at their guns, the riflemen stay in the thicket. They stay, but their nerves are shaken. A man can't help the vibrance of nerves in his knees and the calves of his legs; they aren't really his legs, they are too far away, he isn't too sure they will move when he tells them to move. But they do. The cannoneers go to work on the warehouse. Their hands may not be quite so deft with the flannel cartridges, they may grip the rammers needlessly tight, but they lay the guns well. "A few well-directed shots" drive the rocketmen out of their nest.[11] The rocket fire stops.

But the infantry, filtering through the village, has already accomplished the first vital part of its mission. The steady seepage of
men has saturated the town, it has had the effect of a flood; the village is filled with almost invisible troops. The whole first brigade
has trickled down to the bend of the town and spread northward
behind the houses that face the American lines. The lower town has
turned into a dam with a thousand men gathered behind it. As if
somebody opened a floodgate, a gush of troops bursts from the
dam.

It breaks out from the town at the elbow-bend, where the
road starts down to the bridge. It is the advance guard again, the
leading company of the 85th Foot.[12] It comes down the narrow
road in a compact rush, it comes like the small, solid wave in a mill-
race when the mill pond gate is opened.

With handspikes and dragropes, with fingers gripping the
wheel spokes, with bodies heaving and straining, the Baltimore
gunners wrestle the clumsy guns till the muzzles point toward the
bridge. A gun sergeant, stooping, his hand raised, sees the head of
the running column cross the end of the bridge and the end of the
black iron muzzle. His hand drops, he jumps to escape the backward jump of the gun, the number-two gunner presses the match
to the vent. The piece recoils, it runs back with its trail kicking
dirt, with its matrosses holding it back by the dragropes. A second
gun fires and rolls back. On the bridge, the red column recoils
. . . not as fast as the guns, but uncertain, a churning of men in
confusion, of officers trying to hold the platoons as the gun crews
hold to the guns. Then the company breaks and runs. It leaves seven
men on the bridge and the road. [13]

But it rallies. It tries again. Not a solid wave, now . . . a succession of little waves . . . little clumps of men running, bent over
. . . "small parties at full speed." [14] The Baltimore guns are firing
as fast as the gunners can sponge and load and take aim through
the hanging smoke. They have help, now. Behind them, on the turnpike, the two six-pounders detached from Captain Ben Burch's
Washington battery open fire at long range. Down in the thickets,
the rifles begin to crackle. They cut through the grump of the
guns like the slash of whips, of whips with a long, thin lash. The
shot comes first . . . hard . . . thin . . . then the whine and
sting of the echo. The echo draws out like a whiplash being withdrawn, it coils itself in the hollow between the hills. If it weren't
for the cannon, a man could think he was standing in Market street,

watching the rival stages pulling out from the coachyard of Fountain Inn; he could think he was in the taproom drinking a tall, cool drink, hearing the whips go off like shots and making bets on the drivers. *God, I could use a drink!* My throat's like a flannel cartridge. This gun's getting hot . . . my throat's hotter . . . it's drier, too . . . I could swallow that whole damn' sponge. *Handle cartridge! Charge piece! Ram down cartridge! Prime! Take aim! Fire!*

The six guns behind the embankment are doing the best they can. The two guns on the pike are doing the best they can. But it isn't enough. There are too many motions to make, too many commands. No matter how fast a crew moves, the firing is slow, it takes forever . . . forever. The guns can't keep up with the blunders made hours ago. Eight muzzle-loading, slow-firing guns, throwing pieces of iron no bigger than a man's fist, might stop the rush of those waves on the narrow bridge . . . they might, if the Baltimore guns had been put where they ought to be, not behind a barbette meant for bigger, heavier guns . . . if they had been put where their chunks of iron could sweep the bridge from one end clean to the other. But they can't do that, where they are; they can hit the bridge only obliquely, they can only shoot across it from side to side. They might stop those small parties yet, if they only had grapeshot to spray the bridge . . . if they had case shot or canister . . . if they had shells to burst at the feet of those running men or over their heads. But they have only the solid shot.

And the rush is not coming down only that one neat channel, now. The scarlet, steel-white capped waves are still lapping the bridge, they are breaking across it, but there are others as well. The infantry flood dammed up in the town is beginning to leak through the dam. For a moment, the leaks are nothing but drops . . . a man or two, then three or four men, coming through between houses, running down toward the river above the bridge. The drops multiply and are runlets, the runlets are streams. They gush through the line of houses in strengthening jets. And like jets of water bursting out through a dozen cracks in a dam and flowing down its face, they spread and broaden. The dozen slim streams of red-jacketed soldiers rushing down from among the houses are scattering out, deploying, spreading across the clear ground between the town and the river, flowing together and joining. By the time they reach the east bank of the branch they have formed a line. Not solid. Not thick. Not a drill-ground line. It is loose, uneven; it has sags and bulges. The men are spaced wide apart:[15] this is not Braddock's day, this is not the attack on Breed's Hill: the British soldier has learned a good deal about fighting since then.

This battle line is thick at one end only, the end where the "small parties" are pressing the bridge, where the small clumps of men are following one another down the road to the bridge in spite of the furious guns. The guns are excited, now: the iron balls are going wide: each shot sets the guns rolling backward, they must be dragged back again to the bank of dirt and relaid, and the crews are panting and nervous, they don't like the looks of that oncoming line. Except at the bridge, the line is thin, it is only a skirmish line.[16] But it is a line of veteran British infantry with bayonets fixed, it is a line of the Invincibles attacking. And the guns can't even hold back the attack at the bridge, they can't spare a shot for the skirmish line rushing down to the fords.

From the bridge to the mill, upstream, there are eleven hundred men in this attack. The whole 85th is in it, six hundred men. With them are detachments of three other sturdy regiments—the light companies of the King's Own, the East Essex Foot, the Royal North British Fusilers. With them also are royal marines and the hundred armed Negroes. To meet the attack there are the three Baltimore rifle companies—the Union Yagers, the Sharp Shooters, the Fell's Point Riflemen—a hundred and fifty militia; there are the three infantry companies, another hundred and fifty, perhaps a few more; there are the hundred and fifty gunners and matrosses. In men, this first of the day's three successive engagements is eleven hundred against four hundred and fifty or, at the most, five hundred.

The American batteries change the odds, and the rockets change them also. How much, nobody can say. The guns, in the first few minutes of action, have done more damage than the strange new weapon has done: they have even silenced the rocket fire, temporarily.[17] But both have failed: the rockets have not thrown the weak first line into panic: the guns have not broken up the determined rush for the bridge.

Whatever may be the comparative weight of the guns and the rockets upon the odds of the battle, the blunders outweigh them by far. The results of the long succession of blunders fall with a crushing weight . . . the town abandoned, its houses giving the enemy cover . . . the bridge left standing . . . the guns so placed that they cannot sweep the bridge . . . the guns so placed that

they cannot enfilade the river . . . the line of the river itself undefended . . . the enemy furnished again with cover that gives
them, now, almost as much protection as they had in the town
itself.

Abruptly, the guns have nothing at which to fire. The successive small waves of the advance guard are over the bridge, they
are forming in line, the line is plunging into the thickets and out
of sight.[18] And the rest of the British line, still on the farther side
of the stream, is vanishing too. While it is still advancing across
the open ground between the town and the river, the willows and
aspens on the west bank begin to conceal it; when it leaps down
the east bank and begins to splash through the fords, the trees and
brush hide it completely. The guns can do nothing, the gunners
can only wait. They cannot even fire blindly into the thickets:
the Yagers are down there, somewhere, along with the Fell's Point
men, and the infantry company is down there too, on the flank,
between the guns and the British infantry coming up from the
bridge but still concealed by the brush.

Then the infantry company catches sight of the oncoming
bayonets. The men who carry the bayonets are still too far away
for smooth-bore muskets to do much harm, but the infantry company fires. It lets off one ragged volley and then it runs. Its captain
tries to stop it.[19] Will Pinkney springs down from the top of the
bank and runs toward the fleeing men: he shouts, he commands,
he threatens: the men rush by him and leave him standing alone.

Abruptly, the odds have changed, they have worsened. The
guns cannot fire; the two infantry companies off to the left cannot
fire, they are too far away; even Aisquith's Sharp Shooters are out
of action, they also are too far away. For long minutes, the battle
belongs to the riflemen down in the thickets . . . to the Fell's
Pointers, the Yagers . . . to "somewhat more than a hundred
men." The odds are no longer roughly two to one. They are ten
to one.

The long skirmish line is across the branch. The two rifle companies fight. The whiplike crack of the rifles is lashing the thickets.
The American fire is galling the left the British line, pressing up
through the woods from the bridge. The coiling whiplash shots of
the rifles pluck men out of the ranks of the 85th. The red-jacketed
men go down, they lie still in the yet-green grass of the bottoms or
clutch and pluck at the grass. But the rest press on. The British
begin to fire.

The Tower muskets are loud, they are blunt. They are more
like clubs than whips. They beat at the two small companies. The
British infantry drives ahead through the underbrush like a long
line of game beaters, threshing the thickets with clubs. And the
weight of the blunders continues to fall . . . the first line so weak
and so short that there are no men at all to the south of the bridge
. . . no troops at all to outflank the enemy when he has crossed
the bridge . . . the two companies themselves overlapped and outflanked as soon as the bridge is crossed . . . the Fifth Maryland
Infantry, which Stansbury intended to meet just such a development, now placed far to the rear, far on the opposite flank of
Monroe's inexcusable line . . . the nearest troops four hundred
yards to the rear and held motionless there . . . these nearest
troops of Stansbury's brigade not even visible from where Major
Pinkney stands, but hidden from sight by the orchard[20] . . . these
nearest available troops not even able to see that the first line has
been outflanked [21] and that the guns are in danger.

The rifles are falling back. They can do nothing else; where
they are, it would not be useful even to stay and die. Two companies of militia cannot hold back a reinforced regular regiment.
Even if they could hold back the men just in front of them, they cannot hold back the two ends of the line that is folding itself around
them. The Fell's Point men and the Yagers come running out of the
thickets by ones and twos, by scattered bits of platoons. They stop
and turn and fire at the first scarlet coats bursting out of the brush
behind them. They run, and load as they run, and hang on their
heels to fire. They are in wild disorder, but they are still organized
troops; all adhesion has not been lost. Even now, in the open field,
with the enemy already in force on their right flank, they haven't
made up their minds that they ought to quit.[22] Major Pinkney
knows they can't "hope to make an effectual stand." They are
hopelessly outnumbered; only half of them have bayonets.[23] In a
moment, now, he will have to give the command to retreat. But he
waits, he looks toward the guns.

The six guns are silent. They have targets now, close, in plain
sight. But another blunder is coming home: the guns cannot reach
the targets. The embrasures cut in the too-big earthwork keep the
gunners from swinging their pieces toward the infantry on the
flank. And the impromptu embrasures are still too high: the guns
cannot be depressed far enough to fire on the infantry gathering
now in the low ground down at the foot of the field.[24]

The British are getting ready to rush the guns. You can hear the officers shouting and see them running along the forming line. The line is straightening out. The men in it are unbuckling the straps of their packs and jerking the straps off their shoulders, they are flinging their knapsacks down on the ground.[25] The line moves, the bayonets start to climb. And still the guns can't touch them. From both the front and the right, the British are closing in. The bayonets cross the point of the Y and climb toward the bank where Major Pinkney is standing; more bayonets cross the pike and come into the field. There was something personal about those rockets, but there is something even more personal about those bayonets; there is something positively intimate about those lean, glinting knives on the ends of the slanted muskets. Between the guns and the oncoming, curving, enveloping line there are only those two rifle companies . . . only a hundred men or perhaps a few more . . . only those men already driven back once, not broken yet but not in a firm line either . . . milling . . . uncertain.

The gunners, too, are uncertain. *What do we do about this? What are we supposed to do? There's nothing in Duane about this, there's nothing in drill regulations.* The gunners have no weapons, they have only their sponges and rammers, their handspikes. *My God, do we just stand here? Do we just stand here and wait to be killed? Do they want us to throw six-pound balls with our hands? Let's get out . . . let's get out while we've got a chance. They'll take the guns if we don't get out in one hell of a hurry. Fetch the limbers! Tail onto those ropes . . . snatch that piece back here so we can limber up. Where the hell are those drivers? What the hell do they think they're doing? Move, can't you? Move . . . !*

Major Pinkney, watching the guns, watching his own men, watching the enemy's rush, turning again to the guns, sees the gun teams break from the edge of the orchard, the limbers crazily bounding, men clinging to bridles, wrestling the teams around, backing them up to the gun trails. One gun is hooked up. Whips cut at the horses' flanks. The wheel horses squat to the sudden dead weight of the gun, hoofs dig up the dirt in clouds, the horses scramble like cats and plunge into a maddened gallop.

The two rifle companies break, they begin "at the same instant to move towards the artillery." To Will Pinkney, his command for retreat unspoken, it appears that the flight of his men and of the two batteries is a simultaneous movement. He had hoped that his rifles could "venture . . . another fire," but if they had "remained

much longer, they must have been taken prisoners or cut to pieces."
As it is, Captain Bader is taken. And as the guns and the crews and
the riflemen stream uphill past the north corner of the orchard,
toward the only troops they can see—the Fifth Maryland, with its
left flank on the Georgetown road—the last of the guns is in trouble.
The horses are out of control, the bayonets only a few yards away.
*Leave it! Get that limber away! Spike the gun . . . a file, man
. . . stick a file in the vent! Hammer it in! God damn it, use the*

rammer! Hit it . . . break it off short! The gun stands forlorn, half
in, half out of the embrasure.[26] The last of the gunners run for their
lives.

The flight of the guns that got away becomes uncontrollable
rout. The terrified gun teams tear up the Georgetown road. The
rout pours "in torrents"[27] past the left flank of Stansbury's line,
between Burch's three fieldpieces and Laval's cavalry. One team
swings off to the right of the road, into a farm lane that runs
through the field where the cavalry waits in close order beyond
the fence. There is a gate in the fence, with dragoons massed behind
it. Before the dragoons can clear the gate, the crazed team crashes

through into a jumble of rearing, plunging horses. It topples men out of their saddles. It crushes down others, horses and all. The gun, towing behind, swings from one side of the lane to the other, ripping the swath through the cavalry wider. One spinning wheel strikes Lieutenant Colonel Lavall on the leg and almost knocks him off his horse.

General Winder, on horseback a few yards behind the Fifth Maryland, watches the headlong retreat. He is calm. He is not alarmed by the dispersal of the first line: he did not, in fact, regard it as a first line but as an advanced force only. His army is intact, his two brigades have not yet been in action. Only the advanced detachment has been driven back, and that defeated force is still available. Already "the stream of the running phalanx" is abating. Lavall is getting his disordered troopers into ranks. The panting riflemen are slowing to a jog, a walk; they are rallying and forming on the left flank of the Fifth.[28] If the excited batteries are given time to pull themselves together, they can be brought into action in a new position.

The commanding general's self-control was not shaken earlier today by the ruin of his first conception of the battle—a determined stand in front of Bladensburg, not here behind it. His self-control is not shaken now. He has in mind a new conception. Sound or unsound, his new plan is orthodox. It foresees the eventual defeat of Stansbury's regiments and discounts that defeat; it conceives a final and decisive action at the third line, behind the ravine a half mile to the rear; it contemplates the retreat of Stansbury's troops, under pressure but unbroken, to that third line. Which is to say that Winder's new conception is based on the juncture of the two halves of his army: he still intends to bring his whole force into action as one army, on the line established by Beall, Barney, and the Washington brigade.

What he plans looks simple, in the army's printed regulations. It *is* simple, on a drill field. Under fire, it is less simple; but, for disciplined, tried troops, it is a standard, practical maneuver. What Winder fails to take into consideration is the obvious fact that these troops are neither tried nor disciplined, that they have never practiced any such maneuver, that until yesterday they had never even been a part of a formation larger than a regiment. Even as he watches the stampeding guns and the confused "torrents" of retreating cannoneers and riflemen, he does not foresee confusion.

And he does not see the actual, controlling pattern of the

battle. He has overlooked the Y. He has overlooked, too, the first fatal incident of the battle, the first application of the pattern to the combat.

The action at Bladensburg affords an interesting demonstration of the extent to which a single circumstance, a single flaw, can take possession of a battle. Wholly aside from all the rest of the pre-battle errors, the controlling flaw was the neglect of the terrain *below* the bridge. The controlling circumstance was the resulting advance of the British left wing into the copse south of the apex of the Y—an instantaneous advance against so trifling a resistance that the rifle companies and the batteries were swiftly overlapped and outflanked. The defeat of these troops was not in itself important. Retreat from that first line was almost certainly inevitable, even if it had been held by the whole Maryland brigade. But the consequence of the retreat might have been different.

As Stansbury planned the action, the sturdiest regiment he had —the Fifth Maryland Infantry—was on the right flank of the guns, in close support. It was only fifty yards behind the rifles and its right outstretched them: [29] it was on the turnpike if not actually across it. When driven back, the turnpike would have been the natural, convenient line of its retreat. And retreat up the turnpike would have brought the Maryland troops to the position of the Washington brigade: it would have brought about the union of the two halves of the army. All that, of course, is theory. But what happened isn't.

What happened was that the weight of the British left flank— the heaviest part of the attacking line—bore down upon the unprotected right flank of the rifles and the guns. Their retreat is not significant. The *route* of their retreat is vitally significant. The British pressure from the south directed their flight northward and northwestward toward the Georgetown road. The easy ground along the south side of the turnpike, undefended, gave the British left an opportunity for a rapid, undisturbed advance: [30] it gave the enemy a fulcrum from which he could use his left flank as a lever to pry Stansbury's infantry from its position on the slope behind the orchard. Fortuitiously, this swift advance of the British left flank applied pressure to *both* of the first two American positions in a way that took the utmost tactical advantage of the ground and of the direction of the roads.

This pressure tended to push the whole Maryland brigade nothwestward toward the Georgetown road . . . to make that road the natural route of retreat if the brigade gave way. From the very beginning of the action, the British pressure tended to divide the American army, to drive one half of it toward the upper arm of the Y—the road to Georgetown—and to separate it from the other half preparing to give battle in positions drawn across the lower arm of the Y—the Washington turnpike. The Y shape of the roads had set the pattern for the campaign. It had led the invaders and the defenders to collision here at Bladensburg. It had made

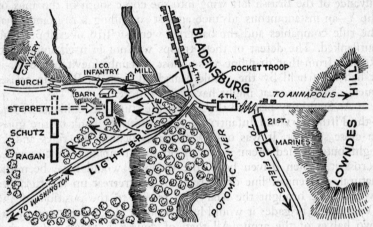

How the British pressure pushed the American left
wing away from the Washington turnpike—and away
from the right wing.

easier the concentration of the American army. Now it was making easier the division and dispersal of that army.

That is the circumstance Winder fails to see. He rides out now into the Georgetown road and tries to give form to his new conception of the battle . . . to his idea of uniting his brigades at last upon the third line for the ultimate, deciding fight. He orders the captains of the two routed batteries to move on up the road and place their guns "on a rising ground . . . in the rear." He points out the new battery position, a hill "immediately in connection with the positions of General Smith's corps"—the Washington brigade, reinforced by Barney's flotillamen and heavy guns, Scott's regulars, and the militia commands of Beall, Kramer, Waring and Maynard. The batteries trundle off. Winder has taken the first step toward uniting his brigades and toward establishing a rallying point for Stansbury's troops if they are driven back—as he expects them to be. But he fails to make sure that Stansbury's troops know where the third line is. He fails to point out that the nearest troops, on whom he expects the Maryland brigade to rally if it is compelled to fall back, are almost half a mile south of the Georgetown road. He fails to make sure that Stansbury's colonels even know that there *is* a third line. Instead of specifying a route of retreat that will bring about a junction of the two brigades, he tells John Law, acting commander of Burch's three guns: "When you retreat, take notice that you must retreat by the Georgetown road."

Here, at this point, when the two rifle companies have rallied and the retreat of the Baltimore batteries has been checked and given direction, the first of the day's three actions merges into the second. The first is over, the other just beginning. And it begins, as the first began, with a blow not dealt by the enemy . . . a blow dealt by the weight of Monroe's blunder . . . by the consequences, suspended for more than an hour, but falling now with crushing, invisible weight.

Take time now to glance at the map. Those three neat blocks in a perpendicular row just to the left of the orchard are Stansbury's three regiments; they aren't as neat on the ground as they look on the map, but they are where Monroe put them. Now notice the shape of the orchard. It stretches along the Washington turnpike, it spreads at an angle across the American front. At no point along the neat row of blocks can a man see all of the ground ahead, the ground where the enemy is: no matter where a man stands, the orchard hides part of the field: in some places, it hides everything, and in these places the men in Stansbury's line can see nothing except the interlaced boughs of the trees.

Winder, trying to see as much of the field as possible, has taken his post at the left of the upper end of the uppermost block in the row of three: he is just behind the flank of the Fifth Maryland. He can see the diagonal sweep of the orchard, he can see the barn, the roof of the mill. He can see all the way down the sloping field to the willows along the river and, over the willows, all the way into the village. But he cannot see through the orchard, he cannot see the open ground southeast of the orchard . . . the long stretch of easy ground leading up from the bridge . . . the ground left undefended when Monroe pulled Stansbury's troops to the rear. Where Winder rides back and forth between the Fifth Maryland and Captain Ben Burch's guns, he can see only half of the battlefield . . . less than half. He does not take time to ride to the other end of the line to see what the situation is there. He knows that his right flank is in the air, but he does not see that the enemy can advance through that unguarded, easy ground with nothing more than a fence to delay the attack. He does not see that the British can come almost up to his flank without being seen by his infantry. He goes into action half blind.

What Winder sees in front, in his less-than-half of the field, seizes his whole attention. The rocket detachment has opened fire again: it is firing on Stansbury's line, but its missiles are wildly erratic: the rockets are flying high over the heads of the men. The ranks squirm. A tremor runs down the line. But the tremor is not fear, yet: it is mostly curiosity: it is caused by men twisting around and craning their necks to look over their shoulders, to watch the fallen rockets darting about in the field behind them like frightened, fiery-tailed lizards. Winder puts his horse to a trot; he rides up and down the wriggling ranks, "encouraging the men to disregard the rockets." But he cannot spend much time in steadying the militia. The British infantry is moving to the attack. Red jackets appear at the lower end of the orchard, pressing on in the wake of Will Pinkney's retreat. They hesitate there, and Ben Burch's three guns open fire. The second combat of the day has begun as the first began, with rocket fire and the racket of field guns.

Patches and flashes of red begin to show in the orchard itself: the skirmishers of the 85th are filtering up the slope through the trees, and the trees give them perfect cover. The British advance, here, is concealed and protected even better than the first rush through the town was concealed by the houses. Thus the second blow of this second, scarcely begun engagement falls on the Maryland troops . . . the second blow dealt by Monroe . . . the second result of his blundering interference. Monroe placed these troops so that they are completely exposed and the British are almost completely concealed. He made the British a gift of an almost perfect position, and they are making full use of it now. Their infantry, running, crouching under the low-bent limbs, infiltrates the orchard and presses through to the edge; it finds excellent cover there. From the long, oblique front of the orchard, it opens a scattering fire.

The orchard begins to bloom. The smoke of the muskets hangs low, it is caught in the trees. The dirty-white smoke gives the apple orchard the shabby look of the morning after a storm in the spring, the blossoms still clinging but no longer fresh, bedraggled and beaten by rain.

But the fire is not heavy yet. The skirmish line is too far away for accurate shooting. The musket balls bury themselves in the dirt or go wailing off overhead. Leaves drift through the smoke of the muskets, lopped branches come flickering down: Burch's guns are pruning the orchard with dull, invisible shears.

At this opening stage of the day's second action, the advantage of numbers is on the American side. On paper, the troops in this second American line muster roughly two thousand men, not counting the crews of the guns and not counting, either, the cavalry off on the flank. Including the cavalrymen (who will take no part in the fight) and the gunners, the maximum paper strength of the Americans is 2,553. Against the eleven hundred of the enemy's first brigade, the odds are little less than two and a half to one.

The enemy is not impressed. To the British regulars, the Yankees drawn up and waiting for their attack on "the brow of a bare green hill" [31] look futile and funny, they present "a very singular and a very awkward appearance." [32] Their order is "tolerably regular," their battle line short and thick; the men are in ranks three deep. [33] They seem to be "sufficiently armed but wretchedly equipped," and most of them "are not dressed in uniform"; they are "clothed part in black coats, others in blue, others in ordinary shooting-jackets and some in round frocks"; they look more like a crowd of spectators than an army. Only a few companies—"perhaps two or at the most three battalions"—are wearing blue jackets; these, and these only, present "some appearance of regular troops." [34] With complete confidence, with a deft professional skill, Wellington's veterans proceed with the business of moving that rabble of armed civilians out of their way.

The fire from the orchard grows hotter. The skirmish line almost concealed in the fringe of the trees is building up stronger and stronger in spite of the three busy guns. Down the slope, past the end of the orchard, the visible British line is lengthening; it is spreading out to the north, toward the mill; it is matching the American front, [35] reaching out for the American left flank as it already has found and outreached the American right. All the troops of the first British brigade are over the river now. [36] Those who crossed by the upper fords have swept aside the two infantry companies and Captain Aisquith's Sharp Shooters and are re-forming under the partial shelter of the big wooden barn. [37]

Winder rides over to Ben Burch's guns and gives Burch an order. The three six-pounders begin to batter the barn. They make a fine smashing and crashing. Splinters fly. The broad planks burst into kindling. Burch, watching, is proud of his guns, he is sure that their fire is "very galling to the enemy." [38] But the enemy's line is unshaken; it is straightening; it is growing steadily stronger as sections and half-platoons, disarranged by their dash through the fords and the thickets, fit themselves into the order of battle. And yonder in Bladensburg, a thick column of reinforcements is moving rapidly down the main street.[39] Winder makes a decision. Now is the time to strike . . . now, before that fresh column can cross the bridge . . . while the enemy's line is still extended and thin. He gallops up to Lieutenant Colonel Joe Sterrett and orders the Fifth to advance.

The Fifth is that mass of blue that has "some appearance of regular troops." It is the uppermost block in that neat perpendicular row of three little blocks on the map. It is only Baltimore City militia . . . it is nine town companies with high-sounding militia names—the First Baltimore Light Infantry, the Mechanical Volunteers, the Washington Blues, the Baltimore Yeagers, the Independent Company, the Baltimore United Volunteers, the Baltimore Patriots, the Union Volunteers, the Independent Blues. The Fifth is a kind of town meeting "comprising some of the most substantial businessmen of the city and some distinguished professional men" . . . a highly respectable meeting. Names on the company rosters are the same names you'd expect to see on the list of subscribers to any respectable cause . . . the solid, old-family names. Here and there the names of the sons and the fathers appear on the rosters together. Here and there in the ranks are the leading merchants and lawyers, the owners of ships and ropewalks, the holders of broad estates whose land grants go back a hundred and fifty years to the days of the lords proprietors. Beside them stand men to whom they pay wages . . . shop clerks and wheelwrights and saddlers, watermen, dock hands, prentice boys, millers and tailors, sailmakers, carpenters. The Fifth is a community in itself. It has annexed, now, another cross section of Baltimore—the Union Yagers and the Fell's Point Rifles. Will Pinkney, retreating on foot with his men, has rallied them well. Without orders, he has formed them again on the left of the Fifth. The two rifle companies, beaten and driven in their first meeting with war, have left wounded behind in the triangle field and the thickets; the Yagers have lost their captain; but they are ready to try it again. Will Pinkney has helped himself to somebody's horse.[40] The British officers, watching the American line, are right in deciding that the body of uniformed troops amounts to "perhaps two or at the most three battalions." It amounts, in fact, to two scant battalions and less than half of a third. It amounts to six hundred men.

Colonel Sterrett is standing up in his stirrups, he has his sword in his hand. The long-drawn command of precaution rings out: "The regiment will advance in line!" The majors repeat it: "Take care to advance in line!" The captains' shouts are echoes. *It surely takes right much talk to get a thing done in the army.* Sterrett raises his sword arm. He raises his voice: "Forwa-ar-rrd . . . " Again the repeating echoes. The regiment stirs, it marks time. All the helmets jiggle. The pompons and plumes and the curling cock feathers are stirred by the small, rhythmic dance of feet lifting and falling in cadence. The colonel's arm drops. " . . . March!" The Fifth Maryland moves down the slope. The rifles move with it.[41]

Sterrett watches a moment, his back to the enemy. His eyes are sharp, his face is taut with concern. Then the tightness relaxes. Pride touches his face and his eyes. The Fifth is marching as if on parade. Its ranks are as straight as they ever were out on Hampstead Hill, on review. The three solid ranks—almost four solid ranks now, with the subalterns and sergeants marching behind their platoons—are precisely two feet apart. They are moving in short, stiff steps, seventy-six to the minute, each step twenty-four inches long. These men have never been shot at until today, there isn't a man in those ranks who knows anything more about war than what he has read in the paper or what he saw a few minutes ago when the Baltimore guns stampeded or what Will Pinkney's men saw just before they ran. Now the rifles are going back into the fight; they didn't have to, the order didn't include them; but there they are, marching as if they belonged to the Fifth, with their ex-ambassador major riding in front on his borrowed horse. The only nervousness Sterrett can see in the marching lines is the nervous twitching of heads to the right, the nervous care to keep the ranks dressed, the nervous hitch of blue elbows keeping the proper touch in the ranks. Lord . . . Lord . . . it's a handsome regiment. [42] The colonel turns his horse and settles himself to the saddle and rides down the hill toward the blossoming smoke. His staff rides behind him.

For minutes, this is war as it looks in the pictures, this is a painted battle.

THE CHARGE OF THE FIFTH MARYLAND—"three solid ranks . . . moving in
been shot a

The Fifth is a moving wall . . . a wall topped with sharp,
splintery flashes of light. (The bayonets glisten like long, sharp
splinters of glass on the top of a garden wall.) The Fifth is a rolling
blue wave . . . a long sea-blue wave with bright foam sparkling
above it. (The thousand sore feet, tramping together, swash through
the susurrant grass with the sound of the surf on the sand.) The
Fifth is a broad blue ribbon across the breast of the hill . . . a
ribbon edged with steel beads and stitched with the white feather
stitching of crossbelts. (The ground is uneven, the ribbon rises and
falls, the hill seems to breathe.) The Fifth is five hundred middle-
aged men and young men and boys four days out of peaceful homes
. . . many from quiet tree-shaded shops where sound is the rustle

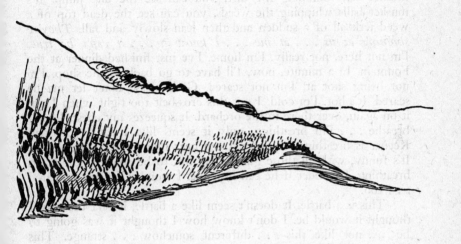

short, stiff steps, seventy-six to the minute . . . these men have never
until today."

of India silk on the counter and soft southern voices of women
. . . from hot-summer somnolent offices where sound is the scratch
of a pen . . . from high-ceilinged courts were sound is the drone
of a clerk and the buzz of a fly at the shutters. The Fifth is five
hundred civilians in coats that are mostly alike, walking down a long
hill in the sun.

It is hot in the sun. *There's a spot in my belly that's cold.* It
is noisy here on the hill. Those cannon back there are making a
sound that is like empty rum casks being dropped one at a time
into the echoing hold of a schooner tied up at Moale's wharf.
*They're our guns, they sound good. But only three guns . . . what
became of the Baltimore guns?* There's a sound overhead that's

silky and soft, it might be silk tearing, it might be sharp scissors shearing through India silk. *It isn't; it's bullets.* There's a sound underfoot that's like a big fly bumping and bumping against the shutters; there's a sound that's like a pen scratching. *It isn't.* It's musket balls bumping the dirt, you can see the dirt jump. It's musket balls whipping the weeds, you can see the dead top of a weed jerk all of a sudden and then lean slowly and fall. *They're shooting at us . . . at me . . . I know it . . . it can't be true.* I'm not here, not really. I'm home. I've just finished dinner at the Fountain. In a minute, now, I'll have to go back to the shop. I'm not being shot at. I'm not scared. God, please don't let me be scared. It's hot. I'm cold. I got this crossbelt too tight when I put it on again, over there in the orchard. It squeezes my chest. I can't breathe . . . I'm breathing, only it seems like I can't. Christian Keener is breathing, all right. I can hear him, right alongside me. It's funny, with all those guns going off, to be able to hear Chris breathing. I wonder if he can hear me. I wonder if Chris is scared . . . too.

This is a battle. It doesn't seem like a battle, it isn't the way I thought it would be. I don't know how I thought it was going to be . . . not like this . . . different somehow . . . strange. This isn't strange. The only thing strange about it is that it seems so ordinary. It's like walking along a strange road, knowing where you're going but not knowing how soon you'll get there or just where you are. It seems like there'd ought to be a sign or a milestone or something to let you know, a sign like "Towson Town, 7 Mi." I don't feel the way I thought I'd feel. I'm not scared exactly . . . I don't think I'm scared . . . it isn't that, mostly . . . I just feel kind of surprised. I've known ever since Sunday that it was going to happen and now it's happening and I feel kind of surprised. One minute you're standing around and talking and then the next minute you're in a battle. It's like getting up out of bed in the night and walking across the room in the dark and knocking your wind half out on the chest of drawers. The chest was there all the time and you knew it was there and yet you're surprised. That's it . . . I feel like my wind had been about half knocked out. I'm awake but I feel like I can't wake up. My legs are working all right but they don't feel right . . . they feel hollow . . . from the knees down they feel about as weak and thin as a hollow barley straw. I feel like I'd maybe be sick and have to lie down. I was lying down just a little while ago. We were over there in the orchard and I was lying face down in the grass and watching a couple of ants and thinking. It was quiet under the trees, it was so peaceful and still. It was even cool . . . anyway, it was cooler, it was cooler than here. I put my arm around the roll of my blanket and thought about Mary Ellen. *Mary Ellen . . . Mary Ellen . . .*

It isn't quiet there now. It looks cool, though. I know it's too hot for snow, but the smoke piled up all along the edge of the orchard looks like a dirty snowbank. It looks the way snow looks after it's laid on the street two-three days and the chimneys have soiled it, after the walks have been shoveled clear and the snow is banked up along the fronts of the houses and stained with the eaves-drip. The smoke is so thick that it makes a dusk for the muskets. The flashes are plain, as plain as if it was evening and not just a little past noon. When the muskets go off, the quick gusts of red light are like lamplight jumping out into the street across the piled snow from doors thrown suddenly open, and then jumping back when the doors are closed again quickly.

We're not in the orchard now. Why didn't we stay there? Those fellows couldn't see us, if we had stayed . . . they couldn't see us any more than we can see them. We could be shooting at them the way they're shooting at us. We're like pigeons . . . we're like passenger pigeons on a limb, all jam-packed together. I shot into a limbful of pigeons once. Just one shot. It killed seventeen. Seventeen besides those that could still flutter a little and flopped away into the brush. I found some of them, but likely not all. It made me feel kind of sick, the shot tore them so. Am I going to be sick again now? I don't want to be sick.

Don't think about it, think about something else. *Gallia est omnis divisa in partes tres.* Don't think about school. Those delph-ware dishes on the back shelf might sell if they were set out on the table up toward the front of the shop. Don't think about father's shop. Think about Mary Ellen.

Mary Ellen's so little . . . she has the littlest nose . . . and the littlest hands . . . and she always smiles when she knows I'm going to kiss her . . . and then the smile goes away, like that, just before our lips touch, and she gets all solemn . . . like a judge or a preacher. *Mary Ellen . . .* Those muskets over there in the orchard sound like the calking hammers, that day we walked down to Harris's Creek to see them building the *Java.* It was hot . . . and you looked so cool. How do girls always manage to look so cool?

*Chris . . . Chris . . . you're out of step. What's the matter with
. . . ?* Oh God, I'm going to be sick.

"Eyes front! Keep your line dressed!" That's Lieutenant Cooke.
That's all right for Lieutenant Cooke. He didn't hear that sound
Christian Keener [43] made just before he went down . . . that
sudden small *uhhh!* as if he'd been hit by a fist in the pit of his
stomach. "Keep your eyes to the front!" My God, do we just leave
him there? Are the men behind just going to walk right over him?
Can't a man even look to see if he's dead or how badly he's hurt?
We do . . . and they are . . . and you can't.

The sag in the line strightens out. The gap closes up. The
charge of the Fifth goes on.

Don't think about Christian Keener. Don't think about home.
Don't think about Mary Ellen. *Don't think*. Keep in step. Keep
your elbow touching the next man's elbow. Keep your eyes fixed to
the ground twelve or fifteen paces in front. That's what it says in
the drill book.

The ground slopes. You're going downhill. You can't keep from
looking at what's ahead . . . the men in red jackets . . . the orchard . . . the smoke.

The Fifth is marching into the obtuse angle formed by the
British line that stretches across the open ground between the barn
and the orchard and joins, at the orchard corner, the oblique, invisible line that crouches and fires all along the edge of the trees.
The hidden part of the enemy's line is the longer part, it is almost
three-fourths of the British front. The Fifth is moving straight
down the slope toward the visible part of the line, it is moving
across the whole front of the long, concealed line in the orchard.
Its right-flank companies come closer at every step to the muskets
they cannot see. At every step, the range for the muskets is
shortened.

There are new gaps in the ranks of the Volunteers, other sags,
other eddies of men confusd by a sudden blue heap on the ground.
With the ranks only two feet apart, you can't stop in time when
the man ahead of you stops as if he'd bumped into a tree. You
bump into him, you can feel him collapsing against your chest, you
can feel him being emptied like a sack that is torn on a nail. You step
over the empty blue sack on the ground, you try not to step
on the sack. "*Dress . . . dress . . . eyes front!*" The book says if
you look to one side you'll pull forward the opposite shoulder, you'll
push the whole company out of its proper direction, you'll "occasion

a continual waving in the march." [44] The books says "carry the head always upright, the eyes directed to the ground." It's all down in the book, it's so neat and precise in the book. But it cramps you, it makes your neck stiff, it gives you a crick in the neck. *If you've got to think, think about that.*

The ranks are not quite so straight now, but they are still going ahead. The long sea-blue wave rolls steadily down the hill, breaking a little, unbroken. That sound as of a wave breaking is the long, roaring *whhssshhh* of the rockets rushing across the orchard. [46]

The rockets are not being aimed at the charge. They are aimed at the drab mass of men left behind on the hill . . . at the two so-called regiments hastily pasted together out of the odds and ends of four drafted regiments-on-paper. The enemy's purpose is shrewd: this new weapon's power to strike terror is greatest when it is used against raw, green troops. And those men in their farm clothes and store clothes are obviously as raw and green as a body of "troops" can be. But the rockets are still going wild, [45] they are only dropping sparks on the huddle of paper soldiers before they plunge into the hill and skitter and burn themselves out.

The charge of the Fifth goes on. There is something gallant about it, something pathetic and earnest. Suppose it fails. There is still something gallant about these dressed-up-alike civilians trying so hard to do what the drill book says. (Give them their moment of honor before they are smeared with dishonor to hide the shortcomings of others.) This is no easy thing they are doing . . . marching in rigid silence, in close-packed ranks, across open ground, into the fire of muskets they cannot see, into fire they are not permitted to answer. (It isn't easy to walk across a bare field toward a man with a gun in his hands, a man who is trying to kill you. It violates every sensible instinct. It makes you feel naked. It blows a cold wind through your bones.) Only the British are firing. The whole American front is silent, except for Ben Burch's three guns. [46] And now one of the guns falls silent: the advance of the Fifth, down the narrowing slope, has come into its line of fire. [47] Sterrett, looking back over his shoulder, wonders how long his men can endure the strain without cracking. (It isn't easy to let a man shoot at you, time after time, and to do nothing about it except keep on walking toward him.) The Fifth isn't badly hurt. The fire from the hidden line in the orchard isn't the kind of fire that the British faced forty years ago on a hill over Boston harbor.

The British aim is unbelievably bad. In three hundred yards, not a dozen men have been hit. (It isn't easy to keep on walking, erect, toward a man who intends to kill you. The wind sucks the marrow right out of your bones, it sucks the guts out of your belly, your belly's too thin for your pants, your pants want to fall down. You want to fall down on your face on the ground and crawl into the ground and pull the ground over your head.) But there is more to it than being hit or seeing another man hit. The Fifth isn't charging a mere line of men: the Fifth is charging a legend. The troops it can see and the troops it can't see are, by legend, the finest troops in the world. If they are not truly the finest they are at least a part of the armies that broke and defeated the finest who carried Napoleon's eagles. They are regulars . . . veterans . . . British Invincibles. In their own moment of time, they are Caesar's legions and Cromwell's Ironsides, the Grecian phalanx, the Spanish pikemen, the Swedes of Gustavus Adolphus. (In another moment of time there will rise a similar legend—the panzerdivisionen.)

The charge of the Fifth goes on, silent, into the angle formed by the British front. It has covered three-fourths of the open ground. It is less than a hundred yards from the lost barbette. The rallied Rifles on the left flank are close to the splintered barn. The companies at the opposite end of the line are close to the smoking orchard: a few paces more will bring them to grips with the British infantry there. Joe Sterrett, storekeeper-banker leading a charge in his first five minutes of battle, knows he must make a decision and make it at once. How far? How far? The shock of six hundred men should break that thin line ahead, recapture the earthwork, retake the abandoned gun. But the earthwork is useless, the spiked gun is useless. How far should he take these men? Where is the border that separates duty from error? The Fifth has left its support behind. It is already outflanked on the right. It is marching into a pocket. The enemy's fire is coming from three directions . . . from the trees, from the line in front, from the heavier body of troops being formed for a new attack near the Georgetown road and the lane that leads from the mill and the upper fords. Ben Burch's two guns are still pounding away at the barn but their fire is slow: it takes a long time to sponge and load and prime: it takes a long time to re-lay, after every shot, a gun that weighs almost a ton. And the six-pound balls, when they come, are doing no serious harm; they are keeping the enemy's skirmishers out of the barn but the barn still shields from the gunners' view the gathering troops in the road and the lane.

Let the charge go on? Close with them? Give them the bayonet? Cold steel is the enemy's favorite weapon, he is skilled in its use; to close with a bayonet charge is the object of British infantry tactics. The Fifth Maryland has found bayonets useful as skewers for broiling its beef, it has found they make excellent holders for candles when stuck pointdown in the sod. And half of Will Pinkney's men have no bayonets at all.

Joe Sterrett checks his horse. He turns, and his arm goes up. "Battalions . . . mark time . . . dress . . . !" The six hundred men go into a shuffling dance. They put their right hands on their hips; their knees rise and fall; their feet beat dust out of the ground; their feet beat the ground like a drum. This might be a tribal ceremony, a final appeal to the war-god, an aboriginal war dance. This might all be a part of a savage ritual that prescribes every motion and gesture—the head rigidly turned, the elbow at just such an angle, the foot raised precisely four inches, each foot lifted thirty-six times to the minute. (This is war of another day . . . the day of the flintlock, the slow firing muzzle-loader . . . a day long before machine guns. Marking time under fire is a part of the ritual of close-order battle; it is the device by which regiments straighten their lines. It will go on and on, as unchanging as any tribal ceremony, through many wars yet to be fought. Men will die performing this shuffling, stationary dance on a thousand fields with names such as Bull Run and Sharpsburg and Chancellorsville. Ritual dies hard. It is easier to kill men than to change the rules by which they are killed.) Now, under converging fire that would cut them to pieces if it were not still unbelievably wild, the eleven Baltimore companies straighten their lines as if this were a dress parade.

". . . halt!" [48] The dance ends. But the ceremony goes on. Command of precaution . . . command of preparation . . . command of direction . . . command of execution. Formal, elaborate, ritualistic commands. "The regiment will prepare to fire." "Battalion . . . prepare to fire." The majors, the captains, the lieutenants, the sergeants repeat the elaborate phrases like acolytes. "Battalion . . . company . . . platoon . . . take care to perform the motions of the manual . . ." *My God, does it take all that chat to shoot off a gun? You'd play hell, shootin' ducks thataway.* The colonel is riding to the rear through the gap between the battalions. There's nothing in front but the enemy now. *If they'd just leave us shoot*

. . . ! Ready . . ." *Ah . . . now . . . now, by God!* All the bayonets leap straight up, the six hundred men raise their muskets
and rifles straight up in front of their faces with "the cock opposite
the nipple of the left breast, the barrel perpendicular in front of
the left eye, the body quarter faced to the right." Six hundred
thumbs pull the gun locks back. "Aim!" The long barrels swing
down; the gleam of the bayonets, suddenly leveled, leaps like a
flash of lightning. "Fire!" After the lightning, the thunder.

It makes its own cloud. Smoke smothers the six hundred men.
As it rolls, it is torn; the hot blasts that produced it rip through
it and tear it apart. Men stare through the rents in the smoke.
Their hands, groping for paper cartridges, raising the cartridges
up to their mouths, stop in front of their chins; their teeth, ready
to bite off the ends of the cartridges, stay wide apart in their wide-
open mouths. Their mouths fill with sound. Not a cheer. A noise.
A sound without shape or intention . . . a roar of amazement and
triumph and disbelief. *By God . . . by God . . . !* The men in red
jackets are going back. The red line is breaking. *We did it!*
We did it! They're running! Some of the British are running.
Some are walking. Some are shuffling backward and loading and
firing and shuffling backward again. Some are sprawled on the
ground; they writhe or they try to crawl or they just lie still.
The dressed-up-alike civilians are yelling the way the crowd yells
when the Liberty Engine Company gets to a fire twenty seconds
ahead of the United Hose and Suction Engine Company, they
are yelling the way apprentices yell at a game of hot cockles. *That
was a dowser! That stung 'em!* The yells are exultant and savage.
Invincibles . . . yea-a-ahhhh! The yells are naïve. The red line
in front is retreating, but not the red column drawn up in the
road nor the invisible line in the orchard.

The yelling is choked by the smoke. The powder fumes
turn it to coughing. The high moment passes.

A change comes over the battle and over the Fifth and the
Rifles. The six hundred men are firing at will, they are loading and
priming and aiming and pulling the tricker [49] as fast as they can.
There is ritual still: between one shot and the next, a man with a
musket must execute twenty-nine separate motions. But after the
opening volley, he must go through the twenty-nine motions alone.
It isn't every man for himself, it is every man by himself. Joe
Sterrett has struck his blow, he has wielded his men as a weapon
for one solid blow. But after the first massed fire the six hundred

men are no longer a single weapon, they are six hundred weapons. Now, when each acts by himself, he loses by ever so little the sense of belonging, of being a part of the whole. By ever so little, the companies lose their cohesion, the men lose the disciplined oneness of will that carried them down the bare slope against every natural instinct. They lose the crowd-comfort, the subconscious counterfeit feeling of being somehow protected by numbers. There is no longer one will, there are six hundred wills. Each man fights his battle alone.

Aim. Fire. Recover. Why the hell do they call it recover? Because the damn' musket kicks your shoulder clear around to the back of your neck? *Port . . . arms. Half cock . . . firelock.* Hook the right thumb over the cock. Pull it back to the half. *Open . . . pan.* Thumb on the hammer, the fingers clenched, the forearm lying along the stock of the musket. Push the thumb hard on the hammer. That's silly. This is a battle . . . I'm in it . . . I guess I'm not scared. If I was scared I wouldn't be thinking of things like that, I wouldn't be thinking about how the army gets everything twisted. Like calling the hammer a cock and then saying the top of the priming pan is the hammer.[50] It doesn't make sense. *Handle . . . cartridge.* Right elbow thrown back, the right hand to the cartridge box. The book calls it a cartouche box and that's silly too. You'd think we could use our own language, you'd think we could load a musket in English as well as in French. But maybe not: those buggers down there are English: it probably wouldn't be right. *Prime.* Grip the cartridge between the thumb and the first two fingers. Bring it up, quick, to the mouth. Bite into it . . . not deep, just to the powder. Pfwah. It tastes foul. It tastes like a tarnished brass candlestick smells when Amanda starts scouring it, green tarnish smell metal smell soap smell all mixed up together and foul. The rough cartridge paper scratches against your tongue. It feels and it tastes like a sock that you've worn till it's stiff. Bring the cartridge down to the pan. Pour powder into the pan . . . *God damn it! It spilled!*

The crash of the big-barreled muskets is more than a sound: it is solid: it falls like a blow: it beats on the ear like a club with a knotty end. The single explosions are harder to bear than a volley. You know when a volley is coming: there's time to take hold of your nerves: you can hold your nerves tight, like reins. But there's no way of knowing when George Golder's musket behind you will blast your left ear or Ben Taylor's explode in the other. After the opening volley the firing is ragged, uneven. Some men load more quickly than others and some men are calmer than others. Some wait for a living target, their faces intent and absorbed. Some fire blindly and wild through the smoke in a frenzy of haste, they pant like exhausted runners, they stare in a fixed fascination at something they cannot see. Their hands shake as they load, they are shaken by something that is not fear but partakes of the nature of fear and can turn into fear: they are shaken by realization, a kind of naïve suprise. *We knew guns made noise. But not noise like this. Why weren't we told how it would be?* After three or four rounds the crashes begin to collide, they run into each other, they blend into hard, ripping spasms of sound like the flam of a fabulous drum. *This isn't how it should be.* This isn't the long roll of musketry, this noise doesn't roll, it jerks like a man in a fit. The whole earth is a drum and the drummer who beats it is drunk. This roar has no pattern nor rhythm; it bursts and subsides and explodes; it breaks but is never quite broken, it never is still. Every now and again you can hear the sticks whack on the rim of the drum—the hard, single shots of the rifles, flat whacks on the rim of the battle.

In the close-packed ranks of the Fifth, one rank firing between the heads of the men in front, the sound is enormous, appalling.[51] It's like all the hammers we heard on the *Java*. It's like being down in the *Java's* hold with the hammers above you, around you. No . . . no, it's not. A frigate's so big you could get away from the sound, you could crouch in the cavernous hull and the sound couldn't beat on your head. It isn't like hammers: a hammer hits quick, but this roaring is bigger and slower than hammers. It squeezes and grinds like two cannon balls grinding the sides of your head: they squeeze the sound into your head till your head can't hold any more. You can't hear, any more.

The appalling sound is a comfort.[52] It covers you, hides you. It shuts the enemy out. Those buggers there in the orchard . . . and down by the earthwork . . . and over there by the barn . . . they're shooting . . . they're trying to kill me. The damned fools, they can't do it. Don't they know they can't do it? Don't they know I can't even hear them? I'm not afraid of those bastards. I'm not afraid any more than I was afraid that time when I was six years old . . . maybe eight . . . and the thundergust beat at the house in the night and I scrooched down deep in the bed with the covers up over my head.

The crashes are woven together, the sound is a thick strong

fabric, the smoke is a smothering quilt spread over a blanket of sound, you can pull them up over your head.

You can't see the red lightning flashes: the quilted smoke shuts them out. You can't hear them strike, you can't hear the thunder. You feel it, you feel the house shake. It feels as if giants with sledges are pounding the walls of the house but you're safe, the blows can't get at you, they only come up through the floor, through the mattress of sound, like a push. . . . Like that. *What was that?* It wasn't a sound: I didn't hear it, I felt it. It felt like the earth had moved underneath of my feet. It felt like somebody pushed me.

The dull shocks of sound that come like a push and a push are two epileptic volleys discharged beyond the right flank of the Fifth and three hundred yards to its rear. The regiments left behind on the slope of the hill when the Fifth advanced have joined in the battle at last . . . first Ragan's, off to the south near the Washington pike, and then Schutz's men holding the center.[53] They are regiments only on paper; even on paper, neither one has so much as its own regimental number. They are a patchwork . . . companies and platoons and detachments from four drafted Baltimore County regiments . . . odds and ends of the Seventh, the 36th, the 15th and the 46th, hastily pasted together.[54] They have never fired volleys before, never stood in a line of battle before. Until last night, when the panicky sentinels turned the whole camp out for nothing, they hadn't known what two regiments looked like in line. And they hadn't seen much, in the dark. Now the volleys they fire are not volleys at all: they are fits and shudders of sound, convulsion after convulsion.

Down the hill where the Fifth is fighting, men turn their heads toward the physical shocks of the sound. They see the smoke of twelve hundred muskets[55] unfold like visible echoes, convulsion after convulsion. It looks like a battle. They yell.[56] *Aa-a-aahhh! Yaa-a-a-aaahhh!*

It's like shouting inside of a barrel. Your head is the barrel, the sound can't get out, it is liquid and sticky like rum, it smarts in your throat and your ears.

Men yell without hearing their yells. They don't look like men who are cheering, they look like men who are startled. Their mouths, rounded for shouting, powder-blackened from biting the cartridges, give them a look of enormous surprise. *Denny . . . Denny Magruder . . . you look like a scared pickaninny.* I wish he could hear me. I'd tell him he looks like a nigra boy caught in a melon patch and scared half out of his wits—so scared and surprised he's turned gray all excepting around his mouth. My God, but Magruder looks funny. *I wonder if I look like that.*

The Fifth is excited but steady.[57] It is still nervous, but not so nervous as when it began its advance. It has moved across open ground under fire, against British regulars; it has stopped them dead in their tracks; it has driven part of them back; it is holding its own. With each minute, its confidence grows.

And now, on the left, to the north of the Georgetown road, the infantry company guarding Ben Burch's three guns pushes down toward Will Pinkney's Rifles and joins in the fight.[58] The whole brigade is in action. Four field guns and nearly two thousand muskets are sweeping the space between the two strokes of the Y. On that narrow front they are pinning the light brigade to the ground. The odds are with them. The odds are about two to one, they are two thousand men to eleven hundred.[59] The two thousand have the four guns; the light brigade had the rockets, at first, but the rocket troop is not in the action now.

The volume of fire from Stansbury's line is impressive and reassuring. It signifies nothing. The reassurance is false.

The two makeshift regiments on the right flank of the Fifth have not stirred from where Monroe put them. They fire where they stand: the only target they have is the orchard: the range is too long for effective shooting: their firing is noisy but harmless.[60] Their own right flank is in the air. The two guns in the turnpike have no flank protection at all. Nobody gives it a thought. Winder is still the piecemeal general: he is completely absorbed in the attack of the Fifth: he is fighting his battle in pieces.[61] Only Will Pinkney is thinking of flank protection, and Pinkney is off at the other end of the line. He is worried about the ford near the mill, he is thinking that enemy troops will be coming from that direction, he has galloped down the mill road to see what is happening there.

What he sees is bad. His own detached rifle company under Ed Aisquith and the two infantry companies that ought to be there have vanished, they have been "withdrawn or driven from their station" which the enemy in the thickets can "reach with his shot without being seen." [62] Worse yet, a "sufficiently formidable" force is feeling its way up the mill road and across the adjacent ground. Already the left of Joe Sterrett's line has "nothing to protect it" against the immediate threat of a British attempt to "gain its rear." [63]

He gallops back under fire. The mill road is in plain view of the enemy's skirmishers, the Georgetown road is in plain view of the assault column forming where the shot-splintered barn partially hides it from Burch's gunners.[64] Will Pinkney's right arm is driven backward by a violent blow, then it dangles, his hand flaps on his thigh. He looks at the arm, tries to raise it: the lower half swings like a pendulum: it is broken above the elbow: a musket ball has gone in at the front, shattered the bone and passed out at the back.[65] He dismounts behind Sterrett's line.[66]

The Fifth is behaving well.[67] Its firing is steady.[68] But it is beginning to suffer. The enemy's fire from the orchard is getting hotter and hotter. The light troops of the British first wave are fighting like Maryland Red Caps, like Pennsylvania Black Boys.[69] They are fighting like Mingoes and Shawnees, taking advantage of all the cover there is: they are lying flat on their bellies in the deep orchard grass, they are kneeling behind the gnarled trunks of the old apple trees, they are shooting through the cracks in the walls of the barn, they are crouching behind its corner and in the weeds that grow thick around barns. Their converging fire is raking the ranks of the Fifth with impunity.[70] All along the line, men are going down.[71] The Fifth fires back at the barn, at the weeds, at the trees, at the hanging smoke; only once in a while there are "single men" to shoot at.[72]

The United Volunteers are taking the worst of the galling.[73] George Clarke has been shot, Bill Williams is hit, Sergeant Murray is hit, Acting Sergeant McCulloch is down with a ball-shattered leg. Oh, my Lord . . . the lieutenant's got it! *Denny . . . Denny Magruder . . . did you see that?* They've got Billy Cooke! *Denny, where are you?* Golder . . . George Golder . . . what's happened to Denny? George . . . ! They've got you, too. *I swore at George Golder a minute ago. I told him God damn you you mind what you're doing next time you fire over my shoulder you shove that damn' musket two feet out in front of my head. I thought he didn't hear me but maybe he did. I wonder if he stepped up closer behind me to do like I said and that's the reason they hit him.* God damn it . . . !

The United Volunteers have lost thirteen per cent of their men in ten minutes. They are still standing up to the British fire. The whole front is standing. The firing on both sides is heavy, but the Fifth and the Rifles are taking the fire of the enemy's hidden troops "without being able to return [it] with any probability of effect." [74] And the odds are beginning to change, they are swinging the other way. The whole British second brigade—1,460 bayonets [75]

—is over the branch, it has re-formed on this side of the bridge, its column is splitting in two. The 44th, the East Essex regiment, is beginning to move up the Georgetown road. [76] And the rocket troop has found another position, immune from the guns. [77] The rocketmen know their business: they have chosen their target shrewdly—not the "two or at the most three battalions" that wear "the blue jacket" and present "some appearance of regular troops," but the mass of "country people who would have been much more appropriately employed in attending to their agricultural occupations than in standing with muskets in their hands on the brow of a bare green hill" and might pass "very well for a crowd of spectators." [78] They open fire now on Schutz and Ragan's men.

The first rockets go wild, the first "three or four" pass "very high over the heads of the line." [79] The British reduce the angle of fire.[80] The next volley is low, it barely skims over the orchard, it barely misses the white straining faces of Schutz and Ragan's men. Sparks fall on their upturned faces. The sweat on their faces turns cold.

Another sheaf. And another. You can't see a cannon ball coming. You can't hear a musket ball coming: if you hear it, it missed you, you're safe. You see these things coming. You hear them. They turn your blood cold. It ain't Christian to fight like that . . . it ain't decent to kill a man that way, to burn him alive. It ain't human. *Those things are human!* You can see 'em hang, like, before they drop. You can see 'em lookin' for you. You can see 'em turn an' come at you. My God . . . *oh, my God* . . . *!* It's like hell-fire. It's judgment an' hell-fire.

The rockets come with a hoarse, whooping roar. They pass close overhead [81] with a roar like storm wind in a chimney . . . the roar of wind across fire . . . the roar of fire pulled by a furious gust. Like wind in a chimney, the rockets suck sparks behind them. They scatter the sparks over the two scraps-of-paper regiments, hastily pasted together.

The paper regiments begin to shrivel. They begin to curl up at the ends and the edges like paper too close to a fire—not on fire yet, not burning, but charring and turning brittle. The two regiments are as brittle as charred paper. Pieces begin to break off. The pieces are blowing away.

Stansbury sees the two regiments going to pieces. He rides down the line,[82] shouting. "Steady! Stand fast! Front . . . face!" His shouts go unheeded. Colonel Schutz, Major Kemp and Stansbury's aide, Major Woodyear, are trying to rally the men. Stansbury roars at his officers: "Keep them in line! Cut them down if they run! [83] *Cut them down!*" Winder comes galloping up from the rear of the Fifth. He, too, is shouting.[84] The company officers shout, they beg and command, they snatch at men's shoulders and arms. They try to hold pieces of companies with their hands, but the pieces crumble and sift through their fingers and blow away. Colonel Ragan gets forty men together, he forms a piece of a line. Captain Gallaway rallies most of his company. Captain Shower holds part of his. A few of Randall's men stick to their captain.[85] Ensign Brewer's detachment out of the 36th stands fast.[86]

Winder sees the groups of men coming back, he sees fragments of companies still in some kind of order, he thinks the rout has been stopped and he gallops back to the Fifth. He can see the field better down there, he thinks that is the critical place.[87]

It is one of the critical places. The Fifth is in a pocket, the stuff that the pocket is made of is getting stronger, the pocket itself is rapidly getting deeper. The assault column on the left front of the Fifth is beginning to move up the slope. And the pocket is already deeper than Winder knows: the first wave of the 85th—the company that led the rush over the bridge—is about to burst out of the woods beyond the Washington turnpike, it is almost up to the two lonely guns in the pike, it is almost up to the remnants of Schutz and Ragan's line, it is already three hundred yards to the rear of the Fifth's right flank.

Winder looks back. The pieces of line he just left are still there. They are fighting again. A flicker of fire runs along their uneven edges. They smolder and smoke. Then they burst into flame—a brief, desperate outburst of firing. And then they collapse like burned paper consumed and collapsing to ashes. Where the two county regiments stood there are only small swirls of ashes—small, furious struggles where a few of the "country people" who stood to the last are surrounded and overwhelmed by the men of the 85th. Two men in the little group around Ensign Brewer are shot, one dead and one dying; others are taken; Bill Brewer escapes.[88] Colonel Ragan is wounded and taken. Stansbury gets away, "raging profanely."[89] (For years, when it thunders, the country people will say "they hear General Stansbury swearing.")[90] But swearing will not bring back his twelve hundred men. Two-thirds of Winder's front has been swept away. He sees, now, that "a strong column of the enemy" has "passed up the road as high as the right of the Fifth."[91] He must do something and do it at once.

Off to the left and the rear, toward the crest of the rising ground, is a patch of woods. If the Fifth falls back on the woods, it will be out of reach of that hidden firing line, it will draw the enemy out of cover. He gives Colonel Sterrett an order to retire up the hill toward the woods.[92] Then he changes his mind. The

Fifth looks steady, it looks as if it can hold on for a little while. If it waits, the British may "issue in a body from the orchard" and risk an attack across open ground into the fire of these still unshaken men. He is afraid that "a movement of retreat" will shake them worse than the enemy's inaccurate muskets. He "instantly" countermands the order and rides over to Burch's guns.[93] But the British aim is improving, their fire is beginning "to annoy the Fifth still more." Winder sees the column "high" on the right deploying to take Sterrett's line "in flank." He changes his mind again.[94] In person,[95] he orders the guns to fall back "to the hill" where he had "directed the Baltimore artillery . . . to halt." He sends the same order to Sterrett.

Ben Burch's gunners are astounded. Not a man in their half-battery has been "touched," they think that the battle is only now "seriously commencing." [96] Burch disobeys the order to limber and retreat.[97] He stays where he is, and his guns continue to fire.

After "two or three rounds," General Winder rides up again and repeats the order "in a peremptory manner." [98] Burch limbers up. The three pieces move off on the Georgetown road. But Winder keeps changing his mind. The guns have gone only "a few yards" [99] when he is at Burch's elbow again. He thinks now that Burch "might venture to unlimber one of [his] pieces and give them another fire." Burch is "in the act of doing so" when Winder countermands that order, too, and hurries the guns to the rear.[100] It is high time, if he wants the guns saved. It is too soon, if he wants the Fifth saved.

The Fifth is obeying his order, it is doing its best to obey. The captains are trying to make themselves heard through the blasts of the muskets, the lieutenants are bawling commands, the sergeants are shouting and swearing. "Cease firing! Cease firing! God damn it, stop! Can you understand that? Stop it, I said! Don't load that piece! Order . . . arms!" *What's happened? Those officers know something. Something's gone wrong. What? We were doing all right. We were holding 'em. Oh, for God's sake, stop that yelling. What the hell do they want us to do? Retreat—* we've got to retreat.

There are ways to retreat, in the book. There are pictures that show how to do it. There are words . . . there are pages of words . . . words like "column formed upon the rear of the center in motion" . . . words like "battalions in echequier" and "augmentation of sections." There are diagrams . . . they look like geometry

. . . they look like a checkerboard, maybe that's what echequier means. But they don't look like war. They certainly don't look like this. They have rows of squares . . . rows of little neat squares . . . there is a square for each man and one of the squares is you. *It don't look like me.* Every square has a neat dotted line to show where it should go, in retreat. *I don't see any dotted line on this hill.*

Anyway, we never got that far in the book. We never practiced retreating on dotted lines. All we can do is do it the way we know. "Order . . . arms! Right about . . . face! Carry arms! Mark time! Forward march!" It is not a good way.

Forward? *Forward, hell.* "Eyes front!" *Front, hell.* I was in front before. That's the rear ahead, where we're goin' . . . that hill's the rear, where the guns are . . . *by God . . . ! The guns have pulled out!* We're pullin' out too an' I'm in the rear . . . the front rank is the rear rank now an' I'm in it . . . it's still in front . . . it's closest to the Britishers . . . my behind is the front an' there's nothin' between my behind an' those God-damn' muskets . . . those bay'nets. . . . *They're comin'! They're comin' out of the orchard!* "The United Volunteers will keep their eyes to the front." *Who says so?* Ensign John Wilmot says so.

Don't look back . . . don't look to one side . . . the book says if you look to one side you'll pull forward the opposite shoulder, you'll push the whole company out of its proper direction. *That's what I was thinking a while ago, we were coming down the hill then.* We were advancing then. Now we're running away. Why in hell don't we *run?* Don't look back . . . keep your head up . . . the high collar digs into the back of your neck . . . it burns, the skin is chafed raw . . . the sweat trickles and stings. But that sting lower down . . . that cold sting in the small of your back . . . like a bayonet point. . . . *I don't want to be stuck in the back.*

Don't look back. The enemy's there. The enemy is no longer hidden. You look . . . and he isn't the enemy . . . he is enemies . . . he is personal . . . he is right behind you . . . he's running . . . he has a gun in his hand and a knife on the end of the gun . . . he is coming fast . . . and we're *walking.* To hell with the proper direction. This isn't drill. To hell with keeping step . . . twenty-four-inch steps. To hell with touching the next man's shoulder . . . the next man was Denny Magruder. I haven't seen Denny since . . . There's the sergeant . . . there's Jim McCulloch . . . he's trying to crawl . . . he's all bloody . . . the ground underneath him is bloody. I don't want to look like that. *I want to get away from here.*

The company nearest the orchard breaks first. It has only one officer left. Surgeon Hanson Catlett is with it, he has been tending its wounded. Now he and the ensign rally it quickly.[101] Then the opposite end of the line goes to pieces. What Catlett just helped to do isn't easy: it says so right in the book: it says "no system has laid down a method of accustoming troops to retrieve a sudden charge, or to rally after being broken.[102] The opposite end of the line does not rally. It runs.[103]

Suddenly six hundred men want to get away from there.

8

TEARS AND IMPRECATIONS

JOHNNY KENNEDY LOST HIS MUS-
ket. It wasn't his fault. He didn't throw it away, he hadn't meant
to lose it. Johnny didn't want to be shot in the back, he didn't
want a bayonet shoved through his back, he wanted to go away
from there as fast as he could. Or faster. But he saw Sergeant Jim
McCulloch trying to crawl, dragging his broken leg.

The enemy was close behind, then.[1] But Johnny stopped running. He laid his musket down on the ground, he knelt in the
bloody grass, he got the sergeant's body over his shoulder somehow.
McCulloch was sick with pain, he wasn't much help. Johnny got
his hand on the musket, he managed to get to his feet, he started
to walk up the hill. McCulloch was heavy and clumsy, the musket
was heavy and clumsy. Private Kennedy's heart battered against his
ribs, his breathing ached in his chest, he didn't want to let go of his
gun but he had to, he couldn't let go of McCulloch. He saw some-

body he knew, he handed the musket over. The enemy was still running but not catching up, the enemy was stopping to shoot at the backs of the running Yankees. The shooting was wild,[2] but a ball found John Kennedy's friend. He dropped his own musket and Johnny's.[3]

Henry Fulford lost his courage. He ran with all his might. There was a woods in the rear. If he could reach the woods . . . the lovely, safe, quiet woods . . . But he couldn't. The bullets and grapeshot flew like hailstones around him.[4] Anyway, that was what he thought. There was no grapeshot to fly, there was only Private Fulford's imagination: it turned him away from the woods and chased him into a swamp. He lay there face down, his heart battered against his ribs, his breathing ached in his chest. He was "fatigued almost to death." He didn't say what became of his musket.[5]

Henry McComas lost the plume off his leather hat. A Britisher shot it right off and left only the stub. Private McComas wasn't too badly upset by his narrow escape from death. But he was right much put out about losing that plume. His annoyance would last for three weeks. Then, in another fight, the British would pay a high price for a curled cock's-feather.

Captain Ben Burch lost his battery. He fell back with his sullen guns but he hadn't eaten for days, he'd been up the most part of three nights,[6] he didn't know what his guns were supposed to do,[7] the heat was making the road go up and down and around. He couldn't keep up with his guns, he tried but he couldn't, he fainted.[8] He lay by the side of the road while the retreat swept around him, over him, past him. When his men missed him they didn't go back, they supposed that he had been captured.[9]

John Law, too, lost the guns. He was disgusted and angry. Burch had vanished again, he didn't know what had become of Burch, this was the second time Burch had disappeared in an hour.[10] It looked as if John Law was in command of the half-battery again but he didn't know. He didn't know what to do with it if he was. Nobody gave him orders. They oughtn't to be retreating. The road was a mess. The road was a boiling porridge of half-human beings and dust . . . a blue-corn Indian porridge of militia jackets senselessly churning and bubbling and blundering into each other. The dust was a smothering smoke, the dust was steam from a boiling kettle. You could hear the fire crackle, you could hear dry sticks being broken to feed the fire. Somewhere off yonder there still was a battle of some kind. Nobody bothered about it. The guns went away from the battle. The dust and the sweat and the sun in his eyes, the disgust in his heart, the senselessly hurrying mob in the Georgetown road got between John Law and his guns. He didn't find them again for three days.[11]

William Winder lost the command of his army—if a man can lose something he never had. The shape of the roads took control. They had interfered before, as Monroe interfered; they could have been overridden. But no longer. Not now. The Y was in full command.

Just as it fixed the pattern of the campaign and of the battle itself, so now the Y fixed the pattern of the retreat. It had brought the two wings of the army together—almost together—but not where Winder chose. Now its convergent force was applying itself in reverse. It became divergent. It split the army apart. Winder could point to a hill, he could tell Joe Myers and Dick Magruder to go there by way of the Georgetown road, he could tell John Law to retreat by that road to that hill.[12] The hill was "immediately in connexion with the positions of General Smith's corps." [13] Smith's corps was the Columbian brigade, reinforced now by Barney's five guns, by Barney's marines and hard-bitten flotilla sailors, by Beall's Anne Arundel men weary but no longer panting, by Maynard and Kramer's militia, by Waring's Prince George's battalion [14] and by Colonel Scott's regular infantry. General Smith's corps was 3,080 men [15] and eleven guns, in order of battle behind the ravines that crossed the Washington turnpike six hundred yards and thirteen hundred yards southwest of the place where Stansbury's men had been. The three thousand-odd men "were not arrayed in line, but posted in advantageous positions in connexion with and supporting each other, according as the nature of the ground admitted and required." [16] Winder's intention to halt his left wing on the hill "immediately in connexion with" these positions was a good intention. His order was not a bad order at all.

But the Georgetown road was not taking orders. It gave them. It carried Magruder's guns and Myers and Burch's "wide" of the place where Winder meant them to be. It threw "the whole mass" of the infantry "off to the right on the retreat toward Montgomery Court House." [17] The "whole of the cavalry, probably from the pressure of the infantry that way, were also thrown wide of the line of retreat" that Winder intended. Winder "had not for a moment, dispersed and disordered as was the whole of Stansbury's command, supposed that their retreat would have taken a different direction." [18]

Now, pushing his horse through the ruck of the flight, trying vainly to stem its headlong current, trying vainly to turn it "more toward General Smith's command," he found the bewildered but obedient Baltimore batteries waiting in the road. But between them and Barney's guns on the Washington turnpike stretched three-quarters of a mile of broken and gullied ground. Smith's nearest troops—a flank outpost two companies strong—were eight hundred yards away. It was "impossible" for the batteries "to get across to the turnpike road or unite with General Smith's brigade." [19] At least, Winder thought it was impossible, and his thinking made it so. He didn't ask the Baltimore gunners to try.

The enemy's light troops were in sight down the Georgetown road, they were "pressing the pursuit," they were coming on fast.[20] Winder looked at the shamelessly hurrying mass of his men in the road—half his whole army—flowing heedlessly past the halted guns, cursing the gunners for halting, trying to unhook the traces and steal the horses and running on when they failed. The sickening sight convinced him that it was "impossible to collect any force to support the artillery."

He had the guns in his hand, but he let them go. He made no attempt to put them into action beside the road, no attempt to check the pursuit with a burst of fire, no attempt to steady and shame and check his own fleeing men with the sight and the sound of their guns. There were fugitives in the fields alongside the road; it would not have occurred to Winder to risk hitting some of them, even to save an army. He "directed the artillery to continue their retreat toward the capital." That was all. No orders to make an attempt to cross the broken ground and join Smith. No orders to find a position from which the guns could cover this flight or cover the retreat of the right wing if Smith, too, should be driven back. No objective, no purpose, no nothing.

The Y had decided what was to happen. All Winder did from now on was to hasten the happening. The Y had broken his army in two. All Winder did from now on was to break up the one strong piece that remained. He kept breaking off little pieces until there was nothing left.

While Winder was hoping and doubting and seeing only impossibilities, the day's third battle had opened. Just as the first battle—Will Pinkney, Joe Myers and Dick Magruder's—had blended into the second, so now Tobias Stansbury and Colonel Joe Sterrett's battle blended into the third. "About half past twelve o'clock," while the troops of Walter Smith's "corps" were going into position, "innumerable rockets thrown from the heights of Bladensburg announced the arrival of the enemy there; and, at this period, Commodore Barney's sailors and marines, in quick march, arrived . . . " [21] The firing of artillery in front "soon commenced"— Magruder and Myers in action, driving the rocket troop out of its nest, raking the main street of Bladensburg, trying to keep the enemy from crossing the bridge, and failing. Then the right wing heard "musketry, in quick and rapid succession" and "in a few minutes the whole right and centre of the front [second] line, with some small exceptions, were seen retiring in disorder and confusion." That was the county regiments, breaking under the rockets; the exceptions were the little groups around Ragan and Randall and Shower, around Brewer and Gallaway, fighting it out gallantly. [22] "The firing continued on the extreme left"—the Fifth and the two rifle companies, standing up to converging fire from three sides—"but shortly after" the men who had made that stubborn last stand of the second line began to fall back and then to fall into confusion.

Those were the day's first and second battles as the men of Smith's corps saw them while they waited to fight the third. They didn't have long to wait, for "mean while, the left of the enemy, in heavy column," was moving up the turnpike. The enemy's left was part of the light brigade.[23] Behind it came half of the second brigade—the Fourth Foot, the King's Own.[24] They came up the same road on which Stansbury's men had made their night march from Lowndes's hill and their countermarch in the morning. They passed through the hot, still woods—the woods blurred again with red dust—and came to the first ravine, to Tournecliffe's bridge and the men who waited beyond it, the last half of the Yankees' army.

"Lieutenant Colonel Scott, with the 36th United States' regiment, was posted in a field on the left of the road, his right resting upon it, and commanding the road descending into the ravine . . . and the rest of his line commanding the ascent from the ravine." [25] Thus were the men of Smith's corps waiting. This is the where and the how of the waiting. "In the same field, about one hundred yards in the rear of the 36th regiment, Colonel Magruder [this is another Magruder] was posted with a part of the 1st regiment of District militia, his right also resting upon the road, the left advanced, presenting a front obliquely to the road, and situated to cover and to co-operate with the 36th regiment. Major Peter with his artillery, six six-pounders; Captain Davidson's light infantry, and Captain Stull's rifle corps, *armed with muskets,* all of the same regiment, were ordered to take possession of the abrupt acclivity . . . terminating the ravine. This was deemed a desirable position, because it commanded completely the ravine and the road crossing it, and a considerable extent of the ground over which the front line would necessarily retire if forced back. But, after a short space of time, report was made [to General Smith] that broken grounds interrupted the approach to it with artillery, but by a circuitous route that would consume much time, and that, in case of retreat, the ground in the rear was such as might endanger the safety of the guns. . . . Near to it was a commanding position for artillery, and easy of access from and to the road."

Smith "yielded with reluctance to the abandonment of the position first ordered, but time did not admit of hesitation." In the "mean while," General Smith had "posted Lieutenant Colonel Kramer, with his battalion of Maryland draughted militia, in the woods, on the right of the road and commanding the ravine which continued in that direction. . . . Upon examining the position taken by Major Peter's battery, it was found that the range of his guns was principally through that part of the field occupied by the 36th regiment. To remove one or the other became necessary, and the difficulty of the ground for moving artillery, and the exigency of the movement, left no alternative. The 36th fell back about one hundred yards, losing, in some measure, the advantage of its elevated ground, and leaving the road. The position of the 1st regiment District militia, from this circumstance, was also necessarily changed. It fell back about the same distance, its right still resting on the road, and now formed nearly in line with the 36th."

The Second regiment of the Columbian brigade had been reduced to three hundred and fifty men by the loss of Ben Burch's guns and their infantry escort, sent forward to Stansbury's line before the first action began. Now the "residue" under its colonel, Brent, was "formed as a reserve a short distance in the rear of Major Peter's battery, and so disposed as to act on the right, or left, or in front, as occasion might require. Near them was posted, in the same manner, Major Waring's Prince George's battalion of militia, about one hundred and fifty." Colonel Beall with his seven hundred and fifty "took a position on the right of the road and nearly fronting it." Beall's post was a low, detached hill; his left flank was two hundred and fifty yards from the turnpike; there was a broad gap between it and Colonel Magruder's First regiment. It was into this gap that Barney's men came "in a trot." [26] His five guns wheeled into battery, the two eighteen-pounders side by side in the road, the three twelves to the right. Barney's "infantry"— his sailors turned soldier—deployed to the right of the guns and formed line with the marines commanded by Captain Miller. The gap had been filled, just in time. The 85th was attacking.

The odds, at that moment, favored the Americans. In number of men, they were as three is to two and a half. Brigadier General Walter Smith had not more than 3,080; the enemy had, on the field and in motion, 2,560.[27] Those figures, however, do not take into account the loss of the light brigade in the first two actions— the dead, the wounded, the stragglers overcome by heat and exhaustion; they do not take into account the men who fell out of Smith's column on its forced march that morning. The stragglers were never counted, the light brigade's killed and wounded were lumped together in the casualty list for the day. Nor do these figures take into account the British reserve—the marine battalion and the 21st Fusiliers—the 1,460 men intact in the third brigade.[28] Walter Smith had no reserve that he knew of, although the Fairfax militia at last was sweating and swearing its way to the front after having its flints counted twice. But including both the Virginia regiment and the enemy's third brigade, the odds in numbers of men are not odds at all. The numbers are almost even: 3,880 Americans; 4,020 British. (The figures mean little or nothing; neither reserve fired a shot; they are set down because so many writers have garbled this battle, seizing this figure or that to prove what they wanted to prove.) [29] Again, the guns weighted the odds. There were eleven guns against one; the British got their six-pounder into this fight, but any of Peter's could match it; three of Barney's were twice its size and two were three times as big. And again, the rockets weighed in the balance against the guns; they did not, in this last engagement, turn the odds as they did in the second.

The first blow of this third battle fell upon Kramer's men, deployed in the woods on the edge of the ravine, to the right of Tournecliffe's bridge. They were "Maryland draughted militia"; there were only two hundred and forty of them; they were six hundred yards out in front of the main positions—six hundred yards out in front of Beall on his hill, six hundred in front of Barney. They were there for a purpose: to stagger the enemy's first attack if they could, to hurt him as much as they could. They were not expected to hold back an army: before they went out they had been given their orders about retreating: when the pressure became too great they were to retire "through a body of woods" on their right and rally on Colonel Beall's line. Against them now burst the advance of the 85th.[30] They fought well. They hurt the enemy. They were driven back, but not routed; they were still firing as they retreated according to orders.[31] According to orders they slipped through the woods, rallied, and re-formed on the Anne Arundel men.[32]

The "heavy column" on the turnpike had halted while its light troops cleared out the copse on the edge of the ravine; now it began to advance straight up the road.[33] Barney swung down from his saddle, ran to the nearest gun, aimed it, ran on to the next.[34] When he had laid the guns, he remounted. The leading company of the British advance caught sight of his battery. The column halted. Barney sat waiting, watching, reserving his fire.[35] The head of the column was moving again. Barney spoke to the gun crew beside him. The eighteen-pounder let go.[36] There was no need to fire the other: the road was "completely cleared." [37] But those men down there were Lord Wellington's men: they had stormed three batteries today:[38] they could storm another. They tried. Barney's guns met them with grape shot and swept them away. They re-formed and tried it again, under a flurry of rockets.[39] The murderous fire mowed them down.[40] Barney thought "all were destroyed." [41]

After three attempts, three failures, even the Invincibles had had enough of those frontal attacks. They abandoned the road, deployed through the broken ground of the shallow ravine, came up into the open field in line of battle and drove for Barney's right flank.[42] Barney's twelve-pounders ripped holes through their line,[43] Peter's six smaller guns tore into them with cross fire.[44] They came on, stubborn and gallant. Barney ordered a counterattack. His infantry charged. The light brigade [45] saw them coming, it halted and fired. The marines and flotillamen fired. For minutes . . . five minues . . . ten . . . fifteen . . . for nobody knows how many minutes [46] . . . this was a stand-up fight, it was two lines of men standing face to face across a few yards of bare ground, slugging it out with ounce balls. "The firing became tremendous" [47] . . .

"an unintermitting exchange of tremendous volleys." [48] The ounce balls killed and maimed, they smashed skulls, they broke bones and tore flesh. Flotilla Captain John Webster, sailorman fighting on horseback, felt his hat knocked off his head. His horse was shot dead. He looked at the hat and saw a hole through the crown, he left the hat where it lay. [49] A subaltern of the 85th went down, instantly killed, a ball through his windpipe, his spine shot through at the base of his brain. A ball hit Lieutenant Gleig's scabbard and broke it, another laid his arm open. In both of those stubborn lines,

the ranking officers were falling. Captain Miller, commanding the American marines, was wounded. Captain Sevier of the marines was wounded. [50] But the British were suffering worse. Lieutenant Colonel Wood, leading the 85th, fell badly hurt. [51] Major Brown, commanding its advance guard, was down with a serious wound. [52] Colonel Thornton of the 85th, commanding the light brigade, was struck and went down with a ball in his thigh, his thigh torn and crippled; [53] he lay on the ground with the musketry crashing above him.

The light brigade wavered. [54] Its senior officers were gone. The guns were making a bloody wreck of its flank. [55] The marines and the sailors ceased firing, they charged with cutlass and bayonet.

The light brigade broke and streamed down the field. The charge swept after it, surged over a fence, drove the enemy back into the woods where Kramer's militia had fought, to the brink of the ravine. Colonel Thornton rolled over and over down the slope,[56] hoping to escape but expecting "every instant" to be discovered and taken.[57] The charge swept past him. But his brigade had been "totally cut up." [58] The flotillamen and the marines left its "shattered remains" [59] in the ravine and "returned to the guns." [60] The Invincibles' disordered retreat to the woods had drawn Barney's men off to the right of their position; now, returning to it, they angled across the field; they missed Colonel Thornton again.[61]

Four assaults, four bloody repulses. Here, in the right center of the American line, Barney was winning his battle. The rest of the line had not been attacked at all—excepting the two hundred and forty "draughted militia" who had not been a part of the line but an outpost six hundred yards out in front. The rest of the line had not been in action at all—excepting Peter's six field guns which had helped to break up the successive assaults against Barney, and excepting Kramer's battalion. Kramer's men had done what was expected of them: they had fought their delaying action, fired as they fell back, rallied, re-formed: they were ready to fight again. Peter's guns had been served "with great animation." [62] They had not been threatened. They, too, were ready to fight again. As far as the actual fighting had gone, it had gone very well. The situation looked encouraging.

In the meantime, however, a less favorable situation had been developing at the left of the line and beyond it. This situation was compounded of two elements. One was the British East Essex regiment, the 44th Foot commanded by Colonel Brooke, the senior among Ross's regimental commanders. The 44th had been pressing the pursuit of Stansbury's routed brigade on the Georgetown road.[63] The other element in the situation was Brigadier General Winder. After giving up all hope of checking the flight of Stansbury's men or of turning them "more toward General Smith's command," and after ordering the Baltimore artillery to continue its retreat without giving it either a purpose or a rallying point, Winder had set out across the broken ground to take command of the right wing, Smith's so-called "corps." He had upwards of half a mile to go and his horse was tired. How soon he started, after he heard the racket of Kramer's fight or the louder uproar of Barney's . . . how fast he rode . . . how long it took him to cover the thousand yards of uneven ground and reach Smith's left flank, nobody ever knew. Winder himself, in his report, said only that he "turned toward the positions occupied by Lieutenant Colonel Beall, Commodore Barney and General Smith." (Historians should not pretend to be mind readers. Even with his official report and all the other official reports before me, I cannot read Winder's mind. I can merely form an opinion concerning his state of mind. The fact is that in his report he listed the positions of Beall, Barney and Smith *in reverse* of the order in which he approached them.")

The situation developed swiftly. Its two elements—the American commanding general and the British East Essex regiment—were active. In combination, they reacted vigorously. So far as the result is concerned, it might be said that they acted in combination. Their mutual reaction did not produce an explosion. It produced a solvent. It dissolved the American army.

The Georgetown road did not lead the East Essex regiment any closer to Smith's positions than it had led the Baltimore guns or Ben Burch's guns. But Colonel Brooke, advancing, was not taking orders from the terrain or the direction of a road. He saw that "the dispersion of the front" [64] that had been composed of Stansbury's regiments had now "caused a dangerous opening" on the left flank of Smith's line. He ordered his regiment [65] to leave the road and strike for the exposed end of that line ahead. The East Essex "advanced rapidly," wheeled by the left, and "soon gained and was turning" Smith's flank.[66] To meet this "alarming movement," Smith ordered Colonel Brent to shift his regiment—the Second of the Columbian brigade—toward the threatened flank. It was a logical countermove: it did not disarrange the troops in combat positions: Brent's regiment had been "formed as a reserve" and had been "so disposed as to act on the right, or left, or in front, as occasion might require." [67] As Brent began to carry out the order,[68] other enemy troops appeared "within long shot" [69] of the center, and Colonel Magruder's First regiment "opened a partial fire, but without much effect." [70]

Winder had not yet reached the right wing of his army. He was "not acquainted with the relative position of the different corps composing" General Smith's command and could "not therefore determine who of them engaged the enemy, nor . . . see how they acted." But before he had time to find out, before he was even close to Smith,[71] he had made his estimate of the situation and issued his orders.

This was his estimate as he set it down in his report: "the enemy had advanced up the road [the Washington turnpike], had driven back Lieutenant Colonel Kramer's command. . . . He [the enemy] had come under the destructive fire of Commodore Barney, which had turned him up the hill towards Lieutenant Colonel Beall, whose detachment gave one or two ineffective fires and fled. . . . The enemy, therefore, had gained this commanding position, and was passing our right flank; his force pursuing on the left, had also advanced to a line with our left, and there was nothing there to *oppose him*."

This was his order: "To preserve Smith's command from being pressed in front by fresh troops of the enemy, who were coming on at the same time, while they were under the certainty of being assailed on both flanks and the rear by the enemy, who respectively gained them; in which circumstances their destruction or surrender would have been inevitable, *I sent to General Smith to retreat*."

Winder's estimate of the situation looks sound. It has the ring of truth. His order to retreat seems timely.

The estimate was unsound, it rings hollow, the truth is not in it. The obvious fact is that it was not an estimate made on the battlefield: it was made *after* the battle. The revealing flaw in his specious report is the timing of the order to retreat. The flaw runs through his own words: "I sent to General Smith . . ." He was not yet there. He had to "send." When he dispatched the order he did not know many of the details he set down in his report as his reasons for sending it. He could not possibly have known that Colonel Kramer had "well maintained his position and much hurt the enemy, and also continued to fire during his retreat." And his statement that Colonel Beall's men already had fled was flatly contradicted by Barney.

Barney, in his report to the secretary of the navy five days after the battle, described the successful counterattack by which his marines and flotillamen repulsed the light brigade and by which the enemy's assault force "was totally cut up." His next sentence said: "By this time not a vestige of the American army remained, except a body of five or six hundred, posted on a height, on my right, from whom I expected much support, from their fine situation." Barney was on the ground; Barney was no more than two hundred and fifty yards from Beall's position, which was of vital concern to him; Barney said flatly that after the rest of the troops had begun to retreat, Beall's men were still holding their hill.

Winder said that when he "reached the road"—meaning the Washington turnpike—he "found Commodore Barney's men also retiring on the road, he having been overpowered by those who drove off Beall's regiment *about the time I sent the order to retreat.*" In other words, Winder was not on the ground; before he reached the turnpike, the British had had time to organize and deliver two more assaults: they had stormed Beall's hill, they had stormed Barney's battery.

General Smith also bore witness to the revelatory timing of Winder's order. Colonel Brent, he wrote in his official report, was "proceeding in the execution" of Smith's directions to move the reserve regiment to the left to meet the threat of Colonel Brooke's flank attack. When the order to retreat came, he said, the troops of the Columbian brigade had been "but partially engaged, and this principally with light troops and skirmishers, now pressing forward, supported by a column of infantry."

Even the Congressional investigating committee, which took the most excellent care to hurt nobody's feelings, made it clear that General Winder ordered the retreat of a force of more than three thousand men and eleven guns from a position hastily occupied but nevertheless chosen with a fair degree of military skill—a force not yet shaken and most of it not even yet seriously attacked —a force that had stoutly and quickly repelled three of the enemy's attempts to advance, and broken the fourth and strongest attempt into a costly, disorderly flight. "The command of General Smith," the committee reported, "including the Georgetown and city militia, still remained in order, and firm, without any part of them having given way, as well as the command of Lieutenant Colonel Scott of the regulars, and some other corps. The enemy's light troops had, in the meantime, advanced on the left of the road and had gained a line parallel with Smith's command, and, in endeavoring to turn the flank, Colonel Brent was placed in a position calculated to prevent it. . . . At this moment, and in this situation, General Winder ordered the whole of the troops, then stationary, to retreat." [72]

These were not beaten men. Even retreat did not shake them. They fell back, in obedience to orders, over broken and difficult ground,[73] without showing what Winder contemptuously called "the usual incapacity of raw troops to make orderly movements in the face of the enemy." [74] Winder himself admitted that "when he arrived in succession" at the "different corps" of General Smith's troops, as he "did as soon as practicable," he could "not recollect to have found any of them that were not in order, and retreating with as little confusion as could have been expected."

Winder accused Beall's Anne Arundel troops of giving "one or two ineffective fires" and then running.[75] Barney, who was depending on them, said they "made no resistance, giving a fire or two, and retired." [76] But there is evidence that Winder was responsible for their failure. Colonel Beall, forthright and blunt, was not the man to higgle and haggle and try to pass blame on to others. "Having marched about sixteen miles that morning," he told the committee of Congress, "my men were fatigued and exhausted. It is not my impression that my command gave way as early as is represented by some." He made, he said, "every exertion to rally the men, and partially succeeded; but they ultimately gave way . . . like the other troops." The other troops fell back under orders. There is another significant sentence in Beall's curt statement: "I have been informed by a gentleman, who acted as one of General Winder's aides, that he brought me an order to retreat; but I do not remember it." [77] The aide who wanted to see justice done to the old Revolutionary colonel and his men was John Eager Howard, Jr., son of another old Revolutionary colonel. He had been a cornet of horse under Captain Henry Thompson, he was a second lieutenant now in Thompson's Independent Company of horse artillery in the Baltimore City brigade.[78] Captain Thompson was in charge of the horse telegraph that kept Major General Samuel Smith and Brigadier General Stricker in touch with the army in southern Maryland.

If Lieutenant Howard carried Winder's order to Beall, as he said he did, this fact emerges from the confusion: *Not one unit of troops in the American third line at Bladensburg retreated except under orders.* And this fact also emerges: with the exception of three or four detached companies, *the only two units that left their posts without orders, out of the entire American army on the field, were the two so-called "regiments" of ununiformed, undisciplined, untrained draft-men from Baltimore county, without even a regimental number to make them soldiers-on-paper.* Historians should at least take the trouble to find out what happened, before they sneer at the men who marched out to Bladensburg to offer their lives for their country and who marched away again *under orders.*

Some of them disobeyed orders—Captain Ben Burch and his gunners, fighting on when they had been told to retreat. Some of them couldn't believe the orders—they fell back a little way and then stopped and waited. It couldn't be true. There must have been some mistake. "The First and Second regiments [of the Columbian brigade] halted and formed, after retreating five or six hundred paces, but were again ordered by General Winder to retire." [79] They obeyed.

Behind them, Joshua Barney was fighting his last fight.

Others have told that story, they have filled it in with suitably picturesque details, they have told how the gunners stood to their guns till they were "bayoneted with fuses in their hands." [80] Barney did not say that, the authors doubtless know more about writing than he did, they knew what would look well in a book. But it was his fight. Let him tell it:

JOSHUA BARNEY

"They pushed forward their sharp shooters; one of which shot my horse under me; who fell dead between two of my guns. The enemy, who had been kept in check by our fire, for nearly half an hour, now began to out-flank us on the right: our guns were turned that way; he pushed up the hill, about two or three hundred, towards the corps of Americans stationed [there] who, to my great mortification, made no resistance, giving a fire or two, and retired. In this situation we had the whole army of the enemy to contend with. Our ammunition was expended; and, unfortunately, the drivers of my ammunition wagons had gone off in the general panic. At this time, I received a severe wound in my thigh; Captain Miller was wounded; Sailingmaster Warner killed; Acting Sailingmaster Martin killed; and Sailingmaster Martin wounded; but, to the honor of my officers and men, as fast as their companions and messmates fell at the guns, they were instantly replaced from the infantry.

"Finding the enemy now completely in our rear, and no means of defence, I gave orders to my officers and men to retire. Three of my officers assisted me to get off a short distance, but the great loss of blood occasioned such a weakness that I was compelled to lie down. I requested my officers to leave me, which they obstinately refused; but, upon being *ordered*, they obeyed; one only remained. In a short time I observed a British soldier, and had him called, and directed him to seek an officer; in a few minutes an officer came, and, on learning who I was, brought General Ross and Admiral Cockburn to me. Those officers behaved to me with the most marked attention, respect and politeness, had a surgeon brought, and my wound dressed immediately. After a few minutes' conversation, the General informed me (after paying me a handsome compliment) that I was paroled, and at liberty to proceed to Washington or Bladensburg; as, also, Mr. Huffington, who had remained with me, offering me every assistance in his power, giving orders for a litter to be brought, in which I was carried to Bladensburg. Captain Wainright, first captain to Admiral Cochrane, remained with me, and behaved to me as if I was a brother. During the stay of the enemy at Bladensburg, I received every marked attention possible from the officers of the navy and army.

"My wound is deep, but I flatter myself not dangerous: the ball is not yet extracted. I fondly hope a few weeks will restore me to health, and that an exchange will take place, that I may resume my command, or any other. . . ." [81]

On the Washington turnpike, the district militia had halted again. Winder had ordered Smith to "collect the troops, and prepare to make a stand on the heights westward of the turnpike gate. This was done as fast as the troops came up. A front was again presented towards the enemy, consisting principally of the troops of this District, a part of those who had been attached to them in action, and a Virginia regiment of about four hundred men, under Colonel Minor" [82]—the Fairfax regiment, its musket flints counted at last. But "whilst the line was yet forming," General Smith "received orders from General Winder to fall back to the capitol, and there form for battle." [83] Smith marched his troops to the Capitol, halted, asked Winder how he wanted the battle line drawn. Winder "gave orders that the whole should retreat through Washington and Georgetown." [84]

Walter Smith, remembering the faces of his men, said that it was "impossible to do justice to the anguish evinced by the troops of Washington and Georgetown on the receiving of this order. The idea of leaving their families, their houses and their homes to the mercy of an enraged enemy was insupportable."

Winder's final order of the day accomplished what the sight of the oncoming Invincibles had failed to accomplish. It shook the brigade to pieces. "Some shed tears, others uttered imprecations

. . . it was impossible for them to comprehend why troops who were willing to risk an encounter with the enemy should be denied the opportunity." [85]

The still-intact regiments began to disintegrate. "To preserve that order which was maintained during the retreat was now no longer practicable. As they retired through Washington and Georgetown, numbers were obtaining and taking leave to visit their homes, and again rejoining; and with ranks thus broken and scattered, they halted at night on the heights near Tenly-town. . . ." [86]

A little before sunset, Ross and Cockburn rode into the abandoned capital of the United States at the head of a few hundred men, only part of their fresh third brigade. A musket went off behind Robert Sewall's house. The general's horse fell dead. The house was destroyed.[87] For the troops who had missed the battle, it was the beginning of a pleasant evening.

Long after dark the two brigades that had fought and won the battle came slogging down the turnpike. They were tired men, but they marched with heads up: this was too good to miss—the Yankees' "federal city" going up in flames. It was a thing to see. It made a gaudier show than ten king's birthdays and a royal wedding, with fireworks on the Thames. The ammunition in the navy yard was letting go now. The explosions crashed like broadsides, and their gouts of fire made giant set-piece vases from which red and orange flowers sprang upward and unfolded, wilted, drooped and darkened and then bloomed again, still climbing, in a writhing foliage of smoke.

Even the tough Invincibles were awed by the great "sheets of fire which quivered through the air" and by "the very waving of the flames, heard in the stillness of the night to an extraordinary distance."

They were awed, too, by their own achievement. Less than a week ago they still had been on board their transports. They had been soft from eleven weeks of idleness. They had been miserable and half sick from being packed together like so many salt fish in a barrel, and from being tossed about in ships that rolled like barrels and stank like enormous privies. Without time to recuperate, without cavalry, without artillery, without a supply train, they had cut loose from their base—the fleet—and plunged into a strange, unreconnoitered country. Now they had spent six days inside that hostile country of eight million people, smashed its army, taken its capital and sent its rulers flying. It was unbelievable. But it was true.

When the British regiments went into bivouac a quarter of a mile outside the burning city, their boats lay sixty miles behind them. Ahead, closer by twenty miles, lay Baltimore—the hated pirates' nest, the "doomed town" long ago marked down for retribution.

The same storm that drenched Queen Dolly drenched the British camp. To Englishmen unused to the sudden fury of a Maryland thundergust, it was a spectacle almost as stunning as the conflagration that it partly quenched. "The effect was magnificent beyond the power of language to describe. Flash after flash of vivid lightning displayed not only the bivouac, but the streets, the houses, nay the very windows in the town, with a degree of minuteness far greater than the beams of the noon-day sun would have produced.[88] The storm was over in less than an hour, and then "there was nothing to break in upon the quiet of the night, except an occasional roar as a magazine blew up, or a crash, as a wall or roof fell to the ground." There was another and more violent storm the next day. A little after noon the sky suddenly grew black until "the darkness was as great as if the sun had long set, and the last remains of twilight had come on, occasionally relieved by flashes of lightning streaming through it." The rain, driven by a "prodigious force" of wind, was like "the rushing of a mighty cataract" and "the noise of the wind and the thunder, the crash of falling buildings, and the tearing of roofs as they were stript from the walls" and "whisked into the air like sheets of paper" appalled the British demolition parties still intent upon the business of destruction. Soldiers threw themselves flat in the muddy streets or huddled behind undamaged houses or the walls of gutted buildings; but walls toppled, dwellings that had been spared by the troops were wrenched to pieces; thirty men were "buried beneath their ruins." Through the dripping bivouac ran a story that two field guns had been "fairly lifted from the ground and borne several yards to the rear." [89]

The hurricane blew itself out within two hours. While the smoldering debris began to smoke again and the sour stench of wet, charred timber and of hot, soaked ashes overpowered the clean smell of the storm-washed earth, another story spread through the rank and file of the Invincibles. The army was advancing. There would be a night march.

It was more than a mere rumor. With it ran a cautious stir of preparation that had meaning to old soldiers. Sergeants checked equipment. Working parties were turned out to gather firewood— a well-worn trick, that one, but still useful: to slip away in darkness, leaving campfires burning to conceal a new blow. Officers were overheard in sober talk about an important movement that must start before tomorrow morning. Men were detailed to patrols, and when the patrols came back to camp there was no doubt left: they had been sent to warn the Yankee civilians who were still in what was left of Washington to keep themselves indoors from sunset until sunrise or be shot.[90] We're not finished with them yet. We're going after them. Sixty miles in six days . . . and sixteen of them yesterday, with a battle thrown in. They say Baltimore is only forty miles, they say it's summat of a town. The boats? Ye'll see no boats this while. It's an advance, I tell ye. Why not? What's to stop us? *Them?*

In Baltimore, a man named David Winchester was writing to a relative in Tennessee, he was telling General James Winchester that the enemy was "in possession of the Capitol of the U.S. and that they did not pay dearly for their temerity is doubly mortifying."

"But to my sorrow," he was writing, "it is not to end here— we expect every instant to hear that they have taken up the line of march for this place and if they do we are gone—we have not a single company of regulars either here or in our vicinity—our own militia, although brave to a fault, are outnumbered by the mercenaries of our enemy, and you known that any raw malitia we can bring in from the country will afford us no protection—under such discouraging circumstances what is to be done. If the town is ravaged which I solemnly believe we have not the power to prevent—I shall be totally ruined to a certainty. To me you may be sure this is the most awful moment of my life, not because, if this place is defended, that I shall put my life at hazard in common with my fellow citizens, but because I am positively sure we shall not succeed. . . . All the valuable goods and women and children are now leaving our city seeking safety in the upper country." [91]

Between the doomed town and the invading army, gathering itself together now for a night march, there was nothing but the fleeing rabble of "malitia." Those who had fled first and fastest, those who had scrounged rides in baggage wagons or had had cash in their pockets to hire farmers' rigs, were already rattling into Baltimore and bringing panic with them. Private Henry Fulford was among the first to reach home. He was safe, he was whole, he was even reasonably clean. When he ventured from the swamp where he had taken refuge, he had found a farmhouse; he had been "hospitably received and got refreshed," and after dark he had set out "with a guide through woods and by-paths" and had tramped five miles to Ross's tavern where he spent the remainder of the night. His personal retreat had been more comfortable than that of most of the defeated army. But his eyes still stared at bayonets, he could not erase from his mind the terrible calmness of the British troops, the inhuman, machinelike advance of the Invincibles. To him they seemed invincible indeed.

He remembered the fire of the batteries concentrating on the narrow bridge and on the men whose bodies filled the bridge. It had been, he thought, a dreadful thing for flesh and blood to face those chunks of flying iron; but the flesh and blood that had faced the guns' fire and survived it seemed more dreadful yet. He was too tired to rest; the awful memories would not let him rest, he poured them all into a letter while they were still fresh. "The fire must have been dreadfully galling," he wrote, "but they took no notice of it; their men moved like clockwork; the instant a part of a platoon was cut down it was filled up by the men in the rear without the least noise and confusion whatever, so as to present always a solid column to the mouths of our cannon, they advanced so fast that our artillery had to give way and fall back upon our line, where they commenced again and fired for a short time." Private Fulford was no weakling. He was a successful man, a strong man in the world with which he was familiar. He owned shares in warships— in the *Diamond*, the *Grampus*, the *Patapsco* and the *Transit*—and the ships that he had helped send out to fight had burned or taken more than fourteen prizes.[92] Perhaps his state of mind would have been described as shell shock at Soissons or in the Argonne. What he said about the Baltimore artillery opening fire again after it was routed from the barbette at Bladensburg is a fair illustration of the confused impressions that men get in battle. Henry Fulford could not have been more than a few hundred feet from the retreating batteries when their flight was finally checked and they were ordered farther to the rear, but he firmly believed that the subsequent cannon fire on the Georgetown road was delivered by those guns; he had no notion that the three fieldpieces which supported the charge of his regiment were Washington guns, not Myers nor

Magruder's. In such ways originate many of the errors perpetrated by history.

Private Fulford, in all honesty, proceeded to give bottom to another error. "The British force," he went on, "was greatly superior in numbers to ours. It is my opinion that not one third of their army came into action at all, any further than by amusing themselves by throwing Congreve rockets at us. They were so strong that we had to give way. I think if we had remained ten minutes longer they would have either killed or taken the whole of us." [93] Now, remembering, he gave up to despair:

"They will be here [in Baltimore] in a few days and we have no force that can face them . . . the only way to save the town and state will be to capitulate."

9

. . . TO PROP UP A FALLING CAUSE

A GROUP OF SOBER-FACED MEN
gathered in a sticky office. It was Mayor Edward Johnson's office,
but Ed Johnson was not there as mayor. The small, sweating group
was not the legally elected government of Baltimore.

The formal processes of politics had been set aside. Government had gravitated to the people. By a kind of natural law, sometimes artificially suspended but released now by the emergency, the
responsibility of government had settled on responsible men and
leadership on leaders. The community had instinctively turned back
to half-forgotten ways—to the spontaneous committee government-
by-common-consent that had sprung up in the old days of stamp
tax quarrels, tea ship burnings and the Sons of Liberty. During a full
decade before Lexington and Concord, committees of correspondence had heated and hammered formless lumps of irritation and
ideas into the weapons of rebellion, revolution, independence. They

had wrought dissimilar, unsympathetic, isolated peoples, scattered through a baker's dozen of colonies, provinces and proprietaries, into a pattern never seen before. Committees of safety had fashioned hundreds of small local governments that took upon themselves the powers of royal governors so gradually and so naturally that many of the governors themselves were scarcely aware that they were becoming expendable.

Government by committee had created a new nation. Now the outgrowth and the culmination of that system—the federal congress and the cabinet—had failed. Small hope of help there. But perhaps the old source had its magic yet. This meeting in Ed Johnson's office was no session of the mayor and the city council. This was "the citizens in town meeting." [1] This was the Committee of Vigilance and Safety. It had chosen Johnson as its chairman.

No group of Maryland men had met to act upon so grave an issue since December 8th in 1774. On that day eighty-five delegates "chosen by the several counties" had assembled in Annapolis to consider putting their several necks into the hangman's noose. It was an interesting topic, personal as well as public; they turned it over on their tongues for four days. Then they resolved, without a dissenting vote, to support "to the utmost of their power" any colony in which Great Britain attempted to execute by force "the assumed power of parliament to tax the colonies." They counted carefully the cost of the decision and prepared to pay it: they voted to enroll into militia every man and boy between sixteen and fifty and to provide each of these citizen soldiers with "a good firelock and bayonet fixed thereon, half a pound of powder, two pounds of lead, and a cartouche-box, or powder-horn, and a bag for ball . . . in readiness to act on any emergency." [2]

Grave as the decision was then, there had been no disagreement. [3] There was none now.

But there was less time for talking. There were no four days to spare for leisurely discussion. The members of the Committee of Vigilance and Safety had no inclination toward it. There were no stump speeches. Nobody twisted the lion's tail or set the eagle screaming. These were men face to face with personal ruin, the loss of their homes and business. They were, in this crisis, the city itself, and the city faced destruction. These were men in trouble—in deep trouble that might possibly be lightened or evaded by surrender, but could not be postponed.

There was no doubt in any man's mind that Baltimore would

be the next objective of the invading army. Long before that army swarmed ashore in Maryland, the London papers had announced its coming and its purpose. They wanted more than victory and more than peace. The wanted punishment. "Chastise the savages!" they cried. "The American navy must be annihilated; their arsenals and dockyards must be consumed; and the truculent inhabitants of Baltimore must be tamed with the weapons which shook the wooden turrets of Copenhagen." If any American cities were to suffer, they declared, the first two should be Washington and Baltimore—the one in order to wipe out the meeting place of Congress, the other to wipe out the "large body of privateer shipping."

Half of that purpose had been realized, half the prophecy had come true. Washington was the symbol and the seat of government, but as a place it was a trifling village; it was nothing but a mud-hole ridiculously bedizened with three or four grandiose buildings. It was no prize at all for a victorious army fresh from Continental wars. John Armstrong had been wrong but logical when he insisted that the British would not strike at Washington, exclaiming: "No, no; Baltimore is the place, sir; that is of so much more consequence."

It was Baltimore the British called "the great repository of the hostile spirit." It was Baltimore they called "a nest of pirates." It was Baltimore they hated. And they had good reason for the hatred and the hard names. In these last two years the city on the upper Chesapeake had developed an uncanny accuracy at hitting the enemy on his two tenderest spots—his pocketbook and his pride in his rule of the seas.

Baltimore had not waited for the war to come close. It had gone out to meet the war—gone three thousand miles to meet it, all the way to the English Channel, right up to the white cliffs of Dover. It was not for nothing that the enemy called Baltimore a nest of pirates. The town had done much more than its fair share of fighting on the sea. It had made this a private war. There was scarcely a merchant in the town who didn't have shares in a warship, and many had shares in a dozen.

Baltimore harbor had spawned more private warships than any other port. Within four months after the declaration of war, Baltimore businessmen had sent to sea forty-two armed vessels carrying three hundred and thirty guns and almost three thousand men.[4] In two years it had sent out no less than a hundred and twenty-six[5] of those small, swift terrors, and the swiftest and deadliest of them all were peculiarly Baltimore's own. They were the Baltimore clippers, with flush decks wide for the deadlier handling of guns, with masts soaring up too high for a sensible ship, masts so slender they bent like a whiplash under sails as big as a Charles street lot, masts so rakishly set that they seemed to be toppling backward and the sails seemed to pick the hull out of the sea like a gull flying off with a fish. The clippers came closer to flying than anything else that hadn't been furnished with feathers. Their speed was the despair of the enemy's frigates and their success the despair of Lloyd's.

For two years they had harried the enemy's convoys, circling and swooping and biting like deerflies. A man never knew where a deerfly would light. It could drive a man crazy, buzzing around his head; and when it bit, it drew blood. The Baltimore clipper-gadflies had driven the Lords of the Admiralty nearabout crazy; they had driven insurance rates up as high as their own crazy mastheads. In spite of the British navy, with six hundred and forty-four ships in commission and nine hundred and thirty-six in being,[6] the Baltimore privateers and letters-of-marque had sunk, burned or captured five hundred and fifty-six vessels. The town that had dealt such painful blows to British pride and commerce could expect no mercy in this war.

It had been a nasty war. There was no need for the members of the Committee of Vigilance and Safety to debate the consequences of resistance. They could count the cost of failure. No one doubted that if Baltimore resisted and was taken by force, it would pay in fire and pillage. And that reckoning of consequences was not grounded on imaginary apprehensions or trumped-up atrocities. They were laid down clearly in the enemy's own rules of war, devised for the occasion and sometimes improved upon in practice. In the United States, every man was subject to militia duty. Ergo, every male of military age was obviously a soldier. Ergo, every house belonging to a soldier was a military barracks. Ergo, it was subject to destruction.

The practical application of that logic added spice to the dull business of blockading. A full century before the Zeppelins dropped their bombs on London, it abolished battle lines and brought war to the doorsteps of civilians. No fishing village, ferry station or plantation along the hundreds of miles of Chesapeake Bay shore could go to sleep without the fear of midnight raiders firing canister and rockets without warning, bursting in doors, burning barns and houses. There were officers in Admiral Sir

George Cockburn's squadron who set down on paper their revulsion at that kind of warfare. One described a foray led by the admiral in person, with General Ross as amateur companion and pupil, to "destroy a factory village which was not only the abode of innocent labor, but likewise the resort of some few militiamen guilty of the unnatural sin of defending their own country." All the men had "fled" or had gone off to their militia rendezvous; the raiders found only women and children. "Therefore," the British officer wrote with angry sarcasm, "we most valiantly set fire to the unprotected property, notwithstanding the tears of the women, and, like a parcel of savages, we danced around the wreck of ruin. Every house which we could by ingenuity vote into the residence of a military man, was burned." [8] And again, when three girls pleaded with Sir George to spare their house, the admiral retorted that their father was a colonel of militia and that they could have ten minutes to remove their personal belongings.

His own subordinate reported that Cockburn laid his watch on the table, counting off the minutes, while the youngest girl, sixteen years old and "lovely beyond the general beauty of those parts, threw herself" at the feet of Sir Peter Parker, captain of the frigate *Menelaus*, clinging to his knees and begging him to intervene. "Never shall I forget that moment. Poor Sir Peter wept like a child. The admiral walked out with his usual haughty stride. . . . In a moment the house was in flames. We retreated from the scene of ruin, leaving the three daughters gazing at the work of destruction, which had made the innocent houseless and the affluent beggars. . . . It was a scene which impressed itself on my heart, and which my memory and my hand unwillingly recall and publish."

If officers participating under orders in the kind of war that had been waged for sixteen months in Maryland were shocked and angered by it and shamed by their own helplessness, there is small wonder that Baltimore expected nothing better than destruction. Nor were these house-burning raids mere isolated cases. In April, 1813, Poole's Island, Sharp's Island, Poplar Island and Tilghman's Island settlements had been attacked and plundered. A few days later, Frenchtown had been raided. Frenchtown was a tavern, a fishhouse, a warehouse or two, some stables and perhaps three dwellings; four hundred men in thirteen barges stormed its "fort"—a pile of dirt equipped with four four-pounder cannon that were souvenirs of the First War of Independence and manned by a handful of stage drivers, stablemen, teamsters and other militia. The wharf, warehouses and fishhouse went up in flames.

Havre de Grace was struck next, then Cresswell's Ferry, then Fredericktown, then Georgetown. The stories that poured into Baltimore from those four little towns were like the stories that had been recounted by the gray-faced fugitives from the frontier stations in the French and Indian War and in the days of Pontiac's uprising. Havre de Grace was a town of fifty houses "built mostly of wood." It was attacked on the morning of May 3rd. "While the great body of the inhabitants were yet in their beds, nineteen barges from the enemy's squadron suddenly appeared before the place, and, without a moment's notice, opened a tremendous fire of shot, shells and rockets." [9] Baltimore could read its future in this eyewitness account:

"On the report of the guns we immediately jumped out of our beds; and from the top of the house could plainly see the balls and hear the cries of the inhabitants. We ran down the road, and soon began to meet the distressed people, women and children half naked; children enquiring for their parents, parents for their children, and wives for their husbands. It appeared to us as if the whole town was on fire. . . .

"The enemy robbed every house of everything valuable that could be carried away, leaving not a change of raiment to one of ten persons; and what they could not take conveniently they destroyed by cutting in pieces or breaking to atoms. The admiral himself was present at this work of destruction, and gave orders for it to his officers. Mrs. John Rodgers [wife to the commodore], Mrs. William Pinkney and Mrs. Goldsborough took shelter at Mr. Mark Pringle's. When a detachment was sent up to burn that elegant building Mrs. Goldsborough told the officer that she had an aged mother in it, and begged it might be spared. The officer replied that he acted under the admiral, and it would be necessary to obtain his consent. Mrs. G. returned with the officer and detachment, and obtained the permission that the house should be spared; but when she reached it, she found it on fire and met two men, one with a sheet, the other with a pillow-case crammed full, coming out, which she could not then notice, but ran upstairs and found a large wardrobe standing in the passage all in flame. William Pinkney, who was with her, and two of the marines by great exertion saved the house; but some of the wretches, after that took the cover from the sofa in the front room and put coals in it, and it was in flames before it was discovered. . . . An officer put his sword through a large elegant looking glass, attacked the windows, and cut out several sashes. They cut hogs through the back, and some partly through, and then left them to run." [10]

Even the stagecoaches in the tavernyard were burned. [11] Only one house was left undamaged. The raiders scattered across the

countryside, plundered and burned farmhouses "a long distance on the Baltimore road," destroyed boats and ferries, smashed out the windows of a church with stones and brick bats, and at Cresswell's "desolated everything within their reach."

The consequences of resistance were plainly evident. The whole vicinity had paid for the crime of Havre de Grace, which had been guilty of attempting to defend itself, when fired on without warning. Militia in two little batteries had returned the fire. At the Potato Battery, after the first few shots, an Irishman named

John O'Neil found himself abruptly left alone with a nine-pounder cannon and two six-pounders. He loaded one of the cannon "and fired her, when she recoiled and ran over my thigh." Badly hurt and limping, O'Neil "retreated" down to town and "joined Mr. Barnes, of the nail manufactory, with a musket, and fired on the barges while we had ammunition, and then retreated to the common, where I kept waving my hat to the militia who had run away, to come to our assistance, but they proved cowardly and would not come back." A British officer on horseback, followed by a detachment of marines, captured the one-man army with two muskets in his hand and sent him on board the frigate *Maidstone*. When he was turned loose four days later, John O'Neil sat down to write a letter to a friend. He began it thus: "No doubt before this, you have heard of my defeat."

If the enemy's policy of punishing civilians for resistance by militia troops required any further clarification after Havre de Grace, it was provided when Cockburn led six hundred men in eighteen barges up the Sassafras River to attack two villages. At Fredericktown, a hamlet of some twenty houses, eighty militiamen had mustered at a breastwork armed with one small cannon. The admiral sent two Negroes ashore with a message "that if the militia would not fire upon the boats, he would only burn the vessels and store-houses." The officer commanding the militia indignantly rejected the proposal. The barges opened fire. More than half of the defenders fled, but thirty-five held out stubbornly behind their breastwork for three-quarters of an hour. When the British charged at last, the little garrison departed and the enemy "with Cockburn at the head, proceeded to the village, and deliberately applied the flaming brand to the houses."

Baltimore could read the consequences of resistance here, too:

"The screaming women and children excited the mirth of these Winnebagoes—(as they were called after a savage tribe of Indians)—deaf to the most humble entreaties to spare the cottages of the poor, Cockburn stood, like Satan on his cloud when he saw the blood of man from murdered Abel first crimson the earth, exulting at the damning deed; treating the suppliant females with the rudest curses and most vile appellations—callous, insensible, hellish. The ruin complete, the savages crossed to Georgetown, a village of about thirty houses in Kent county, where they, in a like manner, destroyed that place, with many houses in the vicinity. It is a satisfaction that some of the wretches paid the forfeit of their crimes—a good number of them were killed and wounded; nine in a single boat, but the whole loss is not known. The property destroyed is estimated at from seventy to eighty thousand dollars.

"While at Frederick Town the admiral frequently spoke of Baltimore, and swore he would never rest until he had burned every house in it." [12]

That sentence of extinction had hung over Baltimore for fourteen months.

For a long time it had seemed unreal, fantastic. Fredericktown and Cresswell's and Georgetown and Havre de Grace might be wiped out, but Baltimore was Baltimore. It couldn't happen here.

Professional peace politicians talked about "the magnanimity and honorable policy" of the enemy. Professional war politicians shouted about "native valor." Taproom strategists proved to their own satisfaction that the town could not be taken. Even the soberer and sounder-bottomed citizens, giving Cockburn credit for the worst intentions, nevertheless reasoned themselves into a comfortable anesthesia. They rationalized the danger until they could scarcely feel it. This war of terror in the Chesapeake, they told themselves, was not war in earnest. Cockburn had to give his crews a little recreation and excitement, he had to let them plunder a clothespress and a hen coop now and then and burn a house or two to keep them happy on their dreary duty of bottling up the bay. He was merely keeping up morale in the blockading fleet.

Yes, the hopeful Baltimoreans answered themselves, that probably was it, that certainly was part of it at least. But there might be another purpose—a shrewd military purpose. The northern states were dead set against this war, they had been sick of it before it started. If Marylanders could be made equally sick of it, their voices joined to those of the New Englanders and the other bluelights might "compel the government to make peace" on almost any terms. Cockburn, they reasoned, was engaged in a deliberate attempt to "render the calamities of war so distressing to the inhabitants of Maryland" [13] that they would tip the scales toward unconditional surrender. This was nothing but a war of nerves.

There had been, for many months, one valid reason for that belief. Cockburn had no army. [14] It was one thing for his marauders to attack a country village; the eighteen bargeloads of marines and sailors that went up the Sassafras had outnumbered the whole polulation of the towns they devastated. It would be quite a different thing to march against a town of forty thousand, the fourth largest city in America. Even the swaggering admiral knew better than to try it.

But that reason had become invalid. On the day the British transports entered Chesapeake Bay, George Cockburn had acquired an army and his threat had taken on reality. It was still fantastic, but it was no longer remote. The glare of flames against the southern sky on Wednesday night had proved that it could happen here.

Now Henry Fulford, who had seen the enemy, was saying that the only way to save the city was to surrender. He was saying there was no force that could face the British army. And he might be right. And he was not alone in his despair; many others thought as he did. The evacuation of Baltimore was beginning. Through the open windows of Ed Johnson's office came the creak of broad-wheels and the clank of trace chains; some of the wagons rolling through the streets might be carrying supplies to the reserve militia mobilizing in the suburbs, but some of them were taking the fainthearted out of town with all their movable possessions. The York road already had its caravan of refugees, straggling north toward Pennsylvania and safety. Perhaps faint hearts and wise heads went together. With the Fifth broken and dispersed, the Rifles scattered, and the two swank batteries of field guns somewhere but nobody knew where, Baltimore had lost the troops it trusted most. Without them—even with them—it could muster a militia force only a little more than half as strong as Winder's routed army.

The "citizens in town meeting" wasted no time on the choice between surrender and resistance. The decision: fight. The question: leadership.

Four men in uniform spoke briefly. They were in complete agreement: what they said had been arranged beforehand. But what they said was none the less amazing. Three of them were regulars. Two had distinguished themselves in hard-fought and victorious battles. One was a national hero. And yet they proposed to offer the supreme command to a militiaman. A clerk copied down the resolution. The Committee of Vigilance and Safety voted. Three men rose to do an errand: Richard Frisby, Robert Stewart and John Eager Howard.[15]

The errand: to ask a man named Sam Smith, sixty-two years old, to take command of the "doomed town" and save it if he could.

10

MAN OF "THE PRECIOUS HOUR"

S<small>AM SMITH WAS A GOOD OAK</small>
beam of a man. This wasn't the first time he had been used to prop
up a falling cause.

He was more than a man: he was part of a gallant legend. He
was part of that thunderous roll call of battles—Long Island, Harlem, White Plains, Fort Mifflin, the Brandywine, Monmouth. He
was part of the old despair, the defeats, the failures, the long retreat through the Jerseys; of Morristown, Valley Forge; of the old

heartaches, the starving, the freezing, the feet wrapped in rags, the bloody tracks in the snow.

He had been one of the first to go in the Revolution—not in the first wild rush of the long-knife men, the scalp-yelling, bare-bottomed, Indian-breechclouted, back-country hellions who followed Mike Cresap to Boston—but with the first regular troops that Maryland sent to the war. He did not hold back, he was simply an orderly man. He had a nice sense of the thing to do: he went when Maryland went.

Sam Smith was born with a silver fork in his hand, in a place and time in which many men still thought of their fingers as table tools furnished of God, and regarded forks, if not as the work of the, devil, at least as the symbol and sign of decadence. He was born on July 27, 1752, in Carlisle, on the great overland trade route that led from Philadelphia—by way of Harris's ferry across Susquehanna River—to the rich fur country beyond Pennsylvania's mountains. His father, John Smith, was a prosperous merchant. When John Smith moved to Baltimore Town on Patapsco River in 1760, he brought with him a capital of forty thousand dollars, no trifling sum for that day.[1] The capital grew. There was money enough to send Sam to the best schools available, to "an excellent academy" at Little Elk and later to Newark, where he "learned much of the Latin and some of the Greek classics." At fourteen he rose in the world—to the top of a long-legged stool in his father's countinghouse. There was plenty to count: John Smith owned ships whose venturesome bowsprits poked into ports with curious names in curious, faraway places. At eighteen, his son Sam was supercargo and owner's agent aboard of a flour-laden, Europe-bound ship. John Smith had ideas concerning his son's education in business: another long-legged stool was waiting for Sam in a countinghouse in London.

But Sam had ideas of his own. He "believed that he would derive no benefit from that plan," so he put ashore at Bristol along with the flour and proceeded to demonstrate that he was either a spoiled, willful brat or a young man possessed of a vigorous mind and the courage to follow his own convictions. Convictions or whims, he made a thorough job of following them: he didn't get home for four years.

He chartered his father's ship out of Falmouth with cargo for Venice, and the pilot conveniently ran her aground in sight of the doges' palace, knocked off her rudder, burst her seams and filled her with Adriatic. Sam got off, safe and satisfied. What could be better? There he was, stranded in Venice—Venice in carnival time. His satisfaction lasted eight months and then he moved on at last —to Rome, to another carnival season. Already he had a sense of the thing to do: he "did" all the public buildings. But he also took in the theaters. A month of Rome, and his appetite was only whetted; he set out on a real "grand tour." Leghorn, Pisa, Genoa, Nice, Marseilles—he saw them all, and he stayed in each "a sufficient time for his purposes." Beyond Marseilles there was Barcelona, and then there were Valencia, Alicante, Granada and Malaga. There was Gibraltar, with a British general treating him like a prince and an officer escort to show him the tunnels hewed through the rock and the great guns crouched in the tunnels. There were Cadiz and Seville and Badajoz and Elvas and Lisbon, with the captain of a British man-of-war to make him an honored guest and take him finally to England as a passenger at the king's expense. It was heady wine for a youngster.

If he sowed a wild oat, at least he didn't confess it. The harvest of his four years' independence was waiting for him in London— not reproof from an angry parent, reward from a proud one. His father, he found, had made him full partner. He came home to America in a ship that also brought Major André; they landed at Philadelphia on the day the first Congress met—the fourth day of September in 1774.

He had covered a deal of ground already, for a young fellow of twenty-two, but now his life gathered speed. The Liberty Boys were bellowing and smashing Tory windows, the committees of correspondence were spreading rebellion as fast as their quills could fly, the "young gentlemen" of Baltimore Town were forming a militia company and the sort of young gentlemen who were permitted to join had money to spend and knew the best tailor in town. Their uniforms were much admired by the suitable young ladies and, perhaps, by some who were quite unsuitable. The young lady who admired Sam Smith was eminently suitable—the "beautiful and imperious" Margaret Speare, daughter of his father's close friend and original hardheaded Pennsylvania business associate, now certainly to be numbered among Baltimore's "men of capital." Sam Smith was a private, then he was a sergeant, and then the town companies of the First Maryland battalion were marching down to the waiting ships at the wharves and the thrums of the enlisted men's purple hunting shirts were fluttering good-bye to the fluttering handkerchiefs on the Long street stoops and in the Market street windows.

Sam Smith was twenty-four, that summer of 1776, a captain in scarlet and buff.[2] His coat fitted more than well; his breeches grew to his legs as smooth as his legs' own skin. When he marched at the head of his company—Eighth company, First Maryland battalion[3]—the leading files could see their own legs in the polished mirrors of their captain's boots. A young gentleman in the ranks could venture to wave when he passed the right window. But a captain couldn't wave. There was nothing about a captain's red coat to flutter; its tails were as stiff as buckram could make them; the man in the coat was as stiff as a wooden soldier. You can't tell very much about the grain of the wood when the bark is still on, no matter how well the bark fits.

The test of the wood in the soldier came quick and hard, on a day when the new nation born at Philadelphia was less than eight weeks old, a day when eight weeks seemed likely to be the whole span of its life. It came at a moment when the battle of Long Island was almost over—when the army of the United States was an army no longer but only a frantic mob that was fighting itself instead of the enemy, fighting itself for room to escape on the narrow dam of a tide mill. There, while the broken regiments fled, the unbroken First Maryland slaughtered itself in five desperate charges that gained "an hour more precious to American liberty than any other in history."[4]

The hour saved the army. Surprised, outflanked, rolled up, dissolved in a chaos of panic, the army escaped from the trap that was closing upon it. But when the hour was over, it was easier to count the living than the dead in the Maryland battalion. Out of less than four hundred who made the first charge, two hundred and fifty-nine were killed, wounded or missing: Not many were missing: "the Hessians gave no quarter on that day."[5] The purple hunting shirts lay in windrows where the musketry cut them down, they lay in piles where the last, lost pieces of companies fought to the end while the bayonets ringed them in and the rings drew tight and the bayonets finished them off.

Three companies chopped their way through. The men who were left of them plunged into the salt-muck swamp that bordered Gowanus Creek. Ahead was the tiderace, full to its slimy brink, too deep to be forded. Behind was Cornwallis's infantry, firing and firing into the squirming mud. Now and again a young gentleman stopped struggling and crawling, his bit of the swamp stopped squirming, blood stained the purple shirt and the ooze slowly rose around him and sucked him down.

The dead marched on in a legend of a nation saved from death. The living marched on to become part of a legend before they died: they became the Maryland Line.

Sam Smith was one of those who emerged alive from the slime of Gowanus swamp. Among the men he had led to the brink of the tiderace, there were some who could not swim. While they crouched in the mud, under the murderous fire, Sam Smith and a sergeant swam across; found, each of them, a slab; and swam back again to save what was left of the company. Two by two, on the ends of the planks, Sam Smith and the sergeant ferried the men to safety.

The scarlet-and-buff was black with muck, the well-fitted coat would never fit well again. But the man in the coat was a man.

The ordeal did not end with the fighting nor with the escape through the swamp and the tiderace. The First Maryland was only a fragment, but it was still an organized, disciplined fragment; its ordeal was only beginning. Through the next day and the next, in drenching rain that was followed by fog almost as wet as the rain, it held quagmire trenches dug out of another swamp; without sleep and without food, it marched and countermarched; it even made a feint of attacking. General Washington, trying to put the pieces of his army together again with one hand, trying to hold the enemy off with the other, used the decimated Maryland battalion as part of the desperate bluff. The battalion bluffed as sturdily as it had fought. The bluff worked: it gave Washington time to pick up the pieces, time to withdraw from Long Island in some kind of order.

The third night came, and still the First Maryland held the post of danger: while the army fled by boat to New York, it held the redoubt that covered the flight. Sam Smith and his mud-smeared, famished, exhausted men held the ditch outside the redoubt. There were outpost lines for a time, but the outposts melted away. About midnight an anxious corporal came panting to his captain. He "had been up and down the lines," he reported, "and not a man was to be seen." Off went both of the Eighth company's lieutenants to hunt for the missing army. They found nothing: the army had disappeared: even the rest of the First Maryland was gone, the redoubt was empty. Sam Smith moved into it. He "presumed that

he had been left as a forlorn hope," and he stayed there; he had
no orders to leave. If dying was what was needed, the Maryland
men had proved that they knew how to die.

But orders came at last and almost too late. Sam Smith was
not the last man off Long Island, but he was as nearly so as a
man could be: he left in the last boat that pulled away from the
beach. It had scarcely shoved off "when the British light-horse
appeared on the hill." They fired their carbines, but they missed
the boat.

That was the first retreat Sam Smith helped to cover, but it
was far from being the last. There was Harlem . . . and the First
Maryland guarding the rear of the beaten army. White Plains
. . . and a cannon ball striking the ground almost at his feet,
bounding over his shoulder, beheading the sergeant who stood behind him . . . a spent musket ball striking him on the arm as he
fired at the oncoming grenadiers, the arm falling helpless, the shot
going wild . . . the last stand behind a stone wall with only two
of his men. Fort Washington taken. Fort Lee given up. Retreat
. . . retreat . . . the battalion worn to a frazzle, worn down almost
to nothing, reinforced by the Blue Hen's Chickens . . . but not
two hundred and fifty men left altogether in the First Maryland
and the good battalion from Delaware that formed the rearguard
with it. Falling back . . . falling back . . . and finally Sam Smith
and a major and another captain riding to Newark to tell Washington that the two battalions could do no more. General Washington saying "I can assign no other regiment in which I can place
the same confidence, and I request you will say so to your gallant
regiment" . . . and the regiment, so small now that it could be
"formed in a circle" to hear what the general said, finding the heart
and the strength to cheer the news that their only relief would be
more "fatigue and danger."

Down through the Jerseys . . . always the last of the column
. . . not even a part of the column, but six miles, twelve miles
behind . . . skirmishing . . . falling back . . . holding a hill or a
patch of woods by day, marching by night . . . floundering on
in the dark over roads torn up by the baggage train and the guns
that had gone ahead . . . the rain falling in torrents . . . the mud
an endless torment, "every step above the ankles and many to the
knee." The Delaware crossed at last . . . and the First Maryland
only a handful . . . only ninety men now out of all the six hundred and eighty-four who had marched with fluttering purple

thrums through the fluttering streets in June. *June!* You could count on your fingers, and June was six months ago. But your fingers are numb with cold, they're no good for counting, put your fingers under your armpits to thaw them out. It couldn't have been *last* June! It was June six years ago . . . six decades ago . . . six nightmare aeons ago.

In June, Sam Smith had a dozen shirts. He still had two in September, but one was lost at the wash. When Christmas came, he had one: there had been no washing to lose it.

He had more commissions than he had shirts. He had one as a major; and then, with the ink scarcely dry on the first, he had another that made him lieutenant colonel. He was second in command of the new Fourth Maryland, one of the seven new regiments Maryland was raising to see the war through. He was riding home to Baltimore to drum up recruits and make love to Margaret Speare. He succeeded in both undertakings. Before the winter was over, he was riding north to Morristown with more Maryland men to stiffen the dwindling army, and Margaret Speare had promised to be his wife.

The fighting began again. Staten Island . . . the blundering night attack . . . the narrow escape . . . the new-made lieutenant colonel escaping again in the very last boat . . . and then taking a flag of truce to the British lines along with a London draft for twenty-five pounds to ease the lot of Major Jack Stuart who hadn't got off in the boat. He was downright fond of Jack Stuart. They'd fought a duel, and having done their damnedest to kill each other had become the best of friends. Then the Brandywine . . . another retreat . . . another last stand without orders . . . the army melting away and Sam Smith left with thirty men . . . a small, hot fight in a cornfield, the enemy going back through the head-high corn but the thirty men going too, dribbling away, disappearing . . . the lieutenant colonel without a regiment helping himself to somebody else's, rallying stragglers, combing them out of the weeds and the brush, forming a battle line with a thousand men that weren't his. He kept them in line until dark and then brought the thousand men out of defeat unbroken, with a pistol held to a surly Quaker's breast to make him a faithful guide.

Disaster followed defeat. Mad Anthony Wayne's division was caught by surprise in a night attack on its camp and was cut to pieces. Congress fled. Philadelphia fell. Billingsport fell, the guns in the batteries spiked and the garrison running away. General

Washington, looking for props to hold up the falling cause, remembered the man who held the Long Island redoubt. He sent Sam Smith to brace the defense of the Delaware River, to keep the enemy's fleet from coming up, to cut off supplies from the enemy's army in the captured capital.

Sam Smith "found himself, at the age of twenty-five years, unskilled in everything relative to the defence of fortifications, having to rely entirely on his own energies for the defence of a Fort walled with freestone on the side opposite the Jersey shore and the approach by the river; stockaded with pine logs, fifteen inches thick, opposite Province-island; and the approach from above flanked by three wooden blockhouses, mounting eight-pound French guns in their upper stories. There was, also, an open platform on which were mounted eighteen-pounders, pointing down the river, with one thirty-two-pounder, being the only piece that pointed on Province-island, where he expected the enemy would establish himself." He had guns . . . but only two gunners. He had two hundred infantrymen . . . but no blankets or shirts for the men. He had two hundred mouths to feed . . . and most of the time no food. He had cannon . . . but not enough powder and ball to fight a single day's action. But he was improvising, he was making cannoneers out of men who had never before heard a cannon go off, he was breaking up the raft that had fetched him to his jerry-built fort on Mud Island, he was turning the logs into embrasures to shield his guns, he was building a dirt-and-log wall to protect his men if the fleet came up the river.

He was writing blunt letters to the commander in chief; he wasn't afraid to speak up when he thought he should. He wrote of "the want of provisions . . . & the Men not being properly Chosen for such an expedition." He told Washington that "few of them have Shoes or Stockings, many of them without Coats or Blankets & scarcely any who have more than one Shirt, without their Clothing it will be very injurious to their Constitution & disagreeable to hear their Constant Murmurings." He sent Washington "a List . . . which I expect your Excellency will order to be forwarded immediately to us." He didn't ask, he *expected*. "I find everything," he wrote, "in the utmost Confusion, not as many Cartouches as will last one day . . . the provisions almost out . . . the Militia refus'd Obedience . . . & have underwent no sort of training." But he added stoutly, "if they will give us Some time to prepare we shall be able to make a tolerable Defence." [6]

The more he saw of the situation, the less tolerable the defense appeared. He was "in Hopes to defend the Garrison if our Ammunition arrives," but his men were sickening in the stinking salt mud of the island. "I have already sent away 6 Men & an officer sick, & this day shall send off 12 & 2 officers besides 7 More in Garrison unfit for duty." On October 11th he was able to write that "last Night the Enemy threw up a Battery in the Rear of the fort Close to the Banks of the Meadow within Musket Shot of us & had already got one p^e. of Artillery in it, we attack'd with the floating Batteries, Block Houses, Gallies & our 32 pounder from the Battery & in short time oblig'd them to hoist the white flag. The party we secur'd consists of 1 officer, 1 Ensign & 56 Serj^s. & privates . . . they belong to 6 or 7 diff^t. Regiments from which I conclude the party set apart for the Reduction of this Garrison is pretty large . . . They will lead us a disagreeable Life."

Life in Fort Mifflin was disagreeable enough. The next night "the Enemy threw up a long Breast work on the high Ground at Province Island, which Enfilades our principal Battery," and to make matters worse Sam Smith by that time had "34 Men sick in Garrison" and "the remaining will soon be worn out with fatigue as I am obliged to keep them on Constant duty." He was begging for more men. He was no longer "expecting," he was writing grimly that "one Chief Reason of my Men being so very sickly is their want of Clothing & Blankets, your Excell^{ys}. order to the Clothier has never been complyed with. I have at least 60 of this small Number without Breeches . . ."

The enemy's shore batteries were churning the mud of Sam Smith's island into an odoriferous batter and knocking his fort into kindling and bits of stone. The commodore of the fleet of American gun galleys in the river was refusing to help him, saying that "the Gallies . . . should not be sent to . . . lay & look at your Garrison." Sam Smith didn't like it and said so. Late in October, instead of reinforcements or clothes to cover his bare-legged, bare-bottomed scarecrows, he got a letter announcing that a foreign officer, the Baron d'Arendt, was coming to take command of Fort Mifflin. He didn't like that, either, and he said so. He wrote to the commander in chief that "there will therefore be no further Occasion for me hear, as the party of Infantry left of what I bro^t . . . does not now exceed 80 Men."

But General Washington chose to keep Sam Smith where he was. The baron duly appeared, "a Prussian, a very military-looking man, six feet high, and elegantly formed." Indeed, Sam Smith concluded, "his whole appearance was that which would commend him to a command, where personal bravery was not required." Sam took him on a tour of the battered fort; when they came to a blockhouse now much the worse for wear, the baron naïvely inquired what had happened to it. "Oh," said Sam Smith casually, "it has been blown up twice." The baron went out the window.

The young lieutenant proceeded to finish the job. "We must frighten him away from the fort," he decided, "or he will do more injury than good." Sam had a knack of succeeding in what he set out to do. The baron developed an "indisposition" and moved off Mud Island to Red Bank. When November came, Sam Smith was still in command. The enemy was having troubles now: the river was rising: the enemy's howitzers were standing hub-deep in water and their outguards were wading up to their knees. Sam Smith was full of hope.

Then the tide turned, literally; a gale drove it higher; on Mud Island the river flowed two feet deep and the only dry spots were the barracks floors and the artillery platforms. The besiegers managed to throw up still more batteries; the defenders could "distinguish 5 Embrasures & Ship Carriages for their Cannon" and while Sam Smith presumed "their Intention must now be to knock down all our pallisades on that side to destroy our Block Houses & then Storm us," a letter arrived from York with unexpected news. Congress, assembled in that little back-country refuge, had voted a sword to the gallant defender of Mifflin. The gallant defender was writing: "The Honorable the Congress have done me too much Honor, perhaps the Enemy may give us an oppʸ. to merit the high Approbation they are pleas'd to express of mine & my officers Conduct."

The enemy was most obliging. Two days later, on November 11th, Lieutenant Colonel Smith sat down to write a dispatch at a table that jarred, every now and again, with the blast and concussion of shells and the solid slam of a round shot striking home.

Fort Mifflin 11th Novr 1777

Sir
    This Morning the Enemy open'd their Battery in the Rear of our N. West Block House about 500 yds. dist. from it of 6 pieces of Cannon & one Howitz & one other Howitz opposite the Right of our Battery, they were so fortunate to strike one of our 18 pʳ. in the two Gun Battery on the Muzzle by which she is render'd unfit

for service. The Shot from the Battery rakes the Pallisades fronting the Meadow & Cuts down 4 or 5 at a time. They have laid
open a great part of that side & destroy'd all that Range of Barracks, they also keep up an Incessant fire from their Hospital, they
have dismounted 3 of our Block Houses & injur'd the Houses
very much. . . . Gen. Varnum has promis'd to prepare for us New
Pallisades, we will replace at Night such as are destroy'd in the
Day & endeavour to keep the fort as long as in our power. . . .
We are determined to defend it to the last Extremity . . .

Sam Smith never finished the letter. He broke off to answer
a message from General Varnum at Red Bank. The brief answer
written, he rose to hand it to Varnum's brigade major. "In the act
of handing it, with his right hand—his left hand being behind
him, and his back to the chimney—a ball came through the stock-
ade, the barracks, and two stacks of chimneys and, nearly spent, it
struck him on the left hip and dislocated his wrist. He fell, covered with bricks, by which he was severely bruised; every joint
in his body appeared to be loosened. The Officers present were covered with bricks and mortar, and so astonished as to give no
assistance. The Colonel did not lose his presence of mind, and
thought fresh air to be essential. He could not rise, but rolled over
and over, until he got to the front door, when the Officers joined
him. Doctor Skinner came immediately, drew the wrist into its
place, and bled him. It was many months before he could use his
wrist. The bruises were numerous; and some, on the bones, gave
great pain. He was carried to the boat, for he could not walk, and
sent to the Jersey shore."

One week later, Fort Mifflin was evacuated.

Bruised and in pain though he was, Sam Smith bought a horse
and rode up to headquarters at White Marsh. "Dinner had just
been removed. He was received by all the General officers, then
present, in the most flattering manner, and by General Washington
in his usual cold manner, at first, but afterwards, with kindness and
sympathy, when he observed his arm in a sling." Washington offered him a place on his staff, but the lieutenant colonel of the
Fourth Maryland believed that he belonged with the regiment he
had helped to raise, and he went back to the Fourth Maryland to
share the hardships of winter quarters. The day the regiment
marched for Valley Forge "it was met by a violent snow storm
. . . the army bivouacked as best it could . . . the officers slept
with a fire at their feet . . . the cover was made with two forked

saplings, placed in the ground, another from one to the other . . .
against this, fence rails were placed sloping, on which leaves and
snow were thrown and thus made comfortable." The elegant young
gentleman from Baltimore, who had known the delights of Venice
in carnival time and Rome in the theater season, had found a new
definition of comfort.

Luck was with him. All his life, whether he always thought so
or not, Sam Smith was a fortunate man; this time he had earned his
luck. Washington had come to depend more and more on the
Maryland Line; he wanted more Maryland men; the hero of Mud
Island siege would be much more useful raising recruits than starving at Valley Forge. Before the first log huts were up, Sam was riding south, he was riding home; he had almost the whole winter
at home, with his fiancée.

It was not a happy winter. Every embrace was a hope deferred,
every kiss was a promise that couldn't be kept. For a year and a half
he had shared the army's humiliating poverty and all its defeats
and frustrations; now, for the first time in his life, he was face to
face with personal frustration and the personal humiliation of his
own poverty. If he had changed from a wooden soldier into a good
oak beam that could be used for a barricade behind a retreating
army or a prop to hold up a flimsy and tottering fort, he had also
changed from a wealthy man to a poor one. When he joined up
as a private in the old First Maryland "he was worth nine thousand pounds of his own and his father was the richest merchant in
Baltimore." But now "their property was almost exclusively in
debts due to them by country merchants" and these debts, when
they were paid at all, were paid "in Continental money which had
become worthless in the hands of his father." Margaret Speare's
father was in a similar plight. Sam Smith might be a hero, he
might have a gift sword from Congress to wear, but he had no
money to furnish a house for a bride or even to buy her food. His
pay as lieutenant colonel worked out to four dollars a month.

His unhappiness and frustration did not interfere with his
duty. The duty was well done: when spring came, with news of
the French alliance, with a swelling hope that the long ebb tide of
the war was turning to flood at last, Sam Smith marched into the
camp at Valley Forge at the head of a column of four hundred
fresh Maryland troops.

A new campaign began, rich in hope and promise. The British
evacuated Philadelphia. At last, after two years of campaigning,

Sam Smith was no longer part of a rearguard protecting a beaten, retreating army; he was part of the advance guard of a strong and confident army, dogging a retreating enemy, snapping at his heels, hanging so close that the Maryland men trampled the enemy's still-smoldering campfires and were blackguarded by the enemy's camp women "who had remained behind to collect, as plunder, anything the officers might have left." He was in the first attack at Monmouth, he was part of the picked brigade that drove ahead on both flanks of the enemy's rear guard and set a trap and was ready to spring the trap. And then . . . frustration again . . . General Charles Lee's astounding, incomprehensible order . . . retreat without fighting . . . confusion . . . complete disgust . . . and the red-coated regiments coming on in headlong contempt for the rebels they'd chased so often.

Sam Smith had his share of the bitter fighting that day and his share of the bitter disappointment . . . the poor half-victory snatched from defeat . . . the barely drawn battle that should have been clean-cut triumph . . . disappointment as black as the faces of the enemy dead who had lain all day in the baking heat. The high hopes dwindled, the confidence ebbed away. Through the bootless summer, Sam Smith marched and idled as the army marched or sat on its backside and watched the enemy's antics around New York. He was one of the players in the tragicomedy of Lee's court-martial, but even that was frustration: they ruled his evidence out. He saw William Smallwood, beloved first colonel of the beloved First Maryland, overpassed to make room for a foreigner, Baron De Kalb, as major general of the Maryland division; De Kalb was a gallant soldier but so was Smallwood, and Smallwood had fought from the first; to a Maryland man, it looked like a shabby business. He listened to all the old bickerings, dragged out afresh: to the old grievance that New England had started the war but the states to the south had been left to fight it: to the denunciation of congressmen who were only too willing to tell soldiers how to fight but who couldn't be bothered to pay the soldiers or give them shoes or a shirt or a chunk of fat-back to chew: to the little cabals for promotions, the petty squabblings about which brigade should do what.

His sense of frustration grew. His purse flattened. When autumn came, he had less than a hundred dollars to his name, out of all the forty-five thousand dollars he had had when the war began. When the army sent him home once more to drum up recruits, it was sending him back to his personal humiliation. When Margaret was in his arms again, when he held her close and knew she was his and knew that he couldn't take her because he had no means to support a wife, the bitter knowledge overwhelmed him. He had offered his life to his country, he had been wounded twice. He loved his country, but a man's country is inextricably mingled with home, a woman, a future. He had lost his hope of a home, his woman was denied him, the life that he knew had been swept away, the future had disappeared. Four dollars a month . . . or Margaret. The decision "was like tearing his heart out." He chose the girl, and resigned, and went to work to prop up the tottering house of Smith.

He did not wash his hands of the war: he remained a soldier, colonel of the Baltimore militia: he did all the things he was asked to do for the army, all the things that had to be done when the fine French army marched into town and pitched its tents on the hill at the top of Charles street, under the ample elms. He never forgot the thrill of those shining white regiments . . . nor the pang that they gave him. But he stuck to the task he had set for himself, and it prospered; the house of Smith did not fall.

Sam Smith had a house of his own, in Water street. He had a wife. He had a son. He had ships at sea, and the ships were fortunate ships. He helped to found a bank. He was honored, respected, elected to Congress. He invested in an ironworks. He began to buy land, putting old grants together into a broad estate .. pieces of Merryman's Chance and Discovery and Ensor's Choice and Orange and Gorsuch's Folly. He built a new house on the land and christened it Montebello. Life expanded along with his acres.

Merchant with the Midas magic, shipowner, gentleman-adventurer trading into the Mediterranean Sea and the Caribbees and the Spanish Main, bank founder, landed proprietor, ironmaster, general of militia, partner in privateers, representative in Congress for ten continuous years and senator now for ten more—this was the man John Eager Howard rode out to Montebello to see, along with Stewart and Frisby.

Past the first tollgate and more than two miles from the town, the three horsemen turned off from York turnpike into a path through the woods, to emerge upon a broad slope of hill swept clean of the forest trees and turned into a terraced lawn. A broad drive circled the lawn to the crest of the hill. There the white mass of Montebello stood behind twelve tall white pillars. Above the pillars, a finely worked balustrade swept back in unusual curves. Montebello was more than a house, it was a position. With the broad white wall of the second story behind them, the pillars and balustrade presented a front that might have been patterned from three of those shining regiments Rochambeau brought to town in 1781—one regiment advanced in the center of the line and one on each of its flanks, a little withdrawn. Over the balustrade, the six broad windows looked away across the town and the

harbor, and they, too, had their flankers—the other broad windows in each of the curving ends of the house. Even the two broad chimneys marching like two platoons had the smaller kitchen chimney to serve as an outguard.

The horsemen rode up to the shallow step and Sam Smith met them there, between the tall pillars, and was not dwarfed by the pillars. Time had touched him a little, but only a little. He had taken the weathering well, the oak was still straight and unwarped. He was still a military figure, he was solid and strong, he was dignified, ample and gracious. So was his house. Servants came for the horses. Sam Smith ushered his visitors in, their heels ringing sharp on the marble floor of the porch, their heels urgent but hushed by the mass of the house as they crossed the great, four-square living room. The living room, only one story high under the portico roof, was warm in the August heat; there was a glimpse, through a pilastered, corniced entrance, of the long oval dining room with its paneled wainscot, its marble mantel brought from Italy, its furniture brought from France, its Stuart painting of General Smith and his wife. The withdrawing room was cool, its windows shadowed by stately oaks, its curved end tempting the breeze from north, east and south.[7]

They sat down in the ample chairs, seeing themselves in the leaded-glass doors of the built-in bookshelves, looking up as visitors always looked up to the odd circular lantern set in the high, coved ceiling. John Howard was an old friend and a neighbor; his own fine estate of Belvedere was just off to the south, through the woods; he knew where the whisky was kept. There were things to be said that were not for servants' hearing; they poured their own drinks while Sam Smith read the paper they gave him, covered with clerkly writing:

By the Committee of Vigilance and Safety
Resolved, That all good citizens be, and hereby requested . . .

Hmm . . . these political job holders were always sloppy and inefficient . . . the clerk had left out the word "are." A businessman couldn't afford to keep clerks like that.

. . . to give this committee any information they may have, relative to suspected persons or places; and that the members of this committee be and they are hereby required to appoint such persons as they may think proper, in each ward and precinct, to search such suspected persons and places.[8]

Well, that was likely all right. Some of the bluelights had come right close to treason. Up north, some of them had gone over the line into outright treason, setting out blue lanterns to tell the blockading fleet that Decatur was coming out from New London to try to slip through the blockade. Yes, the "peace men" would bear with a little watching.

Resolved, That the owners of boats moored or made fast, at or near the wharves of the city, are hereby directed to remove their vessels, immediately to some place below Harris' Creek, for greater security.

Whereas it has been communicated to this committee by Brig. Gen. Stricker, Comm. Perry, Maj. Armistead and Capt. Spence, in person, that it is their wish that Maj. Gen. Smith be requested to take command of the forces, which may be called into service for the defence of the city,— Therefore

Resolved, That Colonel John E. Howard, Mr. Frisby and Mr. Stewart, be appointed to wait on Maj. Gen. Smith, and communicate to him the information this committee have received—to state they unanimously concur with the same; and to request that he would at this important crisis take upon himself the command of the forces. . . .

It gave him a thrill of pride. A man could not help but be proud of a trust like that, he could not help but be proud to be trusted by men like these. John Stricker might have sought this command for himself . . . a good man, John Stricker . . . a good soldier and a veteran . . . commanding general of the Baltimore City brigade. Oliver Hazard Perry . . . hero of the victorious battle of Lake Erie . . . "we have met the enemy and they are ours." Armistead and Spence . . . professionals . . . sound, experienced officers of the regular service. John Eager Howard . . . colonel in the old Maryland Line . . . gallant and able . . . he and John were the same age . . . sixty-two. It was honor indeed to be trusted by men like these, in a crisis like this. And a man must be either more or less than human not to feel a quick, deep thrust of satisfaction. Sam Smith was thoroughly human. He had been passed over when the federal government chose a general officer to command the forces mobilized to defend Maryland against invasion. He was a major general, he had led Maryland troops in action, he had a good record; but the command went to Winder. Sam Smith was commanding general of the Third Division, Maryland Militia, but he hadn't been called into service; some of his best troops had been taken away from him; Winder had dealt with Brigadier General Stricker or with Lieutenant Colonel Sterrett. Now . . .

But Sam Smith felt something that wasn't pride and wasn't satisfaction. This paper he held in his hand brought back the old pang, it brought back the old regret. He had thrown up his commission before the old war was won, he had left the army before its torment was over, he had missed the final, victorious battles. He had had good reasons; there had been few to blame him; even among the men who went on to the end at Yorktown, there had been few to criticize what he had done. But the regret was still there, like the pain of an old healed wound that disappeared most of the time but came back when the weather changed. The pain was there now, not in the Mud Island hip, but somewhere deeper inside him. He envied John Eager Howard . . . Guilford, Camden, the Cowpens . . . John Howard had led the shock troops . . . he had swept the field with his bayonets . . . he had been in at the kill.

The three men sat watching Sam Smith. His face was still intent on the paper . . . a calm, substantial face, almost handsome in profile . . . a solid-looking face . . . a long nose, not too big for the face but a little heavy at the end, slanting up at the bottom with just a hint of a flare at the nostrils . . . cheeks full where they joined the nose . . . a determined mouth . . . a strong, solid chin with a fullness about it that had not softened its strength . . . heavy eyebrows arching down at the outer ends.

Smith had made up his mind on the instant. He would take the command, of course. It was his duty. It was more than a duty, it was a chance to lay the old ghost, to bury the old regret. While his visitors waited, wondering why he was taking so long to decide, he was thinking of something else. His mind was marching firmly toward the first consequence of his decision; his thoughts were deploying to meet it. He was already planning his first battle. His opponent: William Winder.

It was the kind of battle a general ought not to fight. He ought not to have to fight it. But there was no alternative. In asking him to "take upon himself" the command of the defense of Baltimore, the Committee of Vigilance and Safety had taken upon itself a risk considerably more serious, perhaps, than it had realized. It had taken the risk of setting up a divided authority—a command divided against itself. It had put Sam Smith in an untenable position.

William Winder was the commanding general of the Tenth Military District. Baltimore was in that district. Winder was a brigadier general; by title, Smith outranked him. But Will Winder held a federal commission; he had been an officer of the United States army since April, 1812—two months before the outbreak of the war—when he entered the federal service as a lieutenant colonel. Sam Smith was a militiaman. Under law, no mere officer of militia could give orders to an officer of the army of the United States. Under law, Sam Smith could not give orders to Will Winder. It was perfectly clear that Winder was in command of Baltimore and all its forces and defenses, and that if Smith dared to disobey his orders—let alone attempt to displace him—the old militaman would risk the penalties by law provided for a whole platoon of military crimes. Insubordination. Mutiny in the face of the enemy. Treason. Rebellion.

Fantastic? Yes, certainly—if Sam Smith risked and won. But if he risked and lost, the fantastic might become the practical. If disaster at Baltimore followed disaster at Washington, where could the administration find a bigger bucket of whitewash to cover its own shortcomings? How could it devise a gaudier spectacle, to distract attention from its own follies, than the show that could be staged by court-martialing a major general who also was a United States senator? It might be good politics. It might be very good politics indeed.

One thing was certain. A divided command would be fatal. There was no room for two commanding generals. Will Winder might yield a battlefield too easily, but he would defend his personal authority to the last. When the Committee of Vigilance and Safety called on Sam Smith to "take" command, it had used the right word. He would have to take it.

Well, this wasn't the first time he had had to deal with a superior he didn't want. There had been the Prussian baron at Fort Mifflin. After almost forty years, that memory could still prick Smith with a twinge of anger, it could still tug at the corners of his mouth with a pleased amusement. Forty years ago a young officer did not risk General Washington's cold anger by deliberately disobeying orders; but the young officer on Mud Island had found a way to get rid of an unwelcome superior, the Baron d'Arendt. As for William Winder . . . Sam Smith made, now, his opening move. Would the gentlemen of the committee write a letter to the governor of Maryland? The gentlemen would do anything Sam Smith asked. What should the letter say? Well, it might say that in assuming command of the forces defending the city, Major General Smith "wished to be sanctioned in so doing by the Executive of the State and that his powers might be extended." The importance of that mild request would become apparent later.

The three gentlemen lingered only a few minutes longer. Not much more was said. Sam Smith said that he knew he could count on the Committee of Vigilance and Safety. He remarked that there were capable, well-tried officers to prepare the city's defenses . . . Perry . . . Stricker . . . Rodgers . . . Porter . . . Armistead . . .

Spence . . . Howard. Yes, of course; John Howard would do what he could. The gentlemen looked at each other. There would be an ad in the paper that afternoon:

INVITATION

Elderly Men, who are able to carry a firelock, and willing to render a last service to their Country, and posterity; are requested to meet at the *Court House* at eleven o'clock TOMORROW, to form a Company, and be prepared to march in conjunction with the troops, expected to-morrow against the enemy.

It   aug 26

They mentioned the ad to Sam Smith: it was John Eager Howard's ad. They made a little joke about John and his ancient volunteers. But it wasn't a joke to Sam. He envied John Howard. Elderly men . . . a last service. It wouldn't be hard to die: he had had a full life: it was good, but he wouldn't be cheated too much if it had to end now. It wasn't the ending so much: it was the responsibility. He was sixty-two. He didn't feel sixty-two, but John Howard was the same age and John saw himself as an elderly man fit only to captain a company of other elderly men. The responsibility for the future was a terrible thing to put on an elderly man. It was a terrible weight to put on an old oak beam.

They spoke of the danger a little . . . speculating about it . . . guessing whether Wellington's Invincibles would march immediately, straight from the ruins of Washington to strike Baltimore before the militia could clear their heads from the first stunning blow, or whether they would go back to the fleet and attack by way of the harbor, army and warships together. There was no way to tell; you couldn't win battles by guesswork; you had to wait and see.

However much doubt there might be about which way the attack would come, there was no doubt whatever that it was surely coming. There was no doubt whatever that when it came, it would come with the leveling force of a hurricane, with fire and devastation. Nobody knew, as yet, how much of Washington had been destroyed. But when Havre de Grace was attacked last year, the raiders burned forty out of its sixty houses; the farms had been plundered for miles along the road to Baltimore and the farm buildings left in flames.[9] Havre de Grace was a small, inoffensive place; it had done nothing to make itself hated; it was merely American, and handy. But Baltimore was hated in earnest.

Nor was Baltimore only at stake. There were many who believed that the life of the nation itself was in danger; that this war was only the continuation of the War of Independence; that if the war should be lost, independence would also be lost. The *Times* of London had given the warning plain: "Our demands may be couched in a single word,—Submission!" The danger seemed very real, the future was dark.

11

"THAT SINK OF CORRUPTION, THAT SODOM . . ."

Sam Smith saw them off at the steps and watched them riding away. He looked at the trees, at the sweep of the lawn, at the tall white pillars. He put his hand on a pillar: he loved Montebello, it was the stuff of his dreams, it was the work of his mind and his heart, it was his life summed up.

He had started to buy the land in 1793, he had bought it little by little. It had taken him seven years to acquire the land and to build the house. He had lived in the house now for fourteen years, the good ample years at the top of his life. He would hate to lose Montebello, he would hate to see it burned. But if a battle came, it might well come on this ground.

Sam Smith had dreamed dreams, Montebello was proof of that, but he had few illusions. He hadn't been chosen for this new task because he had been a soldier; he knew that. Being a soldier was part of it, but only a part. The town needed someone to trust, it needed someone it knew. It needed a rallying place that meant more than Clem's Lot or a Charles street number. If Baltimore thought that Sam Smith was the man it could trust . . . well, he would hope it was right, he would do what he could. If it thought of Sam Smith as a kind of flag, he would nail himself to the staff.

But he couldn't think only in terms of guns and troops or of so many pounds of beef for the troops and so many pounds of powder and iron for the guns. He had to consider the town and what kind of town it was and what it could do in a pinch.

He knew the town pretty well. He had lived in it since he was eight, he had lived in it fifty-four years. He was a part of the town; his father had been a big part of it; the family roots had struck deep. When John Smith moved down into Maryland in 1760, the moving had been a kind of invasion: he hadn't brought only his wife and his son, Sam: he had brought William Smith and William Buchanan, his brothers-in-law, and William Speare and a friend named Sterrett.[1] They came rolling down to Maryland from Carlisle Town in a sturdy small column of broad-beamed, substantial men and broad-wheeled, substantial wagons.

Some of the Pennsylvania frontier toughness came to Baltimore when the Smiths and Speares and Buchanans moved in. Baltimore wasn't much more of a town, in those days, than Carlisle. There weren't more than eighteen or twenty houses west of Jones' Falls. John Smith and the forty thousand dollars he fetched along and the risk-taking, bold-minded, hard-driving men he fetched along gave a push to the little town. The town hadn't got over it yet.

Even in those early days, when little Annapolis still plumed itself upon being the foremost city of the continent, Baltimore had acquired the reputation of being too big for its breeches. Its breeches had never caught up with it.

The neighbors were jealous then; they were even more jealous now, in 1814. Baltimore had prospered too well; it had grown too fast and too big. It had not been a town at all until 1732, and then it was nothing but a straggling hamlet with the plain, tradesman's-aproned name of Jones Town. It hadn't become a nuisance until 1743, when it first showed its colossal gall by appropriating for itself the title of the lord proprietor of Maryland.

But Baltimore had come a long way in those seventy years. It had come a long way since Sam Smith's father gave it a shove—a long way from the town he moved into—a long way from the pastel village of little frame houses painted pink and blue and apple green, from the cowpath streets rambling amiably from door stoop to door stoop, tucking themselves into the curves of the hills with an unhurrying good nature. Like a prentice on its own wharves, it had had to learn how to hurry, it had learned how to push and shove. It had grown up square-shouldered and chunky—a good deal like Joshua Barney, built solid and close together. It had grown up red-faced with brick. Its belt was already too tight, it was bulging its waistband of hills. It had forty-five thousand people inside its waistband already.[2] It was much the youngest of the seaboard cities, but already it was third in population and fourth in the wealth of its commerce.

It was neither north nor south; it was some of both. Its merchants could drive bargains with a Yankee shrewdness and play host with a cavalier grace. It knew how to use a fork at dinner, but it also knew how to use its elbows in business. Its elbows were always getting into its neighbors' ribs and the neighbors didn't like it.

If Baltimore was unpopular in London, it was almost equally unpopular at home. If the London papers called it hard names, the New York and Philadelphia and New England papers went them one harder . . . "mob town" . . . and "licensed pirates" . . . and "that sink of corruption . . . that Sodom of our country called Baltimore." For the neighbors were more than jealous: they were downright alarmed. Some of them didn't believe in this war; they would rather have peace and trade, and let somebody else have the honor and self-respect. When they saw Baltimore throwing itself wholeheartedly into the war and doing a thriving business in captured cargoes, they went half crazy with envy. When they saw British warships bottling up their own commerce, they gave Baltimore the blame, heaped up and running over with malice and imprecations.

And then, as they saw Baltimore being slowly but thoroughly strangled by the same blockade, they "scarcely concealed their joy of her impending ruin." A Philadelphia paper reported happily that if the British squadron "remains six months as near Baltimore as it now is, many of the inhabitants, and particularly the poor, will have to seek refuge in the country." The squadron remained. The smug prophecy came true. The city's sea-borne commerce was destroyed. The prizes taken by its privateers made up only a small fraction of the loss. When its ocean trade was choked off, its principal reason for existence vanished. Business languished. The cost of living went up like one of Cockburn's rockets, for the enemy had "stopped all intercourse by water, thereby . . . stinting the citizens of even their ordinary supplies of provision." It was a continuing process. "The total annihilation of trade, which threw out of employment all classes of mechanics, and the exorbitant price of most of the necessaries of life, compelled a great number of worthy people to choose between emigration and dependence on charity."

There was more than a suspicion that Baltimore's jealous rivals were fishing industriously and successfully in its blockade-troubled waters. Niles's *Register* reported that "internal foes of the city, co-operating with the enemy, alarm those accustomed to deal with us from the interior, and destroy the whole trade and curtail the supplies for the subsistence of the people of this populous city." But such profitable and stimulating pursuits were not enough; stealing Baltimore's customers and seducing its provisioners could not satisfy its neighbors. For months, in furious columns of newspaper abuse, the city was "pointed out for military execution."

The same Philadelphia paper took pleasure in announcing that "the people of the swindling city of Baltimore are now much alarmed and apprehensive of suffering great injury." But, it demanded, "who would pity such a city and its ill-fated inhabitants? Baltimore has brought the curse of Heaven upon itself. Leave Baltimore to itself and let it make the best of its own situation."

Now these neighborly good wishes seemed likely to be realized. The swaggering small city on the Chesapeake was face to face with extinction. It was going to fight. It might fight well and bravely. But it would fight alone.

When the New Bedford *Mercury* called Baltimore "that sink of corruption, that Sodom," it was speaking with poetic license. There was no truth in the charge, so it must have been poetry—although Baltimore was perhaps more liberal-minded about some things than some other towns were. It was not offended when it read, on page one of its newspapers, that "the late Dr. Warner's method of removing VENEREAL DISEASE . . . subjecting the patient to no restraints with respect to drink or diet . . . may be had at No. 14 East Pratt street, between the new Stone Bridge over Jones' Falls and McEldery's wharf." The town wasn't shocked, and it didn't pretend to be shocked.

And the editor of the New Bedford *Mercury* wasn't concerned with the morality of the goings-on in Baltimore. He probably didn't know that Baltimore wives sometimes ran off with men who weren't legally theirs, although sometimes the husbands were forthright and frank about it in print. There was Charley McCarthy, for instance, who advertised that Lockey, his wife, had "eloped from my bed and board, aged about 27 [the wife, he undoubtedly meant, not the bed or the board] she is tall and slender, of a fair complexion, has black hair and has lost her front teeth." It was supposed, Mr. McCarthy added, that "she went off with a French Fencing Master and Barber, named Philip Houssey, aged about 35, five feet 8, he is well made, has short brown hair, and speaks broken English. He robbed me of a considerable amount of money, and took all the clothing apparel he could lay hands on, not even sparing those of the child, whom my wife has left behind. He has been three times in our own Bridewell lately; he brought from Boston to this city another man's wife, and has left her here in great distress, with her children." Mr. McCarthy offered no reward for the return of his wife, but he offered fifty dollars to anyone who would lay Mr. Houssey by the heels and "lodge him in any prison in the United States."

Charley McCarthy's frankness was not unusual. Baltimore was a forthright town. When Will Warner advertised "elegant wove writing paper," he added honestly that he also had on hand some "writing paper of inferior qualities." And when Baltimoreans itched, they could step over to that same shop at No. 14 Pratt street and buy a box of Wheaton's Itch Ointment, with the printed assurance that "one box cures a person, and there need be no washing after the use of it." Surely an advantage, with the day of bathrooms still to come. On the off chance that Wheaton's one box failed to do the business, the suffering townsmen could fall back on Waites's, at the corner of St. Paul's and Market street. Seventy-five cents spent there would fetch a supply of Dr. Church's genuine patent Scotch ointment, which had "cured half a million of persons in Europe and America of the most inveterate itch in four hours."

Baltimore had been antiappeasement and pro-Madison. It had wanted war. On the day after the declaration of war, a Baltimore paper which called itself the *Federal Republican* and which was proappeasement and anti-Madison, came out with a blast that startled even some of its own Federalist followers. It declared that "without funds, without taxes, without a navy, or adequate fortifications . . . our rulers have promulgated a war against the clear and decided sentiments of a vast majority of the nation." It went on boldly: "As the consequences will soon be felt, there is no need of pointing them out to the few who have not sagacity enough to apprehend them. Instead of employing our pen in this dreadful detail . . . as long as the war shall last we mean to represent in as strong colors as we are capable, that it is unnecessary, inexpedient, and entered into from partial, personal, and, as we believe, motives bearing upon their front, marks of undisguised foreign influence. . . . We mean to use every constitutional argument and every legal means to render as odious and suspicious to the American people, as they deserve to be, the patrons and contrivers of this highly impolitic and destructive war."

If the honest patriots were shocked and angered, the patrioteers were delighted. So were the roughnecks. Here was a chance to show how loyal they were and how brave—and to do it without much risk. Here was a window made for stones. Honestly indignant citizens held meetings in public halls. The pot-valiants held meetings in grogshops. The rabble rousers had the time of their lives. It took them two days to do the job, but they did it well. The roughnecks began to holler in the streets; the braying and the chest thumping brought them reinforcements in hundreds—the congenital witch burners, the bug-wits, the troublemakers and the excitement hunters, the small boys who ran to fires and who trailed a parade, and a fair sprinkling of the merely curious. Only trickles and eddies at first, the crowd grew like a stream in fresh. The fresh rose to a flood and went swirling down into Old Town. A flotsam of bludgeons, hooks, ropes, axes and "other instruments of destruction" bobbed along on the torrent of inhumanity that boiled through Gay street, and the torrent swept away the offices of the *Federal Republican*, wiped them out and obliterated them. The press was smashed and the wreckage thrown into the street. The stock of paper, the type, the furnishings were pitched through the windows; one man in the mob was pitched out—or fell out—and died. Hooks were attached to the doorframes and window sills, the mobsters tailed onto the ropes, the whole building was wrenched apart, the parts were dragged through the town.

This was better than a parade. This was more fun than a fire. This shows how noble we are. This shows how brave we are. Let's have 'nother drink an' find 'nother house. The patrioteers sweated and swilled and brandished their axes and clubs. Find them yellow-livered editors! Get a bucket o' tar! Fetch a pillow! *One pillow's no good. Get a dozen pillows. Snatch somebody's feather mattress. What the hell does it matter whose mattress it is?*

It didn't matter at all to the mob. House after house was burst into, ransacked, plundered. Ships at the wharves were looted, their rigging was slashed, their sails were cut to ribbons: a false story ran through the mob that the ships had British licenses. But the editors escaped. Jacob Wagner and Alexander Contee Hanson, son of the chancellor of Maryland, had fled to Georgetown. For five weeks they published the *Federal Republican* there, and then, somehow grown bolder, they came back to Baltimore and established themselves in a house on South Charles street. With them came a forelorn hope of friends who believed that in America a man had a right to say and write what he believed. Two of those friends had fought in the Revolution; both were generals; one, at least, had been famous.

The paper came out. The mob gathered again. Other men who believed in free speech and free press and the bill of rights walked down to the Charles street house and offered themselves as a bulwark for their beliefs. Some of them came with guns in their hands; an armed sentinel guarded the door. The rabble rousers did their roaring business; the taverns likewise did a roaring business. Somebody fetched a drum to beat up recruits. Boys began to throw stones at the house, men began to throw cobbles. The shutters splintered, the windows crashed with a chatter of glass on the parlor floor. The door burst in, the mob made a rush for the hall, the defenders backed up the stairs. One of them, soldierly-straight, not young, tried to talk to the howling roughnecks. A pistol was thrust close to his breast, the pan flashed, the weapon missed fire; Light-Horse Harry Lee, general in the Revolution, gallant soldier and dashing cavalryman, was spared to die other deaths.[3]

With the mob storming the stairs, the defenders opened fire from the windows; the mob fired back; there were bullet holes in the walls; there was blood in the street. The mob got its hands on a fieldpiece. Before it could knock the house down, mounted militia came on a gallop. The beleaguered garrison surrendered to the militia, was put under arrest and was marched off to jail under a barrage of paving blocks. Apparently nobody thought of putting a few of the roughnecks under arrest; there were thousands of them by now; there were only twenty or thirty defenders of a man's right to say and write what he believed—nobody thought to count them, or even to guard them after the jail door was locked.

The mob sacked the house, but wrecking a house couldn't satisfy patriots now. They roared through the streets and stormed the jail and dragged the prisoners out. A man named Mumma, a butcher by trade, stood at the door to knock each victim on the head as he emerged. The cell became an anteroom of hell, the corridor a gantlet of fiends. The fiends smashed fists into faces already shapeless, smashed clubs down on heads already broken and bloody, thrust knives into bodies already limp as a beef on Mumma's block. They threw the bodies down the steep stone steps of the jail, kicked them as they piled up in a moaning heap, stuck knives in their hands and faces. They fetched lighted candles, dragged heads out of the pile, propped up eyelids with gouging thumbs, dripped candle grease into the eyes. There were cries like the screaming of nails wrenched out of the planks when the mob pulled the house to pieces. Some begged for mercy and got none. Others feigned death; they "sustained without betraying any signs of life, or gratifying their butchers with a groan or murmur, all the tortures that were inflicted upon them. They heard without showing any emotion, the deliberations of the assassins about the manner of disposing of their bodies. At one time it was proposed to throw them all into the sink of the jail. Others thought it best to dig a hole and bury them all together immediately. Some advised that they should be thrown into Jones' Falls . . . . Some that they should be castrated. Others again were for tarring and feathering them, and directed a cart to be brought for that purpose to carry them about town. Others insisted upon cutting their throats upon the spot, to make sure of them. And lastly, it was resolved to hang them next morning, and have them dissected.

"Pointing to Hanson, and jabbing him severely with a stick on the privates, one exclaimed, 'This fellow shall be dissected.' "

Sam Smith knew some of the men who had lain in that tortured pile. He had known Jim Lingan and Harry Lee. Lingan had fought at Long Island, he had been in the Maryland Line on the day it destroyed itself to save the American army. Lying at the foot of the jail-house steps, "the brave General Lingan lost his life by his endeavors to save it. He so much mistook the character of the monsters as to suppose them capable of some feelings of humanity. He reminded them that he had fought for their liberties throughout the Revolutionary war, that he was old and infirm, and that he had a large and helpless family dependent on him for support . . . Every supplication was answered by fresh insults and blows. At length, while he was still endeavoring to speak and to stretch his hands out for mercy, one of the assassins stamped upon his breast, struck him many blows in rapid succession, crying out, '*the damned old rascal is the hardest dying of all of them*' and repeating the approbrious epithet of *Tory!* These blows put an end to his torment and his life."

As for General Lee, his son one day would be a general too. He would be General Robert E. Lee, the stanch hope of the South and almost a god to the Army of Northern Virginia. But on this midsummer night, Light-Horse Harry Lee's "mangled body lay exposed upon the bare earth" while "one of the monsters attempted to cut off his nose, but missed his aim, though he thereby gave him a bad wound in the nose. Either the same person or another attempted to thrust a knife into the eye of General Lee, who had again raised himself up. The knife glanced on the cheek-bone, and the general being immediately by the side of Mr. Hanson, fell with his head upon his breast, where he lay for some minutes, when he was kicked or knocked off. A quantity of his blood was left on Mr. Hanson's breast, on observing which one of the mob . . . exclaimed exultingly, 'See Hanson's brains on his breast.' " Even the mob was satiated at last. A doctor named Hall tricked it into lugging its victims back into the jail for safekeeping until it could get some rest to finish the job. Other doctors appeared; risking their own lives, they tended the mangled victims and then sent for carriages and smuggled some of them out of town. Others crawled away on their hands and knees, hiding in gardens; one was saved by a friend who carried him pickaback; one was fetched off concealed in a load of hay. General Lee was taken to a hospital; he would never be Light-Horse Harry again; he would be a broken old man.

A night like that gave more than a touch of justice to the cry in the London press: "Chastise the savages!" Baltimore had earned most of the names people called it . . . upstart . . . pushing . . . arrogant . . . truculent . . . violent . . . mob town . . . a nest of pirates.

But it was a soberer town now, in late August of 1814, than it had been two years ago when the patrioteers conjured the mob out of a whisky bottle. It had learned a lesson that would last it for twenty years. It had small use now for the patrioteers. The enemy was coming and the enemy was British, but this sobered Baltimore had no silly notions about expunging the word "British" from its vocabulary or the goods with British labels from its shelves. The town didn't deserve too much credit for being tolerant in the matter of labels. Most of the British stuff in the stores now was captured stuff: no credit was involved: the privateers did business on a strictly cash basis: they had paid for the goods on the spot, with powder and solid iron balls.

And that, perhaps, was the reason why William Warner, on Market street, thought it good business to advertise Lord Byron's poem, "The Corsair." A title like that should appeal to a nest of pirates, no matter how British the author. But Mr. Warner also felt free to advertise British Oil; he saw no need to disguise it as Liberty Oil or Victory Oil or General Washington Oil. The troops that had beaten the Fifth and wounded Will Pinkney and wounded and captured Josh Barney were Lord Wellington's troops; he had led them and trained them in Europe; he had picked them himself to "chastise the savages." But Mr. Warner had on his shelves a consignment of books about the enemy's foremost captain and he saw no occasion for making a bonfire of them to prove he was patriotic, or even for hiding them under the counter until the trouble was over. He thought it perfectly proper to offer *"The Life of the* Most Noble *Arthur Marquis and Earl of Wellington, Viscount Wellington, of Talavera and of Wellington, and Baron Douro of Wellesley . . . K. B., Lieutenant General; Marshal General of the Portuguese, and Captain General of the Spanish Armies; Commander in Chief of his Britannic Majesty's Forces in the Peninsula; also Duke of Ciudad Rodrigo, K.C.S. &c &c.*

Baltimore, too, apparently thought it was perfectly proper. The ad kept on running while the disorganized fragments of the Fifth straggled into town with the picture of Wellington's oncoming Invincibles still distorted and terrible in their minds. Neither Mr. Warner nor the editor and readers of the *Patriot* saw anything incongruous about its appearance in the midst of other advertisements that reflected the imminence of danger:

A Substitute

Aɴʏ person who wants a substitute, can get one by addressing a line to A. B. and leaving it at this office, mentioning in it the terms and the time they want one for.

aug. 25   d4t

GUNS

JOHN STEWART respectfully informs his friends and the public, that he has removed from No. 1 to No. 28 Light-street opposite Water-street, where he continues to carry on the Gun-Making business.

                                                                    eo4t

Perhaps there were too many incongruities to give the town time to notice the touting of Lord Wellington. While Baltimore waited apprehensively for the coming of Wellington's veterans, the port warden published a dire threat: "Notice is hereby given to the owners of the several vessels, which are sunk or aground at or near the mouth of Jones' Falls, that if they are not removed within ten days from this date, they will be cut up, or otherwise removed at the expense of the owners, as they obstruct the improvements now progressing in the Cove. By Order—SAMUEL YOUNG, clerk." But this was the masterpiece of contrast:

Brass Barrel PISTOLS

A handsome pair with Holsters complete, for sale at
GEORGE LITTLEBOY'S
No. 115, corner of Market and South Calvert streets
Also, an Elegant Assortment of
MILITARY ARTICLES
and Ladies' Tortoise Shell COMBS

Mr. Littleboy's hope of selling ladies' combs might not be justified. Business was already bad and there were signs that it was getting worse; the enemy was troubling even the drab backwaters of the city's commerce; the *Patriot* announced postponement of an auction and a marshal's sale. But for those newspaper subscribers who were not interested in ladies' combs, or even in brass-barreled pistols because they were thinking more of fleeing than of fighting, there were offers of most timely bargains. The fainthearted had an opportunity to choose between "a second hand family carriage" and one that was "elegant" and "Philadelphia built"; if they lacked motive power, perhaps the "neat saddle horse" advertised for sale in the next column could be impressed to serve between the shafts. And any would-be refugee who had a well-filled pocket might acquire his means of escape in one deal for "an excellent gig, with plated harness and a strong active horse, rising six years old."

But while citizens with a sharp eye for profit offered these temptations to the weaklings, stouthearted men were calling Baltimore to duty:

UNITED HOSE & SUCTION EN-
gine company

IT IS respectfully requested, that during the present alarming times such citizens who are exempt from military duty and whose residence renders it convenient, will immediately on the cry of fire repair to the Engine House of the above Company, and render their assistance. This request becomes the more necessary, as the members generally are engaged in military duty. Such as desire it will be furnished with badges on application to HENRY THORNBERG No. 29, South Liberty-street or

JOHN WERDEBAUGH, *Sec'ry.*
No. 19 North Howard-street

aug. 26   d4i

NOTICE

THE Medical gentlemen of the City, who are not attached as Surgeons to the respective regiments, are requested to meet at Dr. Gibson's, tomorrow morning, at 8 o'clock, for the purpose of organizing a corps, to follow the army in case of necessity.
aug. 26

And here, in five lines, was the essence of a city squirming between business-as-usual and impending destruction. An enterprising shopkeeper rushed into print with the announcement of a new medical work, *Memoirs of Military Surgery*, which had been translated from the French of D. J. Larrey, M.D., inspector general of the medical staff of the French armies, by Richard W. Hall, professor of midwifery in the University of Maryland. Baltimore was about to be delivered of a crisis, but at least some of its tradespeople refused to be dismayed.

The Baltimore packet line to the Eastern Shore, which had kept on running with the utmost disdain for the British warships in the bay, now at last made some concession—but *not* to the enemy. Under its insignia of a frigate and its title, *Rock-Hall Packet*, there appeared this bland announcement:

In consequence of a late change in the mail routes on the Eastern Shore, this Packet will change the days of sailing, and will run in the future as follows:

Leave Rock-Hall on Sundays, Tuesdays and Fridays, at 8 o'clock A.M., and arrive at Baltimore the same days.

Leave Baltimore on Mondays, Thursdays and Saturdays at nine o'clock and arrive at Rock-Hall the same days. . . .

Be it observed that under present circumstances, this is the most preferable route for crossing the Bay, for shortness of distance and safety of conveyance; and that the Packet that now sails on this route, is as fine a vessel for her superior sailing, safety and convenience as any on this Bay. . . .

All Baggage and Goods at the risque of the owners.

That was the kind of town Sam Smith had to save. That was the kind of town he had to use for a tool and a weapon.

It was neither a tool nor a weapon—yet. It was only pieces and parts that were yet to be fitted together. Most of the parts had been fashioned in haste. Some were clumsy and crude. Only a few had been tested, and most of those few had failed; the broken ones must be mended. But a man could make something out of these pieces and parts . . . if he had the time. He might make a right useful weapon . . . if he only knew what kind of weapon he needed. He might make a tool that would do the job . . . if he knew what job had to be done. On the day Sam Smith took command, no one knew how much time was left. No one knew when the blow would come, or where, or from what direction.

Sam Smith, reaching out for the pieces, beginning to fit them together, was certain of only one thing. They were made of good stuff. They were made of the same kind of stuff that went into the old First Maryland, forty years back, and the First had known how to die without being taught. It had saved more than a city, that day on Long Island, before its first bloody lesson was over; too much of it died, but the army had lived, and the nation. These men he commanded now were the same sort of men. They were raw, as the First had been raw. They were mostly recruits and untried, as the men of the Maryland Line had once been recruits and untried.

But the Maryland metal had not changed; it had proved itself in this war. Stansbury's paper brigade may have blown away at Bladensburg, but a new generation of Maryland men had fought like the old Continentals, on the Canadian front. At the storming of York they had plunged ashore from small boats under point-blank fire of British grenadiers, they had driven the grenadiers at the bayonet point. At the battle of Chippewa, Captain Nathan Towson's Maryland battery of six-pounders had engaged an equal number of British twenty-four-pounders, and before the unequal duel was over the British "guns were silenced, their ammunition wagon blown up, and it was with great difficulty that their guns were saved by the dragoons—their artillery horses having been all killed." [4] The Maryland gunners had swung their pieces then in the nick of time: as the enemy's infantry charged with the bayonet, it was swept by a furious oblique fire of canister that broke it and flung it back. Three weeks later, at Lundy's Lane, the Maryland guns under Towson had opened one of the bloodiest, stubbornest battles ever fought by Americans. It had lasted from sunset till after midnight; and when Towson's guns fired the final shot, twenty-seven out of the thirty-six men who served them were down, dead or wounded. The enemy had christened that battery: they called it "the Yankee lighthouse" because it fired so fast that the muzzle bursts seemed to make one continuous flame. [5]

Baltimore, too, had proved itself. The three thousand men who had taken its privateers out to sea through the British blockade and captured five hundred and fifty prizes in spite of the world's greatest navy were proof that the metal was sound. Those three thousand men weren't here to defend their home port; many were still at sea, some were dead, some were crippled for life, some were in Dartmoor and some were in the Mill Prison at Plymouth. But the few who were here would fight, and they knew what hard fighting was like. Captains, mates and sailing masters of Baltimore ships bottled up in the bay when the blockading squadron was reinforced were privates and sergeants now in George Stiles's Marine Artillery. Rank didn't matter; what mattered was that they were men who could handle big guns.

John Cock, who had captained the privateers *Vesta* and *Ultor*, was only a private now. [6] Pearl Durkee, once skipper of the famous *Chasseur*, was a sergeant. David Monsarrat, captain of the privateer *Express*, and Bob Glenn, who had been his lieutenant, were privates together. Joseph Gold, who had sailed as captain of both the *Cora* and the *Burrows*, was the battery's first lieutenant; but in the ranks were the captains of the *Bordeaux Packet* and the *High Flyer*, the *Kemp* and the *Father and Sons*, the *Patapsco*, the *Decatur*, the *Oriental*, the *Daedalus* and the *Halcyon*. Ben Smith, master's mate of the *Joseph and Mary*, wounded in action at sea, was a private. So was the *Perry's* first lieutenant, Freeman Snow. The *Express*, the *Kemp*, the *Oriental* and the *Bordeaux Packet* had furnished two officers each to serve the Marine Artillery's guns. They were more than gunners, these masters of private warships; they were already a legend. The Invincibles might have only contempt for the Yankee militia, but they spoke of the Marine Artillery with undisguised respect.[7]

There were other men who gave even stronger proof of the spirit of the imperiled town—well-to-do men who had in their pockets the means of escape, who had money to hire substitutes to take their places in the militia. Of the two hundred and four Maryland men who owned shares in privateers and letters-of-marque, eighty-seven were serving with troops. Andrew Clopper, part owner of no less than thirteen privateers, was second lieutenant in the Baltimore Fencibles. Levi Clagett, one of the *Comet's* owners, was a lieutenant with Andy Clopper. (He would be killed in the battle.) John Clemm, one of the *Chasseur's* owners, was a sergeant under Clagett and Clopper. (He, too, would die.) George Stevenson, who had been cornet of the Hussars and then captain of the Fell's Point Dragoons, was now aide to Brigadier General Stricker; he had helped to fit out no less than thirteen privateers, and before the war was over they would capture or sink eighty-seven enemy vessels.

Yes, the metal was good. These men might have shirked; the law made it temptingly easy, for men with weak knees and full pockets. This wasn't a week-kneed town. Some thousands of Baltimore's youngest and best were away—on the northern frontier, on the ships of the regular navy at sea or blockaded in distant ports, on the always-wet decks of the little terrier clippers, in prison, or wounded, or dead. But there were more than three thousand names on the rolls of the city militia. More than one-tenth of the city's white population was on those rolls. Half of all Baltimore's men over sixteen years old had fought, or were fighting, or were ready to fight.[8]

Sam Smith knew that Baltimore had come closer to total mobilization of fighting strength than any other American town ever had come—except those small towns of his boyhood, where even the women stood watch at the loopholes with rifles. He knew, too, that is wasn't enough. Baltimore, in the present state of its resources, was as indefensible as Philadelphia had been after the battle of the Brandywine. In another sense, his own position was indefensible. He had no real authority. He had no right to the command he had accepted. In the rigid hierarchy of war, he was a usurper.

Within twelve hours after he assumed command, he was guilty of mutiny.

COMMODORE RODGERS   COMMODORE PERRY   COMMODORE PORTER

12

THE STRUGGLE FOR COMMAND

Brigadier General William Winder had picked up all the pieces he could find. Through twenty-four blurred hours he ordered, argued and cajoled them into something that again resembled a military force. He had lost a battle, he had lost his nation's capital, but he had not lost his confidence in William Winder. He was still in command of himself and of the Tenth Military District.

By forenoon of August 26th, two days after Bladensburg, his sketchy facsimile of an army was plodding northward from its bivouac at Montgomery Court House. Winder was advancing to meet the enemy at Baltimore. The enemy was moving in the opposite direction. The two armies spent the day retreating from each other.

Winder was impatient. His troops moved too slowly. By the time the head of his sluggish column reached Snells Bridge on the Patuxent, he could bear delay no longer. He turned over the com-

mand to Stansbury and rode on rapidly toward Baltimore. He had
a plan. It was a little vague; it had few details; but it was his own.
The fruits of defeat were not all bitter: he had been spared, today,
the hot breath of president and cabinet members on his neck. His

plan was "to bend the whole force of his
power as commander of the Tenth Military
District to bring into activity all the resources" of Baltimore.[1] He did not realize
how badly bent his power already was.

Realization, when it came, was stunning.
A badly beaten general might have premoni-
tions concerning dispatches from the War
Department, but Will Winder had none
when he saw the cavalryman pounding toward him down the road from Baltimore.
He did not know just where the War Department was today, but Baltimore was one

BRIGADIER GENERAL
WILLIAM H. WINDER

place where it wasn't. The courier pulled up.
"From General Smith . . ." Winder took
the sealed and folded paper. He was weary
of papers. He had read so many useless papers in the last three
months—read them and written them and wondered what had been
the good of either the reading or the writing. This would be
one more useless piece of scribbling. Sam Smith could scarcely
have any information that would add to Winder's knowledge of
the military situation or that could not wait for a few hours. But,
of course, Smith didn't know that his commanding general was
on the way to relieve him of responsibility. He rather liked the
old fellow; for an "ancient veteran," Sam Smith had been remarkably helpful and co-operative. Not suitable to be called into the
field, but useful in his place.

Winder broke the red wax wafer, thumbed the paper open.
The words exploded:

Head. Qrs 26 Aug. 1814

Brig. Genl. W. H. Winder
    Sir
    The Enclosed copy of a letter from his Excelly Governor Winder
was received by me this day & I have in consequence assumed the
Command agreeably to my Rank. Do me the favour to send me
information by the Dragoon, of your Situation, the number of troops
with you. We want the tents & Camp Equipage of Stansbury's
Brigade. Some men have come in & I have ordered them to join

their respective Regiments of the General Militia, having called all the Regiments of the 11th Brigade into service, they will give me 1000 Men. Cannot General Stansbury (if with you) come here immy.

SS[2]

It was a shocking letter. Sam Smith had intended that it should be. He had written it deliberately for its shock effect. He was employing, against Winder, the same tactics he would use against Ross three weeks later.

The tactics were based on the same careful estimate of the situation. As Sam Smith saw both situations, each had three identical controlling factors: first, the weakness of his own position; second, his opponent's habits of thought and conduct; third, his opponent's present state of mind. He planned both campaigns accordingly. First, knowing his own weakness, he fortified himself as strongly as his means permitted. Second, forecasting the probable maneuvers of both Ross and Winder, he disposed his forces to meet them. Third, he seized the initiative.

The letter handed to Will Winder had been written in Sam Smith's mind while Bob Stewart, Richard Frisby and John Eager Howard sat and waited in the withdrawing room at Montebello and wondered why Sam was taking so long to accept the command they offered. Now the expression on Winder's face gave proof that Smith had achieved the first purpose of his head-on attack: he had taken his opponent by surprise.

A stronger man than Winder might have reacted differently. The strong course was obvious. Sam Smith had no right to the command; his letter carried no authority whatever; it was a scrap of paper, without meaning unless Winder gave it meaning. Winder himself might be a paper general, but at least *his* paper was official. He could ignore Smith, he could act as if he had received no letter. He could ride straight to military headquarters in Baltimore and assume control as a simple matter of fact under his federal powers as commanding general of the district. He could give orders to Sam Smith and let the old militiaman take on himself, if he dared, the responsibility of overt disobedience. Winder did nothing of the kind. He did what Sam Smith had expected him to do.

For Smith knew his man. He knew little, yet, about what had happened in southern Maryland—the failure to estimate the enemy's strength correctly, the failure to take advantage of his weakness in cavalry, the failure to concentrate all available forces for a bold stand, the final retreat from a position that might have been held or, at least, stubbornly defended. But he knew a good deal about William Winder. Good family. Distinguished in his profession. A nice income—much nicer than the army pay for which he had sacrificed it. A fair politician although a Federalist and therefore, in the opinion of many Baltimoreans, not altogether bright. Undoubtedly a patriot, despite his politics: he had volunteered to fight in a war he had opposed. Undoubtedly, too, a brave man: no one questioned his personal courage. But not, in Baltimore's judgment, any great shakes as a soldier: a little more than two years ago, Will Winder had been merely captain of a company of militia. Baltimore had several dozen captains of militia, not to mention majors and lieutenant colonels: it had failed utterly to comprehend the superior virtues that had transmuted Lawyer-captain Winder into Brigadier General Winder and exalted him above Sam Smith, who had been a captain when Will was born and who had distinguished himself in a famous battle when Will was still dampening his diaper.

Smith's own judgment of Winder was less harsh than that of many of his fellow townsmen. It was a better-informed judgment. As senator, as veteran combat officer and as a housekeeping major general, he was in a position to appreciate not only the difficulties under which Winder had struggled to prepare the Tenth Military District for defense but also the soundness of much that he had tried to do. But he did not see in Winder a man who would strike out instinctively and hotly. As commander of the Tenth District, Winder had been contented with half measures; or, if not contented, he had lacked the strength and vigor to break through the military inertia and the political timidity of Washington. And Winder was a lawyer. He was a good lawyer and he had a good case. That was his weakness.

Sam Smith's curt communication was a shrewd blow aimed precisely at that weakness. The facts were on Winder's side. So was the law. On the point of precedence in command, the law was limpid: the facts could be seen through it clearly. All the legal arguments were Winder's. But disputation meant delay. An argument, as long as it lasted, would leave Smith in command; therefore he was fighting a delaying action. His letter was an invitation to argue. It was a trap baited with a phrase that emphasized the weakest point of his position: he had assumed the command "according to his rank." It was outrageous. It was ridiculous. *It was illegal.*

Winder took the bait. He hurried on to Baltimore, mustering his arguments as he rode, trying the case in his mind. Lawyerlike, he decided that the first thing to do was to cross-examine his opponent's principal witness, the governor of Maryland. He could not believe that the governor was a hostile witness: his name, too, was Winder—Levin Winder; he was Will Winder's uncle.

When the lawful military commander of the Tenth District reached Baltimore, he did not visit military headquarters. Instead, he sat down in his room and wrote a letter to his uncle Levin. Was there any color of authority in Sam Smith's extraordinary conduct? Had it been intended that a major general of militia should supersede an officer of the United States army?

The answer came with gratifying promptness. Its contents were equally gratifying:

> Yesterday, I received a letter from Mr. Johnson as Chairman of a Committee, stating that they desired General Smith to take command at Baltimore and that I would invest General Smith with further powers. I returned for answer, it was proper for General Smith to take command of the militia and make every preparation for the defense of the place, but that I could not invest him with any powers which he did not already possess except to inform him that according to the requisition of the Government of the United States for a Major General, he had been selected for that purpose, but certainly this information was not contemplated to give General Smith command nor neither could it take effect in any respect until confirmation was given to it by the General Government.[3]

Well, that was clear enough. That ought to settle things. Will Winder promptly sent a copy to Sam Smith and waited confidently for the old man to surrender. He waited in vain. The only thing that had been settled was his own hash. For the governor's answer to his nephew had not been entirely frank: it was too thick with words: the words made a smoke screen that concealed Smith's opening maneuver and its complete success.

The Mr. Johnson who had written to Governor Winder was the mayor of Baltimore and the chairman to the Committee of Vigilance and Safety. The letter he wrote was the letter Sam Smith had conceived and virtually dictated when he accepted his dubious command. And the governor's reply, addressed to Smith himself, had enormously strengthened his position:

By request of the President of the United States of the tenth of
July last, one Major General is requested of this State. In compliance to which you have been selected.[4]

That was the letter which Sam Smith had copied and enclosed
in his curt note to Winder. It was simple, innocent, unquestionably
proper. It was also devastating to Will Winder's hopes. It contained none of the qualifying words and phrases that appeared in
Uncle Levin's letter to his nephew. It omitted the "could not" and
the "confirmation" and the "certainly . . . not contemplated." By
a neat technicality, it put the law on Smith's side. The "request" to
which the governor referred was the War Department order fixing
the militia levies for the various states. The order had included, in
Maryland's quota, three brigadier generals and one major general.
When Will Winder summoned part of the Maryland and District of
Columbia militia into federal service, he had sidestepped the question
of rank: he had purposely omitted from his requisition both Major
General Sam Smith of Maryland and Major General Van Ness of
the Washington militia. He had even got a ruling from the War
Department that Van Ness could not take the field because he had
not been specifically included in Winder's call for troops.

Now Winder had been outmaneuvered. Sam Smith had not
been "called" into federal service, but he had been sent; he had been
"selected" by the governor "in compliance" with the War Department's "request." It was all very technical, but a technicality was all
that Sam Smith needed. Instantly he seized the advantage that it gave
him. On August 27th he sent off a dispatch to the secretary of war
announcing that Governor Winder had assigned him as commanding general of Maryland's militia quota in the federal service and
that he had taken command "agreeably to my Rank." Along with
this bold frontal attack on William Winder's authority he delivered
a minor but shrewd flank attack. "General Winder is in the City,"
he informed the secretary, but "I have not seen him. . . . I am
throwing up field work."[5] The implication was plain: Winder, if
not actually sulking in his tent, was doing nothing to justify his
claim to command. The contrast was equally plain: Sam Smith,
with a force that "may be called 4000 effectives," was actively preparing to defend the city, but Winder was doing nothing either to
direct or to help.

Winder was not idle. He was working on a new plan—one that
would put an end to Smith's outrageous conduct. On August 28th

he, too, was sending a dispatch to the secretary of war. He was asking Armstrong to promote him to major general:

> . . . to my astonishment [Smith] still conceives himself in command and persists to exercise it. The manner in which General Smith has placed himself in command in my absence is at least very singular. The immediate and peremptory decision of the Government which can only give me necessary support to enable me to act with effect, is absolutely necessary and although I have never pretended to urge pretensions to increase in rank, yet, I submit it now; for the readiest mode of avoiding all difficulty will be giving me a rank to overreach the possible danger of conflict with any militia officer—as will also to give me the most decisive evidence of the countenance of the Government at this perilous and difficult moment.[6]

It was a good plan. If adopted, it would be effective. But like so many other plans of his devising, it was too late. Again, as in southern Maryland, his opponent had the initiative. Winder once more had been outmaneuvered. Sam Smith was a day's march ahead of him. The secretary of war had received, the day before, Smith's calm announcement that he was now in federal service and had assumed command. And the War Department had not changed its nature: it was still dodging issues, putting off decisions. Armstrong's reply dodged Winder's application for promotion:

> Your letter of Aug 28 has been submitted to the President. . . . The course which under pressure here is thought advisable, is that you return to this place with the regular infantry as soon as possible and that you turn off General Douglas and his Brigade from the road to Washington.[7]

The answer was a bitter disappointment to Will Winder. Vague as it was, it contained one unpalatable order and two equally unpalatable implications. It took him away from Baltimore, where his authority was at stake; and it implied not only that his promotion was doubtful but also that the Virginia brigade was being removed from his immediate control and his command limited to a handful of regulars. Reading Armstrong's reply, he could not be certain that even the Columbian brigade was to remain under his orders. His uncertainty would have been still greater if he had known that Armstrong was no longer secretary of war. Armstrong still had the title but he had been chosen as the administration's scapegoat:

the president had demanded his resignation: Monroe had taken over the War Department.

Winder left Baltimore the next day. If he could not conceal from himself that his departure was a retreat, perhaps he could conceal it from others. Sam Smith was functioning as the commanding general at Baltimore; Monroe was functioning as the commanding general in the District of Columbia; but Winder put on a brave front. In a general order he announced that he had established headquarters of the Tenth Military District in Washington and directed that military reports and returns should be sent to him there. Then he renewed his fight for promotion and supreme command. He wrote to Monroe:

> . . . it is due me in justice and it is due the Government that they should give me the most emphatic support. If they omit to take that step now at every subsequent misfortune, however inevitable, they will be obliged to change their commanding officer and thereby deny themselves the possibility of executing any subsequent plan for defense of the Country at this perilous moment.[8]

It was a forelorn hope, and it failed. The next day Monroe, in effect, recognized Sam Smith as the supreme commander in the Baltimore defense zone and notified him in writing that

> . . . General Winder will unite with your forces such of those under his command as may afford the most efficient aid to the protection of Baltimore.[9]

Monroe's order was unmilitary in its vagueness. It was a typical piece of political double talk and issue dodging. It did not say forthrightly that Winder was to be under Smith's command: if something went wrong, Monroe's alibi was ready. No one could prove, from what he had written, that he had confirmed Smith in the supreme command or had made Winder a subordinate. But the immediate effect was decisive. Even Winder realized that, at least for the time being, he must take his orders from Sam Smith. The only tactic left to him was sniping. He opened on his commanding general a continuous and harassing fire of criticism and complaint. Smith answered the complaints with patient courtesy. He kept a firm hold on his temper—and also on his command.

But even after he had outgeneraled Winder and maneuvered him into grudging obedience, Sam Smith still found himself in a delicate and awkward situation. He was a militiaman in command of regulars, a soldier in command of sailors. His combat experience had been one long succession of defeats. Now, under him, were men whose names were synonyms of victory. He was an unknown. Now, under him, were three of the country's most distinguished officers.

The awkwardness of his position was visible to everyone. It got into print the day after he assumed command—a paragraph tucked away on page three of the Baltimore *Patriot*, a kind of postscript to the news of disaster at Bladensburg:

> Commodores Rodgers and Porter, have arrived in the city, and, with Com. Perry, quarter at the Fountain Inn. They, with their men, join in the defence of the city.

In Baltimore in 1814, no editor's note was necessary to point out the significance of that item. Commodore Rodgers was the senior officer of the United States navy, at the zenith of a career that had included service in three wars. He was the man who had begun this war—the officer whose ship fired the first American shot at a British naval vessel, months before the war began. He was also the man who, with his own hands, fired the first shot of the declared war, from the forecastle of the frigate *President*, his flagship.[10]

John Rodgers was a Marylander, born at Havre de Grace. Strange as it seems, the Maryland man who began the war with ships' guns at sea had come back home to help end it with ships' guns dug into the Maryland earth. And he came with a debt to pay. He owed Sir George Cockburn a little something for the raid on Havre de Grace: his own home had been one of those plundered. Indeed, he had already made a small down payment: he had captured a British warship whose captain was one of Sir George's officers, and the legend was that the captain had in his possession John Rodgers's own sword, picked up as a souvenir in the sack of Rodgers's house.

For the navy's senior officer, return to Maryland was not merely a homecoming, it was also a reunion. Both Oliver Perry and Dave Porter had served under him; all three of them had begun their climb to fame in the old frigate *Constellation*. Baltimore was *Constellation's* home port; she was Baltimore-built, and Baltimore names had crowded one another on her muster rolls. From the windows of the Fountain, the three commodores could see the broad Patapsco reach where she lay at anchor on the April day in 1798 when a boy of seventeen named Davy Porter came aboard her as midshipman. They could look across the Basin to the rise of land where Lieutenant Rodgers, carrying on in the tradition of Josh Barney, had drummed up her crew in his recruiting "rendezvous at the house of Mr. Cloney, at Fells Point." She had carried two of them into their first fight, in the war with France. She had given young Lieutenant Rodgers his first command. And Midshipman Porter, at eighteen, had climbed her wounded, tottering fore-top-mast to his first promotion. Perry, later, had been a lieutenant in the same ship.

Now Perry's fame, if not his rank, exceeded even Rodgers's. He had distinguished himself as an infantryman in the amphibious attack on Fort George, as a cavalryman at the battle of the Thames, and as fleet commander in the battle of Lake Erie. His reward had been command of the fine new frigate *Java*, being built at Baltimore and almost finished, but penned up now by the overwhelming British squadron.

Porter, too, was a Homeric figure, the Odysseus of a fabulous adventure. In command of the small frigate *Essex* he had stretched his orders for a short Atlantic cruise into an invasion of the Pacific Ocean. He had all but swept the British flag from the Pacific. He had made himself the admiral of a squadron of twelve captured ships and the creator and commander of the first United States Pacific fleet. He had fought America's first war in that fateful ocean, established the first beachhead there, made allies, carried out joint land and naval operations, and become the monarch of a tropic kingdom. He had lost his ship at last, in a gallant battle against awful odds. When he came home, after almost two years' absence, he had neither fleet nor frigate; his entire command consisted of one stolen rowboat. But he was still King Apotee of Nooaheevah. He was toasted, feted; songs were written in his honor; he was thanked by Congress and promoted. The promotion meant that three men who had served aboard the old *Constellation* were to meet again, all commodores, to defend the *Constellation*'s home port.

These were the men over whom Sam Smith assumed authority. It was a situation filled with danger. Battles had been lost and battles would be lost again by jealousy, by sticklings over rank, by hagglings about "proper channels." Whole campaigns had failed and whole campaigns would fail again because famous officers could not take orders from superiors at least equally distinguished. General Charles Lee had sneered at Washington, disobeyed him, and twice almost wrecked his army.[11] Robert E. Lee himself would suffer from the disobedience of men he trusted most. Even that great cavalryman, Stuart, would violate Lee's orders and leave him blind at Gettysburg; Longstreet would permit himself to be "irritated and annoyed" [12] with his commanding general, set his mind stubbornly against Lee's tactics and balk them by delay. There had been no doubt concerning General Washington's authority. There would be no doubt concerning Robert Lee's. But Sam Smith had no such authority. He was in command by warrant of a resolution voted by a scratch committee of civilians. He had indeed taken a great deal upon himself.

But if there were jealousies and bickerings in Baltimore, if any of these officers disputed Sam Smith's highly disputable authority, no record of such discord has survived. The outcome itself is evidence that there was none. So is the thoroughness of the preparations for defense, and so is the speed with which those preparations were completed.

These were not little men. They were proud men, but not petty. They had the good sense and the good will to see Sam Smith as his fellow townsmen saw him—the symbol of last-ditch resistance. Patriotism took precedence over precedence. They made themselves into a team, and a situation that might easily have developed into fatal weakness developed instead into strength. It provided the home-town general with an informal staff of battle-experienced officers—men with the habit of command, men not to be rattled by danger or by sudden, unforeseen crises. And Sam Smith had the sense to use them, the tact to get along with them, the self-confidence and the stature to give orders to these much more distinguished officers with no embarrassment and with no sense of inferiority.

Only Winder was reluctant in his obedience—plaintive, critical, sometimes sarcastic. He did not return to Baltimore until September 4th, but it took him no time at all to find fault with Sam Smith. Before sundown he was writing to Monroe that Smith apparently intended to give him a "patched up" brigade put together from the troops of "other Brigadiers who may go away," but that no orders had been issued. Considering the time of his arrival, his impatience seems a little premature. It also seems to have been uncalled for: on September 5th, orders were issued in which he was "charged with the defense of the Ferry Branch" and given command of two small regiments of regular infantry, Colonel Laval's regular cavalry, and two brigades of Virginia militia.

But Winder was not satisfied. He informed Sam Smith of his displeasure in a tart letter:

> After the candor which I have evinced toward you, I cannot for a moment suppose that in the assignment of my command and station, any other motive than a just regard for my rank and other circumstances influenced you—and yet I cannot but believe that in a review of the arrangements you have made, you will be satisfied that it is unjust as relates to my rank and situation and in derogation of the ordinary principles of military service.

Two days later he was complaining again. The garrison of Fort McHenry had not been placed under his command; he wanted it. There were two redoubts on the Ferry Branch shore; their garrisons were not included in the list of troops assigned to him; he wanted them, too. There were, actually, four redoubts in the sector which he had been ordered to defend; apparently he had not yet found the others. Perhaps he was too busy. He was finding more things to complain about. He was reaching out for the command of the troops stationed at Annapolis, thirty miles away. He was again attacking Sam Smith's authority in a letter to Monroe:

> Every moment evinces more and more the impracticability of the present arrangement. . . . Subject as I am to the command of General Smith here, all the force with me is subject to the same command while all the forces in or near the Potomac are subject to your command. This precludes the possibility of my disposing of a man. . . . In truth Sir, it is unnecessary to multiply instances since it is impossible to move a step without violating all military rule and practice or making an impossible impasse. The present state of the Country requires that the command should be arranged without delay.

Patiently Monroe repulsed him. "It was thought improper," he wrote, "to make any change in the command at Baltimore, lest it might cause some derangement there injurious to the public interest." He reminded Winder that he had been offered the command of two brigades of militia called out for the defense of the Potomac, but that Winder had insisted on returning to Baltimore. He also reminded Winder that, as acting secretary of war, he had offered to relinquish the command at Washington to him, but that Winder had declined. Now he renewed the offer. "There is now no obstacle," he said, "to your resuming the command here and in every other part of the district" except Baltimore. But Winder proved more stubborn in controversy than he had proved in battle. He retorted that he apparently had failed to make himself clear. What he wanted, he said, was "some order from the War Department [that] might fix with more precision the Command respectively to be performed by the Major General of Militia and my duties as Commander of the District." And again, in the same letter, he reached out for the command of Annapolis.

His repulse, this time, was overwhelming. Monroe wrote that "there can be but one Commander in every quarter for which any particular force is intended. The force at Baltimore being relied on for the protection of that place, Annapolis and all other places in this District on the Bay, being under General Smith, the movement of troops must be under his command. I thought this idea was conveyed in my last."

Winder had lost his paper battle. But he had devoted to it almost the entire three weeks that had been granted Baltimore to prepare for its fight for existence. On the day Monroe finally put him in his place, the British army landed to attack the city.

13

FAITH WITHOUT FIELD WORKS

I‌t would be almost the middle
of the next month before the guns began to go off at Baltimore. It
would be September 12th before the nervous stutter of militia
muskets opened the three-day battle. But the decisions that controlled the outcome were made on August 25th and 26th. One was
the enemy's. The other was Sam Smith's.

Even while he was using his political and psychological calcu-
lations to work out the problem of command, Sam Smith was struggling to solve a still more dangerous and complicated problem.
Where would the enemy strike? And how? And how soon?

Twenty-four hours after he assumed command, the horse telegraph brought him a partial answer. The British had evacuated

Washington. All their hints and rumors of a "further advance" had
been deliberately planted to conceal their withdrawal. They had
pulled out under cover of darkness. They had passed through Bladensburg at midnight. They had abandoned their wounded, left
their dead unburied, and "at last accounts" had been "retiring to
their vessels."

In the Baltimore *Patriot*, an "intelligent gentleman" who had
left the smoldering capital behind the British rearguard "was confident they would not advance to the attack of Baltimore by way of
Washington" and "supposed they would re-embark for some other
place." Baltimore took a deep breath of relief. The reserve militia
regiments marched back from Elk Ridge Landing. Inevitably, with
danger no longer on the doorsteps, some optimistic citizens talked
themselves happily into believing that the item in the *Patriot* meant
"some other place" besides Baltimore. The optimism was premature,
but the relief was justified. The enemy had made the first critical
decision, and the decision was wrong.

The invading army had not known its own strength. Even
after Bladensburg and Washington, its leaders had not realized the
helplessness of the invaded country; they could not conceive that
their small column outnumbered any American force that could
be mobilized in time to resist a swift advance on Baltimore. Ross
and Cockburn were defeated by their own success. It had been too
easy and too overwhelming for them to believe it. They could not
comprehend its possibilities. They took no advantage of their opportunity. They threw away what they had really won. They lost
Baltimore when they fell back from Washington.[1]

Henry Fulford had been amply justified in his despairing letter:
"They will be here in a few days and we have no force than can
face them." In Winder's demoralized bivouac at Montgomery
Court House, immediate attack seemed obvious and inevitable. The
troops that had been in action were disorganized, dispersed, disheartened. The country militia regiments that had not yet been
called out were, at best, as bad as the two makeshift regiments that
broke and ran before they had been hurt.[2] Distance was no serious
obstacle to the enemy. The beaten Baltimore militia straggled home
in two days. The victorious British could have been there almost as
soon. They had marched sixty miles from Benedict in five days,
with time out to fight a battle. In their camp outside Washington,
they were not much more than half that distance from their real
objective. Supplies and ammunition might be a problem, but it was

not beyond solution. If the British had brought up their full force—the reinforcements which they put ashore at Baltimore three weeks later—and had marched hard on the heels of the fleeing militia, it is highly probable that there would have been no battle in Godly Wood, no attack on Fort McHenry, no "Star-Spangled Banner." Even without reinforcements, the three enemy brigades that fought at Bladensburg were superior to any force Sam Smith could muster against an immediate attack. Baltimore almost certainly must have fallen.

Sam Smith was duly grateful. He was very much obliged to Ross and Cockburn. They had given him some days of grace, and even a few days would be more useful than a whole regiment of untrained militia. The enemy had given him a temporary answer to his problem, but it was also a partial and a suppositious answer. The next decision must be his. The British countermarch toward Benedict might be another feint; they might yet turn and strike overland for Baltimore. Even confirmation of their embarkation, when it came at last, left the problem unsolved. Indeed, it added complications. Was the campaign over? Had the danger passed? Perhaps the threats to destroy Baltimore had been only a part of the war of nerves. Perhaps they had been only a part of the enemy's deceptive tactics—like Ross's feintings on the road from Benedict and like the false rumors of that "further advance," assiduously spread to cover his withdrawal from the capital. Perhaps Washington had been the real target all along, the threat to Baltimore only a distraction. The optimists grew bolder. Hope fed on hope . . . Baltimore would not be attacked . . . they were almost sure of it . . . they were absolutely certain. But Sam Smith could not afford to be an optimist, he could not rely on the supposings of intelligent gentlemen, he could not defend the city with perhapses. If the enemy struck, from what direction would the blow fall? Would it come by water or by land? Or both?

The possibilities were not infinite, but they were much too numerous for comfort. Chesapeake Bay was a broad corridor, every stubby river was an open door, every beach a doorstep. The enemy's troops could disembark at Annapolis and be only half as far from Baltimore as they had been, at Benedict, from Washington. They could disembark at a dozen other places and be closer yet. And no matter where the army landed, the warships could come into the Patapsco to attack the brick fort in the harbor. Baltimore could be assailed from front and rear at once. It could be attacked simultaneously from two directions . . . three . . . four . . . any number of directions. It was a vulnerable city. Except for Fort McHenry and some turned-up sods near by it—two or three small outworks planned but not yet built—Baltimore had no defenses. From the east shore of the inner basin where the *Java* lay unfinished, around Old Town and across Jones' Falls to the bank of the Patapsco River, the perimeter of the city lay open, unprotected. The Patapsco offered some protection, but not much; a little way upstream it ceased to be a river and became a creek. A hostile army landing on the bay shore below the city would have only to repeat the maneuver of the Washington campaign: march up the west bank of the Patapsco a few miles as it had marched up the Eastern Branch of the Potomac to Bladensburg to avoid the broad lower reaches. An army landing a little higher up the bay would be confronted by no such obstacle. There were streams, but they were not barriers. Middle River, Back River and the mouth of the Patapsco itself were invitations to attack.

Sam Smith had neither time nor means to prepare against every possible combination of assaults. He had a few days of grace but probably not many. If attack was coming, it was likely to come quickly. To fortify the whole perimeter of Baltimore would be a task of months. He could hope to defend one point, or two, or three, but he could not defend them all. But which points? Which? *Which?* He must read Ross's mind, and Cockburn's. He must match their moves before they made them, perhaps even before they had planned them.

He thought it out, half soldier and half businessman—a combination of both and therefore neither the one nor the other. The process and the result were a mixture of business methods and principles of war, a mixture of shrewd common sense and of tactics.

He thought of the coming campaign as a business deal. When you're going into a deal it helps to know what the other man's got in mind. You've got to have a right clear notion about what he wants before you can come to a notion about what he'll do. Well, what does this fellow want? What does he really want? You've got to put everything else out of your mind, you've got to see all the way to the end. What he wants is to win the war. That's it . . . to win. Think about that. Don't think about anything else.

Well, then . . . how can he put the deal over? What is he doing to put it over? What has he done? He's been doing a number of things, and some of them are important and some of them aren't.

One way to settle a deal is to make the other man sick of the haggling, to wear him down. We've both of us tried that way. On our side, we've been using our privateers and what few cruisers we've got to make him think that the deal's too expensive. And he has been using his ships to make us sick of the war—blockading us, ruining business, throwing men out of their jobs, pushing up prices, stealing tobacco and nigras and burning the Chesapeake towns. But it hasn't worked. Not with us, it hasn't. Not with him, either. We've worked on each other's nerves and pocketbooks for two years now and the war isn't over, there's no end in sight. Here in Maryland, all it's done has been to make most of us madder and set our teeth harder.

Well, if that sort of bargaining hasn't wound up the deal, what else can the Britishers do to get what they want? What else can they do to win? Why have they failed so far? I've got to clear everything out of my mind except the one thing that counts. Forget the blockade, forget Cockburn's raidings and burnings. Forget Bladensburg. Forget Washington . . . even that doesn't count. The British can't win this war unless they make us too sick to go on . . . unless they make *enough* of us too sick. There, that's it. They can't win the war unless they divide the country. That's been our weak spot ever since the beginning. And the British know it. Some people like to say that the British are stupid . . . and sometimes they do stupid things. Burning Washington was one of them. But they aren't too thickheaded to figure out our weak spot. A blind man would know that the country's divided. His ears would tell him. We've been divided since before the war started and we've got farther apart ever since . . . North and South . . . and New England's farthest of all, New England has come close to treason. That clergyman up in Boston, preaching against the war loans, saying that "the subscribers would be participators in the unholy, unrighteous, wicked, abominable and unnatural war." [3] And that newspaper, reading God's mind: "Let no one dare to prostrate himself at the altar, who wishes to continue the war by lending money; they are as much partakers in the war as the soldier who thrusts the bayonet, and the judgment of God will overtake them." [4] Why, up in New England the government had to promise to conceal the names of the people who loaned it money.[5]

Yes, that's it. It's as plain as a bill of lading. The obvious way for the British to win the war, with a country that's already split at the seams, is to finish the splitting. Divide and conquer—there's the plain sense of it, old as the hills. And it fits in with what they are doing and what they have done.

They tried in the West . . . and young Perry stopped them on Erie and Harrison finished the deal at the Thames. And now this year they've been trying the same scheme that Carleton tried, and Burgoyne . . . sending General Prevost and eleven thousand men down Champlain, on Burgoyne's old track. And they're in Chesapeake Bay where they were in the Revolution, in 1777. They used both the bay and the Delaware then . . . up Chesapeake with their transports to land their troops at the Head of Elk and take Philadelphia . . . up the Delaware with their warships to cover the army and keep it supplied. Maybe they'll try it again. We hear talk that this new army they've fetched is going down to New Orleans. Well, maybe it is. But it's not there yet; it's right here. And New Orleans may be important, but they can take New Orleans and still not have the country, they can take it and still not end the war. They might take Baltimore and still not win the war. But if they went on . . . if they tried the old scheme again . . . if they went up the bay and landed an army at Head of Elk as they did before, while their fleet went up the Delaware . . . Well, they might split us apart. They might rip us apart so completely that at last they would make enough of us sick of the war . . . make enough of us sick enough to be willing to quit.

I don't know. I can't read their minds. But perhaps this deal that I've got on my hands is a bigger deal than it looks. Perhaps there is more at stake than just Baltimore.

One thing's plain. If they come here, they've got to be hurt. We've got to beat them if we can, but whether we beat them or not they've got to be hurt. If we hurt them badly enough, we may keep them from going on.

Well, that looks to me to be the strategy of it. That looks like the military part of the business. I wonder what General Ross would say to that kind of reasoning. He wouldn't think much of it, likely. I'm probably not what Ross would call a soldier. Even figuring about what the British are trying to do, I haven't thought like a soldier. The plain fact is that I'm not one . . . not in the way George Armistead is. I'm not an officer the way Rodgers and Porter and Perry are officers. Oh, yes, I've fought. That's simple enough. Not pleasant, but simple. I can't seem to remember being

worried that day at Long Island. Scared, yes. Sick to my guts. But
not worried about this problem and that. There was only one simple problem: to stay there and fight until you got killed, or to run.
That's a problem that doesn't take thinking. It answers itself: you
either stay or you don't. The answer comes out of your guts, or
your bones, or your instinct, not out of your head. Well, I've run
often enough. Call it retreating, call it withdrawing, call it anything else you like: it comes down to being licked, it comes down to
failing.

I'd like not to fail, this time. It's queer . . . Sam Smith in
command. Sam Smith never won a battle. Perry won his, and he's
been in two more that were won. Armistead knows what it's like to
fight on the winning side. So does Rodgers. Porter's been whipped,
but he's had a taste of the other, he knows how it feels to win.
I've never known. All I've known is being licked and retreating
. . . Long Island . . . White Plains . . . the Brandywine . . .
even Mud Island. Fort Mifflin wasn't abandoned while I was in command; but I was being beaten there, too, when that cannon ball
knocked me out. Monmouth . . . that was another failure . . . we
didn't get licked, but we certainly didn't win. Well, the committee knows all about that. Stricker knows it as well as I do. Perry
and Armistead probably knew it, too, when they voted for me:
there's no secret about it. They certainly didn't decide to give me
the command because I've won battles, they didn't pick me because I'm a soldier who never knew what it is like to win. Maybe
it's just as well that I'm used to defeats. I've learned something. At
least I know some of the things not to do. The committee knows
what I am. I'm a businessman. And maybe that's just as well, too.

War is a business, and you can't run a business the way this
war has been run. You'd go stony in no time, and end up in debtors'
jail. For one thing, you've got to think each deal through; you've
got to have reasons for what you do, and the reasons have got to
be right. For another thing, you've got to study your customers.
Sometimes, maybe, you can sell one pair of overhalls and a whole
shipload of ruffled shirts to the same man—but it isn't likely, nor
often. You've got to know how badly the customer needs what
you've got, and how much money there is in his purse, and how
high he is willing to go.

Take Ross, Cockburn and Company . . . I'd like to know how
set they are on this deal, I'd like to know how set they are on tak-

ing Baltimore. I'd like to know how high they're willing to go. I'd like to know how many lives they're willing and able to pay.[6]

Let's see. I ought to be able to strike a kind of trial balance. How much have they got in their pockets and how much have they got in the bank? Colonel Beall was close to the truth, I'd say, when he made it four thousand men; he was closer to it than Jim Monroe with his figure of seven thousand. The *Patriot* says the odds were ten to one against us at Bladensburg, but that's nonsense; it's bad bookkeeping and bad management. If Winder had used all his men at once, the odds would have been about three to two in our favor. Of course, that's not taking into account the quality of the men: you can't put the same inventory value on a bolt of calico that you put on a bolt of India silk. But it's not taking the guns into account, either. We had twenty-six guns to the enemy's three, and our guns were the better goods. They should have cancelled out the rockets if they had been properly used. Twenty-six guns all pouring it in at once would have made enough noise and fire to balance those rockets.

Well, we've got some guns here in Baltimore, we've got a right substantial lot of artillery. When it comes to the kind of trading you do in a war, artillery is trade goods—and you don't leave expensive goods out in all kinds of weather. You put them into a warehouse, and if there's no warehouse handy you build a shed to protect them. That's all a barbette is, that's all Fort McHenry is: a shelter for guns. When you haven't got forts or barbettes, you've got to build some kind of shelter for your artillery. That's what infantry's for: to cover the guns in a storm. General Stansbury tried to build an infantry shed to protect those two batteries —Magruder and Myers's—but the trouble was that he built it too flimsy. He didn't use enough lumber, he didn't use enough infantry. And then Monroe pulled the braces away from the shed after Stansbury'd built it.

Ross, Cockburn and Company weren't in the market for cannon, they were in the market for Washington. It was like a business deal: the customer wanted a choice Charles street lot, but to get it he had to buy something he didn't want. Our British customers wanted Washington, but to get it they had to get those guns first. They paid a price for them, but the price wasn't high enough. If Winder had driven a harder bargain, if he had been able to make his British customers pay a bigger price, he might not have had to let Washington go. Now Ross, Cockburn and

Company think they can afford to have Baltimore, too. Well, we'll have to try to push the price up. We'll have to try to make Baltimore too expensive for them.

But how can we do it? I don't know where to meet them. I don't know where they'll hit. It's like the beginning of the old war, in a way. It's like Lexington and Concord, and the Minutemen wondering which way the British would come. One if by land and two if by sea. Only it's not quite so simple this time: there's no steeple handy to hang lanterns in.

But here's one thing. It's not as clear as lanterns in a church tower, but it throws some light on this problem. The British have the habit of success—they have it more than ever, now. They can't have much respect for us after we let them burn our capital. I think they were uneasy in Washington and uneasy on their retreat; but nothing happened. They'll be feeling good now; they're likely a little ashamed of how nervous they were; they'll be so sure of themselves and so contemptuous of us that they may not waste time figuring out the surest and easiest way to attack us here.

If I were Ross and knew what I know about Baltimore, I'd attack by land. If Ross knew what I know, he would have attacked already—and whipped us, too. But he doesn't know. I hope he doesn't find out.

They may try a land attack yet, but I doubt it. I don't think they will. Their fleet is too good. It's too good for their good. Their minds are tied to ships. And here's another thing. Ross has two admirals with him, one at each elbow. Cochrane and Cockburn —I'd say they'll tie Ross to their fleet. I hope they do. I'll have a chance, if they do.

Here's something else, too—Fort McHenry. To a military mind, there's something fascinating about forts. They're like a snake's eyes to a bird. That's half the value of a fort, it seems to me: to draw the enemy on to attack you at your strongest point. The Chew house wrecked us at Germantown in the old war. We were driving them until we stopped to clean their troops out of Chew's stone house. That house could just as well have been left untouched, troops and all; it was harmless, but we didn't think so. It made General Maxwell stop and waste time, battering at it. And it pulled back Wayne's division because his men heard the firing behind them and thought that the British were cutting us off from the rear. It ruined our whole attack.

Maybe Fort McHenry will do as much for us now as Chew's

house did against us. Maybe the British will feel honor-bound and rule-bound to attack it. Why they should, I don't know. I'm too much a businessman to understand it. To my way of thinking, it's more sensible to hit the other fellow where he's weakest. But it's probably human nature—plain mulishness, I guess. A fort is a kind of chip on a shoulder. You're not a man if you don't knock it off.

There's still another reason for thinking the British will come by water: they've been here before. Twice before. They threatened us with their fleet in April last year and came back again in August —three ships of the line, five frigates, three brigs, two schooners and Lord knows how many small vessels.[7] But they didn't attack. Why? They certainly would have attacked if they'd thought they could win. What's the difference now? What have they got that they didn't have then? An army, that's what they've got. There! There's the answer! At least it's the biggest piece of the answer. When they come this time, they'll come both by land and by water, they'll use both their troops and their fleet.

Now let's fit in the other pieces. They can use the fleet for two things—to cover the troops and to try to knock out Fort McHenry. There's only one way they can do both of those things at once, there's only one place they can land their troops and support them while they attack the fort with their ships. And that place is North Point.

North Point isn't the best place for a land attack. It's too narrow. There isn't room to maneuver. They can't outflank us there as they did at Bladensburg, they'll have to come at us head-on. *Hmmm* . . . that isn't so. They can't outflank us on land, but they can by water. If we make a stand on the point, they can land troops behind us. Well, there's a way to stop that. So long as the fort holds out, they can't land men within range of its guns; so long as we hold out on land, they can't get around the fort and attack from the rear. But if I pick out a position where I can cover the fort from a land attack and the fort can protect my flanks from a boat attack, the other flank will be out in the open. Well, I can't have everything. I can weight that flank down with earthworks, I can weight it down with guns.

I can't have everything all my own way. I can't do everything that might be done if I had all the time and men in the world. I've got to decide what's the best thing to do and stick to it. I haven't the men or the guns to defend the whole perimeter of Baltimore. But if I've decided that they'll attack up the harbor with warships, I can do something to meet them. If I've decided that they'll attack at the same time by land, I can do something about it—not enough, maybe, but something. But if I have made up my mind that the two attacks will be made close together, supporting each other . . . if I've made up my mind that the troops will attack head-on by the shortest, most obvious route . . . by heaven, I can do a good deal about *that*.

Well, I've made up my mind.

Now for the means. What have we got that the enemy hasn't got? What has he got that we haven't? The answer is simple enough. We've got artillery. Thank God for the privateers, and thank God we've been building warships. The ships can't help us much, but we've got their guns. Ross may have more artillery than he fetched to Bladensburg, he may have more than three grass-hoppers; but he probably hasn't as many guns as we have, and he certainly hasn't any as heavy as some of our ships' guns. He can get some, most likely; he can probably land heavy guns from the fleet, but he'll have to drag them on sledges and that will be slow, hard work. It will take time—and time will be on our side. The longer Ross waits to attack, the stronger we'll be. On the other side of the ledger, Ross has the rockets and Ross has the better infantry. Those rockets are hard on green troops; and even without them, British regulars can't often be whipped in the open field by unblooded militia. It happens sometimes, but you certainly can't depend on it. The Fifth has been blooded; it might do as well, the next time, as the old First did at Long Island. But that wouldn't be enough. The First didn't win the battle, it didn't save Long Island and it didn't save New York; all it did was protect the retreat of the army. General Washington was good at retreating: the British called him a fox. But we can't retreat this time; we've got to stand. If we fall back, Baltimore's gone.

Washington was a fox, right enough, but there's more to a fox than his running. He knew how a fox behaves when the hounds get too close: he knew when to go to earth. He believed in his men, but he knew how much they could do. He knew when to dig in. He knew when to go to earth behind field works; he did it at Morristown and he did it at Valley Forge. The British were strong enough to sweep our poor husk of an army away with a breath, in the open field, but they didn't care to go up against even those scarecrows behind entrenchments.

I believe in these men of mine, too. Give them time, give them the battle training that they can get only in battle, and they'll make soldiers as tough and as steady as any. But I can't give them that. I've got to use them as they are, and this is a case where faith without field works is . . . well, it would be misplaced. I've got to give it its proper place, and its proper place is in trenches. Baltimore isn't a fox, it's more like a wolf, it has been a lone wolf all its life. But it's going to play fox for once. It's going to earth. *This town is going to dig.*

Sam Smith had made history. History would not know that it had been made.

The scene changes again. The setting: a village.[8] The time: midnight of Friday, August 26th. The stage is so dark that what happens cannot be seen clearly. A narrator is required. He is the same man—the English lieutenant—who appeared as both actor and narrator in the first scene in this identical setting. His name is George Robert Gleig. He is disheveled, his scabbard is broken, his arm and his leg sting from wounds. And tonight he is very tired. He is telling why he is tired. He is describing the retreat of the British army from Washington:

"As many horses as could be got together were put in requisition for the transport of the artillery. Even the few wounded officers who had accompanied the column were required to resign theirs; and mine, among the number, was taken away. But the precaution was a very just and proper one. Not only were the guns by this means rendered more portable, but the danger of a betrayal from a neigh, or the trampling of hooves along the paved streets, was provided against; and though individuals might and did suffer, their sufferings were not to be put into the scale against the public good.

"It was about eight o'clock at night [August 25th] when a staff-officer, arriving upon the ground, gave directions for the corps to form in marching order. Large quantities of fresh fuel were heaped upon the fires, whilst from every company a few men were selected, who should remain beside them till the picquets withdrew, and move from time to time, so as that their figures might be seen by the light of the blaze. After this the troops stole to the rear of the fires by twos and threes; when far enough removed to avoid observation, they took their places, and, in profound silence, began their march. The night was very dark. Stars there were, indeed, in the sky; but for some time after quitting the light of the bivouac, their influence was wholly unfelt. We moved on, however, in good order. No man spoke above his breath, our very steps were planted lightly, and we cleared the town without exciting observation. About half a mile in rear of the city, a second line of fires had been established. We looked towards it now, and the effect of the figures, which from time to time moved across the flames, was exceedingly striking. On arriving there we found that the other brigades had likewise commenced their retreat, and that the fires which burned so brightly, had been prepared by them exactly as we had prepared ours. We caused the few men whom they had left behind to join us, as *our* men had been commanded to join the picquets, and pursued our journey.

"We were now approaching the field of the late battle, when the moon rose, and threw a soft pale light over surrounding objects. At first her rays fell only upon the green leaves and giant boughs of the woods which on either hand closed in the road; but as we proceeded onwards other spectacles presented themselves, some of which were of no very cheering or lively nature. When we gained the ridge which had formed the crest of the American position, open green fields lay stretched out before us; every one presenting some manifestation of the drama which had so lately been acted here. Broken arms, caps, cartouch boxes, with here and there a dead body, naked and ghostly white, were scattered about in every direction, whilst the smell, not exactly of putrefaction, but of something nearly akin to it, and mingling with the odour of scorched grass and extinguished matches, rose upon the night air very offensively; yet the whole scene was one of prodigious interest and power. The river and town which lay near us, the former flowing quietly and beautifully along, the latter lifting its modest buildings in the silence of a moonlight night, formed a striking contrast with the devastated and torn ground over which we were marching, whilst the only sound distinguishable was that of the measured tread of feet as the column proceeded down the slope towards the bridge. . . .

"We were in the village; and a halt being commanded, an opportunity was afforded of enquiring into the condition of the wounded. I failed not to avail myself of it; but whilst the men were busied in picking up their knapsacks, which in the heat of action they had cast away, I stepped to the hospital and paid a hasty visit to the poor fellows who occupied it. It was a mortifying reflection, that, in spite of our success, the total absence of all adequate means of conveyance laid us under the necessity of leaving very many of them behind; nor could the non-commissioned officers and private soldiers conceal their chagrin on the occasion. One of these, a sergeant of my own company, who had received a ball through both thighs, actually shed tears as he wished me farewell, regretting that he had not shared the fate of Mr. Williams. It was in vain that I reminded him that he was not singular; that Colonel Thornton, Colonel Wood, and Major Brown, besides others of less note, were doomed to be his companions in captivity. . . .

"Yet no apprehensions could be more unfounded than those of that man; for however unlike civilized nations they may be in other respects, in the humanity of their conduct towards such English soldiers as fell into their hands, the Americans can be surpassed by no people whatever. To this the wounded whom we were compelled to abandon to-night bore, after their release, ample testimony; and they told a tale which hundreds besides have corroborated. . . .

"Reversing the arrangements which had held good during the advance, the third brigade this night led the way; it was followed by the artillery, now supplied with horses, which again was succeeded by the second brigade. In rear of this came the light troops, of whom three companies, which had furnished the picquets during the day, did the duty of a rear guard. Last of all moved the mounted drivers, supported by scattered files of infantry on each side of the way, whilst half a troop of rocket-men marched between the head of the rear-guard, and the rear of the column, in readiness to bring their horrible weapons into play at the first alarm.

"Hitherto our men had moved on in profound silence. The strictest orders had been issued that no one should speak, and no one thought of disobeying the order; but as the night stole on, and the distance between us and the city became hourly greater and greater, a degree of carelessness to the wishes of those in power, became manifest through all ranks. The fact is, that we were completely worn out. The broken rest of a single day had by no means made amends for the toil of the five days preceding, and being followed by a night-march, proved absolutely useless . . . till finally, the only sensation to which we were alive, was one of overwhelming weariness; and the only wish which we cared to form, was, that an opportunity would be afforded of lying down to rest. About midnight, indeed, and for six hours after it, these feelings began to operate very powerfully.

"The men strayed from their ranks; the officers found great

PRELUDE TO "THE STAR-SPANGLED BANNER"—the disorde
led to the incident that brought Francis Scott K

...eat of the British army from Washington. It
...Baltimore harbor to write his country's anthem.

difficulty in urging them on; some dozed upon their legs, and fell under the feet of their comrades; others threw themselves by the wayside, refusing to proceed farther. In a word, by seven o'clock on the following morning [August 26th] it was perfectly manifest that an hour's rest must be taken, otherwise one half of the troops would be in danger of falling into the hands of the enemy.

"We had accomplished a journey of some eighteen or twenty miles, when to the unspeakable joy of every man in the army, the General, finding himself arrived at a convenient spot, commanded a halt. I candidly confess, that I know nothing of the nature of the ground on which the halt occurred, nor of the dispositions which were made to render it secure, for my men were hardly stretched upon the grass when I followed their example. . . . From seven o'clock till a little before noon, I slept as soundly as ever weary traveller has slept, or could desire to sleep. At that period I was awoke to breakfast; and in half an hour after, the column was again in motion.

"The sun had set, and twilight was rapidly closing in. when we found ourselves once more in the vicinity of Marlborough. There it was resolved to pass the night. . . ."[9]

"Though there appeared to be no disposition on the part of the American general to follow our steps and to harass the retreat, the inhabitants of that village, at the instigation of a medical practitioner called Beanes, had risen in arms as soon as we were defeated, and falling upon such individuals as strayed from the column, put some of them to death, and made others prisoners. A soldier whom they had taken, and who had escaped, gave this information to the troopers just as they were about to return to headquarters; upon which they immediately wheeled about, and galloping into the village, pulled the doctor out of his bed, (for it was early in the morning), and compelled him, by a threat of instant death, to liberate his prisoners, and mounting him before one of the party, brought him in triumph to the camp."[10]

But there is also another narrator. His name is Roger Brooke Taney. He will one day become chief justice of the United States Supreme Court. Tonight his only distinction is that he is a successful lawyer and the brother-in-law of young Francis Scott Key, the amateur society artilleryman who "helped" Will Winder to deploy his army. His story of what happened is not quite the same as George Gleig's:

"On the evening of the day that the enemy disappeared [from

the river in front of Alexandria] Mr. Richard West arrived at
Mr. Key's and told him that after the British army passed through
Upper Marlboro, on their return to their ships, and had encamped
some miles below the town, a detachment was sent back, which
entered Dr. Beanes's house about midnight, compelled him to rise
from his bed, and hurried him off to the British camp, hardly
allowing him time to put his clothes on; that he was treated with
great harshness, and closely guarded; and that as soon as his
friends were apprized of his situation, they hastened to the headquarters of the English army to solicit his release, but it was pre-
emptorily refused, and they were not even permitted to see him;
and that he had been carried as a prisoner on board the fleet.

"And finding their own efforts unavailing, and alarmed for his
safety, his friends in and about Marlboro thought it advisable that
Mr. West should hasten to Georgetown and request Mr. Key to
obtain the sanction of the government to his going on board the
admiral's ship, under a flag of truce, and endeavoring to procure
the release of Dr. Beanes, before the fleet sailed. It was then
lying at the mouth of the Potomac, and its destination was not
at that time known with certainty.

"Dr. Beanes . . . was the leading physician in Upper Marlboro,
and an accomplished scholar and gentleman. He was highly respected by all who knew him; was the family physician of Mr.
West, and the intimate friend of Mr. Key. He occupied one of the
best houses in Upper Marlboro, and lived very handsomely; and
his house was selected for the quarters of Admiral Cockburn, and
some of the principal officers of the army, when the British troops
encamped at Marlboro on their march to Washington. These officers were, of course, furnished with everything that the house
could offer; and they in return treated him with much courtesy, and
placed guards around his grounds and outhouses, to prevent depre-
dations by their troops.

"But on the return of the army to the ships, after the main
body had passed through the town, stragglers who had left the
ranks to plunder, or from some other motive, made their appearance from time to time, singly or in small squads, and Dr. Beanes
put himself at the head of a small body of citizens, to pursue and
make prisoners of them. Information of this proceeding was by
some means or other conveyed to the English camp, and the detachment of which I have spoken was sent back to release the
prisoners and seize Dr. Beanes. They did not seem to regard him,

and certainly did not treat him, as a prisoner of war, but as one who had deceived, and broken his faith to them." [11]

The stories told by the two narrators make, together, a good deal more sense than either one makes singly. The second interlude in the campaign—the interlude that was to overshadow the campaign itself because it was the second chapter in the story of a nation's anthem—had been played out to its minor climax.

14

FOR SALE—CANNON BALLS,
MUCH RECOMMENDED

WAR MADE ITS OFFICIAL APPEAR-
ance in Baltimore disguised in whereases. The "resolves" adopted by
the Committee of Vigilance and Safety on August 27th looked as
stuffy and dull as resolutions invariably looked in the *Patriot's*
close-set type. They were full of familiar names—neighbors' names.
The neighbors were right nice people but that was all. They had
decent jobs, and mostly they owned their own homes; they had
children and dogs, and the dogs barked at night and the children
had an annoying habit of scribbling on white stone steps. Certainly there was nothing inspiring about the neighbors, they were
quite ordinary people. There was nothing inspiring about the "resolves" themselves, though they started out well enough:

Whereas the commanding officer has required the aid of the citizens
in the erection of works for the defense of the city, and the committee of

vigilance and safety having full confidence in the patriotism of their fellow citizens, have agreed on the following organization, for the purpose of complying with the request of the major general.

Then they proceeded abruptly to such homely matters as shovels:

The inhabitants of the city and precincts are called on to deposit at the court-house in the third ward, centre market in the fifth ward, market house Fell's Point, Riding-school in the seventh ward, or take with them to the place required, all wheel-barrows, pick-axes, spades and shovels that they can procure.

That the city and precincts be divided into four sections, the first section to consist of the eastern precincts and the eighth ward, the second to comprise the 5th, 6th and 7th wards, the third to comprise the 2d, 3d and 4th wards, and the fourth to comprise the 1st ward and western precincts.

That the exempts from military and the free people of color of the first district, consisting of the 8th ward and eastern precincts, assemble to-morrow, Sunday morning, at 6 o'clock, at Hampstead-hill with provisions for the day, and that Arthur Mitchell, Daniel Conn, Henry Pennington, John Chalmers, William Starr, Thomas Weary, Henry Harwood and Philip Cornmiller be charged with their superintendence during the day.

That those of the second district, comprising the 5th, 6th and 7th wards, assemble at Myer Garden, on Monday morning at 6 o'clock, under the superintendence of William Parks, Captain Watts, Ludwig Herring, William Ross, William Carman, Daniel Howland, Caleb Earnest and James Hutton.

That those of the third district, comprising the second, third and fourth wards, assemble at Washington Square, on *Tuesday morning*, at six o'clock, under the superintendence of Frederick Leypold, William M'Cleary, John McKim, jr., Henry Schroeder, Alexander M'Donald, Eli Hewitt, Peter Gold and Alexander Russell.

That those of the fourth district, comprising the 1st ward and western precincts, assemble at the intersection of Eutaw and Market streets, on Wednesday morning at 6 o'clock under the superintendence of William W. Taylor, William Jessop, Edward Harris, George Decker, William Harkins, Isaac Philips, William Jones and John Hignet.

The owners of slaves are requested to send them to work on the days assigned in the several districts.

Such of our patriotic fellow citizens of the county and elsewhere, as are disposed to aid in the common defence, are invited to partake in the duties now required on such of the days as may be most convenient to them.

Thus the resolution ended, duller than it had begun. A call to arms it might be, but the arms were garden tools. It was not a bugle blast, it was not the long roll of drums. It was not as inspiring by half as the advertisements that offered tickets for sale in the Liberty Engine House lottery. It was a businessman's memorandum. But if there was nothing in it to quicken the pulse, it had certain other merits. It contained not only a plan but also the where and the when and the who and the how of putting the plan to work. Bladensburg might have had a different outcome if the cabinet or the War Department had been equally unconcerned with the public pulse; but the political-minded gentlemen in Washington could hardly have been expected to tell their constituents to get up at five o'clock in the morning and trundle a wheelbarrow to Centre Market by six, they could hardly have been expected to upset the voters by waking them up so early for such an unpleasant purpose. Sam Smith, too, was political-minded. He had got himself elected to the Maryland assembly, he had got himself elected and re-elected to the House of Representatives in Washington five times in a row, he had been a United States senator now for more than ten years. He liked politics, he wanted to keep on being senator, he needed Baltimore's votes. But he did not hesitate to turn his constituents out of bed at five in the morning and set them to digging ditches. A senator-politician might be expected to rip off a peroration. A major general of militia might be forgiven if he indulged in Beauregardian phrases . . . "our beloved country" . . . the enemy's "dastardly feet" . . . "every barn a fortress." Sam Smith called a shovel a shovel.

The resolves brought Baltimore down to earth. They brought the war home. War was no longer a piece in the paper, no longer a glare in the sky, no longer another rumor just off the production line of tongues. War was the Fell's Point market house. War was the seventh ward riding school. War was something a man could hold in his hands. It was the barrow he'd used to wheel manure up from the livery stable to brisken the hollyhocks. It was the spade he'd used to dig up that extra plot and make room for tomatoes: they weren't fit to eat but Mary thought they looked pretty, she liked the name too: love apples, people called them. Those resolves in the paper certainly made a man think, they made him wonder whether he'd be around to put in a garden next spring, they made him wonder whether he hadn't ought to send Mary away. She wouldn't go without him; maybe he'd ought to pull up and leave . . . just leave everything and take her away. But where would they go? Where could he earn their keep? "Away" wasn't a place, there weren't any jobs at "away." If they went . . . and came back . . ..

would there be any house to come back to? He wasn't so young any more. He'd never be able to save enough money to buy another house; if this one was burned they'd have to rent rooms. Or a room. If everybody went away . . . juggins! There'd be nobody left to take care of the town, the whole town would likely be burned. There wouldn't be any rooms. There wouldn't be any shipyards or ropewalks, there wouldn't be any harness shops or any iron foundry or any wagonworks, there wouldn't be anything.

At six o'clock Sunday morning Hampstead Hill—or Loudenslager's, if you preferred the old name—looked like a picnic ground. There weren't many trees, and the grass was brown now with August and worn thin in patches by the feet of drilling militia, but the hill was a pleasant place. It was shaped like the blade of a sickle, curved, with the inner harbor set to one end like a kind of crooked handle. There, at the base of the blade, it slanted steep to the water. In front, toward the harbor mouth and North Point, it sloped down gently to Harris's creek and the shipyard where the *Java* had been building all year. A man could look down on the deck of Commodore Perry's new frigate and count her still-empty gun ports; he could look down the channel to the red-brick fort on Whetstone Point and the white lighthouse at the Lazaretto on the opposite, nearer shore; he could look across the creek and see farm fields and fences and Surrey, the fine home of Colonel Sterrett two miles away, and beyond it Judge Kell's farmhouse. The hill followed the slow curve of Harris's Creek for a while and then bent more sharply north. Behind it, inside of its curve, lay the town. And the town, this Sabbath morning, was moving out to the hill.

But this was a picnic such as had never been seen at Schwartze's Spring or at Rutter's. Part of it was familiar enough—the carriages parked every which way, the horses dozing on their picket ropes, catching up on their own lost Sunday sleep, the coats neatly folded on wicker hampers or laid on the ground with paper-wrapped parcels of lunch bulging out of the pockets, the groups of men in the dignity of broadcloth or the comfort of shirt sleeves. There were even a few women, come to see that husbands got plenty to eat and not too much to drink or to be sure that this man-made occasion for missing church was what the men said it was. There was the inevitable rabble of small boys, shouting, running, playing soldier, playing hot cockles and kit-kat or aping their elders by squatting together in earnest confabulations. But picnics at Rutter's and

Schwartz's produced no such heterogeneous crowds. Not even political meetings brought out such a mingling of frock coats and checkered shirts, of roundabouts and coatees, smocks and ruffles, of gentlemen's elegant truncated-conical hats and mechanics' work-grubby caps, of stable hands, bankers and "free people of color," lawyers' clerks, roustabouts, judges and merchants and slaves.

It was a combination of picnic, fire, political rally, cornerstone laying and drill day. Militia companies marched up the hill to the rowf-rowf-rowf of their drums; they stacked arms to the rowf-rowf-rowf of ecstatic, hysterical dogs. Supply wagons rumbled behind them, tools were tossed out with a clatter. A band played.[1] Flags fluttered. "A well-known, worthy and estimable" Frenchman[2] trotted brisky about, measuring, pointing, nodding his head at stakes in the ground and cords stretched over the grass. His name was Maximilian Godefroy, he was an architect and engineer, and Sam Smith had assigned him to superintend the digging of the entrenchments laid out on the hill.

The crowd grew and grew. On foot with picks over their shoulders, in gigs, in grocers' carts, in surreys and carryalls bristling with long-handled shovels, the men of "the eighth ward and the eastern precincts" came straggling out of the city. With them came the more energetic from districts not summoned till Monday or Tuesday or Wednesday. They looked like refugees; they were men determined not to be refugees. A sense of duty played a part in their coming, but only a part. They were driven also by other, simpler emotions. Apprehension was one . . . the intimate apprehension that what had happened to Havre de Grace, to helpless Chesapeake hamlets and lonely plantations as well as to Washington would soon be happening here. Anger, too, drove them . . . anger at the trouble that had been permitted to burst upon them without preparation to meet it . . . anger at the national government, too weak to help them, too stupid to help itself . . . anger at the federal politicians, busy now with talk of "the cowardice of the militia" to cover their own shortcomings . . . anger at the crude lie about Pinkney's wound, at the things they were beginning to hear about the rancid beef, the lack of knapsacks and blankets and wagons and everything else, the muddling and meddling and the mishandling of Baltimore's troops.

Even with militia companies and flags and martial music and anger, the first wholesale muster of Baltimore manpower was certainly not a military spectacle. There were too many civilians, there were too many militiamen still wearing civilian clothes. There was a good deal of standing around and waiting, a good deal of shouting and arm waving as the eight citizens charged with the "superintendence" did what they could to fetch order out of confusion. The enemy would not have been greatly impressed. But the sight was impressive enough to hearten the man who conceived it. Sam Smith had given Baltimore no high-sounding, appropriate "sentiments," he had given it a job without trying to make the job sound like something it wasn't. He had not dressed it up as a "call to arms." He had issued a call to picks and shovels and asked the town to provide them. The town had responded. In the end, the picks and shovels repulsed the invading army.

The top-hatted gentlemen began to dig. The bankers and the stevedores, the well-to-do merchants and the hostlers, the lawyers and the slaves and the free Negroes and the harness-makers and the coopers and the wheelwrights and the soft-handed shop clerks began to dig. It was no picnic. It was a hot, dirty, backaching, blistering business. They stuck to it all day, grimly. The paper would be able to say with some justification that "the work done demonstrates their power and zeal, to the astonishment of all who behold it." [3] They themselves were astonished. As they dug, two long curving lines of entrenchments began to take shape. [4] The meaningless holes in the ground became rifle pits. Formless heaps of red earth turned into barbettes and fleches, into demilunes and redans. A hard confidence grew, a defiance. They could take a grim satisfaction in hands that were blistered raw. They could put thumbs to sun-scalded noses and waggle stiff fingers in the general direction of Messrs. Ross, Cockburn and Cochrane. It was the same derisive, defiant gesture Tom Boyle had used only yesterday.

The sore-muscled men in the ditches on Hampstead Hill hadn't heard about Tom Boyle's insult. The news would not come for weeks. Even the men who owned shares in Boyle's saucy *Chasseur* didn't know where he was. As they dug, as they drilled with the Eagle Artillerists, as they practiced scouting with the Maryland Hussars and "exercised" the "great guns" in the Water Battery with the Marine Artillery, they had no idea that Tom Boyle was happily using their property to blockade the British Isles. He had been having a wonderful time. For a month or more the *Chasseur* had been in the Irish Sea and the mouth of the English Channel, circling like a deerfly, pouncing on one British merchantman after another, biting and getting away from the swift cruisers sent out to kill her. On the day before Baltimore began to dig, Tom Boyle added sting to the *Chasseur* bites. He had the gall of the devil and a nice sense of the taunt that would hurt. Lying in English waters, under the very noses of the Admiralty, he had written and sent to London, to be posted in Lloyd's, a

PROCLAMATION

WHEREAS, it has been customary with the admirals of Great Britain commanding small forces on the coast of the United States, particularly with Sir John Borlaise Warren and Sir Alexander Cochrane to declare the coast of the said United States in a state of strict and rigorous blockade, without possessing the power to justify such a declaration, or stationing an adequate force to command such a blockade.

I do, therefore, by virtue of the power and authority in me vested (possessing sufficient force) declare all the ports, harbours, bays, creeks, rivers, inlets, outlets, islands and sea coasts of the United Kingdom of Great Britain and Ireland in a state of strict and rigorous blockade, and I do further declare that I consider the forces under my command adequate to maintain strictly, rigorously and effectually, the said blockade.

And, I do hereby require the respective officers, whether captains, or commanding officers, under my command, employed or to be employed on the coasts of England, Ireland and Scotland, to pay strict attention to this my proclamation.

And, I hereby caution and forbid the ships and vessels of all and every nation, in amity and peace with the United States, from entering or attempting to enter or from coming or attempting to come out of any of the said ports, harbours, bays, creeks, rivers, inlets, outlets, islands or sea coasts, on or under any pretence whatever; and that no person may plead ignorance of this my proclamation, I have ordered the same to be made public in England.
Given under my hand on board the *Chasseur*,

Thomas Boyle

By Command of the Commanding Officer

J. B. Stansbury, Secretary

Perhaps Boyle wasn't a deerfly. A horsefly, perhaps, would be nearer the word. He had given the English the horse laugh.

His fellow townsmen in Baltimore would have been proud of Tom and his proclamation. Tired as they were, they would have found breath for raucous, defiant, satisfying laughter. But as August scorched itself out, they found other reasons for pride, other reasons for harsh satisfaction. The more Baltimore heard about the battle of Bladensburg, the more it was inclined to believe that Baltimore men had done most of the fighting. It was hard to get at the truth, it was hard to fit the odd pieces of truth together, but the picture came clear at last. The town could pick out men of whom it could be proud ... Josh Barney and his Baltimore flotillamen ... Colonel Sterrett, leading the charge of the Fifth ... Captain Dominic Bader, firm in the midst of disaster, standing so long that he was surrounded and taken ... young John Pendleton Kennedy carrying crippled Jim McCulloch off the lost field under fire. The town could pick out certain scenes of which nobody need be ashamed ... its own guns and its own rifle companies, fighting an army alone ... the Fifth, drawn back and bewildered, advancing and driving the foe ... the riflemen rallying, helping the Fifth to drive them ... the one Baltimore regiment standing up to the fire of the Invincibles, standing up to the shock of the multiplied errors around it, holding its ground while the rest of the line gave way, while the paper dolls blew away ... Barney and his flotillamen fighting their guns to the last while the army collapsed around them. Men who did things like that were not cowards, there was something in them that wasn't made of blown paper.

Other belated pieces of truth gave the town a grim satisfaction. While the enemy occupied Washington, a detachment of two hundred men had been sent to the navy yard to finish the work of destruction; one of them dropped a lighted match into a well and the well blew up; the navy yard personnel had half filled it with powder and shell. When the debris stopped falling, forty-two officers and men were on the ground, twelve of them dead, thirty wounded.[5] It wasn't a pleasant scene; in ordinary times it would be horrible; but it was less unpleasant than the scene of the capital burning, it was less unpleasant than the field of Bladensburg by moonlight two nights after the battle. There was satisfaction in the story of the invading army demoralized by the hurricane that struck Washington while it still smoldered. Decent men didn't laugh at the killing and maiming of forty-two other men, but they could throw back their heads and roar at the thought of the Invincibles flat on their faces in mud, of the enemy's cannon upset by American wind, of a British officer blown off the back of his horse. The laughter turned scornful when Baltimore heard how Invincibles looked in retreat ... like fugitives ... like refugees ... stolen cattle mixed with the column ... stolen farm carts and wagons and two-wheeled gigs and even one elegant coach[6] filled with plunder and wounded . . . Wellington's veterans breaking ranks, straggling, falling exhausted,[7] being gobbled up by village exempts.[8] Wellington's veterans had acted right much like militia . . . like county militia, at that. There were bitter tones in the laughter. Even the loudest horse laugh rang just a little hollow.

While the four districts dug in relays and the trenches deepened and the first heavy ship guns were dragged up Hampstead Hill to be mounted behind the raw mounds of dirt, life in the town went on pretty much as usual. Mrs. Hayward announced that her School of Young Ladies would be opened "for the reception of her Boarders & Day Scholars on Monday the 4th of September next." Will Alcock advertised his willingness to contract for large quantities of "early Cider." John Love extolled his "patent metallic Columbia cup and saucer" and argued that "the advantages are obvious." Somebody applied for a wet nurse. G. & R. Waites offered "plain green paper for curtains." Other shops still had a few reminders of the days before Baltimore was cut off from the rest of the world—La Guaira coffee and Russia duck, Smyrna madder roots, New Orleans cotton, Muscovado in hogsheads and barrels and Spanish tobacco in bundles.

With the enemy at the door, speculators "and others disposed to seize great Bargains in Real Property" were urged to invest in houses and lots "on the following streets, viz.: Bond-street, Camden ditto, Eden ditto, Franklin Lane and Dock Alley." The blockade and the nearing danger were turned to a good account. Enterprising merchants took Baltimore into their confidence concerning a supply of "choice quality old Port in pipes, quarter casks, half quarter casks, demijohns and bottles" and added that "this port is of the *Minerva's* cargo and now is the only good Wine of the kind to be had in the U. States." John Bier offered "Wheat & Rye Whiskey" and let it be known to his tough-throated customers that he had on hand "a parcel of very nice CORN."

Danger might be very near indeed, but life must go on, teeth could still ache, and people could have halitosis. Dr. Bucknell stood ready to help such afflicted mortals with his "Inimitable Restorative Tooth Powder" which, he said, would not only cure "that painful disease" of toothache "but by a regular use of it will be a sure preventative." Dr. Bucknell was somewhat ahead of his time. He assured the community that his inimitable restorative also "sweetens the breath, takes away scurvy, and makes the teeth firm in the gums—also gives the teeth a delicate whiteness."

Baltimoreans who wanted to get their minds off their troubles could think about other things—about "superb piano fortes," for instance, or copperplate playing cards or "backgammon boards of superior quality" or *Strictures on the Modern System of Female Education* including "the practical use of female knowledge, with a sketch of the female character and a comparative view of the sexes" and certain mysterious "hints" on that subject. The hints could be had for one dollar. And if a young gentleman or a young apprentice lacked the necessary dollar, he almost surely could get it by investing a smaller sum in a lottery ticket. The lotteries did a brisk business, and there was sufficient variety to satisfy the most finicky taste. Anyone with a notion toward investment could choose among the Liberty Engine House Lottery, the Masonic Hall Lottery, the Grand National Lottery, the New York State Lottery and the Internal Navigation Lottery—the last named, perhaps, having special appeal to the samplers of John Bier's "parcel of very nice CORN." The individual prizes—invariably still to be drawn—ran all the way up to $60,000.

Those who craved something besides corn or lotteries to make them forget their anxieties could drop in at No. 37 Market street and browse the new novels—*Rosa in London* and *The Wanderer* and *Rebecca, or the Fille de Chambre*. If they craved more serious fare, Vance's had in stock *Experiments on the Principles of Life, an Analysis of the Differences between Calvinism and Hopkinslanism as well as and Particularly on the Principle of the Motions of the Heart, and on the Seat of that Principle* translated from the French of Monsier Le Gallois, adjunct member of the Society of the Professors of Medicine of Paris. And anyone whose heart did not beat fast enough in his contemplation of oncoming danger could quicken his pulse by purchasing from the Messrs. Vance *The Marvellous Adventures, or Vicissitudes of a Cat; a very Interesting and Instructive Work* by Mrs. Pilkington.

The town made a good show of keeping up its courage. Alex McKim, who had ridden to war at Bladensburg as a civilian because he thought it his duty, boldly declared his faith in the future. He and Robert McKim, his partner, announced that in their factory on French street they had "a quantity of Throssel Yarn, suited to the demand of the season, and their works *now in a state of forward-*

ness, will enable them to keep a constant supply of the article."
They might have been referring as well to the other works now in a
state of forwardness on Hampstead Hill, for they declared stoutly
that "orders from the country will be punctually attended to."
Once more the defiant thumb to the nose for those prospective customers, the firm of Ross, Cockburn and Cochrane!

But there was something more than a show of defiance and a
nose thumbed in print, something more than an eye to the quick
turning of a dollar. There was something stubborn, something positively mulish. With the bay blockaded and the world cut off, Baltimore shipowners and sailing masters were nonetheless tempted with
offers of charts of "the West Indies, Labrador, Guayana, the Sleeve,
the Caribbee Isles, and the Southern Ocean; the Cattegatt and the
Gulf of Finland and the Isles of Sicily, Trinidad, and the coast of
Holland and the entrances of the Scheldt, the North Sea and the
German Ocean, the Coast of Norway including the White Sea,
the coasts of Spain and Portugal, Hispaniola and the Mosquito
Shore." They could also buy *Elford's Polar Tables,* the *Baltic Pilot*
and the *Seaman's Daily Assistant.* And if the captain and shareholders of some privateers were minded to try slipping through the
British cruisers to help Boyle and the *Chasseur* turn the tables of
blockade against the British Isles, they could instantly find charts
of St. George's Channel and "the coasts of England, Scotland and
Ireland and the English Channel" in the shop at the corner of Gay
and Market streets.

Baltimore kept not only its head and its courage and its muley
stubbornness, it kept its sense of humor as well. It chuckled over
the printed "NOTICE—Was committed to the gaol of Frederick
County, on the 8th day of July, instant, as a runaway, a Negro
woman who calls herself ELIZA, alias Ruth." For Eliza and her
"red calico jacket and linen petticoat" belonged to Henry Clark,
who lived "about 5 miles from Bladensburgh." There must be
something to the conjuring and the talking with spirits that went
on in the slave quarters: Eliza had known when to run, she had lit
out from Bladensburg a good while before Jimmy Madison turned
his horse and "fell down into the road" that led away from there.

Morris Leahy, the cooper, volunteered his opinion concerning
the value of some human beings by offering "six cents reward" for
the return of a runaway prentice. And the town got another laugh
out of this:

FOUND

W AS found on Tuesday the 30th inst. on the York-Turnpike-Road
near the first toll gate a large bag containing Spy-Glasses and
one cotton Counterpane.

A boy sometimes fetched along a blanket when he hired a gig to
take a girl friend riding and had ideas about parking. The blanket
was meant, of course, for the horse. A bedspread was going too far.
The fellow who left it behind him must have left in a hurry. He
must have been disappointed. His spyglasses must have misled him,
he must have picked out the wrong girl.

But what Baltimore heard about the doings in Washington
seemed even funnier. Dolly Madison was the real man of the
family: she had saved the spoons: all Jimmy had saved was his
horse, and verse-monger had scribbled a piece of mocking doggerel
about him entitled "The Bladensburg Races." But there had been
one man in the federal government who wanted to fight for Washington. He had had an idea about how to do it, too. He had submitted a plan "to spike the cannon at the gate" of the presidential
palace "and lay a train of powder which would blow up the British
should they enter the house." [9] Like Dr. Bucknell, he was somewhat
ahead of his time, and Dolly Madison had firmly vetoed his scheme
for planting a booby trap. What made the story still funnier—and
more pathetic and shameful—was that this sole tough-minded valiant
would-be defender of the nation's capital was a foreigner and
merely "a faithful domestic" who served as "guardian of the door"
in the president's house. His name was John Sioussat. Queen Dolly
called him French John.

The pay-off was that French John "remained until all had fled
and did rescue the bright-coated, screech-voiced macaw" as the
British advance guard appeared. Baltimore's laughter was sour. The
joke was as bitter as gall. So a servant had wanted to fight when
nobody else had any idea except running. A Frenchy, at that!
Thank God somebody had guts! If French John had been a general
. . . Say, can that parrot talk? Well, then, that's all it needs. Make
it a member of the cabinet! Make it secretary of war!

And then came the final shame, the last indecent exposure—the
federal government stripped to its skin, pilloried in its naked im-
potence. With the enemy only a few miles away, with the six little
Baltimore guns and the three rifle companies facing the shock of an
army, with Barney's flotillamen going into position on a dead run,

seven hundred Virginia militia had stood in the Washington streets while a War Department clerk counted out flints for their muskets, one by one—and then refused to issue the flints until he had counted them twice.

When Baltimore laughed about that, the laughter was savage, it had the wire-edge of a scythe.

Disillusionment was complete. Hope of help was gone. Help? *From Washington?* Send us the parrot! In its angry and desperate mood, the town found a savage satisfaction in the experience of Dr. Samuel B. Martin, who had tended the wounded in "Thorne-cliffe's house" on the field of Bladensburg. Dr. Martin had been a prisoner temporarily and had been severely questioned concerning possible American reinforcements. The British officers had been "particularly anxious," he said, "about the Marine Artillery—the material of which it was composed, the weight of metal, number of men, etc." [10] Fine! That's fine! That's just dandy! The Marine Artillery is a Baltimore outfit. It's got privateer captains serving as privates. It's got forty-two-pounder guns.[11] If the Britishers want to find out about the Marine Artillery, just tell 'em to come to Baltimore. *They'll find out!*

Tom Ryan summed up the town's mood with an ad in the *Patriot:*

Cannon Ball, Double Headed

Do. Grape and Cannister Shot, &c,

THOMAS RYAN has for sale, at his foundry opposite the fish market, a good supply of CANNON BALL various sizes, Double headed ditto, for field pieces, which he much recommends the use of, with Grape and Cannister shot, of all sizes.

N. B.   Cash and the highest price, for IRON as usual.

Let Ross, Cockburn, Cochrane and Company come. We'll do business with them. We'll give them our iron for a price—and the price will be high.

Sam Smith's twelve-year-old nephew and namesake disappeared from his home on Park street. An anxious search of all a small boy's normal haunts was vain. But Sam turned up. His family found him "in the intrenchments, with a shovel, diligently engaged." [12]

15

STARS ON THE BREWERY FLOOR

THE CAPTAINS AND THE KING WERE
gone. With them had gone the *Java's* skeleton crew and the marines,
the seamen and the gunners of the *Guerriere*—the four hundred and
fifty men fetched down from Philadelphia by Rodgers. They were
hurrying south through Maryland by forced marches in the swelter-
ing heat.

For more news had come to Baltimore, and all news now was
bad. The enemy had struck again. A squadron of ships had dragged
itself by main strength[1] through the oyster shoals of Kettle Bottoms
and up fifty miles of the Potomac River.

It was a delayed attack, a joint operation that had come un-

jointed. It was General Winder's belated justification for the fear
that had plucked at his twitching nerves and kept his head jerking
over his shoulder toward Fort Washington while General Ross bewildered him with feints. The movement up the Potomac had
begun on August 17th, the same day Ross's transports stood up
Chesapeake Bay for the Patuxent River and two days before the
troops began to land at Benedict. The oyster banks resisted invasion
more effectively than Winder's army and as stubbornly as Josh
Barney's gunboats. Invisible to the British lookouts and so small
that the leadsmen could not find them, the innumerable shoals
popped up in the middle of apparently clear channels to foul the
frigates' bilges,[2] grip the bomb vessels' keels, and drive their captains crazy with frustration.

Divers fumbled under the ships' bottoms, the heavy guns were
dismounted and swayed into tenders and then swayed aboard again,
sailors toiled at the oars of towboats and the warping hawsers—
and still the fleet was far downstream and out of touch when
Bladensburg was fought.

But on the evening of the 27th, when Baltimore was reading
the resolves in the *Patriot* and looking for shovels in its back-yard
tool sheds and dark cellar corners, the British crews were gazing
curiously at the white pillars of Mount Vernon and the frigates
were dropping anchor just out of gunshot of Fort Washington.
The sun was setting as the bomb ships swung their bowsprits
toward the shore to feel out the strength of the substantial-looking
works and soften them for an assault in earnest the next morning.

The first big shells soared up in lazy arcs and fell. Their bursts
were loud but harmless: they were no more than ranging shots.
Not a gun responded. Suddenly the amazed mortarmen saw
soldiers streaming from the landward gate. A sheet of flame more
vivid than the sunset blotted out the fort, the deck planks of the
bomb ships quivered as if their own ponderous weapons had let
go again, enormous sound slammed against the Virginia hills, a great
cloud of smoke and dust boiled skyward. Fort Washington was
gone, blown up by its own commander.

Once more in this campaign the unbelievable had happened.
The ubiquitous Decius Wadsworth, whose barbette at Bladensburg
lured Stansbury into trouble, had urged the war department to
strengthen Fort Washington. Although his recommendations had
gone the way of Winder's—into a wastebasket or a pigeonhole—
he had still believed that the heavy cannon on the walls "would

enable a well-managed garrison to repulse any number of ships of war that might attempt to pass up the river." [3] But poor bedeviled Winder had told Captain Samuel Dyson, the commanding officer, to destroy the fort if Ross advanced against it with his army. The order may have been warranted: the works could have been taken by storm by an enemy willing to endure the necessary losses: the garrison of eighty men could not beat off an army: neither could the five hundred Alexandria militia Winder had detached from his own inadequate army to "defend the approach." Winder, brave enough when it came to risking his own life, had no stomach for ordering other men to risk theirs in forlorn hopes or last-ditch resistance, no matter how much damage they might do the enemy in dying. And Captain Dyson's stomach was no stronger. He took no chances of upsetting it.

The British could not believe their eyes or ears. A fort armed with twelve heavy guns, supported by two batteries mounting thirteen lighter cannon and flanked by a martello tower equipped with two more,[4] blown up without the dignity of one symbolic shot! Captain James Alexander Gordon, commanding the squadron, could no more comprehend it than Ross and Cockburn had been able to comprehend the fact that the United States possessed no force to resist a swift advance on Baltimore. He kept his men on board and his ships offshore all night. Not until daylight did he venture in to knock the deserted batteries to pieces. When he had "otherwise mutilated" the spiked cannon and destroyed their carriages, there was nothing left to fight, there was nothing left between him and Alexandria. Beyond Alexandria lay Washington, but Washington was already worthless. The capital of the United States was now nothing but a place from which "Queen Dolly," peering through the windows of Colonel Tayloe's house where both she and the parrot had found refuge, could watch the signal rockets of the British fleet. [5] Captain Gordon was not interested: there was neither use nor glory in capturing the enemy's capital twice within one week.

On Sunday evening, while the top-hatted gentlemen were straightening their lame backs and licking their blistered fingers as they rode back to town from Hampstead Hill and the prentices and roustabouts were poulticing their tired belly muscles from the inside with John Bier's corn, the British warships came to anchor off the Alexandria wharves.

What happened next would give Baltimore good cause to think

about those ships. Their names would be remembered for a hundred years—*Seahorse*, *Euryalus*, *Erebus*, *Aetna*, *Meteor* and *Devastation*.

Alexandria was "defended" by a hundred exempts—men too old and boys too young to be enrolled in the militia. The seven hundred volunteers and draftees it had sent to Winder's army were still missing somewhere on the "approach" to a fort that was no longer worth approaching. The pleasant old town had certain vague, mildly exciting memories of war and certain faint, mildly reassuring memories of these people who now came as enemies. A general named Braddock had been here long ago and the Alexandria girls had danced and flirted with his officers. Young Colonel Washington had drilled other Alexandria militiamen for Braddock's army. It was a little hard to realize that such nice people had just burned the city that was named for the young colonel. It was a little hard to realize that the handsome fort, also named for him and built to protect his memorial, had vanished in a puff of smoke. But Alexandria had done what it could to prepare for trouble. It had tumbled bales and barrels of merchandise out of its warehouses, heaved them into wagons and hurried the wagons off to the back country. It had buried the family silver and hidden the clock. It had scuttled ships at the wharves. Now it sent a white flag and a deputation of leading citizens to offer capitulation and a promise of good behavior. But it was not prepared for the kind of trouble the deputation brought back from the *Seahorse*.

The terms were "peremptory and humiliating" [6]—feed the squadron; bring back all the merchandise so carefully sent out of danger; raise the scuttled ships, clean them, caulk them and restore all their "furniture"; empty the warehouses and load all the contents on the ships, to be towed away. The alternative—destruction of the town.

The town was helpless. It went to work under the muzzles of the British guns a hundred yards offshore. The vessels it had sunk were raised; only one resisted salvage, and the British burned her. Down to the wharves and into the holds went sixteen thousand pounds of flour, a hundred and fifty bales of cotton, a thousand hogsheads of tobacco and five thousand dollars' worth "of wines and segars." [7] Four days later the shamed, terrorized townsfolk watched the ransom sail away downriver—twenty-one confiscated vessels filled with plunder—three fine shiprigged merchantmen, three brigs and more than a dozen sloops and schooners. As they watched, they swore and prayed and hoped.

Their prayers were that Rodgers, Porter and Perry would somehow contrive to sink the whole fleet before it reached the mouth of the Potomac. Their hopes were that the furious prophecies in the newspapers would come true: "It is impossible the ships can pass such formidable batteries, commanded by our naval heroes, and manned by our invincible seamen." They wanted to believe the editor who boasted that "we'll teach them how to draw up terms of capitulation." [8]

Baltimore, too, wanted to believe him. But the owners of the cargo vessels lying idle in the Patapsco River, the shareholders of the blockaded privateers, the merchants with their already shrunken assets handy for seizure in water-front warehouses, the bankers with hard money in their vaults, all observed that the enemy seemed to have small need for teaching. When they heard that Captain Gordon had been forced to leave behind at Alexandria two hundred thousand barrels of flour and sundries "for want of transport," [9] it occurred to them that his superiors would be under no such handicap at Baltimore. Gordon had come up the Potomac with six men-of-war—two frigates, three bomb ships and a rocket vessel; the *Aetna*, the *Meteor*, the *Devastation* and the *Erebus* might be dangerous in battle but their holds were small, they had little room for "contribution." [10] Most of the twenty-one ships seized at Alexandria had been even smaller—bay boats, river schooners. But Admirals Cockburn and Cochrane had fifty ships, and if they took Baltimore they would acquire at least as many more unless the owners burned them. If Baltimore fought and lost—and if it could then hope to choose between ransom and devastation—the price would be staggering. It would be enormous, it would bankrupt every business, it would ruin the city for a generation. And there might be no choice. Baltimore was the "pirates' nest," it was the "doomed town." Taken by force, after a futile resistance, it would have good reason to expect both "contribution" and destruction.

Ordinary folk who had deposits in the banks also took notice that the enemy needed no instruction in drawing up terms of capitulation. They hurried to draw out their money. The banks suspended payment.[11]

But neither the bankers nor their customers suspended digging. The "rape of Alexandria" made the town more desperate. The picks bit more savagely into Hampstead Hill. The red dirt flew faster.

The rifle pits were shoulder-deep now; a man stooping to his spade saw only raw earth and his shadow on it and the bent back of the man next to him. But news filled his ears. Through the *ughh!* of pick blows and the scrape of shovels he could hear the crash of sledges and the thud of mauls, the flat whack of hammers and the chuck of axes. He could hear gun locks snapping, wooden drill flints chuckling on the musket pans . . . trace chains clanking and then straining into silence . . . overweighted axles squealing . . . wooden rollers groaning. Now and again somebody slammed a door. No, not a slam, exactly. It was more like the noise a cellar door made when it was dropped, careless. It was kind of hollow, it was deep and hoarse-like. Through and underneath and over all the other noises there were two sounds, saturant, persistent. One was like dogs barking in the night . . . your own dog, and the neighbors', and captain Hanna's out to Fell's Point, and all the dogs for miles around. The other was like hard rain on the roof, it was like a long gust of rain coming up the street and trampling across the shingles of your own roof and going on, and another coming.

A man didn't need to uncrook his back and look out over the parapet to see what was happening. His ears translated the sounds into sense. All along the hill, the town's carpenters and shipwrights were manhandling heavy timbers, fitting them together, hammering them into platforms for the cannon. Draft militia companies were drilling, trying to learn how to fire in volleys by platoons. Wagons that had mostly carried wheat to Ellicotts' Mills and fetched back flour, or hogsheads of rum to Hagerstown and Frederick and fetched back hemp and hams, were jolting up the hill now with loads of iron balls and casks of powder. Long teams of horses were dragging heavy guns on stoneboats and still heavier guns on rolling stages; some of those logrollers had been meant for masts and bowsprits; now they had been sacrificed, sawed into short sections to move the ships' batteries into Monsieur Godefroy's barbettes and demilunes. Over toward the Bel Air road, the Independent Artillerists were "exercising" their guns, firing paper cartridges of powder without ball in the general direction of Philadelphia. They kept dropping the cellar doors, loud and careless . . . sometimes one half of a double door and sometimes both halves together . . . almost together but not quite . . . *bump* . . . *bumbump*. Out on Whetstone Point the Washington Artillerists were using shotted cannon. They had mustered in Hanover Market at daylight, bright and sleek as pigeons on a tree branch in their full-dress summer uniforms, and marched down to Fort McHenry.[12] Now they were firing carronades at a piece of canvas on a raft in the Patapsco, they were trying to knock the raft to pieces with twenty-four pound shot. The shot being mostly underweight and the government powder being what it was, the raft was likely safe. But the guns made a good loud thumping. Maybe it was only the air that shook when they let go, but it seemed like the dirt shook on your shovel, it seemed like the bottom of the trench was shaking.

That sound like barking wasn't dogs, though. It was the officers drilling the militia . . . *hup,hup* . . . *bout,face* . . . *carry, ha'ms* . . . *open,pan* . . . *half cock* . . . *shut pan* . . . *for'd,harch* . . . *hup,hup* . . . *close hup* . . . yap,yap,yap,yap. They sounded like good earnest dogs, all barking because it was their duty. And that sound like rain gusts whushing up the wet street, coming closer, beating across the roof above your head and then diminishing was feet scuffing the burnt grass, tramping across the worn sod, marching past the parapet and going on. There were hundreds of feet, thousands. If a man's back got to aching from the shovel so's he had to straighten up a minute to unkink it, he could see aplenty. Not aplenty of militia, maybe, because maybe there wasn't any such thing as enough militia to stop British veterans, but there were things to look at. Heads, for instance. Along the slope of Hampstead Hill, along its curving crest, there were heads popping up out of holes and ducking down again; there were tired men's heads just looking. Teams. Guns. Wagons. Men swarming in and over and around the whopping big mound of dirt piled up in a three-quarter circle and already christened Rodgers's Bastion.[13] And militia everywhere. Hampstead Hill looked like a better name for it would be the Anthill—except that maybe it didn't look as neat.

The fact was that is was beginning to look right frowsy. It was beginning to smell, too. You couldn't put three-four-five thousand men together in a forty-acre field, days at a time, and keep things like a parlor. You could dig latrines but there were always men that wouldn't use them, there were always men that would rather brace up to a tree or just squat where the notion took them. And war had turned into a twenty-four-hour job: even a militiaman couldn't knock off at sundown and go home: a man had to have a pass to go to his own house. A good part of the militia was camping out on Hampstead Hill and in the fields behind it, and there weren't tents enough to go around. The men who had none had made wigwams out of blankets or patched up huts of stray boards or built half-faced shelters thatched with brush. Over the bivouac hung the odor of unwashed bodies, sweaty clothes and

"A whopping big mount of dirt . . . christened Rodgers's Bastion."

slept-in bedding—the inevitable sour smell of an army in the field.

If the militia smelled like an army, it was also beginning to look a little like an army. Companies of drafted men were all over the place, marching, halting, wheeling, running, pointing muskets at imaginary Invincibles who might not be imaginary in a few days. The draft militia couldn't march like the 27th, and for looks it couldn't hold a candle to the "elegant uniformed" company that Captain Spangler had fetched down from York in spite of Pennsylvania's laws.[14] The drafted outfits couldn't drill the way the Independent Blues were drilling, yonder. But, my Lord . . . ! That surely would be setting your ideas right high. The Independent Blues and the other companies of the Fifth were surely putting their backs into it. They were using their backs like they were ramrods, they were carrying their shoulders like they had chips on them, they weren't taking any nonsense off of anybody. If you want a fight, just mention the word "run" to somebody in the Fifth—you needn't to bear down on it, just say it easy-like and casual. You'd best be set to do some right tall running for yourself. Those drafted fellows, now . . . they're aren't so bad, considering. They're beginning to look a good deal less like farm hands hunting for a strayed cow or like a parcel of 'coon hunters beating up a cornfield. These ditches we've been digging are beginning to look like something, too. The whole business is beginning to look like something.

From the top of Hampstead Hill a man could see a four-mile panorama of preparation. It started a mile away to the northwest . . . away to the left there, where the Bel Air road made a slanting line across the far end of the trenches . . . and it came southward along the curved face of the hill until it touched the harbor. Then it jumped the wide mouth of Harris's Creek and followed the north shore of the harbor eastward to the Lazaretto lighthouse, crossed the narrow channel there and took in Fort McHenry. The low brick fort on the tip of Whetstone looked like the red-painted nail on a woman's finger, pointing toward the Cheasapeake and the "big mouth" of the Patapsco River. On the far side of Whetstone . . . at the base of the long slender finger . . . the shore curved in toward the city and then curved out again. It made a broad, ample cove behind the fort; it made Whetstone Point and the low ground behind it look like the back of a right hand, the forefinger pointing and the other fingers and thumb doubled under and the first joint of the little finger poking out to make the first headland of another, smaller cove called Ridgely's. Westward . . . 'way off to the right and past the mouth of Ridgely's Cove and then southwestward across the wider entrance of the Ferry Branch . . . was Cromwell's marsh.

If Hampstead was an anthill, there were a dozen others not so big but looking just as busy. Tiny figures crawled around the lighthouse and the red-brick fort. Others swarmed over the fresh mounds of earth thrown up at intervals along the shore of the larger cove. Over toward Ridgely's the figures dwindled till they looked like midgets hovering above the redoubt that was being built there.[15] Whole congregations of waterbugs were clustered in the narrow passage between the lighthouse and McHenry, not darting and skittering about but clinging close around a few sticks that protruded from the water like the stakes of pound nets. There was another cluster of them in the mouth of Ridgely's Cove.

If you borrowed a spyglass from that letter-of-marque captain digging in the next trench, you could see toy soldiers playing with toy cannon on the very tip of Whetstone: they would be George Stiles's crack Marine Artillery, drilling at the French forty-two-pounders in the new Water Battery on the shore in front of Fort McHenry.[16] You could make out that the water bugs were small boats . . . barges, gigs and pungeys . . . and that the sticks were masts of sunken ships. The masts made an uneven row part way across the channel, like the end of a pasture fence running down into the water . . . a fence with the posts set crooked, with some of the posts missing. Other ships were being towed out from the inner harbor. Brigs, bay schooners, ship-rigged packets, Jamaica sloops and bugeyes, they were creeping toward the harbor entrance.

There . . . look a' that. That's one of Sam Smith's schooners. See . . . they're warping her into the open space there, inshore by the Lazaretto; they're anchoring her, bow and stern both. She'll be starting to fill, pretty soon; you'll see her going down.

Look a' them barges in the creek . . . movin' out with sweeps. Them's the last of the gun barges that was built for Barney. They weren't finished till it was too late to join him. Jumpin' Judas, I'd rather dig than take a hand at rowin' one o' them! Heavy . . . heavy as the lead in your tail. Clumsy, too. You see them guns? One forrard an' one aft . . . long gun in the bow an' a carronade aft.[17] Fight a spell with one end an' then when the other fellow gets right close they turn around an' fight him with the other.

You know what they're doin' down there? You know what Sam Smith is up to? He ain't satisfied with these here . . . now . . . field works. He's go'n' to have him some water works, too. He's buildin' him a palisade of ships, an' them gun barges are go'n' to sit behind it like a battery in back of a barbette. Yes, sir, they're go'n' to lie there snug as a militiaman in this here rifle pit. You wait 'n' see.

Not all the vessels moving down the harbor were stopping in the narrow entrance. Some were being towed out past the Water Battery and around the end of Whetstone into the broad reach that lay between the fort and Cromwell's marsh.[18] They were anchoring in a long row like a line of battle.

In a way, it was a line of battle. Baltimore was scuttling its merchant ships—not to save them, as Alexandria had done, but to barricade the city. Floating, they were useless, they could not fight mortar ships and frigates. On the bottom, they might whip a fleet. They might keep Cockburn's men-of-war beyond range of the town itself. One by one, they sank. The crooked row of mastheads made a slovenly, forlorn fence from the Lazaretto to the Whetstone shore below the main gate of the fort and from the other side of Whetstone to the marshy shore beyond the Ferry Branch. In the channel that led to the inner harbor, with its wharves and ware-houses, working parties in the clusters of small boats rigged a boom above the sunken hulls [19]—the heaviest chains that could be found in town, spiked to logs and timbers from the shipways. A second boom was being built across the mouth of Ridgely's Cove,[20] where landing barges from the enemy fleet might attempt an am-phibious assault almost two miles behind Fort McHenry and almost in the city streets. In the channel between the lighthouse and the fort, the gun barges were creeping up to the barricade of ships, they were being moored bows-on behind the boom to point their long guns down the harbor.

A man on Hampstead Hill must have a spyglass to make out the details of these preparations, but there was one detail he could see with his own eyes. Fort McHenry had a new flag.

It was the biggest flag the town had ever seen—or any other town, as like as not. Thirty-six feet long, so people said, and twenty-nine feet broad. Big as a house. Bigger. Bigger, anyway, than the house it had been made in. George Armistead's new garri-son flag needed a right good breeze to spread it out, but with a wind to starch it and a bright sun shining it made a kind of flame, like, in the sky. Even two-three miles away, a man could see it plain—a good deal plainer than the fort itself. And when a thundergust came boiling up out of the bay, black and ugly looking, you could take that flag to be a patch of rainbow. It was that big.

But it seemed a smallish matter, times like these. It certainly wasn't important, it was only mildly interesting. Some people said the flag had been Armistead's idea; they said he wanted to be sure he had one that the enemy could see; they said he didn't want old Cockburn taking notions that McHenry had surrendered. Well, he must think the Britishers are right standoffish people, he must think they'll keep their distance. You got to say this for him, though: a man that goes to all that trouble for a flag ain't planning to blow up his fort like Captain Dyson did. What trouble did he go to? Well, he thought up the idea and he figured out the size and he rode in from Whetstone to get the Widow Pickersgill to make it. Maybe so, but Cockburn didn't have anything to do with it. The way I heard, Armistead wanted that flag on account of his wife's go'n' to have a baby. *Get away from here! What's a man's wife bein' pregnant got to do with flags an' such?* All I'm tellin' you is what I heard: it was a kind of present for Mrs. Armistead, it was a special compliment to her.[21]

Like most gossip, the town talk was mostly wrong. Mrs. Armistead was pregnant, her bearing-time was near, and she was waiting for it in her husband's quarters in McHenry; but her husband had not ridden in from Whetstone Point to celebrate by ordering four hundred yards of bunting. The idea of a new flag for his fort had been conceived in sentiment; but the sentiment was not conjugal and it was not his. The Widow Pickersgill had entertained three callers in her house at 60 Albemarle street [22] and one of the three was a regimental officer; but his name was not George Armistead, it was Will McDonald. The other two were "family connections" of the widow [23]—Brigadier General John Stricker and Commodore Joshua Barney, brothers-in-law by Barney's first marriage.

One of these three presumably conceived the notion of providing an enormous flag for Fort McHenry. Which? It was not, in their lifetime, a matter of importance. All that is reasonably certain is that all three had a share in putting the idea into execution.

It sounds like one of Barney's notions. Barney was the lifelong sentimentalist, the incurable romantic. His first great moment was associated with a flag. As a boy of sixteen, second in command of the ten-gun *Hornet* in America's first battle fleet, he had hoisted the first striped banner ever seen in Maryland.[24] As a grown man of twenty-nine, he had seen nothing juvenile about fitting up a fifteen-foot boat as a full-rigged ship, mounting it on wheels, and commanding it as captain" while four horses pulled it through the streets of Baltimore in a political parade.[25] He had gloried in sailing his Liliputian *Federalist* down Chesapeake Bay and up the Potomac to Mount Vernon as a gift to Washington. Barney was the man who could find a tenderly romantic thrill in nursing a young "female"—literally a shipboard pickup, for he caught her as she fainted—who was "suffering the extremest horrors" of seasickness. And although seasickness was "not among the number of those improving maladies" that "add a softening charm to the sweetest countenance," he could remember all his life the "tranquil manner" in which she rested her head on his shoulder and "the soft expression of her swimming eyes as she upraised them to his." [26] Barney was the man who disliked the British so intensely that he was still fighting them twelve years after the Revolution ended. While the United States was preparing for its undeclared naval war with France, he was accepting a commission as a *capitaine de Vaisseau* from the French Republic, he was purchasing three private warships of his own and sending them out to ravage British commerce. Only a little more than two years before the *Constellation* sailed from Baltimore, carrying Rodgers and Porter into battle with *L'Insurgente*, Barney was sailing from Rochfort as *chef de division des armées navales* in command of two French frigates, *La Harmonic* and *La Railleuse*.[27] He would be just the man to yearn for an enormous flag with which to taunt a pair of English admirals.

But the notion also sounds like one of Will McDonald's. Will McDonald was a man of substance—merchant, shipmaster, and commanding officer of the Sixth regiment of Baltimore militia. In his boyhood, his imagination had been tinder for the sparks that flew from Count Pulaski's fiery tongue when that young Polish nobleman swirled into Baltimore, a brigadier general with long, flowing hair, to raise an independent corps of lancers and light infantry for Washington's army.[28] He had joined Pulaski's Legion. Now, past middle age and soberly successful, he still had a tindery imagination that caught fire from new ideas: he had built a steamboat.[29] If Baltimore's clipper captains were amused when their towering sails swept them past his *Chesapeake's* complaining paddle wheel and grubby smokestack, theirs was friendly laughter. Will McDonald was no crackpot; you could chuckle at him and respect him at the same time; he was a good, sound man to have the Sixth. But an imaginative soldier, who had followed Casimir Pulaski's red-silk banner "with the strange device" of an all-seeing eye surrounded by a circle of thirteen white stars,[20] was also a man likely to be intrigued by the idea of equipping Fort McHenry with the world's biggest battle flag.

All this does not exclude John Stricker. Certainly he, too, was intrigued, and his active interest may indicate that he was not merely seconding somebody else's notion. Indeed, the only first-hand evidence includes him and omits McDonald,[31] but the evidence is not conclusive. When the two brothers-in-law went to call on their kinswoman in Albemarle street, it was natural and easy for them to pick up Will McDonald on the way. Natural, because he was the senior of the five regimental commanders in the Third brigade,[32] and the Third was Stricker's. Easy, because he was a neighbor of the window: he lived in Pratt street, only four doors west from the Pickersgill house at the corner.[33]

On a midsummer day when the duties of his divided command gave Barney a brief respite from the weeks of gunboat fighting in St. Leonard's Creek and the Patuxent,[34] the general, the commodore and the lieutenant colonel met in Baltimore. Boyhood scenes were close as they walked up Pratt street together: Barney and McDonald could remember when it had been Queen street, in the days before the Revolution. Over the crowding rooftops loomed the dull-red column of a shot tower. Two squares to the left was Baltimore street—it had been Market street then—where Count Pulaski flew his crimson banner with its misspelled Latin motto [35] over his recruiting office.[36] Down yonder by the wharf sheds, Barney had run up the *Hornet's* colors—"thirteen stripes of red and white, alternately, with the English Union cantoned in the corner." [37] And just over on Front street was the town house of Charles Carroll of Carrollton, who had signed the Declaration that erased the English union from the gridiron flag.

A cellar door, sloping from the red-brick, Flemish-bond wall of the hip-roofed corner house, squeezed the three officers into single file on the meager footwall. They turned left into Albemarle and stopped at the narrow door below the dormer windows. They knocked, the door opened, a woman stood in the doorway. (Thus another thread appears in the pattern. It is a long, strong thread: it weaves the past into the present and into the future as well. It is a feminine thread, it is made of three strands, three women live in the house.

The officers filed in and sat down in the small, neat parlor. They looked at Mary Pickersgill and Mary Pickersgill looked at them. She was a little surprised, perhaps, to receive so imposing a delegation. There is a temptation to dress this scene for the stage, to fill in all the missing lines from the book of the play, to suggest certain suitable off-stage noises. It would be easy to describe Mary's dress, the frilled cap on her head, the quaint little chair that she sat in. A good-looking woman improves any scene: it would be pleasant and possibly useful to say that Mary is lovely. It would be easy, knowing the cast and the set, to furnish the sound effects. There is an old woman, for instance. Old women like rocking chairs; well, then, let her have one. Old women in upstairs rooms like to know what is going on, they listen when visitors come. Rockers creak, so. . . . Off-stage noise of a rocking chair, suddenly silenced: scratch and bump, hitching it two or three inches nearer the bedroom door: the creak beginning again, approving the callers now that their voices have furnished identification. The chair-sound comes and goes as the old woman listens, forgets herself and starts to rock again, and then fetches the chair up indignantly short. There is a young girl, too, and young girls may be heard but not seen. The swish of a broom, perhaps, or the clink of a pot lid, a minor complaint from the crane on the kitchen hearth. It would also be easy to write in bits of mildly humorous business: three not-so-young gentlemen paying a call on a brisk, comely widow should act just a little self-conscious, they should not be too certain about what to do with their hats, they might even indicate that each could have managed this errand much better than three or than two. Even the dialogue would not be too difficult.

Others have written of Mary's "strong womanly beauty." They do not know how she looked. There is no picture of her at thirty-eight. A miniature, made late in her life, shows dark hair parted primly above her nose and drawn down over her temples and under her spectacles' bows. It shows a white frill at her neck and cap ribbons tied under a definite prow of a chin. Her cheekbones make her face broad; either they or the triangle-set of her hair make her forehead narrow. Her nose is as definite as her chin, the nostrils are broad. Under that nose, her mouth looks small, and it turns down at the corners. It is a strong face but, in the miniature, it is not beautiful. It may have been, once.

Artists have made pictures of the scene. They have put uniforms on the men, they have hung epaulets on their shoulders and dangled swords at their belts. They didn't know whether McDonald and Stricker were wearing their uniforms; I don't know, either. Maybe they were, maybe not: the city brigade had not yet been called into service.

Others have written the dialogue. They didn't know what Mary said or what Barney or Stricker said, but they put words into their mouths. They say that when General Stricker asked Mary to make the flag, he spoke "in a tone of voice that he generally used on the battlefield, not in parlors." They say that Mary agreed "with a determined gleam in her eye and cheeks aflame."

I don't know what she said or how she looked when she said it, or whether she wore a frilled cap, or what kind of chair she sat in. They say her widowed mother, Rebecca Flower Young, was visiting at No. 60 Albemarle street that summer; the town directory says that Rebecca Young lived there. I don't know whether Mrs. Young was upstairs or downstairs, or whether she had a rocker. I don't know whether Mary's fourteen-year-old daughter, fatherless now, was doing the sweeping or clinking pot lids in the kitchen. As for John Stricker's battlefield voice . . . well, the parlor is right small for shouting. You can see the house for yourself, but not as it was. The number has been changed and so has the house itself. It is 844 East Pratt street now, and most of the mantels over the fireplaces came from other old homes, and the bathroom and furnace are things Mary Pickersgill never dreamed of. But the ax-hewn timbers and laths are still there and so are the big twin chimneys; there are wooden pegs, not nails, in the window frames; the "odd little cupboards and cubbyholes" still lurk in unexpected corners.

They say that Rebecca Young cut and stitched the striped flag Barney hoisted to gather recruits for the *Hornet.* It is not impossible.[38] The flag was sent down to Baltimore from Philadelphia by Captain Esek Hopkins, who had been chosen commodore of the United Colonies' first battle squadron and was then awaiting his commission.[39] Hopkins has been credited with being the first American naval officer to fly "the flag of America" [40] on an American warship and John Paul Jones, his first lieutenant on the thirty-gun flagship *Alfred,* has been singled out as the first man who actually ran up the "continental" colors to the mizzen peak with his own hands.[41] But it is possible and even probable that the distinctions belong respectively to William Stone, captain of the little

Hornet, and to Joshua Barney, then his second officer "or master's mate." [42] For Baltimore's two contributions to the first American navy, the *Hornet* and the *Wasp,* sailed from the Patapsco in November of 1775 and were "the first regular cruisers that went to sea under the new government." [43] The other five ships of the fleet "were first fitted out" in the Delaware on December 3rd; their officers "did not receive their commissions until December 22," and the Grand Union flag "was probably raised then, or a few days later." [44]

They say that Rebecca Young made the first of those thirteen-striped banners with the red and white crosses of St. George and St. Andrew on the blue field in the corner . . . that she "made the first flag of the Revolution, under Washington's direction" [45] . . . that she "probably" [46] made the flag that Washington raised on Prospect Hill in Charlestown on January 1st or 2nd "in compliment to the United Colonies." [47] This, too, is possible. Even the "probably" may be justified. There is as much evidence to support it as there is to support the Betsy Ross tradition. Furthermore, the evidence contains none of the discrepancies of time and place that cast doubt on the legend of Elizabeth Griscom Ross. [48]

Long before Joshua Barney and John Stricker came to Philadelphia to court Gunning Bedford's daughters, the wife of one William Young had established herself there as a professional maker of flags. Her paid notice was printed in the *Advertiser:*

> COLOURS
>
> For the Army and Navy made and sold on the most reasonable terms.
>
>   *Rebecca Young*
> in Walnut Street, near Third Street, and next door but one to Mr. Samuel McLane's.
> N. B.—Any person having Bunting for sale may hear of a purchaser by applying as above.

In the fall of 1775, Rebecca Young already had five children and was soon to have another. Captain Esek Hopkins was wheedling, arguing and pleading for men, guns and stores for his five ships, lying in the river. Down in Maryland, a young gentleman named Sam Smith was a sergeant in a new militia company; George Stricker was sounding out the neighbors on the matter of going to the war and his son John was watching the likeliest recruits take turns at shooting a piece of clapboard from between one another's legs; and sixteen-year-old Josh Barney was stepping ashore at Baltimore after a nine-month voyage which he had begun as an apprentice and concluded as a captain just in time to volunteer for service in the embryo navy. Up in Massachusetts, an amateur general named Washington was simultaneously beseiging Boston and conferring with a committee of Congress on the multitudinous problems "touching the most effectual method of continuing, supporting and regulating a Continental Army." On November 1st, the committee was back in Philadelphia, full of solutions and resolutions. Among them were the specifications for a flag of the united colonies,[49] to replace the Joseph's coat of colors whose red crosses, pine trees, coiled and uncoiled serpents, anchors, stars and crescents only emphasized the lack of unity.

At least one flag in the new design was cut out, basted, stitched, hemmed and headed and was on its way to Baltimore within three weeks after the return of the committee. Barney was using it for recruiting purposes no later than the last week of November.[50] Early in December—sooner, perhaps—Esek Hopkins's whole fleet had the new "Saint George's ensign with stripes." And by Christmastime the "continental" standard that would greet the New Year in the camp of Washington's army was on the way to Cambridge.

The swiftness with which the multiple birth of the Grand Union flag followed its conception suggests the handiwork of a professional. But the Baltimore tradition that America's first national colors [51] came from Becky Young's skilled fingers rests on something more substantial than suggestion. It rests on one piece of direct evidence—not absolute proof, but the positive testimony of a witness whose competence has not been challenged. The witness is Becky Young's granddaughter, Caroline Pickersgill. There are no reservations in the letter she wrote to George Armistead's daughter, Georgianna: "My grandmother, Rebecca Young, made the first flag of the Revolution, under Washington's direction." [52] Then she added that "for this reason" Commodore Barney and General Stricker "selected" Becky Young's daughter—Caroline's mother—to make the flag that became "the star-spangled banner" when "the dawn's early light" crept over the Patapsco River after two days and nights of battle.

There is other evidence—again, not positive proof, but the corroborative evidence of facts that make tradition plausible. It is in no way remarkable that a Congressional committee in Philadelphia should turn to Becky Young for such a service. She was not a nobody. Her husband might not be a man of note; she might have a houseful of children; hard cash might be none too plentiful. But Becky was a Flower, and in Philadelphia the Flowers were "well connected." They were also at least moderately well-to-do: an "amiable niece" would leave her a legacy of a thousand pounds, no trifling sum in those days.[53] And in a city where many of the first families would welcome the victorious British army with open doors and bottles—and their daughters would welcome the fascinating British officers with open arms—the "sentiments" of the Flowers were above suspicion. Dr. Benjamin Rush, who would sign the Declaration, was a good friend to Becky.[54] Her brother—another Benjamin—was a colonel in the new army and "commissary of the military stores." Charles Willson Peale would paint his portrait.[55] General Washington would send him "a handsome sword" and a letter praising him "for the Masterly Retreat from Philadelphia, when attacked by Howe, September, 1777, and in saving the military stores and magazines of the army, and successfully removing also, the blankets, shoes and clothing, so much needed by the army at that time."[56] In the Peale portrait, Colonel Flower holds the precious letter in his hand, while all around him are symbolic powder casks, ammunition chests, field guns and dismounted barrels for field guns, and one enormous mortar. Tradition says that he not only saved the military stores by concealing them "down the Allentown Road" but also preserved the Liberty Bell by hiding it "in Allentown Reformed Church."

While Ben Flower was winning his citation, his sister was a refugee. The Youngs were fleeing, bag, baggage and six little baggages. The smallest baggage, Mary, was nineteen months old; she had been born on February 12, 1776, three months after the birth of the Grand Union flag.

That flight from Philadelphia was duly entered in the family Bible.[57] On one of the less-torn and discolored pages Becky's husband wrote: "When the British attacked Philadelphia, September, 1777, William Young, his wife Rebecca and family fled in an oxcart. Being closely pursued they hid a chest containing their silver, with this Bible. But months afterward the chest was found broken open and despoiled of its contents. The Bible was found on the ground saturated with rain, and much torn."

In the last week of that same September, a young gentleman named Sam Smith—not so elegant now, and not a sergeant of society militia but lieutenant colonel of Continental regulars—was floundering through the smelly mud of an island in the Delaware, longing

for his own Maryland troops and wondering how he could keep
the British fleet away from Philadelphia with a fort made of pine
posts and loose fieldstones and with a sickly, shoeless, sockless garrison that knew nothing about cannon and preferred not to learn.

The oxcart jolted all the way to Lebanon. Nine months later,
Becky and her brood were still there, and Becky was a widow. The
enemy had evacuated Philadelphia and brother Ben had ridden into
town behind their rear guard. Ben was busy. Washington was
marching from Valley Forge to strike Clinton's army, the battle of
Monmouth would be fought in three days, a commissary colonel
had responsibilities. Besides, Ben was in love with a girl called
Delia, he was making wedding plans; but he also loved his "dear
sister" and he had plans for her, too. On June 25th he was dashing
off a letter "To Mistress Rebecca Young, Lebanon, Favour of
Major French."

"I hope it may be in my power," he wrote, "to provide a house
for you here before many days . . . but many are made so dirty by
the enemy that they are not fit to live in . . . I hope to get two
houses near Mrs. Hobart—one for you and the other for Delia
and Thyrsis [Ben himself, full of hope and romance] who expect
to be united in that tenderest and dearest of all Human ties before
long . . . but how chequered is the Life of man . . . nor can he
command events." Then he turned from love and philosophizing to
the campaign just beginning: "There has been heard very Heavy
firing of cannon all the morning . . . the Enemy have sent their
Baggage on before them to South Amboy, a body of our Light
troops have gone after them." He was as optimistic about war as
he was about real estate and marriage. "There is the greatest probability of that Army being ruined before they get to New York,
but it is the general opinion whether they are or not, this campaign
will conclude all wars in America—then we may be happy."

Another letter followed. Washington had struck, but Clinton's
army was not ruined. Charles Lee was facing a court-martial for the
inexplicable conduct that had delayed and weakened the blow The
war would go on and on through many more campaigns. But Ben
had found "a very pleasant and convenient" house in the neighbor
hood where he had hoped to find it—"opposite Mrs. Hobart." He
had "desired Major Gastelowe to send your furniture," he thought
Becky could be settled in her new home within two weeks. Then,
he said, he intended "to bring little Nancy down." Nancy was his
daughter by a previous marriage—the "amiable niece" who later left

Rebecca the five thousand dollars. "Besides," he added casually, "Delia and I intend to live with you." [58]

Becky came back to Philadelphia with her children and settled down to the business of making "colours for the Army and Navy . . . on the most reasonable terms." The flags were different now; the "Grand Union" had been erased by a resolution of the Congress on June 14, 1777, three months before the flight; where the crosses of St. Andrew and St. George had been, thirteen white stars now represented "a new constellation." The constellation was variable. Sometimes twelve stars formed a circle, with the thirteenth in the center; sometimes they were ranged in rows; sometimes—rarely—they made an arch across the blue field. The army might march itself gaunt, it might be starved until its ribs were racks of bones with skin stretched over them to dry, it might tramp the soles out of its shoes and lose its last shirt at the wash—if any—and burst its overalls until its sharp knees and its meager haunches were scandalously naked. But every skeleton regiment must have its flag, the raggedest battalion must have one piece of whole cloth. Even the militia companies that vanished at harvest time and turned out again after the spring planting must have a muster flag. Not even a blockaded ship could do without its colors. Times were not too bad in the pleasant and convenient house next door but one to Mr. Samuel McLane's.

But Ben Flower's philosophizing had contained more truth than his prophesying. He could not "command events": three years after Becky read his optimistic letter, he was dead, at thirty-three. And so "chequered is the Life of man" that his plans for her were drastically changed. Perhaps the thousand dollars he left her at his death made the change possible. The Flowers had "ties" in Maryland; Becky's father was buried there; in the spring of 1788, her good friend the doctor, Benjamin Rush, was writing to her in Baltimore about a younger Benjamin. [59] "In the present healthy season," he was saying, "I have consented to your son's visiting you, in order to obtain your advice respecting his future settlement in life." Ben Young was studying medicine and his mentor was well pleased with his progress. "I have seldom turned out a young man of one and twenty equal to him," Dr. Rush went on. "I have no scruples in recommending him as equal to the duties of his profession, nor am I afraid of his conduct. He has some follies but no vices, and of them, age and experience will be the only remedies. His good temper and obliging behavior have procured him many friends in my circle of business. All my family love him." The "healthy season" meant fewer patients for Dr. Rush: he could spare his promising apprentice. And he would soon have to get along without him: there was news of an "invitation" received by young Dr. Ben "from several of the leading gentlemen of Northumberland County to settle among them."

It was a heart-warming letter. Life was going on. There was still happiness in living. The Widow Young's son, namesake of her well-loved brother, had his foot firm on the doorsill of success; her youngest daughter was stepping across the doorsill of her own home, a bride. Mary, the girl-child stirring in Rebecca's womb when her flying fingers stitched the stripes of the Grand Union flag, was married at nineteen, in St. Paul's Church in Baltimore, to John Pickersgill. At twenty-one she, too, was mother of a girl-child. The baby died. Two years later another girl was born and died in a few weeks. Mary's third daughter, Caroline, was born on June 12, 1800, but the checkered pattern continued to change: in five years, Caroline was fatherless: John Pickersgill was dead in London. The red-brick house at 60 Albemarle street became the Widow Pickersgill's—a house in which two women lived with their memories and the memories became a small girl's lessons in both history and sewing.

Memories are good, even the bad ones are good, they are better than nothing, they are better than not to have known what life is. But you can't touch them, they don't give the chair at the head of the table a backward shove and stand up to carve the roast goose, they don't drop one boot with a thump and then set the other one down with self-conscious and still louder caution, they don't fill the tub too full on Saturday night, they don't splash the water all over the kitchen floor. You can't warm your feet, chilly nights, on a memory's back.

Women fill houses with talk, they fill them with broom sounds and skirt sounds, sometimes they slam doors and bang kettles; but the houses are empty without their men. They are woman-houses, no matter how hard they try. But there's this: women live longer than men. The women at 60 Albemarle street have outlived their men. Their names are the names the men gave them in marriage, but the men themselves mean nothing, they only married and knew their wives and then died. The names would have died with the men if they had not become woman-names. You would scarcely expect that small woman-house to outlive the imposing man-houses

—Belvedere, Montebello. The dormer window on Pratt street had been looking out at the harbor in time to see the old *Constellation* riding at her first anchor, before she got either her guns or her topmasts: it had been watching the harbor four years when young Johnny Rodgers arrived in town to recruit the first crew for the frigate. The house was built in 1793, the year Sam Smith bought the first parcel of land for his Montebello, miles out on the spacious hills where the town never could crowd it. The town did not crowd Montebello: it merely swept over the broad-shouldered, masculine mansion, merely swept it away and forgot it. But the widow's house . . . woman-house with the sloping shoulders, the slender woman-shoulders crowded and jostled and shrinking and all but lost in the crowd . . . the little-old-lady-house is still there, protected as little old ladies should be, cared for as Colonel Ben Flower had intended to care for his sister.

You would scarcely expect strips of cloth cut out in "the second front room" of the house to outlive the fleet they defied. You would scarcely expect woman-stitches to outlast the iron guns. But the ships are rotted and gone, and the guns are gone. The stitches are still in the cloth. The cloth is shelltorn and faded, but "the star-spangled banner" from 60 Albemarle street is as nearly immortal as anything earthly can be. Perhaps Mary Pickersgill's callers spoke of a "star-spangled" flag. The chances are that they didn't, although the expression had already been invented: young Mr. Key had used it ten years ago in a song, but the song had failed to catch on.[60] Whatever the visitors said, they left with their errand accomplished.

The widow was left with two errands. There was the bunting to buy, and the thread. Let me see . . . It will take . . . Caroline Pickersgill told Georgianna Appleton a good many details about the making of the flag for Fort McHenry, but she neglected to say whether her mother pursed her lips while she figured or whether she frowned or looked at the Wedgwood pitcher or asked Grandma Young's advice. It is too bad. All Caroline said was that she thought the flag "contained 400 yards." To find the material, even in such wholesale quantity, was not a difficult problem. Baltimore with its hundreds of ships was a flag-minded town, its shop shelves were always well stocked with fat colorful bolts; now, with the blockade closed down in earnest, the ships tied up and the market for bunting off, the shops had a plenty on hand. Four hundred yards of stout goods would be bulky and heavy to carry, but that could be managed. The serious problem was space. Thirty-six feet . . . there wasn't a room in the house where even the short upper stripes of a flag like that could be laid out for basting. A warehouse, perhaps . . . there might be one with an empty attic . . . but the warehouses were gorged with goods that couldn't be shipped. Or a sail loft . . . inches deep in dust, as likely as not . . . and a sail loft right under the roof, in this awful heat . . . one of the wharf sheds . . . the mud smelled bad when the tide was out . . . and the rats . . .

Mary Pickersgill found her work room in Clagett's brewery just up the street, across from Charles Carroll's fine house. The brewery's malthouse was ample and cool; they gave her permission to use it. The cutting, however, was done in the "second front room" at home. There is no witness to testify that Rebecca Young sat and watched while her daughter covered the chairs and the pegged window sills and the scrub-veined floor with billows of bunting, there is no one to swear that the old woman talked and talked of the days when she cut the red and white stripes for the first flag of the Union. But even history cannot expect too much: it cannot expect Becky Young not to watch and to talk, although there is negative evidence that she stayed at home when the cutting was finished. The evidence that Mary and Caroline went to the malthouse together is positive and direct.

Day after day and night after night through the hot midsummer weather, the Widow Pickersgill knelt on the brewery floor, basting and stitching the endless rolls, crawling over the blue field—itself as big as a carpet—to lay the fifteen great stars in their rows of three. At night, while the candles did what they could to keep the darkness pushed into the corners, it was like crawling over the sky itself by the light of a clouded moon. "I remember," Caroline told Georgianna, "seeing my mother down on her knees placing the stars in position and sewing them fast." It was like having a hand in creation. "I assisted her," Caroline said.

Night after night it was twelve o'clock [61] when mother and daughter rolled up the unfinished flag and walked down the silent street past the Carroll house to their own. They were tired. It was painstaking, wearisome business: every seam must be as strong as the seams of a frigate's mainsail to bear the sheer weight of the cloth. Tomorrow would be another seam. They had a "given time" in which to finish their work, but they did not know how much time Baltimore had been given. Tomorrow . . . day after tomorrow . . . next week . . . or the next there might be no malthouse at Clagett's, no Carroll mansion, no home. The Clagetts themselves might be dead, the neighbor and the kinsmen who had ordered the flag might be dead. (One Clagett would be killed at McHenry, under the flag. Another would go down, wounded, in Godly Wood. Joshua Barney's Bladensburg bullet would stay in his thigh for four years, and through the last night of his life would torment him with violent spasms.) [62] Mary Pickersgill and her daughter would know these things, in their time. They would never know that their aching fingers had given a nation its anthem. [63]

16

THE LAST DAYS OF GRACE

THE CAPTAINS AND THE KING HAD failed. Prayer, prophecy and profanity had not prevailed against the enemy in the Potomac. Neither had the "formidable batteries" nor the "invincible seamen" who had marched from Baltimore to man them.

The sailors might have done much better if they could have used the editors' forty-two-pound adjectives for ammunition, but the enemy preferred to fight with broadside guns and mortars. The impromptu batteries on shore were pathetically unformidable. The ammunition for Perry's antique Revolutionary gun ran out.[1] The squadron that had put Alexandria to ransom towed and shot its way downriver in a five-day running battle and rejoined the fleet with its whole convoy of twenty-one confiscated ships undamaged [2] and their cargoes of "contribution" all intact.

For a little while the Potomac had looked like a trap with Sir James Alexander Gordon's ships inside it. But the trigger was sprung too soon. The trappers, hidden in a hastily built blind, tried to catch an unimportant *Fairy*, lost her, and so lost the best chance that they had to catch a worthwhile *Seahorse*. The eighteen-gun brig-sloop *Fairy*, miraculously missing every shoal and oyster bank in Kettle Bottoms, was flying up the river with an order recalling Captain Gordon from his profitable excursion.[3] She was cleared for action [4] but the Potomac was as peaceful as the English Avon and her men were loafing, watching the trees on the Virginia shore file past the muzzles of the larboard guns and Mount Vernon slowly spread its white wings on the hill ahead.[5]

Suddenly "a large portion of underwood disappeared." [6] Where the brush had been, five cannon [7] poked their noses over banks of dirt. Smoke burst from them, shot *whfffd* through the rigging. The woods huffed and puffed with smaller smoke bursts,[8] ounce balls beat like hammers on the brig's high bulwarks.[9] Men cried and fell. Their blood made neat pools on the even deck. Then the pools were neat no longer, they shivered and flung out small wet tentacles as the *Fairy's* larboard guns let go. The fight was brisk but brief. The brig stood steadily upstream; in minutes, she was safely past the unfinished battery and she was little hurt; her bulwarks had saved her "from a severe loss." [10] "Early in the morning" of August 31st she was dropping anchor at Alexandria and her captain was hurrying aboard the *Seahorse* to tell Gordon about the trap waiting at the "White House."

Gordon acted promptly. Back down the river went the *Fairy*, reinforced by "the *Meteor* bomb, a gun-boat and a mortar-boat." [11] More underbrush had disappeared, the piles of fresh earth on the Virginia shore had lengthened, there were more guns behind them. The British cut loose with everything they had, and even these small boats had more than the Americans. Militia from the Virginia countryside popped away with muskets; some of the shipless seamen of the *Guerriere* answered the *Fairy's* thirty-two-pound heavies [12] with twelve-pounder field guns,[13] but most of them kept on digging while the mortar shells burst over them and solid shot knocked tons of dirt out of their barbettes. The tons of dirt made little difference, the hasty earthworks had no shape worth fretting over. Captain Baker of the *Fairy* had to send word back to Gordon that "notwithstanding all our exertions" the Yankees had "succeeded in mounting eleven guns and building a furnace for heating shot."[14] (Even Virginians were Yankees, then, to Englishmen.)

Captain Gordon was not happy. The trap was beginning to look serious; the wind was against him; his men were scattered along miles of river, toiling at the towing hawsers of his too-numerous ships. A few miles below Alexandria there was more delay and trouble: the bomb ship *Devastation* went hard aground and the squadron had to anchor to protect her.[15] As she lay there, a flotilla of eight boats came sweeping downstream toward her. Five were rowboats scrounged from the Alexandria water front, three were small craft loaded with combustibles.[16] The crew of the stranded bomb ship tumbled into their own boats and pulled to meet them; gigs and barges pushed off from the frigates. There was a hot skirmish, growing hotter as flames broke out on the fireboats. A midshipman of the *Seahorse* grappled the nearest and most dangerous and towed it ashore, harmless. The *Devastation's* seamen fended off the others and sent them drifting futilely away. The makeshift flotilla fled, pursued "up to Alexandria"[17] by superior numbers.

The attack had been John Rodgers's.[18] The navy's senior officer had failed.

Two days later the *Erebus* and the *Aetna* got down to join the *Fairy* and her consorts. Rockets began to gouge the dirt piles and harass the diggers, the ponderous rain of mortar shells redoubled. In another twenty-four hours the Potomac was choked with the whole convoy of prizes "assembled under Mount Vernon"[19] and the two frigates were pounding at the White House battery with forty-seven more guns.[20] The sailors of the *Guerriere* were pounding back with their eleven, most of them much smaller. The *Erebus* moved in to rake the trenches with her rockets. The gunners wheeled up three fieldpieces; the ships' guns concentrated on them, smothered them and drove them off; but before they went they "did the ship [the *Erebus*] considerable injury."[21]

Five miles upstream the *Devastation* was still aground, and now she called for help: the Americans were preparing to try once more to burn her. The attack came at night. As Rodgers's small boats crept in, they ran headlong upon the whole smallboat flotilla of the squadron hurrying to the rescue. Outnumbered again, the Americans again retreated; but this time they did not lose their fireboats, they hid them in a creek mouth in deep woods to wait for another chance. The British found them there and instantly attacked, pulling on gallantly into musket fire that ripped out from the woods and swept them off the thwarts. The second lieutenant of the *Fairy*, which had found and sprung the first trap, lost his life in this one. Eight or ten other men were dead or dying in the splintered boats when the attack recoiled.[22] But Rodgers had failed again: the *Devastation*, covered by the retreating flotilla, had escaped downstream.

The Potomac was still a trap. Gordon's fighting ships could run the batteries without too much damage, but so long as the guns at the White House were still in action the long train of prizes probably would be knocked into driftwood. Gordon was in the predicament of a man with his fist in a jugful of shillings. He couldn't get his hand out unless he dropped the shillings—or smashed the jug. He made up his mind to smash it.

At noon the next day, with a fair wind behind,[23] the squadron stood down toward the batteries in line of battle. The *Seahorse* and the *Euryalus*, leading, anchored within musket shot and opened with full broadsides. The three bombships, following, steered past the frigates. As they came abreast the gun positions, they yawed; their prows turned briefly shoreward; their huge mortars roared by pairs, the two explosions of each pair not quite together but as close as crash and echo. Three double smoke clouds swirled up. Enormous thunder rolled. Lead rain pelted on the earthworks. No poet's license is required to use that hackneyed phrase. The mortars were crammed with musket balls, with whole kegs of musket balls.[24]

Behind the bomb ships came the *Fairy*, her starboard side ablaze with her gun flashes. Then the *Erebus*, firing sheaves of rockets. Then the gunboats, the howitzer boat, the small mortar boat, the dispatch boat, the tenders and the swarm of prizes—like a parade of little ducks behind their mothers—filed past in the shelter of the frigates. The *Fairy*, *Aetna*, *Meteor*, *Devastation* and *Erebus* dropped anchor in line down the river to extend the shelter. The whole squadron was thundering at the earthworks now. The earthworks were still answering with a puny thunder that was only a faint, exhausted echo of the ships' storm.

It was the best eleven guns could do against Gordon's seventy-five broadside guns and his seven mortars.[25] It was stubborn: it went on for nearly three hours. It was useless: the militia sniping from behind trees did more damage through the gun ports than

the field guns could do against the stout ship timbers.[26] The firing
from the earthworks weakened as gun after gun was silenced. By
midafternoon it was all over, the last gun was out of action.[27] The
frigates slipped their cables [28] and dropped down. The whole convoy followed. Over the plowed, harrowed, bullet-seeded hillside,
a flag still floated as the last ship disappeared. It was David Porter's
old flag, long, white, with his battle motto on it—"Free Trade and
Sailors' Rights." It had swept the Pacific and had hung, limp,
quivering, in the concussion shaken air above the shuddering and
helpless *Essex* in Valparaiso bay. Fifty years in the future, another
David Porter, commanding mortar boats, would run the batteries
at New Orleans and Vicksburg. His father, perhaps, had told him
that it could be done.

For this was David Porter's battle. And he, too, had failed.

The tired men on Gordon's ships "calculated all was over for
that day." [29] They were wrong. The squadron was several miles
below the White House and the sun was low when lookouts on the
frigates saw the smaller ships thrown suddenly into confusion. They
were dropping anchor every which way. The rocket ship, already
punished, was again in trouble. There were cannon on the cliffs of
Indian Head, and the *Erebus* had picked out a shoal in front of
them. She was stuck fast, a target. The guns reached for her,
found her, began knocking splinters out of her. The tough, tubby
Fairy pushed in bravely to save the *Erebus* by drawing the fire
upon herself.[30] *Aetna, Meteor* and *Devastation* flung their bombs
high to burst above the cliffs "with admirable precision." [31] The
frigates elevated their guns to the last notch their quoins could give
them. One by one the guns in the American batteries ceased firing.
Only one, heavier, kept up its pounding.[32] By eight in the evening,[33] when the *Erebus* at last got off the shoal "considerably"
hurt,[34] that one last gun fell silent. Gordon thought that he had
probably done for all of them.

They were done for, but the doing was not Gordon's. In spite
of the "admirable precision" of his fire, not one Yankee had been
hit. In the works on Indian Head, Oliver Hazard Perry was thinking miserably unhappy thoughts about a government that expected its officers to fight battles without decent guns, without
powder for even the one halfway decent gun that he had resur-
rected. The batteries he found at Indian Head were mounted with
useless six-pounders . . . even more useless to stop ships of war than
the Baltimore six-pounders had been to stop the 85th Foot at

Bladensburg . . . worse than useless, because they burned up precious powder to no purpose. He had heard of an old eighteen-pounder, twenty miles away,[35] He had found it, a survivor of the Revolution. He had dragged it to the unfinished earthworks as he had dragged a fleet up the Niagara River, by sheer muscle, nerve and desperation. He had "aimed and fired" it himself [36] until the last powder charge was gone and history could say that he was "overwhelmed" and "compelled to retire" [37] and that his batteries were "completely silenced" [38] by Gordon's "vigorous measures." The batteries were silenced, there is no doubt of that. That Perry was "overwhelmed" by the reason is not beyond belief.

Gordon himself was not so positive as some historians have been that the American guns were permanently silenced and "the whole of the parties on shore" so "satisfied that their opposition was ineffectual" that they would allow his ships to pass "without further molestation." [39] He did not choose to take the risk of running those "silenced" batteries by twilight; he kept his warships and his prizes where they were all night. In the morning, the *Seahorse* led the battle line down to attack again and Gordon was "agreeably surprised at being allowed to pass quietly." [40] It took the captain of the *Euryalus* to do Perry justice. "We ascertained afterwards," he wrote, "that the batteries were hardly finished, and the powder and shot had been expended the night before." [41]

But no matter what the reason, the hero of Lake Erie, too, had failed.

The news that came to Baltimore was astounding. The accumulation of failure was unbelievable. It was sickening. It made a man's heart sink like a scuttled ship.

Then the news was worse. The enemy's fleet was coming up the bay. There was no false alarm about it this time: the horse telegraph had fetched the message. "Twenty-six sail" had passed Point Lookout on Monday, September 5th. By four o'clock Thursday afternoon, thirty more vessels had been counted "beating up the Chesapeake"—twenty-one ships, six brigs, three smaller craft [42] that probably were tenders, mortar boats or gunboats. Fifty-six ships! Battleships . . . the great eighty-gun *Tonnant* [43] . . . the *Dragon*, the *Albion*, the *Royal Oak*, each carrying seventy-four guns or more. Frigates . . . bombs . . . rocket ships . . . transports packed with soldiers . . . gun brigs to run close in to the shore and cover the soldiers' landing with point-blank fire. If Rodgers, Porter and

Perry could do nothing against six ships, what could Sam Smith do against fifty-six?

Sam Smith had done what he could. It was not all that ought to be done. Being a commanding general was a good deal like being Job—if you had Job's patience. It wasn't a matter of waving a sword and leading a charge in a steel engraving, it wasn't shouting commands in a "battlefield voice," it wasn't maneuvering troops in neat blocks of regiments and brigades. It was being afflicted with infinite details of this and that. The details didn't come in neat blocks, they came swarming like country militia, like levies of drafted men, like flies buzzing and buzzing and driving you crazy. You did the best that you could and tried not to go crazy.

Men have to be fed. J. Winchell at 59 South street has an idea about that. He has put an ad in the paper, addressed to "colonels of regiments and captains of companies, now on service in Baltimore." [44] Calling himself "the subscriber," he "respectfully announces to officers of the above description, that he will bake and deliver for the men under their command, Bread of any description agreeably to order—and will receive flour in pay, pound for pound." The ad isn't respectful to the commanding general. J. Winchell probably means well, but he is a civilian, he has gone over the general's head. Mr. Winchell may not be a profiteer; we can't call him that, the word hasn't yet been invented. But flour in payment for bread, pound for pound, looks like a right high price. A commanding general can't let his men go hungry, but he can't let them be gouged. And where is a company commander to get the flour? If all the company commanders in the army spend their time hunting for flour to trade with J. Winchell, their companies will get precious little drill. There must be a better way. There is. On the 3rd of September, there is a contract with Francis W. Bolgiano to bake bread for the troops. [45]

Men have to sleep. You can't tell them to sleep in the streets; but there aren't enough barracks, there aren't enough tents; you've got to do something about it. Sam Smith calls on the Committee of Vigilance and Safety to build sheds. Robert Long, master carpenter employing thirty "exempts," transforms his whole pay roll into a muster roll; he forms his employees into a volunteer company and goes to work, hammer and nails; raw-looking "shed-barracks" begin to spring up overnight in the vacant lots. But they aren't enough. Sam Smith seizes a ropewalk and turns it into a barracks; the owners object; the commanding general receives written notice that the owners hold him personally responsible for depriving them of their property and for any damage incurred in the defense of the city.

British deserters are drifting into town. The constable is keeping an eye on four sailors from Cockburn's fleet, but some of the townfolk are uncomfortable about them. Do something to reassure the jittery citizens. Ask the committee for money to have the deserters "conveyed beyond the Susquehanna" and give them two dollars apiece and turn them loose.

There are other strange faces in the streets. The town doesn't like them; its nerves are on edge. There are rumors that less than a week before Ross marched into Washington, one of his officers visited the capital and even "called on Mrs. Madison in the president's house in the disguise of a distressed woman." [46] Do something about the strange faces. Daniel Conner, for "a compensation to be hereafter agreed upon," is requested "vigilantly to search for all suspected strangers or other persons, and in a discreet exercise of this authority, to report such persons to, or bring them before the mayor." Will Presbury, justice of the peace at Fell's Point, is not a stranger but he is suspected: he is accused of disloyalty and the governor is asked to remove him from office.

No sooner is one problem solved than it comes unsolved. Mr. Bolgiano is baking an enormous quantity of bread, but it quickly develops that quantity isn't enough. Bread will sustain life, but obviously it will not sustain morale very long. This is a free country; free men have a right to be choosy about their menus; the patriots mustering to defend their country choose something to eat besides Frank Bolgiano's loaves. The trouble is that supplies of something else, anything else, are running alarmingly short. The countrymen [47] are no longer coming to market; they have heard that Sam Smith is helping himself to whatever he needs for his war—seizing lumber and ropewalks and ships, impressing horses and wagons, ordering people around and making them dig. You've got to find some means of persuading the farmers to bring their produce to town; perhaps you can tempt them with handbills. The handbills say that Baltimore "reposes unlimited confidence in the disposition of the good people of this and neighboring states who are not employed in a military capacity" and therefore "confidently" calls upon them "to bring to the city *for sale* such supplies as may contribute to the comfort of those to whom, under Providence, the safety of this city is confided." The commanding general has given absolute assurance that "those who visit our city with the laudable intention of contributing to the comforts of its brave defenders . . . shall be permitted to transact their business free from the danger of impressment to their wagons, carts or horses or of any species of interruption to themselves."

The concentration of thousands of untrained, undisciplined men in a small town breeds trouble. Some of them are bound to get drunk. They roar and carouse in the streets, they break windows and get into fights in the taverns. The Committee of Vigilance and Safety orders the grogshops and taverns—"except those for the accomodations of Travellers"—to close up at 9 P.M. and stay closed all night. It is no reflection on the capacity of these patriots to assume that some of them can drink enough between sunrise and 9 P.M. to become "elevated," but even the committee of safety is not so bold as to shut off the liquor in daytime. Instead, it increases the town watch. It also provides the commanding general with a detachment of military police: it orders up three companies of men unfit for combat duty and assigns them to patrol the city every night.

This problem of whisky is not the worst of the commanding general's headaches. Not all the citizens of Baltimore are willing to dig trenches for nothing. Now that Hampstead Hill has been fortified, Sam Smith wants breastworks built across the North Point road; the committee undertakes to hire laborers and to furnish them "with provisions and other necessaries." The other necessaries are "apparently liquor." The laborers, too, believe in being well fortified.

Sam Smith cannot forget for a minute the risk he is taking in concentrating his defenses on the "eastern front." He is not allowed to forget it. Indignant protests pour in from the other three sides of the city. Every citizen, it seems, has become a military expert; every householder is able to see clearly that *his* home is the enemy's prime objective; every man who has helped to dig a redoubt on Hampstead Hill wants an equally strong redoubt in his own back yard and at least one twenty-four-pounder gun, although two would be better.

The anxious clamor is not wholly beyond reason, it is merely beyond Sam Smith's capacity to satisfy it. He knows, better than the signers of the protests, how dangerous it is to leave three-fourths of the city's perimeter unprotected. He knows, too, that even if he had the time and the men to surround the town with redoubts, he would have no big guns to mount in them. He has been a provident military housekeeper. He has mended and improvised, bought and begged and borrowed until he has managed to lay in a right large supply of artillery—more than a hundred pieces. Armistead, down at McHenry, has a respectable number; the trouble is that they aren't the right kind, their range is too short, and the right kind cannot be had. There are enough heavy guns to equip the redoubts on McHenry's right flank and enough to equip the entrenchments on Hampstead Hill; the trouble is that when they are put there they have to stay. Most of them are naval guns mounted on ponderous ship trucks; they have wheels but the pudgy diminutive wheels are fit only for riding out the recoil on a smooth plank deck; they were never intended for roads. Others have no wheels at all; they are cradled on hastily carpentered platforms with pieces of ship spars laid under the platforms for rollers. If the enemy chooses to attack from some other direction, these guns can't be shifted in time.

What Sam Smith needs desperately is more mobile artillery . . . field batteries . . . horse artillery that can be sent at a gallop to any threatened point. Surely the War Department, if it can do nothing else, can find him a few more field guns.

The War Department has a better idea. It decides to take away some of the guns he has. Checking its records, it discovers that Baltimore is preparing to defend itself with nineteen field guns that are the property of the federal government. The War Department orders Major General Smith to return them at once.

It is bad enough to have Will Winder on his hands, it is bad enough to have to use one of his hands to keep Winder from taking away his command. Now he must use his other hand to hold on to his guns. He has no intention of obeying the order. Having defied the federal authority by superseding his superior officer, he has little or nothing to lose by defying it again. And he has not lost his nice sense of the thing to do. In the contest with Winder he had been direct and brutal, he had delivered a frontal attack for its shock effect while maneuvering to outflank him through the Committee of Vigilance and Safety and the governor. He chose, now, different tactics: no attack, no resistance: only maneuver. He did not refuse to surrender the guns. He presented the obvious reason for holding on to them—that they were needed to beat off the enemy—but he did not rely on that reason. It was much too sensible to be effective. He presented another so casuistic that it was bound to appeal to a bureaucrat. He explained that the *barrels* of the guns were, indeed, the property of the federal government, but that the *carriages* were the property of the city of Baltimore. There would be some little difficulty about moving the guns without their wheels; for the time being, therefore, he would be obliged to keep them.

He turned again to the clamoring town. The attack of nerves was serious. If it couldn't be cured, it would spread, it would make the militia too jumpy for any use; he would have to do something to quiet Baltimore's nerves. But more serious was the fact that the town's fears were justified. If it understood fully the weakness of its position, its clamor would be much louder.

Its military position was weak because even its fortified eastern front was split up into pieces by nature. The defenses on Hampstead Hill were cut off from Fort McHenry and its flanking batteries by the long, deep gash of the Northwest Branch and the Basin. The fort and the batteries were cut off from Cromwell's Point by the broad Ferry Branch. It would take hours to move infantry and field guns from Hampstead Hill, through the city streets and around the head of the Basin, to reinforce the garrisons in the redoubts on the Ferry shore.

Sam Smith worked out solutions for both problems and applied them simultaneously. On Saturday, September 3rd, he called on the Committee of Vigilance and Safety to "erect" a bridge of scows across the neck of the inner harbor "from Pattersons Wharf, Fells Point, to the nearest land on the opposite shore." The bridge would shorten his communications. It would reduce by more than three miles the distance between the entrenchments on Hampstead Hill and the field works beyond Fort McHenry. It would multiply his infantry and his mobile artillery by the time saved in shifting them from point to point along the divided front. Within forty-eight hours the committee had requisitioned thirty scows.

On the same day, two hundred citizens were relieved from their digging on Hampstead Hill and were assigned, instead, to "commence works of defence on Camp-look-out-Hill, near the Magazine under the direction of Capt. Babcock." The magazine was on the high ground toward the north side of the city; that part of town, at least, was reassured that its defense was not to be neglected. But the Committee of Vigilance went further, under the commanding general's direction. It divided the city into two districts, east and west, and called on "all exempts" to "turn out and labour on the works . . . *in their respective Districts.*"

Sam Smith's combination of physical therapy and applied psychology was a success. Public clamor was smothered under fresh piles of dirt that would never develop into finished breastworks and would never be supplied with guns or garrisons. Baltimore began to recover from its attack of nerves.

But the strain on Sam Smith's nerves is not relaxed. His problems breed like the flies that swarm around the billets of militia outfits that know little—and seem to care less—about the first principles of sanitation. The situation becomes so bad that the Committee of Vigilance and Safety assigns two of its members "to have the nuisance immediately removed from the Circus, which is at present occupied by our Troops."

The troops need everything—tents, blankets, mess pans, canteens, bayonets, cartridges, even muskets. Hundreds of drafted men are coming in empty-handed. Without weapons they are worse than useless, they are a burden, a danger. Sam Smith requisitions muskets from Annapolis. The requisition gets prompt results: a whole wagonload of arms chests rolls into town from the state capital. When the ordnance officers eagerly pry them open, they find that the chests are not filled with muskets: they are packed to the brim with old records!

The town's nerves quiver again. There is no clamor, now, but there is too much loose talk. When the federal government tries to take away nineteen guns and the state government furnishes documents instead of weapons, it is small wonder that some people fall into the "habit of making use of very improper expressions calculated to produce disunion, and to defeat the preparations making for the defence of our City." The Committee of Vigilance and Safety "most earnestly" urges "the good people of the State of Maryland to be extremely circumspect in their communications respecting the movements of the enemy and our preparations and disposition to resist him." It notes "with indignation" that letters "degrading to our character have appeared in some of the distant papers." For "certain individuals" who are not so distant but who are indulging in the expression of "opinions calculated to inspire a belief that Baltimore will be found wanting" in its resistance, there is something stiffer than indignation. There is a special committee of three to investigate "cases of this kind and make an immediate report." When the investigators report that "a certain man named Maxwell has of late conducted himself in a manner so as to excite suspicion that he has or intends to have some intercourse with the enemy," the Committee of Vigilance takes stern action. It orders Maxwell arrested and thrown into jail for the duration of "the present time of alarm."

The committee itself becomes alarmed by the cost of Sam Smith's physical therapy. Captain Babcock, who is superintending "the works" at Camp-look-out, demands a horse. He is losing time, he says, walking from place to place. He gets his horse; and almost immediately he needs laborers, carpenters and mechanics. The committee permits him to hire a hundred and fifty laborers at "not exceeding one dollar per day, they finding their own provisions and liquor," and carpenters and mechanics at a dollar and twenty-five cents. The laborers object strenuously; the committee is forced to retreat; it rescinds the dollar-a-day limit and authorizes the superintendent to hire workmen "upon such terms as he shall think best." But it is apprehensive about Captain Babcock and his elaborate ideas. It sends a deputation to tell Sam Smith that it fears the captain "contemplates Fortification more complete, more costly and requiring more time than . . . the means of this committee will justify." Sam Smith reassures the committee. He is in so deep now that he might as well get in deeper. He sends back word that "the expence would be met by the United States." He hopes he is telling the truth. The "expences" go on and on.

Some of the men who have been called up for militia service have families but no money. The families are beginning to go hungry. A committee of relief is appointed "to ascertain . . . the situation and wants of the families of those called out on the present emergency . . . and distribute from time to time, with judicious care, such aid and comforts as they shall think proper."

There are sick men: find some place to put them. Men will be wounded: find doctors. The civilian committee assigned to provide quarters for the sick and wounded reports that it has "obtained the use of the public hospital" with accommodations "for about one thousand" and that the cost will be "such as this committee should hereafter deem reasonable." Dr. Colin McKenzie is appointed hospital surgeon and is authorized to engage five other doctors as assistants "to be called as needed."

But these militiamen who are about to face death and wounds still don't look like soldiers, they still look more like a mob. If the regiments had bands . . . Money is found "for regimental music."

Money . . . money . . . money. War drank up money like water. The Committee of Vigilance and Safety called for subscriptions. Then it called again: "The subscription paper is still open at the mayor's office . . . the expences to be defrayed are unavoidably large and are for objects deemed by the military authorities indispensable to our safety . . . the subscriptions have been liberal, yet . . . it is apprehended they will be inadequate." They were. The commanding general pledged his beloved Montebello to raise money for supplies and equipment.[48]

He had done what he could. Thinking back, thinking ahead, he was not satisfied. He could see six dozen things still to be done but he couldn't do them. Being a commanding general is a good deal like being a dog with fleas. The people who own the dog may think he's a right good watchdog, but what they think doesn't give him the legs to scratch in six dozen places at once. A scratching dog never seems to get anything done, he never gets through. I haven't *done* very much. I've thought of things to be done and somebody else has done them. I can't blame somebody else if this deal goes sour. I can't blame the committee of safety. I can't blame the town. The committee has worked like the very mischief, it has done everything I asked it to do, I'm under particular obligations to the committee.[49] The whole town has worked like the mischief. And what has been done has been done on my say-so. I'll get the blame if we fail—and I ought to get it. I'm responsible. The town has staked all it's got on my judgment, it hasn't questioned my judgment.

My judgment is that the British will land at North Point. They shouldn't; plain common sense is against it. That's the odd thing: I'm a businessman and business is common sense, but I've gone against common sense. I've staked everything on the idea that the British will do the wrong thing. It makes a man feel like a gambler. I've staked the town on the turn of a card. And it isn't my deal, it's Ross's and Cockburn's deal. All I can do is wait for the card to fall—and keep a sharp eye on the dealer.

That's one thing I learned in the old war and learned the hard way. Long Island . . . the road not watched . . . Putnam and Sullivan not knowing the road was there . . . letting Clinton march right around our left flank and into our rear. The Brandywine . . . and the same thing over again . . . the hidden road and the ford that shouldn't have been there but was . . . the enemy hitting us where he couldn't possibly be but was. I've tried not to make those mistakes. I've got both my flanks in the air but I can't help that. I wish there'd been time to finish the trenches out on North

Point, I wish there'd been time to finish the rifle pits and the gun emplacements around the north side of the town.[50] But there hasn't been time, and that's that. The field works we've got are good as far as they go. George Armistead's pulled down the houses that might interfere with his fire if Ross tries a boat attack up the Ferry Branch.[51] He's strengthened the weakest spots—the best landing spots—with felled trees.[52] I've weighted both flanks down as hard as I can with redoubts. All I can do now is watch them and not let Ross slip around them and catch me napping.

I don't think he will. We've got boats doing sentry-go down the Patapsco, day and night. We've got signal stations on the high ground at the harbor mouth. I've sent a patrol barge as low down the river as need be to see the top of the Ridgely house on North Point. As soon as she catches a signal from Ridgely's steeple she'll hoist a flag and fire a gun and then pull for the fort to report the signal exactly.[53] North Point . . . I keep coming back to that. I'm sure Ross will come that way. But I'm not going to be *cock*sure about it, I'm not going to let him surprise me. We've got Captain Thompson's horse telegraph, and Major Barney is helping him stretch it in every direction. We've got cavalry watching the roads. We've removed every bridge leading into the town.[54]

If I'm wrong . . . if Ross fools me . . . I've got a way to move the troops fast. That bridge of scows we built at the neck of the inner harbor, from Patterson's wharf at Fell's Point to the opposite shore [55] . . . if Ross tries the Ferry Branch or strikes at the upper river, I can shift troops out of the fieldworks and over the bridge in a hurry to meet him.

But he was only Sam Smith, who never had won a battle. The banks sent their money out of the city.

Rodgers and Porter and Perry came back, heartsore with frustration and failure. Their footsore sailors came with them: they had tramped the deep-dust roads faster than Cockburn's ships sailed the bay: now, tired as they were, they marched out to the guns on Hampstead Hill and the guns in the little redoubts in the cove behind Fort McHenry. But Perry was not only heartsick, he was physically ill—"so indisposed and worn out with the fatigue he had experienced on the Potomac" [56] that he was unfit for "an active command." Some men who had kept a bold front until now sent their wives and children away.

The Eleventh brigade was bivouacked behind the entrenchments on Hampstead. But the Eleventh was the Baltimore County brigade, and three weeks ago Tobias Stansbury's farmers had run like their own silly sheep. The Sixth Virginia brigade marched in under General Douglass. But the Sixth hadn't fought at Bladensburg; only the Fairfax regiment [57] had distinguished itself—by being kept waiting for hours while a clerk in the War Department counted its musket flints twice. A company of volunteers under Captain Quantril had marched in from Hagerstown. Three small Pennsylvania towns had sent men; besides the elegant York volunteers, there was Captain Metzger's smart outfit, and Captain Dixon had brought in his company all the way from Marietta high up on the Susquehanna. They were good men, they had come of their own free will. But there weren't many of them, they'd never been under fire, you couldn't tell how they'd fight. The shops closed. Windows were boarded up.

In and around Baltimore there were seven thousand militia, twelve hundred marines and sailors, seven hundred United States regulars—almost nine thousand armed men. But the city was quiet. It was almost too quiet. The Messrs. Briscoe & Patridge were selling out cheap:

GUNPOWDER

50 kegs Dupont & Co. Powder can be sold low, if applied for in a few days.

. . . as if Baltimore's days were numbered, the last days of grace running out. The September weather lay on the town like a blanket. There was a sense of time standing still, a sense of a weight suspended. The new flag over Fort McHenry was almost invisible, large though it was. It drooped in the listless air, without life. The town was so still it seemed lifeless except for the sudden dry rattle of wheels, the sudden harsh rattle of drums. [58]

17

GUNS BEFORE BENEDICTION

THE CLOTHES AND TRINKETS OF the dead men had been sold at auction on the British transports.[1] Suitable arrangements had been worked out for the dead men's women. The auctions were official, the arrangements voluntary. Both were sanctified by custom. An expeditionary force on foreign service took its women with it—women duly married to men of the rank and file; they washed shirts and stockings, sewed on buttons, and provided other comforts. A lieutenant of the 85th was much impressed by the discovery that "one or two" widows of men killed at Bladensburg "had really loved their husbands." [2] They could not be classed as trinkets. Officers and soldiers took up a collection for them. They were transferred to a homebound vessel.

There were not many dead men. Surgeon Hanson Catlett, who helped tend the wounded of both armies, said a British surgeon told him "they had buried about one hundred on the field," and American details sent to dig graves the day after the enemy withdrew from Washington reported "that they also buried fifty or sixty redcoats." [3] Catlett had seen "all . . . who could walk" set out on the retreat to Benedict, he had counted those who had to be abandoned; he estimated the British dead at one hundred and eighty and their wounded at three hundred "besides forty or fifty left" behind in Washington.[4] An officer of the 85th who had fought in all three of the day's engagements put his army's casualties at "about five hundred men." [5] But the officially reported loss was only half that figure—killed, sixty-nine; wounded, one hundred and ninety-one. None of these estimates included the invading army's loss in stragglers, either captured or not captured. American reports, at variance on many other details, agree that prisoners were taken. Deserters wandered into Baltimore. British accounts of the retreat from Washington describe men straying from the ranks, some falling exhausted under the feet of the plodding column, and others throwing themselves down "by the wayside and refusing to proceed farther." [6]

For a "short scuffle" [7] in which only "fifteen hundred" [8] men got into action, even two hundred and sixty casualties were no trifling loss. On the face of the British accounts, it was a loss of more than seventeen per cent of all the men engaged. The truth behind the false face is that two brigades—twenty-five hundred men, not fifteen hundred—were committed to action and that these brigades suffered admitted casualties a little in excess of ten per cent.[9] Their actual loss in dead, wounded and missing almost certainly exceeded twelve per cent.

General Ross and the admirals went to work immediately to make good the loss and to restore the discipline which "a dashing campaign" and a disorderly retreat had "unavoidably weakened." [10] Knapsacks cast aside in the assault and later picked up in a random scramble were sorted out and given to their rightful owners; lost equipment was replaced; and "the clothing, accoutrements and arms of all were carefully cleaned and repaired.[11] Slightly wounded men rejoined their companies; the seriously wounded were transferred to the *Majestic*, frigate, to be sent to Halifax; the permanently crippled and the probably dying were swung aboard the *Iphigenia* to be taken back to England with the news of victory.[12] Cochrane came up in the *Tonnant* from the British base on Tangier Island.[13] Signals flying from his halyards ordered every ship to "send in a return of the number of seamen, independently of marines, which it could afford to land with small arms," [14] and to lose no time in training them for an amphibious attack.

Unwelcome visitors arrived aboard the *Tonnant*. The general and the admirals became unwilling actors in the third episode of the series that was to give the upstart nation they were fighting its "Star-Spangled Banner." For Francis Scott Key had "readily agreed," on Richard West's appeal, to undertake the release of Dr. Beanes, and the president had sanctioned the attempt. Orders had been "immediately issued to the vessel usually employed as a cartel, in communications with the fleet in the Chesapeake, to be made ready without delay; and Mr. John S. Skinner, who was agent for the government for flags of truce and exchange of prisoners, and who was well known as such to the officers of the fleet, was directed to accompany Mr. Key. And as soon as the arrangements were made, he hastened to Baltimore, where the vessel was, to embark. . . ." [15]

The cartel vessel has been sailing, ever since, under a false name. Like a persistent Flying Dutchman she still drifts occasionally across a printed page as *Minden*. The truth is that she had no name. She did not even have a number. Now she has no identity at all; even her rig is unknown, although there is one contemporary reference to "a beautiful schooner" that may possibly have been Key's cartel. If she is to be imagined, she was probably just one more Chesapeake Bay "work boat" not unlike the low, sharp-prowed schooners that lie at Long Dock in Baltimore in summer with deckloads of watermelons. Almost certainly she reached the mouth of the Patuxent and the anchorage of *Tonnant* on September 6th.[16] Key and Skinner went aboard the flagship and were "courteously received by Admiral Cochrane, and the officers of the army, as well as the navy." Then, suddenly, the air chilled. When Key "made known his business, his application was received so coldly that he feared it would fail." [17]

"General Ross and Admiral Cockburn—who accompanied the

expedition to Washington—particularly the latter, spoke of Dr. Beanes in very harsh terms, and seemed at first not disposed to release him. It, however, happened, fortunately, that Mr. Skinner carried letters from the wounded British officers left at Bladensburg; and in these letters to their friends on board the fleet, they all spoke of the humanity and kindness with which they had been treated. . . . And after a good deal of conversation, and strong representations from Mr. Key, as to the character and standing of Dr. Beanes, and of the deep interest which the community in which he lived took in his fate, General Ross said that Dr. Beanes deserved much more punishment than he had received, but that he felt himself bound to make a return for the kindness which had been shown to his wounded officers, whom he had been compelled to leave at Bladensburg, and upon that ground, and that only, would release him.

"But Mr. Key was at the same time informed that neither he, nor any one else would be permitted to leave the fleet for some days; and must be detained until the attack on Baltimore, which was then about to be made, was over. But he was assured that they would make him and Mr. Skinner as comfortable as possible while they detained them. Admiral Cochrane, with whom they dined on the day of their arrival, apologized for not accommodating them in his own ship, saying that it was crowded already with officers of the army, but that they would be well taken care of in the frigate *Surprise*, commanded by his son, Sir Thomas Cochrane. And to this frigate they were accordingly transferred.

"Mr. Key had an interview with Dr. Beanes before General Ross consented to release him. . . . He found him in the forward part of the ship among the sailors and soldiers; he had not had a change of clothes from the time he was seized; was constantly treated with indignity by those around him, and no officer would speak to him. He was treated as a culprit and not as a prisoner of war. And this harsh and humiliating treatment continued until he was placed on board the cartel."

On September 6th the fleet weighed anchor. It was a striking spectacle of "not fewer than seventy sail," concentrated in a roadstead no more than gunshot wide, shaking out their canvas "all at the same moment." [18] The broad mouth of the Patuxent grew narrower behind them, slowly closed and vanished. On board the ships there was bewilderment and grumbling. Major Peter's gentleman-artilleryman knew more about the vice-admiral's plans than his own crews knew. So far as the troops and sailors were concerned, the fleet was moving southward. It was leaving behind it an objective more delectable than Washington—the fabulous booty of the pirates' nest in the Patapsco River.

Three days later the vice-admiral's armada was still larger. While the fleet beat tiresomely back and forth across the lower reaches of the Potomac and the soldiers and sailors grumbled louder because there was nothing left up that stream now that was worth having, Captain Gordon rejoined with his six fighting ships, his auxiliaries and his long train of prizes, each one with the English ensign flying at the masthead and the Stars and Stripes below it. That was as it should be. A good omen, surely.

A new hoist of signals broke out on the *Tonnant*. Mystery and grumbling ended. The tiresome beat to the Potomac had been nothing but a feint, a trick to fool the Yankees. The signal: make sail, steer for the Patapsco.

A fair wind came brisking in over the larboard rails. The fleet stood up the bay in a majestic column, close in to the western shore.[19] To the watchers in the lookout towers and signal stations, the ponderous line-of-battle ships, the lean frigates, the plump gun brigs, the mortar vessels and the rocket ship, already a terrible legend, the crowded transports and the swarm of gunboats, tenders and dispatch boats were an awesome sight. The whole United States navy could have been swallowed up in that display of English naval power. To the troops on board, the breezy decks were better than the most expensive stalls at the Haymarket—perfect galleries from which to enjoy the rustic comedy that was being played before them on a miles-long stage.

They could chuckle at the puny batteries of the militia yokels in their open earthworks. They could see "beacon after beacon burst into a blaze" and "horsemen mount at every station . . . and gallop towards the interior." They could hear alarm guns sputter. Like every other good comedy, this one had its touch of pathos. As the fleet approached each shore plantation, town or village, the men on deck could see "every house . . . pour forth its inhabitants, while carts, waggons and carriages of all descriptions hastened off, loaded . . . with people and effects." [20] Lieutenant Gleig, misspelling it "Anapolis," made note that the capital of Maryland was stricken with "confusion and alarm . . . to an extraordinary excess." It was a "neat, clean town, surrounded on all sides by elegant villas," and "no task could have been more easily performed than its destruction."

The touch of pathos was not overdone. The war-hardened men in the invasion fleet were not touched too deeply. When the long column of ships stood steadily up the bay and left Annapolis unharmed, they were "not, perhaps, quite satisfied that so fine a prize should be permitted to escape, but hugging" themselves "in the idea that another, and no less valuable one," was waiting for them in the Patapsco River. The pathos was all that was needed to make the voyage pleasant. It was a comfort. It was reassuring. It was final proof of the complete futility of this upstart nation whose capital was now a fire-black ruin. It was the clear omen of an easy victory at Baltimore.

Watching that infection of fear spread along the Maryland shore, it was impossible to credit certain other omens. It was hard to believe that Sir Peter Parker, captain of the frigate *Menelaus*, had lost his life on a pleasant moonlight excursion, chasing one of those silly congregations of militia. While Ross had been landing at Benedict and Cockburn had been chevying the Yankee gunboats, Sir Peter had been sent up the Chesapeake toward Baltimore to distract the Americans' attention. The Yankee general had been properly distracted.[21] The diversion had been most diverting. There had been one fine bombardment: a hamlet by the name of Worten made a handy target. There had been two elegant bonfires—Henry Waller's barns and farmhouse and then Richard Frisby's.[22] Then, to make it perfect, there had been the news that a parcel of rural militia with a few fieldpieces had been foolish enough to pitch a camp within a half mile of the shore. A fox hunt! A paper chase, more likely. Off went Sir Peter with a hundred bayonets and twenty pikemen to surround the camp.[23] He found it empty. No surprise, that. These American yokels had no knowledge of the art of war, they had no pride at all, they would not stand and fight. The bayonets and pikes pushed on—a mile, the landing party's officers said; three hundred yards, so the militia said. The distance did not matter. What mattered was that a piece of one of those Yankee paper regiments had arranged itself in what it imagined was a line of battle in a farmyard.

The British sailors and marines charged gallantly, as usual. The cartridges for the American field guns ran out, as usual. The militia ran, as usual. The guns were left abandoned in the moonlight. But something had gone wrong with this business-as-usual. The yokels had rallied, they were making a stand, they were actually trying to outflank their betters. The landing party had its hands on one of the fieldpieces, but the American militiamen were actually charging; they were coming in a swarm of shadows that multiplied themselves, in the imagination of the startled paperchasers, into five hundred infantry, a troop of cavalry, and finally into a "number much greater." [24] Sir Peter Parker was bleeding his life away in Farmer Caulk's field, thirteen of his men were dead, twenty-seven were wounded.[25] The rest of them retreated to the boats, carrying their captain and most of the wounded. Sir Peter died before they reached the beach.

⋅ But there had been no omen in that costly landing. It had been a mischance; things like that just didn't happen; certainly they didn't happen twice. The rally in the dark and the successful countercharge were the exception that proved the rule: American militiamen won't stand and fight, they can't face British regulars, they always run, when they start to run they always keep on going. Watching that epidemic of panic spreading up the shore now, it was hard for even a pious man to keep from laughing at the funny story of the Yankee parson. There was no omen in that either.

It was a fantastical tall story fetched aboard by soldiers who had been in rest camp down on Tangier Island. An odd fish, the parson. A Methody. Had a sacred grove and all that, like a proper Druid. Came bleating to the admiral that God would be offended if a tree was cut to make room for the tents. Climbed the old man's leg, too, he did . . . it'd cost a man a bloody back to break a twig. He preached to us . . . hell-fire and judgment and thou shalt not kill . . . said God had told 'im it was dangerous for us to go to Baltimore. 'S truth. Said he'd had a revelation . . . said it had been given him from the Almighty that we couldn't take the place.[26] So help me, he's the only Jonathan that thinks so. By the look of things ashore there, the rest of 'em think the British army loads its guns with hell-fire. They think we've all got horns and tails, and brimstone in our pockets. No . . . By the way they run, *they've* got the brimstone and it's in their britches. Go it, Jonathan! *Go it . . . !*

Fair stood the wind for Baltimore—an ill wind that whipped the great fleet northward almost as swiftly as the frantic relay riders could whip their horses over the loose-sand roads. Less than sixty hours elapsed between the completion of the feint in the

Potomac and the delivery of the real thrust a hundred and fifty miles away.

Sam Smith, major general of militia, had only a brief warning. That was all it was—not certain news, a warning. The telegraph riders could tell him that the enemy was coming up the bay, they could tell him that the fleet was larger than the earlier reports had made it. They could not tell him that the enemy, reorganized, was prepared to land an army stronger than the one Ross led ashore at Benedict. They could not tell him when the blow would fall. They could not tell him where. But Sam Smith, shipmaster, knew that this was British weather. Reading two-day-old dispatches, he saw in them more than had been written. He had not seen Cochrane's signal from the *Tonnant,* but he read that also: wind and sky were telescope and code book. This was not another of those clever art-of-war feints. *They've spent days trying to throw us off our guard. They're professionals, they like to do things right. But they can't play tricks forever.* This was not another of those bootless demonstrations. *They've got what they've been waiting for. They've got the men, they've got the guns, and now they've got the wind. They'll be here tomorrow. They'll be landing by tomorrow night . . . or by Monday sunrise, if they wait for daylight. Sometime on Monday we'll be doing business with them.*

The *Seahorse* led the fleet. Captain James Alexander Gordon and his frigate had ripped their way through the Kettle Bottoms and threaded the needle's eye of the Potomac channel all the way to Alexandria; they had frustrated the Americans' "distinguished officers," [27] foiled the fireships and outfought the shore guns. Now the admiral had sent them on ahead to rip their way through the Patapsco shoals, pick an assault anchorage for the transports, and find a channel that would bring the fighting ships within range of the Yankee batteries. Clap on sail! If you strike a mudbank, drive through! If you find booms, break them!

Gordon obeyed orders with a calculated recklessness. By Sunday morning, less than forty-eight hours after Cochrane signaled the advance on Baltimore,[28] the *Seahorse* was dashing into the Patapsco under "a press of canvas." She struck, staggered, shivered . . . and broke through. She struck again . . . and broke through. Captain Gordon "actually sunk his frigate's keel some feet in the slime, and tore through banks by which the progress of almost any other individual would have been arrested—but all would not do." [29] The *Seahorse* struck again . . . and stuck. Her kedging anchors failed to free her. All her boat crews toiling at the towing hawsers could not break her loose. Gordon unloaded "most of her stores" into his tenders, but the mud still held her fast. In desperation, he stripped her of her main-deck guns and got her off at last.[30] She came to anchor just off "a sharp promontory . . . where the Patapsco falls into the bay" and made signal to the *Tonnant*. The line-of-battle ships and the heavier frigates could get no closer to the town. This must be the place.

The promontory was North Point. Captain Sir James Alexander Gordon had picked out the place already chosen for him by a man he'd never heard of. The enemy who might have done a dozen other things had done the one thing that Sam Smith was certain he would do.

It was Sunday morning, and no proper day for business. But Sam Smith, businessman, had customers to meet. The church bells were ringing but Sam Smith, merchant with a city to be sold dear, was working out the details of a business proposition. He was putting the last touches on a scheme to drive the price up and make Baltimore look too expensive for the partners who had come to market, the Messrs. Cochrane, Ross and Cockburn. Like his whole plan of defense, the first tactical move he made was a mixture of business and tactics. There was more of the shrewd trader in it than there was of the soldier. These customers of ours . . . We weren't sure they'd come, but they're here. By the look of things, they're in earnest about this deal. By the look of things, they've fetched the cash with them—the human cash. I wonder how much they've got and how much they are willing to spend. They're poorer now than they were three weeks ago. They spent some of their men for Washington—not many, perhaps, but some. Of course, they may have had more cash in the bank—in those transports of theirs; they may have a good many more men in the fleet than they put on the counter at Bladensburg. But I doubt it. If a man's going to stay in business he's got to study his customers. The more I study Cockburn and Ross, the more I think that they're a little short on assets. The way their Washington deal looks to me, they acted like men who knew they were swinging a big proposition. The way it looks to me, they fetched along most of the cash they had to spend.

The fact is, I've got a half notion they didn't expect to put the deal over. They made bids for two pieces of property—Barney's flotilla and the city of Washington—hoping they might get one or the other. When they got both for the price of one, for a dirt-cheap bargain price, they almost fell over. They acted not only surprised, but scared too—like a colt that has fussed and nosed around the pasture gate at Montebello and finally knocked down the bars and is so surprised that he only sticks his neck through the open gate and is scared by the strangeness—so scared that he whirls around and blasts air and gallops off in a state. That's the way Ross and Cockburn acted—like colts that had scared themselves. Nobody bothered them, there in Washington, but they stayed only one day. Nobody chased them when they left, but they moved as fast as if they were being chased. They didn't stop to bury their dead, they left their wounded behind. An army that's sure of itself doesn't act that way.

I've got a half notion that Cockburn and Ross were right uncomfortable, over there in Washington. The rub was that they started worrying too late—too late for us, that is; by the time they got uneasy, they'd already done the damage. I've got to make them uncomfortable a little sooner, this time. I've got to make the town look right expensive and I've got to do it soon enough so there'll be time for them to do some worrying about the price they'll have to pay. There's nothing like worry to take the edge off a man's appetite for dinner or a deal. So . . . It looks to me as if we ought to start the bargaining ourselves. It looks to me as if we ought to meet these customers halfway. I don't believe they'll be expecting that. After Bladensburg, they likely don't have any high opinion of us; they likely don't expect us to come out and meet them in the open. It might just upset their ideas, it might set them wondering.

There's a risk in going out to meet them. I can't risk too much. I've got to strike a balance . . . I've got to do just enough to make them think that I can do a good deal more . . . I've got to show them enough strength to make them think we're stronger than we are.

If I send somebody out to bargain with these people, the man I send has got to understand that he's not handling the whole deal, he's got to understand that his job is only to talk up the price. If he goes too far, if he gets in too deep, Ross, Cockburn and Company might close the deal right there. I've got to give him just enough troops to put up a good argument . . . enough to give our customers something to think about. He's got to keep himself in shape to come back and help me with the final bargaining.

Who shall it be? It ought to be a man who's had experience.

Winder's been under fire and Winder's here. But Winder's not the man. As near as I can understand what happened, he gave orders to retreat before he had to. If we go out to meet these people on North Point and then give up too easily, we'll do exactly the reverse of what we've got to do . . . we'll only make our customers more confident instead of worrying them. Maybe Winder has learned something. I might trust Winder, but Winder might not trust himself. His neck's been scalded with too many people breathing on it, and a man can get accustomed to that sort of thing, he can get so used to it that he expects it and can't get along without it. A good businessman doesn't hire a manager for his shop or countinghouse and then breathe on his neck; he leaves the fellow alone to do his job. I'll pick out the best man I can and then I'll hold my breath. I'll hold it till I choke, before I'll worry the heart and the life and the self-confidence out of the man I pick. But I can't use Winder for this kind of bargaining.

I can't use Stansbury either. Stansbury wasn't pestered to death with advice—toward the end, maybe, but not at the first. He had positive orders, not advice. He didn't see fit to obey the orders; he held councils of war and did something else. His men broke and he couldn't hold them, but you can't put too much blame on him for that. He tried hard. He's a brave man. His brigade is better than it was three weeks ago; at least, it ought to be. But I can't trust it for a job like this. It needs the heavy guns to hold it down.

I'd like to use the regulars, but I can't do that either. There aren't enough of them to go around. I can't afford to risk John Rodgers's seamen: we've got to save them for the batteries. I can't afford to risk Armistead's infantry [31] or the marines or the flotillamen in this preliminary haggling: we've got to keep them in the lines to see the deal through at the last and clinch it.

Well, that simplifies things. It'll have to be John Stricker and the Third brigade. If anyone can do what I want done, they'll do it. They're Baltimore men. If anybody thinks this town is worth a good stiff price, they are the men who think so. The town's theirs; let them set the figure. They've learned something about this business—some of them, at least. The Fifth and the Rifles did a fairish job at Bladensburg. They should do better this time: they'll be dealing for their own homes this time: they should drive a right hard bargain. And there's something else that's in their favor. They've found out that these customers of ours are human. Joe Sterrett and the Fifth found out that British infantry is not invincible: they stopped them for a while, they pushed them back. They know it can be done. John Stricker knows it too, from the old war. John's a good businessman. We'll see whether John can't make these people stop and count their cash.

In this fashion, by some such reasoning as this, Sam Smith the merchant planned the tactics for Sam Smith the general.

Regardless of his careful reasoning and the soundness of his judgment, the decision to use John Stricker was a decision that pleased him for personal reasons. The relationship between Sam Smith and Stricker might easily serve as the theme of a novel. But truth, being stranger than either history or fiction, does not suffer from their limitations. One of the coincidences which it drops into the plot, as if for sheer good measure, is this: John Stricker and Joshua Barney, born the same year and gallant figures in the first War of Independence while still in their teens, married sisters —the daughters of Gunning Bedford of Philadelphia. Now Stricker and Barney once more had been cast for gallant roles in another war and in the same campaign. And neither a Hugo nor a Tolstoi could have devised a more unlikely denouement, a more sardonic twist to the coincidence.

For Barney, leading the forlorn last stand in a battle so disastrous that it became a scandalous byword, emerged as a national hero. Stricker, fighting as coolly, commanding in a carefully conceived battle that he was not expected to win but doing so well that he had a large share in the ultimate victory, achieved barely a footnote. Barney fought and lost in the series of actions that gave birth to "The Bladensburg Races." Stricker fought and "came off with the profit" in the series of actions that gave birth to "The Star-Spangled Banner." Barney is famous. Stricker is the name of a street.

The relationship between Sam Smith and John Stricker went back a long way. It went back nearly forty years to the bloody slope above the Gowanus tide marsh.

When Brigadier General Stricker spoke up before the Committee of Vigilance and Safety, proposing Sam Smith for supreme command, he was speaking with many voices. He was both the past and the present. He was old comradeship speaking. He was a son speaking in place of his father, and a lieutenant supporting his captain. He had not fought at Long Island, but he was Long Island speaking.

John Stricker was seven years younger than Smith, he was

only sixteen when the Revolution began; but he had been born on the same frontier. He was a descendant of venturesome Swiss pioneers who had settled in North Carolina and followed the lure of the Blue Ridge north into Maryland, to establish themselves in Frederick when that little town lived in fear of the same scalping parties that harried the Lancaster countryside. In 1775 his father, George Stricker, had raised a light infantry company; he had been one of Sam Smith's fellow captains in the old First Maryland; [32] he and Sam Smith together had led their men in the desperate charges that covered the flight of Washington's army through the Gowanus swamp, and George Stricker's company had been all but wiped out. Now George Stricker's son was Sam Smith's right arm; he had been since 1794, when Smith led Maryland's troops in the army that marched to suppress the Whisky Rebellion and John Stricker served as his second in command.

The frontier beyond the Blue Ridge bred sons who liked their own way and had enough gumption to get it. Sam Smith at eighteen had defied his father and stretched an assignment as supercargo and a dull clerk's apprenticeship in London into a four-year grand tour of Europe. John Stricker at sixteen had not shared his father's liking for infantry; his fancy had run to the field guns and he had followed his fancy. When the Revolution ended, he was a captain of artillery and a veteran of Trenton and Princeton, the Brandywine, Germantown, Monmouth, and General Sullivan's seven-hundred-mile fighting march through the Iroquois wilderness, the destruction of forty Indian towns and the furious battle of Newtown. Now he and his father's old comrade were comrades. They were closer than trigger and finger.

And so to John Stricker, sometime gunner in the Continentals, went Sam Smith's order to go out and meet the British army, fight it, hurt it, and then extricate his troops and bring them back intact to fight again on the entrenched line of Loudenslager's hill. It was an order for a holding action only . . . for a battle that could not be won . . . a battle that must be fought to the last useful moment and then broken off before the inevitable defeat became irreparable disaster. (It was an order that has been as little understood as any combat order ever issued.) Stricker understood it.

In the Light street church, that Sunday morning, the Reverend Jacob Gruber prayed that "the Lord would bless King George, convert him, and take him to heaven as we want him no more." [33] Muskets were stacked outside the front door of the Methodist church in Wilkes street. Inside, the preacher was looking down from the pulpit on pews bright with the blue tunics of men of the Baltimore brigade, on the faces of men whose hands felt the desperate clinging of their women's fingers. Somewhere a cannon went off. Then another. And another. *That's it. That's the guns on the courthouse green.* The preacher closed his Bible. "My brethren and friends, the alarm guns have just fired. The British are approaching." He raised his hand. "Commending you to God and the word of His Grace, I pronounce the benediction, and may the God of battles accompany you."

18

HISTORY LOOKS DOWN—ITS NOSE

"... THREE THOUSAND ONE HUN-
dred and eighty-five effective men marched out Baltimore street
upon the Philadelphia road. The troops were full of enthusiasm,
and marched forth with all the glitter of a dress parade. On passing
the outer breastworks and batteries, moving steadily on in brisk step
to stirring music with flags fluttering in the breeze, they were
greeted with enthusiastic cheers." [1]

That is what it says in the book—in the quaint local-history
book. The important, sophisticated books seldom mention these
men. They say little or nothing at all, and the little they say is
said with a patronizing air or an unmistakable sneer. Those men?

Ptuh! What can they do? They're only militia rabble. Anything they do will be "an incident of no importance." No use wasting space on *them*—unless we can think up a wisecrack to show how clever we are and how much we know (and don't know) and how superior we are to a man in a funny hat who didn't have time to finish his Sunday dinner before he went out to be shot.

The significant, dignified books can't be bothered with men like that. Some of them find room for a grudging line about Francis Scott Key and the verses he wrote. Others can't be bothered with even the national anthem: it has no social significance. As for Sam Smith . . . *Smith?* Who is he? They know all about Andrew Jackson: he saved an important city. They find room for long chapters about Andy Jackson and how he did it. But they never heard of Sam Smith. It doesn't occur to the national-history books that these men marching in Baltimore street may have something to do with the course of a nation's life or with the song of a people. They don't wait to see what happens. They never find out that the flag quite probably would not have been there for Key to write verses about if Sam Smith had not read the enemy's plan of battle —and read it correctly—three weeks before the plan was prepared. They never find out who these marching men are or why they are marching or what they are going to do.

It is three o'clock.[2] It is midafternoon of Sunday, September 11th. The street is hot. There was a breeze this morning; it died; the air is dead-still. But there is a sound like wind in the street. (I have heard it before, that sound like slow wind across trees.) It is people, walking together.

The old local-history book is naïve when it calls these men "troops." They aren't. It says they are this-and-that regiment and such-and-such battery. The local-history book adds all the regiment numbers together and says that the sum is an army. It isn't. These men coming down the street are no army. They aren't even soldiers, they're only the City Brigade. They are people, walking together. (I have heard that same sound in the Rue Gambetta in Cherbourg. We weren't soldiers then, either, that day we came off the transport. We were dressed like soldiers, we were a regiment, we had a number to prove it. You couldn't tell, by the number, how many men in the ranks had worn uniforms less than four months. That is one reason, perhaps, why I want to look at these men of the City Brigade. They remind me of men I knew.)

They are going by now . . . the soldiers who never were

soldiers . . . the bright-colored toy paper soldiers . . . the Dres-den-mantlepiece soldiers who look so pretty dancing with suitable Dresden-lamp ladies in lampshade-shaped dresses. The suitable ladies who watch from the footwalks wear dresses with row upon row of ruffles. The ladies are terraced with ruffles. The ladies have no legs . . . they have only dear little feet that steal in and out like mice . . . their feet must be sewed to their petticoats somehow. The men in the street have no necks . . . they have heads and bodies . . . the bodies and heads are connected by unbelievable collars. The stiff tunic collars stand up like cross-sections sawed out of a wooden pump . . . they make the men's chins look like pump spouts in profile. But the buckets are hung the wrong way . . . the handles go under the spouts . . . the absurd leather-fire-bucket hats look all upside down.

That is one way to think of these men. That is one way to see them. But look again. . . .

Some of them glitter. Some don't. There are many who wear the same smock that they wore when they cleaned out the stable last week, the same shirt that they wore in the ropewalk, the same linen coatee a respectable clerk must wear when he sits on his countinghouse stool or sells paper curtains to ladies who have no legs. There are buglers: that's John Buck there, on horseback, with a pompom perked on the top of his cylinder helmet and his trumpet slung over his shoulder.[3] There are men in the ranks who have carried officers' swords but are carrying muskets now; George Eichelberger was a first lieutenant in the 38th United States Infantry once, but today he's a volunteer and a corporal in the Independent Blues.[4] And Jim Davidson, walking beside that gun, was a sergeant of Continentals in 1778; he enlisted the same month the nation was born, July, 1776, and he knows what war is; he was captured in 1780. He's fifty-four years old now and a private—a gunner in the Union Artillery.[5] There are fathers and sons in the ranks. Those are the De Loughreys marching with Captain James Piper's company; the son is a sergeant; the father is "an aged & worthy citizen" who doesn't care much about being exempt when his boy is going to war.[6] Yes, some of those volunteers look right funny. They look out of place. They are going to war in silk hats.[7] But the high silk hats do not look any queerer than General Stricker's, or Sterrett's, or Major Heath's. The field officers' fore-and-aft hats bob along on the current of marching men like so many capsized schooners, their keels sticking up. They also look a good deal like the paper hats that small boys wear when they play soldier.

There are bands; that is true. There are fifes and drums. The bands play "Hail! Columbia," the bands play "Yankee Doodle." The drummers lay into the "happy land," they cock their elbows and give hot licks to the pony when Yankee Doodle comes riding. The squeals that the fifes let out make you think that the licks hurt the pony.

There are flags: that also is true. They don't flutter as much as they do in the book; they ought to, perhaps, but they don't; all the breeze they have is the breeze that they make for themselves when the color-bearers sway them from side to side; they mostly hang limp from their staffs. But there are many flags. Most of them are the Stars and Stripes—the "gridiron flag," to the British —but no two are exactly alike. Some have their stars in a circle. Some have them in zigzag rows; they are the new ones, the ones with the fifteen stars.

The 27th Maryland Infantry is marching behind a flag that has only thirteen—twelve in a circle and one by itself in the middle. The 27th has a high-sounding name; it calls itself the Jefferson Blues. Its thirteen-starred flag is borne by a middle-aged man; his name is Batchelor; he is the junior officer of the eighth company. Ensign Joshua Batchelor has never been in a battle; the flag that he carries has been. His father was a color sergeant in the old, tough Continentals. When the Maryland Line charged at the battle of Cowpens, Bill Batchelor carried the flag; when the charge broke the British front, Bill Batchelor carried a bullet also. He carried it home, and died before the end of the year.[8]

There is another flag, too, at the head of the Jefferson Blues— a bright blue flag with a gold device and a Latin motto in gold.[9] It is new, now; it is clean and whole. It will not be so new tomorrow. By this time tomorrow there will be rents in the silk and the golden threads will be broken. "Non sibi sed patria," the motto says. It says: "Not self, but country."

All down the long column the flags hang like moths . . . like moths that fly only at night and are helpless and blind in the sun. They cling to the slanted staffs like great colored moths with their wings neatly folded together . . . the blue and gold wings . . . the red and white wings with the star-spangled blue at the top . . . the gold and black wings, the scarlet and silver wings of the Maryland flags . . . the arms of the Calverts and Crosslands

. . . the old English arms going out on a new free flag to fight against English arms. (It has its own meaning, that flag. It is still the flag of the Maryland Free State . . . of the only state in the Union that keeps the word "free" in its name as the symbol and sign of its faith . . . of the faith that the best government is the government that intrudes the least on the lives and the liberties of its people.)

But there is another way to look at this column of men moving steadily on, under the bright moth-flags, in the bright blare of the bands. There were banners in Caesar's arena, there were eagles, there was the stridor of trumpets. The trained fighting men who came marching in under the arches saluted the emperor's box, they lifted their swords and their tridents. *Ave, Caesar! Morituri te salutamus!* There is an eagle in Baltimore-street, on the flag of the Jefferson Blues. But these people walking behind the eagle are not trained fighting men. They have Latin words on their flags but not on their lips. And yet we who look at them now can see them as clearly as if we were sitting with Caesar. We can hear what the bands are saying. We can hear the words men do not speak aloud. *Hail, Columbia! We, who are about to die, salute you!* We . . . John Byrd . . . Gregorius Andre . . . Pete Byard . . . we are about to die . . . we salute you. We . . . George Fallier . . . Jake Haubert . . . Harry McComas . . . being about to die, salute you. We . . . Bill McClellan . . . Andy Warner . . . Dan Wells and some others . . . we shall be dead by this time tomorrow. *Ave, Columbia! Morituri te salutamus! Non sibi sed patria!* Not myself, but my country.

Private Byard and the men marching with him are "full of enthusiasm." That is what it says in the old local history book. And the book may be right. But it seems an odd choice of words. A man going up to the front the first time—or the last—is not likely to be full of enthusiasm. He is much more likely to be thinking the thoughts that men think when they know "this is it"—the small creeping thoughts and the dark vague thoughts and the foolish inconsequent thoughts. He is much more likely to be thinking about his feet or his girl or his supper, or what it is going to be like when the fighting begins, or whether he's going to be killed this time and whether it hurts very much and what happens next after that, or what would be the best place to get hit if he's got to get hit. He is likely to look as if he is thinking he doesn't want anyone else to know what he's thinking. He is likely to look as if he is trying to look unconcerned.

The thoughts that flow through the minds of a column of troops going in can't be caught in a word. If they could be, the word would not be "enthusiasm." And these men in the street are not troops. They are only people in trouble. They are men under terrible strain.

The strain is partly fear. It is not sharp, yet. It is a dull, waiting ache. It is a small weight of dread that lies in the pit of the stomach—a knowledge that some of these men walking down the street will be killed, that some will be wounded, that some of the wounded will be crippled for life and that some will linger for days and then die. There is nothing quaint about dying. The museum-piece cut of a coat has nothing to do with the living flesh under the coat. A lead slug or a fragment of iron in the guts hurts as badly in 1814 as it will hurt a hundred and thirty years later. The wounds are as ugly; the chances of living are less. For the men of the City Brigade who are wounded tomorrow, there will be no mercy of anesthetic. There will be, possibly, a little opium or a stiff drink of whiskey, and neither will help very much.[10]

"Anesthetic" is not yet a word. The surgeons who deal with the wounded use other words; they use other means to "counteract" pain and to "equalize excitement."[11] The means that they use is a blister. They multiply pain. They "relieve" it by giving the patient another and different pain.

The doctors of 1814 have a formula—"blister and bleed." They blister a man for pneumonia, for diarrhea, and for paralysis.[12] "It is the most usual practice" in typhus cases "to blister the patient almost from the crown of his head to the soles of his feet."[13] For an overdose of opium the prescription is "eight ounces of blood and a blister"; the unfortunate soldier dies, but the formula is regarded with respect. Bleeding is standard treatment for pleurisy, pneumonia, rheumatism and plain "stitches" in the side, the chest or the belly. It is also the standard treatment for gunshot wounds.[14]

It is not, of course, the only treatment. The army surgeons of 1814 are progressive, intelligent men. They have almost abandoned the theory that "comets . . . and the varying aspects of the planets" have anything to do with infection. Almost, but not quite. For "those remotely revolving orbs, even at this day, are considered as powerful agents, operating upon our globe and through the medium of its atmosphere, diffusing pestiferous influences on animate and inanimate nature." [15]

A man shot through the belly may live, but nine out of ten will die and spend days in the dying. A crushed armbone or leg bone means being crippled for life; it means knives in the conscious flesh; it means being tied to a board with ropes while the saw shudders through the bone. There will be no reprieve of blood plasma. There will be no sulfa to fight the infection in putrefied wounds. The surgeons will not boil either their knives or their saws; they will not wash their hands. They will speak with approval of "laudable pus" and never suspect infection.[16] They will go from one gangrenous wound to another and dabble in pus till their fingers are sore, and yet never suspect that their fingers are spreading death among wounded who might not die if their hands were clean.[17]

Some of the surgeons themselves will die; while they live, they will do what they can with their limited knowledge and means. They will wash the raw stump of a leg with St. Croix rum or harness soap; they will pour powdered cinchona bark into the wound and then cover it over with a "fermenting poultice." If they have charcoal and yeast, they will make the poultice of that; if not, they will sometimes use carrots and sometimes calomel and sometimes the bark of the slippery elm. Many of them have only the vaguest notions about the inside of the body; they have never dissected a body; they slash through nerves without knowing the nerves are there; they are astonished to find how many blood vessels there are in a human leg. A soldier, carried into a hospital with a wound in his foot, develops a cough; the surgeons decide that the wound is inflaming his lungs; they cut off the foot, and are disappointed and puzzled when they find that the amputation has failed as a cure for the cough.[18] In the case of another soldier, they come to the sober conclusion that he died because he was given clean clothes. He has been brought in covered with lice, and some foolish attendant "cleansed" him by "the removal of his dirty linnen, and the hair of his head." When he survives by only twelve hours "the abstraction of this stimulus from the skin," the surgeons decide that the lice had become "necessary . . . to support life" and that the poor soldier perished because they were taken away.[19] A man going into battle in 1814 had reasons aplenty for dreading what lay ahead.

But men in all wars know that kind of dread; they conquer it;

they go on. The men of the City Brigade are entitled to no more credit for going on than is given to other men; but they are entitled to no less, they deserve something better than sneers. The strain that lies on them as they march out to the battle of Godly Wood is not altogether the strain of imagining personal death, of imagining wounds and pain. It is not quite so simple as that. They have in their minds one fear that other American men will not have to endure for a hundred and thirty years—fear for their homes and their women. They will fight with their backs to their homes, with only their weapons and bodies between those homes and a foreign invader.

Baltimore, on this Sunday in 1814, has no expectation of mercy. Cockburn is down the harbor, and Cockburn has sworn to destroy it. For more than a year it has listened to stories of organized vandalism. If its defenses fail, the least it expects is destruction. Some of these men going by are marching in numb despair. That's David Winchester, there. His eyes are fixed on the back of the man ahead, but they do not see the man's back; they are staring at David Winchester's future. He crammed it all into a letter, a while ago: "If the town is ravaged which I solemnly believe we have not the power to prevent . . . I shall be totally ruined to a certainty . . . this is the most awful moment of my life . . . we shall not succeed . . . if I fall those who highly respect and are dependent on me will be left in poverty." His thoughts raced as he finished the letter; his pen couldn't keep up; it left out whole words: "If I survive I shall have the mortification of being a bankrupt . . . than which I could death with much more firmness." [20] In black and white, the future looks mostly black. There are other men whose thoughts are still darker than his. They fear something worse than ruin. Their minds imagine the worst. The worst is the horror of Hampton.

Hampton is an atrocity story. The men of the City Brigade believe that civilians were murdered in the sacking of that helpless Virginia town. They believe that women were raped. Unlike most atrocity stories, this one is true. The British admit it; they themselves use the word "horrors" to describe the "disgraceful" and "revolting" scenes. Colonel Sir Charles James Napier has felt it necessary to state in writing that the "horrible acts" committed there were not done by his 102nd regiment, although its men "almost mutinied at my preventing them from joining in the sack.[21] His detachment of the Marine Artillery has declared that it "blushed" at what it saw when "the British troops, or rather, the foreign troops, for they were the principals . . . commenced perpetrating upon the defenceless inhabitants acts of rapine and violence." [22]

To these Baltimore militiamen whose wives and daughters and sweethearts are watching them march away, it is scarcely a comfort to know that by "unpitying custom" the outrages committed at Hampton must be regarded as "inseparable from places that have been carried by storm." [23] It is scarcely a comfort to know that the British officers "could do no more: they could not be at every man's elbow, as he roamed through the country in search of plunder," or that plunder is something the British soldier "claims as a right, and will have, when the enemy has compelled him to force his way at the point of the bayonet." Baltimore has heard—and believes—that the watchword of Ross's army is "Beauty and Booty"; it is only the swashbuckling toast of an officers' mess, but Hampton has given it meaning. There are men in the ranks of the City Brigade who are sick with fear for their women. They are not alone in their dread. Sir Charles Napier, too, fears that there will be a repetition of those outrages "equally disgraceful to the British name and to human nature." He has taken it upon himself to make representations to Cockburn "in the hope of preventing a second edition of the horrors of Little Hampton."

But Colonel Napier himself has given substance to another dread that gnaws at the minds of these men—the dread of a slave insurrection. For months there have been rumors that the British are arming the Negroes and that their plan of invasion calls for a simultaneous uprising of the slaves behind the American lines. The rumors are not true, but they are believed by many; and there are certain facts which lend them the color of truth. Where British raiding parties have come ashore, slaves have disappeared; nobody —except the enemy—knows whether they ran away or were merely stolen along with the rest of the movable plunder or were taken as recruits for an insurrection. There are Negroes in Ross's army; men who fought at Bladensburg saw a whole company of them, in uniform, under arms; in a region that numbers its slaves by the tens of thousands, the sight was distinctly unpleasant. The Chesapeake country has not forgotten that the royal governor of Virginia "seized and enlisted" several hundred slaves at the beginning of the Revolution—a year before the Declaration of Independence, while Americans were still British citizens. It has not forgotten that Governor Dunmore used the "fear of a servile insurrection" as an excuse for removing the stores of powder from Williamsburg, and that he then proposed "to incite just such an uprising by issuing a proclamation of emancipation." It has not forgotten Dunmore's callous admission that "there is no keeping" such soldiers as his armed slaves "within bounds." [24]

And the remembered dread is not old and remote. Only fourteen years have gone by since the discovery and the last-minute frustration of another plot for a slave insurrection that was to include setting Richmond afire, the seizure of the penitentiary there with its store of powder and guns, and "a general massacre of the whites." [25] Now, in this summer of 1814, Colonel Sir Charles James Napier has submitted to the commanders of the invading forces a detailed plan "to raise a servile war." The same distinguished and humane officer who shuddered at the "horrible acts" committed at Hampton regards the object of his proposed insurrection as "holy." In his mind, the necessary steps have been "perfectly calculated." His plan has been rejected; it has not even been seriously considered by his superiors; but there is an element of British opinion which believes that if he had been "permitted to descant on the iniquity [of slavery] as he desired, a lesson would have been given for the world to admire and applaud." [26]

So . . . Perhaps now you can see them, these men of the City Brigade marching out "in all the glitter of a dress parade" and "full of enthusiasm." Oh, the glitter is there . . . the bright sun on the flowing blue river of men . . . the bright glints on the polished guns and the gilded buckles and chin straps . . . but under the surface, the dark thoughts suspended like silt.

Historians will write fat books about America's wars. They will sneer at "The Bladensburg Races"—without taking the trouble to find out what really happened—but most of them will find no space for so much as a line about the battle of Godly Wood. If they spare it a line, the line will be wrong almost without exception.

A president of the United States will write three and a half pages about the defeat at Bladensburg, but he will write only nine lines about the successful defense of Baltimore.[27] The same author will write a long, enthusiastic chapter about the defense of New Orleans. When he writes of the defense of Baltimore, the attacking army will be merely "British regulars"; but when he deals with the same troops at New Orleans, they will be "the fierce and hardy veterans of the Peninsula War," they will be "trained for seven

years in the stern school of the Iron Duke." The British forces
attacking Baltimore will throw into the battle of Godly Wood "a
brigade of seamen, armed with muskets, and amounting to nearly a
thousand men." Theodore Roosevelt will not mention them—at
Baltimore. But he will specify that at New Orleans the enemy had
"nearly a thousand sailors and marines, men who had grown gray
during a quarter of a century of unbroken ocean warfare.[28] Even
the ships seem to grow after they leave Maryland waters. Admiral
Cochrane's ninety-gun flagship will not be worth mentioning—at
Baltimore. But at New Orleans she will become "the great two-
decker *Tonnant.*"

Private Pete Byard and Lieutenant Gregorius Andre and
Private George Fallier and the other men marching out Baltimore
street to meet death and wounds will receive scanty justice from
history. With rare exceptions, they will be denied even a line in
the books. Why?

What "history" and "historical fiction" have done to the battle
of Baltimore is partly the fault of the uniforms. The temptation to
make the citizen soldiers look quaint has been overwhelming. The
temptation to turn them into puppets in a costume piece has been
irresistible. You will find pictures of some of these men in old
drawings—but the likeness is hardly a speaking likeness. And when
either history or fiction has pretended to furnish that speaking
likeness, it has told only half of the truth. The truth is that these
men speak two languages.

Both languages are English. But they have little resemblance.
One is a quaint parlor language—stilted and high-flown and formal.
The other is plain man-talk, it is tavern or street-corner English.
People sitting in parlors in those days had parlor manners of speaking. They could talk without embarrassment about "drawing the
sword" to defend the "honour of our beloved Columbia," and
about a man's "bosom glowing with patriot flame" and about baring
that bosom to "the foeman's steel." They were as shameless in using
high-sounding phrases to express "noble sentiments" as they were in
using low-sounding, more durable language when that, in its turn,
seemed appropriate. It was a manner of speech that went with
long skirts and with antimacassars. It went out with the skirts and
left the bare legs of the language.

That is another reason why these men seem quaint, why they
seem unreal. Their parlor-talk has been preserved in books, along
with the steel engravings of the ladies who have no legs. But you

can't put their tavern talk into books. You can leave their faces unshaved, you can leave the dirt of the march on their hides and the smell of the sweat in their clothes, but you can't let them speak out in company as they spoke to each other. You can't let the men of Hill 609 or Salerno or Biak speak out in mixed company either. The men of the Baltimore City brigade talk the same language that's spoken in foxholes and Nissen huts, in replacement centers and battlewagons and Flying Forts and PHs and LSTs. Soldier talk doesn't change very much. These men in the fancy coats and the bucket hats use the same four-letter words—the short, ugly, matter-of-fact, satisfactory words. But you can't put the words in a book. You can only take them for granted and, listening with your honesty, recognize these men of the City Brigade as the men you know.

There is still another reason why history has seen these men only dimly. They are men in a changing world. They are the last of an old world that endured long enough to become familiar, they are the first of a new world whose pattern will be distinct for a hundred years before it is broken and blurred by a similar period of sudden transition. These men of 1814 are the hyphen between two epochs. They belong to both and yet are familiar to neither. They are as men suspended between the past and the future.

Everything around them and about them is changing. They have let down their knee breeches and have escaped from the picturesque nonsense of ruffled sleeves; they are wearing long pants, but they still have embroidered waistcoats and feminine frills at their necks. They have taken off the quaint tricorn hat of the Revolution, but the castor they wear looks even more odd; the hats they wear will evolve into Lincoln's stovepipe and then collapse of their own height. The language they talk is changing —not only their parlor talk, which will effloresce into an absurd luxuriance before it goes out of style, but also their plain man-talk. The men of the City Brigade speak of a girl as a piece. A few years ago they would have called her a nice piece of goods.[29] The phrase was complimentary; the word is not yet disrespectful; it will be many years yet before the word takes on a salacious meaning.

Distance also is changing. It is about to shrink into a fraction of itself. Lieutenant Colonel Will McDonald, riding down Baltimore street at the head of the Sixth Maryland Infantry, has built a boat that moves without sails. Somebody else is tinkering with a steam engine that runs on wheels. In one month less than fifte

years, the first locomotive will travel on American tracks. In two
weeks less than sixteen years, the *Tom Thumb* will push a car
filled with thirty people thirteen miles in sixty-one minutes over
America's first passenger railroad, between Baltimore and Ellicott's
Mills.[30]

Even war is changing, in 1814. It is in the midst of one of its
periods of violent evolution. The infantry still fights with spears.
Colonel William Duane's handbook for infantry, published in 1812
and "containing the first principles of military discipline . . . for
the use of the military force of the United States," has diagrams
showing how the spears should be used to protect the men firing
muskets. Part of the British troops who charged at Caulk's Field
carried pikes.[31] And that battery going by now, in the column of

the City Brigade, is the Union Artillery. It has six little four-pound
guns with enormous wheels; they are recognizable as field guns,
but there is something queer about them. They are fitted with
shafts, like so many buggies.[32] The buggy shafts are a hangover
from earlier wars. They are a kind of vestigal tail, not yet cast off
in the process of evolution. Quaint though they look, they are a
sign of progress. When cannon were first drawn by horses, the
horses were hitched in a long single file; the wheel horse was put
between shafts.[33] But the teams were used only to drag the cannon
from place to place; when the time came to maneuver, the horses
were unhitched and the guns were hauled by hand. On the march,
the cannoneers walked; field artillery moved no faster than infantry, on the road; in action, it moved more slowly. It was, in
fact, nothing but infantry equipped with heavier weapons.

The idea of artillery going into the battle line at a gallop had not been conceived until a few years before 1814. Indeed, it was not until 1808 that the United States army made its first experiment with the notion of letting the cannoneers ride on horses or on the caissons and limbers or in a wagon. The experiment was made in Baltimore. Captain George Peter, at Fort McHenry, was ordered by the War Department to prepare "two six-pounders, properly mounted, with one ammunition wagon and one light horse wagon, for conveying four men besides the wagoner." [34] The officers, one sergeant, and three men were to be allowed to ride horseback; with the four men in the light wagon, the outfit was to "proceed at the rate of five or six miles an hour" from Baltimore to Washington and "make some experiments . . . by manouevering the cannon in different directions." Captain Peter was duly furnished with "twenty-six suits of light artillery uniform." The gun carriages and limbers were made in Fort McHenry. The new company—it was called "a new arm"—was the startling novelty of the Fourth of July parade in the capital. Its demonstration "was properly looked upon as an important event" because "artillery moving at the rate of five or six miles an hour was a great advance on anything that had been seen before in this country."

But the Union Artillery of the Baltimore City Brigade has not been "modernized." Its gunners are walking. Its guns already look quaint; they look like toys, between the outsize wheels; they are already out of date. The infantry is not carrying spears, but there are other odd things about it. The infantry companies have third lieutenants and even fourth lieutenants, they have ensigns and "surgeon's mates." Each has its drum and fife—or is supposed to have them.

It must be admitted that to see these men clearly is not easy, that it is difficult to keep from thinking of them as quaint wax dummies in a museum case. They do such strange things. The infantry forms in three ranks: [35] it looks funny, to generations that saw their troops marching in only two ranks. And then, in 1944, the infantry again falls in in three ranks, and the quaintness is not quite so quaint. The infantry has no such thing as a squad; and that, too, seems odd—until America's greatest army abandons the old squad of eight. The demiplatoon of 1814 looks quaint—until the new squad of twelve, in America's greatest war, takes on the size and formation of the demiplatoon. Even the muskets of the City Brigade look funny and clumsy to generations who fight with breech-loading rifles—until you discover that the breech-loader was invented first,[36] and that the muzzle-loader was invented as an improvement upon it—until you discover that the breech-loader looked antiquated and quaint to generations who regarded the musket as a much more efficient weapon.

And the rockets—they, too, look silly. Men actually were afraid of them, in 1814. The rockets went out of style, after a while; they were displaced by the great rifled cannon; they became out of date and useless and foolish—until in the world's greatest war they return as a "new" and terrible weapon—until, in the same Chesapeake waters where the rocket ship *Erebus* sailed to the attack on Baltimore, the new rocket ships dart about on maneuvers that are the rehearsals for landings on faraway beaches. Above them, the rocket planes fly. The rockets are terrible, but they are not new; they were old in 1814; they had been used in Asia for centuries, fired out of bamboo tubes. They will be more accurate in 1944; but their range will not be much greater, then, than it was in 1814.[37]

Quaintness is relative. To say that the men of the City Brigade look quaint does not provide history with an adequate reason for failing to do them justice. It has no adequate reason: it has only excuses.

The best excuse, perhaps, is that the truth was not easy to find. The truth was concealed, first, by an elision of facts. The militia at Bladensburg retreated, some of them fled in a panic. The militia at Baltimore retreated: ergo, they, too, must have fled in a panic.

Second, too many writers with axes to grind used the battle of Bladensburg for a grindstone. The Federalists used it to sharpen their attacks on the party in power; but they were so inept that they attacked the *result* of the administration's blundering rather than the blunders themselves. The blunderers came off with barely a scratch. Other writers used the disaster at Bladensburg to prove that militia is useless; they could not afford to say that militia did something worth while in the defense of Baltimore; to say so would weaken their case.

Third, the truth about Bladensburg—about the orders to retreat and about the troops who did not want to fall back but fell back in obedience to repeated orders—was concealed by a conspiracy of silence. It was concealed and distorted by an administration that hoped to hide its own sins of neglect and confusion. It was concealed even by General Winder, who took no blame for his piecemeal campaign and his piecemeal orders for retreat, but put the whole blame on "the usual incapacity of raw troops to make orderly movements in the face of the enemy." Winder did not mention that Will Pinkney's riflemen, overwhelmed by superior force in an impossible position, rallied after they had been routed; he did not say that they returned to the battle; he did not say that they charged. Winder gave no credit whatever to Joshua Barney, the flotillamen and the marines for their heroic resistance and counterattack that smashed four British assaults. He did not mention the fact that the whole right wing of his army, when he ordered it off the field, was occupying its assigned position—the only half-decent, defensible position held by his men that day. He did not admit that, when it fell back in obedience to his personal orders, it not only was unbroken and unshaken but had not even been seriously attacked. He did not admit that in its retreat it demonstrated its capacity—not its incapacity—to make orderly movements in the face of the enemy. The politicians and officers who heaped all the blame for Bladensburg upon the "raw troops" could not very well admit that the same kind of troops did anything worth while at Baltimore three weeks later. Such an admission might raise awkward questions touching their own skill and conduct. They stood silent while a Congressional investigating committee covered them with a protective coating of whitewash.

The political whitewash was thin. So are history's excuses for not seeing through it. And so are history's excuses for not taking the trouble to look at Sam Smith and his battle plan, or at the City Brigade or even, sometimes, at the calendar. It will care so little that sometimes it will not even bother to see that the date is correct.[38]

The men who were marching in Baltimore street are gone. They have left the street empty and still. They have left the ladies behind and now even the ladies are gone. The ladies have closed the long shutters, they are pressing their knuckles to lips that are stiff from trying so hard not to quiver, they are crushing the bright summer ruffles on beds where they lie alone and will lie alone through an aeon of waiting nights. They don't look quite so much like ladies on Dresden lamps, they look more like women now.

The men of the City Brigade have climbed Hampstead Hill, they have passed between the red mounds of earth piled up on both sides of the Philadelphia road, they have left behind them the cannon that stick out over the crude redoubts. Look at these men once more. Look at them coldly now, without any emotion at all. See them as history would, if it bothered to look. See them as Sam

Smith used them—cash on the counter to drive up the price of a city. See them as blocks on a map.

There are eight of the blocks. Some are larger than others: the five big ones are infantry regiments. The Fifth Maryland is five hundred and fifty men and Joe Sterrett is still in command; you have seen the Fifth charge, you have seen it stand up and fight, you have seen it try to retreat under orders and break and collapse into rout. The Sixth regiment is six hundred and twenty men under Lieutenant Colonel William McDonald, who fought with Pulaski and is interested in steamboats and lives just around the corner from the Widow Pickersgill's door. The 27th Infantry is five hundred men led by Kennedy Long; it has its own flag which isn't a battle flag yet but which will be by this time tomorrow. The 39th is four hundred and fifty men; the lieutenant colonel who leads it is Benjamin Fowler. The largest block is the 51st—seven hundred men commanded by Henry Amey.[39]

There is a small block that is also infantry—another block you have seen before: it is the rifle battalion that fought with the Baltimore guns in that hopeless forlorn-hope stand down at Bladensburg. The battalion and two of its three companies are under new officers now. Captain Bill Dyer has been acting battalion commander since Major Will Pinkney was wounded. His Fell's Point Riflemen and the Union Yagers—the outfits that met the first shock of the British attack in the thickets by Bladensburg bridge—are commanded by first lieutenants. Pete Foy has stepped into Bill Dyer's shoes, and Gregorius Andre has taken the place of Captain Dominic Bader, captured.

The seventh block is the Union Artillery—the seventy-five men with the six four-pound cannon that look like toys. Captain John Montgomery is in command. The eighth block is scarcely a block at all. It is the First Maryland Cavalry under Lieutenant Colonel James Biays. It is four small troops with the high-sounding militia names—the Maryland Chasseurs, the Fell's Point Light Dragoons, the Independent Light Dragoons, and the First Baltimore Hussars. The four troops muster, together, one hundred and forty men. But they will not be together: they will be scouts and patrols.

At eight o'clock Sunday evening [40] the blocks are strung out in a row on a road called the Long Log Lane. Look at them on the map. As they moved out from Baltimore on the Philadelphia road, they have passed through the center of the curving line of entrenchments on Hampstead Hill. They have left behind them the intersection where the Trappe road comes in from North Point, they have passed Colonel Sterrett's house on the left-hand side of the pike, they have turned off the pike to the right into Long Log Lane. The lane has another name: it is also the North Point road. It is a kind of short cut. Seven miles from Baltimore, near the head of Bear Creek, it joins the Trappe road.

The blocks have been moving slowly: this has been no forced march. Sam Smith sees no profit in wasting his assets by wearing them out before the time comes to spend them. By eight o'clock the leading infantry regiment has advanced not quite seven miles. The cavalry, screening the march, reports the road clear ahead. But Brigadier General Stricker has brought his brigade to the place where Smith wanted it brought. His aides gallop down the column, the infantry regiments halt before they have reached the cross-road. Only the cavalry and the Rifles push on. The infantry regiments file off to the side of the lane. They begin to make camp in the pleasant hardwood groves in the valley of Bread-and-Cheese Creek, in the swales where the grass stands half as tall as a man, in the little clearings around Cook's tavern and the Methodist country-church. They unfasten their choking collars, they peel off the smothering tunics, they hang up their bucket hats on convenient branches and on the dead stubs of the scrub pines. They rummage in wagons for kettles and rustle up wood for the fires. The sparks of their supper fires, flying up, mingle with myriad fireflies that rise from the waist-deep grass. While the kettles boil, the men of the City Brigade take the dust-filled shoes off their feet; they lie on their backs in the grass and let the air cool their feet; they look up at the first faint stars and wonder about tomorrow. It's right nice to be lying there, it's pleasant and peaceful. But it isn't the same as the Fifth's first camp on another Sunday evening; it isn't so much like a picnic; the war has come closer since then.

Before the deep dark, the First Maryland Cavalry has tethered its horses in Robert Gorsuch's barnyard and posted videttes in his wood lot. The Rifles have gone into bivouac in the piney woods near a country blacksmith's shop.[41] The blocks are in place for the night.

But why are they where they are? Why have they come to these places?

There are two answers. The first is in Sam Smith's mind: it lies in his reasoned conclusion that the enemy's attack will be a combined operation of army and fleet, that the enemy's troops will be disembarked at the tip of North Point, that the land attack will come up the North Point road. Smith has staked everything on that conviction. The second answer is on the map. North Point is that broad, blunt finger of land that forms the north shore of the Patapsco River estuary; it forms, also, the southern shore of Back River. It is more like a thumb than a finger—like a thumb with a broken nail. Oddly shaped shreds of land curl around it like hangnails; they have been nibbled by tide creeks, they have been bitten half through by the crooked teeth of inlets. There is one place where the thumb itself has been bitten deep. Bread-and-Cheese Creek makes a sharp, clean gouge; Bear Creek makes a deeper one, ragged and ugly. Between them, the peninsula of North Point is chewed almost in two, it is bitten almost to the bone of the road. Between them, there is not much more than a half mile of solid ground.

That narrow place is the place that Sam Smith has chosen for battle. Not for the final, decisive battle. For the preliminaries only, for the first dickering with these people who want Baltimore, for the first hard bargaining with the firm of Ross, Cockrane and Cockburn.

It is not a bad place for the kind of battle Sam Smith wants Stricker to fight . . . a battle in which the objective is to hurt the enemy as badly as possible without hurting his own force too badly . . . a battle carefully planned to make the enemy count the cost of another and harder battle. It is not a bad place at all— if Sam Smith's conclusion is right. There is only one road by which the attack can come. It must come head-on. When Stricker occupies that half mile of ground, his position cannot be turned by a land attack. The two creeks will protect his flanks. Stricker will be defeated. Sam Smith knows it: he knows that he cannot expect three thousand militia—three-fourths of them never yet shot at—to whip three thousand veteran regulars in the open field: he knows that the lowest estimate of the enemy's army at Bladensburg was upwards of thirty-five hundred: he believes that the British can bring against him a force somewhat larger than that. Hurt them. Stagger them. Make them uneasy. Then fall back to the fortified lines in good order, ready to fight again. If John Stricker and the City Brigade do that much, they will do all that Sam Smith expects. This is a good place to do it—if Sam Smith's conclusion is right.

But if his conclusion is wrong, it is not a good place. Even at dusk on Sunday, there is no certainty that the enemy will land at the tip of North Point; the enemy still has several alternatives. The Patapsco estuary is too shallow for the admirals' heaviest ships, but they have a whole fleet of light craft. They had enough gunboats and barges to overwhelm Barney's flotilla and still had aplenty left over to put Ross's army ashore. They have been reinforced since then: they have enough gun brigs and schooners, tenders, dispatch boats and prizes, howitzer boats and mortar boats, barges and gigs and launches to carry thousands of troops up the Patapsco River and land them somewhere on the shores of Bear Creek, or behind it on Sollers' Point, or at Colegate Creek no more than three miles from the city.

Look at the roads on the map. At the narrow place where Stricker intends to give battle, there is only one road. But three hundred yards to the west, the road forks: the Trappe road meets the Long Log Lane. From Bear Creek or from Sollers', another lane leads into the Trappe road; and at Colegate Creek the Trappe road is only a rifle shot from the shore. The enemy can strike at any one of those places . . . or two . . . or all three. He can also strike from the opposite flank: his landing craft can skirt the tip of North Point, enter Back River, and put a whole army ashore above Bread-and-Cheese Creek. If the enemy does any one of these things, his troops will be either on Stricker's flank or behind him. The whole City Brigade—thirty per cent of Sam Smith's entire force, almost half of his infantry—will be caught in a trap seven miles from the nearest help.

19

THE BEACHHEAD

Aᴌᴌ ᴀꜰᴛᴇʀɴᴏᴏɴ ᴛʜᴇ ʜᴏꜱᴛɪʟᴇ ꜰʟᴇᴇᴛ
came in past Bodkin Point. The white topsails passed in endless
flight across the broad mouth of the river toward the ships already
anchored. They swept in among the bare masts like gulls stooping
to the clustered poles of pound nets. In graceful swoops they
rounded to the wind. Their canvas fluttered loose—the last quick
flurry of wings settling to the water. Then the wings were gone,
the sails furled. The masts and yardarms grew into a forest—a

drowned forest rising from the river—and still the ships came in past Bodkin like birds to a rookery. They came slowly and more slowly as the breeze failed, but by evening the whole mouth of the Patapsco had turned into an enormous bird roost.

It was a beautiful evening.[1] Sunset, burning on the low hills, set the bay afire. The river glowed and sparkled, it wore British colors. Dark-red streamers of reflected light ran out across the water, met and mingled to form slowly rippling crosses of St. Patrick and St. George, with shoal shadows darkly blue around them. The ripples drowsed into a mirror stillness, the bay became a placid lake.[2] The long reaches of the river shimmered gold and primrose in the sun's "departing glory." They led straight to Baltimore and a quick, easy victory—a primrose path to glory.

In the gathered fleet there was no doubt of victory. There was no doubt, either, that it would come quickly. This would be no repetition of the campaign in southern Maryland—except in its success. There would be no division of forces. There would be no alternative objectives—a flotilla here, a fort there, a capital city yonder, and an American army scattered every which way. There would be only one objective—Baltimore. Everything was there, in one neat package—the city, its defending fort, the shipyards, the gunboats, the unfinished *Java*. There would be no feinting, this time. There would be two hard, swift blows, so carefully co-ordinated that they would fall with the crushing impact of a single blow. They might even fall with the devastating shock of a complete surprise. The feint to the Potomac had been prolonged; the dash up the Chesapeake had been accomplished with gratifying speed; there was no sign, so far, that the Americans were on their guard—no horsemen on the bluffs to ride alarm, no patrol boats in the river.

The battle plan was simple. A task force of the fleet would move up the river and silence the harbor batteries. A landing force would move up North Point and smash the militia—if the militia would stand long enough to take a smashing. The two forces would advance on parallel lines, so close together that communication could be maintained constantly.

The shallowness of the Patapsco was an inconvenience. But it was not a surprise. It had been foreseen and discounted. Rear Admiral Cockburn and his captains on the Chesapeake blockade had not looked longingly at Baltimore for eighteen months without discovering the conditions under which an attack upon the city must be made. The line-of-battle ships and the heaviest frigates could not join in the bombardment. But that known fact was not a fatal obstacle. It was not even a serious obstacle. It was hardly more than an annoyance. Indeed, the shallowness of the river was a circumstance which an admiral might actually welcome.

An operation such as an attack on the Baltimore harbor batteries involved two risks. The first was military: heavy guns on shore, firing from steady platforms over measured ranges, might knock even a line-of-battle ship to pieces before they could be silenced: valuable vessels might be lost or badly damaged: their attack might fail. The second was psychological: the officer responsible for the attack must stake his reputation and his future on the outcome. Mere soundness of judgment would not be enough. Success at moderate cost would justify a reasoned recklessness; but an equally well-reasoned caution would be no excuse for failure. An admiral who lost his ships and lost his battle too was likely to be broken or, at best, to wait in vain for a command. An admiral who lost a battle by failing to use his ships to the limit of their capacity was in no better case. Either a victory too dearly bought or a defeat resulting from too much risk-taking or too little might well mean a trial before a naval court.

The Patapsco spared Vice-Admiral Sir Alexander Cochrane the hazard of a delicate decision. No court could blame him for not bringing battleships to action through impassable shoals. And battleships would not be needed. Cochrane had at hand a more effective weapon.[3]

The bomb ships *Terror, Meteor, Aetna, Devastation* and *Volcano* had been built for just such work as this. Their ponderous mortars, firing at high angles and long ranges, could drop two-hundred-pound shells from enormous heights. Their bombs, falling, had the crushing, battering effect of solid iron shot fired from the main batteries of battleships, and they exploded "with the destructive effects of a mine."[4] The mortar ships were smaller than the frigates, smaller even than the gun brigs; even when they lay within range of a fort's guns, they made tiny targets; there was an excellent chance that they could carry out their mission and emerge unscathed.

By late afternoon the plan of battle was complete in all its details. The timetable of the attack had been worked out. The vice-admiral shifted his flag from the *Tonnant* to the frigate

Severn.[5] From the whole rookery of ships rose a low, persistent sound . . . the multitudinous and blended noises of ten thousand men in orderly disorder . . . the incessant small sounds of their shifting bodies and their packs and pouches straining at the straps and the incessant stir and scuffle of their feet . . . the stamp of horses restless at the stanchions . . . scuff and bump of small boats being stowed with stores . . . thuds of quilted bags of grapeshot dropped beside the guns . . . louder thuds of iron balls being piled up in the garlands . . . swish of sand strewn on the decks to sop the blood that might soon run across them . . . the harsh grit of boots upon the sand . . . the hushed shouts of sergeants under orders not to make too much commotion. Field guns, limbers, caissons, harness, ammunition carts and powder casks were ranged beside the gunwales to be lowered away. Surgeons' chests, the rocket tumbrils and dischargers, sheaves of rocket staves, rocket carcasses in wooden boxes, handspikes, rammers, the coiled drag-ropes for the cannon, all the odds and ends that clutter up an army like an attic were jumbled on the decks in purposeful confusion.

In the cramped spaces that were left or in the dark "bed places" in the holds, the landing force was mustered by platoons and sections for its last instructions. Every man was told off to his boat place and to the deck station where his boat would load. Every man's equipment was inspected. It was light equipment: musket, bayonet, one spare shirt, one blanket.[6] This was to be a lightning blow: twelve hours from the beach to Baltimore. The packs were stripped of every unnecessary weight, however small. The bit of plunder from that farmhouse on the road to Bladensburg must be left behind. Throw out that clothesbrush: one brush to six men's aplenty. Throw out that candlestick: no matter if you've had it since the raid on Hampton, you can't take it. You . . . you, there . . . you can't take those spoons: somebody else'll get them if you leave 'em, but there'll be more spoons in Baltimore tomorrow. Dump that tobacco out of your knapsack. And no back-chat about it. You know bloody well you stole it . . . and not from the damn' Yankee farmers, from the king hisself . . . the off'cers put the king's broad arrow onto ever' barrel of tobacco that we took at Marlb'rough, an' you thieves that broke 'em open ought to have your backs skinned. *'Shun!* File past an' draw y'r rations.

Every man was issued three days' rations—two and a half pounds of hard sea biscuit and three pounds of boiled pork. Every man was issued sixty musket cartridges to fill his pouch, and then in addition twenty extra cartridges done up in a stout paper parcel.[7] By sundown, more than five thousand men were ready to storm ashore. Every soldier and marine was buckled into his equipment and forbidden to remove it. Every ship's boat was ready to be hoisted out. On the light gun brigs assigned to cover the landing, the carronades were crammed with grape to sweep the beach; the towing hawsers were ready at the bits; the springs were ready to be bent to the anchor cables. But not a boat was in the water. The gun ports were closed. The fleet lay at anchor in a careful camouflage of pretended idleness. Other fleets had been here and had gone away without attacking. Now the Yankees, watching through their glasses, seeing no preparations for a landing, might be cozened into thinking there would be none. At any rate, they'd get no clue to the direction of attack.

The position of the fleet was indeed an indication of its purpose. It was deployed in a great arc across the mouth of Old Road Bay; the inshore ships were lying within cannon shot of Welshman Creek. But that clue might be false; it was almost too obvious; it could not be trusted. When dusk crept over the Patapsco, no visible activity had committed the invading force to any certain course. It could still strike in one or more of a dozen different directions. It could strike tonight . . . tomorrow . . . any time it chose . . . and any place.

The troops lay down in full equipment. The fleet slept under a blanket of men spread upon the decks. In its sleep, it talked: the sentries called the half hours. Near by, their "all's well" was the sharp cry of a man startled by a dream; on the more distant ships it was only an uneasy mutter. The tide, mouthing at the ships' sides, made moist sleeping-noises. Sound hung above the fleet, persistent, multitudinous, strange and yet familiar in this place of swamps and tide creeks—sound of heavy breathing like the sound of swarming insects. All the ships' bells, tinkling, might have been the cows' bells in the salt marsh pastures. Josh Barney, as a boy, had fetched the cows in from the pasture on his father's farm up Bear Creek, not three miles away.

It was after midnight, but the darkness was not absolute.[8] The stars were brilliant in the cloudless sky; in the tide-rippled water their glow came and went like the winking glow of fireflies. The fleet began to stir. Sergeants roused their sections with low-voiced commands. Men, waking, found their faces wet as with a cold sweat and their hair damp; dew lay on their clothing in a clammy film. *Fall in. Quiet . . . quiet, now. No talking. Easy with that butt, you, there. D'ye want to raise the Yankees? A ball in the guts is a good cure for talking.* So is a sergeant's fist against a loose mouth.

The troops shuffling to their loading stations saw the moist bulwarks faintly luminous with starlight and the shapes of small boats rising ghost-like. The blocks dangling from the yardarms made small, eerie noises as the falls creaked through them. The men tailing to the ropes must heave in silence: [9] bosuns had their rope's-ends ready for the rump of any sailor who made too much racket. Soldiers clambering into the lowered boats found their own rumps wet through by the dew-sopped thwarts.

Brig-sloops slid out from among the taller warships; they drifted, silent, moving slowly inshore on the flowing tide. Their port lids, opening, made dark squares in their silvered sides; their bellies rumbled to the wheels of gun trucks; the blunt muzzles of the carronades came out to sweep the beach. A cable's length [10] from shore the covering ships let go their anchors at both bow and stern. With springs to the anchor cables, the brigs' heavy broadside cannon were more mobile than unlimbered field guns. Even if whole thickets suddenly disappeared—as clumps of underbrush had disappeared on the banks of the Potomac—to disclose Yankee batteries along the forest edge, no field artillery could stand up to the crushing fire of thirty-two-pound ship guns.[11]

Small boats swarmed around the frigates and the transports. One by one they pulled away as they were loaded, and were instantly replaced. Others crept out from the gulfs of darkness under the towering sides of the line-of-battle ships, the *Tonnant*, the *Albion*, the *Royal Oak*, the *Dragon*. There was no confusion. Orders had been detailed and specific. Every boat had its assigned position; the anchored ships made lanes, and their ranged masts were guideposts; the crowded landing craft came down their proper lanes, converged and formed divisions. They lay in clusters, waiting, their oars moving softly, holding them against the tide. Armed barges moved into their stations at the head of each division; [12] in the bows of each barge, a gunner crouched beside a carronade, his slow match in his hand; the acrid odor of the burning fuses sifted through the smell of close-packed bodies and wet clothes and foul ship timbers. The brief carrillon of the fleet's bells rang three o'clock.[13] Hushed orders ran from boat to boat. *Give 'way*. The first wave moved toward the black uncertainty of shore.

It moved silently at first, and slowly, and then with quick, short, rushing noises that grew into heavy breathing and then into a loud, rapid panting as the oar strokes drove the boats in surges and the bow waves rose and fell and rose again, each wave the hard-drawn breath and the spent exhalation of a straining runner. The first keel crushed into the beach with the harsh sound of a throat being cleared and its collapsing wave spat softly on the sand.

Men leaped out into the shallows. They hung a moment at the water's edge, a huddle of dark figures suspended in a lighter darkness. Hands, groping, found the next man's arm, his blanket roll, his shoulder; the huddled figures formed a kind of line, rushed up the sloping bank and flung themselves down blindly, headlong upon ground they could not see.[14] Another throaty rattle on the beach, another rush of feet in sliding sand, another half-platoon lay face-down in coarse, rasping grass. Only an officer stood upright, peering forward, feeling his way slowly with his feet. If the landing boats had hit the right place, there should be an open field just here. There was. He whispered a command. The two demiplatoons sprang up and ran. As they ran, they spread. Forty yards in from the beach, they dropped again; their hands groped again to find their intervals; wriggling and crawling through the cutting grass, they formed a skirmish line.

The line built itself up swiftly. All along the beach, the boats of the first wave were landing now. In half an hour, a thousand infantrymen sprawled on their bellies in extended order outlined the perimeter of a beachhead large enough to hold the army.[15] They lay silent, listening and waiting. Even whispers were forbidden. Every fold of ground could hold an ambush, every patch of woods could hide a nest of field guns loaded—in the Yankees' murderous, unmilitary fashion—with old rusty hinges, bent nails, castoff gunlocks, jagged pieces of iron pots, broken pokers, even crowbars.[16] But the only sounds were rustlings of the long grass under restless bodies, the gargling noises of the small boats shoving off to fetch the second wave, the chuckling of the ripples on the shore.

The boats, returning, brought more solid noises—scrape and bump of ammunition cases, grunt of barrels set down on the wet sand, grind of gun wheels, clunk of axles as the carriages and limbers jolted up the bank, sudden flam of shod hoofs on the barges' gunwales, tramp of infantry in columns. By seven o'clock, the army was ashore and there had been no sign of opposition, no sign even of a Yankee picket.[17] Beyond the skirmish line the green fields stretched away in smoothly waving grass unmarked by hoofprints. On the country lane a little to the right, the dust lay undisturbed.

Tense expectancy gave way to easy confidence. The commanding general and the rear admiral who had ridden into Washington rode jubilantly now across their solidly established beachhead. Night operations were always an uncertain business. A night landing with a mixed force on unreconnoitered beaches multiplied the risk immeasurably. Even against American militia, it was an uncomfortable business; it was almost more uncomfortable than a similar operation against trained troops whose reactions could be reasonably foretold. You couldn't tell about these Yankees; they knew nothing about warfare; it was hard for proper soldiers to predict the conduct of such people. They blew up forts that regulars would think almost impregnable, they put their own troops in impossible positions and left the usable positions to the enemy, they retreated when they ought to fight, and sometimes—but not often—kept on fighting when a proper soldier would have known that he was soundly beaten. Who could have imagined that those farmers down at Caulk's, who fled from their fortified camp at the first hint of trouble, would rally and stand fast? Who could have predicted that they would fight in an open field when they had woods to fight in; that they would attempt a flanking movement in the dark and drive it home; that when they had been routed, when they were in full retreat and their cannon stood abandoned, they would rally again and charge and take the guns? Who would have dreamed that the captain of a British frigate would be killed by bumpkins in a farm lot? Poor Sir Peter. His death had proved the risks.

In all truth, there was risk enough in a night landing without opposition. It was a relief to see these regiments forming in the fields in solid masses, in close columns of companies. Putting five thousand men ashore in darkness, from scores of ships, with artillery and gun teams, had been a delicate and infinitely complicated undertaking. It had been accomplished with amazing smoothness. The general and the admirals could congratulate themselves without immodesty. Four hours ago these men and guns and horses had been scattered through the fleet. Sixty hours ago the fleet itself had been a hundred miles away. Now three reinforced brigades, stronger than the army that took Washington, stood in marching order within fourteen miles of Baltimore, and still there was no sign that the doomed town was conscious of its danger. It was an astonishing achievement. British boldness, British skill and British discipline—and British weather—had made possible a military movement of almost unprecedented swiftness. The vice-admiral could take credit even for the weather. He had selected the breeze that would concentrate his fleet precisely where he wanted it, with just enough daylight left to make the necessary dispositions, and then die away into a perfect calm for the touchy work of debarkation.

If the Americans realized their peril, they would be rushing about in the same inept, unmilitary confusion that had made their marchings and countermarchings at Bladensburg so futile. If they had yet to find out that the blow was coming, they would almost certainly be paralyzed by the speed with which it came. In a complete and well-founded confidence, Ross gave the order to advance.

20

THE BATTLEFIELD

IN THE CAMPAIGN AND BATTLE OF Bladensburg, the shape of the roads was the controlling factor. In the battle of Baltimore, the controlling factor was Sam Smith's stubborn conviction. He did not shape the battle. He foresaw its shape and used it.

At eight o'clock Sunday evening the blocks representing the City Brigade on the map were in a tactically dangerous position. The danger passed in the night—at the moment when General Ross committed his troops to a single beachhead at the outermost tip of North Point.[1] By seven o'clock Monday morning General Stricker knew that the enemy had done exactly what Sam Smith expected and wanted.

History has accused Stricker of neglecting reconnaissance and failing to use "ordinary caution." [2] It is an accusation unsupported by factual evidence; indeed, the known facts refute it.[3] Colonel Biays had not confined his reconnaissance to Robert Gorsuch's farm. He had pushed out his patrols at least three miles farther, down the narrow neck between Old Road Creek and Denton's. They had gone far enough to find out that the British were landing "from and under cover of their gun vessels which lay off the bluff of North Point, within the mouth of Patapsco River." [4] They had stayed long enough to ascertain that the enemy was coming ashore in force and that this was no barn-burning raid and apparently no mere diversion, but an attack in earnest. About the time the last of the British landing boats were being unloaded on the beach, cavalrymen sent back by Colonel Biays were galloping into the bivouac by Bread-and-Cheese Creek with some reasonably intelligent intelligence.[5]

General Stricker began to move the blocks.

The City Brigade, mustered for stand-to before daylight, was already fed and under arms and ready for the road. Its baggage train moved first—to the rear "under a strong guard." [6] The Fifth came tramping out of the woods into Long Log Lane and moved off in the opposite direction. After the Fifth came the 27th, the Union Artillery, the 39th.[7] Ammunition carts swung into the road behind their regiments. But the last files of the 51st, closing the column, looked back over their shoulders and saw the Sixth Maryland Infantry turn toward Baltimore and march away, following the white-topped baggage wagons to the rear.[8] *What the hell . . . ?* The 51st was a drafted regiment; it was also a "precinct" regiment,[9] which is to say that it had been drawn from the thinly settled suburbs of the city. *What are those buggers back there doin'? They're goin' home, that's what they're doin'. Goin' back to Hampstead.* It seemed like a right good notion. To these miscellaneous civilians, home seemed wondrously attractive. Home was familiar. Home was breakfast at a proper table. Home was your own bed and your own dormer window and the slanted ceiling that you had waked up to nearabout as long as you remembered. It was better than lying on the ground all night, thinking about what was going to happen . . . better than feeling the dew gather on your face in beads like sweatdrops and your hair turn sticky with it . . . better than the touch of the wet blanket clammy on your face and the feel of your own flesh cold and clammy, like a dead man's. Home was safe . . . it always had been . . . it was safer, anyway . . . it was the safe-feeling trenches along Hampstead Hill with the dirt piled up thick in front of them . . . it was the reassuring cannon and the assured-acting sailors in the batteries. *I wisht I was home. I wisht to God I was.*

But the Sixth was not going home. It marched only two hundred yards to the rear, across the plank bridge over Bread-and-Cheese Creek, and halted near Cook's tavern.[10] The other infantry regiments and the six small field guns and the three or four ammunition carts moved slowly down the lane in the direction of the enemy. Seven miles away the British army was moving up the lane.[11]

The head of the American column approached the intersection where the Trappe road came in from the right. The Fifth looked at it, uneasily at first and then with relief as it went by. *That's one road we don't have to travel.* The Fifth had its memories of Bladensburg. They were confused and blurred; they varied with the individual, they were streaks and patches; but some of them, like Henry Fulford's, were uncomfortably vivid. The regiment also had its memories of the forced march from Elkridge Landing and of the night countermarch and of the counter-countermarch next morning. These were not quite so vivid, they were somewhat more confused and blurred because the marching had dragged itself out into one long brain-numbing torment of heat, dust, thirst, hunger, pain and apprehension. But of the two memories, the recollection of those endless roads had become the more unpleasant. *Sure, we can march. We did, didn't we? Faster 'n' farther'n any other outfit. But we don't have to like it.*

Thank God, this wasn't starting out like Bladensburg, all panting hurry and confusion, red-eyed weariness and belly cramps and the sick, belly-deep suspicion that whoever was managing things didn't know his backside from an anthill. By the way the generals had jumped around at Bladensburg you would have thought they had been sitting first in one anthill and then in another. This was different. Nobody had worn anybody's legs off, this time, nor kept everybody awake all night because he couldn't make his mind up. If anybody had laid awake last night, it was his own fault. It was a man's own business if he couldn't sleep for worrying about what was going to happen.

The air was fresh and cool. The lane ambled along through pleasant, open woods. Slanted shafts of sunlight slid down through

the oaks to dapple it. The road was easy to the feet. The dust
that padded it was thick but it was also dark and heavy with the
dew; it did not rise in blinding, choking clouds; it did not make a
cloud at all, it was more like a stream with men wading in it. The
disturbed dust made a kind of flowing, like a shallow creek with
silt suspended in the sun-filled water and small, aimless currents
moving every which way. In the shaded stretches it looked only
ankle-deep; where the sun sifted through, it lay in knee-deep pools
like eddies with slow currents weaving. The men's legs darkened
in it. The silty dust, settling, clinging, fitted all the legs with red-
brown gaiters.

There was little talking in the ranks. There was no loud talk
at all. There wasn't anything much to complain about, there
wasn't anything to criticize. But nobody seemed to feel like joking,
either. On the easy road, in the cool of the morning, men's minds
were not nagged by discomforts of their bodies. They could
think about what was coming or they could try not to think about
it, they could set their minds deliberately to a thousand other
things. If you thought hard enough about the first time you saw
Anne, or about the white Marseilles waistcoat you'd bought and
hadn't worn yet because the United Volunteers had been called
out the next forenoon, or about going fishing with Walt Muschett,
you could keep your mind off what was going to happen. It was
like counting sheep. In a way, it was. You couldn't stop. You had
to keep on finding things to think about or else it didn't work.

And it was a caution how some of the things you thought
about reminded you of what was happening now. Like thinking
about Walt Muschett and the times you had gone trouting. You
hired a gig and you drove out to Western Run and you put up
at a farmer's house and got up early the next morning. This wasn't
very different; you had the same sick-sleepy feeling and the same
feel of strangeness about having been up before dawn in the cool,
moisty dark; and there was Walt now, walking ahead of you along
the path that led down to the run—only it wasn't a path, it was
Long Log Lane and Walt had a gun across his shoulder instead
of a fishing pole. But the sickish-empty, early-morning feeling
would ease off, pretty soon. It always did; you always got to feeling glad that you weren't down at Waites's, selling ink wafers and
paper curtains and, in between times, climbing up on the high
stool in the back room to work on the accounts. You'd feel fine,
pretty soon. Only this *was* different no matter how much it

seemed like other mornings, this was considerably different. No matter what you thought about, there would be a time afterwhile when thinking wouldn't work. There would be a time afterwhile when you'd have to start griping or making jokes to show that you weren't nervous. It had been like that the last time, on that hill at Bladensburg, when Walt Muschett told you for God's sake to shut up. You hadn't even known that you were talking. But it was all right yet. Nothing was going to happen for a good while yet. Not for hours yet. Maybe not until tomorrow. Maybe not at all.

A clapboard meetinghouse without a steeple [12] squatted in a weedy clearing and stared blindly toward the lane, its windows dazzled with the sun. Beside it spread a dusty wallow, stamped out of the sod by the hoofs of tethered horses while the preacher and the flies had droned together through interminable Sabbath sermons. You'd meant to wear that Marseilles waistcoat when you went to church with Anne. Now you didn't know whether you'd ever have the chance to go to church again, or see Anne again, or . . . *Stop it.* A hitching rail, worn slick, stretched over the dust wallow like a one-log footbridge over a dried pond; dry rivulets of ruts came meandering down across the clearing and trickled into the road. When you looked back at the church, over your right shoulder, it had changed expression. The light didn't hit the windows the same way; the windows had gone dull; the meetinghouse looked as if it had closed its eyes and drowsed off, unconcerned. It gave a man a kind of lonesome feeling, shut out, unimportant and forgotten.

Who cares what happens to you? Who cares whether you ever come back up this lane? Who cares if you get killed this afternoon? Somebody. Perhaps. She said she did. I don't know. She's a long way off. She's away back in Baltimore. Maybe she isn't even awake. Maybe she's gone. She ought to go; she oughtn't to have stayed. I wish I knew where she is. I wish I knew what she's thinking. How much will she care, if I don't come back? How long will she remember? There's that fourth sergeant in the Fencibles, in Captain Nicholson's battery. She used to like him right well. The Fencibles are down in Fort McHenry. They've got good thick brick walls around them. The fourth sergeant of the Fencibles will come back safe enough. Oh, damn. . . .

When you turned your eyes front again, you could see the woods ending a little ways ahead. You could see the lane slipping out between two braced fence posts, and the rail fences stretching off to right and left along the straight edge of the woods. You could see the lane going on. But the mounted officers at the head of the column were not going on, they were reining in their horses. An arm lifted, pointing. You could hear a command begin to travel down the column—the same word repeated, over and over, passing from one captain to another. It was queer how your mind kept running to familiar things. The officers' cries, drawn out and suspended and left hanging, sort of, made you think of the high-pitched, expectant-sounding cries of the old free nigra that came trundling his cart full of soft-shelled clams up Albemarle street, mornings, calling "mano . . . mano-oo . . . mano-o-ooo. . . !" They sounded homey and peaceful and everydayish, excepting that the officers were calling "company . . . comp'nee . . . comp'nee-e-eee. . . !" The second word of the command fell off the end of the suspended note. "Halt!" You could hear it dropping, bump, bump, all along the column. "Halt . . . halt . . . halt-halt!"

It didn't seem right. It was too soon to be halting. Rest? No, can't be that. It ain't time for that yet. And then, up the road: "Right wheel. . . ." It was not repeated: it concerned only the head of the column. "For'rrd. . . ." All the captains and lieutenants went to work on that word. ". . . ha-arrch!" The leading sections of the foremost company turned off into the woods. The rest of the column moved forward, stopped, jerked forward, stopped again. Here and there a man began to talk. *Flank patrol, that's what it is. John Stricker knows his business. He's not taking any chances.* That's right. He's a banker, ain't he? Catch a banker taking chances! *Well, what's wrong with that?* Nothin'. Nothin' at all. Seems like a right good idea, considerin' that it's us he would be takin' chances with. Those Britishers ain't g'on' to catch John Stricker with his flanks unbuttoned. *Sa-ay, hold on a minute. That's a right big patrol.*

Company after company, in column of sections, was peeling off the road. The column in the lane was still moving forward, slowly, jerkily, but more than half the regiment was already in the woods. The rest of the companies began to take a sharper interest in the proceedings. There go the Union Volunteers. The Patriots, too. There's only the Independents and the Mechanicals left between them and us. *What's going on here, anyway? If it ain't a rest . . . an' it ain't a patrol . . .* I'll tell you what's goin' on. What's goin' on is that we looked too comf'table. Off'cers on horseback just natcherly can't endure to see men walkin' along easy on a good road. Ain't you found that out yet? *Oh, well, the woods don't look so bad.* No, not here, they don't. But up ahead a ways they're thicker than your granpa's whiskers.

The last company of the Fifth turned off into the woods. It had scarcely cleared the road when it was halted. Oh, my Lord . . . again? March-halt. March-halt. Who said this was going to be so all-fired different? It's the same as last time. Start-stop. Start-stop. Giddiap-*whoa!* I wish to God they'd make their minds up.

The whole regiment was halted. It was standing, waiting, strung out in a column that resembled nothing in the drill book; it turned and twisted back and forth among the great oaks, as crooked as a snake. In the lane behind it, the 27th was coming up. The rear companies of the Fifth looked backward, suspicious and prepared to be indignant. *Godamighty, they're puttin' the Jeffersons ahead of us! Of all the low-down. . . ! Where's the colonel? Joe Sterrett ain't g'on' to stand for anything like that!* The men of the Fifth were not full of enthusiasm for being killed; they were, individually and collectively, self-conscious. The regiment did not admit, to outsiders, that it was not entirely pleased with its behavior at Bladensburg. Indeed, it had almost convinced itself, with a measure of justice, that it had done very well. We charged, didn't we? We charged the Britishers and pushed 'em back and held 'em. We didn't give an inch till Winder ordered us to fall back. How many other outfits did that? One—just one. And that one was Barney's. Even Barney's men had to fall back after they had charged. Oh, I know: they rallied, and we didn't. Sure. Sure, we ran. What else could we have done? The flotillamen still had their guns to rally on. We didn't; Winder had pulled all our guns away. The flotillamen still had their own troops on both sides of 'em. But what did we have? We had Britishers on both flanks, and some of 'em working round behind us. Even Barney had to give up when he got in that fix. But regardless of the self-esteem it had recovered, the Fifth Maryland was still acutely sensitive. It had acquired a prickly pride that would resent the slightest slur upon its conduct. And it watched, now, the approach of the 27th with its resentment at full cock. Then it relaxed. No-o-oo. No, they aren't putting the Jeffersons ahead of us. I don't know what they're doing, but it's not that.

When the leading company of the 27th was still a few paces from the edge of the woods, it too turned off the road. But it

turned left. The long column of the Jefferson Blues began crawling away among the trees on the opposite side of the lane, moving
in the opposite direction from the way the Fifth was headed. *Now
what's all that about? Spreading out like that . . . two regiments
. . . it looks as if . . . you don't suppose . . . ?* Na-ah. Not yet. It's
too soon for that, yet. We just started. Good Lord, man, we
haven't come much.more'n a half a mile. *That's right. That's a fact.*
It was too soon.for anything to happen. When you went to war,
you had to march for hours to get to where the war was. You
hadn't marched for even half an hour this morning. And you'd just
passed that church. Nobody'd fight a battle in a churchyard. Bladensburg . . . there must have been a church in Bladensburg . . .
it's funny . . . I don't remember any church . . . there must have
been one, though.

Oh, well, it didn't matter. Nothing was going to happen in a
place like this. These woods were just like Howard's Woods at
home, on the hill beyond the end of Charles street, where people
were talking about putting up a monument to President Washington and where you went walking Sunday afternoons with Anne.
They were just like the woods at Rutter's Spring. You didn't fight
a battle in a picnic grove. These woods even sounded like the
grove at Rutter's. That shouting, up ahead there, sounded like a
politician ripping into an oration. The hollering would probably
turn into a command of some kind; there were a plenty of fanci-
fied commands, in the back half of the drill book, that were nearabout as long as speeches.

It was going to be a command, all right. Richard Heath, first
major of the Fifth, was riding down the crooked column, his
horse stepping high and dainty over the dead leaves and brittle oak
twigs buried in the deep grass. He checked the horse and rose up
in the stirrups. You could see his throat swell. "Battalion . . .
atten-*shun!*" Well, anyway, we aren't going to stay here. We're
going to march some more . . . and halt some more . . . and
march . . . and halt . . . and . . . "The battalion will take care
to form front by wheeling on the left of sections!"

A sudden tenseness quivered through the column. You could
see it tighten in the backs of men already rigid at attention. You
could see the muscles bulging at the hinges of Walt Muschett's
jaws, you could see his leather hat jerk as the muscles stretched the
chin strap. You could feel a small, cold hollow in your belly. It

hadn't been there; it was there now; it was round and empty, like a bubble.

"Sections . . . upon your left . . . *wheel!*" The stirring of a thousand feet upon the dead leaves made a sound like sighing, like the sound your breath made when you'd held it and then let it out because you knew the thing that had made you catch your breath was going to happen and you couldn't help it. Abruptly, the thick column was a thin line and the line was moving forward. It became more crooked; it was sags and bulges. It moved quickly, but the sound it made now was a slow, crawling sound. It was in the edges of the woods, the great oaks were ending, the cool shadows ending. Sun and warmth came pushing. The regiment, in double ranks, emerged abruptly into open ground. There was a narrow space of weeds and grass, a post-and-rail fence, a strange feel of space and emptiness beyond. There was a sergeant-major standing like a fence post, marking the position. "Guides . . . !" There were sergeants running, stopping, shuffling, stiffening. "Mark ti-i-ime . . . dress . . . !" The crooked line bulged into the straight line of sergeants, the ten companies fitted themselves into it like panels. "Dress . . . dress . . . dress it up, men . . . b'tallyun-nn . . . com'nee-e-eee . . . p'too-o-oon . . . *hult!* Or'rrr . . . *hmmms!*" The Fifth Maryland stood in line of battle. It could not believe it. There was some mistake. There must be.

But there wasn't and you knew there wasn't. Even standing at attention, with your eyes front and the sun blind-bright against them, you knew that this was the place where it was going to happen. It looked the way a battlefield had ought to look.

There was the rail fence, with the creepers swarming up the posts and crawling out along the top rail, and the bottom rail half hidden in the rank grass. Beyond the fence there was a farm field and, fifty yards ahead, an old log-built house beside the lane, and then more fields that stretched away for maybe half a mile, and then another oak woods with the sky behind it. To the left, across the road from the log house, there were six or seven haystacks strung out in a hit-or-miss row.[13] Halfway between the haystacks and the distant woods there was a cluster of frame buildings in a rail-fenced farmyard—a substantial house, sheds and a stable and a little outhouse. That was all. Excepting for the old cabin and the peaked stacks, the farmstead and its corn patch, there was nothing but the empty fields all rimmed around with woods.

It was the woods that gave the fields their look of having been laid out a-purpose, not just for farming but for something else too —for a race-day meeting or a county tournament of beauty. The open ground was shaped like that—like an arena, sort of. It was half a mile across and half again as long, with straight edges on the front and back sides like the stretches of a race course, and the two ends rounded where the woods curved in.

The woods were different at the two ends, right and left: they were more raggedy and crowded-looking than the clean oak groves, and the trees were mostly spindlier and close together, rising out of the young growth and underbrush that sprang up where there was water near by. Bear Creek should be over yonder to the right, close, and Back River off the other way but not so close. You could see the sun glint on the waist-high grass along the edges of the ragged woods, at the beginnings of the low ground. You could hear a long, dry rustling like the sound the grass made, this time of the year, when it was harsh and stiff against the wind. There wasn't any wind now, though. The harsh rustling was the 27th wheeling from column into line in the woods on the other side of the lane and coming out in pieces, its long double rank disordered by the trees, to form behind the fence.

Even when the Jeffersons had dressed and halted and stood motionless, the dry, crawling sounds continued in the woods. The other infantry regiments had turned off from the road, to right and left. The 51st was going into line three hundred yards behind the Fifth. The 39th was going into line three hundred yards behind the 27th.[14] The Union Artillery was filling the lane itself with purposeful confusion. Shafts of limbers dropped and clattered; gun teams trotted to the rear with trace chains clinking; gun crews, straining at the prolonges, dragged the four-pounders up into the gap between the two front-line regiments. The blue gunners swarmed around their pieces, seized them by their stubby trails and high wheels and manhandled them into position in the lane and in the weeds on either side. The six small guns stood almost hub to hub.

It was nine o'clock. The blocks were all in place.

The deployment did not take full advantage of the ground. The right of the Fifth Maryland rested "on the head of a branch of Bear Creek"[15] and was thus protected against a flanking movement by troops advancing up North Point. It was vulnerable to attack by troops coming up the creek in boats or landing somewhere on the western bank, but Sam Smith had taken precautions against both of those possibilities. The "light corps" under Major

Randall, which he had pushed out to Sollers' Point on Sunday afternoon to cover Stricker's bivouac against a night attack from the Patapsco, was three miles downstream.[16] In darkness, hostile barges might have been able to slip by undetected; now, in daylight, Randall's detachment had full observation of the river and the Bear Creek estuary. The "light corps" was scarcely strong enough to repel a landing attempt in serious force on Sollers' Point or on

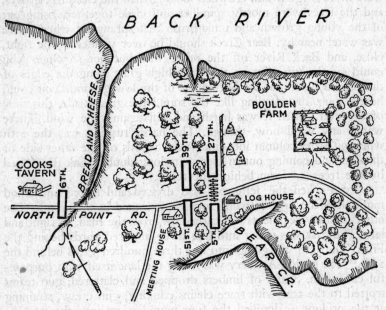

STRICKER'S ORDER OF BATTLE, about 9 a.m., September 12.

the river shore behind it; and, having no artillery, it could not prevent British boats from passing up the creek. But it could give Stricker ample warning of any amphibian movement that might threaten his right flank.

The left flank of the City Brigade's first line had no such protection. The deployment of the 27th extended "towards" a branch of the Back River,[17] but there was a considerable stretch of firm, open-wooded ground between the left of the regiment and the pondlike arm of the river. Stricker knew it. He decided, for the time being, to leave that flank exposed.

It was a calculated risk. Twice, at Bladensburg, the British light brigade had flung itself against the American positions by the most direct route. Twice, it had been checked—first by the counterattack of the Fifth under Sterrett, and later by the furious charge of Barney's men. In both attacks, the core of the American resistance had been finally broken by a flanking movement; but the fact was that in both instances the British had delivered their first attack head-on, without attempting to maneuver. It seemed probable, to Stricker, that they would try the same bludgeoning tactics again. There was only one road by which they could advance. It would lead them straight against the center of the brigade front. It might well tempt them into a frontal attack. If it did . . . well, Stricker's mission was to hurt them.

With his troops formed in depth—two regiments in front, two more in close support, and the Sixth under the veteran McDonald in reserve—he should have three chances at them. He could fight three successive actions. But if he extended his first line now, before it was necessary, by moving the regiments of the second line into that gap beyond the left flank of the 27th, he would lose at least one of those three chances. He might lose two of them. A frontal attack in concentrated force might throw an unsupported first line into such confusion that it could not rally on McDonald. The enemy might break through on the road and drive ahead so swiftly that the first-line regiments, retreating in deep woods and over swampy ground without roads or paths, would find themselves divided, cut off and trapped between the British and the long arms of the tide creeks.

There was risk in leaving that left flank uncovered. There was risk in facing an attack with one extended line. Stricker, seeing both, chose the one that seemed to offer the less danger and the greater profit. If the British moved against that unguarded flank, he could shift his second line to meet them. He would stick to this orthodox, old-Revolution deployment in depth until he saw that it would not do.

Deployment in depth had failed at Bladensburg; but it had not been, there, a sound deployment. The three lines at Bladensburg had not been co-ordinated; they had not even been planned; they had only happened. The second line, which might have given the first line support, had been withdrawn before the fighting started; the only portion of it that advanced had not been ordered forward until after the first line had been destroyed. And the second line had not known that there was a third line.

At the least, Stricker would see to it that those blunderings were not repeated. His orders were brief, precise, uncomplicated. The Fifth and the 27th were "to receive the enemy, and, if necessary fall back through the 51st and 39th, and form on the right of the Sixth or 'reserve regiment.' " The two supporting regiments —the second line—were ordered to fight where they stood, after the first line retreated through them; and then, if they were forced back, they also were to rally on McDonald's third line behind the little valley of the Bread-and-Cheese Creek.[18]

With his infantry deployed and his guns in battery, Brigadier General Stricker made one more preliminary move. His cavalry reconnaissance was still well out in front, its headquarters at the Gorsuch farm two and a half miles distant. His night outpost screen was still in position, a mile closer to his battle line. Now, when he was ready to fight, he could afford to use the rifle battalion for a mission more aggressive than security.

In another and earlier time, the woods and thickets east of Bear Creek would have offered opportunities for ambush. But this was not the Seven Years' War; British columns did not go plunging blindly into unreconnoitered forests as Braddock's men had gone at the Monongahela. Ross, marching unopposed through southern Maryland, had felt his way cautiously with his impromptu cavalry and combed his flanks with infantry patrols; now, advancing on the fourth largest city in America, he would certainly be no less careful. Against even rudimentary precautions, an attempt at large-scale ambush would be naïve. It might be disastrous. But there was one place . . .

South of the blacksmith shop that marked the overnight position of the rifle companies, a "low thick pine wood" [19] thrust out in the direction of the enemy. Beyond lay open ground, a broad expanse of sedge on both sides of the road. Something might be done there. A stiff stand . . . a small holding and harassing action . . . would begin the application of Sam Smith's trader-soldier tactics. *Haggle with them. Make them buy something they don't want before they get a chance at what they do want. Screw the price up. Make them think that Baltimore is too expensive. But don't risk too much of your capital for too small a profit.*

The pine wood had already been considered and discarded as being an unsound investment—an unfavorable position for a general engagement that was expected and intended to end in a withdrawal. The growth was too dense to permit maneuver or even deployment in close order; green troops, scattered through the tangle, would lose touch, cohesion, courage and themselves. To keep them in hand would be difficult; to extricate them, in condition to be rallied and renew the fight, probably would be impossible. Under such circumstances, retreat might degenerate into a rout as hopeless as the chaos on the Georgetown road three weeks ago.

But a position fatal for a large force might be useful for a small one. Concealment . . . surprise . . . a clear field of fire . . . rifles outranging the Tower muskets . . . Captain Dyer's three companies, hidden in the fringes of the pine woods, could make Ross pay dearly for that sedge field. The hundred and fifty riflemen should be enough to stop the enemy's advance guard in its tracks, hurt it, force Ross to reconnoiter and deploy more troops, make him lose time and men and possibly a little of his easy British confidence. The profit would be small; but the investment also would be small, the risk slight. Properly handled, the rifle battalion could stay long enough to punish even an overwhelming force advancing through the sedge field and still slip away before the British infantry could drive home a charge or work through the woods and get around its flanks. Stricker sent a mounted messenger to Dyer with an order: *move your battalion forward to the skirts of the pine wood; the cavalry is still in front and will inform you of the enemy's approach; take advantage of the covering of the wood and annoy his advance.*[20]

There was ample time to execute the order. The rifle battalion and the enemy's advance guard were still four miles apart. Ross was moving slowly. In the two hours or more that had elapsed since his last troops came ashore, he had marched only a little more than two miles. His column, squeezed thin by the narrow lane, was longer and less compact than was desirable in a strange and hostile region. Now, at about the time General Stricker sent orders to Captain Dyer to move forward, the invading army was strung out for a considerable distance on the long curve of the North Point road where it arched around the head of Old Road Creek. [21]

And one of its officers had just suffered an embarrassing repulse.

21

BEAUTY AND BOOTY

FOR THE SHIP-WEARY BRITISH troops in column on the country road, the advance up North Point from the beachhead was a pleasant march, reminiscent of other early morning marches up the valley of Patuxent.[1] For the platoons on flank patrol, it was not so pleasant. Thick woods crowded close

on both sides of the road; brush and brambles laced them; only an occasional small clearing broke the tangle. "Little lakes . . . abounded" and were too deep to be forded. Small streams "landing" in broad tide creeks thwarted and confused the unhappy infantrymen struggling through the thickets. As these veterans' discomfort and disgust increased, so did their contempt for Yankee military skill. Here were "a thousand defensible posts"—not one of them defended.

The British army, its march slowed to a crawl by the frustrations of its flanking parties, had been on the road an hour or more before it discovered the first evidence that its night landing had not taken the Americans by surprise. The discovery was mildly disappointing but not unexpected, and the evidence itself was not dismaying. On the contrary, it was merely fresh and quite unnecessary proof of American ineptness and stupidity; it was reassuring; it was downright funny.

The evidence consisted of a patrol of Yankee troopers—three of them, in well-cut, dark-green uniforms—sitting their fine horses in plain sight at the edge of a patch of timber on a small hill.[2] They were obviously supposed to be videttes and they were doing what they supposed videttes were supposed to do. They were watching the British column marching up the road, and they were so absorbed in trying to count the soldiers in the column that they apparently had forgotten that the enemy might also have patrols and outguards.

A flank platoon of the 85th Foot, scratching through the underbrush, caught sight of the three horsemen on their hillock. Perhaps the American army—if indeed the Americans still had an army—had not been taken unaware by the invasion; but those three oblivious dragoons were surely begging to be taken. The platoon promptly spread itself out to surround them. Before it could close in, the videttes got a glimpse of scarlet tunics slipping through the woods; they whirled their horses and went crashing off into the thickets. The patrol assumed that the Americans knew their way in their own woods; it did not pursue them. As it turned back, it heard the British bugles signaling a halt.

General Ross had been attracted by the imposing mansion of the Shaw plantation near by. An army must have a headquarters, and while the comforts of home were not a military necessity for headquarters in the field, neither were they so common as to be despised. The general, with his staff in support, had undertaken a reconnaissance in person while the army waited.

The right flank patrol of the 85th Foot, however, was interrupted in its enjoyment of the halt. What it had failed to accomplish, geography did for it. The elegant dragoons who had escaped from its attempt at envelopment were three citified young gentlemen of Baltimore: the wilds of North Point were as unfamiliar and bewildering to them as to the enemy; in plain truth, they were lost. The road, filled with British troops, skirted a deep arm of the Back River; the three gentlemen-volunteers, in their excited flight from the patrol, found themselves trapped between the water and the halted column. They plunged back into the woods, tethered their horses, and began to search the creekbank for a boat. They had just found a log canoe when the underbrush began to thrash and crack around them. Britishers! Confound them, they were better scouts than they were credited with being! British patrols were supposed to hug the roads, just as the scarlet infantry regiments were supposed to fight only in close order; but frequently they failed to live up to the American traditions of Breed's Hill and the Monongahela. One of the British scouts had failed now to live up to the dragoons' most reasonable expectations; he had found them again, had slipped away unnoticed, and was bringing a whole section down upon them.

They leaped into the canoe and paddled furiously, but they were only in midstream when a dozen British soldiers burst out upon the bank with leveled muskets and a British voice called on them to surrender. One of the embarrassed cavalrymen waved a pocket handkerchief. The canoe turned back. The amused and jubilant subaltern in command of the patrol began to think about finding his commanding general. It would be a feather in his cap to present to Ross, in person, his impressive-looking prisoners and his more impressive-looking booty—the Americans' "three beautiful chargers."

In the meantime, Ross had found the Shaw house to his liking. His staff officers, politely enough, had taken possession of the lower floor and ordered the family to retire upstairs. On the stairway one of the British lieutenants came face to face with Eleanor Shaw.

Perhaps the lieutenant had drunk so often to the toast of "Beauty and Booty" that, like many Americans, he had swallowed it whole. Perhaps he was a rounder. Perhaps he was merely lonely and impulsive. It was one of those "meeting engagements" in which, as young officers are taught, reaction must be instant and instinctive. The subaltern's instant and instinctive reaction was to throw his arms around Eleanor—or try to. She pushed him away and, so the legend has it, jumped out through a window. There was no pursuit. Ross took prompt action to convince his young men that "Beauty and Booty" was not an official expression of the policy of his Britannic Majesty's government at war. He put the frustrated lieutenant under arrest and sent him back on shipboard in disgrace.[3]

Ross did not remain long at the Shaw plantation. He rejoined the column. The march quickened.

It was a march under surveillance—close, constant and, for a time at least, unsuspected by the commanding general.[4] Not all of Colonel Biays's dragoons had got themselves cut off and captured. In thicket after thicket, American videttes dropped out of treetops or crept from coverts in the roadside underbrush, untied their waiting horses, mounted in haste and made off through the woods at fox-hunt speed. The British advance guard had pushed on nearly a mile and a half when it caught a glimpse of horsemen scampering away. Two hundred yards farther up the road, it "arrived at a piece of ground which appeared as if it had been lately in possession of the enemy." [5] Across a narrow neck of land between two tide creeks ran a sketchy line of trenches: stakes marked the outlines of a ditch and parapet: on a low rise of ground, the sod had been torn up in the beginnings of a battery.

The column halted again. The advance guard reconnoitered. In relation to the visible terrain, the position was impressive. It had been skillfully selected, and the line as laid out indicated at least rudimentary knowledge of field fortification. The flanks were protected both by water and by thick woods; musketry from the unfinished trenches could have swept the open fields in front; cannon in the intended battery could have enfiladed them. But there were no cannon, and the half-dug rifle pits were empty. This had been, apparently, another case of the Americans' too little and too late. The bugles blew again. The invading army marched in solid column through the uncompleted and abandoned field works.

At this point, between the head of Humphrey's Creek and a blunt, nameless arm of the Back River, history begins in earnest its unnatural labor of distortion. The outlined ditch becomes a "line of intrenchments and abattis." It acquires a garrison of "American dragoons and riflemen." The troops "stationed there" break and flee "without firing a shot," [6] and the untrue story of the battle of Baltimore as one more example of "disgraceful warfare, redeemed only by the naval exploits of American seamen and the decisive victory of Andrew Jackson at New Orleans," [7] is off to a good start.

This first of many falsehoods, like most of the other falsehoods that distort the story, has a flimsy camouflage of truth that will be plausibly deceptive for more than a hundred years. It is true that there are American riflemen on North Point, but they are not "stationed" in the unfinished trenches; the nearest riflemen are at least two miles away. It is also true that there are dragoons in the neighborhood, but they are not a garrison; their mission is observation and liaison, not combat. The horsemen seen galloping away are part of Colonel Biays's chain of outposts; they are obeying orders by fetching back the information they were assigned to get.

They have not been surprised; but they would be as thoroughly surprised as their comrades in the log canoe if they could know that in a few years an eminent historian will reproach them for not giving battle, in an unfinished ditch, to an army of five thousand.

The Gorsuch farm, headquarters of the cavalry detachment, was less than half a mile west of the "intrenchments." Biays, carrying out his mission, fell back as the enemy approached; Ross took possession of the farmyard. Lieutenant Gleig of the 85th, coming in with his three prisoners and their "chargers," found his general in a mood to appreciate the comical aspects of his report. Ross and Cockburn were sitting in the front yard of the farmhouse, with their staff officers glittering around them and their orderlies walking their horses slowly back and forth.[8] Both the general and the admiral were in a high good humor. Everything was going splendidly. Baltimore was only ten miles distant; the first troops had been ashore six hours and still there was no sign of resistance except those halfhearted, half-begun entrenchments and those pathetically clumsy costume-ball dragoons. Long before the hour set for the combined attack by land and water, the army would be in position to assault the city. It was time now for breakfast, there was time to spare, and breakfast for the general and the admiral was cooking in the farmer's kitchen.

Other breakfasts squawked and squealed around them. Calves were bellowing in terror. Pigs were shrilling, hens were scurrying and flying. Ducks had lost their dignity in panic. The air was full of noise and feathers. There was a long gap in the column halted on the road: the regiment of seamen had broken ranks without orders. In spite of "all the threats, orders and entreaties of their officers," the bluejackets were running wild in the Gorsuch barnyard, killing pigs and poultry, plundering the roosts and stables. Being sailors, they of course "knew nothing about discipline on shore, and they were not now going to learn it." They were so completely out of control that "the very endeavor to bring them back was abandoned."[9]

Beauty might have the general's protection. Booty was another matter. The officers found it impossible "to refrain from laughing at the singular behaviour of these men . . . nor did anyone appear to enjoy the joke more than General Ross." He was "laughing heartily, as were the admiral and the rest of the group" when Lieutenant Gleig appeared with his prisoners. Here was another topping joke: American scouts outdone at their own business in their own woods: Yankee dragoons squatting helpless in a hollowed log: cavalry run down by infantry. It was almost too good to be true, but it was of a piece with the whole delightful morning. The commanding general "with difficulty suppressed his mirth" and "proceeded to cathechize them respecting the number and position of the force appointed for the defence of Baltimore."

The three dragoons did their best to make up for their failure as videttes, and their best was good enough to be preserved in history as fact. When the truth seemed adequate, they told the truth: that in artillery the strength of the defenders was "prodigious," with "upwards of one hundred pieces of cannon" in batteries manned by regular seamen of the fleet. But the truth about the infantry was not nearly so impressive. They multiplied it by their imagination and assured Ross that no less than twenty thousand men were waiting for him. Their imagination improved as they went along. When Ross remarked that the American forces doubtless were militia, they multiplied the Fort McHenry infantry by five and produced three thousand regulars.

The British staff officers "took it for granted" that the garrulous prisoners were trying to alarm them, and decided that the information was "neither very distinct nor very satisfactory." They did not realize, then, how unsatisfactory it was: the dragoons had limited their garrulity to the fort and fieldworks on the outskirts of the city and had carefully neglected to mention that part of the garrison had come out from the defenses.

It was, for Ross, a fatal omission. His advance almost certainly would have been conducted differently if he had known that an American brigade supported by artillery was preparing to give battle only a little more than two miles up the road. But he was not impressed by the tall tale of the hundred cannon, the imaginary regulars and the fabulous army of "twenty thousand men" ten miles away. Lieutenant Gleig observed that "the general heard all this with a countenance which never once varied in its expression." And legend has it that Ross, when the questioning was finished, announced with a gay confidence that he would take Baltimore "though it rain militia."

More reliable evidence as to his state of mind and that of his subordinates is the delay at the Gorsuch farm and the prolonged indulgence of the seamen. The army had pushed into strange and hostile country without cavalry reconnaissance; the trusted officer who had commanded the advance guard through southern Maryland had been left behind at Bladensburg, severely wounded; [10] the picked force which had constituted the advance guard had been "dissolved" after the loss of its commander. Protection of the march, today, was under the direction of the officer "who chanced to be senior" among those attached to the three companies assigned to that duty. Ross was "ignorant of the talents of those on whose sagacity the welfare of the whole column so much depended." [11] And now, with the column halted and vigilance relaxed, forward reconnaissance was neglected; patrols were not pushed out to any useful distance beyond the Gorsuch farm: the outguards failed to flush the American cavalrymen watching the proceedings in the farmyard from the shelter of the woods ahead.[12] The naval brigade —almost a fifth of the whole army—was in wild disorder, defying or ignoring its own officers. But the commanding general was not disturbed by the military implications of his situation. Neither was he embarrassed by the immediate circumstances. He enjoyed his breakfast while the whooping sailors "continued to amuse themselves" at the expense of his involuntary host.

Two and a half miles away, the implications of a different situation were bringing acute embarrassment to Captain William Dyer.

22

A BAD BEGINNING

Two and a half miles away, Brigadier General John Stricker waited for the crash of the collision he had planned. On horseback, with his staff around him in the lane behind Montgomery's guns, he listened expectantly for the sound of Captain Dyer's skirmish. The gunners of the Union Artillery and the infantrymen of the four deployed regiments, knowing nothing about Dyer's orders, merely waited.

BRIGADIER GENERAL
JOHN STRICKER

They had listened, for a time, with an expectancy as taut as Stricker's. The rifle battalion was out yonder somewhere, behind the green horizon of the woods. Well, anyway, it was supposed to be; somebody'd said it was. Well, anyway, the cavalry was out there. You could see that for yourself; every now and then one of the dragoons came bursting out of the far woods and galloping up the lane as if he aimed to jump his horse right over the four-pounders. It was funny, the first two-three times, to see how annoyed those buggers acted when they found the road blocked. They acted like they had been done a mean trick. It surely took the starch out of their importance when they had to slow down and pick their way around the guns. Maybe, though, they had cause to feel important. Maybe they had reason to be in such a tearing hurry, maybe they knew something. The enemy was out yonder somewhere, too . . . *yeah, iffen he ain't somewheres else . . . iffen he ain't behind us* . . . Ah, shut up!

You couldn't go on forever listening for something when you didn't know what you were listening for exactly. You couldn't just go on forever listening to nothing. Not with everybody jabbering, you couldn't . . . *right now* . . . *those dragoon fellows could be fighting right now and we wouldn't know it* . . . Hell we wouldn't. Day as still as this is you can hear a man choppin' wood far as you can see him. *How far can you see him?* Mile. *You can't* . . . *not to tell what he's doin'.* You could hear a musket farther'n that, though; musket shot's a damn sight louder than an ax is. *Pistol ain't* . . . *the cavalry's got pistols.* That's dandy. You got things fixed up just dandy, only our side firin'. I suppose the British ain't got muskets. *A-a-aahh* . . . *!*

The regiments stood at ease in ranks. The men draped themselves over their long weapons. They clasped their hands on the muzzles and rested their chins on their knuckles; they used their muskets like crutches, they used them for props; they rested the muzzles on tree roots and rested their chests on the butts; they stood humpbacked and swaybacked, they stood first on one foot and then on the other. Their buttocks, in the tight drab breeches, protruded like bustles; their hips canted sidewards like the hips of outrageous dancers. In the narrow space between the rail fence and the edge of the oak grove, the two first-line regiments made a long hieroglyphic sentence, a human alphabet hopelessly scrambled. But the sentence could be read. The hieroglyphics could be translated.

The sentence spelled out by the unconsciously posturing bodies was a universal idiom. It expressed the universal instinct of men to hide their innermost feelings, to disguise their emotions. It expressed the need of these men to conceal from themselves and each other their thoughts of what lay concealed behind the woods half a mile ahead. It was an idiom never, intentionally, spoken aloud. Its meaning was never, intentionally, put into words.

The literal translation was boredom. The meaning was subtler than boredom. It was compounded of many meanings—of men's fears and their fear of fear; of the infinitely various natures of all these men and of their infinitely various experiences; of their childhoods, their homes and their women; of the remembered past and of wondering whether the past would be all; of their hopes for the future and of wonder concerning the imagined immediate future; of a nonexistent monotony, of the sense of repetition that comes even to inexperienced soldiers as the first of all soldier experience—the real unreal feeling of having been here before, of having done all this before in just the same way, in places precisely like this.

There was something familiar about this place, something annoyingly familiar. You couldn't for the life of you figure out what it was. You almost had it; then you didn't have it. The place wasn't like Bladensburg, it didn't look like Bladensburg at all. There wasn't any town. There wasn't any stream downhill in front of you, with a bridge across it. There wasn't any hill. The open ground was nearabout as level as a floor—as level, anyway, as the floor of an old barn, with the fields for planks and no two planks exactly the same width or the same color and some of them warped a little. The lane ran out across the fields as straight as a crack between two planks and it was dirty-brown the way a crack was in a barn floor. The log house sat beside the lane like a shabby feedbox in a stable; the flat roof was a lid, and the curled, broken shingles looked as if a horse had gnawed it trying to get at the grain inside. Maybe that was why the place looked familiar; maybe it reminded you of the livery stable where you went to hire the gig to take your girl out riding . . . *oh, for God's sake . . . !* Why did you have to think about *that?* It wasn't any time to think about a thing like that when maybe you were going to be killed and come to judgment.

You'd thought the same thoughts last time, though. You'd laid on your belly in the grass and put your arm around your rolled-up blanket and imagined that it was a girl. You'd written a girl's name in the dust on the flat top of your leather hat. The sergeant made you wipe it off; but you hadn't been killed for what you had been thinking. You hadn't been shot, even for what you thought about the sergeant. It was the sergeant that got shot. *Funny.* . . . Things had changed considerably. Sergeant McCulloch wasn't here to holler at you. Chris Keener wasn't here. George Golder wasn't here to let his musket off in back of your left ear. Everything was different. The sun didn't scald you, it was just warm and comfortable. You weren't tired and you weren't hungry. There wasn't any apple orchard. There wasn't any town.

*You thought that before . . . you thought about that just a few
minutes ago . . . maybe that's why all this seems familiar, because
you're thinking the same things over and over. . . .* No, it can't be
that. It's something, though. There's something that's the same as
last time. What are we waiting for, anyway?

Wait . . . wait . . . wait. . . .

It's the waiting that's hard to take. It's the waiting that's the
worst. No, it's not . . . that's not true. It maybe was true the last
time, it isn't true now. I didn't know, last time, what it was going
to be like . . . the noise . . . and Chris Keener falling down and
the noise he made . . . *uhh* . . . sick and kind of surprised . . .
we left him there, we just went on and left him . . . George
Golder all bloody . . . and Jim McCulloch trying to crawl . . . I
wasn't mad at Jim any more . . . the dirt turning to mud in
streaks where he'd dragged his leg . . . and puddles where he'd
had to stop crawling . . . and the noise . . . the godawful noise.
I didn't know. I know now. That's what makes the waiting bad.
I know what it's going to be like when the waiting ends. It's
going to be worse. Those fellows across the road there . . . those
fellows in the 27th . . . they're lucky . . . they don't know. They
wouldn't be acting so brash and easy if they knew. I wish I didn't
know. I wish to God I didn't. *Did I say that?*

You must have said it. You must have said *something* out loud.
It seemed like the whole section was looking at you, looking you
over, not disapproving exactly but just looking. Somebody said
shucks, if you're going to make a wish you might as well make it
a good one. Might as well wish this fence was a creek and you had
a fish pole. Might as well wish that tree was a bar'l full of whisky.
Might as well wish this here patch of grass was a featherbed and you
had a . . . *With a whole brigade of chaperones? Thanks just the
same.*

They weren't nervous. They weren't afraid. You were the only
one that was scared. You had to say something to prove that you
hadn't been scared, you had to show them you'd been thinking
about something sensible and important. This looks like the same
old story. Yes, sir, it surely does. It's the same as Bladensburg. It's
the apple orchard and us in it—only the orchard is this oak woods—
and the rifle battalion somewhere out in front by itself. The Rifles
have been out in front by themselves all night. And we've got the
same number of guns that we had before. Six. You watch, now.
You'll see. Pretty soon now they'll stick the guns out in front by

*them*selves. And then they'll move us out of here to a worse place, same as they did at Bladensburg, and . . . *Wait a minute, can't you? It hasn't happened yet. What you so touchy for?* I'm not! I'm not touchy!

But you were. Walt Muschett knew it; he was turning his head, grinning at you. And Jake Haubert, standing next to you, was looking at you with a kind of curious expression. Just because a man happened to stand next to you in ranks didn't give him any right to ask you questions. Not that kind of questions. You could maybe tell Walt Muschett why you had been talking. You could maybe tell Walt that you had been talking loud because you couldn't help it, because you had to do something to fill up that hollow feeling that was digging itself deeper in your guts. But you couldn't tell Jake Haubert. It was too soon for a man's nerves to be getting crawly.

Three or four files away, somebody else began to talk. *It isn't like Bladensburg. . . .* The hell it isn't! The voice was calm and slow. You hated the man with the voice with a sudden fierce hate, the way you'd hated Golder when he fired his musket in your ear. *. . . except for one thing.* Well, now. Well, that's more like it. *That log house reminds me of the barn at Bladensburg. It's too close to us. The Britishers can make us trouble if they get that house. They can form up a whole column back of it, same as they did behind the barn. We ought to hold that log house, or tear it down, or burn it.*

Presently it developed that the officers—the general or somebody—had got the same idea. Colonel Sterrett came riding along behind the line of the Fifth Maryland. A drum burped. Captains and lieutenants shouted. The human alphabet erased itself; the hieroglyphics of the lounging bodies became two blank, ruled lines; the regiment stood at attention. Then a piece of it broke off. A company climbed the rail fence and moved across the field toward the log house.[1] The remaining companies higgled and jiggled, faced right, marched, faced left, dressed, poked elbows into ribs until the gap left by Captain Sadtler's Yeagers had been filled and the regimental front was smooth again and unbroken. The captains shouted "Fall out!" The sergeants came in with their own bawlings: "Fall out! You can fall out, but that don't mean you can go wanderin' around. You can set down or lay down, but mind you stay right here."

The stiff ranks disintegrated. Some men sat down; some

sprawled out in the sun; some eased back into the fringes of the woods and lay down in the shade. A good many hung themselves across the top rail of the fence and watched the Yeagers. A small company advancing on an empty log house wasn't such a much to look at, but it was something; it was better than nothing; it was something to talk about, to keep your mind off other matters. You could talk about the way they marched—not loud enough to make Ensign Wilmot tell you to shut up but loud enough to burn the Yeagers' ears. You could watch the insects boiling up in puffs, like, out of the grass around the striding legs. You could watch the resentful jumpings of the grasshoppers. You could make jokes. You could say well, anyhow, those fellers are g'on' to have themselves a proper privy. Yes, sir; private, too. That's what I call g'on' to war with all the comforts of home. You could say I wonder how them Yeagers come to get first chance, I wonder if we're g'on' to get turns at it.

One big fat grasshopper took off with a spiteful whirring that was almost like the sudden, run-together squawking of a scared hen. You could almost see the way he kicked his heels, indignant. The kick gave him a good start; he shot across the faded, feathery weed tops with a long, brittle buzzing, and he stayed in the air so long it seemed as if he didn't mean to come down ever. He lit, finally, in the weeds just beyond the rail fence, with a stiff, rustling plop. You'd heard a sound like that before . . . somewhere . . . sure you had, you had heard other hoppergrasses lighting . . . no, not that . . . something else. . . . It was the sound a woman made when she sat down abruptly in a chair . . . a rustly plop, stiff silk and starchy petticoats being crushed . . . a little old lady sitting 'down. Why did she have to be an old lady? Girls wore stiff silk, girls wore petticoats, they rustled . . . why did you have to think about girls again?

Somebody was down on his knees beside the fence, reaching through between the rails. Head and shoulders through the rails . . . peering into the grass . . . hand pouncing . . . *got him!* The militiaman pulled back, grinning, his hand closed into a loose fist. He squatted by the fence and spread his knuckles just a little, carefully. He had the big hopper in the cage of his fingers, he was immensely pleased about it. He was showing two-three other men and they were looking pleased, too, squinting through the cracks between his fingers. *Wish I had a hook an' line . . . wish we were going fishing.* . . . They fell to arguing about whether the hopper was too big to be a good bait. *Scare any ordinary fish, he would.* I don't want no ordinary fish. *Spit tobacco juice right in a fish's eye, he would . . . look at him chew, that's quite a cud he's got . . . what he needs is a sandbox to spit in . . . or a fish's eye. . . .* He's satisfied, though; he's makin' out all right; he's g'on' to spit! *Hail! Columbia, happy land . . . spit it out in papa's hand!* They were laughing, rocking on their hunkers, their heads close together over the bunched fingers. What was so funny about that? That was a hell of a way to talk . . . turning the soaring music of the bands, yesterday, into a joke like that . . . making fun . . . when pretty soon a man might be dying for Columbia. . . . Why do they call it Columbia? There isn't any such thing . . . *hail, heav'n born band* . . . the militia bands weren't born in heaven . . . they weren't any angel choir and that was certain. But the song didn't mean that kind of band. It meant people. Those people on their knees, arguing about hoppergrasses, didn't look heaven born; they looked downright foolish.

A dozen of them were crawling on their hands and knees, parting the grass with their fingers, hunting for more hoppers. They were gabbing *race day . . . race day . . .two to one on this here gelding . . . how you know he's a gelding? Well, he will be if I lose my bet.* A whole platoon was crowding around now . . . half a section of them had caught hoppers. They were laying wagers, laughing, yelping at each other, making conditions. *Got to clear the top rail or it don't count. Ought to have a bugle . . . can't, you might start a war or something . . . got to have a starter . . . Jake, you be the starter . . . you count one, two, three . . . .* Sure, Jake can count up to three. *No, a flag. You got a handker-chief?* Won't do . . . a gentleman jockey can't watch his horse an' watch a flag too . . . these here leppers are right high-spirited; you better count, Jake. When Jake says three, you can tickle your horse with a grass stalk. Line up, here! *One . . . two . . . three . . . !*

The race didn't last long. When it was over, it was a kind of letdown. Nobody suggested having another hopper race. They just sat.

The sun soaked through them. The two first-line regiments simmered in it, their talk like the low humming of a kettle boiling gently. Underneath the talk there was another humming. It was light, almost too light to hear—a gauzy fabric of sound, thin and delicate. The sound of a thousand men talking came through it, but the thin gauze of insect sound was always there . . . like a delicate lace shawl over solid silk.

A cicada shrilled and shrilled. It sounded like a fiddler tightening a string with reckless turns, not caring if the string broke. It ought to break. It surely would, the next turn. But it didn't. The sound went on and on, the undertone of insect sound went on and on. It would be the same tomorrow. It wouldn't matter whether you were there to hear it. Everything would go on and on without you. *Oh, hell, stop it.* Far off, a mourning dove was moaning. Rain, somebody said, it's going to rain. There was another argument about that.

One after another, three fat white clouds came up over the line of the far woods. It was hard to say whether they rose up from behind the woods or were just born there. You couldn't see them move. They were moving, likely, but you couldn't see it any more than you could see the hour hand of a clock move. The clouds stayed there like three old gentlemen in powdered wigs and fluffy white stocks, looking over a green wall, mildly interested in the crops in the half mile of fields.

One after another, with long empty waiting intervals between, the cavalry videttes came riding up the lane. Each time one of them came, the dirt rose up in little rounded plops to match the *plop* sounds of his horse's hoofs. The puffs of dirt weren't like the feathery loose dust that had pursued the express riders' horses up the road past Lowndes's hill and into Bladensburg and up the turnpike past the apple orchard. These were neat, plump swellings of moist dust. The damp-powdery surface of the lane rose up in precise patterns of small splashes underneath the hoofs, the way water rose up when you dropped a stone into it. *That's queer . . .* you dropped the stone . . . it didn't make a hole into the water, the water stood straight up as if to meet it . . . and then when the little straight-up spout of water had subsided, there was the hole . . . if you were quick enough to see the hole before it slid into the surface and was gone. The dirt in the lane was like that, only different. The dirt rose up under the dropped hoofs; it settled quickly, almost as quick as water; you could see the hole where the hoof had dropped. The difference was that the hoof splash stayed there in the road—a long line of patterned splashes, four by four, as far down the lane as you could see.

But nothing happened when the videttes rode up to the clump of mounted officers behind the guns. Nothing happened except talk, and not even much of that. It looked as if it was the horses that were holding council, not the staff officers. The horses, fighting flies, shook their heads and hacked them up and down in violent disagreement or agreement. The officers just sat there, waiting.

It seemed as if it didn't make any difference what you expected war to be: it would manage somehow to be something else. Looking across the fields, you expected war to come bursting out of the still woods beyond that cluster of farm buildings—Boulden's place, somebody said it was—or to come poking cautiously out of the dark hole the lane made in the woods. You expected anyway a flash of scarlet, like when the British skirmishers broke through the thickets in the river bottoms by the bridge at Bladensburg, or like when they came pushing through the edges of the apple orchard, running, crouching. But it didn't happen that way. War didn't come with a rush.

When war came to the City Brigade, it was only a few men walking up the road.

They were not Britishers. The men who came out of the woods had blue coats on. They walked along the lane in a little straggly group, like men who happened to be going in the same direction at the same time—to market, maybe, or to church. The only thing that wasn't like that was the way they looked back, every now and then, as if they were expecting somebody to catch up with them.

Pretty soon there was another little group of men walking across the fields a hundred yards or so to one side of the lane. They had come out of the woods like men that had been hunting and had got tired and were starting home. They, too, kept turning their heads, looking backwards. But there wasn't anything for them to see except the woods they had come out of. Watching those men, you got a feeling something had gone wrong; you got a feeling something had happened in the woods. *That's foolish.*

Nothing had happened. There hadn't been any shooting. There hadn't been a single shot, there hadn't been a sound. And yet the rifle battalion was coming back. It was retreating, straggling, walking up the lane and through the fields in little groups and looking backward every now and then.

The hum of talking ceased. The hum of insects ceased: the sudden stirrings of men's bodies hushed it. You felt naked in the sudden silence. You felt as if you had been lying in the warm sun with the gauzy fabric of sound over you and now, without warning, it was gone. Somebody had stripped it off of you and left you bare. It made you feel self-conscious . . . no, conscious of yourself. There was a difference. You didn't know what the difference was, but there it was: you felt it. You got up off the ground. You stood up, feeling naked that way, feeling awkward and exposed, feeling slow and heavy and light at the same time, the way you felt when you had taken off your clothes and waded out into the Patapsco shallows and the water rose up slow around your body, warm as air but stiffer than the air, resisting, pushing, making you feel partly heavier and partly lighter. Standing here now, you felt the way you felt in water—as if you were standing in a different element. That was foolish, too.

Other men were beginning to stand up. They were getting up from where they had been lying, sitting. The crushed grass and the crushed weeds held the imprints of their bodies. When they stood up, the pallid shapes of their bodies, of their heads, their legs, lay on the ground like prone ghosts. *I wonder if my body* . . . You looked. It was. The shape of your body was lying there, plainly marked in the sun-faded grass, in the desiccate gray undersides of the pigweed leaves. A place marked out, waiting for your body . . . quit it . . . *quit it!*

Without orders, the two regiments were forming. It was a formation of their own devising. Their line was straight because the fence was straight and they were packed against the rail fence like a race-day crowd. The talk began again. It was not a hum, now, low and silken. It was hoarser, louder. It moved. You could feel it moving, you could feel it tightening around you. *What . . . ? What in hell . . . ? Why . . . ? What's the matter with those fellows?* Question . . . question . . . doubtful answer . . . wonder . . . back . . . forth . . . what . . . what . . . The clacking shuttle of a thousand men's talk wove a cloth of sound to cover their alarm. It was thick and rough, like homespun. It was thicker than the gauzy fabric of the insect sound. The insect sound was smothered . . . *last time . . . running, that's what . . . same as Stansb'ry's men last time . . . no . . . no . . . the Rifles ain't drafted men, they ain't county m'litia* . . . The thick fabric swelled. You could almost see it rising, swelling, like the cloth of the balloon you'd seen once, spread out on the ground and being filled with hot gas. You could feel the talk rising, filling up with apprehension . . . *Britishers behind 'em . . . must be . . . beating the woods . . . combin' 'em out of the woods like rabbits.* In the tall weeds around the log house, you could see the heads of Sadtler's Yeagers popping up and down like rabbits.

The sound-fabric tore. The drums ripped it with long, tearing noises. The long roll pulled the crowd of men back from the fence and into ranks. The double ranks were not quite as straight as the thick line had been along the fence. They were merely tauter, stiffer. They felt, somehow, more exposed: when the drums stopped beating and the officers stopped shouting, there was no sound to cover them: they stood naked in the silence. The empty hollow in your belly was a bubble, swelling.

The scattered groups of riflemen were drifting together, the men walking in the fields were drifting over toward the lane. They made, along the road, a strung-out and shapeless column, and then a column that had shape in places, where a half-section or a platoon had gathered itself together and got into step. You could hear somebody calling cadence . . . *hup* . . . *hup* . . . *hup* . . . *hup*. It sounded like a dog barking monotonously, a long way off. It sounded as if maybe the Bouldens' dog was still on guard in the barnyard. You wondered if the Boulden family was still there in the house. You expected any minute to see somebody run out of the house. You expected any minute to see scarlet jackets in the lane where it bent past the barn . . . there . . . *there* . . . *!*

But it wasn't what you had expected. It was another man on horseback, it was another of those dragoon fellows. No, it was three of them together. They weren't in a hurry like the others had been; they were only trotting their horses; they were looking around, backwards, sidewards. You got a feeling they were looking for something that they thought should be there for them to see but wasn't. They pulled their horses to a slow walk, close together, as if they were puzzled about something and uncomfortable about it and were talking it over. Then they came on at a gallop, past the strung-out column. You could see the color of their jackets now— not dragoon green, but blue. You could see the curled cock's feathers on their tall hats, you could tell that they were officers in the Rifles. Dyer . . . that's Captain Dyer . . . and that's young Will Pinkney with him . . . young Will's the adjutant. The third one's Dr. Martin. But what were they doing back there a minute ago? Stopping that way . . . looking . . . talking . . . they didn't act like they were being chased . . . I don't understand it.

Brigadier General Stricker did not understand it either. For two hours he had been prepared for battle; he had been ready since nine o'clock. For almost two hours he had been hoping to get in the first blow—not a blow that would do the enemy great damage but one that might give his own men a surge of confidence at sight of the Invincibles' advance guard taken by surprise, halted, perhaps scattered, hurt at least a little. He had not expected too much, but he had been hoping that Dyer would hurt the enemy enough to make Ross cautious in the final action, make him choose a formal parade-ground advance across the half mile of open ground instead of an instantaneous charge. It was the possibility of a swift, headlong assault that Stricker dreaded most. A charge, launched promptly and pressed firmly home, could cross the fields before his little battery could get off more than four or five rounds; it would be within a hundred yards of his brigade front before his musketry could hurt it. The sheer overawing power of a British charge might snap the nerves of the militia regiments and break their lines before it came close enough for decent shooting. He had been hoping that Will Dyer would persuade Ross to advance slowly, to give the City Brigade time to steady itself after the first shock of seeing the Invincibles advancing.

It had not seemed an unreasonable hope. Ross had been co-operative: already he had given Dyer ample time to get into position. More than an hour ago Colonel Biays had sent back a message that the British troops were "moving rapidly up the main road." Since that message came, vidette after galloping vidette had "continually announced their progress." Minute after tightening minute, Stricker had waited for his riflemen to "proclaim by a galling fire" the "still nearer approach of Ross's columns." [2] Now, without a shot fired, he saw the whole rifle corps falling back on his main position—saw his hopes dribbling away in a thin dribble of retreat. [3] It was unbelievable.

If Stricker had difficulty in believing what he saw, Will Dyer had even greater difficulty in explaining it. The explanation was not incredible. It was merely discreditable.

The explanation was credulity. Captain Dyer had been routed by a rumor. He had "too credulously listened to groundless information that the enemy were landing on Back River" [4] to cut him off. He had believed that he was outflanked and about to be surrounded. Instead of obeying orders to advance, he had withdrawn his whole battalion.

The quiet fields, the waiting guns and the long lines of deployed infantry were disconcerting to an officer in precipitate retreat. Will Dyer knew, as he rode up to Stricker, that he had erred —erred badly. His report, now, was helpful neither to himself nor to his general. He had no facts, he had nothing but an untraced rumor. What he had listened to meant nothing; what he had done provided the one piece of direct evidence available to support the charge of history that Stricker had neglected "ordinary caution." If the accusation means anything, it means that Stricker was careless or incompetent.

The justice of the charge is questionable. The justice of using the conduct of the rifle battalion as evidence to support the charge is also questionable. Two facts are obvious: the unauthorized retreat was Dyer's: the immediate responsibility was Dyer's. Two alternative conclusions are almost as obvious. One is that Dyer neglected to protect his left flank by stationing patrols where they could observe the whole sweep of Back River. The other is that the patrols, if they were sent out, failed to do their duty. Indeed, it is not improbable that the false alarm originated with a nervous outpost. But when the baseless rumor came to Dyer, he made no adequate effort to confirm it or disprove it. He made no attempt either to warn Stricker promptly or to ask for orders. He retreated forthwith.

Captain Dyer's blunder was primarily a reconnaissance failure by a man whose commanding officer had risked his life on personal reconnaissance at Bladensburg. Will Dyer, trying to fill Will Pinkney's shoes as commander of the Rifles, had been filled with a concern about his flanks that was as great as Pinkney's had been. But apparently he was not filled with an equal sense of personal responsibility.

True, there is no evidence that Stricker had given Dyer specific orders regarding proper observation on his flanks. Neither is there any evidence that Stricker failed to give them. But Dyer was on outpost duty; his battalion was the advance guard, the covering force for the main body of Stricker's combat team; it was in the presence of an enemy whose direction of attack was yet unknown. Until Stricker sent him orders to advance, Dyer's obvious and primary responsibility was adequate reconnaissance and observation. Under the circumstances, specific instructions should have been unnecessary.

There is no direct evidence that Stricker himself had taken precautions to watch Back River for a possible amphibious attack designed to get behind his left flank. Neither is there any direct evidence that he had not taken such precautions. The testimony that now appears is Stricker's own, and it is not conclusive. It can be interpreted to mean that he was careless and overconfident of his safety from a water-borne assault against his left flank or behind it. It can also be interpreted to mean that he knew, from his own security measures, that no such assault was threatening, and that his reconnaissance on the left was as adequate as on his right, where Major Randall's light corps watched Bear Creek and the Patapsco River. Stricker, in his official report, said curtly that Dyer's information had been baseless. He did not say that he took steps to establish the truth or falsity of the alarming rumor. The implication is that he knew instantly that it was false—that he already *knew* there were no British landing barges in Back River and no hostile troops ashore there. His course of action gives weight to the implication.

Listening with chagrin and anger to Will Dyer's explanations, Stricker was so little concerned about a British landing from Back River that he sent the rifle battalion to the opposite end of his brigade front. "I threw the riflemen," he said in his report, "on the right flank of my front line, thereby, with the addition of a few cavalry, very well securing that flank." To conclude that this was the action of an overconfident or careless man is to make an unwarranted assumption. It was, in fact, a calculated, reasoned action.

One of the reasons was the road. It divided Stricker's chosen battlefield into two unequal parts. South, the head of Bear Creek was only a few hundred yards away; between lane and road, the open ground was only a little longer than the front of the Fifth Maryland. North, the arm of the Back River was more than twice as far away; Stricker could not cover all the open ground there except by deploying four full regiments in one line. His left flank was in the air; he could not anchor it without destroying his deployment in depth. But this deployment in depth was based on the expectation that the enemy, advancing up the road, would attack head-on. The arrangement of his troops was, he believed, the best possible measure of defense against direct attack. If he could make his right flank so secure that he need not be much concerned about it, he could devote his attention—and his supporting regiments, if need be—to the naturally weaker left flank. The thickets to the south, around the head of Bear Creek, offered cover for the Rifles and an opportunity for flanking fire against an attack upon the right flank of his line. To the north there was no similar opportunity.

Another reason for ordering the rifle battalion to the right instead of the exposed left was his loss of confidence in Dyer.[5] He was unwilling to trust, in what might become the most critical position, the officer who had upset his plans by fleeing from a rumor. Probably he did not trust the battalion itself. It had retreated twice—at Bladensburg where part of it had rallied and advanced, only to be absorbed and dissolved in the final panic, and again today. And not only was, its regular commander absent, wounded: two of its three companies were in the field without their captains—Dyer himself, now leading the battalion, and Dominic Bader, captured at Bladensburg. Stricker, calculating the risks, preferred to cover the left flank—if the battle moved in that direction—with troops under their normal command and not involved in a silly and disorganizing retreat.

But he knew, as the riflemen tramped off toward the Bear Creek thickets, that the risks he faced were greater than he had intended them to be. They were not, perhaps, much greater; but he had failed in his effort to reduce them. Instead of stiffening the morale of his militiamen by giving them a chance to strike the first blow, the attack he planned had almost certainly had an opposite effect. His first maneuver had turned into a fiasco. The enemy would come on unchecked, unhurt. If Ross decided on headlong assault, the charge he dreaded would burst upon regiments already shaken by the spectacle of Dyer's flight. The whole brigade knew, now, that things had gone wrong. It had been a bad beginning.

23

THE PRICE OF A FEATHER

THE FIRST SEEPAGE OF MEN FROM
the retreating rifle companies had begun to trickle out of the woods
beyond the Boulden farm a little before eleven of the clock. It

was eleven and a half or later before Stricker got the disorganized battalion into decent order. It was almost noon [1] before he knew that there was still a chance to retrieve the opportunity that Dyer had thrown away.

Stricker listened with amazement as an excited young dragoon blurted out the news from Biays . . . yes, sir . . . at Gorsuch's . . . the advance party [2] . . . halted in the road, in column . . . except the sailors . . . running wild, sir . . . they're all over everywhere, chasing pigs and chickens. Colonel said to tell you it looks like the officers are figuring on breakfast. Yes, sir; in the front yard. They've had chairs fetched out and they're sitting in the front yard, laughing.

Stricker's temper was already edgy with the waiting and the disappointment. Now the dragoon's story rasped it like a whetstone. *Laughing.* . . . British contempt for American troops was understandable. It was also unendurable. He could imagine the laughter: it would not even be contemptuous, it would be merely indifferent, unconcerned. It would not have anything to do with these men of the City Brigade who were putting their flesh and their lives between their homes and the enemy; the Baltimore militia were not worth a thought. That was the essence of contempt. That was the insufferable insult.

But he did not have to suffer it. By the Lord, he didn't. He could do what he wanted to do. (If it seems odd that a man should feel so insulted—being a sensible man and a general and having such things on his mind as a battle—well, he said that he felt insulted. He said so officially, in his report of the battle. He ought to know how he felt.)

There was a kind of savage satisfaction for Stricker in realizing that sound tactics justified an action that suited his personal resentment and anger. Sound tactics not only justified an attack, they demanded it.

Ross had given him back his lost opportunity. The enemy had given him back the time that he thought had been gone forever, the time that should have been gone forever. The day had moved slowly, slowly—but not as slowly as Ross. Now it had stopped, it was actually moving the other way. Ross had turned the clock back with a careless finger. John Stricker was much obliged.

"Colonel Sterrett . . ." He started to give an order, and saw Joe Sterrett's strong, handsome face instantly kindle with eagerness. But it was not to be that kind of order. Stricker could let loose his anger without letting loose of his judgment. He would not risk, in a small attack, the only brigade officer who had commanded a full regiment in action. Sterrett must stay behind.

The same considerations that had shaped and limited Stricker's plan for a stand by the rifle battalion in the pinewoods applied now to this new situation—the difficulty of deploying a large body of inexperienced troops in the dense growth, the greater difficulty of withdrawing them, the risk of confusion, disintegration and panic. His instructions from Sam Smith were clear: he was to fight only a holding action: he must break off the battle before he was overwhelmed: he must bring his brigade back to the Hampstead lines in good order and ready to fight again. His main action today must be fought here, on this carefully chosen ground. Any attack on the Gorsuch farm must be a small one; it must not risk too much. It could be only a warning blow—hard enough, if possible, to make the enemy cautious—hard enough, if possible, to dissuade Ross from a headlong charge.

How many men could he afford to risk? Not so many that their loss, if they were cut off and destroyed, would mean a fatal weakening of the brigade. He could use the videttes sent back by Colonel Biays; there were enough of them to form an adequate advance guard. He could use one of Montgomery's six guns to cover the withdrawal; it would be a risk, but it might enable the infantry to get back to their lines. Sterrett . . . ? No, the colonel of the Fifth could not be spared for such a mission. Sterrett could be permitted only to call for volunteers and to select the officer to lead the attack.

Sterrett's choice for command was Major Richard Heath, his senior battalion commander.[3] Then he found that he had to pick out the troops as well: there were too many volunteers. Every captain clamored to have his company chosen. The whole regiment wanted to go—or felt, rather, an inescapable obligation to want to. The men of the Fifth were still militia, they were a long way from being veterans, but they had gone through one of the experiences that produce veterans. Their failure at Bladensburg—not the retreat, but the manner of it—was a rankling memory. Now they were undergoing another of those experiences: in the presence of the other, greener regiment watching them from across the lane they felt an inescapable obligation to behave like veterans. Their clamorous eagerness might be counterfeit; but a spurious coin, undetected, passes at its face value. Counterfeit, unsuspected by either the spender or the taker, deceives both.

There is no balance in which to weigh the proportions of mint metal and base metal in the apparent eagerness of the Fifth Maryland to attack. There is no means of measuring the extent to which it was self-deceptive. The Fifth's manifestation of fighting spirit was taken at face value, and it purchased something worth having. Real or counterfeit or partly both, it had the psychological effect of strengthening the confidence of the regiment itself. It also had the psychological effect of stiffening the morale of the 27th by giving that unblooded regiment a standard of conduct to be matched.

Sterrett's choice of volunteers fell on the smallest and the strongest of his companies—Captain Ben Howard's fifty Mechanical Volunteers and Captain Aaron R. Levering's hundred-odd Independent Blues.[4] Then a new clamor rose. There were men in the rifle battalion who felt exceedingly foolish; they itched with shame for their flight. Edward Aisquith, captain of the Sharp Shooters, was hotly embarrassed and angry; he had been snatched away from the battalion at Bladensburg and sent to the opposite, distant flank; the battalion, already too weak for its task, had fought and been broken without him. The recollection smarted. So did this morning's blunder. Lieutenant Gregorius Andre, commanding the Union Yagers in Dominic Bader's place, remembered his captain at bay in the Bladensburg stubble field, standing alone there, a stubborn and sturdy figure, trying to cover the Yagers' retreat while the bayonets penned him in. Andre's stubbornness now equaled Bader's. His anger was equal to Aisquith's.

Stricker welcomed their anger. It was a reassurance: the foolish retreat had not wrecked the morale of the Rifles. Let them go, he said. Seventy went.[5]

The riflemen came striding up the field just in front of the fence, along the line of the Fifth. They looked right good as they passed. They didn't look like men who had run from the shadow of something that wasn't there. A few had grins on their faces. Some of the grins were don't-care and jaunty and some were the stiff kind a man used to cover his scare and some, you could say, were sheepish and mad all together, as if the Rifles had an idea what the Fifth had been thinking about them for running. There were other men who looked sullen and sore, and some who looked blank as if they would rather not think, but most of them just looked determined. They even sounded determined. They marched at attention, their legs swung in cadence, their legs ripping through the weeds made a sound like scythes. Their feet made tough sounds on the earth . . . *uff* . . . *uff* . . . like the grunts a man made when he h'isted a rum keg or heaved at a loaded wagon that had buried itself to the axles in mud . . . like it couldn't be done but he'd do it.

The two infantry companies clambered over the fence and fell into column behind them. The column turned into the lane and halted. It waited there while the cavalry formed, up ahead. Then it waited another while. One of Montgomery's crews seized a gun by the trail and trundled it down the lane past the fence and turned it around.[6] The drivers fetched up the team from the woods and backed the near wheel horse into the shafts of the limber and hooked up the chattering trace chains. The four horses came trotting out through the battery line, the limber slewed into the ditch past the waiting gun and came up again into the lane, the trail was hooked to the limber. Heath rode to the head of the column. *For-rr-rrd . . . !*

The column began to move. In the moving ranks, young Dan Wells looked at young Henry McComas:

"Here we go."

"Yuh."

"Remember what you said?"

"What'd I say? I've said lots o' things."

"When they busted your feather. After they'd shot it off and I told you. Gees, you looked funny. You said . . ."

"Yuh. I remember, all right. It was better'n this one I got now. You don't find a rooster 't's got feathers like that, every day."

"Well, you might get a chance to collect."

"Yuh, I might." Henry McComas felt cheerful about the prospect. He felt pretty good about everything. Being in a war didn't bother him much. Even the march down to Bladensburg hadn't bothered him very much; he was young and tough; he'd had a pretty good time on that trip. It hadn't been fun, exactly; his belly's got empty and sour; he'd got tired, all right, but no worse tired than he'd got in old Jenkins's saddlery shop. One thing was sure, there'd been a lot more excitement, along toward the end. Being in a war was better than being a prentice to Felix Jenkins. Being in the Yagers was something . . . the uniform was a thing to see, on a proper man . . . a man eighteen years old and more than six feet high . . . it was a long ways better than wearing over-halls in a stinking leatherworks. And the hat was a something, too. It was like gentleman's castor. A man could feel like somebody when he had on a hat like that. He didn't feel like a prentice; he felt like a gentleman.

Henry McComas liked the feeling. But he didn't like the so-and-so that had shot the plume off his hat. It had been a kind of deliberate challenge, like knocking a chip off his shoulder. People didn't go around knocking chips off Henry McComas's shoulder: a husky Baltimore apprentice knew what to do if they did. But there hadn't been much he could do about the spoilt feather. It had been like hearing somebody make a dirty noise at you out of a crowd and not being able to tell which one made it. It was a personal matter, but he hadn't been able to make it personal. He hadn't hated Britishers until somebody in the crowd of them shot off the plume on his hat; he hadn't had much feeling about them one way or another. Now it seemed as if he'd taken a right down dislike to them. Not to *them*, exactly. Not to any one of them. It was their insides he hated. He hated their guts. For three weeks now he'd wanted to see somebody in a scarlet jacket over the front sight of his rifle . . . anybody . . . any body. His sense of having suffered a personal affront was no more illogical than John Stricker's sense of having been insulted by the enemy's contemptuous carelessness. The private's resentment was no more childish than the general's. Both were instinctive.

Henry McComas was not a philosopher. He did not know that he had undergone the transmutation that turns a green soldier into a fighting man. He did not trouble to analyze his feeling. If he thought about it at all, he considered it wholly proper and was quite untroubled by it. He was not concerned with the process by which the desire to kill had germinated and developed within him. It did not occur to him that the desire sprang from a vague realization of the immense impersonality of war and from an in-stinctive resentment that this impersonal immensity had violated its own rules of the game by suddenly becoming intimately personal. He could not get even with the personal entity that had in-jured him, he could only get even with the immensity itself by simplifying it into another personal entity—into any other entity in a red coat. He would have been amazed if Dan Wells had told him that it was an oversimplification and that it ignored such important matters as loving your country and protecting it. Dan told him nothing of the sort:

"You know what that dragoon fellow said?"

"What dragoon fellow?"

"The last one that came in. The one that said he'd watched 'em chasin' pigs at Gorsuch's. He said Ross has got a white horse.[7] He said the vee-dettes had seen Ross ridin' on it."

"Yuh. What of it?"

"If we see an off'cer on a white horse it's Ross, ain't it?"

"He could change horses."

"If we was to get Ross, that would be something. It'd be a feather in our hats. Sa-ay, that's a good one. Feather in your hat, huh, Henry? That'd sort of make up for the one they shot off."

"Yuh. I guess so."

"They'd make us off'cers, maybe. Sergeants, anyways. They'd have to."

"I dunno." It sounded reasonable, though. "I know a white horse when I see one. Here goes for a gold epaulet or a wooden leg." [8]

From somewhere in the rear a horse—not white—came jogging along the edge of the field beside the lane. The rider jounced up and down; his mouth was pursed with clucking at the horse. Heads turned and lifted. Remarks that were intended to be very funny followed Dr. Samuel Martin [9] as he hurried toward the head of the column. The riflemen were not surprised to see their battalion surgeon going into action with them, but they were pleased. Their talk disparaged and concealed their pleasure . . . *doc's got his mind on business . . . looks like he's huntin' for trade. . . . *Well, he's got a nose for it; he's headin' in the right direction. *Got a call already, looks like . . . must be somebody's go'n' to have a baby . . . how 'bout you, Dave?* Not me. I'm empty, I am. It's past nooning, and I like my dinner. *'S why we're in a hurry . . . go'n' to Gorsuch's to help Ross eat his dinner . . . step along . . . ain't polite to keep the gen'ral waitin'. . . .*

At Gorsuch farm the general already had been given evidence of American politeness. His meal—breakfast, from his viewpoint, though he did not finish it till after noon—had been quite satisfactory. The food had been good. The Yankees were undoubtedly a backward people, but it must be admitted that they did themselves well at table. They did themselves very well indeed. His host's attitude also had been satisfactory: not cordial, but correct. A certain constraint of manner was understandable. One could hardly expect open-handed welcome from a backwoods farmer, in particular a Yankee farmer who stood likely to be emptyhanded by the time his guests departed. After all, a deal of constraint had been applied to him. Those sailors . . . they had been a sight to see. It had been a good day so far, it had been a splendid morning.

Breakfast aside, the halt had been a useful interlude. Even the sailors now seemed to be—for sailors—reasonably content and reasonably in hand. The barnyard hunt had done the business. Discipline need not be always harsh. For animal spirits—animals. It was an excellent formula. It might not be accepted as a new principle and written into the regulations for the government of his Majesty's forces, but it would furnish at the least a humorous anecdote for future dinner tables.

Ross gave the order for the bugles to sound the advance. An orderly brought his horse. Ready to mount, he found his host beside him.

"You will be returning this way, general, this evening? Shall I have supper ready?"

Ross missed the sharp point of the question—the insinuation that his army would be in retreat by sundown. He found the farmer's courtesy almost disappointing. It was one thing to provide hospitality for an enemy under compulsion; to offer it unasked was quite another. Was there no pride at all in these Americans? Had they no loyalty, no self-respect? Probably not. They had nothing to be proud of, God knew. Three or four flukish victories at sea, won by disguised ships of the line over honest frigates, could not offset abject surrender at Detroit, panic at Bladensburg, and the final shame of Washington. He had rated this fellow too high: restraint had not been dignity, it had been merely sullenness. Now the essential truckling spinelessness of Yankee character was revealing itself. Small wonder the Americans made so poor a showing in the field. There was little credit to be had in beating them.

He was aware, for a moment, of a faint feeling of revulsion, a sense of staleness and futility, of being spent in an unprofitable business. The splendid veteran army, the ponderous fleet, the enormously complicated mechanism of an overseas campaign—all devoted to the object of dispersing a mob or two of chicken-hearted, rabbit-footed militia. Egypt, Portugal, Spain, France—campaigning there had had a certain dignity, it had seemed worth the effort and the cost. One did not grudge the lives spent at Talavera and Vittoria or the bodies broken in the brilliant charge at Salamanca and the gallant storming of Badajos. This was different. He would have missed Colonel Thornton, if Thornton had been shot down at the crossing of the Douro; he would have missed Major Browne, too. But he would have missed them in a different way. Sir Peter Parker, dead in a petty backwoods skirmish, was not gloriously dead: he was merely wasted. There was always that off chance of being so foolishly and futilely dead. But no faltering, ever. Duty and devotion always. That was what other peoples seemed never able to get through their heads—the British devotion and determination that could not be broken. Ross made, now, a phrase to answer Robert Gorsuch:

"I'll sup tonight in Baltimore, or hell."

That is the legend.[10] The fact is that he had less than an hour to live.

Major Richard Heath and Surgeon Martin rode past the Boulden house. The lane bent to the right, there; the column bent with it; the woods were just ahead. The mingled treetops made a tunnel for the road, shadowy, splashed here and there with sun. The small cavalry advance guard was disappearing down the tunnel.

Heath pulled off to one side of the lane. The column halted, waited while a platoon of riflemen broke away and followed the cavalry at a shuffling trot. A section of riflemen slipped away into the woods to the right of the road, another section took the other side. The twig-snapping, bush-rustling, dryleaf-stirred commotion of their progress dwindled. The column moved on again.

It was quiet in the woods, and warm. The air hung motionless, it was close and heavy and there was a feel of thickness in it, as if the still air and the dense foliage were mixed into a single substance. Distant sounds were muted by it; smaller, nearby sounds were magnified. The harsh calling of the English bugles was not even a faint vibrance, but the click of a brass sleeve button on a musket stock was sharp and clear. All along the column men could hear the little cannon talking to itself behind them. The axles of the gun carriage and the limber made a low, smooth *chuck-chuck-chuckle* over the soft road, as if the four-pounder knew a secret joke. The weeds, tall and close on both sides of the lane, had hard stalks, woody with September. When the outside files brushed against them with their elbows, you could hear the dry rattle of the seeds falling through the brittle leaves and down the hard stems. The seeds sounded like shot spilling from a pouch. The sound made a man want to put his hand to his cartridge box to make sure that the top flap hadn't come unbuckled.

It seemed strange to be walking down this quiet country lane— not strange to be walking here yourself, but to be in a crowd this way. The lane wasn't meant for crowds. It was meant for a smocked farmer and a cart piled with wild hay from the salt-creek meadows; for children with wooden buckets in their hands, hunting berries; for a boy with a long willow switch, driving the cows home from pasture.

The water bucket hanging underneath the limber of the cannon swung like a big bell dangling at a cow's neck. The trace chains made a dull *tunk-tunking* like a muffled bell, like a cow's bell when the cattle had been feeding in the marshes, legdeep, to get away from the flies that plagued their udders, and the herd leader's bell had got plugged full of mud. It didn't sound warlike, it was just a sound that seemed to belong here. The sun-tawny lane and the brooding woodland were not meant for war—except an Indian war, maybe. But the Indians had been gone for a long time. There had been white people in Maryland almost two hundred years, there had been people in Baltimore about a century. It seemed queer that after almost a hundred years there should still be woods as thick and wild as this, so close to Baltimore. It was remarkable how little difference it made whether there were people or not. They didn't change things much . . . only in spots, here and there . . . back yonder was Baltimore, the fourth biggest city in America, and here were woods just as they'd always been. People didn't get very far away from being wild. . . .

A sound clanged against the stillness. It was not a war sound. The first startled, broken-off note of the English bugle sounded like as if a bell cow, coming up out of a salt marsh, had struck her mud-filled bell against a stone. And then it sounded like the stone had jarred the mud out of the bell and scared the cow at the same time. The cow was running, the bell clanging crazily . . . not swinging, shaking . . . the clapper-bumps all ran together into one sound . . . the bugle up ahead was going crazy . . . the whole herd was running . . . you could hear the hoofs. The hoofbeats in the lane were soft explosions; they were like the bugle notes, all run together; they were one continuous cottony explosion, coming closer. Down the lane, a mass of horsemen exploded into sight.

The cavalry advance guard was retreating. It was not defeated: it had not fought. It came at a mad gallop. It was not panic-stricken: it was merely stricken with excitement. The elegant chasseurs, the green-jacketed dragoons, the gentleman-volunteer hussars knew how to ride, they knew how to shoot their pistols, they had practiced swinging their long sabers at innumerable milkweed tops and cattails; they did not know what to do when they collided head-on with an enemy advancing.[11] The sheathed sabers banged against their legs, the pistols were still mostly in their holsters. The cavalry had not lost cohesion: with the infrangible cohesion of a single idea, the whole American advance guard was rushing back to tell what it had seen. It burst upon the advance platoon of riflemen and scattered it into the woods.

The column stopped, recoiled, and ceased to be a column. It became a pudding, lumpy where men tried to keep formation. The excited horses stirred it and the lumps broke. A musket went off, somewhere in the woods . . . another . . . and another. Heath was standing in his stirrups, shouting. Between shots, men heard him. Some obeyed. The companies began to form along the ditches. The cavalry, crowding them off the road, helped form them. The first whip cracks of the rifles helped, too: they were reassuring: they were thin and distant. The muskets did not sound so close now, either; they were not coming closer, they were going back.

Aisquith and Andre got their riflemen into their hands and shook them out into a long, thin line across the road. They laid the line out as a stagecoach driver laid the long lash of his whip along the ground before he made it curl and crack. Ed Aisquith's voice lifted the line. It curled a little as it began to move. It was longer than a whiplash; it took longer for the whip sound to come out of it. The advancing skirmish line was out of sight among the trees before the infantry behind it heard the rifles crackle. The firing sounded far off—farther off than ever. *My God, we're driving them . . . !* Shake foot . . . get into line, here . . . let's go, boys . . . Mechanicals, atten-nn-*shun* . . . for-rr-wurd . . . *Ed Aisquith's driving them . . . !*

Ed Aisquith was not driving them. Ed Aisquith was playing hide-and-seek with a few British skirmishers—with a half dozen of them or a dozen or two dozen. He could not tell; he could not see more than three or four at any one time, and those three or four behaved like jumping jacks—like store-new wooden jumping jacks with their top halves painted bright red. They moved quickly, darting from behind one tree trunk to the shelter of another, but they moved stiffly, jerkily; they were still burdened with their packs and awkward with their extra load of ammunition in stiff paper parcels. The top half of them was all that he could see: the bottom half was hidden by the underbrush: the drab breeches of the 85th Foot blended with the drab brush. The same troops that began the battle by the bridge at Bladensburg were beginning this new battle. The rifle battalion was fighting the advance guard of the 85th.

Presently Captain Aisquith was playing hide-and-seek with his own men as well. He could see no more than half a dozen of them. His firing line was not a line, it was clumps of two or three men running forward, running hunched over, huddling behind trees to fire and load, running on again after the retreating enemy. But the retreating soldiers of the 85th were only part of the advance guard. The British army was coming on behind a screen of three companies of infantry. The three companies themselves moved behind a screen of twenty men a hundred yards ahead, the men in files on each side of the lane and wide apart, one man behind another.[12] Even this small section had its own screen—two scouts far up the lane. Ross might not have confidence in the commander of his advance guard today, but that officer was not being as careless of security as Ross had been of time. His flank patrols were well out and well forward: they were abreast of his leading company: they were moving in skirmish line, with broad intervals between the men, on both sides of the road. The line was a great rake dragging the woods, with skirmishers for teeth and the main column for a handle, pushing it.

The British advance guard, halted momentarily by the appearance of the cavalry, moved on again. Within minutes, the flank patrols collided. The two sections of American riflemen, pushing forward while the cavalry retreated, came into contact with the hostile skirmish line.

The two sections were small: they did not cover nearly so much ground as the wide British rake: they struck it near its handle. American and British, the reaction was again instantaneous: both sides attacked. Momentarily, at the point of contact, the riflemen were more numerous and more compact; they gained a little ground; red-coated figures, darting from tree to tree but each time to a tree a little farther toward the rear, gave them confidence. Then the British rake began to sprout teeth: the files in the lane spread out into the woods, the leading company of the route column was coming on the run, deploying as it ran. The riflemen began to look across their shoulders, to pick out another tree, to dart back. Aisquith's skirmish line, advancing, mingled with them and absorbed them. They took back a few trees.

But trees did not grow in lines of battle. The tangled woods absorbed the fight into its own orderless confusion. There was, in minutes, no line of riflemen, no line of British infantry;[13] there were only a few red-painted and blue-painted jumping jacks making stiff, jerky motions, popping up from bushes, disappearing. There was only the glimpse of an arm in a red sleeve cocking itself at an awkward angle from behind a tree trunk, ramming down a bullet; there was only another arm in a blue sleeve cocking itself at the same awkward angle from behind a tree a hundred feet away. When the arms disappeared, the trees blew puffs of smoke, white bullet scars sprang out like weals upon their bark. Now and again a red-coated body or a blue one jerked more violently; now and again a body was snatched from behind its tree trunk, to spin and wobble like a top almost run down or to stand stiff, wooden for an instant, and then soften and collapse and fall. Some of them continued to jerk and wriggle, to make the rattling, squeaking, straining noises of a disarranged mechanism. Some of them just lay there.

Aisquith's men began to drift back. There were only seventy of them; there were, in the woods now, twice as many British. The riflemen were being beaten, but not badly. They ran hard when they ran, but they went back by twos or threes or singly, and they did not go far. The effect of their retreat was a continuous slow shifting from one covert to another. The skirmishers of the 85th pressed on persistently and closely, but their advance was the same continuous shifting, the same gradual filtering through the woods. It was too slow to be called pursuit, it was resisted by too brisk a fire. The riflemen were not being routed, they were merely fighting like Indians; in that kind of fight the loss or gain of a few trees meant nothing; one oak or poplar thick enough to shield a man while he fired and loaded was as useful as any other oak or poplar of the same size. The spontaneous, instinctive tactic was effective: the 85th was not being hurt badly, but it was losing more men than the Rifles. Here in the center, near the road, the advance was very slow.

It was so slow that it gave the automatic mechanism of British march security a chance to function. The patrols, stretched out through the woods like a line of game beaters, extended beyond both flanks of Aisquith's force. While the riflemen were holding up the center of the enemy advance guard—never quite stopping it but making its progress gradual and moderately expensive—the two ends of the British line were meeting no resistance. They pushed ahead rapidly, slowed only by the difficulty of keeping some sort of alignment in the confusing undergrowth. With the center delayed, the rapid progress of the flanks soon drew the formation of the advance guard into an approximation of a V.

Heath's two companies of infantry, deployed now and advancing on both sides of the road to support the Rifles, could see nothing of the fight; they could only hear it. The racket of the firing and the commotion of their own threshing struggle through the thickets kept them from hearing lesser, similar commotions in the woods around them. There was, here, another failure of reconnaissance, more dangerous than Dyer's. The Mechanical Volunteers and the Independent Blues, hurrying toward the sound of fighting, were moving toward the apex of the V. Before they saw an enemy, before the first bullet-severed leafy twigs came twirling down upon them, the two companies were outflanked. They attacked without knowing that they were almost enveloped.

Their attack was ragged, their fire ineffective. It was impossible to keep formation in the brush-choked woods, impossible to do much damage to an enemy who hid behind the trees and crouched among the bushes and was nothing but a puff of smoke and, now and then, a twitch of color like the flicker of a scarlet tanager in flight from bush to bush. They lost, almost at once, their forward motion: the smoke of the British muskets made a barrier that thickened quickly: the British skirmishers were being reinforced, the rest of the advance guard was coming into action. The hostile line was thicker but it was not, physically, a line at all; it was a scattering of men by themselves and men in little clumps that could be connected mentally by an imaginary line. Nevertheless, there was an actual line. It was not physical, it was not imaginary: it was merely invisible: the disconnected clumps and solitary skirmishers were connected by an invisible tough wire of discipline and habit.

The militiamen had no such discipline or habit. Physically, they were more compact than the enemy's deliberately loose formation; but they were held together by a dread of loneliness, they bunched up instinctively for comfort. Yet they were not solid. Only sound was solid. The dense woods did not diffuse sound as they did the men who made it. They compressed it, hardened it into a weapon. The blended crashes of Levering's hundred muskets and Ben Howard's fifty suddenly became more deadly than their ounce balls and their buckshot.

Ross was riding near the head of his main column. The three companies of the advance guard were out of sight, but he was only mildly interested in the wooded terrain that concealed them. It was strange ground, but it was sufficiently familiar: it was of a piece with all the rest of this unkempt America. His interest sharpened when the bugle sent back its warning blast, but even the first spattering of shots gave him no more than casual concern. They meant, probably, a few more videttes or such a parcel of militia bumpkins as had ventured, once, within musket range of his patrols in the woods north of Benedict. It was advance guard business. The main column could halt briefly while the advance guard got on with it.

But the business moved with an unwonted slowness. When the firing should have slackened, it grew louder. For a minor skirmish, it was beginning to sound "tolerably hot." [14] Ross felt a slight uneasiness. What was happening up there? A platoon of the regiment that had stormed the bridge at Bladensburg should be enough to send those amateur dragoons scampering off in no time. A company should be ample to brush away an outpost of militia. But the firing was "more heavy and more continued than it ought to be." It was too heavy for a brush with outposts. By the sound of it, all three of the advance companies must be engaged.

Concern grew into apprehension. Could it be an ambush? He missed Major Browne. If the advance guard had its regular commander, he would not feel so apprehensive. Browne would have known what to do. But he could not be sure, now. Had the three companies blundered into a serious ambuscade? [15] He could not trifle with the safety even of "a few companies." He had to know.

He touched his horse's white flank with the spur and set out at a gallop. With him rode Colonel McNamara [16] and two aides, Captain M'Dougal and Lieutenant Hamilton.[17] Two enlisted men galloped after them—a courier and Sergeant William Sannford of the Enniskillen Dragoons, chief of couriers. They had four hundred yards to go before they reached the woods.

The riflemen had lost all order. They had not had too much order to begin with; now they were hopelessly scattered. Some of them knew it and were heading earnestly toward the rear. Some, knowing it, were still stubbornly reluctant to give up. They had retreated once today unnecessarily. A man could do a thing like that once and find reasons for it, but if he did it twice in the same day his reasons might wear thin: a man could feel right naked, people looking through his thin excuses and knowing what he'd done: he could feel right naked and uncomfortable, knowing it himself.

A few of the stubbornest had tired of playing hide-and-seek. They had not joined in the slow drifting backward. Now they were tucked away in various small pockets they had found in the complicated garment of the woods; they were kneeling behind windfalls, squatting in hollows, shrinking themselves tight as bark against the bigger trees, loading, waiting, firing at the targets that were easier to find because there were now so many more of them.

One of these pockets was not far from the lane. In it were men of both Aisquith's company and Bader's; young Lieutenant Andre, living up to the example of his captured captain, had pulled together out of the confusion a few men of his own Gray Yagers and a few of the Sharp Shooters. They were in a good place. Just in front of them the woods thinned out a little; well-concealed themselves, they had a clear view of the road. Their rifles, so far, had kept the British skirmishers away from their small covert. The place had one disadvantage: to get away from it themselves might not be easy. There was open ground behind them—a tiny meadow with a rail fence running through it; there were Britishers in front of them, close—well hidden, but within short musket range. To go back meant running across that meadow, climbing over that fence. Just within the trees beyond the fence, a man on horseback watched the pocket. Doc Martin had no business being there, but there he was. Or maybe he did have business. He had picked out a likely spot. Somebody was going to get hurt there in that little swale.

It was beginning to look as if getting away was a matter that would have to be attended to almost immediately. The Britishers weren't bothering them too much, just now, but there were a plenty of them in the woods—in front and on both sides. The ones in front weren't shooting, just now; they were waiting for somebody to stick up his head or else they were getting themselves set to try a rush. But musket balls were thwicking through the brush from somewheres else. It was good and plain that the war was working itself around behind. It was a whole lot plainer than it was good.

Come on, somebody said. *Come on* . . . lieutenant says to move [18] . . . Sergeant MacKensie says he says so . . . where's Adam Wilhelm . . . *bugle* . . . *if we're goin' to retreat we ought to do it right* . . . *Adam oughtta blow his bugle.* . . .

Adam Wilhelm did not blow it. The only sound was the slam-banging of the muskets. It was coming from the rear now; anyway, it seemed so. Through it or underneath it you could hear men squirming, you could hear them taking deep breaths, you could hear their feet go past you, you could hear the brush snap. Henry McComas and Dan Wells got ready to run too. It was about time; they were about the last ones. Then Henry hesitated. There was something down the lane there. Horses . . . horses coming at a gallop . . . four of them bunched up together . . . sudden glint of sun . . . gold epaulets . . . a white horse . . . He eased back to his tree.

"Dan. I see a mark."

"So do I." [19]

Dan Wells went back to his tree. They looked at each other. Henry cocked his rifle. Dan cocked his. They waited, standing back a little from their trees, steadying the long barrels on the rough bark. *Say when? Yuh. Wait* . . . *wait* . . . *ready* . . . *now!*

The two rifles went off like a single shot. Major General Robert Ross leaned forward.[20] The reins dropped from his hand. His hands groped for the pommel of his saddle. His body was a great unstable weight, like water in a sack; he rested the weight of it on his hands. His horse lunged forward. His hands lost their hold. He sagged, swaying sideward, the life draining out of him like water. Colonel McNamara's arm caught him as he fell.[21]

In the still air the smoke of the two rifles hung, wavering, thin as cobweb spun upon the bushes. Through it Dan Wells saw British soldiers spring up from the thicket thirty yards in front. He turned to run. Henry McComas was reloading with desperate haste. He had poured a charge down the barrel, he had sprinkled powder in the pan, the powder horn was still swinging violently to its string. He was pressing a ball into the muzzle of his rifle, snatching the ramrod from its bands. Forcing the ball down the barrel was an awkward business. With one shoulder pressed against the tree it was too slow and awkward. He stepped out to use the full strength of his arm.[22] The British soldiers fired. An ounce ball smashed through his ribs into his heart.[23] Another struck the back of Dan Wells's head and crushed his skull.[24]

Dr. Martin saw them fall.[25] But there were other riflemen still nearer. Most of Lieutenant Andre's men had reached the woods in safety. They had stopped and turned there, waiting. The last three or four were running hard across the little meadow. They were throwing themselves at the fence now, squeezing through between the rails, scrambling over. One of them was Andre, another was MacKensie. The sergeant was over the fence, they were all clear of it but Andre. The lieutenant had been loading as he ran. He turned now astride the top rail, looking back.[26] The British skirmishers were breaking through the thicket where McComas and Dan Wells lay dead, they were breaking out into the meadow.

Andre hooked his knee across the top rail of the fence, hooked his right foot underneath the bottom rail. He took careful aim and fired. His body jerked to the recoil. Then it jerked again. He toppled backward, dead.

MacKensie, too, was down. The same volley that killed Andre wounded his third sergeant badly. The riflemen in the edges of the woods were firing at the British rush, holding it off, lashing at it with their whipcracks. Martin rode boldly toward the fence, sprang down, got his arms around MacKensie, lifted him into the saddle [27] . . . *hold on . . . can you hold on . . . ?* Walking slowly, he led the horse into the shelter of the trees.

Heath knew that he was beaten. The only shape that his detachment had now was the shape imposed upon it by the enemy and by the ground he fought on.

The two arms of the V were closing in. He was certainly outflanked, perhaps almost surrounded.[28]

His cavalry was useless: it could not charge through the thickets: it had never heard of cavalry that fought dismounted. Milling in the lane, it served only to help keep the four-pounder out of action. The service was superfluous. John Stiles, first lieutenant of the Union Artillery commanding gun and gun crew, was already frustrated and defeated. The stiff underbrush and the close-growing saplings made a barrier against him. It was impossible to haul the gun into the woods with horses, impossible even to drag it by hand without cutting a path with axes. There were not enough axes, there was not enough time. In the narrow lane it was almost impossible even to get the team, the limber and the clumsy fieldpiece turned around. When he accomplished that, the lane was clogged with horsemen. Then it was empty, there was nothing to shoot at. Then it was clogged again with men on foot, coming toward him.

Heath had given the order to retreat. That, too, had been almost superfluous.

24

WHEN FREE MEN SHALL STAND

HEATH'S BEATEN MEN SPILLED OUT
into the fields. Montgomery's gunners, standing to their pieces,
watched them. The 27th, standing in ranks, watched them. *So
that's what it looks like.* It didn't look like much of anything—like
militia drill day, maybe, when the drill was over and everybody
tore out for the whisky barrel, or like the United Hose and

Suction Company rehearsing for a fire and a whole crowd of neighbors running along with them. The cannon jouncing up the lane could be the engine, only you didn't hitch up horses to the suction engine. It might be a good idea though.

The Union Artillery and the Jefferson Blues, the dressed-up-alike civilians and the last-minute volunteers in their white linen coatees and their roundabouts, their go-to-meeting frock coats and their Sunday beavers, felt a little disappointed. They felt let down. War was a fraud. There had been a battle over there past Boulden's, in the woods somewhere; they'd heard it. But it hadn't sounded like a battle. It had sounded, at first, like a farmer fixing up the loose boards of a cowshed—sort of looking the shed over and hitting a loose nail when he saw it and once in a while driving in a new one. The distant shots hit like a hammer . . . *whack* . . . and then a wait and then *whack* again . . . and pretty soon *whack whack whack whack*, like a fresh nail being driven. It had been all wrong. A man didn't potter around, doing chores like that, on a fine day like this: he waited for a heavy, dull day after a night of rain, when everything was sopping and the fields were too wet for farm work. The sounds themselves had been all wrong: they hadn't been bright and sharp and dangerous, they had been dull and heavy. The shots fell like a hammer on a wet plank, with now and then a thump as if a plank had come loose and fallen down. Only once or twice there'd been a drawn-out crash that sounded like a battle. Even that sound could have been a pile of lumber falling over, like when Bob Long and his company of carpenters were building the shed-barracks on the vacant lots in Gay street. And now—just a crowd of people running. *It ain't right. It's diff'rent. This ain't what we came for.*

The Fifth Maryland, watching, knew that this was different. The Fifth had a gauge by which to measure this retreat: it had a guilty knowledge of retreating. It also had a guilty conscience: no matter how well it had done at the beginning of its first battle, it had done badly at the end: no self-justification could quite gloze the panic on the Georgetown road. Being composed of human beings, the regiment could hardly have escaped a kind of satisfaction, a secret sense of being justified, if other human beings did no better under similar conditions. The retreat streaming toward them now was similar to theirs—the men running helter-skelter, the quick backward apprehensive looks, the thickening confusion in the road, gun, gun team, riflemen, dragoons and infantry all mixed together. But it was not the same. There was no panic in it. You knew that. Almost half a mile away, you knew that. Those men weren't running blindly. They ran as if there was a purpose in their running. They weren't just trying to get away from some place that had terrified them, they were trying to get quickly to another place they knew of. When they got there, they would stop.

They did. Heath's men came back to the brigade lines panting, streaming sweat, exhausted, but not panic-stricken. Some were bloody with their own wounds or the wounds of others helped along, half carried. The cannoneers stared at them curiously as they filtered through the battery. They looked somehow changed: they didn't look like the same men who had gone out: they didn't look like the Jefferson Blues standing neatly there behind the fence or like the United Volunteers standing neatly at the other end of the short row of guns.

They passed: faces red as if with sun-scald, faces blotched white with fatigue, sweat-beaded, swollen looking, hollow looking, pinch-mouthed, slack-mouthed, dull-eyed, incurious, uncaring. So that's what it's like, that's what it does to you. What happened, anyway? What did they see to make them look like that? There was a body hung across a saddle like a pair of grist sacks, there was blood on the pommel of the saddle; blood dripped from the stirrup, from a small lump on the stirrup that was like the blunt beginning of an icicle. Under the slow, swelling, pendulous drops, the lump of thickened blood was turning black. *Second gunners . . . light your portfires . . . !* The slow matches, fixed in notches in the two-pronged linstocks, began to glow in pairs. The second gunners drove the iron butts of the three-foot linstocks hard into the dirt in front of the axle of each gun, between the left wheel and the barrel of the gun. Thin wisps of smoke stood up. The smell of the burning matches pricked the nostrils with thin needles. Beyond the Boulden place, the flash of scarlet jackets showed against the woods.

There . . . there they are . . . that's them. . . . As if you didn't know. As if you couldn't see them for yourself. That sudden needless need to talk, to say something to the man next to you . . . that sudden needless need to shift your feet, to ease the crossbelt on your shoulders, to look at your musket, to make sure that the flint was screwed tight in the lock, that it hadn't worked loose somehow. . . . The talk made a sound like sighing, like a deep breath. The involuntary minor stirrings of a thousand bodies made a kind of shudder in the blue ranks. Middle-aged man in the high-crowned castor, talking . . . *there aren't many of them . . . I thought* . . . peach-down-faced boy talking . . . *you wait . . . that's how they do* . . . *that's how they did before* . . . *there'll be a plenty of them soon* . . . *you'll see* . . . not talking to each other, talking to themselves mostly . . . reassuring themselves, each in his own way, the ways precisely opposite.

The first British skirmishers, spilling out into the fields, caught sight of the two regiments and the row of guns. They stopped abruptly. In their own minds they had been "in full pursuit" of a demoralized enemy "flying with all precipitation before them." But the pursuit had not been so rapid as they thought it was; it had been ineffectual; now it ceased entirely. To the officers of the advance guard, coming up, the American line of battle looked surprisingly substantial. It did not look like the crowd of "awkward . . . wretchedly equipped . . . country people" that they had seen three weeks ago "on the brow of a bare green hill." It looked very much like "a regular army." [1] The British officers thought that they could see, behind the foremost line, the "heads of columns" in reserve. [2] They thought that they were seeing, in the first line alone, no less than "six or seven thousand" Yankees. [3] And one officer thought that he could see an opportunity.

He was a captain in the 85th Foot—the same man who had led the rush across the bridge at Bladensburg. He prepared, now, to lead another. That cluster of farm buildings two hundred yards ahead was an objective to be seized immediately. The Yankees might be there in force, concealed and waiting; from his point of view they should be, but they probably had been too stupid. If the enemy's main body attacked while the British army was breaking from march-column into line of battle, the stout-looking farmhouse and its barns and stackyard would become important: in British hands, they would cover the deployment.

General Stricker had no notion of attacking. Sam Smith and he had chosen this ground for one purpose only: to compel the British to attack across it. The Boulden farm was useless to him; it had no importance whatsoever. He watched the scarlet patches multiply and run together. They made, finally, a streak against the woods. *Captain Montgomery* . . . Yes, sir. *You might see whether you can reach those people.* Yes, sir!

It was long range for the four-pounders of the Union Artillery.

To throw an iron ball nearly half a mile and drop it in the general vicinity of that short skirmish line would be remarkable shooting; to hit the line and knock men out of it would be a miracle. The range was extreme for canister or grapeshot. Using it would probably be wasting ammunition, but there was at least a chance of hitting something: grape would scatter like a handful of thrown

gravel.[4] Montgomery put into motion the complicated human mechanism required to fire his guns. *Number One piece . . . number Two piece . . . with grape . . . !* Firing two guns at once, without a sighting shot, would probably waste twice as much of his precious powder. But two guns were more than twice as good as one gun: the mingled pattern of shot flying from two small guns could do far more damage than the discharge of a single cannon twice their caliber.[5]

Three yards behind the trail of each four-pounder stood a pair of gunners—ammunition passers. At the feet of each pair lay the two side boxes, lifted from their places on the axle and set down there when the gun had been unlimbered.[6] Now the two gunners stooped. One plucked out the cartridge—the bag made of flannel boiled in sizing and hard-packed with powder; [7] the other picked out of the box the cylinder of grapeshot. The grape came in bunches, in bags made of coarse cloth quilted stiff with pack thread.[8] The second gunner, standing between wheel and barrel, took the cartridge. The gun sergeants were reciting from the drill book . . . *handle cartridge* . . . *charge piece* . . . The second gunner slid the flannel bag into the muzzle . . . *ram down cartridge* . . . the first gunner, on his right and facing him, pushed it with the wooden rammer; the quilted bag slid after it, the rammer drove it home . . . *prime* . . . the first gunner set his flask upon the touchhole and poured in a tiny rill of powder . . . *take aim* . . . the corporal stooped, peering up the slanted barrel, seeing the red streak against the distant woods.

The streak was small, it was a long way off. But it was moving now. You could see it better. The red jackets made a flicker now like the small flames of candles, like a crooked row of candles on a shelf against a green wall; a draft blew upon them, all the small flames leaned and wavered in it. Shooting at them would be trying to snuff candles with a rifle. *Fire!* Even after that, it took time. It took endless time. The second gunner blew the slow match into a clean glow, he poked the linstock toward the corporal's face, he pressed the glow upon the vent, the corporal jumped back, the gun jumped after him. The two guns fired together—or almost together. The explosions, blended, made a slamming sound as if a spar had fallen from a great height to a ship's deck and one end of it had struck the planks a split second before the other end had finished falling. Under the low branches of the oaks, the crash was hollow-sounding. The smoke hung beneath the branches, curling in slow convolutions. Through the smoke the leaning candles flames were dimmer. They were also closer. Of a sudden they were taller: the British soldiers rushing toward the farm were climbing Boulden's east fence. *Tend vent* . . . *sponge piece* . . . Now they were over the fence and they were not so tall. But they were plainer, nearer. *Fire!*

Smoke blotted out the road. It hid the farmyard. The gun-pointers could not see what they had done. They had done better than could be expected. The grape had left a bloody juice in Boulden's yard. Three men were down.[9] The rest had reached the stables and the house.

There were no more useless rushes. There was no powder to be spared for useless firing at the blank walls of buildings. There were only empty fields and silence and the waiting . . . and the waiting . . . *waiting* . . . It wasn't reasonable. It wasn't decent, scarcely, after what had happened. It gave you a strained, pulled-together feeling, like there was a wire inside you, in your guts, tight. You felt like you had been hung up on a thin wire so your feet just barely touched the ground and then you'd been let down . . . and then pulled up again . . . let down, pulled up. You felt like you couldn't stand much more of it. But you weren't nervous like you had been; not the same kind of nervous. You weren't calm exactly, but you weren't scared either. You were only tight and drawn together, like, inside, the way you got sometimes when you wanted a thing badly and were waiting for it and were getting tired of waiting . . . getting impatient . . . getting so damned tired of waiting that you ached inside. Those damned Britishers! Where are they? What's keeping them? Why don't they come? *I didn't mean that. I don't want them to come. I do . . . and I don't.*

They came.

The solid column of the light brigade flowed out upon the lane. The head of it protruded from the woods like the blunt head of an enormous scarlet caterpillar crawling. It crawled smoothly, purposefully. It had innumerable light-colored legs; its legs grew in rows, twelve legs in every row; the rows came on endlessly, all close together, one behind another. It had stiff, shiny spines upon its back, in rows; they rippled as it crawled. Undulations rippled its thick body; you could see the skin creep on its body, wrinkling and unwrinkling. The smooth-flowing undulations were legs moving and arms swinging and you knew that, but you felt your own skin creeping. You knew what that thing was: it was only men in step together, men about your own size; but there was something monstrous and unnatural about them, in a mass there, crawling. You've seen them before: they're the same men, likely: they look different somehow.

The enemy, seen for the second time, almost always looks different. Only when he has been seen many times does he become familiar, natural, expected.

The scarlet caterpillar turned abruptly. It turned north, off the road, before it reached the bend. Its head passed out of sight behind the Bouldens' big barn and the house and reappeared beyond them while its body was still crawling from the woods, its tail still hidden in them. Then the tail, blunt like the head, was dragged out of the woods and off the road. The undulations ceased, the body lay motionless for minutes on the fields between the woods and Boulden's. Then it wriggled. It grew thinner, longer. While the tail still lay motionless, the body stretched itself, the close-set rows of legs began to separate. It was too long now to be a caterpillar: it was almost a quarter of a mile long. "The Eighty-fifth regiment, in beautiful regularity, spread itself at extended order over the whole of the enemy's front." [10] That is what will be said in the books.

But the 85th looks like a snake with legs, a thin snake with a pale-colored belly and a red back. There are spots on its back; you can see them—pale spots and black spots, in pairs: they are faces and leather hats. The thing makes a noise. It is the wrong color for a rattlesnake, and it isn't coiled; but you can hear the faint, harsh, rattling noise that it makes. You can see the rattles now, on its tail: carts, and men pulling the carts: ammunition tumbrils. The carts, too, turn off the road. They go bumping and rattling across the fields behind the deployed 85th; they pull up somewhere behind the Boulden stables like farm carts returning from market. The stables conceal them.

A mass of blue shows on the road. That is different, too. It is not smooth, not rhythmic: it does not flow: it overflows, filling the lane, bulging into the fields on each side. The naval brigade, under discipline now but under its own kind of discipline, not in neat ranks but a mass, swells past the bend of the lane and comes on toward the row of American guns. Then it stops, almost out of range but perhaps not quite. [11]

Well, it's time . . . somebody talking again . . . *'bout time to start* . . . chirpy, irreverent . . . peach-down-faced boy showing off, being big and brave . . . *they've got the body laid out.* My God, what a thing to say! Then you think: why not? You think: that's how it is, that's the crazy thing about war, that's one of the crazy things. That's the difference between dying in a war and dying at home in your bed when you're old and being laid out in your Sunday clothes. In a war they lay everybody out beforehand, neatly, just so, all dressed up in their best. And when they're laid out, they can die. It's time, now. It's time. The preacher can start any time, he can clear his throat. I wonder why preachers do that. I wouldn't, if I was a preacher; I'd think that God wouldn't like it, a noise like that made in His ear. I wonder what time it is.

Somebody drags a fat watch out of his pocket and looks surprised. He says: going on two and a half.[12] He says: we been standing here more than five hours. It seems fifty. It seems . . . *aa-agghhhh!*

The harsh, tearing sound is a throat being cleared. Not a preacher's throat: a giant's. The sound is a prelude to prayer. Not a preacher's prayer: yours. *Oh, God.. . . rockets again . . . not rockets . . . God, don't let them use rockets.* . . . There's no sense to your praying. You can't stop the rockets, they're coming, it's too late now, you'd ought to have started sooner. You cringe, you want to be small. There's no sense to that either. The rockets can't hurt you, they aren't coming your way at all. You can see them, plain, arching up from in back of Boulden's and skimming across the fields to the left. They don't look much bigger than insects, they don't look any bigger than grasshoppers taking off on the other side of the fence.

They look like grasshoppers jumping, they move as if they had legs and had kicked them, they whir like grasshoppers' wings. They're gone. You can't see where they light, you can't hear them light. You could hear the big hoppers land when Captain Sadtler's company routed them out of the weeds as it moved towards the old log house: they went *plop* in the grass, the grass stirred. The ranks of the Fifth are stirred like grass now by the distant and harmless rockets. The ranks rustle with quick, startled talk . . . knew it . . . that's what they had in them carts . . . ain't decent to use things like that . . . low, it's lower than low . . . worse'n Indians . . . *bastards!* Pshaw, them things don't do no hurt; all they do is curdle your guts. *Hell they don't . . . man in Barney's flotilla . . . Patuxent . . . rocket went clean through his body . . .* Were you there? *Major Will Barney was there; he's Josh Barney's own son, ain't he? He saw it . . . took the man fair in the belly an' came out his back . . . came through him still burnin' an' lit in a barrel o' powder an' set it afire . . . an' a barrel o' ca'tridges caught an' went off. . . .* [13] I seen a cat once. Some boys had put turpentine on it and set it afire. It went crazy. It screamed like a woman in labor. It ran crazy, sidewards and backwards, and then it ran under a shed and burned the shed down. *By God,*

*it's worse'n a turpentined cat if they hit you . . . like havin'
a red-hot poker shoved through you . . . .* They're bigger
than pokers. They're big as your arm, they're near as big as a fence
post. It'd be like having a burning fence post rammed through your
guts. *Shut up, will you? For God's sake, shut up!*

Again the harsh sound tears phlegm from a giant throat. More
rockets leap into the air beyond Boulden's, they come in low
arching flight, with a snarling whir, with smoke trailing behind them
like legs, with fire blurring vague in the sun like the blur of wings
beating too swiftly for seeing. They dart down into the woods,
away off to the left again. You listen. But nobody screams. Nobody's been hit: a man gouged by a burning fence post would have
to scream. It's all right, the rockets are harmless, they're only intended to scare you. Even if that were true, the truth would be
hard to believe. And it isn't true.

The rockets that jump and fly like monstrous and horrible
insects are leaving behind them a row of cocoons from which they
sprang. The cocoons are long metal tubes; they, themselves, look
like enormous insects; they, themselves, look as if they were going
to spring. They crouch low to the ground on four legs, on two
pairs of stiff spraddled legs. One pair is short; set close to the tail
of the long, hollow body, it lifts the rear end of the tube not quite
to the height of a soldier's knee. The other pair, close to the opposite end, raises the head of the tube not quite to the height of his
hip. The metal tube, with its two unequal bipods, is known as a
bouche à feu.[14] A hundred and thirty years hence it will go into
battle again; it will lose its legs but, otherwise, it will look very
much the same. Even its name will look much the same—not *bouche
à feu,* but *bazooka.*

The rocket troop manning the tubes is also a new device—a
cross between cavalry and horse artillery. It is intended to go into
action on horseback and then dismount. Its rocket dischargers are
carried in leather buckets that hang from the saddles; its reserve
ammunition is carried in cases strapped to the backs of pack horses.
But it can campaign on foot. Its weapons are light: one man can
carry a *bouche à feu* without trouble: two others can carry, each
in a pouch on his back, enough six-pound rockets to keep the discharger in action for several minutes. A rocket troop eighty strong
can put its twenty-four tubes into action within half a minute. Each
tube can fire four times a minute. Given a tumbril or two to bring
up reserve ammunition, a troop can fire four hundred and eighty

six-pound shells in five minutes. Man for man, the troop's volume
of fire is something that field artillerymen will not dream of for
generations.

The rocket troop is made up of teams of three. The center
man of each team—Number 2—carries the *bouche à feu*. When the
team goes into action, he runs forward fifteen or twenty paces and
sets up the tube, with its four legs thrust solidly into the ground.
His two teammates, each helping the other, unfasten their pouches,
unbuckle the straps that hold the long sticks of the rockets in a

close sheaf over their shoulders, and look to the screw that fastens
the stick to the shell. Number 2 lights his portfire—a paper case
packed with a composition of mealed powder, saltpeter and sulphur
and fixed to a six-foot stick. Number 3 comes up on a run with a
shell in his hands and trusts it into the open rear end of the tube.
The tail protrudes; so does the base of the shell, with its fuse exposed. Number 3 runs back; Number 2 steps aside and touches the
fuse with his burning portfire. The shell spouts a fiery tail; the
sparks scorch the grass; the wooden stick shivers and beats the
earth and the flaming tail drives the rocket out of the tube and
lifts it up into the air. It flies where it will, after that.

That is the weakness of rockets: their flight cannot yet be
controlled. But the rocket barrage, scarcely aimed, is not aimless.

The British are using it shrewdly—as shrewdly now as they used it last month to cover the river crossing, to cover the deployment of the army, to soften with apprehension the Yankee flank that seems to have no protection. They let loose the rockets in sheaf after sheaf toward the left of the American front. The damage they do can't be seen. Stricker, watching, decides that the rockets are useful—to him. They are proving their own futility, and he thinks that the visible proof should reassure nervous men. The hoarse, strangled, whooping-cough roar, it seems to him, is having "no other effect than to prepare his line for the sound of the artillery." [15] But he waits. The range is still long for good shooting —almost half a mile. He sits his horse in the lane behind Montgomery's guns and continues to watch. He is not at all concerned with the rockets; he is soberly weighing the mass of the naval brigade, but he is much more concerned with what is coming behind it. Artillery . . . horse-drawn guns . . . four . . . five . . . more guns than Montgomery has . . . seven . . . eight . . . howitzers, too, by the look of those last two pieces . . . mortars on wheels. That means grapeshot in bunches bigger than ours and more deadly, it means we're outgunned. Not too badly, though, if Montgomery's men can stand what they're going to get. I wonder . . . They've never been under fire, they don't know what it's going to be like. I wish those were six guns of Proctor's. If the Union Artillery was a battery out of the old regiment, I'd know how much it could stand. I wonder whether there's any truth in that rumor of Heath's . . . Ross shot . . . that's something else I'd like to know. Heath's a good man, he didn't say it was so, all he says is that some of his men say it's so. It might make a difference. But what kind of difference? I had something to go on, with Ross. I thought he'd come at us quick, hard and straight ahead; I tried to persuade him not to. If somebody else is commanding, I don't know what he'll do. But even if Ross is alive and still in command, I can't tell whether he's been persuaded, I don't know what to expect. So it doesn't matter, it doesn't make very much difference. I've waited this long, I can wait awhile longer until I can see what those people intend to do. They've halted the guns . . . they're waiting, too . . . more infantry . . . now we'll see . . .

Another scarlet caterpillar is crawling out of the woods, creeping up the lane. Its undulant rhythmic body has white streaks upon it, a gleaming white pattern of crossbelts. Its blunt head has two slanted feelers. The feelers don't match: the flags of the Fourth

Foot are fashioned of different colors—one scarlet, the other light blue. The flags cling to their staffs, barely stirring; the staffs barely sway to the stride of the color-bearers like bright but incurious feelers. The column is leaving the road. It turns, half-right, before it reaches the halted British battery. It begins to move north behind the Boulden fences, behind the thin line of the light brigade. It marches as if on parade, in colmun of half-companies [16] with precise clean spaces between them, each half-company in close double ranks; you can see the subalterns and captains, small figures marching alone and precisely, spaced just so in the spaces.

The men of the Union Artillery stand in stiff, waiting poses; their nerves are drawn tight; they strain like men harnessed to drag-ropes against the invisible harness of discipline. They look at their captain, Montgomery looks back at Stricker and Stricker nods.[17] Montgomery's arm goes up.

The guns are already laid. Their blast shakes the leaves on the oak boughs. Their smoke swirls in tight, churning eddies that loosen and roll and unfold and spread into one and hang and grow slowly still. The gunners swarm to their pieces and wrestle them back into line. *Tend vent! Sponge piece!* You see . . . you can't see for the smoke . . . you think . . . down the lane there . . . another small, violent eddy somewhere in that mass of blue. It spreads and grows quickly still, it is gone, you're not sure that you saw it. *Ram down . . . !* You saw it. *Prime . . . !* But a man or two hurt means nothing to British seamen. The space where they stood is filled. *Fire!*

There's no mistake this time. You see it—the sudden tight swirl in that neat double rank of scarlet just wheeling half-right off the road. But the ranks don't stop, they go on, they are neat again. In spite of the guns, the regiment marching as if on parade is moving toward the left of Stricker's line, pushing briskly across his front toward the flank that he purposely left exposed. And it is not deploying. It is drawing the British front out toward Back River, drawing it longer and longer. The brisk column is not coming nearer; it is marching parallel to the American front; there is still half a mile between the armies. But the British front is overlapping the American front by two hundred yards . . . by three hundred . . . four hundred. Already the head of the column is beginning to disappear in the clumps of trees by Back River.[18] The guns try to reach it. They can't.

But Stricker's doubt, too, disappears. *Major Calhoun . . . Cap-*

tain Stevenson. . . .[19] Here, sir. *To Colonel Fowler* . . . the 39th
will extend the front line at once . . . form on the left of the 27th.
To Colonel Amey . . . the 51st will take position on the left flank
of the 39th . . . line of battle at right angles to the front of the
brigade . . . cover the flank . . . is that clear? Yes, sir. Brigade
major and aide-de-camp are off, their horses lifted into a gallop.[20]

Critics who weren't on the field will find fault with that order
to Amey. They will say that deploying the 51st on a line perpendicular to the line of the three other regiments was an odd
maneuver. They will say that Stricker committed his largest regiment to action with its flank to the enemy and its front facing nothing but empty space. They will say he exposed the 51st to enfilading artillery fire. They will say he sent his poorest troops to the
post of greatest danger. They will say that he should have known
better. And they will put into their fault-finding just enough truth
to make their conclusions seem weighty and weighed. A little
truth, mixed with much ignorance, produces delightful magic: it
swells up the critics until they look bigger, at least to themselves,
than those whom they undertake to diminish.

The critics of Stricker's decision are in the pleasant position of
having no responsibility; they are in the even more pleasant position of not being overly bothered by facts. The facts are that the
maneuver was not odd: it was orthodox. It was not difficult: it was
simple. If, in theory, it exposed the 51st to flanking artillery fire,
the casualty lists show that the fire was, in fact, almost harmless.
Numerically, the regiment was the strongest unit in the City
Brigade. On its record, it was not untrained.[21] If it was untried,
so were the other regiments with the exception of the Fifth—and
the Fifth had fled from its first field in panic. When Stricker ordered
the 51st to the left flank, the only evidence that it was different
from the other untried troops on the field was the fact that it was
the "precinct" regiment. The critics use the word "precinct" as
epithet, argument and proof. It is none of the three: it meant
nothing except that the 51st was drawn from the Baltimore suburbs
that had not achieved the political status of wards.

Stricker had reasons for giving the order. One was the British
deployment: it showed plainly an intention to envelop his left. By
refusing that flank he expected, with reason, to prevent the enemy
"right column" from carrying out the envelopment and rolling up
his line; he applied, there, the principle of the British square. His
other reason was the terrain: by deploying Amey's regiment at a

right angle to the rest of his front, he gave it a stronger position: to attack it, the enemy must advance across swampy ground at the head of the Back River tide creek or else flounder through thickets and through the deep creek itself. But there was a weak spot—the corner where the right flank of the 51st would join the left flank of the 39th. The real risk was there; Stricker knew it and acted to meet it. *Major Barney* . . . tell Captain Montgomery to detach two guns . . . send them to the left flank of the 39th . . . between Colonel Fowler's regiment and Amey's.[22]

The two guns cease firing, the cannoneers haul them back out of the coiling smoke, they coil up the dragropes, the teams come at a trot to the limbers, the two guns go weaving away through the oaks. Stricker's eyes turn to the British again. The first thing he sees is the enemy battery, moving. Its horses have been unhitched, they are going back to the rear. A howitzer and two six-pounders are coming straight toward him,[23] the crew of each hitched to the dragropes by bricoles and dragging the piece. The short, straining rows of red-jacketed men are bent double in pairs at each gun; others heave and shove at the trails. Four more guns and another howitzer—ten more rows of bent-over men—are moving across Boulden's stubble field, spreading out into battery front toward the left of his line. Shrewdly or fortuitously, the British are throwing the weight of their long-range fire power—their rockets and their artillery—against his untested troops;[24] the Fifth, which at least knows the sound of battle, is being spared.

Stricker could not foresee this move. But, fortuitously or shrewdly, his countermove has already been made: he sent those two fieldpieces off to the left in the nick of time. Two guns against five aren't enough; he knows it; he cannot spare more. The four guns in the lane, with three heavier weapons against them, must stay where they are. When that column of seamen advances, the four will not be enough either. The battle is taking shape, he can see it now. The attack, when it comes, may be either a frontal assault on his center and right or a blow to crush in his left. It may also be both together: the British have men enough. Either move they have made, so far, may be real or a feint, but it makes little difference which. The massed naval brigade in the lane may be only a threat, the regiment out of sight now in the Back River groves may be only a feint to draw troops from his right; but he cannot move to meet either threat without making the other threat worse.

Without even a shot from their guns, the British have pinned him down.

There is a group of mounted men behind Boulden's east fence line now. Their field glasses flash in the sun. Stricker looks at his personal antagonist without being able to see him, he cannot tell one from another. Is Ross there? The sureness and skill of the British deployment gives no hint whatever of doubt or incompetence. If not Ross, who? Stricker's personal antagonist is Arthur Brooke, colonel of the 44th Foot, commanding the third brigade until Ross fell dying and left him command of the army. It will be days before Stricker finds out who he is, or knows that Ross is dead.

All that Stricker knows now is that he is facing a greatly superior force. Already, infantry and seamen and artillery, the enemy commander has more men on the field than he has. And the British army is still pouring out of the woods. A third regiment of infantry in route column of half-platoons is turning off into the fields behind the long skirmish line of the light brigade.

Montgomery's guns are firing as fast as the gunners can load. Their smoke has grown into a dirty-brown toadstool above them; at every discharge of the guns, the toadstool turns pink underneath. The grapeshot is slashing the British column and doing "considerable execution," but it is not shaking the column. That regiment coming on now is Arthur Brooke's own 44th; it cannot be shaken by four little four-pound guns. And in the edge of the stubble field, close to the lane, the British battery is almost ready to fire. The gunpointers talk to the men at the handspikes, a captain named Carmichael watches the six-foot wooden levers give the last delicate heave to the trails: one howitzer and two six-pounders are trained on the toadstool of smoke and the scurrying ants underneath it. The five other guns have a broader, easier target—blue infantry standing behind the long panels of fence as if it had needed the fence to get itself into straight lines.

The infantry, watching, is not alarmed. It is much more concerned with the rockets. The Fifth thinks it knows about guns: it remembers the British infantry filtering down through the back yards of Bladensburg, jogging down toward the river untouched, the clumps of men running across the bridge, the batteries helpless to stop them. It remembers Ben Burch's guns in the Georgetown road: the solid shot knocking the barn planks to pieces and scattering kindling but failing completely to scatter the infantry swarming up through the orchard. The men of the 27th have never seen cannon firing in earnest until today, but they have seen the town companies of artillery "exercising"; they have seen prankish gunners play catch with the four-pound balls, scooping them up in their hands while the balls are still rolling along the ground, almost spent but not quite. And Montgomery's furious firing is only confirming their notion that cannon aren't such a much. You can see a solid shot skipping and bouncing and kicking up pieces of sod; but you can't see grapeshot flying, you can't see them hit. You can only see that the enemy's column comes on: it merely quivers now and again, but no more than a horse's flank quivers to shake off a troublesome fly.

And the British guns, at this distance, are not impressive. They sit in a row in the stubble like so many hound-dogs enjoying the sun. *That there one's too chunky to be a houn' . . . it's got bow legs. . . .* The howitzer squats like a mongrel dog on its haunches, its stub of a tail out behind and its broad blunt muzzle lifted and snuffing the air; its wheels hunch up into bony shoulders, the hubs stick out on both sides like the joints of bowed legs. When its muzzle jerks, it looks like a dog that had let out one bark and then settled back on its haunches.

The howitzer lets out a puff of smoke—a great whuff of soft smoke but no sound. It takes time for the sound to travel across the fields but it looks like it ought to be soft, it ought to be *whuff* when it gets here. It isn't. It's hard, it's like iron, it's hollow and hard, it's an iron pot hit by an iron sledge. The pot is your head. It is crushed, it is broken to pieces, the pieces fall in heap. But your head is still there: it rings. Look . . . *look* . . . *!*

The brown toadstool of smoke over Montgomery's guns is enormous. It's no longer flat, it's round like a puffball—a puffball as high as the trees. There's a sound in it somewhere, a crying, a hurt child's strained terrified wailing. What happened? *What happened?*

It happens again. Red light tears the puff ball to pieces. The pieces clang . . . *smoke can't clang.* But it does. It rings like thin metal, it's loud but it's empty, an iron kettle smashed into pieces. Something burst, over there in the lane, among Montgomery's men. But *what* . . . ? Are the powder chests blowing up? Or the guns? Oh, my God, did they send us out with guns that explode when they're fired?

The iron sound bursts again. And again. And again. Not on the battery now: to the left, just in front of the fence, just in front of the 27th. Something raps on a rail like a hard-thrown stone: the earth smokes, just in front of the fence; there's a scorched place, the grass is on fire. The ranks of the 27th buckle and sag as men shrink from this unknown thing.[25]

The British are using another new, terrible weapon. The eight guns are firing shrapnel.[26] The name is the name of the British subaltern who thought up a missile more deadly than rockets, combining the terror of rockets with the murder-potential of grapeshot. "The Shrapnel is a hollow globe of iron, the cavity . . . filled up, not with powder only, but with . . . musket balls." [27] The British guns use it like round shot and "being supplied with a fuse, more or less short according to the distance to be traversed, it bursts just in front of its object, and throws the whole of its murderous contents forward."

The raw troops of the City Brigade who have never heard shots fired in anger until today don't know they are facing war's newest and deadliest killer. Few veterans ever have faced it. Fewer have faced it unbroken. The Jefferson Blues do not break. They shrink back and stand and stare at the circles of char in the grass, at the grass blown flat, scorched brown to the roots, cut short as if sheared by a scythe. They throw up their arms to ward off the new crashes that burst in their faces. There are men on the ground; they squirm, clutching their bodies; blood dribbles between their fingers. There are men who stand looking at nothing, blind from the flashes, and men who lean dazed against trees. The Fifth does not break. It is startled and tense, but most of its units are out of the zone of fire; only its left flank companies, close to the guns, have been hit. But the guns have been badly hit . . . five men down at the first burst [28] . . . a row of men lying now in the weeds at the side of the lane. There aren't four guns now, there are three and a wreck.[29] The three are still firing. The tattered smoke catches fire from the flashes; its edges burn, briefly red, like a loose heap of smoldering rags.

The dressed-up civilians behind the rail fence stand fast. The Dresden mantelpiece-ornament infantry hasn't been broken; its rows aren't as straight as they were, but the rows are still ranks. The holiday-dress-parade gunners are doing so well that the enemy thinks there are five guns in action, not three.[30]

But the British infantry regiment that was coming out of the woods when Carmichael's battery opened is still moving in perfect and rigid precision. It has cleared the lane. it has left one field behind. Now it halts, and the half-platoons of its column begin to swing like so many paneled doors swinging on hinges—the top panel painted bright red, the lower panel drab-dull. The doors swing shut, they are locked in a solid wall; the regiment stands in attack formation, solid, closed up. And the lane behind the massed seamen is filled again. Another column turns, half-right, into the field left vacant. It is a shorter column: it is like the infantry regiment but it is not the same: when its sections wheel into line like closing doors, their upper halves are the same bright scarlet but their lower halves are even brighter, they are made of the white breeches of Royal Marines.

A soldier cannot help admiring those splendid regiments, an old soldier commanding green militia cannot help envying an antagonist who wields that disciplined perfection. Suddenly, for Stricker, it is more than envy: it is a sharp pang of apprehension. Without a casualty in its ranks, with the 39th and the 27th between it and the enemy, his strongest regiment has collapsed into wild confusion.

The 39th, under shell fire, is carrying out its orders: it is forming in line of battle beyond the 27th, not with the precise perfection of the British regulars but with some sort of order, with its captains and lieutenants shouting at it and its sergeants herding it into position. The seven hundred men of the 51st are in no kind of order. They are willing, but they have no notion about what is wanted of them; neither has their colonel. Companies are marching every which way; bewildered officers are swearing and waving their arms; men are halting without orders, sullenly suspicious that the other men who lead them do not know their business. Even the British officers half a mile away can see that something has gone wrong. Stricker, with Dyer's senseless retreat in his mind, knows only too well that the confusion can lead to insensible panic. *Major Frailey . . . !*

Brigade Major Leonard Frailey knows his business: he has been an officer of regulars, commanding a battalion of the 38th United States Infantry.[31] He rides swiftly and acts calmly. With Calhoun and Stevenson, he gets Amey's milling men under control.[32] The column begins to move. But the rocket troop and the British gunners know there has been a blunder—some kind of "mismanagement" somewhere; the "marching and counter-marching" do not "augur very favourably of the determination which on that flank at least" the Americans will "exhibit."[33] They go to work to weaken what determination there is. The rockets are sweeping the woods with a fiery broom, but the bursting shells are worse. At each glare and crash, the companies falter and stop. When they move again, they move slowly, they stare at the smoking earth and avoid each spot as if there is "something deadly in the very soil." They hang back and then rush past the torn-up sod;[34] the next company does the same thing; the gaps between companies lengthen.

Frailey and Calhoun and Stevenson put the 51st into line with their hands. It hasn't been hurt: its whole loss is one per cent.[35] In line, it looks as steady as the other regiments, and Barney is there with the two detached guns to weight down the weak spot—the joint where the flank of the 51st meets the flank of the 39th. But there are other weak places now; the knee joints of seven hundred men whose confidence in themselves and their officers has been shaken. Neither the brigade majors nor Barney's guns can undo what was done by those minutes of aimless confusion. The men of the 51st feel awkward and out of place, not facing the enemy, facing almost away from the enemy troops they can see. By what they can see when they look back across their right shoulders, most of the British army seems to be behind them.

And the British army is still coming, there is still no end to it. Another regiment in column is pouring out of the woods—not turning off as the others did but coming straight on up the lane, growing steadily wider as the open ground affords space for its sections to spread out into column of platoons. When it halts behind seamen, it is a mass more than forty ranks deep, twenty men abreast in each rank.[36] It makes, with the naval brigade, an assault column of almost two thousand men—a blunt missile aimed at the center of Stricker's original front. The center now is forty-five amateur gunners and three small guns. On one side of the guns—on the right—is the Fifth Maryland Infantry; on the left is the 27th. The Fifth and the guns and a part of the 27th must meet the attack of those two thousand men. They must meet it with less than a thousand.

Stricker can give them no help. The only reserve he has left is the Sixth, more than half a mile to the rear. If he orders Mc-Donald forward to strengthen the line . . . He gives the temptation only the briefest thought and rejects it. McDonald's six hundred men cannot avert the inevitable. But, left where they are, they can cover the retreat of the other regiments, give them time and a place to rally. They can prevent the retreat—Stricker hopes—from becoming a rout. A rout in these woods, in this narrow lane, can become a complete disaster. He sees, in his mind, the lane choked with panicky men, the teams trampling them, wagons and guns abandoned, the road blocked, massacre, wholesale surrender. He leaves the Sixth where it is. He will hold on as long as he can with twenty-five hundred men against seven thousand, eight thousand.[37] The odds, he believes, are three to one against him.

Over there in Boulden's north field, Colonel Brooke and his staff have arrived at different figures. They believe the numerical odds are six or seven to five against *them*. They are wrong; so is Stricker, but Stricker's countinghouse mind has come closer to striking an accurate balance. There are, in Brooke's line of battle, a few more than five thousand men. There are, in the American line, a few less than twenty-five hundred. There are eight British guns to five smaller American guns. There are the two new and terrible weapons—the rockets, the shrapnel. And there are discipline, confidence, habit.

You can't weigh discipline in a greengrocer's balance. You can't measure confidence by a carpenter's rule or the length of a dry-goods clerk's arm. You can't add up on your fingers the long British habit of winning. There's no need to measure or add, you can guess the result. Your fingers are stiff, they're gripping the musket so tight. Standing here in the ranks of the Fifth, you can't even count the men in that ponderous mass on the road or the men in those triple lines back of Boulden's place. You try, and you can't. But you know there's a godawful lot of them. There's a lot more of them now than the last time. They whipped us the last time. Now they've got more men, we've got fewer. They chased us the last time . . . *God . . . it was awful . . . being chased . . . running. . . .* God damn it, don't think about that. And stop swearing. *I wasn't . . . I didn't mean to . . . Chris Keener . . . George Golder . . . Jim McCulloch all bloody . . . I'll see that again . . . I've seen it again already, those men by the guns, falling down . . . I wonder who next time . . . me?* Your fingers are numb, the bubble is cold in your belly. *I don't want to be killed . . . I don't want to be hurt . . . our Father which art . . . I don't want to be scared . . . I don't want to feel that way again. . . .*

But you do. You can't help being scared. You feel guilty because you can't help it. You're not an old soldier, you haven't had time to find out that fear is a thing that you live with, a thing that you wear like a sweat-filthy, clammy shirt. You can't change your shirt every day, in a war; it's not a disgrace, it is only an intimate, personal misery when it itches and clings and crawls. It's no disgrace to be scared of those men over there. They are old soldiers; they know this business of killing, they know it much better than you do. They are shrewd at their trade. Those sailors have practiced their business of killing for twenty years, there are men in that mass of blue who fought at the Nile and Trafalgar. That regiment massed behind them is almost a century older than the republic it has been sent to conquer: it is the 21st—the Royal North British Fusiliers: it stood its first muster in 1678 and its battle record goes back through a hundred and thirty-four years—Bothwell Bridge, Steenkerke, Blenheim and Malplaquet, Sheriffmuir, Dettingen, Fontenoy, Culloden. In these last few years it has fought in Egypt and Sicily, Italy and Holland, and fought so well that it was chosen to march in the great Lord Nelson's cortege. And four years ago the Royal North British cut off a French amphibious task force, cut it to pieces, and captured a thousand men.[38]

There is another name, too, on the roll of the 21st's battles—a name that might make you feel better. The 21st tried its hand at invading America forty years ago: it was beaten at Saratoga and laid down its arms with Burgoyne. But you don't know that. All you know is that some of those men are the same men who beat you the last time.

The men in the long skirmish line back of Boulden's farm are the same ones who crouched in the orchard and shot Christian Keener and George Clarke and Billy Williams and Sergeant Murray. They are the 85th, fresh from the siege of Bayonne and Wellington's final triumph. And the regiment drawn up behind them in double ranks is the 44th, the East Essex. It has more American traditions than the Americans facing it now. George Washington himself once commanded the 44th. It fought under Braddock at the massacre of the Monongahela; its colonel, Sir Peter Halket, fell in the first blast of fire, and young Colonel Washington led its retreat. There is a sentence in the regimental record that says: "It was in this action that George Washington first gave promise of that military talent which was, in after years, displayed against the British army, in the American war, in which the 44th regiment was employed."

The 44th fought the French at Ticonderoga in 1758 and again the next year at Niagara. It came ashore from its transports in

Boston harbor just after the fight on Breed's Hill. (Thus again the old threads come together: Sam Smith knows this regiment well, and John Stricker's father knew it.) At Long Island, in 1776, the 44th formed part of the column that General James Grant led against the American army's right wing to distract attention from the main British attack that rolled up the other wing. James Grant was the man who rode through Sam Smith's boyhood town to attack Fort Duquesne after Braddock failed, and to give his name to another massacre. It was the 44th which, under Grant, gave Sam Smith his baptism of fire at Long Island. It fought again at White Plains, where a musket ball numbed Smith's arm and a cannon beheaded the sergeant who stood behind him. And today is not the first time it has taken part in an amphibious invasion: it was in the landing boats at Aboukir Bay thirteen years ago. It fought at Alexandria and at the siege of Cairo; five years of campaigning in Sicily have whetted its fighting edge; it took part, last year, in the siege of Tarragona.[39]

You don't know these things, and it's probably just as well. It's just as well that you can't see all the enemy's troops. The regiment hidden now in the Back River groves is the Fourth, the King's Own. It is old: it was mustered in 1680 and called, then, the Second Tangier. Its reputation is high and its hardest service is recent; it has been in the field for six years, in the deadliest fighting in Spain. It led the right wing of the British invasion in 1808, under Sir John Moore, and bore the brunt of the French assault at Corunna. In its headlong pursuit of the French from Almeida it plunged into the gorge of the Barba del Puerco, turned that grim chasm into a slaughter pit, and emerged with three hundred prisoners. At the storming of Badajoz it led the fierce attack on the bastion of San Vincente, charged up the mined slope, hacked down the outworks with axes, leaped into the moat below the thirty-foot walls, put up its scaling ladders—and found the ladders too short. But the Fourth took the wall.

Two years ago, its brilliant charge at Salamanca swept up eleven French cannon, two eagles and six stands of colors, and won Major Faunce a decoration for valor. (Faunce leads it today.) Last year, at Vittoria, it charged into point-blank artillery fire, drove the French from their bridgehead across the Zadora, took their guns, and then charged three times over the bridge itself. Two months later, at San Sebastian, it stormed a breach under a "tempest of shells and grape-shot which blazed in the air, tore up the ground, and menaced the brigade with instant destruction." Not a man in the first wave lived to reach the top of the wall; the survivors clung to the rubble while heavy guns pounded the breach a few feet above their heads; then they charged again, took it, fought for three hours to hold it—and held.[40] What can militia do against troops like these? Militia already outnumbered by two to one?

And the odds are not merely a matter of numbers nor of tradition or habit. These British troops are not merely veterans, they are not merely so many regiments of Wellington's Invincibles: they are a machine. Three of Brooke's regiments have fought side by side in Europe. The Fourth was brigaded with the 44th in the lines of Torres Vedras; it fought with the 85th at the siege of Bayonne.[41] They are used to each other, they know how to work together. You've seen how they work: you saw how they did it the last time: working up through the orchard, working around you, working around behind you. They're doing the same thing now. You can't see, but you know. What else can it be? What else are they waiting for? Come on . . . oh, for God's sake, *come on!*

The British are taking their time. They are taking the fire of Montgomery's guns. Where the small quilted bags of grapeshot break in the ranks of the 21st, Montgomery's fire is "destructive."[42] And yet the ranks barely stir; they close and are solid again. The two guns on the left come into action at last, trying to reach the thin line of the 85th. Their grapeshot begins to smash windows in Boulden's house. Look a' that! *Will you look at that?* A section of the British skirmish line leans suddenly forward and disappears like a fence panel blown flat by a wind. Another falls flat, and another. The whole light brigade disappears. It is lying down.[43] *Bastards* . . . thin, cool voice in the ranks of the 27th . . . *I hope Boulden's cows have been feedin' good* . . . thin and cool as skimmed milk in a springhouse crock . . . *I don't wish Boulden hard luck but I sure hope his cows had the scours* . . . hot personal tumult of fear strained and chilled now into cold impersonal anger . . . *I hope that pasture's got plenty of cow flops in it. Bastards. . . .*

The two guns on the left have only a poor target now. The three in the lane still have the blue mass and they still have the red mass behind it. All five of Montgomery's guns have the enemy guns for a target. That is what's wrong: twenty rounds of grape have been futile. They have probably done some damage but, so far as

Stricker can see, they have not done enough to matter; every piece in the British battery is still firing, not one crew has been put out of action or even thrown off its stride in the smooth, measured pace of the firing; the masses of men in the lane look as solid and steady as ever. The range is too long, it is more than three hundred toises; the infantry back of the naval brigade is four hundred toises away. At that range, the grape is no longer a tight, deadly bundle; it spreads and loses its pattern,[44] few shots take effect; each shot is a random pebble.

Case shot might be more effective than grape; Stricker is tempted to try it. But even at half that distance—even at four hundred yards—a canister loaded with twelve iron balls can't be counted on to put more than four to six balls into a space the height of a man and ninety feet wide.[45] It's more likely to do worse than better. At six, seven, eight hundred yards it is likely to miss altogether. Stricker knows that he ought to wait. Distances under three hundred yards are the deadliest ranges for either case shot or grape.[46] But it isn't an easy decision. He dreads letting the enemy's battery play undisturbed on his waiting and helpless men, he can't know how long they will stand there and wait while the shells explode at their feet and behind them and overhead. He makes the decision . . . cease firing . . . wait for close canister range.[47]

The American guns go silent. The British guns fire with the spaced, measured strokes of a bell—a slow, ponderous bell—an enormous, cracked bell without clangor. The strokes of the clapper are loud, but they're flat; they don't ring. It's your ears that ring when the sudden red flashes of shell bursts leap from the empty air; your eyes wince, your whole body winces. You feel alone, and you are. You've shrunk back, you're behind the ranks, you're back here in the file closers' ranks, you don't know how you got here. *Dress* . . . that's the sergeant . . . *dress* . . . *steady* . . . *keep dressed now.* . . . You feel undressed. You also feel foolish: that shell burst was fifty yards off. But you can't feel your legs at all when they walk you back up to your place in the line: they're stiff, they're like wood, they're as stiff as the legs of a stool. You look at Jake Haubert but Jake doesn't know you are there or know that you weren't; he looks straight ahead and he's sweating, the sweat makes a slick greasy streak on his face and his face looks sick. Not pale-sick: yellow. You lift your hand up to your face to wipe at your own running sweat and the fingers are yellow: the air is half smoke: the light that sifts through it is tarnished.

The British guns fire and fire. They don't look like they're firing, they look like they're tossing out bundles of dirty clothes. The clothes scatter; they'd ought to fall, but they don't; each new dirty bundle bursts as it leaves the gun and spreads out and floats on the smoke of the other guns. The smoke seethes like boiling suds in a kettle of dirty clothes. And then *flash* in your eyes . . . and then *k-kkram-mn* in your ears . . . *rra-aakkk* in your head . . . the soiled smoke in the grass . . . as if kettle and dirty washing and suds and the fire underneath the kettle had all been thrown at you together.

Whole platoons cringe back where the flashes break. The front of the City Brigade seems to writhe as the ranks recoil and are dressed again and recoil. To the British it seems that the American infantry is being "mowed . . . down by whole sections." [48] The firing is bad enough but it isn't that bad. There are gaps, men are being hit, but most of the gaps are not dead men's or wounded men's places. The lines of the 39th and the 27th waver and bend in a dozen places but do not break; there is a toughness about them that Stricker had hoped for but hardly had dared to expect; the bends straighten, the gaps are filled. The left flank of the Fifth shudders back when the shells come close and a musket falls and the man who held it stoops as if picking it up and falls slowly as if undecided and lies in a heap on the musket. The United Volunteers suffered most of the Fifth's loss at Bladensburg; they are suffering most of it now, on the flank by Montgomery's silent guns. Their line sags and recovers, sags and re-forms and stands fast; it clings to its place at the fence.

The shells come . . . rockets . . . shells . . . and more shells. Minute on minute, a dozen red crashes a minute. *Why don't we lay down?* If we laid down like the British they couldn't see us any better'n we can see them, we'd be hid in the grass. There's thick grass there, along the fence . . . I wonder why it grows thicker by fences than anywheres else . . . I wish I was down there in it, scrounged close to the ground . . . man's days are like unto leaves of grass . . . that's not right . . . in the Bible somewheres . . . *God! That one was close.* The guns got it again . . . there's a bundle of clothes in the road underneath that gun but it isn't one of the gunners . . . it's one of the Jefferson Blues . . . the shell knocked him right out of ranks into the road . . . there's a piece of him caught in the wheel, running down . . . but the rest of him's squirming, he's still alive. You see how it is now. The British battery isn't throwing iron spheres that break with the awful red noise, they're not throwing dirty clothes either: they're throwing men . . . pieces of men . . . chunks of flesh partly undressed: they're throwing men's bodies across the field, six hundred yards, and dumping them down like raw meat. Good God Almighty, the roustabouts down at Moale's wharf don't treat bales of dried hides like that, the teamsters that drive the commissary wagons don't throw quarters of beef off their wagons like that.

The rockets aren't flying so wild now. They're lower, they're swooshing low over Boulden's barns, they're skimming the haystacks, they're falling in front of the 27th. One strikes at the edge of the lane and lies still in a fur of smoke. Then it shakes and goes into convusions. Its tail beats the ground, its long wooden pole of a tail threshes the dirt like a dying man's frantic legs. *One* leg . . . that man underneath the gun has one leg, the other was stuck in the wheel of the gun until somebody pulled it away and carried it to the side of the road and laid it down in the ditch . . . like the ditch was a grave and part of the man was buried while part of him is still alive.

A rocket falls short. It darts past the Boulden house and plunges into a haystack.[49] The hay catches fire. In the British lines the bugles begin to blow.

The light brigade springs to its feet. The whole front line of the British army suddenly stands erect, as if it had sprung from the earth.[50] The whole British army stands like a Meissonier painting of war. All the colors are brilliant, the brush strokes are strong, the sun glows on the splashes and slashes of color. There is just enough smoke in the foreground to give a suggestion of battle, just enough fire in the stackyard to hint very politely at war's desolation. The smoke wreathes the British guns with conventional, stylized curls. The haystacks burn neatly. You can't see the cannoneers, you can't see the soldiers crouched at the sills of the broken farmhouse windows and choking now in the smoke of the burning stacks, you can't see the men who will die or be torn and maimed. You see only important and suitable people—commander and staff on their horses; the "common" men, soldiers and sailors, are lost in those masses and streaks of color. There is no realism about it at all. Now, at ten minutes before three o'clock, the British army looks as unreal as a painting hung on a wall.

But the painting is not yet finished. The brush is still busy. It dabs at the smoke, red flashes dart out and are wiped away with a thumb, the smoke thickens and hides the guns. The British battery is firing faster—or maybe it only seems to be firing faster because time has stopped. Time, too, hangs suspended, a clock that has suddenly stopped. It waits for the British to move. Your breath waits. *Will they never move?*

Only the smoke and fire move. The flames of the haystacks are real now, they make their own wind and are blown from one stack to another, the whole yard is burning, the smoke of smouldering straw is an ugly black spreading smootch. Pieces of fire are torn loose and whirled up through the smoke and float down: at this distance the swirling wisps are no bigger than sparks from a rocket. The hay in a loft door catches, flames quiver along the eaves, the whole loft seems to explode. Sheds, stables, even the privy are burning.[51] Fire runs up the side of the farmhouse. Away to the left, toward Back River, sparks glow in the rank tall grass and a long streak of red like a grass fire brightens behind them. The "right column" of the British army is starting its advance upon the American left behind its own screen of skirmishers.[52] The painted war comes to life, it begins to turn real. In the middle background two tiny figures break from the cluster of horsemen.[53] They gallop: they don't look like officers mounted on galloping horses, they look like two bright birds darting, like two scarlet tanagers skimming across the fields in opposite directions. The bugles are blowing again. The army steps out of the painting.

Attensh . . . *hahhn!* You can't stand any stiffer or straighter, you can't pull your belly in flatter, the thin wire inside you is pulling it tight to your backbone, your insides are up in your chest. *Fix bayonets . . . !* Your arms are as stiff as the musket, they move like two wooden sticks. Shoulder . . . *humms!* Carry . . . *humms!* The iron strip on the butt of the musket feels warm to your hand, it is warm from the earth, it feels good: your fingers are cold. Your tongue feels stiff in your mouth and cold . . . *my mouth's open.* You close it, immensely surprised. *Gaping. . . .* There's nothing to gape at, you've seen British troops before, you feel like a fool.

But you've never seen them like this . . . like brick walls suddenly stirring . . . like wall after wall solidly moving . . . coming nearer and solidly nearer and bigger. They'll fall on you, smother you, crush you. It's like a dream. I'm not dreaming. I'm wide awake. I'm wider awake than I've ever been in my life, but it's like a dream . . . like a dream that keeps coming back every so often . . . the one about something falling, something high up above me and falling and getting bigger and bigger until it fills the whole sky and I'm underneath it and can't get away and it's going to crush me unless I wake up in time. I can't wake up now because I'm already awake.

It's silly. You know it's silly. And yet it's real. It's more real than the shrapnel. The shells jerk the wire in your guts, your whole body jerks. But that's not the same: the shells aren't all aimed at you, they walk up and down the three regiments hunting for someone but not always you: the red splintering crashes don't last, they don't stay in your mind. But those moving walls come like the doom of the ponderous personal weight in that awful childhood dream. The fear stays in your mind like a sound that won't stop . . . a thin sound . . . a cicada shrilling and shrilling . . . a cicada stuck to the bark of your brain and boring . . . boring. . . . Cicadas don't bore. Or do they? That's funny . . . I'd ought to know that. When I get home I'll find out. It won't matter then but I'd like to know, I'm going to find out just the same—if I wake up in time, if those walls don't fall on me and crush me before I wake up.

There are flags on the moving walls. You think wildly: an army with banners. You think: they're the color of blood. They're not all that color, but those are the ones you see plainest; they drip bright as blood from their staffs, they pulse to the stride of the bearers like blood pulsing out of a wound. Those are king's standards—the red ones. Each has another beside it, a different color—a dark-blue one down the lane there, like the flag of the 27th—a yellow one swaying above the close double ranks of the regiment crossing the stubble.[54]

You can see what the walls are made of; you already know but now you can see, you can pick out small separate figures of men fitted neatly together in patterns. The patterns are mostly the same, they are made of white crossbelts above and legs moving below; the legs make a herringbone pattern that changes, now light and now dark. The wall that is nearest is also the thinnest—one line of men with thin spaces beginning to show now between them. This line is not straight, it curves in and out like the serpentine wall that you saw in Virginia once when you traveled three days in a stagecoach to go to a Charlottesville dance. But it, too, is bonded with crossbelts in white streaks like mortar—a design that is half a mile long, a thousand St. Andrew's crosses. They gleam. They go dull in the smoke of the "conflagration" at Boulden's. They gleam. They go dull again as they pass through the battery smoke. The British guns cease firing. The crossbelts are whiter and bigger and nearer.

Montgomery's guns take up where the British left off. But they are not nearly so dreadful, they have no exploding shells. They have small tin cans filled with musket balls, bolts, rusty nails, scraps of old iron, pieces of broken gunlocks.[55] The two cannon in the lane begin to hurl cans of scrap iron straight down the road at the oncoming naval brigade and the Royal North British Fusiliers forty ranks deep behind it. The two cannon away to the left hurl tin cans at the line of the light brigade. But the cans don't explode, all they do is spill, you can't tell for sure where they hit. For all you can see, you might as well take a can in your hand and throw it.

The first line comes on "cool and orderly." [56] The blue mass in the lane comes on, and the forty-deep ranks come on, and the long double ranks of Marines and the 44th. The four-pounders can't stop them, can't hurt them, they can't even make them hurry. There's something inhuman about that advancing army, nerveless, insensate, machinelike.

But even the British have nerves, even the tough Invincibles wince when the canister whines and the wind of it brushes their faces and men go down. The seamen are suffering "some loss." The Fusiliers' loss is "severe." [57] The steady pace never falters, it never quickens.

There is a rush from the farmhouse. The company hidden there bursts through the smoke, a huddle of blurred, running figures. A fence stands in their way. They begin to swarm over the fence and Montgomery's guns catch them there and sweep "five or six men" off the rails.[58] A solid shot tears away one man's shoulder and shears off his ribs, and an officer sees his lungs bulge through the bloody hole. The officer thinks of shooting him: "Might not the blowing out of a man's brains, under such circumstances, be not only justifiable but praiseworthy?" [59] He wonders but does not shoot. The man lingers for days, is carried six miles, laid into a boat, hoisted over the rail of a transport, and dies at last. His death is remembered because he has been "by far the most skillful maker of fires" in the 85th.[60] They remember that, but they do not remember his name.

His death is a trifle and so are the other deaths. The parade-ground advance rolls on. But it is beginning to change. The last

time you looked at the shapeless blue mass, part of it was in the
road and part in the field alongside, you could see that part of it
over the roof of the old log house. Now all of the naval brigade is
in the field and it is not coming straight on. It is slanting off to its
left, moving diagonally toward the right flank of the Fifth; it leaves
a widening gap between itself and the road and the infantry regiment coming behind it fills up the gap. The regiment isn't deployed
like the others, it isn't a series of walls: it's the Royal North
British in dense assault column, a column twenty men wide, forty

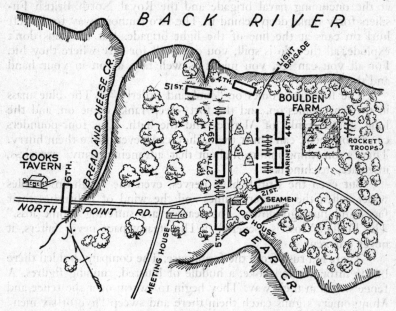

The situation just before the flight of the 51st.

deep. It looks like a balk of timber, a short squared beam. It looks
like a battering ram and it is.

This is the head-on attack that Stricker foresaw, the blow to
crush in his center. The log house stands in its way. Captain Philip
Sadtler's Yeagers also are in its way. Now, at long range, they open
the infantry battle. Their muskets slam like old hewn-slab doors
slammed shut in the enemy's face.

The storm column aimed at the center has all the appearance
of being intended to strike the knockout blow, but all the im-

pending attacks will be heavy. Wherever he looks now, Stricker sees almost his whole front menaced by unshaken bodies of troops that outnumber his waiting militia. Only on his extreme left flank are the odds running even. The 51st, there, has only one regiment coming against it; the British flank column has, probably, no more men than the 51st's seven hundred. And Amey's men have the two guns to help them, the tide creek to cover their left, the soft ground to hinder a charge at their front, and the 39th to protect their right. The British enveloping movement is aimed at the strongest part of the flank it is meant to roll up; its skirmishers, swashing waist-deep through the rank swamp grass, dot the whole front of the 51st with their heads and shoulders, but the main body clings to cover. Major Will Barney ignores it: the attack may be dangerous soon but it isn't yet, and the skirmishers make a poor target: he keeps his guns trained on the bigger, more dangerous target—the impervious steady advance of the light brigade and the heavier lines behind it.

The British flank column breaks through the thickets and comes to a doubtful halt. Its officers knew there was water ahead, but they thought it was only "a little inland lake." [61] The creek is an ugly surprise. It is wide, it looks deep. On the other side, within musket shot, stand long double ranks of infantry. The British have reached the American flank but they haven't turned it: the flank has turned into another front. Unless they can find a ford, the enveloping movement is finished: the Fourth Foot will have to swing to its left past the head of the creek and deliver a frontal attack. While men sqush through the border of muck and wade into the sluggish stream, hunting for shallows, the column begins to pile up on the bank. In the swamp grass, the skirmishers open fire. They are too few and too far away to do any serious damage; all they can do is discourage the Yankees from trying a counter-attack while the Fourth is held up. A determined charge now might throw the British attack off balance. Even militia might, with a little luck, pin the Fourth back into the angle between the creek and the river.

The opportunity passes. Good troops might have used it. So far as the 51st is concerned, the opportunity never existed. Attack is the last thing the regiment thinks of. It lets off "one random fire." [62] Then its frayed nerves break. The whole regiment breaks and runs. And the panic spreads. The 39th sees its protection dissolving, its left flank exposed, the enemy almost behind it. The

second battalion begins to fall back in confusion.[63] The officers try
to hold it; they fail. The guns stand deserted by all but their
crews. But the gunners are stubborn men and Will Barney has
fought guns before against hopeless odds, he has fought British
frigates with rowboats. The cannoneers stick to their pieces. They
can't check the British charge but the fact that they stick helps to
check the incipient rout of the whole 39th. The first battalion stands
fast, a few men of the second rally.

The British flank column has found a ford through the creek.
It goes cheering and splashing across, in full cry on the heels of
the 51st.

At both ends of the field, Stricker sees his men giving way.
The Yeagers also are running—the seventy men sent to hold the
log house fifty yards in advance of the Fifth. They have done
what they could: the storm column of the Royal North British
Fusiliers is a bare hundred yards from the house: the Yeagers have
knocked a few chips off that squared human timber grinding in-
exorably toward them, but they have neither delayed it nor swerved
it. Smoke seeps through the cabin walls, the chinks glow, the shingles begin to curl; the roof goes in a roar of flame as the Yeagers
come tumbling over the fence. Captain Sadtler has obeyed his order
to set the house afire as soon as he "should be compelled to leave
it." [64] The order was necessary, but it was also a blunder.

The blunder was Stricker's. The house was useless to him—too
small to be garrisoned strongly. Not a third of Sadtler's small company could jam themselves in, not ten muskets could fire through
the chinks. But it was extremely useful to the enemy: left standing,
it masked the advance of a column along the south side of the lane:
through three-fourths of the last vital hundred yards—extreme
musket range—it would give an assault column almost complete protection. It was also a potential strong point from which a few men,
under cover, could fire on the American line while the charge
closed in. The house should have been torn down or burned when
Stricker decided to fight on the line of the oak woods. The decision had not been hasty, it had been made days ago. There had
been time last week, and last night; even after the troops deployed
there had been ample time. Now it had to be done, too late, when
the battle was turning against him, the odds growing worse.

The odds are not two to one now. They are three to one.
Stricker's left flank is gone, his largest regiment gone and with it a
part of another; the Fifth has been weakened, the Yeagers are

rallying back of its line but they are confused and excited, Heath's detachment has been re-formed but the men are still "much exhausted." The British right column already is in Stricker's rear; it is still well off to the left, it is not actually behind what is left of his front; but it *can* be behind him in minutes. It should be. Stricker expects it. Facing Wellington's veteran regiments, only a fool would count on a British blunder to save him.

The miracle happens. The British flank column blunders. The Fourth Foot misses its chance to roll up the American front. It rushes ahead pell-mell in pursuit of the 51st and is lost till the battle is over.[65] The two regiments cancel each other. Now, at the climax, the battle has taken the shape Stricker hoped it would take: the slow, formal frontal attack. But he has fewer men to meet it than he had expected to have. The shock of the British assault will fall upon fewer than seventeen hundred men. More than four thousand are moving against their front.

You can see the men plainly now in the fields to the north of the lane where the smoke of the burning cabin does not conceal them. You can see little things about them—the bright yellow facings on scarlet jackets, the bright yellow slashes of chevrons, the sun-glint on gilded chin straps. The white belts have buckles that glint. *When we fire, don't aim at the buckles . . . aim under them . . . keep your aim low. . . .* A man's body is soft there, the buckles lie just at the tip of the breastbone, the ribs slant away. You know, because that is where your buckle lies. *Aim at the officers first . . . get the officers first . . . steady . . . steady . . . not yet . . . not yet . . .*

The officers, marching in front, have their sabers tucked up to their shoulders; the sabers make quick curving flashes of light that keep time to their steps. A scarlet sash flaps and flaps against a captain's left knee, a shiny black leather haversack swings by a strap and dangles against his right hip. He looks back at his company quickly, his shoulders half turn, you can see the small wooden keg hung around his neck, hanging down his back and jiggling between his shoulder blades.[66] Something trips him, he falls, his hands catch him. He crouches on hands and knees and the front of the company opens and closes and hides him. Another ten paces: you see him again past the heads in the oncoming line, he is lying down. *The wall crushed him.* It didn't, you know it didn't. But there he is, flat on the ground. Your mouth's dry, you swallow . . . you try to but it hurts your throat like the swallow'd gone up

and not down, your throat aches. The bubble inside you swells up
into your neck and bursts in the back of your mouth and your
mouth isn't dry . . . it's wet, the wet burns, it is hot and bitter
as bile . . . there was a man last time, I don't know who he was
. . . he threw up . . . I don't want to throw up. . . .

There's a retching sound: *kwaugh* . . . hard and brassy . . .
all sound has been turned into metal . . . *kwaugh* . . . *kwa-kwaugh*
. . . John Buck blowing his trumpet. And somebody bawling something that sounds like bah blah, blaah, bah bah blah. All the officers
bawling . . . Major Heath on a horse again . . . he's got him another
horse . . . Fifth Mur'lunnn . . . pr-wrrr wrrr . . . rrr . . . nnk
. . . oooo-oon . . . ! *All right now, Uniteds!* Thank God, there's
one voice you can hear. Ensign Wilmot is standing backed up to
the fence, with his back to the burning log house and the redcoats. The red coats are brown through the smoke. The white
crossbelts aren't white, they're yellow, they're dirty-looking.
We're going to fire . . . Johnny Wilmot's face is as white as a crossbelt had ought to be . . . *by platoons from the right* . . . *mind you
wait till I tell you* . . . he licks his lips, he's scared but he doesn't
act scared . . . *up to you after that* . . . *aim* . . . *take it easy* . . .
aim low. . . .

The company cheers him. Ya-aaah! You're yelling, you don't
know why. The whole regiment's yelling. Yaa-aaah! Waa-aaa-
aaahhh! Waa-aaa*slam!* The first volley hits you across the mouth.
It crams the yell back in your mouth. *Slam. Slam slam slam* . . .
slam k-rr-*rruk!* The volleys march down the line, the echoes
come crashing behind them. The echoes don't march, they run,
they jostle each other and stumble and fall in a racketing heap.
Slam! That's the Patriots firing. K-rrr-*rruk!* The heaped sound is
piled higher and higher. We're next. First platoon, poise arms.
Present arms. Aim . . . there's nothing to aim at but smoke and
brown ghosts in the smoke . . . *fire!*

You fired. Did you? You must have, your shoulder hurts. But
you can't remember, you heard all the other muskets but not your
own. Load . . . load now . . . you've got to load. Your fingers don't
feel like yours, they are clumsy and stiff and slow and the paper
cartridge is clumsy, it tries to fall out of your fingers. The cartridges aren't the same. They're top-heavy. No, bottom-heavy.
They're not loaded today with a single ounce ball, they're loaded
with ball and three buckshot.

The volleys are marching away down the line of the 27th.

Between them you hear the first separate ploppings of muskets away in the other direction. They don't sound like shots, they are small ineffectual noises. You've made sounds like that: you've thrown stones at the neighbors' privy, you've pounded a stick on a fence rail.

The sound grows, it comes hurrying toward you. The Fifth is firing at will and more muskets are pounding, they beat now like clubs on the fence rails. You can't see the fence: it is hidden in gushes of smoke and your shoulder feels numb and your arm feels numb. There's no single sound any more, there's a crazy roaring that jumps like the kick of a musket and splits like a bursting shell and is fitted together again and is solid and splits and collapses and falls on a sliding enormous pile. The musket roar punies the cannon. *That there was a cannon.* It didn't sound like one, it sounded like somebody up and said "Boh!" in a serious tone. *It sounded like somebody spit.*

Hand to the cartridge box. Bite through the paper. You can't taste the powder, your tongue's dry as powder, you couldn't spit if you tried. Prime. Shut pan. Cast about. Cast the butt of your gun to the front and left side . . . let it slide through your hand. Butt to the ground in front of your left foot. Right hand to the muzzle. Load. Raise the elbow as high as the wrist . . . pour the powder into the muzzle . . . shake the cartridge, get the last grains . . . force the empty cartridge paper into the muzzle. Draw ramrod. Seize it with thumb and forefinger . . . push it up briskly about a foot . . . keep your thumb pointing upwards. Reverse the right hand . . . keep the back of your hand to your face, little finger on top . . . seize the rod, draw it clear . . . reverse it, turn its head outwards and down . . . *there's so much to do and it takes so long and they're coming, the brown ghosts are big in the smoke now, they're solid, the brown wall is coming to crush you.* . . . Place the head of the rod in the muzzle . . . run the hand half up the length of the ramrod, hold it between the thumb and the first two fingers. Hurry . . . hurry . . . ram down. Tap the heel of the butt on the ground to level the powder. Ram the wadding well down the barrel. Return ramrod. Poise. Present. Aim . . . The sweat blurs your eyes. You can't see the front sight for the sweat and the smart of burned powder that flashed from the pan, that last shot. But you can see the brown wall turning red, coming out through the smoke. *Fire.* . . .

They've stopped! By God but they have! We've stopped 'em!

We did it before and we've done it! Yaa-aaaah! Yaa-aaa-aaahhh!
Look out . . . ! They're going to shoot . . . !

The first British volley explodes like the world blowing up.
The world shakes, you can feel it shake in your knees. A great piece
of the earth has been wrenched away, the whole British army is
gone, there is nothing left but the place where you stand on a
small strip of earth like a shelf that is hung over nothing. You
can't see the edge of the shelf: where the enemy stood and fired
there is only the dark rolling smoke of the volley: the field ends
there, all the rest has been torn away and there's only a chasm,
a great hole that has swallowed the rest of the earth and the
British army.

And then the smoke thins and you see them. They haven't
been swallowed, they cling to the edge of the shattered world, they
lean toward you as if they are trying to drag themselves up onto
all that is left of the world. What is left is yours and they want it.
There's not room for both of you on it, they'll hurl you off. And
they're coming, they're leaning because they are running. Fire!
Stop them! *You've got to stop them. . . .*

They stop. They take aim. What is left of the world blows up.
There is not much left, the explosion is not so loud. The British
are firing by half-battalions. All along the half mile of front, each
alternate half-battalion has run forward fifteen paces, halted and
aimed and fired. At the instant it halted, the other halves started to
move. They are coming now through the regular gaps in the line,
past the halted ranks where men's arms pump up and down at the
ramrods; they stop fifteen paces in front; as they aim and fire, all
the half-battalions behind them trot forward at double time. The
British front moves like the squares of a checkerboard, moving.

The firing is almost unbroken. The volleys crash into the
echoes. The smoke is a dense, rolling cloud that is blown by the
wind of the muskets. It rolls toward the other smoke that hangs
in a dense low cloud all along the American lines. The red flashes
spring from the rolling cloud like sheet lightning, in level streaks.
Through the other cloud, the red flashes flicker like lightning that
runs along fences. There is nothing to see but the smoke. There
is nothing to fire at but flashes.

Flags stir in the smoke. The bright moth-flags can fly in the
dark. The blue flag of the 27th is swinging in long, slow swoops,
and Bill Batchelor's son is swinging the flag with the circle of
stars. *It didn't go back at the Cowpens . . . they killed pa . . .*

he came home to die, but he didn't run . . . they can kill me, I'm not going to run. . . . Ensign John Lester feels the staff of the blue flag tug in his hands: there are holes in the silk where the bullets went through: some of the gold threads are broken. He knows what the letters say. They say: Not myself, but my country. Maybe he thinks of the Latin words, maybe he doesn't. He thinks: *I won't run . . . I won't. . . .*

The smoldering musket wads wink in the long matted grass like fireflies deceived by the premature twilight of smoke. Where they fall, the grass catches fire; the grass by the rail fence is speckled with little brown circles of scorch. There are other small spattered circles that are not brown yet; but they will be, the blood will dry. Sergeant Elisha Lewis feels his hand sting to a sudden blow. He looks down at it, puzzled, and sees that a bullet has shattered the stock of his musket; under his fingers the wood is a fuzz of splinters.[67] A private lies dead, face-down, by the bottom rail of the fence. Sergeant Lewis stoops . . . *it's gettin' on to be autumn . . . the leaves on those creepers are turnin' a'ready . . . those spots on the rail aren't leaves. . . .* He drags the musket from under the dead man's body and looks at the priming. There's blood on the stock. He wipes it off with his sleeve and fires through a rift in the smoke at the British skirmishers running for cover behind a haystack. *We'd ought to of burnt those stacks.* Every haystack in the stubble in front of the 27th has a dark clot of infantry swelling behind it.[68] *They're hurt . . . they don't like what they're gettin' . . .* They don't, but that isn't important: skirmishers scatter to let the assault troops come through: the regiments running and firing by halves of battalions are steadily closing in, they are already close, they are not more than sixty yards now from the lines of the City Brigade.

What is left of the City Brigade is not lines. It is separate huddles of men. It is men getting down on their knees to see under the smoke. It is men climbing up into trees to see over the smoke. The kneeling men press themselves close to the fence, they are firing between the rails and the rails drip smoke. The men in the trees twist their legs around boughs and fire past the trunks, they stand on the thick low boughs with legs braced and their backs to the trunks of the trees. This is the useless militia. These are the holiday-dress-parade soldiers. These are the quaintly decorative Dresden mantelpiece-ornament soldiers. These are the paper soldiers.

They are the crossed-sword Dresden. They are the tough cartridge paper. Give them this hour of honor.

They have stood more than an hour under the rockets and shrapnel, erect, in close ranks, without shelter.[69] They have stood up to the murderous fire of the veteran British infantry. They are standing up to it yet. Make small of them, sneer if you like. But Napoleon did not sneer: the soldier who conquered a continent said he had never seen "anything more terrific than the fire of a British line of infantry." [70]

Many are broken and torn. Fifty-three men of the 27th are wounded or dead; Major Moore, the senior battalion commander, is wounded; the adjutant, James Lowry Donaldson, has been shot from his saddle and killed. Captain Tom Quantrill is wounded, Captain George Stewart is wounded, Lieutenant John Reese has been hit. In the Fifth, forty-nine men are down.[71] Major Heath's second horse has been shot, Heath himself has been struck on the head by a spent ball and painfully hurt.[72] Major Barry's horse has been killed under him.[73] The Fifth's adjutant, too, has been wounded. The United Volunteers have lost seventeen per cent of their rank and file. John Byrd has been killed, Bill McClellan is dead, Elie Clagett is streaming blood, Henry Brice has been hit and Jim Gibson and Reverdy Hays, Denny Marsh, Jack Swann, Charles O'Rourke, Holly Hollingsworth, Stedman Van Wyck.[74] Jake Haubert is dying. Walt Muschett lies in a writhing heap at your feet and the grass is slippery there and the butt of your musket is slippery. *I wonder if Walt's going to die . . . it hurts him . . . we used to go fishing together . . . I used to sell paper curtains to ladies at Waites's . . . I sat on a stool in the office behind the shop to work on the accounts . . . a high stool . . . it was hot in the back room this summer, it's cool here . . . it wasn't a minute ago, it's cool now, there's a breeze. . . .*

The air stinks and your mouth is foul. You can't taste the breeze but you feel it across your face, you can see the smoke like a curtain that slides on a pole. The wind pulls the curtain aside and you see them—that solid mass like a block made of layer upon layer of men and the men in the front layers moving their arms up and down.[75] They're so near! You can see their closed fists going up and down . . . like they're pounding and beating on something . . . *like they're beating in somebody's face.* They're so close you can see the dark ramrods slide up and down. They're loading. *I'm going to be killed.* You know it. They're going to shoot at you again and they're close, they can't miss.[76] *I don't want to be killed . . . what's it like to be dead?* Your musket is empty, you can't get it loaded in time. *I don't know what it's like to live, yet . . . I don't want to die when all that I know about living is twining my legs around the thin legs of a stool . . . the guns . . . why don't the guns stop them?*

You look and the guns are gone.[77] There's only the wreck of one, left by itself in the lane. Your legs quiver, the tendons let go. They don't snap, they just ooze and crawl. You can feel them crawl up through your loins and up into your body and leave your loins trembling with weak, uncontrollable shudders.

The guns haven't gone far but they're going as fast as they can, they are trying to get away. The gunners are dragging them, pushing them, hooking them up to the limbers; the drivers are struggling with terrified horses. The confusion looks like the rout on the Georgetown road. It is not a rout yet, it is a retreat under orders that came when the clearing smoke showed the enemy momentarily halted, re-forming, preparing to charge. Stricker knew that was the end. He had fourteen hundred men left, he had held on as long as he could and still save them to fight again, he had held on almost too long before calling Montgomery off and sending orders to Fowler to start falling back. But he has a plan and the plan is beginning to work. The "ordered retreat" of the 39th's single battalion [78] is drawing a screen of still-stubborn men between the retreating guns and the British right. The worst danger is there. Stricker's front, shortened now, is outflanked; but Fowler's three hundred men—if they do not break—will cover the line of retreat long enough for the guns to be saved. Brigade majors already have spurred off with orders to Sterrett and Long: keep on firing, hold on to the last thin minute, but don't try to meet the charge.

You don't know about that. All you know is that Wilmot is shouting. *One more . . . we've got time for one more . . .* the shouting sounds more like a whisper . . . *one more shot and fall back . . . rally . . . creek . . .* Then the British volley lets go, the red flame reaches out for your eyes, the sound tears through your loins, and a cheering comes out of the smoke and the bayonets come and your stomach heaves into your throat. Your arms are as weak as your legs and the musket is suddenly heavy. You fire at a wide, yelling mouth and you want to run but your legs won't move and you strain at your tendonless legs. They are moving, they only seem not to; you're running; an oak bough is just over your head, there's a man standing on it, the heel of his boot has brass nails in a five-pointed star. As long as you live you'll remember that pattern of nails.

All but one of the guns gets away. The last piece and "one tumbril alone" [79] are cut off by the rush of the Fusiliers up the lane. The lead horses are shot in the traces,[80] the cannoneers overwhelmed as they fight with their handspikes and rammers. Jim Davidson, sergeant of Continentals, makes the last stand of the battle with John Lamb, who once was the battery's first lieutenant and rejoined last week as a private. The bayonets ring them in, they go down, both are badly hurt. Old Man Davidson's second war ends as the first one did: he is captured again.[81]

Only a "few" are captured. Most of those taken are wounded men, left behind; most of the others are men who got lost in the woods in the flight of the 51st. But firing continues. As long as you live you'll remember the muskets still going off far behind you—the dull single explosions, the two or three shots close together. The men who climbed into trees to see over the smoke are not being allowed to surrender. They are being shot.[82]

25

THE BOMBS BURSTING IN AIR

There was no pursuit. That fact emerges plainly from the confusion of retreat. It stands as solidly, if not quite as plainly, in the confusion of conflicting narratives and contemptuous descriptions.

Stricker's force had been driven from the field "in fifteen minutes"[1] or had fought for "more than two hours."[2] It was "routed."[3] It retreated "to a wood" from which it was "quickly expelled, chiefly by the bayonet."[4] The whole American army "fell into confusion . . . as soon as their left gave way."[5] One British officer had never seen "a more complete rout . . . infantry, cavalry and artillery huddled together without the smallest regard to order or regularity . . . numbers actually trodden down by their countrymen in the hurry of the flight . . . desperate and unintermitting efforts made to overtake and cut off such as were hindmost . . . with loud laughter and tumultuous outcries."[6] The battle was a "brilliant" action[7] won after "an hour and a half of pretty severe fighting."[8] But the American militia committed "nearly the same blunders" which had made their fight at Bladensburg so futile. The American commanders were guilty, at the same time, of two opposite offenses: they had "risked a battle with part of their army, when there was no necessity for it," and they had "neglected numerous favourable opportunities of harassing" the enemy's advance.[9] The battle also was a trifling matter of driving in "the American advance guards" and a day of "desultory skirmishing."

The contradictions are to be expected. The disparagements and slights, however, are somewhat surprising: they come from Americans as often as from Britons. Many American critics have uncritically followed the convenient and imaginative versions and ignored their own source records. In the excitement of battle, British officers imagined that they saw "fearful gaps"[10] torn in the American lines by their exploding shells, that the American loss "at the most moderate computation" was "at least one thousand hors de combat" and that "the 5th Regiment of militia in particular" had been "nearly annihilated."[11] The loss of the City Brigade, sworn to by Brigade Major Leonard Frailey, was two hundred and thirteen—twenty-four killed, one hundred and thirty-nine wounded, fifty captured. The Fifth Maryland had not been annihilated: it had lost almost exactly ten per cent in dead and wounded—six privates killed and one captain, one lieutenant, three noncommissioned officers and forty privates wounded.[12]

The implications of such phrases as "complete rout" and "trodden down" and the "loud laughter" of the British infantry in "desperate" pursuit are as misleading and inaccurate as the word "annihilated." The British versions contradict themselves. Brooke's bugles sounded the recall. The troops were "checked, not without some difficulty, in the midst of their ardour, the different regiments collected round their colours, and formed into close column . . . fires were then, as usual, lighted . . . and there, but a short space removed from the bodies of the slain," the victorious army prepared to pass the night.[13]

For a victorious army, the note of apology that runs through its records also is surprising. The day was "now considerably advanced." The troops were "exhausted." The "thick woods quickly screened the fugitives." The British had no cavalry, not even "mounted drivers," to pursue them. "No effectual pursuit could be attempted." The imposing muster of excuses shows a consciousness of failure. A defeated army which was "flying" after suffering "enormous" losses was permitted to escape destruction. If the picture of confusion, flight and panic is correct, the failure is incomprehensible and the excuses are not valid.

Stricker's final orders for retreat were issued "about fifteen minutes before four o'clock" when the first battalion of the 39th already was withdrawing and the Union Artillery was limbering up its guns.[14] All resistance at the rail fence ended minutes later. Sunset was still more than two hours away.[15] Even after his regiment had gone into bivouac, Lieutenant Gleig found he had "some hours of daylight" to explore the battlefield.[16] Undoubtedly the British army was fatigued: it had marched seven miles and fought a battle. But three weeks ago it had marched twelve miles by midday through choking dust and hotter weather, fought a battle with a larger army, and pressed on to Washington. It had no cavalry worth mentioning at Bladensburg: even its artillery there was dragged by hand. Now junior officers, uncomfortable over the loss of time, told one another that if Ross had lived "the chances are that we should have fought two battles in one day." [17] Their opinion was based on "the celerity of his motions" although it was Ross who moved so slowly up the North Point road that it was half past one before his advance guard collided with the American delaying force under Major Heath. Ross had taken more than six hours to advance six miles. Brooke got the blame for being dilatory; Ross had set him the example.

The contradictions are important for one reason only: they establish as fact John Stricker's version of what happened.

Stricker's troops ran. But, with the exception of the 51st and part of one battalion of the 39th, they were not routed. When they fell back under orders, they had held on to the last thin minute when the British charge was twenty yards away.[18] Retreat, under the circumstances, was disorderly. Prompt, vigorous, organized pursuit might well have turned it into rout and panic. But there was no panic. The fact is that the Baltimore brigade retreated only to the west bank of Bread-and-Cheese Creek, where McDonald's reserve regiment was "well posted to receive the retired lines." [19] The disordered troops "mostly rallied well" [20] and re-formed in line of battle.

Stricker let his tired men rest, although he watched uneasily for signs of organized pursuit. His left and center were protected by the creek but on his right the open country offered opportunity for a quick British turning movement.[21] Nothing happened. No enemy patrols came close enough to see that the "complete rout" had been transformed, within a half mile, into an army waiting to be attacked again. It was not a broken army. Reinforced now by the Sixth, it was actually stronger than the force that met the British onslaught after Amey's men fled. And it was waiting with an "increased confidence." [22] The men who had stood up to rockets, shrapnel and the British musketry, and held their ground until the orders came to fall back, had learned much about war and more about themselves. They had looked into hell and had returned alive. Battle might be just as terrifying next time but the shock would never be so stunning: sight and sound at least would be familiar. For an hour [23] the army that had just been beaten waited to give battle within half a mile of the superior army that had driven it from the field.

The fact is that the Invincibles had won the field but the militiamen had won the battle. The City Brigade had merely moved into the next field. It undoubtedly would lose that also if attacked in force. But Stricker, left undisturbed to reorganize his troops, had attained all three of his objectives. The battle, conceived and planned as a delaying action, had achieved its purpose; the enemy's advance had been effectively delayed; if there had been a timetable to co-ordinate the combined operation of the fleet and army against Baltimore's defenses, the land attack had been thrown off schedule. [24] Stricker had succeeded in the difficult business of breaking off a general engagement and extricating the bulk of his command intact. He had done it with an undue degree of co-operation from the enemy, but it was done. And "the great object" had been accomplished. The brigade had given "the Enemy a specimen of Baltimore bravery and Sharp Shooting, an earnest of what he might expect, when he came to the great encounter where our force and strength would as far exceed his—as his did that of Genl Stricker's." [25] As Sam Smith's agent, Stricker had not only given notice that the city would be sold dear; he had also taken a down payment.

The price of Boulden's farm, a burned log cabin, a few fields and haystacks and a strip of oak woods had not been light. The invading army had paid more than two to one in dead and almost three to one in wounded. The "earnest" exacted by the militia marksmen had been heaviest in officers. The commanding general had been killed, a major and eight captains wounded. [26] At least two of the fallen captains had commanded infantry battalions. [27] Six junior officers were wounded, another was dead; fourteen non-commissioned officers were dead or hurt. The loss in seamen and marines had totaled fifty-five. [28] The storming column of the

Fusiliers had left ninety-seven killed and wounded in the lane and in the field beside it.[29] The sum of the down payment had been forty-six lives and the wounding of three hundred officers and men.[30] In less than three hours, the command of one brigade, one regiment, three battalions and many companies had passed into new hands. When the army advanced to attack the city, two brigades,[31] three regiments and at least five battalions would be led by officers who had not commanded them at the beginning of the Maryland campaign. The army itself would be led by a man thrust suddenly into responsibility and impressed so deeply by the stubbornness of the American militia and his own losses that he failed to follow up the advantage for which he had paid nearly seven per cent of his entire strength.

Toward sunset, Stricker began a deliberate retreat. He left behind, at intervals, details of axmen to fell trees across the road.[32] By midnight the campfires of his regiments were blazing in the fields around Worthington's mill.[33] Behind them and to their right the works on Loudenslager's hill drew a long arc of redly winking light; where it came closest to the hasty bivouac of the City Brigade, the Philadelphia road passed through the fortified lines between redoubts and batteries; the entrenchments bent there, curving sharply westward. To the left flared the watchfires of General Winder's brigade, Douglass's Virginia militia, which had marched through the town at nightfall from their encampment along the Frederick turnpike in the northwestern suburbs.[34]

The Philadelphia road ran at a sharp angle to the northeast across the front of Stricker's troops; his pickets watched it.[35] On the Trappe road, a mile and a half outside the lines, Major Randall's light corps was on outpost duty; it had been withdrawn at sundown from its similar task at Sollers', at the mouth of Bear Creek, where it had guarded Stricker's left flank against a waterborne attack.[36] A mile and a half farther to the northeast, a small squadron of United States light dragoons under Captain Bird was pushing its videttes down Long Log Lane and challenging the road-block details as they came in.

Behind these outguards, the City Brigade held the post of greatest danger: both roads leading from North Point would bring the enemy's column into the Philadelphia turnpike and the pike would lead them to the sharp bend in the field works and the short left flank of the position. But it was a "veteran" brigade now, at least by comparison with the country militia levies in the trenches and with the Virginia and Washington militia commanded by the general who would not let the Columbian brigade fight when it wanted to at Bladensburg. Sam Smith had sent Stricker's regiments straight from battle to his vulnerable left flank, where three converging roads came into town behind the westernmost redoubt of the continuous entrenchments.[37] The colonel of the Fifth could look into the darkness to the northeast where his home stood on its pleasant hill a mile away; he could see, in his mind, the tall white pillars of Surrey; he could think of the Boulden house. If the British army moved by way of Long Log Lane tomorrow, Surrey would be almost in its line of march;[38] if the battle broke along the Philadelphia road, the house would almost certainly become a British strong point. In a few hours, now, the guns of his own brigade might be battering at the stately portico, the pillars might have new clinging vines of flame. It gave a man a strange, lost feeling to stand in the dark and stare at his invisible home, not seeing it but seeing every well-loved detail clearly—the deserted rooms, the favorite armchair, the serving table stripped now of its silver, the fresh brickwork in the cellar walling up the entrance to the wine vault, the empty stables and the rustling pigeons. Thank God, he had been able to get the stock away.[39] There had been nothing he could do about the birds. If Surrey burned, he hoped the fire would spare the pigeon loft. It might rain tomorrow.

The rain came a little after midnight, without wind or thunder but in drenching torrents. It beat with a low, unbroken roaring on the fields and roads. Fires sputtered and went out. The trenches became flooded ditches, the militia garrisons stood ankle-deep in muck. The redoubts were pools, the gun platforms were like decks awash, the swearing frigate gunners heaved up ammunition chests on blocks of wood and spread their own jackets over them to keep the flannel cartridges from being soaked. The weary men of the City Brigade who had escaped guard duty slept in thin sheets of running water and woke shuddering with cold and slept again. The pickets hunched their shoulders and endured the downpour.

The same silent deluge roused the British in their bivouac and made their night an equal misery.[40] It drowned out most of the sounds that came from the small church [41] in the woods where surgeons worked all night over the tight rows of wounded of both armies. Only a scream could be heard through the solid pounding of the rain; there were screams, now and then; there was a pile of amputated arms and legs outside the door by morning.

The bugles roused the sodden army for stand-to at five and a quarter o'clock.[42] The regiments stood as they had slept, or tried to sleep, in close columns of companies, waiting for the sunrise. Even dawn was thin and washed-out and the puddled fields were dull, the woods dripped but they did not sparkle as the troops formed column in the road. The infantry was in good spirits: a day's march and another battle—if there were any Americans left to fight—would be better than the night had been, and at the road's end there was a city to be looted.[43] The seamen were as damp as any soldier but, perhaps, more used to drenchings; their high spirits were undampened. While the column formed, they skylarked. Infantry might stand in silly rows, stifflegged, but "no man ever set this technical arrangement so completely at defiance." To them it was "a matter of the most perfect indifference how or where they stood; whilst their garrulity exceeded all conceivable bounds, and their laughter made the very woods ring." [44] While the sailors laughed, the infantry laughed at them. The army moved out in a "merry and light-hearted" mood.[45] It was hours late, but that did not matter. As the march began, a dull thump far away signaled the opening of the attack on Baltimore's defenses.[46]

All day long on Monday, while the army marched and dawdled and finally fought, and all through the evening [47] while it lay in bivouac, the fleet had been working cautiously and slowly up the river. The line-of-battle ships and the heavier frigates had been left behind, off North Point; but the lighter frigates, the gun brigs, the mortar vessels and the rocket ship had felt their way through the tortuous shallows for six of the eight and one half miles that separated Fort McHenry from the anchorage off Old Road Bay Creek. Now, by the dawn's early light, the garrison in the red-brick star fort on Whetstone Point and in the mud-wall batteries on the shore below could see sixteen ships [48] ranged in two concentric arcs across the river. The nearer, shorter arc was six small ships—the bomb ships *Meteor*, *Terror*, *Aetna*, *Devastation* and *Volcano* and the rocket ship *Erebus*.[49] They were still standing up the stream,[50] their sails set and drawing; but behind them, two and a half miles downriver from the fort, the other arc of ships was anchoring, the canvas creeping slowly upward, disappearing. At that distance the bare masts and yards sketched the suggestion of a rail fence built crookedly across a farm pond.

Biggest of the ten ships in the anchoring line were the frigates *Euryalus, Hebrus, Severn* and *Havannah*.[51] *Euryalus* was Charles Napier's ship; with *Erebus* and three of the bomb ships she had broken through the gantlet of John Rodgers's fireboats, David Porter's battery and Perry's antique cannon in the ten-day running battle down the Potomac River after holding Alexandria to ransom. *Severn* flew the pennant of Vice-Admiral Cochrane, who had shifted from the *Tonnant* to direct the attack in person.[52] The other ships were smaller—ship-sloops and brig-sloops mounting eighteen guns. They had covered the landing of the army, but were useless for bombarding such strong works as those on Whetstone. Their mission now was to protect the bomb ships against attack, in the same way infantry was used to cover field guns against hostile infantry. Cochrane had reason to believe that it might be a vital mission.

Even a rudimentary intelligence service had sufficed to provide him with a good deal of information: all that was necessary was a handful of Yankee newspapers. Barney's flotillamen were there in Baltimore; so were their foolish "gunboats"—puny imitations of the Spaniards' *garda costas*—in considerable number. Fragile and clumsy as those barges were, they could make trouble when tough seamen manned them. And the flotillamen had amply proved their toughness. The three top sea dogs of the American navy were there also—Rodgers, Porter, Perry; and they probably had with them crews for the three men-of-war that lay unfinished in the inner harbor—*Java*, frigate, and *Ontario* and *Erie*, ship-rigged war sloops. The very names made Cochrane itch to batter his way in and take or burn those ships: the Yankees had a nasty way of rubbing other people's noses in their naval victories. But he could not be careless with such people. With three commodores, the flotillamen and seamen from the fleet at hand, he could not disregard the possibility of a sudden dash of armed barges to overwhelmn *Erebus* and the lightly armed bomb vessels. The frigates' long guns might give the mortar ships a little help in smashing the American defenses, but the gun brigs were far more important: they would be ready to beat off the barges if the Yankees ventured to attack.

The ships moving up the river had left behind them more than half the fleet—the line-of-battle ships, the transports, and the nameless cartel. Francis Scott Key and the exchange agent, Skinner, had been aboard *Surprise* during the dash up the Chesapeake and while "preparations were making for landing the troops." But when the army was ashore and the mortar vessels stood up the Patapsco to attack the works on Whetstone Point, both Key and Skinner were "sent on board their own vessel, with a guard of sailors or marines to prevent them from landing." They had been "permitted to take Dr. Beanes with them, and they thought themselves fortunate in being anchored in a position which enabled them to see distinctly the flag of Fort McHenry from the deck. . . ." [53]

While the inner arc of British ships still moved upstream, [54] closing almost imperceptibly upon McHenry, a cloud of smoke gushed over one blunt prow and the first two-hundred-pound shell [55] soared up from one of the two mortars on the foredeck. It climbed steeply, swiftly. Dark smoke trailed behind it thinly, barely visible. The shell almost vanished. Then it lost momentum. Far up, it seemed to hang, a round black speck suspended in the pale sky. But it moved a little, slowly, in a lazy arc that bent and bent as if a great weight pulled it. The slow arc became a steep slant and the shell fell faster and grew larger. Twenty-eight seconds after it was hurled upward from the ship's deck, it was a rushing black doom shrieking down upon the thousand upturned faces of the men on Whetstone. In one second more, it burst behind the fort. [56] The earth seemed to shake. The air was shrill with fragments.

There were more gouts of smoke above the bomb ships now. More specks were soaring upward, hanging, turning, rushing downward. The explosions were not thunder, they were lightning without thunder—blinding, stunning, rending crashes. And the ships were taking in sail. The British captains, watching—Samuel Roberts, *Meteor*, Richard Kenah, *Aetna*, John Sheridan aboard the *Terror*, David Price in *Devastation*, Thomas Alexander in *Volcano* [57]—saw the shells burst and the smoke spread until it was a dark ring on the finger of the point. The ring fitted loosely; it was only part way down the finger; they could see the red fort like a rouged nail with the ring behind it on the first joint. *Anchor . . . let go the best bower* [58] *. . . mains'l sheets, there . . . small bower . . .* The first shells either reached or overreached the target. [59] No hits, likely; that would be expecting too much with the ships under weigh. But the bombers were already well within range. They had stood in even closer to the fort than necessary. At two miles, they were almost a thousand yards inside extreme range of their mortars. They would not have to use full charges: twenty pounds of powder would throw a thirteen-inch shell two and a half miles with reasonable accuracy: at thirty-five hundred yards, no more than twelve pounds would be needed.[60] The anchored ships began to fire. The McHenry batteries began to answer.[61] Whetstone Point became a finger with a dirty nail.

Fort McHenry was not merely a fort. It was not solely and exclusively a concentration of artillery walled in by permanent defenses. It was a small town, with a village green and story-and-a-half red-brick houses for its population. Life went on within it. There were women, carpenters and blacksmiths, there were clerks and sick men and a doctor, nurses (but no women tolerated) and cooks and a baker and people who washed clothes and mended them, wiped dishes and made beds and emptied slops. There were rail-fenced gardens. Horses cropped the grass in pastures. Haystacks wandered across fields of stubble.

The place also was an anchronism, a survival, a vestigial appendage of a way of life, a hyphen between past and present. It was a medieval walled town whose chief function was survival. It was at the same time the pleasant suburb of a modern city, suitable for family excursions of a Sunday—a quite normal place with certain mildly curious customs and a fine view of the river. It was a pentagon. From the higher ground, as you drove toward it out the two-mile dirt road from Baltimore, it looked like a big five-pointed star that had fallen neatly and precisely on the tip of Whetstone. On hot summer days, with the sun burning on the red-brick walls and the heat haze shimmering, the star looked as if it had not yet quite cooled.

You rode up to it past a long rail fence and tied the horses to a post and crossed a plank bridge hung on chains above a dry ditch [62] and walked under a brick archway through a shadowy cool passage that was like a tunnel in the thick wall. Steps led downward from it, in small tunnels that looked dark as cellars. As you walked by, your footsteps sounded hollow; cellar smell came from the small, dark tunnels. Then the hollow sound stopped, your shoes crunched on gravel, and you were standing at the edge of the village green. It wasn't called a green; they called it the parade, but only very small parades could have been managed. The Jeffersons or the Fifth would have been badly cramped there. Whatever you called it, the space inside was not a match

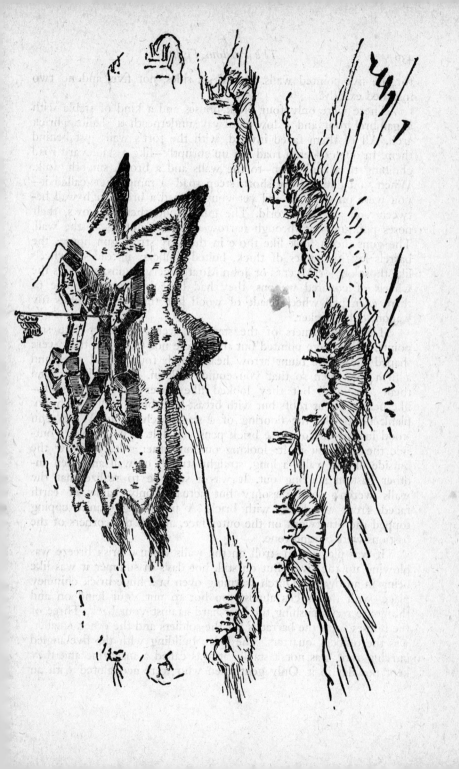

for the five-pointed walls. It had six sides, not five, and no two matched exactly.

There were only four brick houses and a kind of stable with a gambrel roof and a low doorway underneath a shallow brick arch. All of them faced inward, with the fort's walls just behind them. In one corner, a road ran up abruptly—like a stableyard road climbing to a bank barn—to the walls and a broad, smooth walk. When you climbed the short, steep road—a ramp, they called it—you were on the wall and yet you still had a breast-high wall between you and the world. The guns stood there in rows, their noses pointing out through narrow slots like gutters in the wall. The guns didn't look like those in the Gay street gun house: the barrels lay in cradles of thick, bolted timbers: instead of wheels like those on Joe Myers's or John Montgomery's guns, as big as the wheels of covered wagons, they had little iron ones.[63] Some of them even had wheels made of wood like those on a child's toy wagon, only thicker.

The five corners of the star-fort were not sharp like star points. They were pointed but they were not triangles: they were shaped more like blunt arrow heads, with four walled sides and a fifth side open so that you could walk in. The soldiers called them "bastions" but they looked like queer-shaped box stalls—like pens without roofs but with breast-high brick walls and heavy plank floors like the flooring of a stagecoach stable. When you stood in any one of these brick pens you felt as if you were outside the fort, not in it: looking out on either side, you saw the outside of the walls—a long, straight stretch of wall and then another bastion sticking out. It was a surprise to realize that the walls weren't solid masonry but actually only banks of earth faced, front and back, with brick. A projecting granite coping topped the brickwork on the outer face, and all the corners of the bastions were of sandstone.

It was pleasant to stroll on the walls when a brisk breeze was blowing up the river. But on still, hot days in summer it was like being in an oven—a Dutch warming oven in a huge brick chimney place—with the bricks almost too hot to put your hand on and the house roofs pushing the heat hard against your back. Three of the houses were the barracks for the soldiers and the other, smaller, was the officers' quarters. The brick building with the five-angled curving roof was not a stable: it was called a magazine and they kept powder in it. Only gentlemen who were acquainted with an officer were let to look inside it; and sometimes they came out talking loudly and then lowered their voices quickly and stood looking at the roof and talking earnestly in low tones. Sometimes, in the carriage driving back to Baltimore, somebody said he'd heard the magazine wasn't bombproof; but almost invariably somebody else said that such talk was nonsense. Weren't the walls of it ten feet thick, and weren't there six feet of earth and timber in the roof? Six feet ten, to be exact about it.[64] There was always gossip. Nobody paid a great deal of attention to it.

When the bombardment opened at dawn Tuesday, the 13th of September, the community on Whetstone was much over-populated. It was filled with strangers. Its normal population of less than two hundred [65] had grown to more than a thousand.[66] There were white tents in the pasture and, in the opposite direction near the shore, great heaps of muddy earth into which men had dug shallow burrows and stuck odds and ends of lumber to make hutches. The slopes all around were littered with crude shelters like a refuge camp—tarpaulins spread over handspikes, rain-sopped blankets sagging on the ramrods that had served as tent poles, planks laid over empty biscuit barrels. The whole place was wet and bedraggled from the night's storm, the sod trampled into paste, the rain standing in the deep holes made by boot heels, the brick facing of the fort's walls streaked with seeping water. The walled village was almost deserted: there were only cooks and women and the doctor and the sick men in the houses: there were nearly forty sick men.[67] All the rest, amounting to "one thousand effective men," [68] were in the batteries and outworks.

The American defenses, where they faced the arcs of hostile ships, were ranged in layers—three tiers of men and guns. The innermost tier was the star fort itself; but of its twenty-one guns only those along two curtains and a part of those in three of the five bastions pointed down the river; the rest faced the rear, the Ferry Branch of the Patapsco, or the channel to the inner harbor. The fort's guns were manned now by one company of United States artillerymen under Captain Frederick Evans and some seventy militia gunners—the "very fine" Baltimore Fencibles commanded by a judge, Josh. Nicholson.[69] The second tier was infantry, the oddments of four regiments of regulars, stationed in the "outer ditch." But the so-called ditch was not a ditch at all: it was a crooked strip of open ground between the fort's walls and a zig-zag parapet that faced downriver and curved backward at the ends to guard the shores of both Patapsco branches against possible attempts to land troops on the point and take the fort by storm. The open ground was thirty feet across in places, fifty feet in others.[70] The parapet was banked earth, shoulder-high, and sloped to keep it from collapsing; it afforded stout protection against solid cannon shot or musketry but none at all against shells bursting in the space between it and the fort walls. And the six hundred men who lined the parapet were regulars only in the same sense that the position they were occupying was a "ditch." Both terms were technical; both were misleading and, for practical purposes, almost entirely meaningless. Many of the "regulars" were green recruits; few, if any, had been under fire until this morning.

The outmost tier of the defenses was a continuous low mound of earth that curved around the tip of Whetstone a few feet above high-tide mark. The dirt wall was muddy now and oozing and rain-gullied; it was sawtoothed with embrasures. Behind it were the timber platforms for the Water Battery [71] of thirty-six guns.[72] Fifteen of the pieces there were "of the largest caliber" [73]—ponderous weapons with ten-foot-long barrels that weighed more than three tons and threw forty-two-pound shot from seven-inch bores.[74] These guns had been Napoleon's: Sam Smith had borrowed them, while France was still at war, from the French consul.[75] The rest of the cannon in the Water Battery were smaller—twenty-four and eighteen-pounders;[76] and a few were howitzers.[77]

The assortment of guns was no more motley than the assorted gunners. The artillery in the "lower works" was manned by two companies of United States Sea Fencibles [78]—coast defense troops in the federal service but distinguished from the "regulars" by the fact that they were temporary units;[79] two companies of Baltimore militia—the Washington Artillery commanded by John Berry and the Independent Artillerists under Charlie Pennington, whose captain's epaulets were store-new; [80] and fifty-four flotillamen commanded by Lieutenant Rodman who had been Josh Barney's sailing master.[81] To the left, the Water Battery became a floating battery: outside the boom [82] that stretched across the channel from the tip of Whetstone to the Lazaretto lighthouse lay the barges that were left from the original flotilla. They were under the command of Solomon Rutter,[83] the lieutenant who had been Barney's right-hand man. He had been commodore of the Patapsco gunboat squadron since July, when Barney had divided the command of the flotilla and, incidentally, dropped in at the Widow

Pickersgill's in Albemarle street, with Stricker and McDonald, to leave an order for an outsize flag.

The flag was flying from its staff now, high above the bastion that looked toward the Lazaretto. It seemed bigger than the barracks far below it, and the men who stood along the "outer ditch" were dwarfed both by the flag and by the sixteen-foot walls of the fort behind them. The thousand square feet of bunting in the flag were heavy, they weighed too much for the breeze that blew in from the bay. Now and again the breeze wearied of holding out the fifteen stripes; it let go, and the stripes hung in folds and the drooping flag was a stick of striped peppermint candy. Now and again the folds shook in the sudden hard gusts of hot wind that fell out of the sky in black iron globes to make their own sudden storm clouds and blow unpredictably, up, down, north, east, south, west. Sometimes the red-lighted thundergusts blew four or five ways at once. "Four or five bombs were in the air at a time" [84] when the mortar ships fired in salvo. Now and again, when no shell had burst, the folds of the flag still trembled: you felt a tremor in the earth and in your knees: the breeze stood still in the concussion of the cannon as the Whetstone batteries began to answer.

But only a few guns were firing—the borrowed French guns and the howitzers, land mortars. All the others, more than two-thirds of the batteries, were hopelessly out of the battle, the nearest British ships far out of range. Even to the veteran artilleryman, George Armistead, the cannonading from the Water Battery seemed satisfactorily "brisk." [85] And yet the guns fired slowly: it took time to aim a three-ton cannon at a flyspeck. [86] The American gunpointers had to train their clumsy weapons on a mark that was all but invisible by contrast with the enemy's convenient target. Whetstone Point was six hundred yards wide and the works there stretched from shore to shore. The fort itself was more than six hundred feet wide as it faced the bay; there was room upon its small parade ground for all five of the attacking bomb ships and for the *Erebus* also. But at a distance of two miles the ships were mere specks, and the specks were separated from each other by broad reaches of the river. It was one thing to drop bursting shells upon a fortification that was almost a quarter of a mile across and more than a quarter of a mile in depth. It was another thing to hit, with a solid iron ball, a ship no bigger than Tom Boyle's privateer, the *Chasseur*, not one-third the size of a small frigate.[87] It was like shooting at a beaver hat adrift upon the river.

The first spouts of water thrown up by the solid shot were short—alarmingly short. Rodman's gun crews knocked the last coin [88] from beneath the breeches,[89] raised the ponderous barrels to their maximum elevation. The brief specks of splashes appeared closer to the specks of ships, but they were missing yet by several hundred yards. Rodman increased the powder charges and increased them again and yet again. Another ounce of power and the breeches probably would burst and leave him only dead men, but he took the risk. The shot-jets were still futile white spots in the dull gray river, cable lengths short. And the howitzers were just as futile: the bursts of their shells were dark spots that hung longer on the surface of the river but were even farther from the target than the useless splashes.

Armistead, watching, felt apprehension closing like a hand upon his heart. He had been ill for days; now he was sick with the knowledge of failure. His howitzers could not be expected to match naval mortars: the land mortars were made shorter, lighter: bore for bore, the British mortars certainly were twice as heavy, their extreme range twice as great. They might even be four times as heavy.[90] His only hope, at two miles, was the French guns. If they failed . . .

They tried again, and failed. The only damage they accomplished was the damage they did to themselves. The barrels had not burst, yet, from the dangerous charges with which Rodman crammed them, but the cast-iron wheels could not absorb the enormous shock of the recoil. Three guns already were dismounted, tipped at drunken angles, out of action.[91] Sick at heart, Armistead gave the order to cease firing.[92] There was nothing he could do, now. He had fifty-seven cannon, but not one with which to fight. All he could do was wait, his thousand men "entirely exposed" [93] to the "constant and tremendous shower of shells." [94]

He waited, dreading what would happen. He could see it— the mud walls of the Water Battery disintegrating, the bastions swept clean of guns and men, the magazine blown up, the ditch a slaughter pen. There was good reason for his dread. No overwrought imagination was required to picture the result of a few hours' bombardment by skilled gunners undisturbed by even one answering shot. Neither the infantry in the open ditch nor the artillerymen in the temporary earthworks had the slightest shelter from the scything fragments of bombs bursting in the air above them or behind them. The casemates just behind the brickwork facing of the fort's walls offered no protection against thirteen-inch shells. Not even the magazine itself was bombproof.[95] One direct hit would destroy it: a two-hundred-pound shell would batter in the roof: even if the bomb did not pass entirely through the inadequate layer of dirt before it burst, the explosion would reach to the powder chamber and touch off the ammunition. The magazine itself would be a bombshell. It would level every building, pile the guns in heaps of wreckage on the ravelin, blow the gun crews off the walls or smash them into pulp against the parapets. That was his failure. He had failed before the battle opened.

Armistead had been defeated by the War Department. It had paid no more attention to his warnings and appeals than it had paid to Winder's frantic pleas for soldiers. James Piper, captain of the United Maryland Artillery militia battery, was wrathful over Washington's bland lack of interest in "the most urgent solicitations . . . to the Govt to put this great Arm of defence in order by our Committee of Safety, Col⁰ Armistead, our member of Congress & by our leading influential citizens." [96] The result had been "unsatisfactory." Captain Piper, who had done "a tour of duty of some weeks" with his battery in Fort McHenry, declared angrily that "the invading Army of the North seemed almost exclusively to engage the attention of Govt & to absorb its funds—which left but little to be expended on home defenses." He blamed "the pervading sentiment of Fancy politicians" who believed that "Republican Govts cannot prepare for war before war is commenced" and who therefore insisted that "the necessity to strengthen our Fort could not exist & ought not to be made, as it might prove a useless expenditure until the enemy should clearly indicate his intention by some overt act or by some public declaration." Captain Piper was indignantly convinced that the fort "never could be rendered a safe & reliable place of defence without being made bomb proof" and that in justice to the men called to fight there "it ought to have been done promptly."

Now the shells were falling, and neglect and penny pinching and the cowardice of fancy politicians must be paid for with men's lives and broken bodies. The shells fell and fell. The British mortar fire was "incessant and well-directed." And *Erebus* also was in action now, her rockets patterning the sky with smoke trails. The streaks that they left behind were higher and more steeply curved than the arcs traced by missiles fired from mobile rocket-troop dischargers. The ship rockets made the same harsh, strangled whooping; it was even louder; but it lacked some of the terror of the others: it was not so personal and close, it was high over-head until the last few seconds. The fire-spouting things seemed, now, not quite so awful: they did not dart straight at men's eyes and faces: they fell, and their downward plunge was not quite the erratic, crazy jumping of land rockets skimming low across the fields and fences. They had a different purpose.

The function of *Erebus* was not solely to spread terror. Her mission in the attack was not solely or even primarily to demoralize the garrison on Whetstone. She might cause a panic, but the panic would be incidental. Her prime mission was destruction. She was firing carcasses—incendiary shells. The hollow war heads of her rockets were packed solid with combustibles, saltpeter, pitch and sulphur and corned powder.[97] She was reaching out with fiery fingers for the houses in the fort, the ready ammunition in the batteries and bastions, the plank platforms and revetments, and the gunboats moored across the channel.

The long cylinders flung up from her dischargers looked indeed like flaming fence posts as they swooped down and the sparks of burning fuses touched the war heads. But their flight was wild; the navy's rockets were as unpredictable as ground troops'. Some dove into the rain-softened earth and stuck there, upright. Some fell far short. Most of them plunged hissing into the Patapsco; where they sank, the water boiled and smoked; their scorched wooden tails came up and floated like dead fish.

The mortar shells were worse, their screaming splinters far more dangerous, their rending crashes harder on men's nerves. And they were far more accurate. Only a few were falling short, some dropping in the fields behind the fort.[98] But they came unceasingly, now singly, now in clusters, at the rate of one shell every minute. And "a large proportion" [99] of them burst above exposed men who could only stand erect and face them or crouch under the gun barrels, hug the carriages or press themselves against the walls and wait. Every three or four minutes [100] one of the black spheres came hurtling down inside the works, digging itself out of sight into the muddy earth or lying half buried in the firmer ground and smoking from its fuse holes, while men threw themselves face-down or ran desperately to get away before it burst. Some sputtered out,[101] the others threw up fountains of mud filled with deadly splinters.

One bomb fell among the tents behind the fort; a whirling fragment of two-inch thick iron [102] sliced through a soldier's wife and left her body lying in two pieces.[103] Another struck the magazine roof, crushed it, stuck there—and did not explode.[104] Armistead organized a working party and set it to moving kegs of powder and the chests of flannel cartridges out of the magazine and out of the fort.[105] One miracle had happened, but there might not be another. Chests and barrels strewed the slopes, with wide intervals between them. While the working party toiled, the colonel wrote a letter. Henry Thompson, ubiquitous and indefatigible, had established his horse telegraph between the fort and Baltimore; [106] now Armistead sent off one of Thompson's riders with a message to Ed Johnson. The chairman of the Committee of Vigilance was de facto chief of commissary, provost marshal, wagon master, surgeon general and chief quartermaster; he could send help more quickly now than Sam Smith, waiting for the British army in the works on Loudenslager's hill. The major's scrawled note begged Ed Johnson to send "two hundred shovels one hundred Pick axes and five hundred Pieces of Timber eight feet long and one foot square, for the purpose of erecting bomb proof covered ways for the protection of the soldiery." [107]

The appeal had every aspect of a futile and despairing gesture, one more instance of too little too late. It would be many hours, a day, perhaps days, before Johnson could provide the timbers and find volunteers to risk their lives on wagons creeping through the British shell fire. The covered ways would be built late but not, perhaps, too late. The bombardment might go on for days. Admiral Cochrane had devoted twenty-two days to the expedition against Alexandria; he had risked eight vessels on that unimportant mission. By comparison, the capture and destruction of the port of Baltimore, with its forts, its merchant fleet, its privateers and gunboats and its unfinished warships, was enormously important. And as Cochrane chose to fight the battle, he was risking not a single vessel. Armistead could see no reason why the British fleet should not lie in the river, out of range, for days or weeks until it battered the defenseless works into the Whetstone mud. It could knock out the heavy batteries at leisure, then close in to short range safely, finish off the gunboats and silence the redoubts. So much destruction might not be accomplished quickly, but it seemed inevitable. Open works could not endure indefinitely the pounding of thirteen-inch mortars. When the lighter batteries along the Ferry Branch shore had been put out of action, hostile troops could land almost at will on Cromwell's Point. Indeed, they could come even closer to the city: without the enfilading fire of big guns raking it, the barricade of sunken ships across the entrance to the Ferry Branch would be no serious obstacle to landing barges. A successful amphibious attack there would put troops ashore two miles from Baltimore and on its unfortified flank.

The situation called for just such tactics. In the enemy's combined operation, the strength of his two forces was unequal in proportion to American resistance. On the water, the British were overwhelmingly superior by reason of the long range of their battering artillery. On land, the British army was outnumbered and outgunned. Paradoxically, sound tactics demanded a division of the comparatively weak land forces—maneuver, deception and diversion. A landing on the almost undefended south side of the city would compel Smith to withdraw troops from the lines that fronted North Point. As the lines there were weakened, the chances of outflanking them or taking them by storm would be proportionately greater.

Armistead set his mind against the weakness of his position and the weakness of his own sick body. He would hold on while he had a gun left and a man to fire it. Timbered shelters, even though inadequate, would help prolong resistance; they would postpone the day when Cochrane could land troops in the cove behind McHenry; they might save some of the men and guns to meet the storming parties on the tide flats. That was all that he could hope for, if the enemy persisted. All that he could do now was set an example of calm courage for the garrison and fire a single cannon, now and then, to let Vice-Admiral Cochrane know his time had not yet come.

Hour after hour, from Loudenslager's hill, Sam Smith had watched the torment of McHenry. Even through field glasses, he could see but little: the fort was a mile and a half from Rodgers's bastion at the extreme right flank of his position. There was only the low dark smudge that thickened slowly over Whetstone Point, the incessant wink of flashes, and the rocket trails that hung across the sky in windrows of unnatural, thin cloud. Only the widow's flag showed bright, at intervals, above the rolling smoke. Sam Smith was deeply troubled. He admired and liked the young major of artillery who commanded at McHenry. Regular though he was, independent in his command of the fort, Armistead had been more than loyal to the old militiaman. He had stretched his authority and used his garrison to turn out musket cartridges for Smith's ill-provided troops,[108] sacrificing time that might have been spent building bombproof shelters for his own post. Now he would be paying for that generous co-operation. It was midforenoon, and still the harbor batteries were the sole target of the enemy's attack.

A merchant-politician-general who had staked a city on his trader judgment could not help but wonder. Had he been mistaken? Was the landing on North Point a mere diversion? Stricker's oral report last night had been almost too cheerful: he had held his ground for two hours, fallen back only half a mile without being pressed, rallied his men, and waited for a new attack that did not come. What did it all mean—the sluggish movement of the British column from its beachhead, the strange dawdling at the Gorsuch farm, the failure to pursue an inferior and beaten force, and now today another sluggish march? The British were advancing up the North Point road now, but the reports of Bird's videttes made it plain that they were moving slowly. For almost four hours the fleet had been bombarding Whetstone, but the army had not traveled four miles. Was it the British army or was it only a part of the army? The best officers often overestimated the strength of the troops opposed to them. Had Stricker overestimated the force brought against him? Was there still a strong force aboard the transports, waiting to deliver the main blow on the undefended south and west sides of the city when the fleet had neutralized the batteries on Whetstone?

These were questions which Smith could not answer. But he knew how weak his flanks were. He had staked everything on his own forecast of the British tactics—on the North Point landing, on direct assault against his field works. He had concentrated almost his entire strength in this one small sector. He had left no troops at all on the west side of the city. On the south side there was only one small regiment of Virginia militia—Griffin Taylor's [109] —and a smaller detachment under Captain Hancock on the marshy ground of Cromwell's Point at the south end of the line of sunken hulks across the Ferry Branch.[110] Well, he had been right so far. The apparent lack of co-ordination between fleet and army was surprising but not necessarily significant. If it meant anything, it meant a breakdown of liaison quite as probably as it indicated some maneuver that was yet to be developed. Whatever else Sam Smith was, he was not a weathercock. He would stick to his plan and wait and see.

He waited until ten o'clock to see the British army.[111] It came as he had expected it to come, debouching from the North Point road into the Philadelphia pike [112] and moving up the turnpike toward his lines. It halted "at the distance of two miles" [113] with its leading regiment a half mile southwest of the Kell house. While the column stood in "full view" [114] on the road, patrols pushed westward cautiously toward Surrey and south toward the Trappe road, but they also halted while there was still a mile between them and the pickets of the Baltimore brigade and Randall's outguard. A group of horsemen rode rapidly up the "eminence" [115] north of the turnpike and dismounted on Judge Kell's lawn. Minutes later, field glasses in the works on Loudenslager's picked up gleams of scarlet at the upstairs windows.

Colonel Brooke had had his troubles in the last several hours. He had been moving through a region that seemed "even more wild" [116] than any through which the army had yet marched—a strange, uncomfortable sort of country to find on the outskirts of a major city. The trees felled by Stricker's axmen had delayed him.[117] They suggested ambuscades, and the repeated halts while sappers cleared the way had given him concern for his close column jammed up in the narrow road. His flank protection had not been as good as flank protection should be under such conditions. Patrols had got themselves lost. Now, with the army in the presence of the enemy, some of them were still out of touch and wandering in "the interminable wilderness." [118] But the view from an "upper window" [119] of the Kell house made Brooke's troubles of the morning seem small.

It was instantly apparent that the "corps" which he had beaten yesterday was only a detachment—and a small one [120]—of the troops mustered for the defense of Baltimore. The town itself was hidden by a curving ridge of hills [121] but the American "grand army" [122] was in plain sight on the crest and slopes, entrenched "in the most formidable manner." [123] He could see "the whole face of the heights" covered with "a chain of field redoubts, batteries, breastworks, fleches and traverses." [124] Where the works had not yet been completed, there were "deep ditches . . . stakes and palisadoes." To the left, above the sheen of water, a substantial-looking circular "fort" [125] protected one flank with "some twenty guns." [126] To the right, just where the hills bent back upon the town,[127] the cannon in another formidable redoubt looked down the turnpike toward his waiting column.

The fantastic figures rattled off by the captured Yankee troopers in the farmer's dooryard yesterday seemed less fantastic now. There must be a hundred cannon in those field works: count them: someone counted and stopped at one hundred twenty.[128] Troops behind entrenchments could not readily be counted but they could be guessed at. Officers guessed and came to the conclusion that they faced no less than "two-and-twenty thousand men, with upwards of a hundred heavy cannon" many of which were "twenty-four and thirty-two pounders." [129] It was to be expected that "the greater numbers" of the "twenty thousand infantry" would turn out to be militia, but the prisoners had spoken of three thousand regulars; the British officers decided now that the American commander must have "full five thousand troops of the line" besides "the choicest seamen from the fleet" manning "all" the guns.[130]

Sam Smith had won a victory—preliminary, bloodless, but important. He had persuaded the enemy to strengthen his army by five thousand nonexistent regulars and multiply his total force by two. He had, within the Loudenslager works and in the fields north of them, not more than eleven thousand men. He probably had less.[131] He had no regular infantry at all: the six hundred sent to reinforce him were at Fort McHenry. And not all the hundred cannon in his batteries were manned by Rodgers's seamen; many of them were small field guns of the First Maryland Artillery, manned by the militia companies with fancy names—the Franklins and the Americans, who had fought and fled at Bladensburg, the Columbians, the Washingtons, the Uniteds and the Independents and the Eagles.[132] But what Sam Smith had accomplished was sufficiently impressive. It was an enormous change since Bladensburg. In three weeks he had concentrated some twelve thousand troops and somehow sheltered them and fed them. He had found muskets, blankets, mess pans and camp kettles for militia levies who came empty-handed. He had found shoes for men who came barefooted. He had somehow filled their cartridge boxes—or their pockets—with thirty-six rounds of ammunition. He had turned them into something that at least resembled a "grand army" and the low hills into "heights" which looked "naturally strong" and had been "rendered doubly so" [133] by his entrenchments.

Brooke's junior officers admitted to themselves that "it would

be absurd to suppose" that the sight of the American position
"did not in some degree damp the ardour" of their seniors and
that it would be simply "madness to storm such works without
pausing to consider how it might best be attempted." [134] Brooke
paused. His glasses turned to the approaches: they were equally unpleasant. The whole countryside within cannon shot of the American lines had been swept clean. Woods and underbrush were gone.
Attacking infantry must cross a mile of open ground where
shrivelled corn still standing in the fields afforded only trifling
cover and the pastures and mowed fields none.[135]

Brooke shifted his glasses to the terrain beyond the Yankees'
left flank. The chain of redoubts seemed to end abruptly. He could
make out two or three small outworks but no trenches. Three
roads ran together and seemed almost undefended. A weak spot,
surely: there should be a chance there. A demonstration would at
least reveal something of the quality of the American commander.
It might tempt him into blunders. A movement in force toward that
vulnerable flank might draw troops out of the entrenchments.
Militia suddenly deprived of cover would feel naked and uncertain.
There was always the chance that green troops, trying to maneuver,
would become confused: Brooke had seen, yesterday, a sample
of confusion and its consequences: the American left wing, un-
settled by its own awkwardness, had fled the moment it was
threatened. If he could tempt enough troops out of the defenses
and bewilder them, a quick attack might send them scampering.
A rush of panic-stricken men back to the trenches would confuse
the troops remaining to defend them: a mob of routed infantry
would give his own troops cover: they could be in the works before
the Americans could open fire without killing their own fleeing men.

It was well worth trying. Aides went galloping down to the
road with orders. The column began to move. It turned west, off
the pike, toward Surrey. Then it turned again, northwestward,
moving steadily "as if with the intention of making a circuitous
march and coming down on the Harford or York roads." [136]

Sam Smith did not blunder. Neither did his brigadiers. Orders
went to Stricker and Will Winder "to adapt their movements to
those of the enemy so as to baffle" the British commander in his
apparent purpose to strike at the city's unfortified north flank by
way of the converging highways.[137] The City Brigade struck out
"across the country" [138] and Brigadier General Douglass's Virginia
brigade moved out behind it with Winder in immediate command.

Both Stricker and Winder carried out their orders "with great skill and judgment." By the time the British column reached the Perry Hall road where it crossed a creek called Herring Run,[139] some three miles from the junction of the three roads, the two brigades already stood between it and the city. They were deployed in "an advantageous position" [140] and their line of battle stretched from the last redoubt at the west end of the continuous fortifications, past

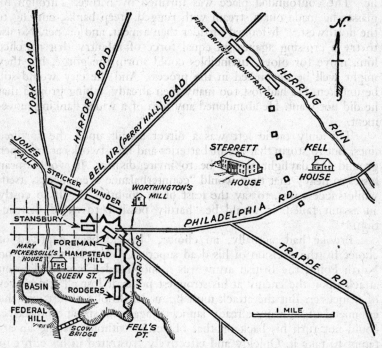

BROOKE'S FIRST MANEUVER, noon, September 13.

two small detached works and beyond a third one on McKim's hill on the east side of the York road.[141]

Brooke's first demonstration had failed. It had drawn no troops out of the trenches. The American commander had made the proper countermoves and made them promptly, and his troops had changed front quickly and without confusion. A mobile army equal to his own stood waiting for him.[142] He had no doubt that he could rout it, but the effort might be costly: the attack would have to be delivered under cross fire of the guns in the detached works: when the American line broke—as he was sure it would—before a bayonet charge, his troops would be caught in an enfilading fire of heavy cannon in the redoubts. And they would still be confronted, he believed, by fresh troops which enormously outnumbered them.

He considered the alternatives. He could push his demonstration farther and try coming in upon the Yankees' rear. Or could he? The confounded place was fortified by nature. Through his glasses he made out a stream with rugged, steep banks, curving to the northwest.[143] It looked broader than a moat, and deeper. No use to try a crossing against an equal force of infantry that matched him, move for move. Invincibles could storm the gorge, but they might well be decimated in the process. And the city would still be untaken. He had lost too many men already, taking ground that he did not want. He abandoned any idea of a wider flanking movement.

The only tactic left was a direct assault upon the fortified lines. But to storm that arc of batteries and breastworks across open ground by daylight would be to invite disaster. It would mean losses so heavy that they would "counterbalance even success itself, while success was, to say the least of it, doubtful." [144] If so costly an assault failed, it would be "hardly possible to avoid destruction." [145]

Brooke had, actually, no choice. He had been deprived of choice by the decision of his dead superior. When Ross landed on North Point, the British army was immobilized. Committed to an attack upon the enemy at his strongest point, it lost all real power of maneuver. But the attack must be made. Brooke, thrust into the command of an army already launched against a specific objective, could not turn his back on that objective without making an attempt to take it. Quickly and effectively frustrated in his effort to maneuver, he made now the only decision that offered any prospect of success without ghastly, crippling losses. He would storm the works tonight, under cover of the darkness.[146] The fleet should support him, either by direct fire or by a diversion.[147]

He recalled the column from its futile flanking movement.[148] While it marched back, he studied the American position and worked out the details of the night assault. The south end of the fortified ridge looked almost impregnable: it could not be turned: the harbor channel flanked it. The circular battery [149] there was probably the strongest in the whole chain of defenses, and the slopes below were steepest. At their foot, the broad mouth of the creek [150] was probably impassable for infantry. The west end of the curving ridge was much less formidable: the approaches were gentler: there were no natural obstacles to protect it against a quick, short turning operation. But unless the Americans became careless, there was little prospect of achieving a surprise at that point, and Brooke saw nothing that encouraged him to count on carelessness. The American brigades that had moved out to meet his demonstration were now matching the march of his returning column as closely as if they were another column of his own troops. They were like a shadow, inescapable, keeping their distance but moving always as the British army moved, keeping themselves persistently between it and the town. The American commander showed every intention of maintaining that mobile force between Brooke's troops and the weaker western end of his own fortified arc.

Once more Brooke tried to throw Sam Smith off balance by maneuver. A feint against the east face of the "heights" might cozen the defending general into thinking a daylight assault was coming; a new demonstration, vigorously pressed there, might alarm him into withdrawing more infantry into the entrenchments to reinforce the garrison. At the least it would distract attention from the point that Brooke had chosen for the night attack.

A little before one o'clock he issued orders that would concentrate his whole force on the Americans' front.[151] His column, swinging down the Herring Run valley past the Kell house, crossed the Philadelphia pike and turned south. By two o'clock the British army was in line of battle on the high ground overlooking the broad, shallow valley of Harris's Creek. It was still some two miles from the American defenses; between it and the fortified ridge ran the creek, an obstacle but not so serious an obstacle as the Potomac branch had been at Bladensburg. Brooke's front was impressive. His right flank lay across the Philadelphia pike, a few hundred yards west of his headquarters at the Kell house. His left extended a short distance to the south of Trappe road.[152] With normal intervals between his regiments and battalions, he had enough troops to present a battle line more than a mile long in double ranks.[153]

The bugles blew. The British troops moved forward. In the Loudenslager batteries, the frigate gunners stood with lighted matches. Two miles straight southward from the left flank of the British army, four ships of the bombarding squadron weighed and stood in toward McHenry. Three were mortar vessels and the fourth was *Erebus*.[154] They were closing in on Whetstone while the other bomb ships covered their advance with a continuous fire. It was a little after two o'clock.[155] By land and water, the attacking forces at last were advancing in what appeared to be a co-ordinated attack.[156]

The American cavalry videttes fell back as the British troops came on. Their withdrawal was a series of spasmodic semicirclings—little groups of horsemen in the wet fields, waiting, turning suddenly and galloping off to the rear and swooping back again in meaningless short dashes toward the enemy, and then reining in again to wait. To the men behind the breastworks, watching without glassses, the dragoons' retreat looked little like a military operation. It looked, at this distance of a mile or more, like small packs of wild dogs scuttling off from something that they dreaded, gaining courage as they gained safe distance, circling back to show their teeth and snarl and stand momentarily at bay before they ran again. The only difference was that you could have heard dogs yapping. There was no sound at all as the advance rolled on.

The British army left a quarter of a mile of sloping fields behind it, half a mile, three-quarters of a mile. In the American redoubts, the gunners blew their matches. In the low ground near Worthington's Mill, two columns of American infantry began to move: Sam Smith once more was matching Brooke's maneuver. He was drawing the Virginia brigade in toward the Philadelphia turnpike where it entered the sharp angle of his field works; he was swinging the City Brigade north around the mill, then eastward toward the pike.[157]

The tough-minded old militiaman was not convinced by Brooke's imposing demonstration. He was certain that the enemy was bluffing: the advance would come on boldly a few hundred yards more and then stop abruptly: no man in his right mind would attempt to storm these works by daylight.[158] If an assault was coming, it would not come until after sundown. But he did not intend to sit and wait for it. When the attack came, he would meet it with a counterattack. He was maneuvering the two brigades into a position from which they could fall upon the British "right or rear"[159] while the assaulting regiments were struggling through the creek.

Brooke saw the danger. The right wing of his line of battle was advancing into an obtuse angle formed by the east face of the fortified ridge and by the deploying infantry northwest of the turnpike. This was Bladensburg again—reversed. There the Americans had thrown away the advantage of superior numbers, abandoned the defense line of the river, and presented to the British the invaluable cover of the orchard;[160] the one attack they risked had been made into an obtuse angle, under flanking fire.[161] They

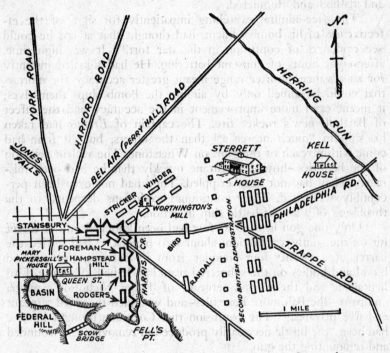

BROOKE'S SECOND DEMONSTRATION, about 3 p.m., September 13.

had committed no such blunders here. The American commander, whoever he was, seemed to know his business; he had made no mistakes at all, so far as Brooke could see.[162] He had the advantages of both ground and numbers, and he was guarding them tenaciously and shrewdly. If the British move had been intended as a serious attack and not as a demonstration, the countermove would have meant check and, probably, checkmate as well. It was, now, nothing but a warning. Brooke's troops halted where he had intended they should halt, a mile short of the entrenchments.[163] But Sam Smith's maneuvering, about two o'clock, shaped Brooke's plan for the assault at midnight.[164]

As the British army halted, the slow, distant firing down the river erupted suddenly into furious cannonading. Every big gun at McHenry was in action.[165] Mortar shells were bursting over and around them, rockets trailing fire across them. The point smoked and flashed and thundered.

The vice-admiral, watching impatiently for signs of the effectiveness of his bombardment, had thought that at last he could see evidences of confusion in the star fort.[166] It was high time, after eight hours of constant battering. He had signaled instantly for an advance. Shorter range meant greater accuracy for mortars that could be aimed only by aiming the bomb ships themselves; it meant even more improvement in the accuracy and the effect of Bartholomew's rocket fire. The captain of *Erebus* had taken his ship in "much nearer" [167] than the others, but all four had come within reach of the guns on Whetstone. The violent reaction of the batteries showed Cochrane quickly that he had been mistaken. They had not been crippled. They had not even been perceptibly weakened. Their continuous explosions deepened to the throbbing of a line-of-battle ship in action.

Only one gun in the star fort had been knocked out. A direct hit on the southwest bastion, about two o'clock,[168] had hurled the barrel of a twenty-four-pounder from its carriage and strewed blood and bodies on the splintered planking. It had killed the third lieutenant and the second sergeant of Judge Nicholson's militia company—the Baltimore Fencibles—and wounded the third sergeant and five privates.[169] The confusion that Cochrane thought he saw had been "the bustle necessarily produced in removing the wounded and remounting the gun." [170]

But now forty guns were firing. Their solid shot were churning the Patapsco white around the British ships. One of the mortar ships was struck, and then another.[171] The Whetstone gunners were sure that they saw "several shot take effect." [172] Cochrane became alarmed.[173] The small vessels of the bombing squadron were more important, in this operation, than his battleships and frigates.[174] He could not afford to lose them. If he left them where they were, it would be a miracle if some of them were not destroyed or crippled. A hoist of signal flags soared up to *Severn's* peak—the vice-admiral's order to withdraw. On the three bomb ketches, seamen swarmed around the capstans, hauling up the anchors; the bows began to swing; through dangerous minutes, the ships lay broadside to the Whetstone batteries. Then they were tacking down the river. But the rocket vessel, nearest to the enemy, was not yet under weigh. As the mortar ships drew out of range, the guns were concentrating upon *Erebus*. Perhaps David Ewen Bartholomew, her captain, had Lord Nelson's blind eye and was deliberately failing to understand the signal. If he was not in difficulties, his stubbornness made the withdrawal of the other ships seem hasty

and unnecessary. Cochrane was in no mood to tolerate either disobedience or sacrificial gallantry; he chose to "imagine that Captain Bartholomew could not maintain his position." [175] A division of small boats pulled away from *Severn* with the vice-admiral's orders to tow *Erebus* out [176] whether her commander wanted to retreat or not.

In half an hour the last ship was again beyond the reach of Armistead's guns. [177] The batteries ceased firing and the garrison "gave three cheers." [178] Far out of danger, the five mortar ships reopened their bombardment.

The ordeal of helpless waiting had begun again. It would go on for nine hours.[179] Now and then "a single gun" would answer, useless as a muttered oath and not much louder in the crash of shell bursts. Now and then a man would scream, a gunner crumple silently, a fragment slam a body back against the mud wall to slide down and roll in agony. Not many men were hit: enough to make those not yet hit expect the next shell to be theirs, and then the next, the next. In the forty-two-pounder battery, a flotillaman lay dead beside his gun, three others had been wounded.[180] Two of the Sea Fencibles were down at Bunbury's guns. Fourteen more militiamen were hit. In the Washington Artillery, one man was killed, two mangled, and five others wounded. The third lieutenant of the Independent Artillerists was bleeding, a shell tore off Emanuel Kent's arm, two men beside him had been badly wounded and two others slightly.

Historians would count the cost and say disgustedly that it was "insignificant." Another man who was not there would say that "there was something exceedingly picturesque and beautiful about the silence of that fort!" [181] To the men who were there, it was hell.

But it was also victory. The enemy's most dangerous attack had ended in repulse.

26

THE ROCKETS' RED GLARE

Sir Alexander Cochrane was confronted, in mid-afternoon, with a situation far more serious than a mere tactical repulse. He was face to face with a disastrous [1] failure. And he knew it.

The realization was as unexpected as it was unpleasant. London would find it difficult to understand why a vice-admiral should fail just after the captain of a minor frigate had succeeded in a similar operation. Fort Washington on the Potomac had been deserted, its twenty-seven guns spiked and its magazine blown up, at the first threat of an attack by only six ships. Captain Gordon had knocked out a permanent fortification, held a town for ransom, beaten off small-boat attacks and fireships, anchored under the point-blank fire of Porter's batteries and put them out of action, and brought his long train of twenty-one booty-laden prizes safely down the river. Cochrane had been provided with the strongest fleet yet concentrated in American waters for a combined offensive.[2] He had forty men-of-war, including four ships of the line, a dozen frigates and a score of ship-sloops and bomb vessels. If that powerful armament turned back, frustrated, from a brick-and-sod fort and a mud-wall battery, the contrast would be most unfortunate.

The American army had been driven from the field at Bladensburg by less than half its numbers.[3] The capital of the United States had been abandoned without pretense of resistance. If the veteran British army that had achieved so much without the fleet's support turned back now, frustrated, the contrasts would become embarrassing. The War Office would see instantly and plainly that there had been no attack, but it probably would not see the reasons either quickly or plainly; it might never see them. The Lords of the Admiralty would read the most plausible dispatch from Cochrane with tight-lipped displeasure. They would ask stern questions and want explanations—good ones. Failure was unwelcome. Through the late afternoon and early evening, Cochrane and Brooke worked earnestly to retrieve the situation.[4]

Much nonsense has been written about what they did. More —and worse—nonsense has been written about why they did it. The result has been confusion and distortion. Both were needless.

The confusion and distortion, carelessly accepted, have minimized the seriousness of the attack on Baltimore, disparaged the skill and foresight and courage of the defense, and falsified the facts.

One obvious fact, invariably perverted, is that by midafternoon Sir Alexander knew he had failed. The form of the perversion is invariably the same. It consists of two parts. The first is the acceptance, as the sole reason for his failure, of one distorted circumstance. The second is the complete overlooking of one obvious and vital circumstance. The distortion is concealed in the accepted statement that "as the entrance to Baltimore by sea was entirely obstructed by a barrier of vessels sunk at the mouth of the harbor . . . a naval co-operation against the city and intrenched camp was found impracticable." [5] This statement appears and reappears in many forms —"the heavier British ships feared to approach within range, owing to a barrier of sunken vessels" [6] and "none except the very lightest craft could make their way within six miles of the town and even these were stopped by vessels sunk in the channel, and other artificial bars, barely within a shell's longest range of the fort" [7] and the British ships "could not run past the defenses or get closer to them because of the shoals and a line of hulks . . . sunk across the channel." [8] The sense of the assertion never varies: the fleet attack failed because the sunken hulks prevented it from coming to effective range.

The "sense" is nonsense. Contemporary charts of the defenses show the barriers of sunken vessels—one across the channel between Whetstone Point and Lazaretto light, the other across the entrance of the Ferry Branch between Whetstone Point and Cromwell's. The only other barrier was a mile and a half farther in—the boom across the mouth of Ridgely's Cove. The fact is that no British man-of-war—not even *Erebus*—approached within a mile of any of these "artificial bars."

Like most of the other distortions that appear in secondhand accounts of the whole Maryland campaign, the false excuse for British failure is made plausible by an admixture of the truth. The Patapsco shoals did prevent the line-of-battle ships—*Tonnant*, *Dragon*, *Royal Oak* and *Albion*—from engaging the American defenses. But they did not prevent the frigates from engaging. The fact is that there was depth enough in the McHenry channel and the river for such ships as *Constellation*—a fair match for the forty-gun frigate *Severn* or the thirty-eight gun *Seahorse*. There was depth enough for the heavier *Java*, which the British themselves rated as a line-of-battle ship misrepresented as a frigate.[9] The fact is that the captains of *Havannah*, *Hebrus*, *Severn* and *Euryalus* volunteered to "lighten their ships and lay them alongside Fort McHenry." [10] The gallant offer was rejected. The reason for rejection was a simple one: the proposal involved a desperate risk of ships and lives without offering any reasonable prospect of success. It was, in fact, a proposal to send weaker forces into action after stronger forces had completely failed.

There is the truth about the battle. There is the key to its

BRITISH BOMB SHIP with mortars in tandem, on pivots—with cross-section of ship showing great timber supports under the mortar beds; views of mortar beds from above and from one side; cross-section of mortar; and shell showing handles and fuse.

outcome. It has been obvious since 4 P.M., September 13, 1814. But it has been ignored.

The vital circumstance that has been overlooked is this: Cochrane had already used the full power of his most effective weapons. Sea mortars were designed specifically to perform the mission he had given them today. Mortar ships had been designed specifically to bring these highly specialized weapons into action at effective ranges with a minimum of exposure to hostile fire.[11]

Neither the size nor the appearance of the bomb ships was impressive. They were small—smaller than a gun brig—ninety feet long on deck and twenty-seven feet broad. They were low: their gun ports were but four feet and eight inches from the waterline: a man standing in a gig alongside could rest his elbows on a mortar ship's deck. Their guns were puny and they carried only eight of them and a few swivels. They looked odd and out of date and awkward, and their masts looked misplaced.

There were two masts, one aft, one amidships. From the mainmast aft, a kind of poop deck rose six feet above the main deck and was reminiscent of the days of caravels and galleons. From the mainmast to the bowsprit, the range of the deck was naked, without mast or superstructure. For half her length, a mortar ship was nothing but a platform for artillery, with a breast-high bulwark like a wooden wall around it. The bulwark made her look scooped out and hollow, and the abnormally long poop deck finished her absurd appearance. She looked like something you could put your foot in. At a little distance she looked like a Dutchman's wooden shoe adrift upon a pond.

Not even the piratical long yard that slanted rakishly across their mizzenmasts—the lateen rig familiar in the Barbary ports of Tripoli and Tunis and Algiers—could give the mortar ships a dangerous look. Their very name diminished them. The French called them *galiots*, a term suggestive of small galleys. And the British called them ketches.

Appearance, name and size were all misleading. That, perhaps, is history's excuse for giving them one casual glance and then dismissing them. But it is not a valid reason: the truth was readily available.

Small though they were, the mortar ships were timbered like a frigate and they had the staunchness of a fifty-gun ship. And they needed it. The mortars that they carried were the most powerful fortress-battering artillery afloat. Some of them were armed with two thirteen-inch mortars—more than five feet long and weighing more than four tons—set side by side in fixed beds on the forward deck. Others carried a thirteen-inch mortar and a ten-inch, one behind the other, set in circular beds that could be turned on pivots. The beds were made of ponderous timbers bolted solidly together. The trunnions of the mortars lay in semicircular notches in the timbers, and their bellies rested on another great beam called the bolster. Beneath them, in the ship's hold, upright timbers stood like the thick pilings of a wharf, supporting the enormous weight of beds and mortars.

The shells matched the weapons. They were iron spheres filled with powder and equipped with two iron handles, one on each side of the fuse hole. To handle them was difficult: booms must be rigged, hooks thrust into the handles, and the shell raised with block and tackle to the muzzle of the mortar. To fire them safely took elaborate precautions. So great was the risk of premature explosion from a flying spark that until recent years the mortar ships had not carried their own ammunition. The shells were brought up in tenders, and especially trained details of marine artillerymen "fixed" them in the small boats lying alongside. "Fixing" was the process of driving the fuse—a conical tube of beech or willow wood —into the fuse hole. The large end, protruding, was kept sealed with tallow until the last moment.

Loading a mortar was like filling a trash barrel. Five to twenty pounds of powder went in first. Then came a layer of hay and then a wooden plug and then a layer of sod. The squealing tackle lowered the shell into the barrel. Over it and around it the mortar-men packed hay or straw or chunks of turf. The tallow cap, made stiff with pitch or beeswax, was cut off or broken open. One man touched a slow match to the fuse, another laid his slow match to the priming powder.

Fire spouted from the vents at each discharge; sparks shot up toward the rigging and rained on the deck; the touch-hole blast was like the fiery trail of a small rocket. Plank screens, five feet square, must be hung above the vents to take the flame; even then, the booms must be kept drenched; details of seamen manned the fire pumps and long rows of leather buckets were kept filled with water; the smallest bolt hole must be plugged to keep out flying sparks.

The shock of firing, in those small ships, was terrific. The mortars had no recoil mechanism, the hull took the whole blow.

Bulkhead doors must be kept shut "to prevent the cabin being injured by the explosions." Every discharge wracked the ship and drove her two feet down into the water. She could stand it; she was built to stand it. And the shells she threw were six times as heavy as the largest solid shot thrown by a British line-of-battle ship.

Erebus, too, was a special engine of destruction. She had been a twenty-gun sloop of war—a stout, hard-hitting cruiser. On the day she moved in to attack McHenry, she still had her twenty

CROSS-SECTION OF GUN-BRIG converted into rocket ship. Scuttles cut in brig's side, below gun deck, for rocket tubes.

cannon; outwardly, she was still nothing but a cruiser. But Sir William Congreve, the inventor of the rocket, had converted her into a new and unique weapon for attacking land defenses. Along both sides, just below her gun deck, he had cut a row of small square holes. He called them "scuttles" and the name was fitting: they looked a good deal like the square hole cut into the side of a frame dwelling for the convenience of the coal man. Inside each scuttle was a boxed-in frame—a kind of coal chute carefully enclosed to keep the dust from spreading through the cellar. In *Erebus*, the long boxed frames that slanted down into the hold had been designed to serve a similar purpose: they kept the burning fuses of the rockets from spreading flame and sparks throughout the ship.

Inside each coffin-shaped box, the metal tube of a discharger thrust its round nose just up to the square hole in the ship's side. The tubes of the rocket battery on *Erebus* were larger than the dischargers with which rocket troops had been equipped for land campaigning; they fired thirty-two-pound missiles—five times the weight of the land rockets normally employed. The tubes were equipped with gunlocks and could be discharged by lanyards. They could be loaded, aimed and fired more easily and quickly than a cannon; the frames that enclosed them could be raised or lowered or traversed. *Erebus* could throw a rocket-broadside horizontally against a hostile ship or almost straight up—at an eighty-five-degree angle—to come hurtling down on buildings, forts or batteries ashore. Iron shutters, built into the frames, confined the sparks and flame. The rockets' flight carried their fiery tails beyond the rigging and eliminated the danger of sails catching fire. The sailors on the deck above could work the ship and man the guns "without the least risk" to the crew or vessel. And the warheads of the rockets could be suited to the target. They could carry a twenty-four-pound solid iron shot, or an explosive shell, or an incendiary carcass—a fire bomb—filled with a furiously inflammable mixture of pitch, powder, tallow and saltpeter.

To say that Cochrane sent six small vessels to attack McHenry means exactly nothing. To say that shoal water or the hulks of sunken ships prevented him from using his most powerful weapons is a plain distortion of the truth. The truth is that he had sent against the Baltimore defenses the most powerful naval siege artillery in existence. The truth is that he had been given two-thirds of the British navy's whole supply of special fortress-battering equipment. He had with him five of Britain's eight bomb vessels and the only rocket cruiser on the high seas of the world.[12]

He had been using them for nine hours under ideal conditions —in smooth water, at medium range, and without the slightest danger of retaliation. The bombardment had been target practice, not a battle. But after nine hours of incessant, unresisted pounding, the American defenses had been able to pour such a storm of fire upon the ships when they advanced that Cochrane almost instantly recalled them. He did not dare to risk, within range of that cannonade, the only weapons with which he could hope to crush the batteries. He knew that if he lost those vessels, he lost Baltimore.

This testimony is not biased or incompetent. It is expert, scientific and impartial. It is British. And there are five witnesses. The first is Henry Wilkinson, whose treatise on *Engines of*

War remarked that "many foreign writers affect to treat [rockets] with contempt, and endeavor to impress on the minds of their countrymen the belief that rockets owe their efficacy more to the moral effect produced on an enemy than to their own destructive powers, by inspiring confidence on the one side and terror on the other; but this is a very erroneous opinion, as they possess many advantages over cannon in certain circumstances. . . . They are capable of projecting almost every variety of shot and shells that can be thrown from cannon, howitzers and mortars. . . ." The second witness is Lieutenant Colonel Fyers of the Royal Horse Artillery, commander of a rocket corps, who certified that a twelve-pounder rocket shell penetrated "not less than from twenty to twenty-two feet in a solid bank" of earth before exploding. The penetration was "nearly double that of any ammunition now used in field service, which makes it peculiarly applicable to the attack of all field fortifications, lines, redoubts, &c; even against twelve-pounder field artillery, we should consider ourselves safe behind a sod work of twelve feet in thickness."

The third witness is Sir William Congreve: "It is possible to equip a gun-brig so as to discharge twenty thirty-two pounder rockets in a broadside, firing them as quick as may be desired in succession." Each shell, he testified, was "equal, or rather superior, to a ten-inch spherical carcass." And ten rocket vessels such as *Erebus* could discharge two hundred of them "in the space of a few minutes." Ten mortar ships equipped with ten-inch weapons would require two hours to deliver the same volume of fire. One gun-brig, Congreve told his government, using thirty-two-pound rockets, was the equal of ten mortar vessels. Taken at face value, Congreve's testimony makes the *Erebus* equivalent to ten *Aetnas*. It gives to Sir Alexander Cochrane's bombing fleet the fire power of no less than fifteen mortar ships—a volume of fire equal to that of thirty pieces of the most powerful siege artillery afloat.

The fourth witness is Robert Simmons, another English expert whose *Sea-Gunners Vade-Mecum* was a naval bible: "Mortars are used in the attack of a fortified place, by sea, to discharge bombs or carcasses amongst the buildings" and the great shell, falling "into the works of a fortification, &c., destroys the most substantial buildings by its weight; and, bursting asunder, creates the greatest disorder" while its splinters "flying off circularly, occasion incredible mischief."

The fifth witness is Sir Howard Douglas, the acknowledged

British authority on naval gunnery. Thirty-seven years after the bombardment of the Baltimore defenses, England was experimenting with new ten-inch guns and Sir Howard Douglas was concluding that they might prove "useful in shelling towns, roadsteads, open batteries, and troops on shore at great distances." But he was adding that "how far they are fit to supersede mortars in the attack and bombardment of large fortresses and arsenals is another question." In bombarding forts, he pointed out, small elevation was a disadvantage. "There is too much horizontality in the trajectory," he said, "to produce the crushing effect of bomb-shells. The shell wants that tremendous force which can only be acquired by the descent of mortar shells fired at the elevations which produce their greatest range (42 or 45 degrees) when they fall with force sufficient to penetrate into any building, and finish their course with the destructive effects of a mine. Shells fired horizontally from any ordnance, however useful in shelling places of minor importance, are not efficient substitutes for mortar-shells for purposes of bombardment. A bomb-ship may, without much exposure, do great damage to an extensive fortress or arsenal, which, being a large object, ought to be struck at every discharge at upwards of 4,000 yards, whilst she is a mere speck on the sea at that great distance."

Neither shoals nor sunken hulks were keeping Cochrane from bringing the full power of his most effective armament to bear upon the target with impunity. The fury of the American fire, a little after three o'clock, was shocking. It meant that he had done his utmost for nine hours and that his best was not enough. To send in frigates armed with thirty-two-pounder, flat trajectory guns against fortifications that had stood up under the prolonged, unopposed pounding of two-hundred-pound mortar shells would be useless folly. To use even their long eighteen-pounders, they would have to close in to within half the distance that separated the bomb vessels from the nearest batteries. The smallest frigate was three times as large as any bomb ship. At any range at which their fire could be effective, Cochrane's frigates would be targets to be knocked to pieces. They would sacrifice themselves in vain.

It is true that "on the evening of the 13th" Cochrane told Brooke that "a naval co-operation" with the army was impracticable because the channel was "entirely obstructed by a barrier of vessels sunk at the mouth of the harbour" [13] and "defended inside by gunboats." [14] But he was not saying that the sunken hulks were interfering with his bombardment of the works on Whetstone. Obviously, they were not. The vice-admiral was dealing with an entirely different problem. He was replying to Colonel Brooke's request for an attack on Rodgers's bastion, the redoubt that guarded the extreme right of the American entrenchments.[15]

For Brooke had completed his plan for a night assault and had communicated it to Cochrane.[16] The confusion and distortion which have obscured the British preparations, and thereby minimized the danger, disappear when the plan for a combined and co-ordinated attack is understood. The operation can be traced step by step, and almost hour by hour, from its conception through its execution to its failure.

It was conceived by Brooke in the late afternoon, when his two maneuvers had failed to disclose any weakness in the American commander or his dispositions. Studying the curve of Loudenslager's hill, the erstwhile colonel of the 44th believed he saw a weakness in the fortified position. The American lines could not be turned from either flank; they could not be carried by daylight assault except with ghastly losses. A general attack on the whole front, in darkness, might succeed; but it involved the risk of units losing their direction, of mistakes in timing, of attacks delivered piecemeal, their combined shock dissipated and the advantage of surprise lost. Brooke's hope lay in concentration, and he thought he saw the place where it could be applied successfully.

Where the ridge curved backward sharply, the main highway entered the American position.[17] A little to the left, as Brooke faced the fortifications, a lane crossed the creek at a sharp angle,[18] climbed the slope diagonally, and united with the turnpike just behind the line of earthworks. Both roads were strongly guarded. He could make out seven guns in a redoubt between them, two more emplaced to sweep the lane, and six others in two batteries close by.[19] But the redoubts certainly were not impregnable, for "of the field works begun, not one had arrived at completion." [20] Brooke's long experience told him that troops placed but little trust in "works only half defensible." [21]

His hopes grew; he was almost confident. In a night operation "a compact body of veterans, well-disciplined and orderly," was certainly "an overmatch for whole crowds of raw levies." [22] A surprise attack, in darkness, would deprive the enemy of almost his whole advantage in superior artillery.[23] And there, at the bend of the entrenched lines, was the one place where cross fire could not sweep attacking infantry. It was unlikely that the Americans would have a force there strong enough to hold out even momentarily against a solid storming column crashing into them with no more warning than their pickets would have time to give. A battering ram of regiments that had stormed fortress walls at Tarragona and Badajoz and Bayonne should smash through those field works quickly, split the fortified position, cut off the two segments from each other and outflank both. The storm troops should be on the crest in minutes. They would be behind the batteries and trenches. It would be a miracle if American militia, in the darkness and confusion, rallied and attempted to dislodge them. Even for regulars, it would not be easy.

Even for British regulars, the risk of disorganization caused by success itself was so great that Brooke set limits to the operation. He would penetrate the Yankee lines, gain the summit of the ridge, reorganize and hold on there till daylight, and then "taking the whole of the works in flank . . . carry them one by one." [24] The thing might be done. It could be done! It must be!

But he could not do it all, alone. He did not feel that it should be expected of him.[25] The fleet must help him, and the place for its co-operation appeared obvious to Brooke. There was one obstacle that troubled him—the "strong post well supplied with heavy ordnance" [26] on the extreme right of the American position. It was protected by the harbor channel on one side and by the broad mouth of the creek in front. To attempt to carry it by escalade would be "too hazardous." Even a demonstration there would require troops that he needed for his storming column. But to leave it undisturbed would put his whole attack in jeopardy. The earthwork bastion commanded the entire east face and summit of the ridge. When daylight came, its guns could play at will upon his storming column; they might mean repulse, disaster; they might even mean destruction.[27]

The bastion must be knocked out. At the very least, it must be neutralized. And the attack there, either by bombardment or by diversion, should begin before the storming column struck.[28] The Americans' attention must be distracted from the bend in their lines where the assault would come.[29]

Brooke sent an officer hurrying away to "open a communication with the fleet" and present his battle plan to the vice-admiral.[30] It was, in principle, a sound plan. Although the infantry attack would be a *coup de main*,[31] it was not a forlorn hope; it offered at least some prospect of success. British troops had taken greater risks on many fields, and won. But in its demand for the fleet's co-operation, it was based upon inadequate knowledge of the situation. It asked Cochrane to do the impossible. But Brooke's lack of information does not indicate a British failure in liaison: Cochrane himself did not realize, until the middle of the afternoon, that his bombardment had not seriously damaged the McHenry batteries. Colonel Brooke's plan was transmitted to him aboard *Severn* some time after his unpleasant discovery that his lighter ships could not close in toward the harbor at least until the mortar ships accomplished more than they had yet accomplished. Knowing that nine hours of concentrated mortar fire had failed, he could not count on putting the American guns out of action in time to give Brooke the support he wanted.

Brooke had called for naval bombardment of the "fort" at the south end of Loudenslager's hill. His plan of operation indicated that he wanted it for two reasons: first, to cripple the battery there so that it could not play[32] upon his troops at daylight and, second, to provide a diversion that would draw the Americans' attention to the south end of the ridge, away from the point chosen for the infantry assault. It was this request that the vice-admiral was answering when he sent word to Brooke that "a naval co-operation" was impracticable. He was referring specifically to the co-operation for which Brooke had asked. But he was going further: he was telling Brooke not only what he could not do, and why, but also what he could and would do.

The bastion on which the army wanted naval fire was twenty-six hundred yards northwest of Fort McHenry. To reach it with mortar shells at maximum range, the bomb ships would have to move up to within a mile of Whetstone and within less than a mile of an American battery at the Lazaretto. Cochrane did not limit his reply to a rejection of Brooke's request for a bombardment. The second purpose of bombardment—a diversion to distract the enemy's attention—could be achieved by a small-boat attack. The army commander, not knowing all the circumstances, might expect at least that much assistance.[33] Cochrane thought about it and decided quickly that it was impossible. His message to Brooke said so and explained why: the line of sunken hulks across the channel was "defended inside by gun-boats."

The gunboats had been one more of the unpleasant afternoon's surprises. They lay "close in, under the banks at the water's edge"[34] below the Lazaretto battery, and Cochrane had not noticed them until the mortar vessels and the rocket ship moved closer to the fort.[35] The flotilla barges were at least half a mile downriver from McHenry;[36] when they opened at close range, their guns and the batteries on Whetstone caught the British vessels in converging fire. It had been a warning. A small-boat expedition, if it were discovered trying to approach the sunken hulks and the armed ships behind them, would come under the same converging fire; if it reached the barrier, it would be swept by enfilading crossfire.

Both a bombardment and a demonstration against Rodgers's bastion were impossible. But Cochrane did not give up easily. An amphibious attack at some more vulnerable point, he decided, should give Brooke the diversion that the army wanted. Signals flew from *Severn.* The vice-admiral was ordering small boats prepared to make a night attack, timed to precede the infantry assault and draw the enemy's attention.[37] Then, when he had given the preliminary orders, he put a messenger [38] ashore to tell Brooke that the diversion he had asked for was impossible but that there would be another.[39] It was nearly sundown.[40] The messenger had several miles to go—a mile by ship's boat to the nearest shore, at least a half mile across country to the nearest road, and then two miles by the most direct route to the British lines. By the longer and more likely route—the road from Sollers' Point—the distance to Brooke's quarters at the Kell house was almost six miles.

There was a bustle in the fleet—unnoticeable ashore—as men were told off and equipped for the attack, boat guns and rocket launchers checked, and ammunition loaded. The mortar shells fell ceaselessly on Whetstone Point. But on Loudenslager's hill and on the gentle slopes that curved around it beyond Harris's Creek, the late afternoon was peaceful. The British troops lay where their simulated push against the works had halted. Pickets watched each other curiously. Only Brooke's staff and the British foragers were busy. Mounted officers and orderlies went trotting from one idle column to another, carrying the detailed orders for the night attack. Off toward Herring Run, hungry soldiers were ransacking Furley Hall,[41] and the colonel of the Fifth Maryland could see scarlet jackets on the portico of Surrey.

An outpost of the 85th had made itself at home in Sterrett's house, but it had a grievance: the pantry shelves were empty and so was the barnyard. "There was not a pig, fowl or other living creature" except pigeons.[42] The lieutenant and his four men, hunting for a supper better than salt pork and stony biscuit, tried their hands at catching pigeons but "they were a great deal too wary not to baffle every effort . . . to surprise them." The disgusted poachers were "preparing to quit the inhospitable domicile, when a whole crowd of stragglers, artillerymen, sappers, sailors, and soldiers of the line, rushed into the hall. In a moment the walls of the building re-echoed with oaths and exclamations, and tables, chairs, windows, and even doors, were dashed to pieces, in revenge for the absence of food." A shout of joy broke in upon the uproar. It came from the cellar; and the riotous foragers, jostling down the stairway, saw "through a chasm in a brick wall . . . the interior of a wine cellar, set round in magnificent array with bottles of all shapes and dimensions."

Colonel Sterrett's camouflage had failed. A soldier had noticed the new brickwork and by the forthright method of "applying the but-end of his musket" had smashed through the false wall. "In five minutes the cellar was crowded with men, filling, in the first place, their own haversacks and bosoms, and then handing out bottles, with the utmost liberality, to their comrades." They did their work so thoroughly that "in less than a quarter of an hour, not a single pint, either of wine or spirits, remained of all this magnificent stock." [43] The lieutenant came back to his sputtering picket fire, through drenching rain, with a flask of cognac and two magnums of Bordeaux. The biscuits seemed not quite so flinty and the government-issue salt pork tasted just a little less like tarred rope. The cognac even made up for the blankets left behind this morning when the march began. "In a state of excessive moisture" the British army watched its own fires and those of the enemy draw two redly flaring arcs across the darkness.

The British campfires were a part of Brooke's preparations for attack. In their normal night formation, the brigades went into bivouac in close columns of companies. Tonight, in an attempt to make the American commander think that his whole front was threatened, the fires were "stretched out in a single line . . . far more imposing than if they had been confined as usual" [44] to the three or four rectangles of brigade camps. The company officers knew, by this time, what was coming. One regiment would hold the front and keep the camp fires burning. All the rest would move silently to the right and form in storming column opposite the sharp bend in the enemy's position. The point of attack was plainly visible, the "whole face of the hill" ablaze with the Americans' fires. They made "a sort of semicircle, only the horns of their crescent, instead of advancing, fell back on both sides from the center." [45] At least one subaltern, in spite of his flask of cognac and his two magnums of Bordeaux, was soberly impressed by the contrast between the "dense arrangement" of the hostile bivouac and "the scattered and somewhat irregular disposition" of his own.

In the American lines, the same contrast had impressed some of Sam Smith's brigade commanders. They were urging him to make a night attack, and the old man was listening. His mind was made up. He knew the arguments already. But it did no harm to let these younger fellows whet themselves keen on the solid grindstone of his patience. They told him that he had superiority of numbers, that John Stricker's fight had given the whole army confidence, that the risk of a night attack was small because his troops knew every inch of ground. Here was the chance, they argued, to annihilate the enemy: he could surround the British army, cut the roads behind it, drive it back upon the harbor and compel it to surrender. That would be indeed a famous victory.

Sam Smith heard them out. "Yes," he said. It would be a fine thing. Then he added earnestly: "But when you fight our citizens against British regulars, you're staking dollars against cents." [46]

That was the philosophy on which his whole plan of defense was based. His mission was to keep the enemy from getting Baltimore. He had undertaken to fulfill the mission by convincing the invaders that the price would be too high for them to pay. When he sent the City Brigade out to meet superior numbers, he was risking some lives to save many. To the British, it seemed reckless and unnecessary. To Sam Smith, it seemed to be the best way to give them "an earnest" of what they might expect to pay if they attacked his field works. All day the behavior of the British army had increased his confidence that his trader tactics had been right. If the enemy attacked him, he would hold his lines as doggedly as he would hold a dollar. But he would not spend one life to buy a few cents' worth of glory by attacking when he did not have to.

The brigadiers gave up their arguing. Sam Smith had silenced them with one unmilitary sentence. As they went back to their posts, he turned again to the problem that had troubled him increasingly since morning. The grump of shells exploding over Whetstone was a dull, intermittent throbbing in the heavy air. A fort that was not bombproof, open batteries and human nerves could not endure that hammering forever. The horse-telegraph couriers had been coming in all day, at intervals, galloping across the bridge of scows with reassuring messages from Armistead.[47] The batteries had proved, at three o'clock, that they had not been crippled. From Loudenslager's, it seemed like a miracle. Twelve, thirteen, fourteen hours, and still the single gun growled now and then, and still the messages were reassuring. Such luck could not last. Unless the law of averages had been suspended, the persistent mortars must get some hits on the open batteries. It would not take many. They were searching for the gunboats too, now, and the three-gun Lazaretto battery.[48]

There must be some way to put a stop to that relentless pounding, at the least to interrupt it, to give Armistead some respite. The flotilla barges? No. The channel must be guarded closely: a small-boat attack might try to break into the harbor, past the line of hulks, to burn the warships in the Basin. It would be a suicidal mission. Certainly it should be. But the destruction of *Java*, *Erie* and *Ontario* would justify a high price. If the barges could not be spared for an attack upon the bomb ships. . . . Sam Smith sent a verbal requisition to Ed Johnson for two fireships, any sloops or schooners that he could lay hands on and cram full of tar and lightwood and deliver "with all possible dispatch" to Rodgers.[49]

The rain still fell. It had lost some of its sullen violence, but a rising wind[50] was whipping it across the faces of the militiamen who stared across the breastworks at the awful spectacle of the night bombardment. They could trace the shells' flight now—the gout of light that seemed to stab straight upward when a mortar fired, the red spark of the burning fuse that climbed and climbed and hung and turned and fell, and then the gust of flame above McHenry. Brief, fierce flashes showed the torn smoke like a ragged cloud rack, tossing wildly, flung in all directions. The red glare of rockets lighted up low storm clouds that were also torn and ragged, rushing, driven by the high wind.

Men who watched from the redoubts and trenches in the Loudenslager lines would long remember Whetstone burning, smoking and exploding in the rainstorm like a sodden Roman candle. They would say that what they saw was "terribly grand and magnificent." [51] They would say that "if the firing had not have been all on one side" they would have felt better.[52] They would recall that "from our elevated position we could see every Bomb & Rocket fall, & happily they generally fell short or went beyond the Fort." They would recollect the quick glimpse of a courier, a moving speck against the shell glare, and tell how Captain

Thompson's riders dashed "at full speed to & fro" on duty that was "perilous in the highest degree amidst a shower of Bombs & Rockets."

But they would think, too, of a verse not written till the night was over—a line, seldom sung, that would have a meaning for them that ít would not have for others. They would long remember waiting in the rain and staring, not toward Fort McHenry, but across the valley where the picket fires blazed and the dark beyond the fires was solid. "Where the foe's haughty host in dread silence reposes" would bring back the silence in the trenches and the silence of the unseen British army, and the waiting, and the slow dread.

All the British regiments were moving silently through the blacker darkness behind the screen of fires.[53] The 21st was deploying into a thin line of outposts, stretching across the whole front to conceal the disappearance of the army.[54] A detachment, probably not more than a battalion strong, was marching toward the left flank.[55] Brooke, as yet uncertain of the fleet's co-operation, was preparing a diversion of his own—a feigned attack with heavy firing to distract the enemy's attention.[56] A small outguard held its post near Surrey.[57] All the other troops were slogging through the muddy fields, converging toward the right flank of the bivouac area to join the storming column.[58]

The attack was forming along the Philadelphia road.[59] Its spearhead was the 85th, the old reliables who led the way at Bladensburg and North Point. Behind them was the naval brigade.[60] When the 85th broke through the enemy's first line, the sailors would know how to deal with other sailors in the Yankee batteries: the clearing of the redoubts would be boarding-party work, familiar. It would also be a settling of old scores. The guns emplaced to guard the turnpike and the Sparrow's Point road were manned by seamen of the *Guerriere* and *Erie*. And *Guerriere's* marines were in the trenches to support them.[61]

The Fourth Foot formed behind the naval brigade. The last regiment in colmun was Brooke's own, the 44th. Sailors and infantry, the storming column was a compact mass of some three thousand men—a battering ram three times as heavy as the one Brooke drove against the center of John Stricker's line. A single regiment, the 21st, had formed the assault column that charged across a half mile of open ground in daylight under the fire of Montgomery's guns and Sadtler's Yeagers at the log house, to overwhelm the battery and break the left flank of Joe Sterrett's regiment. Now Brooke was using three regiments and a thousand seamen as a ram to break Smith's center.

His plan of attack was simple. It would begin with the diversion on the left, a half mile to the south. He would give the feint a little time to make an impression on the Yankees with its deliberate

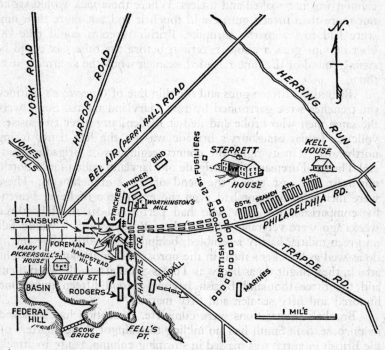

BROOKE'S ORDER OF ATTACK, night of September 13-14.

commotion and its rapid firing and then send the real attack in. There would be no firing on the right. The storming column would go forward "silently and with the bayonet" to penetrate the works.[62] "Having overcome all opposition" in the breach it made, it was to "wheel up upon the summit of the ridge, to remain stationary until dawn, and then, taking the whole of the works in flank, to carry them one by one in detail." It was to be essentially the form of attack that would seem new and terrible when it was used a century and a quarter later—the German army's "wedge and kessel" tactics.

Darkness had concealed Brooke's concentration; wind and rain had smothered the sound of his marching columns. Dark and storm should cover the advance until it struck the pickets. The Yankee gunners might have time to fire once—if the priming in their cannon was not soaked and useless. Where the attack would strike, not more than fifteen guns could touch it and not more than nine were laid to sweep the turnpike. British veterans could take the blast of nine guns without faltering; before the other six could be swung round or the nine reloaded, seamen would be swarming over them.

Behind the fifteen guns and the thin line of *Guerriere's* marines, the trenches were garrisoned by raw Maryland militia. Some were the same men who broke and fled at Bladensburg after two useless volleys: Tobias Stansbury's brigade was on the left flank, facing northward.[63] On its right, the county regiments of Brigadier General Thomas Foreman's first brigade of Maryland militia faced north, northeast and east round the bend of the entrenchments. These were men who had not had even the experience of being beaten; by comparison, the men who had performed so shabbily three weeks ago were veterans. The shock of Brooke's attack would fall on green militia, hastily assembled; behind breastworks, they might do as well as Stricker's men; in the uproar and confusion of a night attack, they might do as badly as Tobias Stansbury's. Between them and the three thousand British bayonets stood fifteen guns, one hundred and fifty seamen and fifty marines.[64]

Brooke's preparations were complete. Deception had achieved its purpose. Sam Smith had no inkling that almost three quarters of the British infantry was massed in storming column, ready to attack him.[65] Surprise was at least a possibility. But Brooke waited. He had asked for the co-operation of the fleet; no answer had yet come from Cochrane; he did not intend to move without it. The rain lashed the waiting column, drenched men shivered in the cold wind.[66] The bombardment matched the night with its spasmodic growling, like dull, distant thunder. Brooke's staff fidgeted and wondered. Precious time was being lost; delay risked discovery. Miles of hostile country lay between the army and the river. A courier from Cochrane might have been picked up by "wandering parties of the enemy."[67] Brooke's own concern became anxiety.

He sent off a mounted officer to find his way down to the shore beyond the Yankee lines and try to reach the fleet.[68]

The officer was lucky, by the story that gained credence in the army. "Having delayed a few minutes till the moon rising gave light enough to distinguish objects, he pushed forward" with a cocked pistol in his hand until he "heard the sound of voices through the splashing of the rain . . . listened . . . and discovered that they came from two American soldiers." Whether they were

"centinels" or stragglers he did not know, but he "called out to them to surrender." They ran. He "overtook one who instantly threw down his rifle . . . commanded him to lay hold of his thigh and guide him directly to the river, threatening, if he attempted to mislead him or betray him into the hands of the Americans that he would instantly blow out his brains." They "gained the brink of the river" in half an hour and there found "a party just landed from the squadron and preparing to make their way towards the camp" and "by them he was conducted to the Admiral, from whom he learnt that no effectual support could be given to the land force."

It is one more story whose origin appears to be the place from which so many soldier rumors come. Why "a party" presumably

on a mission from the vice-admiral to Brooke should waste time
going back to let the officer hear Cochrane repeat himself is not
readily apparent; Sir Alexander might not have been pleased. A
much more serious obstacle to credence is the "moon rising." The
moon did not rise that night; it was a new moon, and it set sixteen
minutes after the sun did.[69]

There is no reason to doubt, however, that Brooke sent an
officer to "open a communication." Under the circumstances, it
would be surprising if he had not done so. But whether his one-man
liaison expedition saw the admiral and what he "learnt" is not important. The fact, obvious enough from Brooke's own actions, is
that sometime before eleven o'clock,[70] somehow, the commander
of the army was informed that Cochrane had made certain necessary changes in his plan of battle. He knew that there would not be
an attack on Rodgers's bastion. He knew that there would be an
alternative diversion. And he also knew the signal that would tell
him the diversion was beginning—the mortar ships would suddenly
increase their rate of fire.[71] For half an hour or more, the fire would
be intense. Then it would cease, and Brooke would know that the
assault boats were so close to shore that shells from their own ships
might hit them or the glare of shell bursts, lighting up the river,
disclose them to the Americans and prevent surprise.

The army waited. "About eleven o'clock" the signal came.
"The bomb-vessels seemed to renew their fire with redoubled
energy."

A division of armed boats, manned by seamen and marines, was
pulling up the river toward McHenry through the blinding rainstorm.[72] A brave and efficient officer was in command—Charles
Napier of *Euryalus*.[73] He was the captain who had helped James
Alexander Gordon break the Potomac trap by laying his light
frigate alongside David Porter's battery and anchoring her there,
within musket shot, to slug it out with eighteen-pounders against
earthworks. The force he was leading was as motley as the string
of captured ships that he had helped to bring through the Potomac
gantlet. It was made up of at least twenty [74] barges, launches, gigs
and pinnaces, a rocket boat and, by the testimony of an American
battery commander who faced the attack, a "long schooner" pro-
pelled by sweeps and mounted with a gun as big as those in the
main battery of *Euryalus*.[75]

Napier's objective was to give the army the diversion that it
wanted. But "diversion" could mean much or little. It might be a

bluff—a quick feint and a quick withdrawal. It might also be a
desperate affair—a landing on an unreconnoitered shore, a blast of
fire from unseen batteries, a rush to storm them in self-preserva-
tion, hand-to-hand fighting in the darkness against overwhelming
numbers. Cochrane had not chosen Napier for nothing: the captain
of the *Euryalus* was a fighter. And he had, tonight, a mission that
was difficult as well as dangerous.

His orders were to find—or cut—a passage through the barrier
of sunken ships, get his miscellaneous flotilla past it, and effect a

landing on the shore behind McHenry.[76] For the last mile and a half
of his approach, his boats would be within range of the converging
fire of the McHenry batteries, the Lazaretto and the Yankee gunboats. The line of hulks was enfiladed by the fort's guns, and the
Lazaretto and the barges could reach most of it with cross fire.
What he would face when he had passed the barrier, he did not
know. There was at least one battery in Ferry Branch; there might
be more, with infantry in close support. The cove could be a trap
much worse than the Potomac. He might get in, by stealth. But he
might not get out.

Two batteries were waiting for him in the Ferry Branch. A substantial earthwork called Fort Covington had been laid out by Decius Wadsworth "a little below Spring Gardens" [77] at the mouth of Ridgely's Cove. Its guns not only guarded the boom across the entrance to the cove but also covered the narrow mouth of the Patapsco River. It was garrisoned by eighty seamen of the *Guerriere* commanded by her third lieutenant, Newcomb.[78] A quarter of a mile north, on an indentation of the Ferry Branch shore, a new breastwork had been thrown up and named for Captain Babcock, the weary-legged superintendent of "the works" who had applied to the Committee of Vigilance and Safety for a horse and got it.

Fort Babcock was a mud wall four feet high,[79] with platforms behind it for six guns but with no pretense of protection for the gunners against either shells or weather. If the term "fort" gave it undue dignity, it nevertheless was an important part of the chain of defenses: its battery could enfilade the shore of Ferry Branch in two directions: any attempt to take McHenry from the rear by an amphibious assault must reckon with Fort Babcock. "Open and exposed" as it was, the mudbank fort had one thing that Fort McHenry lacked—a bombproof magazine. The magazine was "composed of a hole dug in the side of a hill" some twenty yards behind the guns,[80] but it was safe from everything except a shellburst in its narrow entrance. The garrison was fifty veteran flotillamen,[81] most of whom had helped smash British barge attacks in the Patuxent and had fought with Barney in his last stand on the road to Washington.[82] The commanding officer was John A. Webster, sailing master, whose proud record included "all the engagements with Commodore Barney."

He had been the third lieutenant of Josh Barney's famous *Rossie*. He had fought with rowboats against British frigates. His horse had been killed under him at Bladensburg. John Webster was the man who summed up that battle by remarking, after a musket ball went through his hat and knocked it off, that he "did not take time" to pick it up. He had lost his hat that day, but not his head. As Winder's bewildered and disintegrating army fled through Washington, it passed four eighteen-pounder field guns standing deserted in the street in front of the capitol.[83] Nobody from the general down had time to bother about saving the field guns—not even the kind of guns that had been more useful, that afternoon, than any general present. With one petty officer, John Frazier by name,

Webster "ran down" to the navy yard, found eight harnessed horses there and helped himself, hitched them to the cannon and marched off, a two-man battery. In front of the presidential mansion he found still another gun abandoned. He "attached that to the others and continued on," spiking one piece when it broke down, collecting survivors of the flotilla until he had a force of fifty, and arriving at Montgomery Court House with the only heavy artillery left in Winder's army. The militia showed their gratitude at once. They immobilized the precious battery by stealing all eight horses.

Webster was not done with trouble. But he was a calm man. It was raining "quite fast" when the rapid firing of the bomb ships tautened the alertness of the Babcock garrison. Webster ordered his guns "double shotted with 18-pound balls and grape shot." [84] Then he spread a blanket on the breastwork and lay down in the rain to rest until the enemy got around to disturbing him. Charles Napier, frigate captain, and John Webster, sailing master, were a good match.

A little before midnight [85] the bombardment ceased abruptly. After almost eighteen hours of firing, the silence was unnatural, unreal, impossible. Webster sat up on his puddled blanket, listening. Presently he thought he could make out "a splashing in the water." It was hard to be sure, in that torrential downpour. But the faint, straining sough of muffled oars was different from the sough of rain across the sodden parapet; he heard it now and recognized it. "Very soon afterwards" he could "discern small gleaming lights in different places." Some were higher up the branch "next to Fort Covington" but some were very close.

Charles Napier was living up to his fine reputation. He had brought his boats two miles upriver past the Lazaretto and the gunboats, found a practicable gap in the barrier of hulks, and brought part of his force through undetected. But eleven of his boats had gone astray. [86] They had vanished in the rainy darkness before he reached the barrier. Napier had searched and waited for them as long as he dared, but now he was delivering his attack with less than half his strength. To concentrate what force he had left, he was risking discovery and destruction by ordering his barges to show guiding lights. [87] Skill and courage almost won the gamble. In spite of storm and darkness and strange currents, he was closing in unerringly upon both of the batteries. The barges pulling for Fort Babcock were "not more than two hundred yards off" when Webster and his men detected them.

A less experienced or more easily excitable officer might have blundered in his eagerness to open fire. John Webster took no chances with wet priming powder; he took time instead. A glow of linstock matches in the gun embrasures or the tramp of feet on timbered platforms would tell the attacking force that it had been discovered; the assault boats would come with a rush, and guns that misfired could not stop them. His disciplined flotillamen stood motionless and silent as he climbed astride each gun, hunching his body over the vent to shield it from the rain while he looked at the priming. The aprons—eight-pound lead plates tied across the vents with two eighteen-foot strings of white marlin [88]—had kept the powder dry; every gun was ready. Webster aimed each piece himself and then stood back. *Fire . . . !* The six guns exploded like a broadside. For a second the embrasures stood out in the red glare, sleek and black, with mud crumbling down their sides and the rain water streaming in a shiny patterning of gullied rivulets. Then the dark snatched them back.

Webster had touched off the battle.[89] The brief glimpse of his flame-lighted mud wall gave the British crews a target. The men at the oars ceased rowing. Flashes darted from the bow guns, and their muzzle flare spread sudden pools of red light on the water, with the prows of barges in them. Webster saw the boats "distinctly . . . by the explosion of their cannon." Not all of them were ships' boats: one was "a long schooner." She was being worked by sweeps and she was mounted with an eighteen-pounder gun that "should have done much execution." But she was firing high. Her shot were whistling overhead and going *thuck*-waa-at in the cut bank of the hill behind the battery. Webster's guns were doing better: he could hear the crash of round shot striking British barges and his men believed that they "could hear the shrieks" of wounded.[90]

The battery at Covington came into action. The cannon on the bastions at McHenry opened. Napier's rocket boat slashed streaks of fire across the cove.[91] The sheaves of rockets arching up from *Erebus* far down the river laced the night like tracers. The shells of the bomb ships fell in clusters and the clusters now were coming close together. Whetstone shuddered as they ripped themselves to pieces. This was *Terror*, this was *Devastation*. This was *Meteor* by night, shaking the earth, exploding, burning, stinking with hot gases. This was *Erebus*, the darkness between earth and Hades, with the fires of Hades glowing. *Aetna* and *Volcano* had

transferred themselves to Whetstone. Great belches of fire-reddened
smoke shot up, spread as they darkened, and the next burst blew
the thick cloud open like a crater. Hot fragments rattled on the
barrack roofs and cracked against the brick walls—stones and debris
from a crater in eruption. Water spouts sprang from the river in
white, fiery-hearted fountains, hidden instantly by darkness while
they stood erect. You never saw them fall. You only heard the
water hissing, sometimes, and collapsing; but not often, there were
only seconds when no gun was firing and no mortar shell exploding.

In Baltimore the windows rattled. Houses shook on their foun-
dations.[92] Men who watched "the heavens lighted up with flame"
and felt the trembling of the solid earth believed that "never . . .
from the time of the invention of cannon" had so many guns been
firing "with so rapid succession." [93]

Webster's fellow officers of the flotilla were trying hard to
help him. Frazier at the Lazaretto swung his three guns to fire past
the tip of Whetstone; the fight in the Ferry Branch was out of
range but he could try to pen the British up there, he could sweep
the shore above McHenry and perhaps smash landing parties before
they could get a foothold. Rutter turned his barges: more flotilla
guns began to beat the water into foam behind the British boats and
rake the line of hulks to cut off Napier's retreat.

But Napier was not retreating. He was fighting. He was half
surrounded, he was in the curve and on the barb of a great fishhook
of gun flashes, with the enfiladed barrier of hulks behind him. But
he was fighting stubbornly and shrewdly, firing, shifting his boats
quickly, trying to baffle the American gunpointers. He was trying
hard to silence Covington and Babcock, but it was too big a task
for nine boat guns. He was angry and chagrined. The rockets had
set something on the shore afire: he could see no sign of troops
there, and no other batteries: Fort McHenry was defended from
the rear by only these two earthworks. His thoughts scorched the
boat crews who had gone astray. There . . . and there . . . and *there!*
Confound them! He could have landed "with ease" on "several
parts" of the cove shore if he had had his whole force with him.[94]
But the crews he had were probably outnumbered by the gunners
in the two mud forts,[95] and surely there were infantry supports not
far away. An attempt at landing, he decided, could accomplish
nothing worth the lives that it would cost.

Yet he fought on. While he stayed there, drawing the fire of
thirty, forty, perhaps fifty guns, he was carrying out his mission.

And the Yankees were co-operating nobly: the cannonade was making his diversion sound convincing. To the militia army in its trenches, this must sound like a pitched battle. The longer he could hold on, the more chance there was that the Americans would think this was a real attempt to break into the city or to storm the star fort from the rear. Armistead himself believed that this was an attack in earnest—an attempt to land "twelve hundred and fifty picked men with scaling ladders" to assault McHenry.[96] Rodgers, too, believed that it was serious.[97] The American guns "kept up a continued blaze for nearly two hours."

The man who would not be convinced was Arthur Brooke. "From midnight . . . up to the hour of two" he listened and did nothing. "That all things went not prosperously was manifest enough."[98] There was too much firing; it was lasting too long. It slackened: Napier was breaking off the fight. Blue rockets soared up: Napier was signaling the fleet that he was pulling back into the zone of shell bursts.[99] The mortar ships and *Erebus* ceased fire, but the cannonading from the shore burst out again as furious as ever: the boats were slipping through the barrier of hulks to run the gantlet of converging fire.

One by one, the batteries went silent. Napier was gone, and so was Brooke's chance—or at least he thought so, and thereby destroyed whatever chance he had. To the "inexpressible astonishment"[100] of the troops, he gave the order to abandon the attack and fall back. The outpost line pushed forward to conceal withdrawal.[101] The flank guards were called in.[102] The storming column faced about. Toward three o'clock,[103] behind a screen of blazing outpost fires[104] and covered by "the extreme darkness and a continued rain,[105] the retreat began.

The troops marched to the dull throbbing of the mortars and the sullen rumble of the bombshells again falling on McHenry. An hour before dawn, the last pickets followed the defeated army. The adjective "defeated" is used deliberately. The invasion had been "not merely an empty, but, considering what had been lost by it, a highly disastrous 'demonstration.' "[106] The conclusion is not biased. It is not American, but British.

Brooke's planned attack might have succeeded without Cochrane's help and without Napier's diversion. If it had succeeded, the fleet's failure would have been of no importance. Fort McHenry would have been of no importance. The harbor batteries probably could have held out for days against bombardment from the river.

They might even have held out against a land attack; although, with Smith's militia routed and his heavy batteries on Loudenslager's taken, Brooke almost certainly could have overpowered McHenry by storm or hauled up captured guns to cover a more leisurely attack. But there would have been no need to take the fort. The whole object of the expedition was destruction of the port of Baltimore—the "pirates' nest"—with its new men-of-war, its merchant fleet and its "immense quantities of naval stores." [107] Success in the night attack would have exposed them all. But Brooke lacked the confidence to attempt it.

He was not his own man. His hands had been tied by the original decision to land on North Point, where Sam Smith was so sure that the attack would come. If Brooke possessed initiative and ingenuity, he had no opportunity to use them. Cochrane, Ross and Cockburn had not seen the weakness of the city, the south and southwest sides unfortified and lacking natural defenses; their original conception had committed them to an offensive at the strongest, not the weakest places. Now Brooke's mind, too, was tied to Cochrane's ships. When they failed, his confidence in his troops and in himself failed. He dared not use the only chance he had.

His army was not beaten. It was driven from the field by one man. It was defeated by the habit of thought on which Sam Smith had based his whole defense—the British habit of believing in the fleet.

27

BY THE DAWN'S EARLY LIGHT

. . . THE TROOPS IN THE LOUDEN-
slager trenches saw the fields in front of them deserted. Camp fires
still burned wanly. Surrey's broken windows were black holes behind the pale loom of its pillars. The mortar ships still lay at anchor
in the river and their shells still crunched at Fort McHenry. But
the British troops had vanished.

Sam Smith "consented" to immediate pursuit.[1] Winder took
the North Point road with the Virginia brigade and Bird's dragoons.
Major Randall hurried out the Trappe road with his Pennsylvania
riflemen and the Maryland cavalry.[2] To the weary men who made
the march, the effort to catch Brooke's retreating column was a

vigorous pursuit. To Sam Smith it was a formality—a conventional, expected, mildly useful gesture.

Its usefulness was psychological, not military. The unusual wording of Sam Smith's report suggests that he regarded the operation as superfluous or tactically unwise and, in either case, unlikely to achieve results. It even suggests that the command went to Winder as a harmless poultice for his injured feelings. But pursuit was a psychological necessity. Failure to follow the retiring enemy would damp the spirits of his already damp militia and give every rear-rank strategist a theme for oratory. The officers who had been so hot last night for an attack upon the British bivouac were even hotter now for a pell-mell chase by the whole army. Sam Smith, soldier, did not choose to risk the army.

He could not be certain that the enemy was abandoning completely the attempt to take the city. The retreat might be a ruse to draw him out of the entrenchments. It might also be the first move of a new attack—a shifting of the army to the south side of the river. The fleet showed no intention of withdrawing. The attack in Ferry Branch had failed—as an attack—but it might have been a vigorous reconnaissance; it showed, at least, an inclination to probe other sectors of the town's defenses. Armistead believed that it had been intended as an escalade. Rodgers believed that there had been two boat attacks, not one; he had rushed Randall's riflemen to beat off barges which he thought were trying to land men to storm Lieutenant Frazier's three-gun battery at the Lazaretto.[3]

In those circumstances Sam Smith, general, would not commit his whole force to a pursuit that would deprive him of his two prime advantages—his heavy batteries and trenches for his inexperienced militia. That might be precisely the objective of the enemy's maneuver. An all-out pursuit by the Americans would reverse the situation. It would give the enemy commander a chance to select his own position, to make full use of his better-disciplined and more skillful troops on open ground, and perhaps to fight behind entrenchments. Five thousand men could quickly turn the unfinished ditch across North Point, from Humphrey's Creek to the Back River, into a stout line of breastworks.

But Sam Smith, practical psychologist, would do what seemed practicable to keep the spirits of his men up and the undue enthusiasms of his staff down. He "consented" to pursuit by a limited force. Sam Smith, politician, would do what seemed useful to improve the morale and the unity of his hodgepodge army. Some thousands of his men had come from other states; their pride was sensitive; their officers were trigger-quick to notice or imagine slights. Therefore to the Virginians and the Pennsylvanians went the honor and excitement of pursuing the retreating British.

If Smith had believed that a serious blow was desirable and feasible, it is unlikely that he would have picked Will Winder to deliver it. Winder had shown neither taste nor talent for close, stubborn fighting. No question of his personal courage was involved; he simply had not shown the toughness of mind necessary to send other men into desperate action. It is also unlikely that Smith would have chosen the untried Virginia brigade. He probably would have turned again to Stricker and the Baltimore brigade. The city regiments had done the army's only fighting, but they were no more exhausted than the others; the whole force had been under arms for three nights under miserable conditions. Stricker himself was sure that his brigade was not only ready for another fight but would go into it with increased confidence. It was Sam Smith's surest weapon, but he did not choose to use it.

The pursuit was as ineffectual as he expected it to be. The tired troops moved slowly. The enemy had a three-hour start. Winder found it "impracticable to do anything more than pick up a few stragglers." [4]

On the deck of the cartel ship at anchor in the river, Francis Key was scribbling earnestly on the back of a letter "which he happened to have in his pocket." [5] He and Mr. Skinner had been up all night "watching every shell, from the moment it was fired, until it fell, listening with breathless interest to hear if an explosion followed." When only the bomb ships were firing, they could pick out the separate explosions; but that they could do so when McHenry and the Water Battery, the Lazaretto and the gunboats, Napier's barges and Fort Covington and Webster's guns were all in action is, to put it mildly, doubtful.

"While the bombardment continued, it was sufficient proof that the fort had not surrendered. But it suddenly ceased some time before day; and as they had no communication with any of the enemy's ships, they did not know whether the fort had surrendered, or the attack upon it been abandoned. They paced the deck for the residue of the night in painful suspense, watching with intense anxiety for the return of day, and looking every few minutes at their watches, to see how long they must wait for it; and as soon as it dawned, and before it was light enough to see objects at a distance, their glasses were turned to the fort, uncertain whether they should see there the Stars and Stripes, or the flag of the enemy. At length the light came, and they saw that 'our flag was still there.' "

Even a chief justice of the United States Supreme Court may fall into error. Roger Brooke Taney, author of the quoted passage, stands reversed by the identical testimony of both of the contending parties in the case.

No doubt Francis Scott Key paced the deck all night. But his intense anxiety was not caused by the cessation of the battle. He was not wondering whether Fort McHenry had surrendered. He knew that the flag above it was the Stars and Stripes and not the British ensign. For the bombardment had not ended "some time before day." The bomb ships were still battering away at Whetstone when the first "few faint streaks of dawn" [6] sent Brooke's rearguard hurrying up the Philadelphia road. They were still bombarding when the sun came over the horizon. And they kept on firing through at least an hour of daylight. It was seven o'clock when they were finally "called off." [7] The sun had been up for an hour and thirteen minutes.[8]

"As the day advanced" Mr. Key and his companion "discovered, from the movements of the boats between the shore and the fleet, that the troops had been roughly handled, and that many wounded men were carried to the ships. At length he was informed that the attack on Baltimore had failed, and the British army was reembarking, and that he and Mr. Skinner, and Dr. Beanes would be permitted to leave them, and go where they pleased, as soon as the troops were on board, and the fleet ready to sail."

The generally accepted supposition is that Key dashed off the words of "The Star-Spangled Banner" in a rush of relief and joy and patriotic fervor in the early light of dawn and that they appeared in print under that title the next morning. For it is "the morning of September 15 when Samuel Sands, the apprentice, is popularly supposed to have set the poem as a broadside." [9]

The fact is that the title under which Key's poem first appeared was the matter of fact "Defence of Fort M'Henry." And the date is doubtful.

The fact is that the British army did not finish its re-embarkation until after noon on September 15th. Sam Smith said that "the enemy commenced his embarkation that evening [Wednesday, the 14th] and completed it the next day at one o'clock." [10] Lieutenant

Gleig, who was with the rear guard, said that it was considerably later when the last troops cleared the shore. "The evening was as yet very little advanced," he said, "when the whole army, with all its material and stores, found itself again lodged on board of ship." [11] Roger Taney said that Key told him he "commenced" the verses on the deck of the cartel ship "in the fervor of the moment, when he saw the enemy hastily retreating to their ships, and looked at the flag he had watched for so anxiously as the morning opened; that he had written some lines, or brief notes that would aid him in calling them to mind, upon the back of a letter which he happened to have in his pocket; and for some of the lines, as he proceeded, he was obliged to rely altogether on his memory; and that he finished it in the boat on his way to the shore, and wrote it out as it now stands, at the hotel, on the night he reached Baltimore, and immediately after he arrived." If Key was not permitted to depart until "the troops were on board, and the fleet ready to sail," it was the evening of the 15th when the cartel brought him at last to the dock at Baltimore. If he began to write his verses before seven o'clock on the morning of the 14th, the nation's anthem was not born in the aftermath of certain victory; it was born while the mortar bombs were still "bursting in air" and the American commanders did not yet know that the battle had been won and the attack abandoned.

It was nine o'clock before the British ships got under weigh and the retreat of the naval force began.[12] It was after noon when the last shots were fired.[13] The fighting ended, as it had begun, on land. The last blood was shed on the same ground where the first was spilled in Major Heath's fight, beside the lane and near the patch of woods where Ross was killed.[14]

While Key was waiting anxiously for sunrise, Brooke's retreating column had halted and was resting after marching three miles.[15] While the bombardment was still thundering across the river, the rear guard caught up;[16] by the time pursuit began, the army was again in motion. It was making the same early-morning march that Stricker's troops had made two days ago. The day was pleasant; the storm of wind and rain had "died away"; the road was good and "the late moisture rendered it better than it had been before, by hardening it."[17] But the heat increased. By eleven o'clock, when the army halted once more on the battlefield, the sun was beating down upon it "somewhat powerfully" and the bodies strewn along

the rail fence and across the stubble "were beginning to emit an odour."

The bodies had not been stripped like those at Bladensburg. They lay as they had fallen. "Both the sight and smell were too familiar to affect" the veteran Invincibles very deeply,[18] but there was one sight that struck the officers as curious. The bodies of several Americans hung lifeless in the branches of the oak trees. "They had been riflemen who chose, during the battle, to fix themselves in these elevated situations, for the combined purposes of securing a good aim, and avoiding danger. Whatever might be their success in the first of these designs, in the last they failed; for [the British infantry] discovered them and, considering the thing as unfair, refused to give them quarter, and shot them on their perches." [19]

The halt lasted for an hour while the troops ate their rations and sorted out the blankets they had cast aside the day before. Toward noon the column formed again. It was "passing the wood" where Ross fell dying from his saddle when the rear guard's bugle spluttered an alarm and musket shots slammed futilely against the smother of the thickets. They were futile also against the sudden rush of cavalry that burst around "an angle of the road." [20] Bird's United States dragoons had overtaken the retreating army. [21] The rear files had time to fire only "a couple of muskets" before the horsemen were upon them with their sabers swinging. [22] The North British Fusiliers who formed the rear guard threw themselves into the woods. [23] The charge spent itself on the empty lane, recoiled, and clattered back. The army halted. To right and left, the regiments wheeled into line. Up the road at full speed came a field gun and a howitzer to support the Fusiliers. [24]

The dragoons were re-forming. There were only "twenty or thirty" of them. [25] They had outridden the militia cavalry; Randall's weary riflemen were far behind; Winder's plodding column was still miles away. But the handful of regulars did what they could to pin Brooke's army down. They charged again, and the guns slashed at them with canister. The charge broke against the abatis of underbrush. "One or two" of the dragoons attempted "with great bravery" to force their horses through the thickets and their sabers cut down two men in the British firing line. [26]

There were empty saddles when the cavalry turned back. [27] There were dragoons on foot, running. There were dead and dying horses in the lane behind them. To try again was hopeless, in that canister-swept road. But Bird had one tough and stubborn sergeant and he tried again. Only three men followed Sergeant Keller, but he led them with a reckless courage. [28] At half-canister distance, the two guns blazed at them. But they lived. They plunged into the thickets, broke the rear guard's line and got behind it, scattered it with hacking sabers, and rode back through the woods with six Fusiliers as prisoners.[29] In a campaign in which the cavalry had worn itself out running errands, some useful and some silly, Sergeant Keller and his three light dragoons had won at least the comfort of citation in division orders for "bold and intrepid" action.

The campaign was over. More than Keller and a few dragoons were needed to bluff Brooke into thinking that this was a serious pursuit. Brooke indeed prepared to fight "a general action" but, after waiting to see whether infantry was following the reckless cavalry, he ordered the retreat resumed behind a "recognizance" screen of two guns and an additional infantry battalion. He camped that night behind the unfinished line of trenches[30] and at 9 A.M. on the 15th the column reached the beach where it had landed. Boats were waiting; gun brigs covered the re-embarkation. The artillery went off first. Then "brigade after brigade fell back to the water's edge." But this was no victorious army returning to its ships. There was "no hearty cheering" from the crowds of sailors. "On the contrary, a solemn silence prevailed . . . and even the congratulations on the safe return of their individual acquaintances were accompanied by an expression of deep sorrow for the loss of General Ross, and the profitless issue of the inroad."[31] There was no attempt at self-deception. A British fleet and army were retreating. This had been a costly failure. It had been defeat.

Sam Smith had won, but he did not know it until late that afternoon when a vidette came back from North Point with the certain news that the boats were taking off the last troops of the British rear guard. Even then he would not let himself believe it until, one by one, the ships began to spread their canvas and stand down the bay. He had been preparing to beat off a new attack, and he had had proof of his weakness if the enemy forced him to fight outside his batteries and trenches. He had begun to shift troops to the south side of the city on the night of the 14th, withdrawing them from the strongest part of the defenses—the right of the fortified works near Rodgers's bastion. What happened had been ample evidence that he was right when he refused, the evening of the 13th, to order a night attack upon the British bivouac.

First Lieutenant Bartgis of the Frederick volunteers set down the story in his diary:

"Received orders to strike our tents and take up the line of march to a hill near the Magazine and near Forts Covington and Patapsco, and on the road to Fort McHenry, as it was understood (or rumored) that the enemy might possibly attempt a landing somewhere at that point to attack the town. The night was cold, and raining lightly, made it very disagreeable, but the few days and nights previous, of fatigue and want of rest, made the inclemency of the weather of but little object. . . . There was an unfortunate incident happened, during our march this night. . . . After we struck our tents and joined the Regiment, the whole was moved off for the new position we were to occupy that night. On the march, as our company had just passed the Eastern bridge in Baltimore street, a great confusion was discovered in front of us—the night was very dark, and until lights were placed at the windows, we could not discover what position we occupied or how to dispose of ourselves, therefore halted to await the issue.

"The 3d Regiment, in front of us, became confused in consequence of a team of horses approaching them in full drive, were ordered to file out to the right and left to let the wagon pass; when, some of the officers and men, in that and our regiment, becoming alarmed, not knowing what was meant by it, while the women, who took alarm from the confusion in the street, came running out of their houses crying the British! the British! the British! and officers and men whom fear had operated on, *supposing* it to be an attack from the British took to their heels for safety.

"All the companies to the right and some on the left of us broke, but our company, not knowing and not caring, what was the matter, stood the shock with firmness and not a man moved from the ranks, with the intention of leaving them . . . In the retreat, as we call this disgraceful affair, some lost their muskets, some their knapsacks and some their bayonets; and if our company had been permitted, they would have bayonetted many and shot others, it was with difficulty the officers could restrain the men— one Captain got his thigh broke and sixteen others were so severely wounded that they were sent to the Hospital—a number of others were injured slightly.

"The 3d Regiment soon had its first company formed, but many of its men never returned, and as they had no orders to strike their tents, they were left standing, and a guard placed over them for the night, to which place some of the deserters fled and reported that the enemy had attacked the whole line on *Horseback* and they were flying in all directions—as it was, some were never seen in Camp afterwards."

The panic might afford some comfort to the county regiments

that fled at Bladensburg. It gave none to Sam Smith, waiting hourly for some indication of a new offensive. He was busy with a hundred details—requisitions for "Hacks or other Carriages" to bring in the wounded from John Stricker's battle and for details of civilians to provide for the "internment" of the dead; with inquiries to Armistead concerning a need for more ships to be sunk in the barricades of hulks; with shifting laborers from "the Fortifications at Camplook-out" to help strengthen Fort McHenry. There was the matter of a deputy commissary who was absent from his duty. There was a dispatch to be sent off to Washington:

H. Quarters, Hampstead-Hill
Balt., Sept. 14, 1814—10 a.m.

Sir—I have the honor of informing you, that the enemy, after an unsuccessful attempt both by land and water, on this place, appear to be retiring.

We have a force hanging on their rear—I shall give you further particulars in the course of the day.

I have the honor to be, your obedient servant,

S. Smith, Major General Commanding

P.S. The enemy's vessels in the Patapsco are all under way going down the river. I have good reason to believe that General Ross is mortally wounded.

Honorable James Monroe, acting Secretary of War.

Particulars came slowly. There were only driblets coming back that day and the next day from Will Winder's troops moving cautiously and slowly in the rear of the retreating British. The enemy had burned the century-old homestead of the Todds.[32] At Lodge Farm, the old home of the Eagers, the wall had been adorned with a Union Jack design cut out with bayonets. The home of Judge Jones near Welshman's Creek had been used as a hospital, and the "featherbeds had been ripped up and the cases used for oat bags and dragged on sledges to the ships." The Stewart house had been looted. And Colonel Joe Sterrett, his boots crunching on the broken window glass that strewed the floors of Surrey, had found bureaus broken open, bedding plundered, and his wine vault empty. He had also found a note, scrawled jovially on the back of a piece of paper on which an epitaph for Mrs. Sterrett's father had been written. The note, lying on the sideboard, said: "Captains Brown, Wilcox and M'Namara, of the Fifty-third Regiment, Royal Marines, have received every thing they could desire at this house, notwithstanding it was received at the hands of the butler, and in the absence of the colonel." [33]

The particulars were trifling, but they were an earnest of what Baltimore had been spared—if, indeed, it had been spared. It was evening of the 15th before Sam Smith felt justified in telling James Monroe that the attack apparently had been abandoned. His dispatch began with an apology:

> Headquarters, Baltimore, 15th September, 1814.
>
> Sir—I have been so incessantly occupied, that it has been impossible for me to convey to you the information respecting the enemy, which it would have been proper for you to have received from me. A detailed statement will be forwarded as soon as it can be made out; in the mean time, I have the pleasure to inform you that the enemy embarked their rear guard about 1 o'clock, and that their ships, a few excepted, are out of the river; their destination unknown.
>
> I have the honor to be, your obedient servant,
> Samuel Smith, Major General Com'g.

If the British had exacted literal obedience to the conditions they imposed upon the cartel ship, Francis Scott Key was then sitting in his hotel room, writing out his poem from the rough draft on the back of the letter he had happened to have in his pocket. Several days later he told his brother-in-law that "on the next morning he took it to Judge Nicholson, to ask him what he thought of it, that he was so much pleased with it, that he immediately sent it to a printer, and directed copies to be struck off in hand-bill form." [34]

Captain-Judge Nicholson was one man who was certain to be pleased. He and Key had married sisters, but the family relationship was the smallest of his reasons for delight in these sonorous lines. He had seen "the rockets' red glare" leaping toward him. He had felt the plank floors of the bastions shudder to the shock of "the bombs bursting in air." He had lived this poem. He and his militia Fencibles had endured that "constant and tremendous shower of shells" for twenty-five hours. One of his guns had taken a direct hit. Two men of his loved company were dead and six were wounded; two of them might die. He "had been relieved from duty, and returned to his family only the night before Mr. Key showed him the song." And "you may easily imagine," Taney said, "the feelings with which, at such a moment, he read it, and gave it to the public."

Judge Nicholson made one change—an addition.[35] He was a "musician and something of a poet" and he "no doubt took but a few minutes to see that the lines could be sung" to the music of an air long popular "and, in all haste to give the lines as a song to the public, he thus marked it." [36] The air was "To Anacreon in Heaven."

The printing shop to which he sent the verses was the office of the Baltimore *American and Commercial Daily Advertiser.* The paper, along with all the other papers in the town, had suspended publication and "the editors, journeymen, and apprentices able to bear arms" [37] were with the troops. Thomas Murphy, one of the proprietors, had been with Captain Aisquith's Sharp Shooters [38]—the company in which young Dan Wells and his friend Henry Mc-Comas had marched out to die. Murphy had just come back to the shop when Nicholson's messenger arrived; the counting room was open for such business as there might be; but the only printer in the place was a "devil"—Samuel Sands, apprentice, fourteen years old.[39]

Sam Sands set Key's lines by hand, picking out the letters one by one, and struck off galley proofs.[40] Key's name was not on them. When the Baltimore *Patriot* helped itself, four days later, and published "Defence of Fort M'Henry" just below its masthead, it too omitted Key's name. The author was still anonymous the next day when Murphy's *American* got around to publishing the verses in its columns. It had been scooped on its own story—unless the galley-proof handbills that it issued may be counted as a wartime "extra." By the time his verses got into the papers, Key had left town.[41] Had he heard his song sung? No one knows.

No one knows, either, who first sang it, or where it was first sung. There are many legends. One that seems most plausible of all is that a Pennsylvania volunteer named Ferdinand Durang sang it "in front of the Holliday Street Theater" with twenty other soldiers.[42] The witness is his brother Charles, one of the twenty soldiers. They had missed the battle; they had come too late even to get a glimpse of the British topsails dwindling down the river. Charles Durang's story has one plausible, disarming detail: the Pennsylvania volunteers gathered in front of the theater for their "libating mornings" because there was a tavern next door and its juleps pleased them.[43]

The tavern occupied "a small frame one-story house" and was run by "a Colonel MacConkey." [44] Among its patrons were Leonard

Frailey, brigade major of the gallant City Brigade, Captain Ben Edes of the 27th, and a captain in the 39th, Tom Warner.[45] Mint juleps in the morning, a colonel for their host and, for their drinking companions, officers who had fought the British—small wonder that men who had missed all the excitement liked MacConkey's tavern. It was also a rendezvous for actors who played at the theater, and the

Durangs were actors.[46] Charles Durang's story has the ring of truth. But there is no proof.

Positive evidence of the singing of the nation's future anthem does not appear for thirty-five days after Francis Scott Key saw the Widow Pickersgill's flag flying over Fort McHenry by the dawn's early light of Wednesday, the 14th of September. In the meantime, on October 12th, the managers of the theater offered to the Committee of Vigilance and Safety "the profits of a night's performance . . . in aid of the fund for the defense of the City." Ferdinand

Durang, whose brother said he sang Key's song, was on the program. But he did not sing it that night: his performance was a "military hornpipe." [47] It was the next week before the Baltimore papers published advertisements of a play called *Count Benyowski* to be staged October 19th. The advertisements had a footnote:

> After the play, Mr. Harding will sing a much admired *New Song*, written by a gentleman of Maryland, in commemoration of the GALLANT DEFENSE OF FORT M'HENRY, called, THE STAR-SPANGLED BANNER.

And on November 12th an advertisement of "a brilliant military entertainment" announced that "The Star-Spangled Banner" would be sung "for the second time." [48] In two months, two performances. Key's song was not a hit. It was only unconquerable.

Not a marching song. Not a quick-time song. Not a song to sing on the road, but a song to beat in the heart. A route-march kind of song, slow and slogging and stubborn . . . a song to stay deep in your guts on the dusty roads, on the muddy roads, the long bone-aching roads where the infantry goes . . . a song written before the battle was over, before the ordeal was done.

Well, it was over in Baltimore now. The toasts had been drunk. The lines had been written, and sung to a borrowed tune. The dead men had been buried. The battle of Baltimore soon would be. Had it all been, indeed, an "incident of no importance"? Had the dead died in vain?

The impact of the news in a small town not far from Waterloo suggests the answer.

28

THE NEWS REACHES GHENT

Go back. It is August 24th again.
On the field of Bladensburg, the left wing of the American army
has collapsed in panic. It is a terrorized mob, running. The commanding general is making certain that the right wing will not
stand and fight, he is pulling it apart as fast as he can issue orders,
he is dragging the pieces away while Barney's sailors die beside their
guns. The president of the United States is a fugitive. In a few
hours, the victorious invading army will take possession of the
capital of the republic.

At the moment when Will Winder's paper army crumples and
is torn to pieces, five other unhappy Americans are sitting at a table
in a room in Ghent. They are crumpling sheets of paper, they are
tearing them to pieces. The table and the floor are littered with the
wads and pieces. But there is one paper that they neither tear nor
crumple. They would only like to.

The paper is an ultimatum.[1] Its terms are as humiliating and
disastrous as the rout that streams along the Georgetown road,
three thousand miles away.

The five men around the table are the American peace commissioners—Henry Clay, Jonathan Russell, Albert Gallatin, James
Bayard and John Quincy Adams.[2] For months they have been trying to find some way to end the war. One of them, John Adams,
has been trying for almost two years. Now they have come to the
end of hope. The document handed to them by his Majesty's commissioners presents two alternatives. If they reject it, the war will
go on and on. If they yield, they will bankrupt their country of
honor. They will also bankrupt its whole future.

Reduced to plan language and plain meanings, the terms are these:

1. Abandonment by the United States of its impudent and preposterous claim to immunity from search and seizure of its ships and impressment of its seamen.

2. Complete American disarmament, both naval and military, on the whole frontier of the Great Lakes—the dismantling of all United States forts and bases there, a pledge never to maintain an armed force on the shores or waters of the lakes or on any of the rivers that flow into them, and an acknowledgment of Great Britain's exclusive right to arm and garrison the frontier.

3. Surrender—for annexation by Great Britain—of the north half of Maine, the whole south bank of the St. Lawrence River from Plattsburg to Sackett's Harbor, the region around Fort Niagara, and the bastion island of Michilimackinack.

4. Agreement that the Mississippi shall be forever not an American but an Anglo-American river, with a guarantee of British rights of free navigation.

5. As a corollary to the internationalization of the Mississippi, the surrender of another large segment of the original territory of the United States—the region between Lake Superior, the Canadian border and the headwaters of the Mississippi.

6. Creation of an "independent" Indian state north of the Ohio River, as a permanent buffer between the United States and the possessions of Great Britain and as a permanent barrier against the growth of the upstart American republic.

It is this last astonishing demand that gives the British terms the nature of an ultimatum. It has been presented as a *sine qua non*. The Americans, "dumbfounded" and "enraged," [3] have been informed that until they yield on this point there can be no talk of peace.

The buffer state would be, in fact, a British protectorate. It would be a wedge driven between the United States and the vast region recently acquired by the Louisiana Purchase. It would be a constant source of danger, a constant threat of invasion; it would outflank the disarmed and helpless northern frontier; it would be a knife thrust deep into the vitals of the nation. His Majesty's ministers had even selected the boundary of the new buffer state, they had drawn the line across which the United States must never dare to step. That they had drawn it through the heart of the existing nation did not trouble them at all. That they had thereby amputated a large part of the republic, as established by the Treaty of Paris at the close of the First War of Independence, gave them no small satisfaction. Beyond the "Greeneville Line" [4] that they had chosen lay most of Ohio, Indiana, Michigan and Illinois. Beyond it lay the towns and farmsteads of a hundred thousand citizens of the United States.

The American commissioners asked a question: What is to become of those hundred thousand Americans?

The British commissioners had a quick and callous answer: Let them shift for themselves!

Disarmament. Dismemberment. Dishonor.

Between national emasculation and continued war, there could be but one decision. At the moment when the flames burst through the windows of the halls of Congress, and the fleeing president of the United States turned in his saddle to watch the glare above his burning capital, the American commissioners at Ghent were "sifting, erasing, patching and amending" their answer to the ultimatum. They were writing defiantly that the British terms would never be considered "till the people of the United States were ready to give up their liberty and their independence." [5]

They had not the smallest doubt as to the consequences of their answer: the war would go on. They had had fair warning as to the consequences of continuing the struggle. The *Times* of London had been frankly brutal: "Our demands may be couched in a single word,—Submission!"

The unpleasant facts were plainly visible to the Americans. The international situation had changed enormously since the war began in June of 1812. Then all Europe had been fighting. England had been straining every resource in the desperate struggle with Napoleon. The conquering French eagles had been sweeping on toward Moscow. The British troops in Spain had not yet become Wellington's Invincibles; they had been only Wellington's "scum of the earth," outnumbered and retreating.

Now everything was changed. The great Napoleon was in exile. Europe was at peace. The puny strength of the disUnited States confronted, alone, the whole might of the British Empire. And now Britain was undertaking to abate the American nuisance. Less than ten days after Napoleon's abdication, the London *Courier* had announced that twenty thousand of Wellington's victorious veterans would sail from France to settle the business of the United States. The Iron Duke himself was "quite sure that all the

American armies of which [he had] ever read would not beat out of a field of battle" the troops that were being sent against them.[6] The *Times*, with psychic prescience, reported that the Americans were "struck to the heart with terror for their impending punishment." It prayed devoutly

. . . oh may no false liberality, no mistaken lenity, no weak and cowardly policy, interpose to save them from the blow! Strike! chastise the savages, for such they are!

On the day the American commissioners prepared their answer to the British ultimatum, the punishment was no longer merely impending. Nothing had interposed to save the savages from the first blow. The American army defending its own capital had demonstrated its inability to "beat out of a field of battle" the smallest of the converging forces sent to administer chastisement. And the next blows were about to fall.

The operations of the British expeditionary forces had been worked out on a grand scale. They were intended to be overwhelming and decisive. In mid-June the London press was printing rumors heard "in the diplomatic circles" that the "naval and military commanders on the American station have no power to conclude any armistice or suspension of arms," but that "they carry with them certain terms which will be offered to the American government at the point of the bayonet."

The bayonets were coming from three directions. On August 24th, one army held the capital of the United States, and "after the capture of Washington, that of Baltimore seemed but holiday sport."[7] A second expeditionary force—eleven thousand men under Sir George Prevost—was concentrated on the northern frontier, ready to invade New York along Burgoyne's old route and split off dissident New England from the rest of the United States. A third expeditionary force was at sea, moving toward its rendezvous at Jamaica; its objective was New Orleans.

A fourth blow also was about to fail. It would not be a military operation but a diplomatic maneuver co-ordinated with the threefold invasion. The British government already had decided on the fundamentals of the postwar settlement. The basis of peace with the United States would be the *status uti possidetis*—diplomatic jargon which, translated, becomes *winners keepers, losers weepers*. England, in plain English, meant to keep whatever it could take. Even the ultimatum delivered in late August did not reveal this ultimate objective. But the American commissioners could see straws in the wind that blew from London, and the wind itself was chilling. They could feel the purpose of the enemy to prolong the war while going through the motions of negotiation.

For the British government was playing for high stakes. It was investing a great deal of money in the new campaign in America; for a nation already strained by the Napoleonic ordeal, the cost of the three expeditionary forces was enormous. His Majesty's ministers had no intention of sacrificing both the prospective profit and the capital investment by making peace before the profit was in pocket. The Americans had been prepared to open negotiations early in the summer; but for four months—ever since the new campaign had been decided on—London had been stalling and postponing. August had come before the British commissioners arrived in Ghent. Even then, it could not be said that they had come as peacemakers. They had not come to seek a cessation of arms. They had come to impose terms.[8] And it was as evident to the Americans as to the British that the terms could be made harsher after the three impending military blows had fallen crushingly upon the United States.

The rejection of the British ultimatum was neither surprising nor displeasing to his Majesty's ministers. Automatically, it prolonged the war. But it did not have the further effect which the Americans had expected to be automatic: it did not put an end to the negotiations. It prolonged them, too. For it suited the purposes of the British government to have the American peace commissioners available at the psychological moment. And the psychological moment would come with the arrival of dispatches from the expeditionary forces. No one doubted that the dispatches would bring news of overwhelming victories. On September 2nd, Lord Liverpool, war secretary in the British cabinet, was writing to Lord Castlereagh, the foreign secretary, that before the Ghent negotiations were resumed "we shall know the result of the campaign."

The first dispatches reached Ghent on October 1st. They brought news of "the cruel humiliation at Bladensburg and the burning of Washington."[9] To the American commissioners, it was "a grievous stroke."[10] It "caused British and Americans alike to expect a long series of British triumphs."[11] In Canada, the governor general was so sure that General Ross would continue his victorious invasion that "the proposed public rejoicings at Montreal because of the capture of Washington were postponed, so that they might celebrate that of Baltimore at the same time." [12] And in England "no one seemed to doubt that [the] army from Canada would meet that of Ross on the Susquehanna or the Schuylkill as conquerors of the country, and that Baltimore would be their base for future operations." [13]

The psychological moment had arrived. Victory, complete and crushing, seemed certain everywhere. The British government prepared to show its hand. To the commissioners at Ghent went orders to let fall the fourth of the impending blows—formal diplomatic notice that America could have peace only on the principle of *winners keepers*. The notice was drafted. On October 21st it was presented to the Americans in its ornate Latin dress—the *status uti possidetis*. But something had happened to it. The phrase was there, nonetheless arrogant for its antique language. The principle was there, nonetheless brutal for its adorning rhetoric. Phrase and principle, they meant conquest and submission. But they no longer meant what they had meant three weeks ago. They had undergone a change so great that they were hardly recognizable. *On October 17th fresh dispatches from the expeditionary forces had arrived in London.*

The British fleet had failed in its attack on Baltimore. The British army had recoiled from Sam Smith's batteries and earthworks. Ross's Invincibles had retreated to their ships, carrying a grievous load of wounded and the body of their general. Four days earlier, the British fleet had failed in its attack at Plattsburg; it had been smashed to pieces, its commander killed. The British army striking south from Canada had recoiled from the American defenses. Sir George Prevost's Invincibles were in full retreat across the border.

Overnight, the situation had reversed itself. The "result of the campaign" had indeed been overwhelming, but it had overwhelmed the wrong side. There would be "public rejoicings," but they would not take place in Montreal or London. The Americans had called the tune, and it sounded very much like the music played at Yorktown when "the world turned upside down." And this time they had had no help, no allies. They had upset the world by their unaided efforts.

The unexpected, unimaginable bad news "threw confusion into the [British] ministry and their agents in the press and the diplomatic service throughout Europe." [14] To the American commissioners it came "with the effect of a reprieve from execution . . .

Gallatin was deeply moved; Adams could not believe the magnitude of the success." [15] The news reached Ghent on October 21st, the very day the British commissioners presented their summary demand for settlement based on the *status uti possidetis*. The moment was *not* psychological. The Americans were infuriated. In their anger and their enormous relief, they could not realize immediately that the British cabinet was merely trying to save face. The arrogant assertion of the *uti possidetis* was pure bluff and camouflage. Behind it, his Majesty's government was in full retreat.

The British note was not nearly so remarkable for its assertions as for its silences. When the Americans emerged from their mood of mingled rage and exultation, they discovered that Great Britain had abandoned the humiliating terms included in the August ultimatum. Gone was the demand for wholesale annexations, gone the demand for disarmament, gone the scheme for setting up an Indian buffer state to block the growth of the republic. Of the positive demands, nothing remained but a British claim to Moose Island in Passamaquoddy Bay, a "right of way across the northern angle of Maine, Fort Niagara, with five miles circuit, and the Island of Mackinaw." [16] True, the silences included the specific causes of the war—search and seizure of American ships and the impressment of their seamen. True, there were certain "mutual accommodations" to be worked out by negotiation—American rights in the Canadian fisheries, and British rights to free navigation of the Mississippi. But the note, in sum, was a confession of defeat—a confession reluctant and concealed as carefully as possible, but nonetheless as frank as the carefully concealed night retreat of the British army from the lines of Baltimore.

The enemy was falling back: *pursue him!* The American commissioners were not hampered by the considerations that caused Sam Smith to refrain from throwing his militia against the British regulars on the night of September 13th. They were not militia: they were skilled negotiators: they were abler men than their antagonists. [17] They pressed their advantage now. Their answer to the British note was a curt rejection of the *status uti possidetis*. In the British cabinet, the rejection had much the same effect as a vigorous pursuit by confident troops pressing after a retreating army; it "created a feeling akin to consternation." [18]

For in the practical psychology of defeat, elements that once were friendly or neutral appear suddenly to turn hostile, burdens that were not too heavy in victory seem suddenly to become unbearable, the future that was bright with promise darkens. The

British ministers suddenly felt new weight upon their backs. The expeditionary forces had been costly: now they felt, in anticipation, the galling burden of a new and "prodigious" expense. Lord Liverpool estimated the cost of carrying on the war against America at not less than ten million pounds, and other estimates were even higher. The ministers in power saw the political future dark with the consequences of increasing taxes. In Vienna, where the post-Napoleonic map of Europe was being drawn, the British diplomats found themselves embarrassed, their position weakened and their prestige waning. They were no longer spokesmen of a conquering England, mistress of the seas and of an invincible army. They could shrug off the surrender of a few British frigates, they could explain—with logic if not with pride—that the treacherous Yankees had won their naval victories with battleships disguised as cruisers. But they had more difficulty in explaining what had happened to the invincibility of the Invincibles. They had been so contemptuous of America and its militia mobs that the almost simultaneous defeats of two British armies left a most unimpressive impression. The "liberated" French, with an unbecoming lack of gratitude for the removal of Napoleon from their necks, let loose a roar of cheers for the American successes. The great Wellington, invited to take command in America, replied that he could not promise himself "much success." [19]

Suddenly it was Britain that yearned for peace—not peace at any price, but at a price that had gone very low indeed. Within weeks, the remarkable silences of the October note had spread and deepened until they included the fisheries and the free navigation of the Mississippi.[20] Fort Niagara was forgotten; so was Michilimackinack. If his Majesty's commissioners could be so forgetful, the Americans also could afford a lapse of memory. With Europe at peace, Britain would no longer be concerned with blockades: it had no enemies to be blockaded. And it would have more sailors than it needed: there would be no occasion for grabbing other people's sailors. There would be no more search and seizure and no more impressment. The causes of the war had disappeared. There was nothing left to talk about.

The treaty of peace was a Christmas gift to the United States. It was signed on Christmas Eve. It would not be delivered until February 11th, when a British sloop-of-war sailed into New York harbor. But it had been purchased in September. Sam Smith, merchant, had helped to buy it.

29

THUS BE IT EVER

ONLY THE PROUD HOME-TOWN
orators, flushed with triumph and the whisky necessary to wash
down innumerable toasts, ventured to describe the defense of Baltimore as a decisive battle. History ignored them. Military com-
mentators scoffed. Jealous neighbors sniffed and said that they were
drunk. Perhaps they were.

Few battles are decisive. Few wars in modern times have been
decided by the issue of a single action. On June 18th in 1815,
Wellington and Blücher wrecked Napoleon's army at Waterloo;
less than four weeks later, Napoleon surrendered himself as a

prisoner to the captain of a British warship. But Waterloo is the exception.

Other battles, called decisive, are in truth only turning points. They are historians' landmarks. They are surveyors' stakes marking the high tide of a cause—the point at which the flood ceased and the ebb began. The battle of Gettysburg is one such landmark. When the spent waves of Pickett's charge sank into the earth of Cemetery Ridge, the tide began to fall; it never rose so high again. But Gettysburg was not decisive in the sense of being final and conclusive. After it came the Wilderness, the Bloody Angle, Spotsylvania, Cold Harbor, Chickamauga, Lookout Mountain, Franklin, Nashville, Mobile Bay, Fort Fisher. The simultaneous Confederate defeats at Gettysburg and Vicksburg make, together, a turning point as logical as any. But after them came twenty-one months of death and blood and tears. After them came almost half the war.

One hundred days after the almost simultaneous British defeats at Baltimore and Plattsburg came peace on terms acceptable to the United States. Thirty-three of the hundred days had been consumed in carrying the news to London, thirty-seven in bringing it to Ghent. Peace came just sixty-seven days after the first impact of those battles. It came, with honor and with no small profit, just four months after a disaster that had seemed as overwhelming as it was humiliating, and four months after the American commissioners had risked everything by rejecting an ultimatum that involved disarmament, dismemberment, dishonor.

The battle of Baltimore was not *by itself* decisive. But that dignity has been assigned to many other battles whose effects were slighter. It was the climax of a long series of events and circumstances that dulled the enemy's will to fight. It was the final frustration, the last disappointment. To the British government in office, it was the last straw. The back of aggressive policy was broken.

Five days after the news of Baltimore and Plattsburg had reached Ghent, Commissioner James Bayard was writing to his cousin Andrew:

> I expected when I wrote you by the *John Adams* to have been at this time near the coast of America.
>
> Not one of us then expected that the negotiation would have continued ten days. . . . It has clearly been the policy of the British Government to avoid a rupture and to protract for that purpose the discussions. With the same views she created the delays which attended the opening of the negotiation [*sic*].

She was influenced by two motives. Ist, To see the effect of the armaments she had sent to the U States; 2d, To ascertain the probable result of the proceedings at Vienna.

They certainly did expect that the force sent to America would in the course of the campaign strike a blow which would prostrate the nation at her feet. Whether in that event she would have been satisfied with dictating the terms of an ignominious peace I think very doubtful. *It is more likely that she would have been encouraged to aim at complete subjugation.* The Capture of Washington was a source of great triumph and exultation and inspired a belief that their troops could not be resisted. This error has been sadly corrected by the repulse in the attack upon Baltimore, by the destruction of their fleet on Lake Champlain, and by the retreat of Prevost from Plattsburg.[1]

And G. B. Milligan, an attaché of the American peace mission, was writing to Bayard from London that "the public mind has been very much influenced by these disasters . . . the people now begin to call as loudly for peace as six weeks ago they did, for the continuance of hostilities. . . .this country has been so long accustomed to success, that they are entirely unprepared for adversity, and it is ten times more galling in being produced by us, where it was least expected."[2]

On December 6th, Bayard himself thought that he had "intelligence . . . of great consequence." He set it down on paper:

. . . in August not one of us had the remotest idea that a pacification would result from our negotiation and we had fixed the time when [we] would embark for America. The negotiation has been designedly spun out by the British Government in order to have the benefit of any favourable events which might occur before the closing of the year. But the time has arrived which has obliged them to decide upon a new campaign in America or to make peace. And they have chosen the latter. They have given up all the material pretensions with which they set out. . . .[3]

Months later, Henry Clay came home from Ghent. His fellow citizens of Lexington, Kentucky, gave him an admiring welcome and a public dinner. The toastmaster lifted his glass:

"Our able negotiators at Ghent—Their talents for diplomacy have kept pace with the valor of our arms in demonstrating to the enemy that these States will be free."

Clay rose to his feet in a storm of cheering.

"I feel myself called on by the sentiment just expressed," he began, "to return my thanks, in behalf of my colleagues and myself. I do not, and am quite sure they do not, feel that in the service alluded to, they are at all entitled to the compliment which has been paid them. We could not do otherwise than reject the demand made by the other party, and if our labors finally terminated in an honorable peace, it was owing to causes on this side of the Atlantic, and not to any exertions of ours. Whatever diversity of opinion may have existed as to the declaration of the war, there are some points on which all may look back with proud satisfaction.

"The first relates to the time of the conclusion of the peace. Had it been made immediately after the treaty of Paris, we should have retired humiliated from the contest, believing that we had escaped the severe chastisement with which we were threatened . . . We should have retired unconscious of our strength, and unconscious of the utter inability of the enemy, with his whole undivided force, to make any serious impression upon us. Our military character, then in the lowest state of degradation, would have been unretrieved.

"Fortunately for us, Great Britain chose to try the issue of the last campaign. And the issue of the last campaign has demonstrated, in the repulse before Baltimore, the retreat from Plattsburg, the hard-fought action on the Niagara frontier, and in that most glorious day, the 8th of January, that we have always possessed the finest elements of military composition, and that a proper use of them only was necessary to ensure for the army and militia a fame as imperishable as that which the navy had previously acquired." [4]

The "most glorious day" of which Clay spoke was the day of Andrew Jackson's victory at New Orleans—a victory won two weeks after the war ended. But the battle of New Orleans was as unnecessary to prove Clay's point as it had been to win the war. The point, like the peace, already had been made.

On Christmas Day,[5] the morning after the signing of the treaty, James Bayard had written to his son:

"The war has raised our reputation in Europe and it excites astonishment that we should have been able for one campaign to have fought Great Britain single handed . . . I think it will be a long time before we are disturbed again by any of the powers of Europe."

AFTERWORD

IT IS NOT OFTEN AN AUTHOR FINDS that someone else has finished his book for him.

The most important part of this conclusion to *The Perilous Fight* was written in North Africa two years ago by Relman Morin, a war correspondent of the Associated Press. It is included in this book, by special permission, because it contains the essence of what I want to say. Relman Morin wrote:

"It was the Fourth of July in this joint British and American officers' training camp and the day was not very old before the American quartermaster sergeant and the British stores sergeant were angrily comparing notes.

"The American said: 'Some so-and-so busted into the storeroom last night and stole thirty pounds of sugar and a whole hell of a lot of bread and, cripes, how much coffee!'

"The British sergeant replied sadly: 'Our whole month's ration of whiskey has disappeared!'

"Meanwhile, as the day wore on, the American officers began to be a little disgusted, too. No announcement was posted about a Fourth of July celebration. The camp was to follow its usual routine. There would be a route march at 5 o'clock. They said:

"'That's a fine way to spend the Fourth.' And: 'Marching around those goldarned mountains—that's just fine.'

"At five o'clock they fell in and started up the trail. They noticed that the American general was making the march with them, but they did not see any British officers around. They murmured among themselves:

"'It's *our* holiday, and *they* get the day off. Can you beat it?'

"The trail then led through a grove winding up and down the slopes of the mountain, and the sun was nearly down when they emerged into a clearing.

513

"At the same moment they heard singing. They came rigidly to attention, saluting.

"Just ahead in an open space among the trees the British officers were lined up in two files. They were singing 'The Star-Spangled Banner.' An American flag waved above their heads.

"Nearby was a long table covered with dishes and glasses and some large pitchers. When the anthem was ended they all crowded around the table and drank the first of many toasts to America's most important national holiday.

"A British officer said: 'We had to steal some sugar from your stores last night—didn't have enough to make whiskey sours for you.'

"And then he apologized for making the whiskey sours with scotch.

" 'But that's all we had,' he added."

There it is—everything that I would have liked to say. Except this:

History implies truth. Search for truth implies impartiality of motive. Yet it is true that truth itself may be used to serve motives that are not impartial.

I am unwilling that my motives in writing this book should be either misunderstood or misinterpreted. I am also unwilling that any of the truth which it contains should be put to the service of any special purpose.

Specifically, I am unwilling that this book or any passage in it should be interpreted as being anti-British. Such an interpretation would be not merely unwarranted but deliberately biased. I have not forgotten—I cannot forget—the music of "The Star-Spangled Banner" thundering from the deck of the British transport that carried my regiment to war. I cannot forget the British officer who became the best friend I have ever had: he died to save his ship.

It is my firm conviction that the one tangible hope of a decent, peaceful world lies in the continuance and the further development of sympathetic understanding and determined cooperation between the United States and the British Commonwealth of Nations.

Specifically again, I am unwilling that any statement in this book should be regarded as supporting a continuation, after the end of this war, of our haphazard and dangerously inadequate preparedness for national defense. The United States has won its wars in spite of its criminal neglect of its defenses. The adjective "criminal" is used deliberately. The United States has been preserved by the blood and agony of thousands—tens of thousands—of men who need not have died if their country had been prepared for war. In 1814, men who had never stood in military ranks were asked to die to save their country. In 1918, men who had never held a live grenade in their hands were sent into trenches, unprepared, to die. In 1941, men went on maneuvers with dummy tanks and wooden guns because their country still was blind to all the lessons of history. Men died on Bataan and in the hell of prison camps because the country that expected their lives of them had not been willing to prepare itself to defend its way of life, its ideals, or even its existence.

The United States must not be guilty of that neglect again. Of all my convictions, this conviction is the strongest:

The United States, for its own sake and for the sake of decency and a peaceful world, must maintain always the world's most powerful navy and the world's most powerful air force, and it must adopt at once a policy of universal military training *in peace to preserve peace.*

To do less is to risk the loss of everything we love.

NEIL H. SWANSON

ACKNOWLEDGMENTS

Mᴀɴʏ ᴘᴇᴏᴘʟᴇ, ʟɪᴠɪɴɢ ᴀɴᴅ ᴅᴇᴀᴅ, have had a hand in the writing of this book.

He who seeks to re-create the past owes his first obligation to those who made its re-creation not only worth while but also possible. He has, in common honesty, the obligation to deal with them truthfully and fairly. To some of the men in this book, that debt of history was long overdue. It could not have been paid at all without their help; and the author, therefore, acknowledges his obligation to them for their letters, diaries, reports and memoranda. Much of the story has been told not merely from their own point of view but in their own words, set down while the events were fresh and vivid in their minds.

But it would have been impossible, without much help, to bring these living records of the past together in one place. The author gives grateful thanks to Louis H. Bolander, associate librarian of the library of the United States Naval Academy at Annapolis, for his generous and invaluable help in finding the answers to numerous difficult questions of fact—for example, the armament of *Erebus* and the time when fixed beds gave way to pivot mountings on bomb vessels in the British service. This book probably could not have been written without the equally generous and valuable co-operation of Dr. Joseph L. Wheeler, until recently the librarian of Enoch Pratt Free Library in Baltimore. The author's sincere thanks go to him and to many members of the library staff—to Miss Kate Coplan, director of exhibits; Miss Elizabeth C. Litsinger and her assistants in the Maryland Room; Miss Dorothy Sinclair, head of the department of history, travel and biography; and Miss Harriet P. Turner, head of the civics and sociology department. Warm thanks are due also to Dr. Lloyd A. Brown, librarian of the Peabody Library, to Samuel E. Lafferty who recently retired as senior members of the staff, and to H. C. Kaufmann; to Miss

Edith Lenel, Ph.D., in charge of the reference desk in the Division of Manuscripts in The Library of Congress, and to Robert D. Fisher and Robert M. Agard, General Reference and Bibliography Division, Library of Congress; to Miss Josephine P. Etchison, librarian of the C. Burr Artz Library in Frederick, Md.; Miss Cordelia B. Hodges, cataloguer of the Washington County Free Library in Hagerstown, Md.; and Miss Margaret M. Williams, reference librarian of the Martin Memorial Library in York, Pa.

And to the many friends who have given generously of their time, their encouragement and their practical helpfulness—sincere thanks. That means you, Bruce Earnest. It means you, George Carter; you, Francis Bierne; you, C. H. Meredith and H. B. Hostetter; and you, Lloyd Stratton.

Last, but most gratefully and admiringly, the author acknowledges the help and encouragement of the girl to whom this book is dedicated—his wife. She has been a good soldier.

NOTES

CHAPTER 1

1. American State Papers, XVI, Military Affairs, I, 565.

2. Based on a letter written by Miss Polly Kemp, published in *Maryland Historical Magazine*, vol. I, p. 206.

3. Life and Letters of Dolly Madison, by Allen C. Clark, p. 167.

4. *The Constitution of the United States*, compiled by David C. Mearns and Verner W. Clapp, p. 15. Library of Congress, 1944.

5. The cabinet was widely scattered in its flight. The president and Attorney General Richard Rush fled by a roundabout route to Brookville, Md.; Secretary of the Navy Jones reached Loudon County in Virginia; the secretary of war and the secretary of the treasury went to Frederick, Md.

6. Grasshoppers—small brass fieldpieces throwing three-pound shot.

7. Letter of Lieutenant Colonel Joseph Sterrett, Fifth Maryland regiment, dated Aug. 22, 1814, with an endorsement by Major Richard K. Heath, published in *Maryland Historical Magazine*, V, 342-343.

8. Dispatch from R. Patterson, director of the horse-telegraph station at McCoy's tavern, to Brigadier General John Stricker, Aug. 24, 1814.

9. *Maryland Historical Magazine*, V, 343.

10. Names of officers and men of the Maryland troops, appearing in this book, are taken from the official muster rolls as printed in *Citizen Soldiers at North Point and Fort McHenry*, published by James Young on the occasion of the seventy-fifth anniversary of the battle of Baltimore, and from the "Maryland Roster, War of 1812," prepared by Louis Henry Dielman and published as an appendix to *The British Invasion of Maryland*, by William M. Marine, in 1913, under the auspices of the Society of the War of 1812 in Maryland.

11. This statement of time is based on a horse-telegraph dispatch to General Stricker, signed by James Carroll and endorsed by R. Patterson at McCoy's tavern half an hour after midnight, Aug. 25, 1814.

12. The text of the dispatch referred to in the preceding note. *Maryland Historical Magazine*, V, 346.

13. *Maryland Historical Magazine*, V.

14. *Maryland Historical Magazine*, V.

15. "Blue-light" was a term of reproach, an approbrious epithet born of the political passions of the time. Its origin was an incident of the British naval blockade of the American seaboard. Commodore Stephen Decatur, commanding a United States squadron of three ships—the frigates *United States* and *Macedonian* and

the sloop of war *Hornet*—prepared to slip through the blockading fleet off New London on the night of Dec. 12, 1813. As he was about to weigh anchor, his guard-boats reported signal lights burning on both sides of the Thames River. They were blue lights. Commodore Decatur was convinced that they had been placed by spies or traitors to warn the enemy fleet that he was coming out. While the guilty never were traced, the blame was speedily placed on the "peace men" opposed to the war; and because the Federalist party had opposed war, it too was blamed. "Blue-light Federalist" became one of the prime political catch phrases and insults of the day.

16. *Growth of the United States*, Ralph Volney Harlow, p. 295; *History of the United States*, Henry William Elson, p. 446.

17. Polly Kemp's letter, dated in December, 1814, appears in *Maryland Historical Magazine*, vol. I, pp. 206-207. I am fully aware that in following Polly's version of Dolly Madison's unhappy experience I am diverging from other versions which have had general acceptance. Two of these versions appear in *Life and Letters of Dolly Madison*, by Allen C. Clark. One is that Mrs. Madison "slept in a tent in the encampment [at Tennallytown, two miles north of the heights of Georgetown] under guard" on the night after the battle and "the next day [Thursday] crossed into Virginia"; that "on the Virginia side of the Potomac she arrived at the place of Mr. Love" and that "she pushed on to a tavern" where "the tavern mistress, for a fancied grievance, reviled her; and that from the tavern she moved further on to Mrs. Minor's." That version is similar to the tale recounted by the valet, Paul Jennings, who declared that "Mrs. Madison slept that night at Mr.

Love's, two or three miles over the river. After leaving that place she called in at a house and went upstairs. The lady of the house learning who she was became furious, and went to the stairs and screamed out, 'Miss Madison! you come down and go out! Your husband has got mine out fighting, and D—— you, you shan't stay in my house; so get out!' Mrs. Madison complied and went to Mrs. Minor's, a few miles further, where she stayed a day or two."

Jennings related this story forty-nine years after the event—and secondhand, at that. He admitted that "all the facts about Mrs. M. I learned from her servant, Sukey" (*Life and Letters of Dolly Madison*, Clark). In the same work it is related that Mrs. Madison and the president met at Georgetown late on the day of the battle and "at the meeting Mr. and Mrs. Madison agreed on the routes and rendezvous of retreat."

There is no doubt that Madison himself crossed into Virginia. Richard Rush, the attorney general, said in a letter to Colonel J. S. Williams: "We were on horseback, attended by servants, proceeding on the Virginia side of the Potomac, which we crossed at the Little Falls, intending to recross at the Great Falls that night or the next morning, so as to be again on the Maryland side." On Aug. 27th, Madison was at Brookville in Maryland, as evidenced by his letter to Dolly. Lossing says he was there on the 26th. Brookville lies only a few miles north of Great Falls.

Various circumstances cast doubt on the Jennings version—it came secondhand from a servant; it was related half a century after the occurrence; and the panic prevailing in Washington on the evening following the battle of Bladensburg, together with the complete disintegration of the American troops, makes it seem highly improbable that the president's wife spent the night in a tent at Tennallytown. Polly Kemp's account was written less than four months after the incidents which it records, and Polly was positive about her details; her letter has nothing in it of the vagueness and implausibility that characterizes the other, legendlike versions. Circumstantial evidence indicates that the tavern she describes was in fact the rendezvous agreed upon by Mr. and Mrs. Madison when they met in Georgetown.

CHAPTER 2

1. Files of the Baltimore *Patriot*, and dispatches published in *Maryland Historical Magazine*, V.

2. The numbers of troops engaged, at various stages of the battle, are stated in later chapters dealing with the action at Bladensburg. In some instances, in which supporting evidence is cited, the figures given in this book are at variance with those commonly accepted.

3. "Narrative of Brigadier General Winder," in *American State Papers*, XVI, *Military Affairs*, I, 559.

4. This statement is based on General Winder's narrative, dated at O'Neale's, Sept. 26, 1814, and on the official reports of other officers, cited in detail in later chapters dealing with the battle.

5. General Philip Stuart, representing the First Maryland District. *History of Maryland*, J. Thomas Scharf, III, 60.

6. *History of Maryand*, J. Thomas Scharf, III, 60.

7. *Pictorial Field Book of the War of 1812*, Benson J. Lossing, p. 917. (This work will be referred to in subsequent notes as Lossing.)

8. Lossing, p. 919.

9. Lossing, footnote, p. 918.

10. *American State Papers*, XVI, *Military Affairs*, I, 526.

11. *History of the Invasion and Capture of Washington*, John S. Williams, brigade major and inspector, Columbian Brigade, in the War of 1812, p. 173.

12. *Memoirs of General James Wilkinson*, I, 754.

13. Scharf, III, 66.

14. Winder was captured at the battle of Stony Creek in June, 1813.

15. "Winder's Narrative," *American State Papers*, XVI, *Military Affairs*, I, 552-553.

16. Winder's narrative, reference above, p. 554.

17. Letter of General Winder to the secretary of war, dated at Piscataway, July 27, 1814.

18. Secretary of the navy.

19. Winder's narrative.

CHAPTER 3

1. *Subaltern in America*, 22.

2. Williams, 137.

3. *Maryland Roster, War of 1812*.

4. *Ibid.*

5. These two units were not regiments in fact; they were a conglomeration of detachments from several militia regiments. See Chap. VII.

6. Report of Brigadier General Walter Smith, Oct. 6, 1814.

7. Letter of Colonel Monroe, Nov. 13, 1814. He did not know how many men he had in his own patrol: he said "twenty-five or thirty."

8. Monroe's dispatches, published in *American State Papers*, XVI, *Military Affairs*, I, 537.

9. Williams, 158.

10. General Winder's narrative.

11. *Ibid.*

12. Williams, 159.
13. Winder narrative.
14. *Ibid.*
15. Letter of John Armstrong, Oct. 17, 1814.
16. The quotation is from Colonel Allen M'Clane's so-called journal of the Maryland campaign. M'Clane apparently acted as "a volunteer aid to General Winder": Williams, 142.
17. *Ibid.*
18. *Ibid.*
19. *Ibid.*
20. Subaltern, 42.
21. Winder's narrative.
22. The quoted passages in the description of the departure of the Baltimore troops are from Henry T.

Tuckerman's *Life of John Pendleton Kennedy*, reprinted in Marine, pp. 105-113.
23. The Columbian brigade from Washington marched ten miles from its first camp to join the detachments of marines, regular infantry and militia cavalry at the Wood Yard on Aug. 21.
24. Statement of General Walter Smith.
25. *Ibid.*
26. Based on Major Richard Heath's statement of the time of departure, and on John Kennedy's statement that the column reached Bladensburg "about five in the afternoon"; Marine, p. 109.

CHAPTER 4

1. *Subaltern in America*, 43.
2. Scharf, III, 75-76.
3. The inaccuracy of these "professions" becomes evident upon comparison with Roger Brooke Taney's account: see Chap. XV.
4. Winder's narrative.
5. Colonel Allen M'Clane's "Jour-

nal of the Campaign" in Williams, 145.
6. *Ibid.*
7. Winder's narrative.
8. Stansbury said Winder ordered him to march "slowly" toward Marlborough. Winder, in his report, did not use the adverb.
9. Winder's narrative.

CHAPTER 5

1. Winder's narrative.
2. Stansbury's report.
3. Winder put Stansbury's strength at not more than fourteen hundred; how many of the Baltimore County militiamen had fallen out on the difficult march was not recorded.
4. Kennedy, in Marine, p. 111.
5. The circumstances of General Stansbury's disobedience of orders, as set forth in this chapter, are drawn from Stansbury's own report and from that source only, except as specifically noted. The other source is Winder's official report. Winder was positive about the details of the order he sent by "an aid" to Stansbury in

midafternoon of August 23rd; he described it as "directions" to Stansbury to "take the best position in advance of Bladensburg, and unite Lieutenant Colonel Sterrett with him . . . and should he be attacked, to resist as long as possible, and if obliged to retire, to retreat toward the city." Stansbury, in his report, admitted receiving Winder's order attaching Sterrett's troops to his command; he made no mention of the other, vital portion of the order. He did not deny receiving it, he merely said nothing about it. Winder did not say that the order was sent in writing; but Stansbury said that the order concerning Sterrett's troops was contained in "letter No. 4." Since Winder definitely described his orders concerning Sterrett and his orders concerning a position in advance of Bladensburg as parts of a single order carried by an aide, and since Stansbury acknowledged receiving *half* the order *in writing*, it would be reasonable to conclude that he received the whole order. However, the description of his conduct as disobedience of orders does not rest solely on that one order. Stansbury's own report makes it clear that he subsequently disobeyed two later orders from his commanding general to "resist the enemy as long as possible." He himself pointed out that the second of these orders apparently was written "without a knowledge" of his movements—that is, of his retreat from Lowndes's hill. Even without Stansbury's statement, it would be obvious that Winder fully believed that his subordinate brigadier was holding his position "in advance of Bladensburg."

In justice to General Stansbury it should be noted that if his report is a full and accurate statement of the facts he knew, it immediately appears that he was not informed concerning Winder's retreat from the Battalion Old Fields to Washington until at least six and a half hours after the retreat began, and that Winder did not send him this vital information until he himself had traveled six or eight miles from the Old Fields. Winder's report said nothing about dispatching this intelligence to Stansbury. Stansbury said that Major Bates, who reached him with the information at 2:30 a.m. on the 24th, had come from Washington; Winder said that he himself was "at the bridge [in front of Washington] about eight o'clock." The delay is amazing, the liaison was unbelievably bad.

Taking Winder and Stansbury's reports together, it appears that there was more than a failure of liaison. There was a cavalry failure also. Winder said that on the afternoon of the 23rd, while on the Bladensburg-Upper Marlborough road, he "left orders with Lieutenant Colonel Tilghman's cavalry to continue their observation on the Bladensburg and Marlborough *roads*, and in case the enemy should move on that road, to give General Stansbury immediate notice and fall back on him. In proceeding to the Old Fields [which Winder reached about five in the afternoon] I met Lieutenant Colonel Tilghman himself, and renewed these directions. Captain Herbert was also between General Stansbury and the enemy with the same instructions." But Stansbury said that Tilghman's cavalry came into Bladensburg "a little after dark for refreshments." In other words, the cavalry had not carried out the orders Winder said he gave. The contrast between Winder's positive assertion and the cavalry's conduct is not quite so definite in Captain Herbert's case; the context of Stansbury's report gives room for suspicion that Herbert's troop, too, had fallen back and that on the night of August 23rd it was not "between General Stansbury and the enemy."

In the light of these circumstances, Stansbury's acute discomfort is understandable. Whether the circumstances excuse his retreat, after the acknowledged receipt of Winder's positive orders to resist the enemy as long as possible, is another matter.

6. General Walter Smith's statement.

7. Winder's narrative.

8. Monroe admitted, in his state-

ment to the Congressional investigating committee, that he advised Stansbury to make the night march and the night attack with raw, exhausted troops "although it was then 12 o'clock at night."

9. Statement of Major William Pinkney, Nov. 16, 1814.

CHAPTER 6

1. Scharf, III, 76.
2. *Ibid.*
3. Statement of Major William Pinkney, Baltimore Rifle Battalion, Nov. 16, 1814.
4. Stansbury's report.
5. *Ibid.*
6. Pinkney's statement.
7. Roosevelt, I, 99, put the short weight of American solid shot at 7 per cent.
8. Stansbury's report.
9. *Ibid.*
10. Major Pinkney described the position of the Fifth Maryland, before it was moved, as being "about fifty yards in our rear" and "outstretching the line of his rifle companies." General Stansbury, describing the shifting of the Fifth without his approval, stated that it "was taken out of the orchard." These two statements do not contradict each other. The reasonable interpretation is that the Fifth, just before Monroe moved it, was in line in the lower edge of the orchard, with its right flank protruding into the open ground south of the orchard and extending to the Washington turnpike if not actually across it. Pinkney was positive in saying that the position of the Fifth "gave confidence to my companies and the artillery." His testimony bears out the judgment that General Stansbury was aware of the vulnerability of his first line to attack against its right flank and had placed the Baltimore infantry in a position to meet just such an attack as that which developed. It also indicates that Stansbury had taken advantage of the orchard not only to conceal the strength of this supporting force but to give it the very cover which the enemy used to excellent advantage later.

11. Armstrong's letter.
12. Ingersoll, II, 174.
13. See Chap. XIX.
14. *Spangled Banner*, Victor Weybright, p. 69. Farrar and Rinehart, New York, 1935.
15. *Ibid.*, pp. 69 and 86.
16. *Ibid.*, 87.
17. Barney *Memoir*, 265: the flotillamen came up "in a trot."
18. Major Pinkney's statement.

CHAPTER 7

1. The figures are based on official reports, rosters, regimental records and Gleig's *Narrative*.
2. Subaltern, 65.
3. Gleig's *Narrative*.
4. Subaltern, 70.
5. *Ibid.*
6. Winder's narrative.
7. Subaltern, 70.
8. *Projectile Weapons of War*, J. Scoffern, p. 168. London, 1859.
9. *Naval Gunnery*, Sir Howard Douglas, 324.
10. *Projectile Weapons*, 170.
11. Stansbury's report.
12. Subaltern, 71.
13. *Ibid.*
14. Stansbury's report.
15. Subaltern, 71: "the advance was quickly scattered into skirmishing order."

16. *Ibid.*, 72: "each file being full ten paces apart from the other."

17. Major Pinkney's report.

18. Subaltern, 72: "upon the left of the road, where the copse happened to be more thick."

19. Pinkney's report.

20. *Ibid.*

21. Subaltern, 72. The left of the British first line "moved on for several minutes without seeing any enemy." This passage makes it clear that the British advance to the south of the Washington turnpike was invisible "for several minutes" to the officers and men of Stansbury's brigade.

22. Winder's narrative.

23. Pinkney's report.

24. *Ibid.*

25. Gleig's *Narrative*, 119.

26. Stansbury's report: "but one of the pieces was lost, and this was rendered harmless before it was abandoned."

27. Statement of Lieutenant Colonel Laval.

28. Pinkney's report.

29. *Ibid.*

30. Subaltern, 72.

31. *Ibid.*, 67.

32. *Ibid.*

33. *Ibid.* The statement that the infantry of Stansbury's brigade was formed in three ranks is a conclusion based on several items of evidence. First, "the habitual order of formation of the battalion is in three ranks"—The System of Infantry Discipline According to the Regulation Established for the Army of *The United States, 19 March, 1813*, p. 103. Second, the reference in *Subaltern in America*, p. 67, to "the three motley lines of infantry." It is possible that "subaltern" was referring to the three positions into which the American army was divided; but at the stage in his narrative at which the passage occurs, he was not yet in sight of

Barney's flotillamen and the Washington and Virginia troops beyond Tournecliffe's bridge, and at no time did he refer to the two Baltimore batteries and their slim support as the American first line. Third, the Fifth Maryland numbered about five hundred men, and the two Baltimore County regiments were somewhat larger. The entire front occupied by the three regiments and Pinkney's two rifle companies—totaling about 1,953 men—was little more than four hundred yards. Allowing regulation distances between companies and battalions and regiments, it seems reasonable to conclude that on the narrow front allotted to it, the brigade formed in the three lines which were "the habitual order."

34. Subaltern, 67. This passage is undoubtedly a description of the Fifth Maryland; the subaltern, at that stage of his narrative, was much too far away to see the few United States regulars beyond Tournecliffe's bridge.

35. Gleig's *Narrative*, 119.

36. Subaltern, 72.

37. Winder's narrative and statement of John Law, temporarily in command of the three guns of Burch's battery at the left of the Fifth Maryland.

38. Report of Captain Benjamin Burch, Washington Artillery.

39. The British second brigade, made up of the 44th (East Essex) Foot and the Fourth Foot (the King's Own).

40. Pinkney's report.

41. The precise moment at which this movement began is elusive. General Winder said he ordered the Fifth to advance "and sustain the artillery." His memory probably was at fault: no other eyewitness account of events in that part of the field, just preceding or during the advance of the Fifth, coincides with Winder's

version. Captain Burch and John Law, who commanded three of Burch's guns until Burch himself came up after seeking and finding Winder, agreed that these guns opened fire before the Fifth was ordered forward. Winder said he gave the order to the Fifth; the Fifth was next to the guns; he could not have given the order until he arrived in the immediate vicinity of the guns *after* Burch found him. And the guns could hardly have opened fire while the road was choked with the retreat of the Baltimore batteries. Furthermore, the two rifle companies which *followed* the fleeing batteries had rallied on the Fifth and advanced with it. The only reasonable conclusion, therefore, is that Winder did not order the Fifth to attack until after the retreating artillery had cleared its flank.

42. General Winfield Scott, order of Nov. 18, 1814.

43. Names and units of American soldiers in action at Bladensburg, North Point or Fort McHenry are from the Maryland Roster, War of 1812, published in Marine, or from the company rosters in *Citizen Soldiers.*

44. *A Handbook for Infantry.* William Duane, lt. col., U. S. A., 1812.

45. Winder's narrative.

46. Stansbury's report says positively that the Fifth opened the infantry fire-fight, on the American side, in this second of the day's actions. It did not open fire, however, until it had halted after its advance. Therefore, during its advance, "the whole American front is silent," except for Ben Burch's three guns," although there may have been scattering shots fired by some of the militiamen of the companies originally detached to protect the left flank of the Baltimore batteries and which were driven back about the time

the batteries fled. What happened to them after the retreat of the guns is not disclosed in any official report.

47. Captain Burch's report.

48. Several secondary accounts of the battle of Bladensburg turn this advance of the Fifth into a headlong bayonet charge. They halt it only in the thickets on the bank of the Eastern Branch. And they are wrong. These exaggerated versions, as persistent as they are erroneous, are based on George Gleig's *Narrative of the Campaigns of Washington and New Orleans.* Gleig suffered elisions of memory; his battle scenes ran together; the result, while interesting, is undependable. Speaking of one scene which can only be the advance of the Fifth Maryland, he says that the Americans "advanced to recover the ground which was lost" and that "against this charge, the extended order of the British troops would not permit them to offer an effectual resistance, and they were accordingly borne back to the very thicket upon the river's brink." It is dramatic, but it is not true.

Gleig was not the only British writer to give American military skill and courage more credit than was due them that day. In James's *Naval History*, the gentle slopes occupied by the divided American army become "commanding heights," and the implication is that the position was wisely chosen. There is no doubt that the steady advance of the Fifth checked the onrush of the first British brigade *on its front*—that is, along the line of the orchard and in the open ground north of the orchard. Obviously it did nothing to check the advance of the left wing of that brigade. And not one American officer, no matter how anxious to put the best face on the matter, made any claim remotely resembling Gleig's description of an American charge that swept the enemy back to the "river's brink."

To have done what Gleig said they did, the men of the Fifth would have had to advance six or seven hundred yards. They would have left the orchard on their exposed right flank —and the orchard was full of the enemy. They would have had to advance beyond the barn behind which the British were re-forming. They would have been in a pocket from which veteran British infantry should not have let them escape. The charge described by Gleig and improved on by American writers is a charge of five hundred men upon eleven hundred British regulars—a charge that drove them back almost half a mile. It is dramatic, but it is purely imaginary. Considering the situation—the flank of the Fifth exposed to raking fire from the orchard, the position of Burch's three guns and Burch's statement that only one of his guns was masked by the advance of the Fifth while the other two "continued the fire with much effect"—it is certain that the Fifth moved no farther forward than the barn, on the left, and the lower end of the orchard, on the right.

49. Duane's spelling.

50. Duane's *Military Dictionary* is indignant about the nomenclature.

51. Only men who have gone into action without being prepared, in training, for the noise of battle, will understand the full meaning of the word "appalling."

52. The correctness of this statement is reflected in the advice given by Major General William H. Rupertus, USMC, to his officers on the eve of the attack at Cape Gloucester, New Britain, in December of 1943. As quoted in an Associated Press dispatch by Murlin Spencer, General Rupertus said: "Don't permit the men to fire promiscuously to create noise and build up a sense of false security."

53. Stansbury's report.

54. The presence of men from all four of these regiments has been established by checking the rosters.

55. On paper, the two county regiments mustered 1,353. At least two companies had been detached to the left flank of the Baltimore batteries before the battle began. The unidentified company that fired one fusillade on the right of Pinkney's riflemen, and then fled, may have been from one of these regiments. Allowing for these and for straggling, it is doubtful whether even 1,200 men were in line, in the ranks of these two regiments, at this stage of the fight.

56. Subaltern, p. 68, said that "the Americans, from the instant that our advanced guard came in view, continued to rend the air with shouts." Perhaps they did; but the subaltern's memory suffered elision in numerous instances. It is reasonable to conclude that the Americans did shout, however, when they had something to shout about.

57. Stansbury, in his report, spoke of its "steady and well-directed fire." It was not his regiment, his statement may be accepted as impartial.

58. Major Williams's map shows this company in position north and slightly west of the barn—across the Georgetown road and the run on which the mill stood. He said it did good service.

59. The British figures are from Gleig the American from Winder's report and Williams.

60. Surgeon Hanson Catlett, in his report, spoke twice of the range as too great for effective fire.

61. The passages of Winder's report dealing with this phase of the action are confused, the narrative jumps back and forth, it gives an

impression that he was almost every-where at once. For that reason, ap-parently, Scharf, in a footnote to Gleig's exaggerated description of the advance of the Fifth Maryland, speci-fically put Winder "at the head of the Fifth regiment." Winder himself did not say that he led the charge, no other officer said that he did. It was not his duty to lead single regiments. My statement that Winder was fight-ing his battle piecemeal will be borne out by successive incidents as they de-velop in this chapter and the next.

62. Pinkney's report.

63. The words are Pinkney's. Either Captain Doughty's company had fal-len back or Major Pinkney regarded it as part of Sterrett's command.

64. Statement of John Law.

65. The evidence on which I have based the statement that Major Pink-ney was wounded on his return from his ride down the mill road is cir-cumstantial. It is contrary to asser-tions in several secondary sources. Scharf, for instance (III, 83), says flatly that Pinkney was wounded in the opening fight around the Balti-more batteries. He was misled, ap-parently, by General Stansbury's report; the general, praising the con-duct of the riflemen, inserted a paren-thetical note that "this gallant officer in the course of the action was se-verely wounded." He did not say in the action in front of the Eastern Branch bridge; so far as his note is concerned, Pinkney might have re-ceived his wound at any time be-tween 1:00 and 2:30 P.M. Pinkney himself did not specify time or place. But he did say that the wound "dis-abled me from further service," and he mentioned it *after* describing his "going to, and returning from, the mill road."

66. The evidence here, too, is cir-cumstantial but valid. Pinkney, in his report, said that he "left the field,

with (or a little after) the last of our friends, about five or six in num-ber, among whom, I believe, was Mr. Meredith of the Fifth."

67. Pinkney's report.

68. Stansbury's report.

69. Maryland frontier rangers serv-ing against the Indians sometimes wore red kerchiefs bound over their heads: hence the name: Red Caps. The Pennsylvania Black Boys were originally volunteers recruited by Captain James Smith to protect the Conocoheague settlements against Indian raids. His men campaigned stripped to breechclout and mocca-sins, their faces and bodies blackened with grease and soot, and their faces painted like Indians'. Later, when he led his uprising against the British military authorities because of their toleration of the sale of arms and ammunition to the savages, his men once more adopted their Black Boy disguise to reduce the likelihood of identification. See *The First Rebel*, Neil H. Swanson; Farrar and Rine-hart, 1937.

70. Pinkney's report.

71. The American casualty records are so incomplete that it is impos-sible to state figures with any degree of confidence. For instance, Major Pinkney stated that his rifle com-panies suffered "some small loss in wounded," but the records fail to show more than one man in his command wounded; indeed, they fail to show Pinkney himself as wounded, although there is no doubt about it. In the confusion after the battle, no one knew who had been shot, who had been captured, who had fallen exhausted and would turn up later; it is entirely probable that some men never reported their wounds. As to those captured, there seems to have been a conspiracy of silence. The roster of prisoners taken at Bladens-burg seems to be fairly complete, but

in almost every instance there is the notation: "command unknown." Officers apparently were not anxious to have it known how many men of their units had been captured, although certainly many of those taken prisoner were captured because they stood and fought longer than many of those who escaped.

72. Winder's narrative.

73. The evidence is the "company book" of the United Volunteers; the casualty figures taken from it appear in *Marine*, p. 113. Incidentally, they do not agree with the Maryland Roster, War of 1812, in the appendix of the same volume: they include the name of Francis H. Davidge, a volunteer, wounded, and omit the name of Christian Keener, Jr., listed as wounded in the Maryland Roster.

74. Winder's narrative.

75. Gleig.

76. Williams, 232—"the 44th regiment, continuing up the old Georgetown road in pursuit of the routed troops."

77. No report mentions any artillery fire against the rockets after the opening engagement. It is probable that the rocket troop, at this stage of the battle, was still in or near Bladensburg and out of range of the guns on either road. The extreme range of six-pounder field guns was from 1,000 to 1,300 yards, according to firing tables in Duane's *Military Dictionary*, published in 1810; their effective range was much less. Sir Howard Douglas, in his *Naval Gunnery*, speaks of three-pounder rockets traveling 1,800 yards and six-pounders 2,300 yards.

78. Subaltern, 67.

79. Winder's narrative.

80. Douglas's *Naval Gunnery*—a six-pound rocket burst at 2,300 yards when discharged at an elevation of 37 degrees, a three-pounder at 1,800 yards when fired at an angle of 25 degrees. The length of the fuse used also affected the range.

81. Winder's narrative.

82. Stansbury's report.

83. Stansbury himself so stated in his report.

84. Winder's narrative.

85. Stansbury, largely confirmed by Winder.

86. The evidence is the casualties in the Maryland Roster, War of 1812.

87. Winder's narrative.

88. The recurring notation "command unknown" makes it impossible to state how many were captured. It is probable that a considerable percentage of the total list of prisoners was taken at this point.

89. *Old Baltimore*, Annie Leakin Sioussat, p. 181. The Macmillan Company, 1931. (Hereafter referred to as Sioussat.) The author was a daughter of Captain Sheppard Church Leakin of the 38th United States Infantry, seriously injured by a falling tree while building abatis for the defenses of Baltimore.

90. *Ibid.*

91. Winder's narrative. If he meant "right," as he said, the column was already "higher" than the flank of the Fifth: it was actually considerably in the rear of the Fifth. His account is confused. For example, in dealing with this stage of the action, he made one of those unintentional errors that fill the contemporary accounts of this whole campaign like booby traps. He referred to the two Baltimore County regiments as "composing the centre and left of Stansbury's line." They formed, of course, the center and *right*. This is one of the more obvious errors. How effective such mistakes have been in trapping the unwary historian is evident in even a casual reading of the secondary accounts.

92. Winder's narrative.

93. *Ibid.*

94. *Ibid.*
95. Burch's report.
96. Statement of John Law.
97. Burch's report.
98. *Ibid.*
99. *Ibid.* Law said "about a hundred yards."
100. Burch and Law.
101. Catlett's report. My statement that the company nearest the orchard broke first is based on three items of circumstantial evidence—Catlett's presence, indicating that he was needed; the probability that the heaviest casualties were suffered by the unit closest to the firing line in the orchard; and his reference to "another officer and myself." The United Volunteers had suffered the heaviest loss, including their acting company commander; their only officer, when they retreated, was an ensign.
102. Duane's *Hand Book for Infantry*, 92.
103. Catlett's report.

CHAPTER 8

1. Pinkney's report.
2. *Ibid.*
3. Johnny's own letter, quoted in Marine, p. 112.
4. Burch's guns were retreating; the British had none in action, at that time and place.
5. Based on Henry Fulford's letter, quoted in Marine, p. 114.
6. Based on the official report of Brigadier General Walter Smith, commanding the Columbian brigade of Washington and Georgetown militia.
7. Law's letter.
8. Burch's report.
9. *Ibid.*
10. Law's letter. The first time Law couldn't find his battery commander, Captain Burch had been hunting for Winder to ask for orders.
11. Law's letter.
12. Winder had instructed Law to retreat by the Georgetown road. Law said no rallying point was designated; Winder said specifically that he "directed the artillery to retire to the hill"; presumably he gave that instruction to Burch.
13. Winder's narrative.
14. Walter Smith's report.
15. This figure is based on the estimated strength of component units as listed by Winder and Williams. It is made up as follows:

Columbian brigade	1,070
Kramer	240
Waring	150
Maynard	150
Beall	750
Regulars	380
Flotillamen	400
Marines	120
Total	3,260

From this force, however, Captain Burch's battery and Captain Doughty's infantry company had been detached from the Columbian brigade; eighty of the regulars had been left at the Eastern Branch bridge near Washington; and there had been some loss by straggling. The figure used in the text deducts the eighty regulars and one hundred men for Burch's and Doughty's units; it makes no allowance for stragglers.
16. Winder.
17. *Ibid.*
18. The quotations are from Winder.
19. *Ibid.*
20. Williams, p. 232, said the British right wing was "continuing up the old Georgetown road."

21. Walter Smith.
22. Stansbury's report.
23. Subaltern.
24. *Ibid.*
25. The description of the positions of General Walter Smith's troops is taken from his official report, with minor omissions of superfluous punctuation to make reading easier. These changes do not alter the sense of his report in the slightest degree.
26. Barney *Memoir*, 265.
27. The figures are based on Williams and Gleig and on the regimental records of the British regiments engaged.
28. This figure is probably not exact: Gleig described the third brigade as "equalling in number the second brigade," about which he was specific.
29. Even Williams exaggerated on this point: he said, p. 232, the enemy outnumbered the troops in Walter Smith's positions "nearly two to one." Obviously, he was counting the British reserve brigade, which did not come into action.
30. A "charge" was not necessarily a bayonet charge; it was more likely to be a succession of advances between halts to fire; its objective was to come to close quarters with the bayonet, but the word did not, at that time, imply a single headlong rush.
31. Winder.
32. Walter Smith.
33. Letter of Joshua Barney to the secretary of the navy, dated from his farm at Elk Ridge, Md., Aug. 29, 1814; *American State Papers, XVI, Military Affairs*, I, 579.
34. Barney *Memoir*, 265.
35. Barney's letter.
36. *Ibid.*
37. *Ibid.*
38. From the British point of view —two companies of Baltimore artillery in line as a single battery, Burch's two guns in the Washington turnpike, and his three guns in or near the Georgetown road at the opposite end of Stansbury's line.
39. Barney *Memoir*, 265.
40. *Ibid.*
41. Barney's letter.
42. *Ibid.*
43. *Ibid.*
44. Walter Smith.
45. It is impossible to tell how many men of the light brigade were in this action. The brigade almost certainly was considerably weaker at this point than when it crossed the Eastern Branch; probably some of its men, even whole companies, had become separated from it during the pursuit of Stansbury's troops and continued to operate on the British right rather than on the left where Colonel Thornton, commanding the brigade, was leading its advance in person.
46. Subaltern thought it was half an hour. Barney thought that half an hour would cover the whole period from the enemy's first attempt to advance up the road toward his guns to the launching of its fifth attack on that end of the line—the assault that drove Beall's command off its hill.
47. Walter Smith.
48. Subaltern, 75.
49. Captain Webster's account, published in Marine, 177-181.
50. Barney *Memoir*, 266.
51. *Ibid.*
52. Gleig.
53. Subaltern, 75.
54. *Ibid.*: "our people, a little disheartened, retired."
55. Barney *Memoir*, 265.
56. Subaltern, 75.
57. Barney *Memoir*, 266.
58. Barney's letter.
59. Subaltern, 78.
60. Barney *Memoir*, 265.
61. *Ibid.*, 266.

62. Walter Smith.
63. Williams, 232.
64. The quoted words are General Walter Smith's.
65. Brooke probably had more men than those of his own regiment. See note 45.
66. Walter Smith.
67. *Ibid.*
68. The report of the Congressional committee of investigation went farther; it said, "Colonel Brent was placed in a position calculated to prevent" the flanking movement. The language used implies that Brent had taken up the new position.
69. Report of the committee of Congress investigating the causes of the defeat at Bladensburg; *American State Papers*, XVI, *Military Affairs*, I, 530.
70. *Ibid.*
71. This statement is substantiated later in the chapter.
72. See note 69.
73. Walter Smith.

74. Winder's narrative.
75. *Ibid.*
76. Barney's letter.
77. *American State Papers*, XVI, *Military Affairs*, I, 571.
78. *Maryland Roster, War of 1812*, Marine.
79. Walter Smith.
80. Gleig.
81. Barney's letter to the secretary of the navy.
82. Walter Smith. Incidentally, this regiment had shrunk to about half of its estimated force.
83. *Ibid.*
84. *Ibid.*
85. Williams, 238.
86. Walter Smith.
87. Lossing, 933.
88. Subaltern, 82.
89. Gleig.
90. Subaltern, 85-86.
91. Sioussat, p. 192.
92. From data in *Men of Marque*, Cranwell and Crane.
93. Marine, 114.

CHAPTER 9

1. *Citizen Soldiers of Baltimore*, frontispiece and p. 69.
2. Resolutions of the Annapolis Convention, Dec. 12, 1774.
3. The words "resolved, unanimously" appear at the beginning of both resolutions mentioned.
4. Scharf, III, 32.
5. *Men of Marque*, John Philips Cranwell and William B. Crane, p. 34. W. W. Norton & Company, Inc., New York, 1940.
6. Abstract of the ships and vessels belonging to the British navy at the commencement of the year 1814, appendix, *Naval History of Great Britain*, William James, vol. VI. London, 1859.
7. *Men of Marque*, 401.
8. Lossing, footnote, p. 945.

9. Scharf, III, 41.
10. One of the British officers who confirmed American charges of plundering as well as burning was Sir Charles Napier, commanding the 102nd regiment and a "brigade" of marines. He remarked that one or two officers in Admiral Cockburn's expedition had fathers "living in the very towns we are trying to burn"; that "at Ocracoke I put a stop to plunder"; and that "strong is my dislike to what is perhaps a necessary part of our job, viz. plundering and ruining the peasantry . . . we drive all their cattle and of course ruin them; my hands are clean, but it is hateful to see the poor Yankees robbed, and to be the robber." His

testimony on the outrages at Hampton, Va., appears in a later chapter, as published in *The Life and Opinions of General Sir Charles James Napier, G.C.B.,* Lieutenant General Sir W. Napier, K.C.B., I, 225. London, 1857.

11. Scharf, III, 42.
12. Niles's *Register*, IV, 182-196.
13. Scharf, III, 51.

14. Except for sailors and marines, Cockburn's force during 1813 and much of 1814 appears to have consisted of the 102nd under Charles Napier and a detachment of renegade Frenchmen enlisted as "Chasseurs Britanniques"—Napier, I, 220.
15. Resolution of the Committee of Vigilance and Safety, published in the Baltimore *Patriot*, Aug. 26, 1814.

CHAPTER 10

1. Except as otherwise noted, the details of Samuel Smith's early life and his military service are taken from his own third-person autobiography, published in part in the *Historical Magazine*, second series, vol. VII.
2. From Graydon's account of the court-martial of Lieutenant Jack Stuart (later major) of Smallwood's First Maryland battalion.
3. Roster of officers elected by the Maryland Convention, 1776.
4. *Battle of Long Island*, by Thomas W. Field.

5. Smith autobiography.
6. *Maryland Historical Magazine*, V, 205.
7. Description of Montebello from sketches and photographs published in the *Sun* of Baltimore and from an article by Lawrence Hall Fowler, illustrated with floor plans and with photographs by Julian A. Buckly, in the *Architectural Review*, November, 1909, XVI, 146-149.
8. Resolves of the Committee of Vigilance and Safety, Aug. 25, 1814.
9. Lossing, 672.

CHAPTER 11

1. Smith Autobiography.
2. The federal census of 1810 recorded the total population of Baltimore as 46,555.
3. The composite narrative sworn to by Peregrine Warfield, Richard J. Crabb, Charles J. Kilgour, Henry Nelson, Ephraim Gaither, Robert Kilgour, John H. Payne, H. C. Gaither, and Alexander C. Hanson as "some of the surviving persons who were devoted, or meant to be devoted, to the brutal and murderous fury of the mob in the late massacre in the jail at the City of Baltimore." They made their deposition under oath before John Fleming, justice of the peace for Montgomery County, at Rockville, Md., Aug. 12, 1812.

4. Scharf, III, 97.
5. *Ibid.*, 98.
6. The military service records of Baltimore privateer owners have been compiled from two sources: the lists of share owners as published in *Men of Marque*, by John Philips Cranwell and William B. Crane, W. W. Norton & Company; and the Maryland Roster, War of 1812, prepared by Louis Henry Dielman and published in Marine's *British Invasion of Maryland*.
7. Lossing, footnote, 948.
8. The total white population of Baltimore in 1810 was 36,212. The city's white males over sixteen years of age totaled only 11,311.

CHAPTER 12

1. "Controversy Over the Command at Baltimore," Ralph Robinson, in the *Maryland Historical Magazine*, vol. XXXIX, no. 3, p 179.

2. From a copy in Sam Smith's letterbook, in Smith MSS, Library of Congress; photostat by courtesy of Ralph Robinson. The initials which appear as the signature on the letterbook copy do not necessarily indicate that Smith did not sign original letter with his full name and rank—the style he used after assuming the command.

3. Winder mss. in the Library of Congress.

4. Smith mss. in the Library of Congress.

5. *Ibid.*

6. Winder mss.

7. *Ibid.*

8. *Ibid.*

9. Smith mss.

10. To conserve space, other specific footnotes for this chapter have been omitted. Following are the principal sources used:

Naval Documents, Quasi - War With France.

United States Naval Chronicle.

Life and Letters of Admiral D. G. Farragut, Loyall Farragut. D. Appleton and Company, New York.

Journal of a Cruize Made to the Pacific Ocean in the Years 1812, 1813 and 1814, Captain David Porter. Abstract of ships of the British navy at the commencement of the year 1814.

The Naval War of 1812, Theodore Roosevelt (2 vols.). Review of Reviews Company, New York.

History of Maryland, J. Thomas Scharf (3 vols.). John B. Piet.

Field Book of the War of 1812, Benson J. Lossing. Harper & Brothers, New York.

11. The two instances in which General Charles Lee's disobedience almost wrecked Washington's army: first, his refusal to cross the Hudson to support his commander in chief in November of 1776, thus forcing Washington to retreat across the Jerseys with only a fragment of his force; second, when he ordered the retreat at the beginning of the battle of Monmouth.

12. *R. E. Lee*, Douglas Southall Freeman, III, 89.

CHAPTER 13

1. James, VI, 187. Even this notoriously partisan British historian, ever on the alert to make the best possible showing for his countrymen, says that "had it [an overland attack on Baltimore] been risked, and had the fleet made a simultaneous movement up the bay, there is little doubt that Baltimore would have capitulated."

2. Letters of Henry Fulford and David Winchester, quoted in Chap. VIII.

3. Scharf, III, 39, footnote.

4. *Ibid.*

5. Ingersoll, I, 62.

6. A direct clue to the personal philosophy that shaped Sam Smith's thinking and his tactics appears in the unpublished diary of one of his militia officers. It is quoted in Chapter XXVI.

7. Scharf, III, 49.

8. Upper Marlborough.

9. Subaltern, 86-92. A few phrases and sentences have been omitted, without indication, to avoid retarding the narrative.

10. This paragraph is from the *Narrative of the Campaign of the British Army at Washington and New Orleans*, by the *same author*.

11. From Roger Brooke Taney's in-

troductory "letter" published in *The Poems of the Late Francis S. Key,*   *Esq.,* edited by Henry V. D. Jones and published in New York in 1857.

CHAPTER 14

1. Scharf, III, 100.
2. Letter of Captain James Piper to Brantz Mayer, 1854, *Maryland Historical Magazine,* VII, 378.
3. *Citizen Soldiers at North Point and Fort McHenry,* p. 70, quoting Niles's *Register* of Sept 10, 1814.
4. Scharf, III, 100.
5. James, VI, 180.
6. James, VI, 181.
7. *Subaltern in America,* 92.

8. Letter of Roger Brooke Taney, 1856.
9. *Life and Letters of Dolly Madison,* pp. 164-165, quoting a letter written by Mrs. Madison to her sister, Aug. 23, 1814.
10. Lossing, 948, footnote.
11. Scharf, III, 101.
12. Frederick M. Colston, in the *Maryland Historical Magazine,* II, 112.

CHAPTER 15

1. James, VI, 182.
2. Napier, 76.
3. Lossing, 938.
4. Napier, 80.
5. *Life and Letters of Dolly Madison.*
6. James, VI, 182.
7. Lossing, 940, footnote.
8. James, VI, 183.
9. Napier, 82.
10. Napier, 82.
11. Scharf, III, 103.
12. Baltimore *Patriot* advertisement.
13. Lossing, 949. Designation of the entire system of field works on Hampstead Hill as "Rodgers's Bastion" is erroneous.
14. *Citizen Soldiers at North Point and Fort McHenry,* 72.
15. R. E. Lee Russell's map of the battle of Baltimore.
16. Scharf, III, 101.
17. *Biographical Memoir of Commodore Joshua Barney,* Appendix, 315.
18. Russell's map.
19. Marine, 167.
20. The boom is shown on R. E. Lee Russell's map.
21. Weybright mentions this legend, p. 122, and quite properly discounts it.

22. *Star-Spangled Banner Flag House Guide to Historic Landmarks of Baltimore,* Mrs. Arthur B. Bibbins, p. 50.
23. Letter written by Caroline Pickersgill to Georgianna Armistead Appleton, daughter of Lieutenant Colonel George Armistead.
24. *Biographical Memoir of the Late Commodore Joshua Barney,* edited by Mary Barney, p. 30. Gray and Bowen, Boston, 1832.
25. *Ibid.,* 157-158.
26. *Ibid.,* 103-104.
27. *Ibid.,* 194-196.
28. Scharf, II, 345-346.
29. *Flag House Guide,* 22.
30. In collection of the Maryland Historical Society.
31. Caroline Pickersgill to Georgianna Appleton.
32. Scharf, III, 129.
33. *Flag House Guide,* quoting the Baltimore *Sun* of Nov. 11, 1928.
34. Barney *Memoir,* 262. The pertinent passage is this: "On the 1st of July, he [Barney] received a letter from the Secretary of the Navy, requesting his presence at the seat of government, which he immediately obeyed. On his arrival there, the subjects of consultation, on which

his views were required, were the situation of the flotilla, the probable intentions of the enemy, and the measures necessary to be taken by the government for the protection of Washington and Baltimore. The result of their deliberations was, that he should keep his thirteen barges and sloop *Scorpion*, with five hundred men, in the Patuxent, and that his first lieutenant, Mr. Rutter, should be despatched to Baltimore to take command of the fourteen barges and five hundred men remaining there. . . . He returned to his command, as soon as this decision was made known to him, having been absent only two days, and immediately despatched Mr. Rutter to Baltimore. After this, to place himself more conveniently within reach of either city in the event of invasion, he moved his flotilla up to Nottingham. . . ." The memoir then records "a short consultation" with General Winder at Nottingham and continues: "Thus things remained, until about the 16th of August. . . .'" The passage has been quoted almost in its entirety because it contains one of the reasons for my conclusion that Barney was in Baltimore, on at least a brief visit, sometime during the period covered. It shows that from the first week of July to the middle of August, except for the "short consultation" with Winder, there was nothing extraordinary to keep him at Nottingham, while there was an excellent reason for him to go to Baltimore to see Rutter established in command of the other half of the flotilla. While the evidence is indirect and circumstantial, it coincides with Caroline Pickersgill's positive statements that Barney (she named him first) and Stricker selected her mother to make the Fort McHenry flag, and that Mrs. Pickersgill had a "given time" in which to complete the work. The time limit imposed, and Caroline's testimony that her mother "worked many nights until twelve o'clock," indicate that the task was completed under pressure. A reasonable conclusion is that the pressure was due to either the increasing aggressiveness of the enemy's naval force in the Patuxent or positive news of the reinforcement of the fleet by troopships on the way from the Garonne. Positive information that the transports were on the way reached the United States "near the close of June" (Lossing, 917).

35. The motto was obviously intended to be "Unitas Virtus Fortior" —unity strengthens valor—but the last word was spelled "forcior."

36. *Flag House Guide*, 12.

37. Admiral Lord Howe's description on July 25, 1776, quoted in *The National Flag*, by Willis F. Johnson, p. 21. Houghton Mifflin Company, Boston, 1930.

38. The *Flag House Guide* goes so far as to say "probably."

39. *The National Flag*, 19.

40. John Paul Jones's phrase.

41. Johnson, 23.

42. Barney *Memoir*, p. 30, says that master's mate was "the second rank in the sloop." Scharf, II, 201, refers to Barney as "second officer," which technically would have made him third in rank but which undoubtedly was intended to mean that he was second in command.

43. Scharf, II, 202.

44. The clauses in quotation marks are from Johnson, p. 19. Unless the *Hornet* sailed from Baltimore without her new flag—an improbability, in view of the excitement caused by its arrival—Mr. Johnson's reasonable conclusions indicate that either Stone or Barney raised the Grand Union flag on an American warship before Jones raised it on the *Alfred*.

45. Caroline Pickersgill to Georgianna Appleton.

46. *Flag House Guide*, 11.

47. Johnson, p. 19, quoting Washington's letter to Joseph Reed.

48. These discrepancies are set forth in detail in Johnson's *The National Flag*, 39-41.

49. *Ibid.*, 18-19.

50. The *Hornet* and the *Wasp* sailed from Baltimore "towards the latter end of November," Barney *Memoir*, 30; "late in November," Scharf, II, 202.

51. They became "national colors" with the declaration of independence and were not supplanted by the Stars and Stripes until June 14, 1777, when Congress "Resolved: That the Flag of the thirteen United States be thirteen stripes, alternate red and white: that the Union be thirteen stars, white in a blue field, representing a new constellation." After that, the transition to the new flag was gradual.

52. It is posible, of course, to read different meanings into this sentence. It can be tortured to mean that Mrs. Young made the flag under Washington's direction *in person*, and thereby be discredited by known facts of time and place. But it does not say *in person*; taken as it stands, it coincides with the conclusions of.

historians of the flag, in so far as they believe Washington was consulted by the Congressional committee. It can also be interpreted to mean that Mrs. Young made flags according to the pattern of the first Grand Union flag. Caroline's leter is matter-of-fact; it contains no evidence of desire to "dress up" the circumstances; indeed, when Caroline was not certain, she said "I think." The tone and spirit of the letter seem to indicate that if Caroline had believed her grandmother merely made *some* flags or *a* flag of the first design, she would have said exactly that.

53. Letter of Dr. Benjamin Rush to Rebecca Young, Dec. 11, 1795.

54. *Ibid.*, and letter from Dr. Rush to Mrs. Young, May 30, 1788.

55. In the Pickersgill house, Baltimore.

56. *Flag House Guide*, 44.

57. Preserved in the Flag House.

58. Quoted in *Flag House Guide*, 46.

59. Preserved in the Flag House.

60. Weybright, 146.

61. Caroline Pickersgill to Georgianna Appleton.

62. Barney *Memoir*, 296.

63. "The Star-Spangled Banner" did not become the national anthem officially until March 3, 1931.

CHAPTER 16

1. Dutton, 235.

2. Napier, 85.

3. James, VI, 184.

4. Napier, 84.

5. *Ibid.*

6. *Ibid.*

7. James, VI, 183.

8. Napier, 84.

9. *Ibid.*

10. *Ibid.*

11. Napier, 84. Gordon's squadron was stronger than the list of his ships'

names indicates; his tenders were armed, some as gunboats, at least one as a mortar boat, one carried a howitzer, and one of the vessels seized at Alexandria was a gunboat. Lossing, p. 940, speaks of "war vessels, ten in number."

12. The normal armament of the British 18-gun brig-sloops.

13. Lossing, footnotes, 940.

14. Napier, 84.

15. *Ibid.*

16. *Ibid.*
17. *Ibid.*
18. James, VI, 184.
19. Napier, 84.
20. The normal combined broadside of two frigates, one rated at 38 guns but actually carrying 48, the other rated at 36 but carrying 46. Roosevelt, I, 81.
21. James, VI, 184.
22. *Ibid.,* 185; Napier, 84-85.
23. Napier, 85.
24. *Ibid.*
25. Lossing, p. 940, says 173 guns, but he was speaking of the squadron's total armament, not the number of guns that could be brought into action simultaneously. Counting the guns available in one broadside only, and crediting the bomb ships with their usual equipment of eight small deck guns each and the auxiliaries with the weapons mentioned by either James or Captain Napier of the *Euryalus,* the figure used in the text is very nearly correct.
26. Napier, 85.
27. James, VI, 185.
28. James says "cut." Napier, who was there, says "slipped."
29. Napier, 85.
30. *Ibid.*
31. James, VI, 185.
32. Dutton, 235.
33. James, VI, 185.
34. Napier, 85.
35. Dutton, 235.
36. *Ibid.*
37. Lossing, 941.
38. James, VI, 185.
39. *Ibid.*
40. Napier, 85.
41. *Ibid.*
42. Lossing, footnote, 941.
43. Barney rated her at 92 guns.
44. *Patriot,* Sept. 5, 1814.
45. Marine, 145. Except as otherwise specifically noted, details of activities in Baltimore in the first ten days of September are based on the text of resolutions of the Committee of Vigilance and Safety.
46. Clark, *Life and Letters of Dolly Madison,* p. 169, quoting the *National Intelligencer.*
47. In Maryland, even to this day, the word "countrymen" means people living in the country—that is, in rural areas. I am including this explanatory note because I used "countryman" in *The First Rebel* just as Colonel James Smith used it in his memoirs, in its almost immemorial colloquial meaning. A metropolitan-provincial critic seized it as a cudgel to belabor me for distorting history by trying to make it appear that James Smith's Black Boy insurgents, in 1765, thought of themselves as citizens of a new and independent country. The critic merely paraded his ignorance.
48. *Flag House Guide,* 23.
49. General Orders, dated at the headquarters of Major General Samuel Smith, Baltimore, Sept. 19, 1814, by order of the commanding general and signed by William Bates, assistant adjutant general of the Maryland Division.
50. Scharf, III, 100.
51. Sioussat, p. 186.
52. *Ibid.*
53. Written message from General Smith, quoted in full in Sioussat, 187.
54. *Ibid.*
55. Marine, 145.
56. Commodore Rodgers's report to the secretary of the navy, Sept. 23, 1814.
57. Letter of Brigadier General Hugh Douglass, Sixth Brigade, Virginia Militia, to the investigating committee of the House of Representatives, dated at Ellicott's Mills, Md., Nov. 20, 1814.
58. *Citizen Soldiers,* 70.

CHAPTER 17

1. Subaltern, 101.
2. *Ibid.*
3. Catlett's report.
4. *Ibid.*, postcript.
5. Subaltern, 116.
6. *Ibid.*, 92.
7. James, 177.
8. *Ibid.*
9. This percentage is based on acceptance of General Ross's figures; it is hardly to be expected that a general would make a false casualty return. His figures and Catlett's can be reconciled by assuming—as Lieutenant Gleig stated—that many of the slightly wounded rejoined their commands.
10. Subaltern, 100.
11. *Ibid.*
12. *Ibid.*
13. James, 188.
14. Subaltern, 103.
15. Taney's narrative.
16. James, VI, 188: "On the 6th of September came a flag of truce from Baltimore." It seems unlikely that two cartel ships from Baltimore visited the British fleet almost simultaneously. James's account, without evidence, implies some connection between the arrival of the flag of truce and the departure of the fleet from the Patuxent on the same day. It also raises a question as to whether *Tonnant* was then lying off the mouth of the Patuxent. But the confusion is no more confounding than the others which obscure and distort the whole campaign, and when one source fails another sometimes clarifies the issue; in this case, Subaltern's narrative at least suggests the possibility that if

the cartel arrived on September 6th, as James says, *Tonnant* was with the fleet. In that case, Taney erred in saying that Key found the British fleet in the mouth of the Potomac; but Taney's narrative was based on his recollection, after forty-three years, of what Key had told him. Errors of detail would not be surprising.
17. Taney's narrative.
18. Subaltern, 102.
19. *Ibid.*, 106.
20. This description of the movement of the British fleet up the bay is based on Subaltern.
21. Chapters II, IV.
22. Marine, 117.
23. Report of Captain Henry Crease, in Marine, 121-122.
24. *Ibid.*
25. The American and British reports agree.
26. This passage is based on *The Parson of the Islands*, a biography of the Rev. Joshua Thomas, by Adam Wallace; published by the author, 1861.
27. Both the words and the sarcastic quotation marks are James's.
28. The timing is based on Subaltern, 105.
29. *Ibid.*, 108.
30. *Ibid.*
31. The regular infantry attached to Winder's command during the southern Maryland campaign was detached and assigned to Armistead.
32. Scharf, II, 192.
33. This passage is a paraphrase of Marine, 147.

CHAPTER 18

1. Scharf, III, 107.
2. *Ibid.*
3. From a contemporary drawing.

4. Dielman's Maryland roster of the War of 1812.
5. *Ibid.*

6. Major Piper, in *Maryland Historical Magazine*, VII, 382.

7. Frederick M. Colston, in *Maryland Historical Magazine*, II, 113.

8. *Flag House Guide*, 47.

9. The flag is preserved in the museum of the Maryland Historical Society.

10. *History of the Medical Department of the United States Army*, Colonel P. M. Ashburn, pp. 37-38, Houghton Mifflin Company, Boston, 1929.

11. *Medical Sketches of the Campaigns of 1812, 13, 14*, James Mann, hospital surgeon of the army, p. 78. H. Mann and Co., 1816.

12. *Medical Sketches.*

13. *Ibid.*, 163.

14. *Ibid.*, 212, 225, 226.

15. *Ibid.*, 29.

16. *History of the Medical Department*, 38.

17. *Ibid.*

18. *Medical Sketches*, 227.

19. *Ibid.*, 79.

20. Sioussat, p. 192.

21. Life of *Charles James Napier*, 222.

22. James, VI, 94.

23. *Ibid.*

24. *Virginia, The Old Dominion*, Matthew Page Andrews, pp. 288-289. Doubleday Doran, New York, 1937.

25. *Ibid.*, 390-391.

26. *Sir Charles Napier, Life and Opinions*, Lt. Gen. Sir W. Napier, I, 216.

27. Theodore Roosevelt.

28. *Naval War of 1812*, Roosevelt.

29. The author is indebted to H. L. Mencken for his confirmation of the evolution of this expression.

30. *The Story of the Baltimore and Ohio Railroad*, Edward Hungerford, p. 104. G. P. Putnam's Sons, New York, 1928.

31. Report of Captain Henry Crease, who succeeded to the command of the landing party after Parker's death.

32. Models of field guns of the War of 1812, carved from bone by prisoners of war, show shafts for the near wheel horse; hitching the teams tandem had been abandoned, but the shafts remained.

33. *Historical Sketch of the Artillery of the United States Army*, William E. Birkhimer, first lieutenant, Third regiment, p. 230, 1884. Lieutenant Birkhimer said that the substitution of the pole for shafts was among the changes "made before 1807," but much of the matériel used in the War of 1812 antedated the adoption of the changes.

34. *Ibid.*, 34-35.

35. *A Hand Book for Infantry*, Colonel William Duane, 1812; and The *System of Infantry Discipline According to the Regulation Established for the Army of the United States, 19 March, 1813.*

36. *Field Artillery Manual*, Captain Arthur R. Wilson, vol. I, chap. XL, p. 10. George Banta Publishing Company, 1929.

37. Sir Howard Douglas, in a footnote in his *Naval Gunnery*, mentions 3,700 yards as the range of a 24-pound rocket with "full length fuze" at an elevation of 47 degrees and 3,000 yards for a 12-pounder at 40 degrees.

38. In his *Naval War of 1812*, Theodore Roosevelt gave September 13th as the date of the action at North Point, vol. II, p. 47.

39. The strength of the regiments is based on Sterrett's report.

40. *Ibid.*

41. *Ibid.*

CHAPTER 19

1. Subaltern, 109.
2. *Ibid.*
3. Sea mortars: see Chap. XXVII and footnotes.
4. *Naval Gunnery*, Sir Howard Douglas.
5. James, VI, 191. Roger Brooke Taney's account of Francis Key's experiences in the British fleet says Cochrane shifted to the frigate *Surprise*, commanded by his son.
6. Subaltern, 110.
7. *Ibid.*
8. *Ibid.*, 112.
9. *Ibid.*
10. In the British service at that time, "all cables were made 120 fathoms in length"—The Old Wooden Walls, *Falconer's Marine Dictionary, 1769-1859*, p. 40. Then, as now, a fathom was six feet.
11. The largest field guns mentioned in American records of the Maryland campaign are eighteen-pounders.
12. *Narrative*, 170.
13. *Ibid.*
14. Subaltern, 114.
15. *Ibid.*, 113.
16. *Ibid.*, 179. Commodore Joshua Barney was the officer who once fired crowbars into an enemy ship.
17. *Ibid.*, 113.

CHAPTER 20

1. The actual danger; in theory, the brigade's flanks were still exposed to amphibious assault, but none was intended.
2. *The War of 1812*, Henry Adams; *Infantry Journal* edition, p. 236.
3. Stricker's report says that he received information of the enemy's landing "from the advanced videttes" at seven o'clock. The landing was not completed until seven, according to Gleig; the videttes who brought the information had to come seven miles; they might have come sooner, but they brought the information before the British advance began. The charge that Stricker did nothing to protect himself except to send a detachment of cavalry and riflemen "a mile or two" out falls flat. If the cavalry videttes had been no more than two miles to the front, they would not have seen the enemy until nearly noon.
4. Stricker's report.
5. *Ibid.*
6. *Ibid.*
7. The order of march is assumed from the order of deployment.
8. Stricker's report.
9. Louis Henry Dielman.
10. Stricker's Report.
11. The British advance did not begin until after seven o'clock: *Narrative*, 170.
12. The description is from a sketch reproduced in Lossing, p. 950.
13. From a contemporary painting.
14. Stricker's report.
15. *Ibid.*
16. Smith's report.
17. Stricker's report.
18. *Ibid.*
19. *Ibid.*
20. *Ibid.*
21. This is a conclusion, the result of working out a timetable of the day's events from the known times, and fitting into it the incidents and situations of which no actual time record has survived but whose relationship to the sequence of events can be established.

CHAPTER 21

1. This passage is based on Subaltern, 116-117.

2. *Ibid.*, 117-118.

3. Sioussat, 183-184.

4. Stricker's report: "the cavalry continually announced" the progress of the British column.

5. *Narrative*, 171.

6. James, VI, 189.

7. *Medicine in Virginia In The Nineteenth Century*, Wyndham B. Blanton, M.D., p. 317. Garrett & Massie, 1933.

8. Subaltern, 119.

9. *Ibid.*

10. Major Browne.

11. Subaltern, 116.

12. The evidence that the American videttes were watching is contained in Stricker's report, although Stricker apparently was unable to believe that the whole British army was then at Gorsuch's: he thought the men there must be "a small marauding party."

CHAPTER 22

1. Stricker's report.

2. *Ibid.*

3. *Ibid.*

4. *Ibid.*

5. Stricker not only sharply criticized the retreat of the rifle battalion in his report, he also pointedly thanked Captain Aisquith while omitting any mention of Dyer by name except in his statement of his total force.

CHAPTER 23

1. This statement of time is based on the time of Stricker's countermove "about one o'clock." It fits into the timetable of events which can be definitely established.

2. This was Stricker's impression, as stated in his report.

3. Smith's report.

4. Stricker's report.

5. *Ibid.*

6. Stricker's report: "one 4 pounder with 10 men under Lieut. Stiles."

7. Based on a passage in the Life of *John W. H. Hawkins*, by William George Hawkins, quoted in Marine, p. 191: "Early in the day the word had passed along the lines, 'Remember boys, General Ross rides a white horse today.'"

8. The quotation is from Marine's account of "the tradition of the Mc-Comas family," p. 193.

9. The presence of Dr. Martin, mounted and accompanying the fore-most elements of Heath's detachment, is substantiated in *Old Baltimore* by Annie Leakin Sioussat, who as a child heard Dr. Martin tell his story of the fight of the detachment.

10. Recounted in Marine, p. 191, as having been related to Dr. Martin by Robert Gorsuch "a few days after the battle."

11. The account included in *Citizen Soldiers*, published for the seventy-fifth anniversary celebration of the successful defense of Baltimore, says that Heath's advance guard was attacked "before they expected it."

12. Subaltern, 30.

13. This passage is based on Subaltern's description of the fight "from thicket to thicket, and tree to tree."

14. Subaltern, 122.

15. *Ibid.*

16. Marine, p. 192, paraphrasing Sannford's *Experiences of a Sergeant*

in the King's Service in America, London, 1817.

17. Subaltern, p. 124, names Captain M'Dougal as Ross's aide-de-camp.

18. The order to retreat had been given: Marine, 193.

19. Marine, 193.

20. Subaltern, 123.

21. Based on Sannford's account. Subaltern says M'Dougal caught Ross as he was falling. Both can be correct.

22. Marine, 193.

23. *Ibid.*

24. *Ibid.*

25. Sioussat, 188.

26. *Ibid.* Dr. Martin "also saw Lieutenant Andre of the Union Yagers fall from the fence from which he fired his last shot."

27. *Ibid.*

28. From the Hawkins narrative, quoted in Marine.

CHAPTER 24

1. Subaltern, 125.

2. *Ibid.*, 127.

3. *Ibid.*, 125.

4. Stricker did not mention, in his report, the "two discharges of grape" described by Lieutenant Gleig. The omission, however, is not remarkable; there is no reason to disbelieve the account in Subaltern, 126.

5. Duane's *Military Dictionary*.

6. The description of the handling of the guns is based on Lieutenant Birkhimer's *Historical Sketch of the Organization, Administration, Materiel and Tactics of the Artillery, United States Army*, pp. 312-313.

7. Duane.

8. *Ibid.*

9. Subaltern, 126.

10. *Ibid.*, 127.

11. *Narrative*, 178.

12. Stricker's report.

13. *A biographical Memoir of the Late Commodore Joshua Barney*, edited by Mary Barney, p. 257. Gray and Bowen, 1832.

14. Congreve; see note 11, chap. XXVI.

15. Stricker's report.

16. Subaltern, 128.

17. Stricker's report: he ordered the artillery to open on "the enemy's right column then pushing across towards my left."

18. Subaltern, 128.

19. Stricker in his report cited both

Calhoun and Stevenson for courage and efficiency in the action.

20. The orders are virtually verbatim from Stricker's report.

21. The Smith mss, in the Library of Congress include several returns of the 51st on summer training duty.

22. Stricker's report. The evidence that Barney transmitted the order and served with the guns on the left of the line is circumstantial: Stricker commended Barney in his report for his "great service" in "aiding Captain Montgomery," and since Montgomery had only four guns left in action in the lane the place where Barney could have been most useful was with the detached pieces on the exposed flank.

23. Subaltern, 128.

24. *Ibid.*, 130: "their extreme left . . . in the course of the cannonade . . . received more than its due proportion of salutations" from the British artillery.

25. Subaltern, 129.

26. *Ibid.*, 128. Shrapnel was invented in 1784 by Lieutenant Henry Shrapnel. Captain Arthur Wilson's *Field Artillery Manual* states that it was then known as "spherical case shot" and that its name was changed to that of its inventor in 1852. However, it is called Shrapnel (with a capital S) in Lieutenant Gleig's account published in 1833. Captain Wil-

son states that the new shell did not come into use until sixteen years after its invention. It was still so new that Lieutenant Colonel William Duane, author of the *American Military Library,* did not mention it in his exhaustive *Military Dictionary* published in 1810.

27. Subaltern, 128.
28. *Ibid.*
29. *Ibid.*
30. *Narrative,* 178.
31. Maryland Roster of the War of 1812, in Marine.
32. Stricker's report.
33. Subaltern, 127.
34. *Ibid.,* 129, and *Narrative,* 178.
35. Three killed, four wounded.
36. *Narrative,* 177: "the 21st remained in column upon the road."
37. Smith's report.
38. *Historical Record of the Twenty-first Regiment.*
39. *Historical Record of the Forty-fourth Regiment.*
40. *Historical Record of the Fourth Foot.*
41. *Ibid.*
42. *Narrative,* 178.
43. Subaltern, 129.
44. Duane.
45. *Ibid.*
46. *Ibid.*
47. Stricker's report.
48. Subaltern, 128.
49. *Narrative,* 177.
50. *Ibid.,* 179.
51. *Ibid.,* 177.
52. From a contemporary painting.
53. Subaltern, 129.
54. The regimental color of the 44th.
55. *Narrative,* 179.
56. *Ibid.*
57. *Narrative,* 180.
58. Subaltern, 132.
59. *Ibid.*
60. *Ibid.*
61. *Narrative,* 175.
62. Stricker's report.

63. *Ibid.*
64. Stricker's report.
65. Subaltern, 135: the Fourth "arrived not in time to take much share in the action." Its whole share, in fact, was the rounding up of stragglers from the 51st—"about half of a battalion," Gleig said, although the record of prisoners does not include so many.
66. From the description of officers' equipment in Subaltern and *Narrative.*
67. Lossing, 674.
68. From the painting of the battle by Thomas Ruckle, who was a corporal in the Washington Blues of the Fifth Maryland.
69. Stricker said the British opened fire with rockets at "half-past 2 o'clock," that the British line advanced "about 10 minutes before 3 o'clock," and that after infantry firing began it was "incessant till about 15 minutes before 4 o'clock."
70. Subaltern, 134.
71. The casualties are taken from Brigade Major Leonard Frailey's report, of which he said "I pledge myself for its correctness."
72. Stricker's report.
73. *Citizen Soldiers,* 76.
74. The casualties of the United Volunteers are from the memorandum made by John Pendleton Kennedy from the company book.
75. Subaltern, 133.
76. Subaltern, 133: the last British volley was fired "within less than twenty yards of the American line."
77. *Citizen Soldiers,* 73. The guns had fired 130 rounds.
78. Stricker's report.
79. Gleig reported two American guns and one tumbril taken. The Americans admitted the loss of only one gun. Again, the seemingly conflicting claims may both be correct—if the Americans did not count the gun wrecked by the enemy's fire.

80. *Narrative*, 181.

81. Maryland Roster of the War of 1812 and Surgeon James H. McCulloch's list of wounded American

prisoners of war "paroled at the meetinghouse." Both Davidson nad Lamb are on the list.

82. *Narrative*, 194.

CHAPTER 25

1. *Historical Record, Twenty-first Regiment, Royal North British Fusiliers*, p. 41.

2. *Narrative*, 180.

3. *The War of 1812*, Henry Adams: *Infantry Journal* edition, 237.

4. James, VI, 189.

5. *Narrative*, 180.

6. *Ibid*.

7. Colonel Brooke's dispatch.

8. Subaltern, 135.

9. *Narrative*, 197-8.

10. *Ibid.*, 177.

11. Brooke's dispatch.

12. Marine, 170.

13. Subaltern, 137.

14. Stricker's report.

15. Sunset was at 6:19 P.M.

16. Subaltern, 138.

17. *Narrative*, 197.

18. *Ibid.*, 180.

19. Stricker's report.

20. *Ibid*.

21. *Ibid*.

22. *Ibid*.

23. The "hour" is an approximation based on the time probably required to re-form, collect stragglers, reorganize the small train, and assign details to block the road and equip them with axes. Stricker said he left the position after "due deliberation." He may have held it longer than an hour.

24. There is no direct evidence indicating a timetable in the literal sense. Cockburn's presence with the army indicates a considerable degree of co-ordination; and in two services accustomed to working together, some co-ordination must be assumed.

25. Major James Piper, who was captain of the United Maryland Ar-

tillery battery, City Brigade, during the defense of Baltimore; letter to Brantz Meyer, *Maryland Historical Magazine*, VII, 382.

26. *Historical Record, Twenty-first Regiment*; and James, VI, 190.

27. Because the regular battalion commanders were leading regiments.

28. James, VI, 190.

29. *Historical Record, Twenty-first*.

30. James, VI, 190. The casualties may have been higher. James, for example, does not include Major Robert Kenny of the 21st among the wounded. In the light of the discrepancies in the British casualty reports after Bladensburg—that is, the omission of all wounded who were able to continue duty or who quickly rejoined their units—it is not unreasonable to think that the official return of casualties after the battle of Godly Wood was reduced by similar omissions. Only the admitted casualties have been used in the text.

31. Thornton and Brooke's.

32. *Narrative*, 186.

33. Stricker's report.

34. Smith's report.

35. The positions of the American troops as given here are taken from contemporary maps, superimposed upon an accurate scaled map generously given to the author by George Carter, deputy city engineer of Baltimore.

36. See Chap. XXI.

37. From east to west: the Bel Air or Perry Hall road, the Harford road, the York road.

38. Surrey stood about a mile and a half straight west from the junction

of the Philadelphia and North Point roads, but only half a mile from the Philadelphia road itself.

39. Subaltern, 152.

40. *Ibid.,* 141.

41. *Ibid.,* 136.

42. Half an hour before sunrise.

43. References to looting in this narrative are in no sense reflections on the British army; looting was an established custom in most armies of the time.

44. Subaltern, 142.

45. *Ibid.*

46. Armistead said the bombardment opened "about sunrise," which was at 5:46. He also said it lasted, with two slight intermissions, for 25 hours and ended at 7 A.M. Wednesday. The first shot, therefore, was fired about 6 A.M. Tuesday.

47. Armistead's report.

48. *Ibid.*

49. James, VI, 190.

50. Armistead's report.

51. Roosevelt, II, 47-8.

52. James, VI, 181.

53. Taney's narrative.

54. Armistead's report: "finding that his shells reached us, he [the enemy bomb vessels] anchored."

55. Scharf, III, 120.

56. At 3,500 yards, the flight of a thirteen-inch mortar shell lasted 29 seconds: Duane's tables of English sea-service mortars.

57. James, VI, 190.

58. The "best bower" and the "small bower" anchors, a little different in size, were so named because they were carried in the bows: The Old Wooden Walls, Falconer's *Marine Dictionary, 1769-1815,* p. 4.

59. Armistead's report; the first shells "reached us."

60. Duane's tables.

61. Armistead's report.

62. The ditch has been filled in.

63. Minutes of the Committee of Vigilance and Safety.

64. This passage is based on the proceedings of the Committee of Vigilance and Safety and on detailed drawings prepared by F. A. Smith, captain of engineers, from dimensions furnished by Captain Henry Thompson.

65. Marine, 86.

66. Armistead's report.

67. *Ibid.* Thirty-five men of the three regular artillery companies alone were "sick and unfit for duty."

68. *Ibid.*

69. *Ibid.*

70. From army engineer drawings of the fort, 1819.

71. Rodgers's report.

72. *Fort McHenry, National Monument and Historic Shrine,* published by the United States Department of the Interior.

73. *Ibid.*

74. Duane's tables.

75. Scharf, III, 101.

76. *Fort McHenry,* note 72 above.

77. Armistead spoke of them as mortars.

78. Armistead's report.

79. Duane.

80. He had been a first lieutenant, and had been recently promoted.

81. Rodgers's report.

82. This statement seems to contradict James, VI, 191, although James's reference to "gunboats" *inside* the barrier of hulks may be to vessels other than flotilla barges. At least some of the barges apparently were outside the barrier, because Lieutenant Rutter of the flotilla was thanked by General Smith for his conduct of "the highly important duty of advanced night guards" for the fort.

83. Rodgers's report.

84. Niles's *Register.*

85. Armistead's report.

86. The testimony is British: the word is Sir Howard Douglas's.

87. *Chasseur* was 356 tons; the tonnage of the eight bomb ships in the

British navy in 1814 totaled 2,845, an average of 355 tons. *Constitution* rated 1,576 tons; *Old Ironsides*, p. 7. Light British frigates armed with eighteen-pounder cannon rated better than 1,000 tons: tables in James, VI.

88. Coin—the 1814 spelling of quoin, a wedge for varying the elevation and range of a cannon.

89. The term "breech," strange as it may seem to the layman, applied to muzzle-loading cannon. It was "the solid piece of metal behind, between the vent and the extremity of the base-ring, and which terminates the hind part of the gun, exclusive of the cascable"—Duane. The cascable was defined as "the hindermost part of the breech, from the base-ring to the end of the button."

90. Duane's tables.

91. Minutes of the Committee.

92. Armistead's report.

93. Smith's report.

94. Armistead's report.

95. Minutes of the Committee: a special committee was named "to erect three bomb proof Magazines, and two bomb proof barracks at Fort McHenry, agreeable to the requisition of the Major General [Smith] of this date." The roof of the magazine was not strengthened to a thickness of thirteen feet until long after the bombardment.

96. *Maryland Historical Magazine*, VII, 377.

97. Duane.

98. Armistead's report.

99. *Ibid.*

100. Armistead said 400 fell within the works in 25 hours.

101. Duds were dug up after the battle and found to weigh, with their explosives in them, 210 to 220 pounds. The regulation weight of thirteen-inch mortar shells, loaded, was 194 pounds.

102. The iron casings of the mortar shells were 2.05 inches thick: Duane.

103. Lossing, p. 956.

104. *Ibid.*

105. *The Flag Is Still There*, Swanson. G. P. Putnam's Sons, New York.

106. Piper, *Maryland Historical Magazine*, VII, 384.

107. Minutes of the Committee.

108. Smith mss., Library of Congress.

109. Lieutenant Colonel Taylor's regiment was thanked by Smith in general orders. Its position was specified in division orders issued by Winder on Sept. 15: "left in charge of the defences in part on the Ferry Branch."

110. The position of this detachment appears on some maps. Neither the identity of troops composing it nor the identity of the commander is mentioned in reports. There is one officer named Hancock on Dielman's roster of the Maryland campaign: Captain Francis Hancock, 22nd regiment, Maryland militia. The 22nd was an Anne Arundel regiment.

111. James, VI, 190. Smith said the British "manoeuvered during the morning towards our left." Gleig said "we did not come in sight of the main army of the Americans till evening." Gleig implied that the whole British army did not come within sight of Smith's lines until evening, and the implication has misled the historians of a number of British regiments. The timing and the sequence of events in this portion of Gleig's account are jumbled and useless.

112. Smith's report.

113. *Ibid.*

114. *Ibid.*

115. Frederick M. Colston, *Maryland Historical Magazine*, II, 119.

116. Subaltern, 144.

117. *Narrative*, 187.

118. Subaltern, 144.

119. Colston, above.

120. *Narrative*, 187.

121. The phrase is Gleig's.

122. *Narrative*, 187.
123. *Ibid.*
124. The quoted words are from both *Narrative* and Subaltern.
125. Rodgers's bastion.
126. Subaltern, 148.
127. *Ibid.*
128. *Ibid.*
129. *Ibid.*, 149.
130. *Ibid.*
131. It is impossible to arrive at an accurate figure. Scharf said seven thousand "occupied the trenches," but he put the City Brigade in the trenches—where it was not. James, surprisingly conservative in this instance, spoke of 4,500 at North Point "backed . . . by at least 8,000 more, and these hourly augmenting." In addition to the Baltimore brigade, Smith had two other Maryland brigades and one from Virginia, plus the garrison of Whetstone Point and the batteries in the Ferry Branch and at the Lazaretto, plus Rodgers's seamen and marines in the Loudenslager works, plus the crews of the flotilla barges, plus various other units. Records fail to show whether Griffin Taylor's Virginia regiment was a part of the Virginia brigade, whether Randall's Pennsylvania riflemen were attached to one of the Maryland brigades, or whether Hancock's men were counted in the strength of any of the brigades. I have preferred to err—if there is any error in my estimate of Smith's force—on the side of greater numbers.
132. Scharf, III, 104.
133. Subaltern, 149.
134. Narrative, 188.
135. *Ibid.*
136. Smith's report.
137. *Ibid.*
138. *Ibid.*
139. Colston.
140. Smith's report.
141. Colston.

142. The Baltimore City Brigade and the Virginia brigade.
143. Jones Falls.
144. *Narrative*, 192. The quoted words applied to the night attack; they apply with even greater force here.
145. *Ibid.*
146. James, Subaltern, and *Narrative* agree that the night attack was definitely planned.
147. The wording of this sentence is deliberate. Whether Brooke conceived the possibility of a diversion by means of a boat attack against some other part of the American defenses is a question that cannot be answered. The relationship between the plan to carry the works on Loudenslager's hill by night assault, and the boat attack in the Ferry Branch, apparently has escaped notice. The fact is that the water-borne attack was made—preceded by an unusually heavy fire from the bombarding ships —at the time Brooke's troops were awaiting orders to go forward in a silent bayonet assault on Smith's works. The fact is that the retreat began *after* the failure of the boat attack, and that the orders for retreat were not given until *after* the storm of firing from the encircling American batteries gave proof that surprise had failed and that the attack, too, probably would fail. The fact is that the *two* night attacks were coordinated as to time, and that the prime characteristic of the boat attack was diversionary. The reasonable conclusion—indeed, the only conclusion that makes any sense—is that the boat attack was intended to distract the Americans' attention from the impending assault in the vicinity of the Philadelphia road, and that Cochrane decided on it as the only practicable means of supporting the land assault (James, VI, 191). The corollary conclusion is that Gleig's excited

account is wrong in respect to timing, and that there was in fact liaison between fleet and army sometime in the afternoon or at the latest by early evening of Sept. 13th. This does not eliminate Gleig's story of his friend's adventures in attempting to open communication with the fleet later that night. It does not eliminate even his description of the anxious waiting, in the British lines, for the fleet to open fire; obviously, what Gleig meant was that the troops were waiting for the fleet to *reopen* fire. There was a period of especially furious bombardment shortly before the boats were discovered in the Ferry Branch; and there was—as there must be—a break in the firing when the boats entered the zone of shell bursts.

148. Smith's report.

149. Rodgers's bastion again.

150. Harris's Creek.

151. The timing and the place of the British concentration are based on Smith's report. Smith said that the movements of Stricker's and Douglass's brigades "induced the enemy to concentrate his forces [between one and two o'clock] in my front."

152. The right flank of the British deployment is fixed approximately by the fact that Colonel Sterrett's home, Surrey, was within the British lines, although possibly only within the lines of outguards on the right flank. The conformation of the harbor channel made the southern end of the American position unassailable —by land—on a front of approximately a quarter of a mile and perhaps more, if allowance is made for deep water in the mouth of Harris's Creek. Including proper flank guards, the British lines need not have extended more than a mile and a half to cover the whole assailable part of the east front of the American position.

153. It should be noted that this narrative undertakes no description of the British formation; no record of it, apparently, has survived, if any ever was set down. The front of the British concentration was covered by an extended outpost line later in the day; but in the early afternoon, presumably, the infantry did not deploy into the line of battle but advanced, probably, in columns of half-companies. The context of Smith's report indicates, although it does not say so positively, that he felt no apprehension of immediate attack; he might have felt some concern if the enemy had advanced in line of battle.

154. James said "*the* four bomb-vessels" and *Erebus*. Armistead mentioned only three ships, but at no point in his report did he refer to *Erebus*. James's phrase obviously is an error: there were five bomb ships in the action. The reasonable conclusion is that Armistead was correct in his reference to three bomb ships taking part in the close bombardment, and that James confused the four ships engaged at close range (including *Erebus*) as *the* four bomb vessels.

155. The incident which encouraged the British ships to advance occurred, according to Armistead, "about two o'clock." The aggressive movements of the ships and army were in progress at about the same time. It is not intended to imply that they began at the same moment; to establish the exact timing of the two movements is impossible.

156. There is no evidence of deliberate co-ordination at this stage. The movement of the ships at about the same time the troops advanced seems to have been wholly opportunistic.

157. Smith's report: "I immediately drew Generals Winder and Stricker nearer to the left of my entrenchments and to the right of the enemy."

158. *Ibid.:* "showing an intention of attacking us that evening."

159. *Ibid.*

160. The orchard not only covered the British firing line but also screened the rapid advance of the enemy's left flank from Winder's observation.

161. The advance of the Fifth Maryland. The charge made by Barney's men in the final phase of the battle was a countercharge or a pursuit of a defeated British charge rather than an advance.

162. British criticisms, right or wrong, apply only to Stricker's battle and to the absence of resistance along the North Point road from the battlefield to the Baltimore lines.

163. Smith's report.

164. "Midnight" is an approximation. Its use as the intended time of the land attack is justified by the evidence that Brooke's night assault and the boat attack in the Ferry Branch were planned as a co-ordinated operation.

165. Armistead's report: "I immediately ordered a fire to be opened, which was obeyed with alacrity through the whole garrison." Since the ships were within what Armistead believed to be "a good striking distance," the conclusion that he used every gun that had a chance of reaching them is warranted.

166. Armistead's report.

167. James, VI, 190.

168. Armistead's report.

169. Marine, 173.

170. Armistead's report.

171. James, VI, 191.

172. *Citizen Soldiers,* 75.

173. James, VI, 191, says Cochrane became concerned about *Erebus;* the fact of withdrawal, in the immediate presence of the vice-admiral, is sufficient evidence of his anxiety about the other ships.

174. See Chap. XXVII.

175. James, VI, 191.

176. *Ibid.*

177. Armistead's report.

178. *Ibid.*

179. Until the bombardment temporarily ceased just before the boat expedition entered the zone of fire.

180. The casualties are from Marine, 173.

181. Scharf, III, 116.

CHAPTER 26

1. The word is James's, VI, 192.

2. Other commanders had had as many ships at their disposal, but they had been dispersed for blockade purposes.

3. The full strength of the British army was not used at Bladensburg.

4. Based on James and Gleig.

5. James, VI, 191.

6. *War of 1812,* Adams, 237.

7. *Narrative,* 192.

8. *Men of Marque,* 298.

9. *Naval War of 1812,* Roosevelt, I, 85.

10. James, VI, 192.

11. The sources of the descriptions of the mortar vessels and the rocket ship are these:

A Treatise on the General Principles, Powers, and Facility of Application of the Congreve Rocket System, as Compared with Artillery, Major General Sir W. Congreve, Bart., M.P., F.R.S. Longman, Rees, Orme, Brown, and Green, Paternoster Row, London, 1827.

The Elements and Practise of Naval Architecture, David Steele. Steel and Co., Chart-Sellers to the Admiralty, at their Navigation-Warehouse, 70, Cornhill, London, 1812.

The Sea-Gunners Vade-Mecum,

Robert Simmons. Charles Wilson, 157, Leadenhall street, London, 1812.

Engines of War, Henry Wilkinson. Longman, Orme, Brown, Green and Longmans, Paternoster Row, London, 1841.

A New and Universal Dictionary of the Marine, originally compiled by William Falconer, modernized by William Burney, LL.D., master of the Naval Academy, Gosport, 1830.

A Military Dictionary, by William Duane, late lieutenant colonel in the Army of the United States. Philadelphia, 1810.

The Naval Gunner, Lieutenant T. S. Beauchant, Royal Marine Artillery. James Gilbert, Paternoster Row, London, 1828.

12. James, VI, appendix; table of "the ships and vessels belonging to the British navy at the commencement of the year 1814." The table for the next year shows only seven.

13. James, VI, 191.

14. *Ibid.*

15. The reference is unmistakably clear: Subaltern, 156.

16. This is a conclusion, but every detail of the evidence supports it.

17. See end paper map.

18. The road from Sparrow's Point.

19. Rodgers's report.

20. Subaltern, 158.

21. *Ibid.*, 159.

22. *Ibid.*

23. *Ibid.*

24. *Ibid.*, 156.

25. The evidence is Brooke's own conduct.

26. Subaltern, 156.

27. *Ibid.*

28. *Narrative*, 189.

29. Subaltern, 156.

30. A conclusion warranted by the accumulation of evidence.

31. The term "in military affairs, implies a desperate resolution in all small expeditions, of surprise . . . the very name . . . implies risk,

hazard, precarious warfare, and a critical but desperate operation": Duane.

32. The word is Gleig's.

33. That Brooke expected some form of assistance, even after he knew that fire on Rodgers's bastion was impossible, is obvious.

34. From a letter, in diary form, written by M. E. Bartgis, first lieutenant, Frederick volunteers.

35. *Ibid.*

36. See end paper map.

37. James, VI, 191.

38. *Ibid.*

39. *Ibid.*

40. That is, it was "after the boats had been ordered upon this service" (James, VI, 191) and therefore after the repulse of the mortar ships and *Erebus* from their advanced stations in midafternoon.

41. Colston, *Maryland Historical Magazine*, II, 119.

42. Subaltern, 153.

43. *Ibid.*, 154.

44. *Ibid.*, 155.

45. *Ibid.*

46. Diary-letter of Lieutenant Bartgis.

47. Major Piper.

48. Rodgers's report.

49. Minutes of the Committee of Vigilance and Safety.

50. Subaltern, 154.

51. *Citizen Soldiers.*

52. Major Piper.

53. A conclusion, obvious upon the evidence.

54. This is a conclusion drawn from the fact that the 21st did not appear in Gleig's listing of the order of attack.

55. The attack "was to begin with a heavy fire on the right" of the American position: Subaltern, 156. The conclusion as to the strength of the diversionary force is based on two pieces of indirect evidence: first, the omission of the marine battalion

from Gleig's order of attack and, second, the obvious fact that Brooke could not spare many men for such a diversion but that, in a force whose companies did not much exceed fifty or sixty men, a single company could hardly have produced a heavy enough fire to create an effective diversion.

56. *Ibid.*

57. Gleig's own outpost, stationed near Surrey, was called in just before the retreat began: Subaltern, 158.

58. Gleig found the column formed on the road: *ibid.*

59. Not necessarily *on* the road.

60. Subaltern, 156.

61. Rodgers's report.

62. Subaltern, 156.

63. From contemporary maps.

64. Fifty was the normal marine complement of a United States frigate; since Rodgers specified that the marines were from *Guerriere's* crew, the force did not exceed fifty.

65. At least, Smith made no mention of any concentration that night.

66. Lieutenant Bartgis is the witness as to the cold nights.

67. *Narrative,* 189.

68. *Ibid.,* 190. The account is from the *Narrative.*

69. J. M. Clemence, Director *Nautical Almanac,* United States Naval Observatory.

70. A conclusion, warranted by the evidence: Brooke was waiting for an outburst of firing from the ships: the "redoubled" bombardment began "about eleven o'clock," according to Sailing Master Webster.

71. They did. *Ibid.*

72. James, VI, 191.

73. *Ibid.* Testimony to his efficiency appears, *ibid.,* p. 181.

74. *Ibid.,* 191. Webster said the British had twenty-two barges and "a long schooner."

75. *Euryalus* was an eighteen-pounder frigate. Webster, who dug the schooner's shot out of the bank

behind his battery, said they were eighteen-pounders: he used them in his own guns.

76. James, VI, 191, says Napier "could have landed."

77. Rodgers's report.

78. *Ibid.*

79. Webster, in Marine, 179.

80. *Ibid.*

81. Rodgers's report. Webster, himself, said he had 45 at the time of the action.

82. See Chap. VIII.

83. Webster's narrative, in Marine, 177-181.

84. *Ibid.*

85. "About midnight" Webster was able to hear oars.

86. James, VI, 191.

87. A conclusion, based on the fact that Webster, a flotilla veteran, certainly would have recognized gunners' matches and presumably would have referred to them as such.

88. Duane.

89. Fort Covington did not open fire until after Fort Babcock.

90. Webster's narrative.

91. James includes a rocket boat in Napier's force.

92. Citizen Soldiers.

93. *Ibid.*

94. James, VI, 191.

95. Babcock had a garrison of 45, Covington had 80. James puts Napier's force in the Ferry Branch at 128.

96. Armistead's report. The precise truth concerning the strength of Napier's expedition probably never will be known. The force as stated by James seems remarkably small, if the eleven boats that "pulled, by mistake, directly for the harbour"—that is, toward the Lazaretto channel—carried no more men per boat. British boat expeditions, on other occasions, were stronger in proportion to the number of boats used; for example, the Brit-

ish barges sent into the Penobscot in 1814 carried 740 men, and in the attack on the privateer General Armstrong at Fayal, seven boats from H.M.S. *Plantaganet* and *Rota* contained 180 men. In the first instance, the figures are from Roosevelt, II, 68; in the second, from James, VI, 224. The British version of Napier's strength has been used in this narrative.

97. Rodgers's report recounts how he sent Major Randall's detachment, which was under his command that night, "to dislodge a party of men in the enemy's boats, which it was supposed intended landing near the Laz-

aretto, to take possession of our little three-gun battery." A reasonable assumption is that Rodgers mistook the part of Napier's force which went astray, pulling toward the Lazaretto channel, for a deliberate attempt to attack the Lazaretto's battery.

98. Subaltern, 158.
99. James, VI, 191, and Webster.
100. Subaltern, 158.
101. Bartgis diary.
102. Subaltern, 158.
103. *Narrative*, 193.
104. Bartgis diary and Webster.
105. Smith's report.
106. James, VI, 192.
107. *Ibid.*, VI, 188.

CHAPTER 27

1. Smith's report.
2. *Ibid.*
3. Rodgers's report.
4. Smith's report.
5. Taney's narrative. Also the following paragraph.
6. Subaltern, 159.
7. James, VI, 192. The quoted phrase is his.
8. United States Naval Observatory.
9. *The Star Spangled Banner*, Oscar George Theodore Sonneck, chief of the division of music, Library of Congress, p. 76; United States Government Printing Office, 1914.
10. Smith's report.
11. Subaltern, 163.
12. Armistead's report.
13. *Narrative*, 194-195.
14. *Ibid.*
15. James, VI, 191.
16. Narrative, 194.
17. Subaltern, 160.
18. *Ibid.*, 162.
19. *Narrative*, 194.
20. Subaltern, 161.
21. Division Orders, Sept. 15, dated at Winder's headquarters in New Church street.

22. Subaltern, 161.
23. *Ibid.*; and Winder's division orders, which identified the rear-guard detachment as "fusileers." The identification probably was correct; it confirms the conclusion in the preceding chapter that the 21st regiment had furnished the screen for Brooke's front when he drew the bulk of his army to the right to form his storming column.
24. Subaltern, 161.
25. *Ibid.*
26. *Ibid.*
27. *Ibid.*: "Then was a fire opened, which in a trice brought men and horses to the ground."
28. Winder's division orders.
29. *Ibid.* The British admitted that two prisoners were taken: *Narrative*, 195.
30. Smith's report contains this implication; its correctness is confirmed by the timing in Subaltern, 162: the army did not halt for the night until "about four o'clock."
31. Subaltern, 163.
32. This sentence and the three immediately following are based on An-

nie Leakin Sioussat's account in her *Old Baltimore*, pp. 183-184.

33. Lossing, footnote, 958. He said he had seen the note.

34. Taney's narrative.

35. This was the view which Mr. Sonneck thought "absolutely correct —provided that Key himself did not propose the tune of 'To Anacreon in Heaven,' or any of its then current American equivalents."

36. The belief of Judge Nicholson's granddaughter, quoted by Sonneck, p. 81.

37. From a letter written by Samuel Sands under date of Jan. 1, 1877, and quoted in Sonneck, p. 82.

38. *Ibid*. Thomas Murphy's name does not appear on the muster roll of the Sharp Shooters, but its failure to appear means nothing; few volunteers are listed either in the Maryland roster or on the rolls of the units with which they served.

39. Marine, 188.

40. Sands' letter, in Sonneck.

41. Weybright, 150.

42. *Historical Magazine*, 1864, VIII, 347-348; an article signed "C. D." and presumably written by Charles Durang; quoted in Sonneck, pp. 72-73.

43. *Ibid*.

44. *Historical Magazine*, 1867, II, 279-280; a paper read by Colonel John L. Warner before the Pennsylvania Historical Society; quoted in Sonneck, p. 73.

45. *Ibid*. Warner's identification of these officers was correct.

46. *Ibid*.; and Sonneck text, p. 73.

47. Sonneck, 77.

48. Marine, 188.

Note: "The Perilous Fight" was written to present, in one place and in proper perspective, the events which preceded and attended the writing of "The Star-Spangled Banner," and the author's research has been directed to that purpose. The doubts and confusions which long obscured the details of the printing of Key's verses, how and by whom the tune was chosen, and where and by whom the song was first sung, have been largely cleared away by the careful research of Oscar George Theodore Sonneck. His summary of his findings, published under the auspices of the Library of Congress and under the imprint of the United States printing office, 1914, is readily available to anyone interested in the detailed story.

CHAPTER 28

1. The word "ultimatum" is used deliberately. It is justified by the fact that at least one of its demands—the setting up of an independent Indian "state" as a buffer—had been presented as a *sine qua non*.

2. As United States ambassador to Russia.

3. *A History of the People of the United States*, John Bach McMaster, IV, 265.

4. Made by General Anthony Wayne about a year after the battle of Fallen Timbers, in 1795.

5. McMaster, IV, 266.

6. Letter from Lord Wellington to Castlereagh, Nov. 9, 1814. It is quoted out of sequence to indicate the confidence placed in the troops sent to America.

7. Lossing, 959.

8. *History of the United States of America During the Second Administration of James Madison*, Henry Adams, III, 17. Charles Scribner's Sons, New York.

9. *Ibid*., 31.

10. James A. Bayard to Levett Harris, Dec. 6, 1814; in *Papers of James A. Bayard*, published as the Annual

Report of the American Historical Association, 1913, II, 357.

11. Adams, III, 31.
12. Lossing, 959.
13. *Ibid.*
14. Adams, III, 35.
15. *Ibid.*, 37.
16. *Ibid.*, 34.
17. McMaster, IV, 263, describes

the British commissioners as being "in rank, in notoriety, and ability, a good indication of the contempt with which [the British ministry] regarded America."

18. Adams, III, 38.
19. Wellington to Castlereagh, Nov. 9, 1814.
20. Adams, III, 52.

CHAPTER 29

1. *Bayard Papers*, II, 348.
2. *Ibid.*, 353-4.
3. *Ibid.*, 357.
4. *The Life and Speeches of Henry*

Clay, Vol. I. Greeley and McElrath, New York, 1843.

5. *Bayard Papers*, II, 365.